User and Reference manual

stylevision™

2004

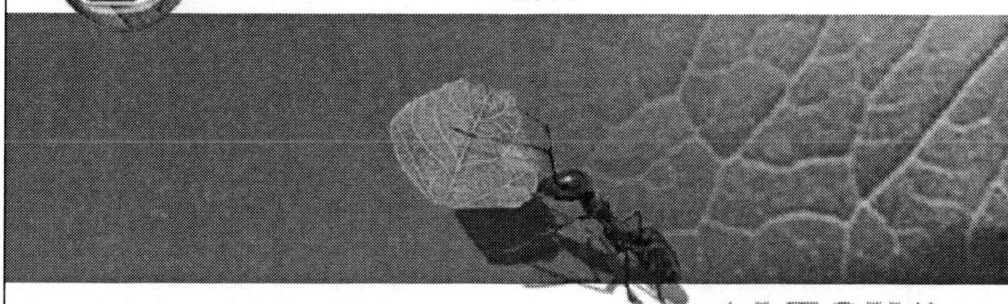

ALTOVA®

www.altova.com

STYLEVISION 2004

Published: 2003

Printed in the United States of America

5 4 3 2 1

ISBN 0-9723-5595-2

Table of Contents

Part I Introduction to Stylevision 1

Part II Welcome... 4

1 Introduction to XML 5

2 What is XML 6

Why XML 9

The XML Standards Puzzle 11

3 User interface 13

XML Editing 14

Schema Editing 15

XSL Editing 17

Project Management 18

Part III Tutorial 20

1 Overview 21

2 Creating a schema from scratch 22

Creating a new Schema file 23

Adding elements to a schema 26

Adding elements with drag and drop 29

Completing the basic schema 30

3 Making schema components reusable 33

Globals, extending simple and complex types 34

References, attributes and enumerations 40

Navigation shortcuts in schema documents 43

4 Creating an XML document 46

Creating and completing a new XML file 47

Editing in Text- and Grid view 50

Validating and entering data 53

Manipulating data - Entry helpers 57

Database/Table view 59

5 XSL Transformation 65

Transforming XML to HTML 66

6 Creating a project 69

Adding files to a project 70

7 That's it! 72

Part IV User Reference 74

1 Windows 75

Main Window 76

Enhanced Grid View 76

Database/Table View 79

Schema/WSDL Design View 82

Schema design content model 85
Schema, Content model 88
Text View 92
Authentic View 95
Browser View 96
Project Window 98
Entry Helper Windows 99
Element Entry-Helper 99
Attribute Entry-Helper 100
Entity Entry-Helper 101
2 Info Window 103
3 Menus 104
File Menu 105
New... 105
Open... 107
Open URL... 108
Reload 110
Encoding... 110
Close 110
Close All 110
Save 111
Save As... 111
Save to URL... 111
Save All 112
Send by Mail 113
Print... 114
Print Setup... 115
Most Recently Used Files 116
Exit 116
Edit Menu 118
Undo 118
Redo 118
Cut 118
Copy 118
Paste 119
Delete 119
Copy as XML-Text 119
Copy as Structured Text 119
Copy XPath 121
Pretty-Print XML Text 121
Select All 121
Find... 122
Find next 122
Replace... 123
Project Menu 124
New Project 124
Open Project 124
Reload Project 125
Close Project 125
Save Project 125
Source control 125
Open project 127
Enable Source code control 130

Get Latest Version ... 130
Check Out ... 130
Check In ... 131
Undo Check Out... ... 132
Add to Source Control ... 132
Remove from Source Control ... 134
Show History ... 134
Show Differences ... 135
Properties ... 136
Refresh Status ... 137
Run Native Interface ... 137
Add Files to Project... ... 137
Add URL to Project ... 137
Add Active File to Project ... 138
Add Active And Related Files to Project ... 138
Add Project Folder to Project ... 138
Add External Folder to Project ... 138
Add External Web Folder to Project... ... 141
Project Properties ... 143
Most Recently Used Projects ... 145
XML Menu ... 146
Insert ... 146
Insert Attribute ... 146
Insert Element ... 146
Insert Text ... 147
Insert CDATA ... 147
Insert Comment ... 147
Insert XML ... 147
Insert Processing Instruction ... 147
Insert DOCTYPE ... 147
Insert ExternalID ... 148
Insert ELEMENT ... 148
Insert ATTLIST ... 148
Insert ENTITY ... 148
Insert NOTATION ... 148
Append ... 148
Append Attribute ... 149
Append Element ... 149
Append Text ... 149
Append CDATA ... 149
Append Comment ... 149
Append XML ... 150
Append Processing Instruction ... 150
Append DOCTYPE ... 150
Append ExternalID ... 150
Append ELEMENT ... 150
Append ATTLIST ... 150
Append ENTITY ... 150
Append NOTATION ... 151
Add Child ... 151
Add Child Attribute ... 151
Add Child Element ... 151
Add Child Text ... 152
Add Child CDATA ... 152

Add Child Comment ... 152
Add Child XML ... 152
Add Child Processing Instruction ... 152
Add Child DOCTYPE ... 152
Add Child ExternalID ... 152
Add Child ELEMENT ... 153
Add Child ATTLIST ... 153
Add Child ENTITY ... 153
Add Child NOTATION ... 153
Convert To ... 153
Convert To Attribute ... 154
Convert To Element ... 154
Convert To Text ... 154
Convert To CDATA ... 154
Convert To Comment ... 154
Convert To XML ... 154
Convert To Processing Instruction ... 154
Convert To DOCTYPE ... 155
Convert To ExternalID ... 155
Convert To ELEMENT ... 155
Convert To ATTLIST ... 155
Convert To ENTITY ... 155
Convert To NOTATION ... 155
Table ... 155
Display as Table ... 155
Insert Row ... 156
Append Row ... 157
Ascending Sort ... 157
Descending Sort ... 157
Move Left ... 158
Move Right ... 158
Enclose in Element ... 158
Evaluate XPath ... 158
XPath Visualizer options ... 159
XPath examples ... 160
Check Well-Formedness ... 162
Validate ... 163
Validate XML ... 163
Validate Schema ... 164
Update Entry-Helpers ... 164
Namespace Prefix ... 164
DTD/Schema Menu ... 166
Assign DTD ... 166
Assign Schema ... 166
Include another DTD ... 166
Go to DTD ... 167
Go to Schema ... 167
Go to Definition ... 167
Flush Memory Cache ... 167
Schema design Menu ... 168
Schema settings ... 168
Zoom ... 169
Display all Globals ... 169
Display Diagram ... 169

XSL Menu **170**
XSL Transformation 170
Assign XSL... 170
Assign XSL:FO... 171
Assign sample XML file 171
Go to XSL 171
Authentic Menu **172**
Assign an Authentic Stylesheet 172
Hide markup 172
Show small markup 172
Show large markup 172
Show mixed markup 172
Append row 172
Insert row 173
Duplicate row 173
Move row up 173
Move row down 173
Delete row 173
View Menu **174**
Enhanced Grid View 174
Schema/WSDL Design View 174
Text View 176
Authentic View 177
Browser View 177
Synchronize 177
Expand 178
Collapse 178
Expand fully 179
Collapse unselected 179
Optimal widths 179
Word wrap 179
Go to line/char... 179
Go to File 180
Browser Menu **181**
Back 181
Forward 181
Stop 181
Refresh 181
Fonts 181
Separate Window 181
Tools **182**
Spelling... 182
Spelling options... 184
Compare open file with... 187
Compare directories 189
Compare options 191
Customize... 193
Commands 193
Toolbars 194
Keyboard 196
Menu 200
Options 203
Customize context menu 203
Options 205

File 205
File types 206
Editing 207
View 208
Grid fonts 208
Schema fonts 209
Text fonts 209
Colors 209
Encoding 210
XSL 210
Scripting 212
Window Menu **214**
Cascade 214
Tile horizontally 214
Tile vertically 214
Project Window 214
Info Window 214
Entry Helpers 214
All on/off 214
Currently open window list 215
Help Menu **216**
Table of contents 216
Index... 216
Search... 216
Registration... 217
Order form... 218
Support Center 218
FAQ on the web 218
Components download 218
Altova on the Internet 218
Training 218
Japanese distributor... 218
About... 219
4 Dialogs **220**

Part V HTML to XML Conversion **224**

1 Description of the Interface **225**
2 HTML to XML Tutorial **226**
Saving an Internet page locally using XMLSPY 2004 .... **227**
Importing an HTML file into Stylesheet Designer **230**
Building the XML document tree **231**
Generating the XML, DTD or XML Schema, and XSLT files **237**
3 HTML to XML Conversion Reference **240**
Save HTML file with XMLSPY 2004 .... **241**
Import HTML file into Stylesheet Designer **242**
Building the XML tree: pop-up menu **243**
Building the XML tree: HTML Import menu **245**
Context menus **247**
Help **249**

Part VI Authentic View **252**

1 Introduction **253**

Authentic View and Authentic Stylesheets 255
Authentic View terminology 257
Authentic View features 258
2 Authentic View interface 260
Overview of the GUI 261
Authentic View toolbar icons 262
Authentic View main window 264
Authentic View entry helpers 267
3 Authentic View Tutorial 272
Opening an XML document in Authentic View 273
Entering data in Authentic View 274
Adding document content and elements 275
Inserting an element 278
Applying and clearing elements 279
Entering attribute values 280
Adding entities 281
Printing the document 282
4 Authentic View: How To 283
Using tables in Authentic View 284
SPS tables 284
XML tables 285
XML table editing icons 288
Using context menus 291
Using the Date Picker 292
Part VII Stylesheet Designer 294
1 Introduction 295
Uses of Authentic Stylesheets 296
Stylesheet Designer and Authentic View 297
Stylesheet Designer and HTML / PDF output 299
Stylesheet Designer concepts and terminology 300
2 Getting Started 302
Setting up Stylesheet Designer 303
Stylesheet Designer interface 305
Document design process 307
3 Stylesheet Designer Tutorial 309
Setting up the Authentic Stylesheet 310
Processing attribute values for output 314
Including an image 316
Processing element content for output 318
Formatting the components 323
Inserting a dynamic SPS table 328
Inserting a static SPS table 332
Inserting bookmarks and hyperlinks 337
Using Auto-Calculation 340
Using Conditional Templates 347
Creating the Table Footer 356
Text formatting with global templates and text state icons 360
Using Additional Validation 362
Completing the stylesheet 364
4 Stylesheet Designer How To Use 368

Data-entry devices **369**
Lists **371**
Tables **375**
Creating static tables 377
Creating dynamic tables 378
Formatting static and dynamic tables 380
XML tables 381
Conditional templates **384**
Date Picker **386**
Input Formatting **388**
Global Templates **396**
PDF processing and page layout **401**
FO Processing for PDF Preview 401
PDF page definition 404
PDF layout elements 405
5 Stylesheet Designer User Reference **409**
Symbols and icons **410**
Text and Block Style Windows **413**
Formatting **414**
File **416**
Open 416
Save 416
Save as... 416
Assign working XML file... 416
Save generated XSLT file as... 417
Save generated XSL-FO file as... 417
Most recently used files 417
Exit 417
Edit **418**
Undo 418
Redo 418
Select all 418
Insert **419**
Image... 419
Paragraph 419
Format 419
Bullets and Numbering 419
Horizontal Line 420
Contents 420
Rest of Contents 421
Date Picker 421
Page 422
Bookmark 422
Hyperlink 422
Auto-Calculation 423
Condition 424
Table **425**
Insert Table... 425
Delete table 425
Append row 425
Append column 425
Insert row 426
Insert column 426
Delete row 426

Delete column 426
Join cell left 426
Join cell right 426
Join cell below 426
Join cell above 426
Split cell Horizontally 427
Split cell Vertically 427
View cell bounds 427
Table properties 427
Cell content alignment 427
Authentic 429
Node Settings 429
Text State icons 431
CALS / HTML Table properties 432
Assign Template XML file 433
Auto-add Date Picker 434
HTML Import 435
Open HTML file 435
Add to Parent 435
Insert 435
Append 436
Settings... 436
Properties 437
HTML Page... 437
PDF Page... 437
Table... 437
Bullets and Numbering... 437
Selected object 438
Tools 439
Spelling 439
Spelling options 440
Customize 442
Commands 442
Toolbars 444
Keyboard 444
Menu 445
XSL-FO Options 447
Help 448
Table of contents 448
Index... 448
Search... 448
Registration... 448
Order form... 449
Support Center 449
FAQ on the web 449
Components download 450
Altova on the Internet 450
Japanese distributor... 450
About Stylesheet Designer 450
Context menus 451
Change to 452
Change... context menu 456
Create... popup menu 457
Insert Contents 459

Part VIII Technical Background Information 462

1 XML Parser ... 463
2 Schema Dialects ... 464
3 OS & Memory Requirements ... 465
4 Internet Usage ... 466
5 Unicode Support ... 467
Windows NT 4.0 & Windows 2000 ... 468
Windows 98/ME ... 469
Right-to-Left Writing Systems ... 471
6 RichEdit Component ... 472
7 License Metering ... 473

Part IX Licensing and Distribution 476

1 Electronic Software Distribution ... 477
2 Copyright ... 478
3 Software Product License ... 479

Index 487

Part I

1 Introduction to Stylevision

stylevision™ 2004 allows Web designers with little prior knowledge of XML to easily create advanced XML websites. New intuitive visual editing and conversion tools effectively eliminate the complexities of XML.

Writing even the simplest XSLT stylesheets by hand is a truly daunting task, requiring an understanding of XSL elements, XPath query language, and complicated rules-based document processing models. By abstracting away the underlying error-prone semantics **stylevision™ 2004** allows anyone to write stylesheets using considerably less time, and resulting in substantial cost savings.

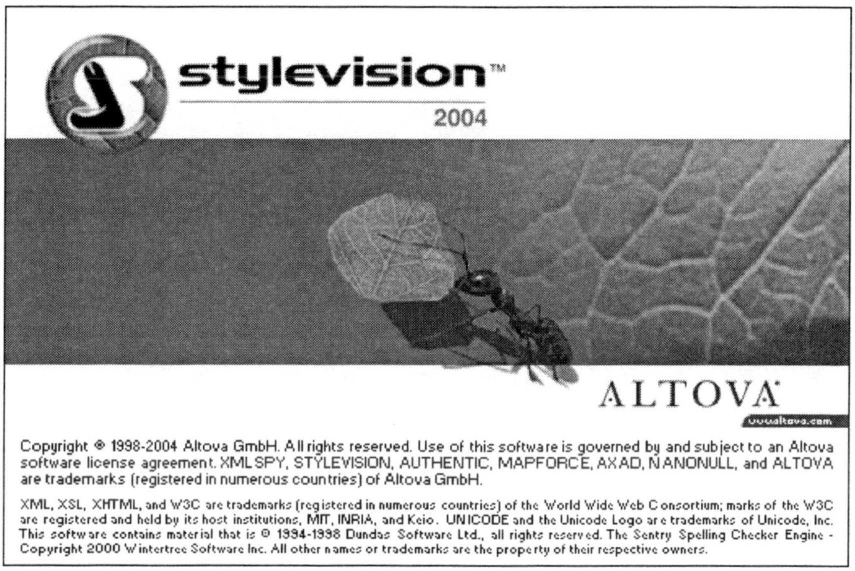

Part II

2 Welcome...

STYLEVISION 2004 is a comprehensive and easy-to-use product family that facilitates all aspects of XML Application Development.

Stylesheet Designer is a new approach to automate the writing of complex XSLT Stylesheets using an intuitive drag-and-drop user interface. Stylesheet Designer creates advanced electronic forms for use with Authentic View.

AUTHENTIC 2004 Desktop Edition is a word processor type editor, supporting electronic form-based data input, graphical elements, tables, as well as real-time validation using XML Schema.

STYLEVISION 2004 is the industry-leading solution for XML-based application development, allowing easy creation and management of XML documents, XML schemas, as well as XSLT Stylesheets.

STYLEVISION 2004 includes a Tutorial that shows you how to use STYLEVISION 2004 for the major aspects of XML:

- **XML editing & validation**
- **Schema/DTD editing & validation**
- **XSL editing & transformation**

The Reference section explains each window and menu command in detail and can easily be accessed through the Contents, and Index tabs of the help file.

You may also want to periodically check our Altova web-server for news, updates, and new examples. Please note that the complete STYLEVISION 2004 documentation is available in printed form, and can be purchased from http://www.altova.com/bookstore in the USA or Canada. To order from other coutries please go to the Resources page and select the specific link for your region.

Available now on **Amazon.com**, the definitive "**XMLSPY Handbook**".

The handbook explains XML, Namespaces, XSLT, XPath, XML Schema, SOAP, and WSDL using a wide array of relevant examples, while introducing the various features of XMLSPY. This is also the official textbook for XMLSPY training and certification.

If you encounter an occasional error or, perhaps, some incomplete information in this online help or the printed documentation and you need help with STYLEVISION 2004, please don't hesitate to visit our Support Center on the Internet, where you'll find additional links to the FAQ pages as well as our online Support Form. Also, please feel free to send us any feedback regarding the new documentation.

We will also be providing periodic free updates to the online help system and the printable documentation on the Download page on our web server.

Introduction to XML

The eXtensible Markup Language (XML) is a subset of SGML (the Structured Generalized Markup Language) that has been defined by the World Wide Web Consortium (W3C) in 1998 (see http://www.w3.org/TR/REC-xml). Its goal is to enable generic SGML to be served, received, and processed on the Web in the way that is now possible with HTML. XML has been designed for ease of implementation and for interoperability with both SGML and HTML.

The STYLEVISION 2004 online help and printable documentation contain a Tutorial section that give you a general overview of XML and STYLEVISION 2004.

To learn more about XML and its associated protocols, please also visit our list of recommended links to various XML-related information resources on the Altova web server.

We will take a short tour to discuss the various aspects of XML and the other related W3C standards, before explaining the various features of STYLEVISION 2004 that will help you make the most of XML.

If you are already familiar with XML, you may wish to skip to the User interface section.

What is XML

If you are new to XML, perhaps the most confusing aspect is it's similarity to HTML, which makes XML seem familiar at first, but also tends to obscure the view for the finer details of what makes XML tick.

We will, therefore, start by looking at what XML really is and why you need XML.

The XML Specification
The W3C specification defines XML as a subset of SGML, so to properly understand XML, it is useful to take a closer look at SGML first.

SGML stands for Standard Generalized Markup Language, and was developed for large scale applications, aircraft maintenance or power plant documentation, and intended to be maintained over the long term.

The reason why XML seems to be so similar to HTML lies in the fact that HTML is defined as a subset of SGML. XML is actually a lot more similar to SGML than to HTML, because HTML is only one specific subset of SGML used to describe web pages.

As XML was created to simplify SGML, it is no wonder that the W3C has now decided to redefine HTML 4.0 as an XML application, thereby creating XHTML 1.0. But this shall be of no concern for us at the moment, because we are still faced with the fundamental question "What is XML?".

To answer this, let us define what XML is **not**:

- It is **not** a programming language.
- It is **not** the next generation of HTML.
- It is **not** a database.
- It is **not** specific to any horizontal or vertical market.
- It is **not** the solution to all your problems, but it can be a very powerful tool in building such a solution.

XML is a clearly defined way to **structure, describe,** and **interchange data.**

Data in this context really means every conceivable kind of data! You can use XML for such diverse things as describing mathematical formulas, chemical compounds, astronomical information, financial derivatives, architectural blueprints, annotating Shakespearean plays, collecting Buddhist wisdoms, or voice-processing in telephone systems!

To get a feeling for XML, let us take a look at a simple XML document:

```
<product>
  <name>Apple</name>
  <price>0.10</price>
</product>
```

The < and > angle brackets are used to distinguish between the so-called "markup" (between the brackets) and the actual data of the document (outside of the brackets).

The XML document consist of individual *elements* that are marked by start- and end-tags (hence the term markup). Tags contain the name of the element, so that they can be distinguished from one another more easily.

The start-tag is bracketed by < > and the end-tag by </ > - both the start- and end-tag must always occur in pairs. The example XML document contains one element called "product", which consists of two elements: "name" (which contains the data "Apple") and "price" (which contains the data "0.10"). Unlike HTML, XML does **not** enforce a predefined set of element names (such as "body", "h1", and "p") - you can make up your own to suit the particular needs of your data.

This simple XML document also shows a very important aspect of XML - it is "self-describing". In addition to structuring the actual data, the XML element names (sometimes also called *tag names*) serve to describe the information provided in the document (in our case the price of an Apple). If you compare this to the way such data is traditionally exchanged between different applications (e.g. comma-separated value or CSV files), you can easily see the benefit:

"Apple";0.10

This is even more obvious, if you look at a slightly more complicated XML example document (as shown as in the Text View of STYLEVISION 2004):

```
<invoice due="2000-09-22">
  <product>
    <name>Apple</name>
    <price>0.10</price>
  </product>
  <product>
    <name>Orange</name>
    <price>0.08</price>
  </product>
  <product>
    <name>Strawberries</name>
    <price>0.20</price>
  </product>
  <product>
    <name>Banana</name>
    <price>0.14</price>
  </product>
  <total currency="US$">0.52</total>
</invoice>
```

You can immediately see another crucial property of XML here: the elements can be nested in any way that is useful to show the semantic structure of the data contained, and elements can be repeated, if more than one item of data of the same kind needs to be listed. Our example now describes an invoice with four products and a total.

Also note that some elements contain additional information within the start-tag: *attributes* always have a name and a value and are written as `name="value"` (E.g. `currency="US$"`). Attributes are used to further specify additional information that augments the data of the element (in our example, the currency of the total).

A disadvantage of XML is that the bigger an XML document is, the more markup it contains. This can make it difficult to find the data contained in the document. This slight disadvantage is typically more than compensated by the flexibility of XML, and by the fact that XML is inherently suitable for reading by both humans and machines.

STYLEVISION 2004 offers a concise presentation of an XML document - called the Enhanced Grid View. This view allows you to see and directly manipulate elements in your XML document, such as the actual data it contains:

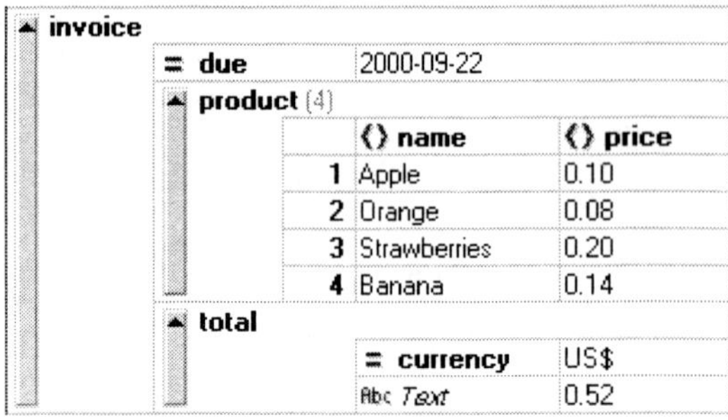

This is the same XML document as show in the Text view above. The product names and respective prices are shown as columns of a table - just as you would expect to see in a grid view.

Editing in this view is infinitely more comfortable, since you can simply:

- drag & drop elements
- insert new rows
- copy/paste your data to and from other applications (e.g. Excel, etc.) and
- manipulate data in a graphical way that is not possible in views offered by other products

You now have a first impression of an XML document and have learned about the two most important features of XML: **elements** and **attributes**. We will explain the other concepts of XML in the tutorial when we look at the specific features offered by STYLEVISION 2004.

Before we continue, let us first consider the ever-important "why" question...

Why XML

The reasons for using XML typically are as diverse as the different forms of data that exist today. We will, therefore, not consider specific benefits for certain vertical markets - such as engineering, e-commerce, mathematics, or others - but will instead try to focus on several individual properties of XML that are of universal advantage to all applications.

XML is easily readable by both humans and machines
Until now, most formats for storing data were either suitable for interpretation by software programs (e.g. dBase, GIF, etc.), or human readable (text or CSV files) - but not both.

XML defines a set of rules that make interpretation by computer very simple. It thus satisfies both needs, because XML documents remain text-based and can still be easily manipulated by a human being.

XML is object-oriented
While the relational data model is very successful for processing large amounts of table-like data, manipulation of other kinds of data - such as hypertext (i.e. text plus hyperlinks), multimedia, graphics, mathematical or chemical formulas, hierarchical information - are not so straightforward.

In contrast, XML is object-oriented in the sense of being suitable for describing objects of the real world or any abstract problem domain by modeling their properties as they are, instead of enforcing a normalized decomposition into various tables linked by relations. This makes XML documents more intuitively understandable and thereby reduces both the time required to design and implement computing systems based on XML.

XML is being widely adopted by the computer industry
One key factor in the success of the Internet was the wide adoption of the TCP/IP protocol suite by many corporations. This resulted in huge sales volumes and consequently ever decreasing prices for all network components used.

XML is widely accepted and implemented by many vendors, this fact will result in higher volumes and lower prices for software components. This is why XML's predecessor, SGML, was never successful on a broad scale. SGML products were typically priced in the ten-thousand dollar range, whereas XML products are today priced in the hundreds.

XML is global
To better understand the attention that XML has received, it is useful to recall another widely-adopted data standard that everybody takes for granted today: ASCII, the American Standard Code for Information Interchange.

While ASCII was restricted to a certain alphabet and writing system, it was still crucial in allowing different computer types and operating systems to freely exchange data. With the adoption of Unicode 1.0 and its continuing evolution. The idea of ASCII was expanded to encompass *all* languages and writing systems of the world.

Today, it is taken for granted that computers are capable of reading and processing text documents based on ASCII or Unicode. XML takes this approach one step further, by building on Unicode and defining a universal way to describe *structured* data for all different purposes.

All XML documents are per definition Unicode-based, but may be stored on disk or transmitted over the network in various different "encodings", such as ISO-8859-1 or UTF-8 . This is, why some people today call XML the "ASCII of the future".

Now that we have investigated some of the reasons why XML makes sense, we will turn to the XML "Acronym Puzzle".

The XML Standards Puzzle

In addition to XML, you will also encounter one or more of the following standards or acronyms closely associated with XML:

DTD
The "Document Type Definition" is a part of the original XML 1.0 specification that allows a developer, or standards body, to specify what elements and attributes may be used in a particular type of XML document and what their structure and nesting may be. This is also called the *content model* or *schema* of an XML document.

If an XML document conforms with the content model defined by a DTD, it is said to be *valid* with respect to that DTD.

XSLT
The "eXtensible Stylesheet Language Transformation" is a programming language that allows XML documents to be transformed from one schema to another or into entirely different forms, such as HTML pages, WML cards, or PDF files.

XPath
The "XML Path Language" is a language for addressing and querying the content of XML documents.

XPointer
The "XML Pointer Language" is a companion standard to Xlink and describes mechanisms for addressing particular parts of a document.

XML Schema
The "XML Schema" is an ongoing effort by the W3C to supplant DTDs with a more flexible and powerful system to describe the structure of conforming XML documents, including provisions for defining datatypes.

XHTML
The "Extensible HyperText Markup Language" is the reformulation of HTML 4.0 based upon XML and will soon supplant HTML as the de-facto standard of the Internet.

WML
The "Wireless Markup Language" is used for WAP phone systems to enable a mobile Internet environment and is entirely based on XML - it is described by one particular DTD, which is part of the WML specification.

SVG
Scalable Vector Graphics. SVG is an XML application used to describe 2D vector graphics, text and raster images. This enables vector graphics to be defined solely in XML.

SMIL
The "Synchronized Media Integration Language" is an XML document type designed to describe multimedia presentations.

DOM
The "Document Object Model" describes how some XML parsers return the information contained in an XML document. The elements of the XML document are described as nodes of a tree that can be traversed by a programmer.

SAX
The "Simple API for XML" provides another programming model used by some parsers,

which is based on events instead of a traversable tree.

This list does not attempt to be a complete list of all XML-based standards, as there are new proposals emerging on an almost daily basis and many standards are very specific to a certain market or problem domain. Please feel free to visit our Home Page to learn about recommended links, news, and other XML related information.

User interface

This screen shot shows the STYLEVISION 2004 application window.

The Enhanced Grid View  is enabled, and the ipo.xml file is the active document.

The Database/Table view has been activated for the Division element. This view is available wherever the **Enhanced Grid view** can be activated, and can be used when editing any type of XML file - XML, XSD, XSL etc.

Clicking the "Display as Table" icon,  activates the Database/Table view.

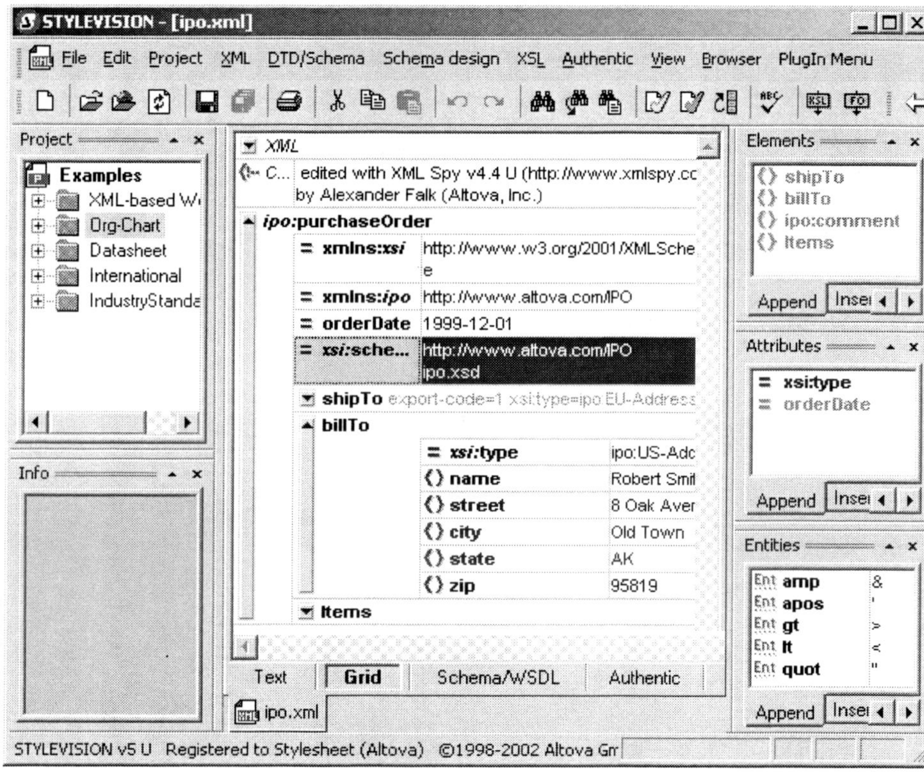

XML Editing

This screen shot shows the main window containing an XML document, and the same document in Browser view.
Click on the Browser tab, to open the Browser view of an XML Document.

For the Browser view to display/render an XML document correctly:

- The XML Document must contain a reference to an XSL stylesheet, or
- An XSL Stylesheet has to be assigned to the to the XML folder or project.

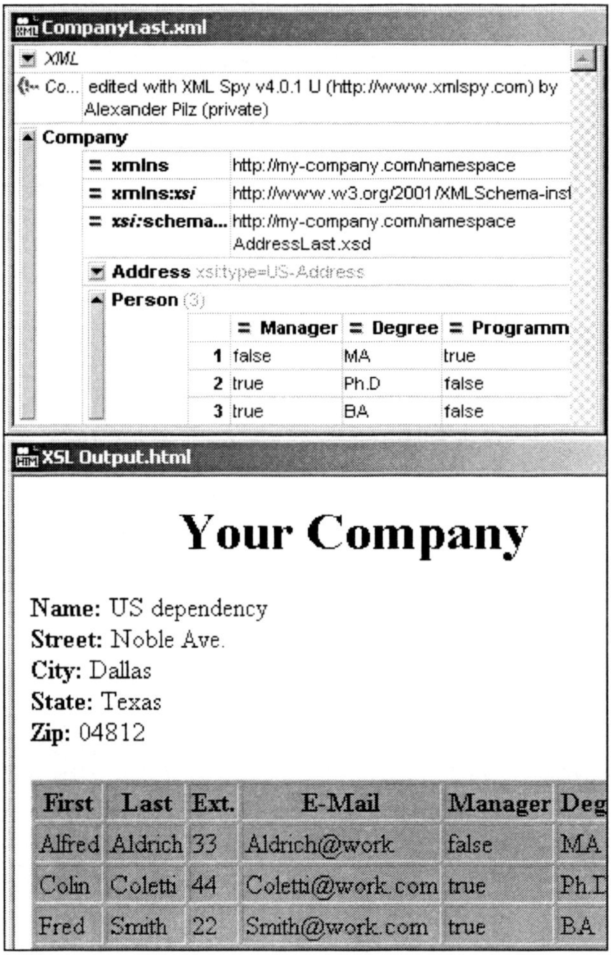

Schema Editing

This screen shot shows the main window containing an XML Schema document (XSDL - XML Schema Definition Language).
Click on the Schema/WSDL tab to open Schema Overview. The main window then displays all Global "definitions" (elements, complex types etc.) in list form.

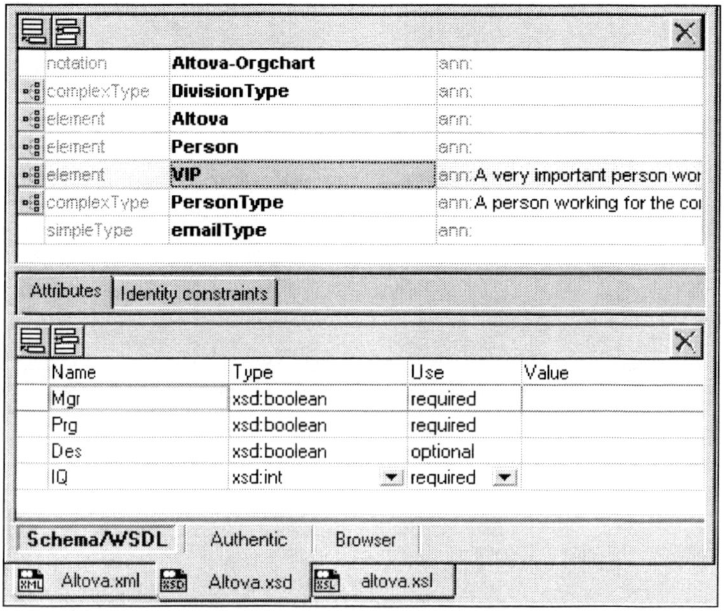

To see the content model in graphical form:

1. Click on the icon next to the definition you want to display.
   The *content model* for that component appears in a tree view.

To return to the Schema overview:

- Click the "Show Globals" icon to return to the Schema Overview.
- Select the menu option **Schema design | Display All Globals** to return to the Display All Globals view.

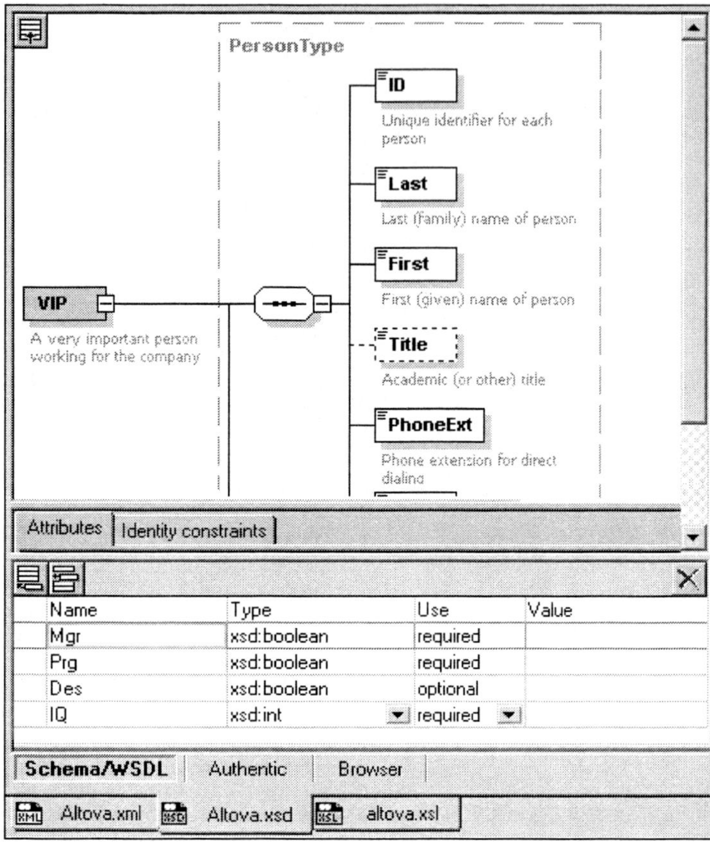

Please note:

Global definitions (global elements, complex types, etc.) can be moved or copied to other schemas visible in the schema overview, using drag and drop. You can of course, reposition definitions in the currently open schema. Right clicking a definition opens the context menu in which you can select the standard cut, copy, paste commands, to achieve the same thing.

The drag and drop method also allows you to move or copy **attributes** as well as **Identity constraints** between schemas.

XSL Editing

This screen shot shows the main window containing an XSL (eXtensible Stylesheet Language) document, in Text view.

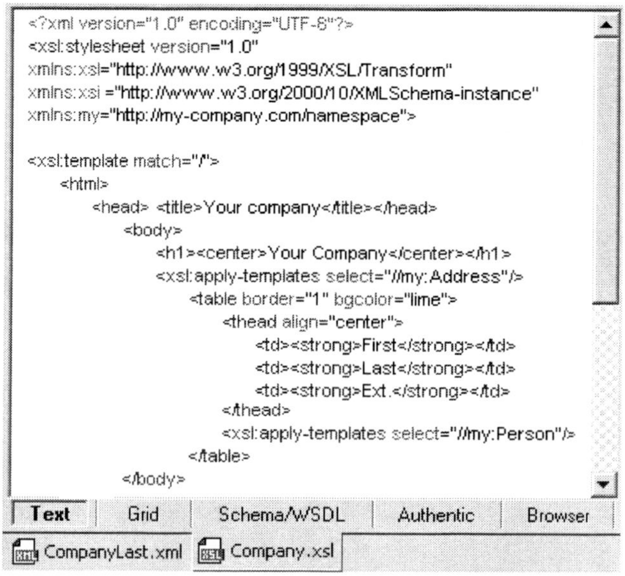

Clicking on the Grid tab, displays the same XSL document in grid form.

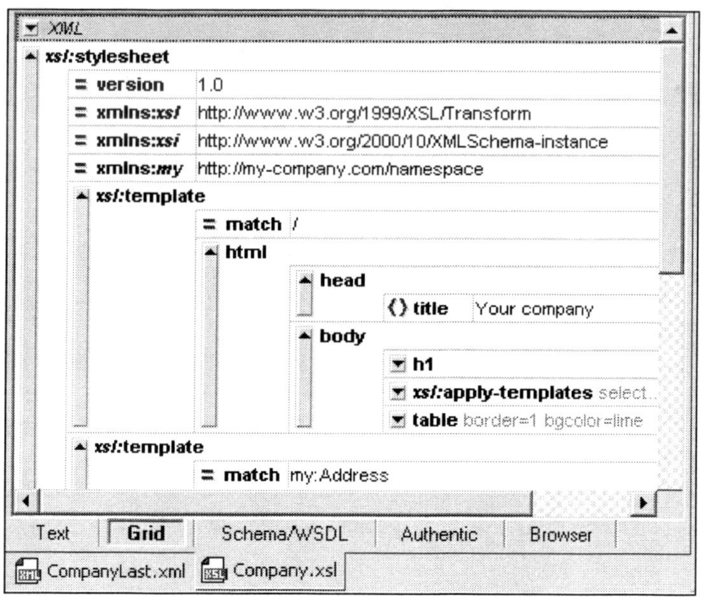

Project Management

STYLEVISION 2004 uses the familiar tree view display to manage your XML projects. Please note the Project window is not available in the Home Edition.

Project folders allow you to:

- Group XML files by their extension
- Assign XSL transformation parameters to specific folders, enabling you to view XML documents with "default" stylesheets
- Validate XML files by assigning DTDs or Schemas to specific folders.

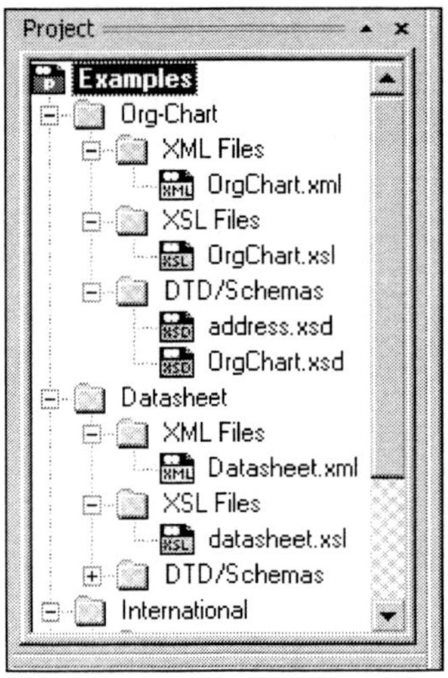

Part III

3 Tutorial

This tutorial gives a short overview of XML, and takes you through several tasks which provide an overview of how to use STYLEVISION 2004 to its fullest.

Please note that there is separate documentation (tutorial and reference) for Stylesheet Designer, which allows you to create XSLT Stylesheets using a drag and drop interface.

You will learn how to:

- Create a **simple schema** from scratch
- **Generalize** the schema using simple and complex types
- Create schema **documentation**
- Create an **XML document** based on the schema file
- Copy XML data to a **third party product** (Excel) and reinsert it in STYLEVISION 2004
- **Validate** the XML document against its schema
- **Update** Schema settings while editing the XML document
- **Transform** the XML document into HTML using XSLT, and see the result in the Browser view
- Create a STYLEVISION 2004 **project** to organize all your XML documents

Installation and configuration
This tutorial assumes that you have successfully installed STYLEVISION 2004 on your computer and received a free evaluation key-code or are a registered user.

The evaluation version of STYLEVISION 2004 is fully functional but time-limited to 30 days. You can request a regular license from our secure web server or through any one of our resellers.

Tutorial example files
The tutorial files are available in the **...\Examples\Tutorial** folder.

Tutorial example files:
AddressFirst.xsd
AddressLast.xsd
CompanyFirst.xml
CompanyLast.xml
Company.xsl
Company.html

The **Examples folder** contains various XML files for you to experiment with, while the **Tutorial** folder contains all the files used in this tutorial.

The **Template folder** contains all the XML template files that are used whenever you select the menu option **File | New**. These files supply the necessary data (namespaces and XML declarations) for you to start working with the respective XML document immediately.

Overview

STYLEVISION 2004 provides several windows that show various aspects of your XML document:

- The left area consists of the **Project** and **Info** windows.
- The central area, called **Main** window, is where you edit and view all types of XML documents.
  You can choose from different views: Grid view, Schema view, Text view, Authentic View or Browser view. The Grid view incorporates a special view, called the Database/Table view, which collapses recurring XML data into table form.
- The right area contains the three **Entry helper** windows which allow you to insert or append: elements, attributes, and entities.

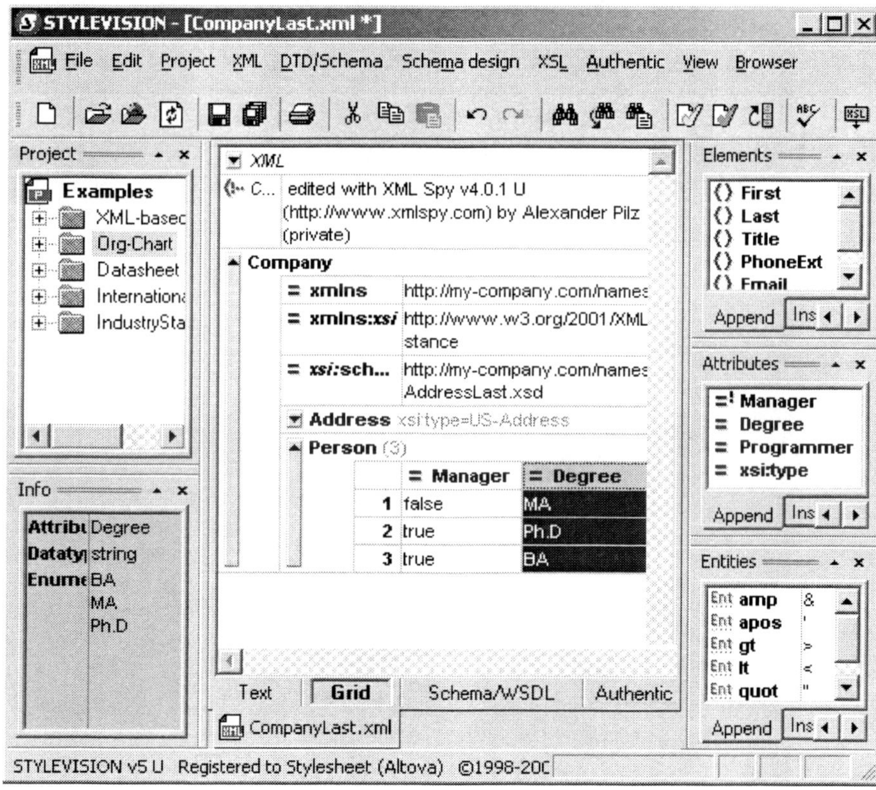

Creating a schema from scratch

A schema describes what one or more XML documents can look like,
and defines:

- The elements the document contains, and the order in which they appear
- The element content, and element attributes if any

The purpose of a schema is to allow machine validation of document structure. Instead of using the syntax of XML 1.0 DTD declarations, schema definitions use XML element syntax. A correct XML schema definition is, therefore, a well-formed XML document.

Goal of this section:
The goal of this section is to **create a simple schema** describing a company and its employees. The company is to consist of an **address** and an unlimited number of **persons**.

This will be achieved by:

- **Adding** elements to the schema
- Defining element **sequences**
- Adding **sub-elements** to an element (child elements)
- Creating elements using **drag and drop**
- **Configuring** the schema view
- Making an element **optional**
- Defining an element **facet**

Functions (and their icons) in this section:

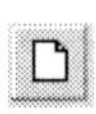

File | New creates a new type of XML file.

Schema design | Display diagram displays the content model of the selected global component in the top part of the main window. To display the content model of a component, click the "Display diagram" icon located to the left of each component in the "Display all globals" view of the Schema overview. The "Display diagram" function toggles with the "Display all globals" function.

Schema design | Display all globals displays all global components of the schema in the top part of the main window. The "Display all globals" function toggles with the "Display diagram" function.

TAB Takes you to the next field and automatically opens a drop-down list if one exists.

CTRL + **Drag&Drop** enables you to copy existing elements.

Append icon, allows you to append an element to the schema.

Creating a new Schema file

To create a new schema file:

1. Start STYLEVISION 2004 by double clicking on the STYLEVISION 2004 icon on your desktop.
   You are presented with an empty environment. There are no XML documents in the main window.

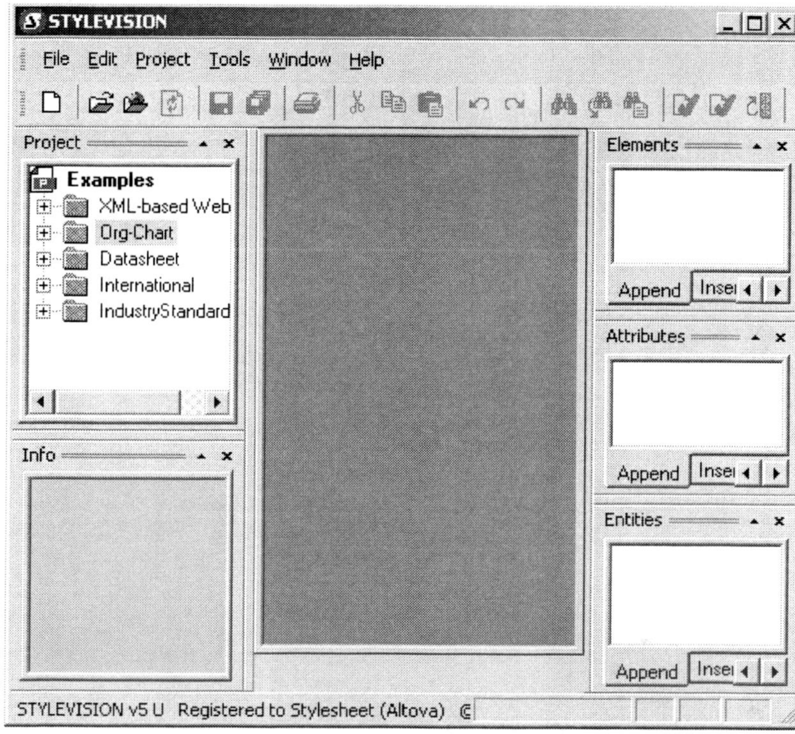

2. Select the menu option **File | New** and select the **.xsd XML Schema** entry from the dialog and confirm with OK.

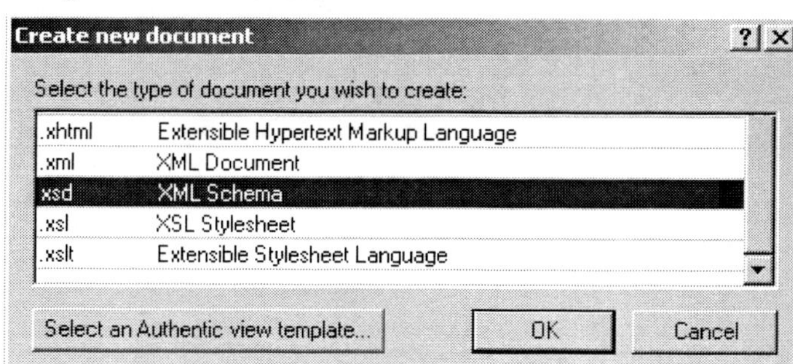

An empty schema file appears in the main window. You are prompted to enter the name of the root element.

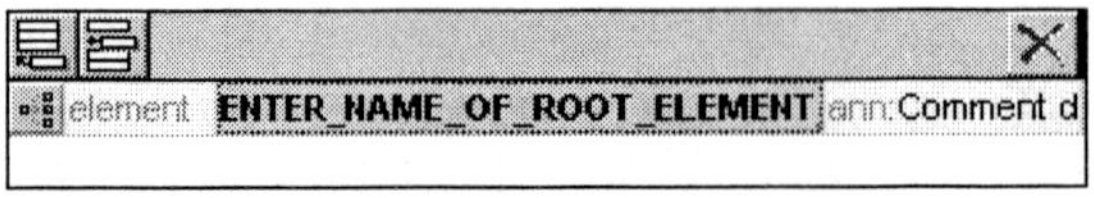

3. Click in the highlighted field and enter "Company", confirm with Enter.
   Company is now the "root" element of this schema and is automatically a "global element" as well.

   This view is the **Schema overview** and displays the **global components** in the top window and the **attributes** of the currently selected component, in the lower one.

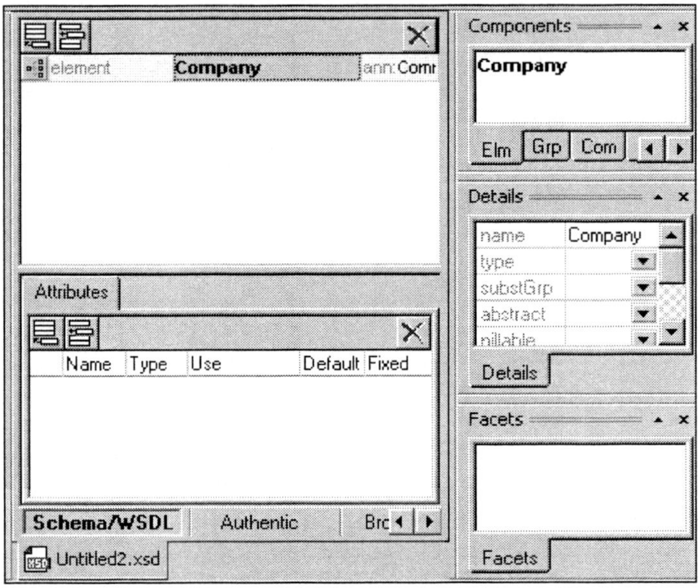

   The top entry helper window, the **Component Navigator**, displays Company in the "Elm" tab. The entries in these tabs can be used to navigate your schema by double clicking on them.
4. Click the menu option **File | Save**, and name your schema (**AddressFirst** for example).

Defining your own namespace:

1. Select the menu option **Schema Design | Schema settings.**
2. Click the Target namespace radio button, and enter **http://my-company.com/namespace.**

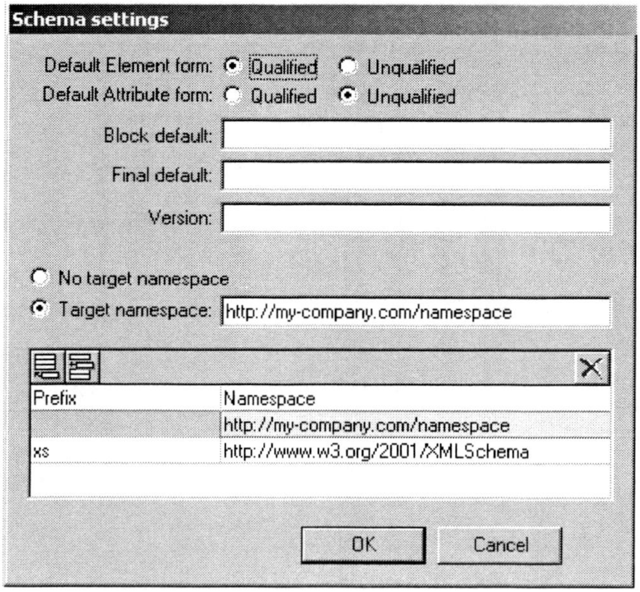

3. Confirm with the OK button.

Adding elements to a schema

To add elements to a schema:

1. Click the component icon next to the **Company** element, in the main window, to display the content model (or double click the Company entry in the Component Navigator - top entry helper).
   The text below the company element is annotation text. Double click the text if you want to edit it. (shortened to "Root element" here.)
2. Right click the Company element to open the context menu, and select **Add Child | Sequence**.

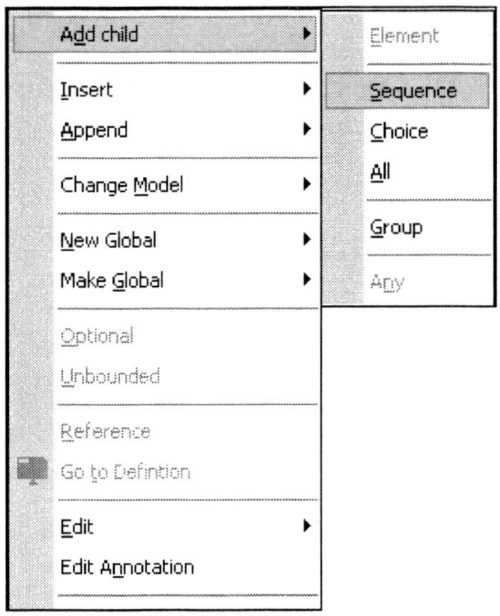

This inserts the **Sequence compositor**, and defines that the following elements must appear in the same sequence (in the XML document).

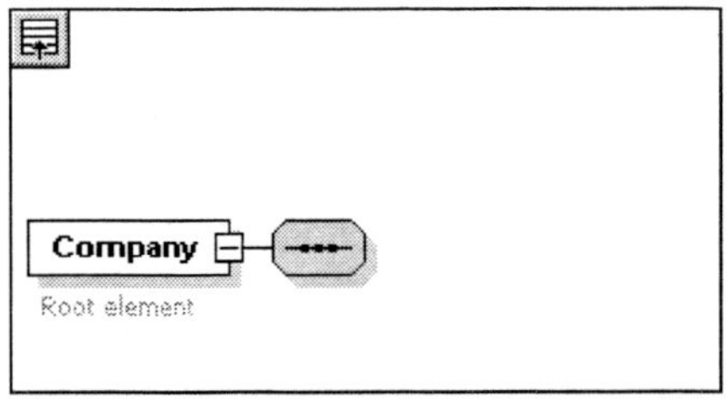

3. Right click the Sequence compositor and select **Add Child | Element**.
4. Enter "Address" as the name of the element, and confirm with the Enter key.

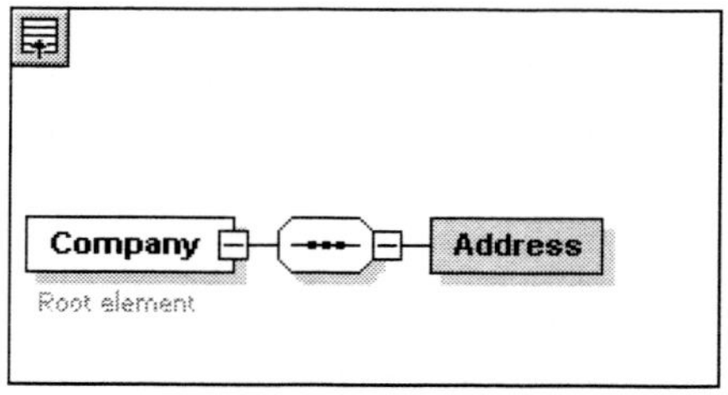

5. Right click the Sequence compositor again, select **Add Child | Element**, and enter "Person" as the name of the element.

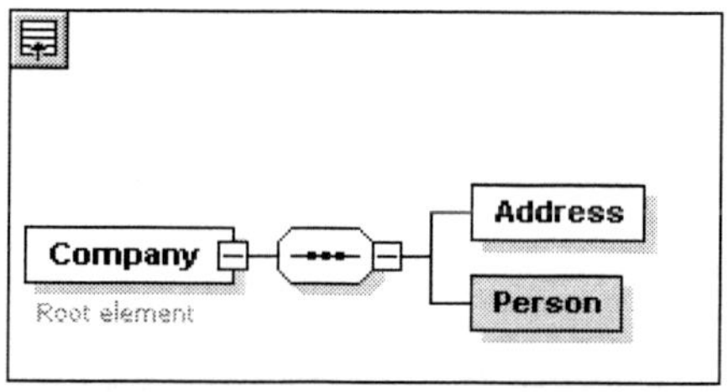

We have now defined a schema which allows for one address and one person per company. As this is too restrictive, we want to make sure that we can include as many persons per company as necessary.

6. Right click the Person element, and select **Unbounded** from the context menu. The Person element changes at this point, showing the range in which it can occur, in this case 1 to infinity.

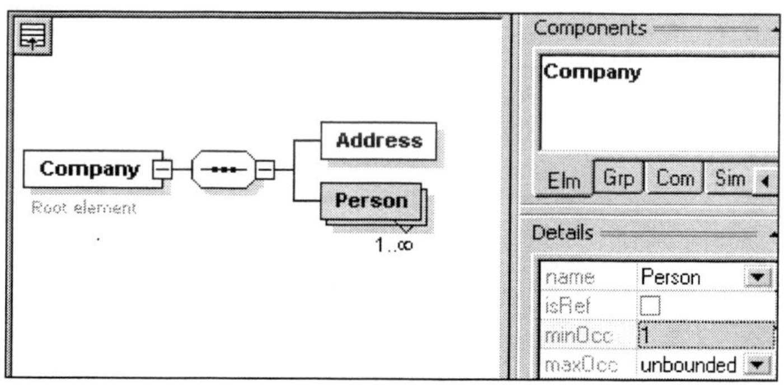

Please note:
You can also edit the **minOcc** and **maxOcc** fields in the Details entry helper directly.

We will now add the sub-elements which define the address structure.

To add sub-elements to an element:

1. Right click the **Address** element to open the context menu, and select **Add Child | Sequence**.
2. Right click the **Sequence** compositor, and select **Add Child | Element**. Enter "Name" as the element name.

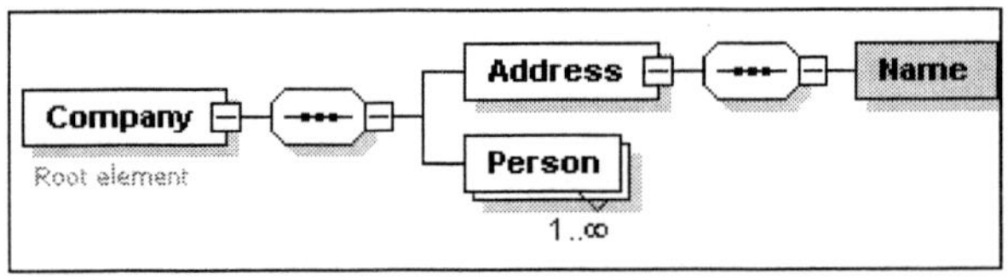

Defining element parameters:
At this point we want to define that the Name element is to occur only once, and contain only textual data.

1. Click the Name element, if not currently selected.
2. Click on the **type** combo box of the middle entry helper, and select the entry **xs:string** from the drop down list.

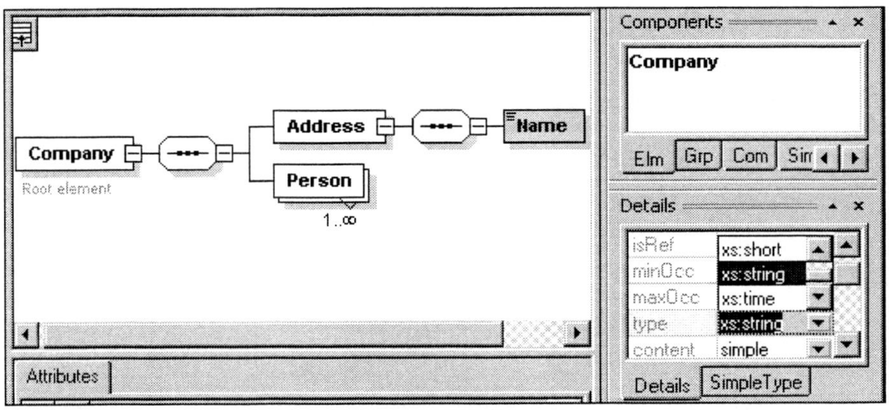

This entry helper is called "**Details**" in the Schema/WSDL view, and provides information on the currently selected element. **All data can be edited directly in the Details window!**

An icon appears in the top left of the element Name, indicating that this element contains text.

Both "minOcc" and "maxOcc" fields contain 1, showing that there is only one occurrence of this element (this is the default setting when creating a new element).

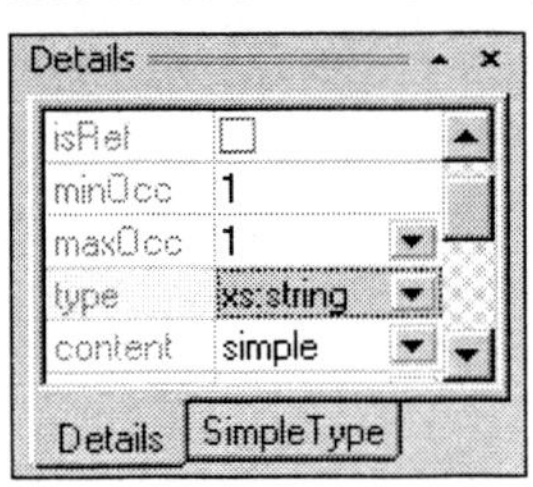

Adding elements with drag and drop

To add elements using drag and drop:
There is a quicker method of adding new elements to a schema, which avoids multiple menu commands:

1. Click the Name element, hold down the **CTRL** key, and **drag** "slightly" with the mouse. A marquee with a small "plus" icon appears, showing that you are about to copy the element.

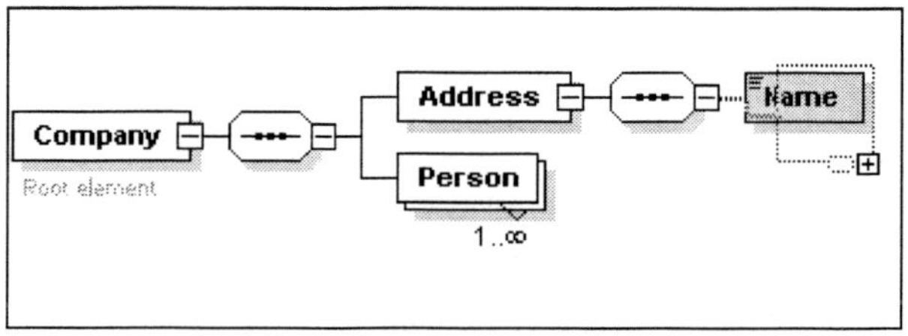

2. Release the mouse button to create the new element. If the new element appears somewhere else, just drag it near to the Name element and drop it there.
   This method creates an element of the same type, with the same settings as the one copied.

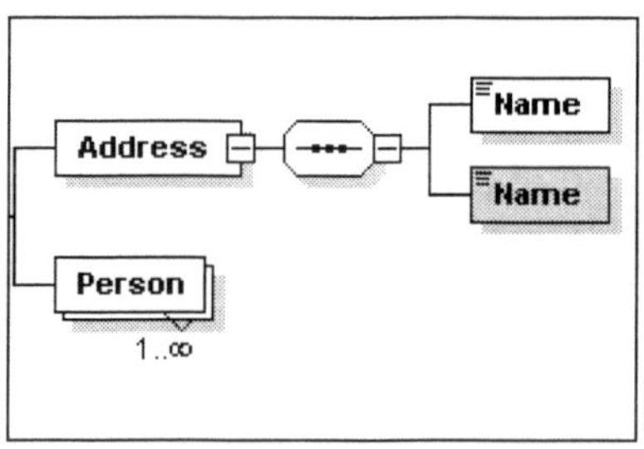

3. Type "Street" to change the element name.
4. Use the same method to create a third element, "City".
   The content model should now look like this:

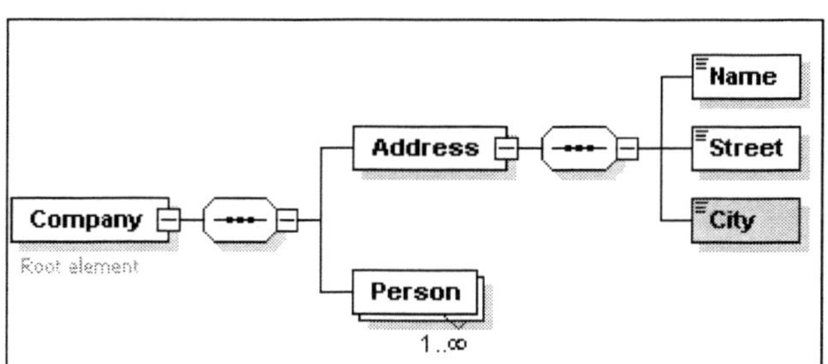

Completing the basic schema

At this point we want to add those sub elements to the Person element, which make up the personal data. All these elements will be **simple types** (with **simple content** models).

Person sub-elements: First, Last, Title, PhoneExt, and Email.

Requirements:
Title element: should be **optional**
PhoneExt: should be an **integer** and limited to **2 digits**

1. Right click the Person element to open the context menu, and select **Add Child | Sequence**. This inserts the Sequence compositor.
2. Right click the **Sequence** compositor, and select **Add Child | Element**.
3. Enter "**First**" as the name of the element, and hit the "**Enter**" key.

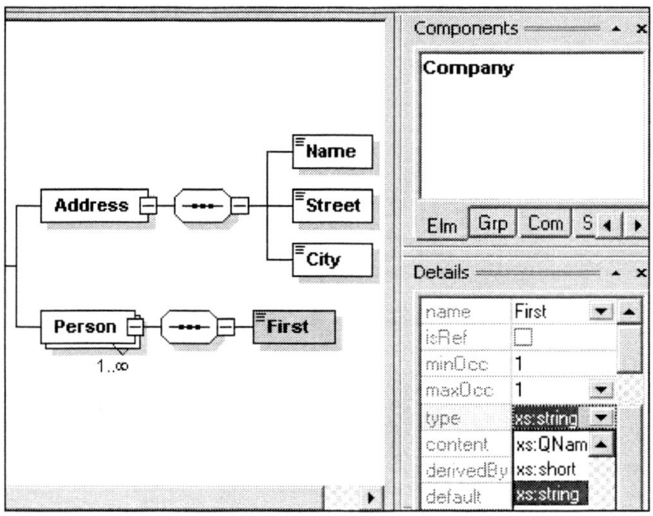

4. Click the **type** combo box in the Details entry helper, and select (or enter) the **xs:string** entry from the drop down list.
5. Use the drag and drop method to create **four more elements**, and name them: Last, Title, PhoneExt, and Email respectively.

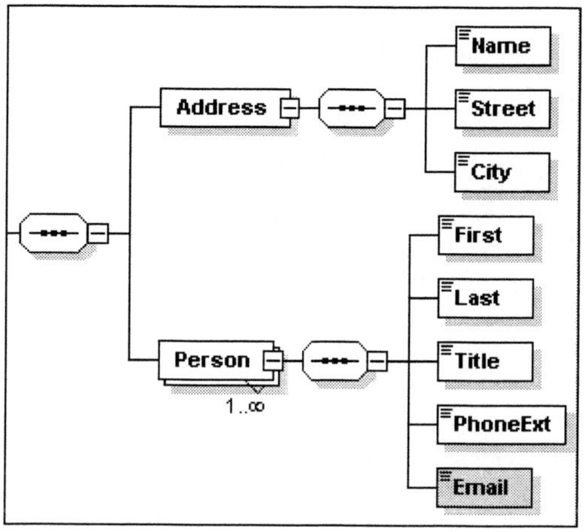

Please note:
You can select multiple elements by holding down the CTRL key, and clicking each one.

To make an element optional:

1. Right click the **Title** element, and select **Optional** from the **context menu**. The solid element frame changes to a dashed one; this is the visual display that an element is optional.

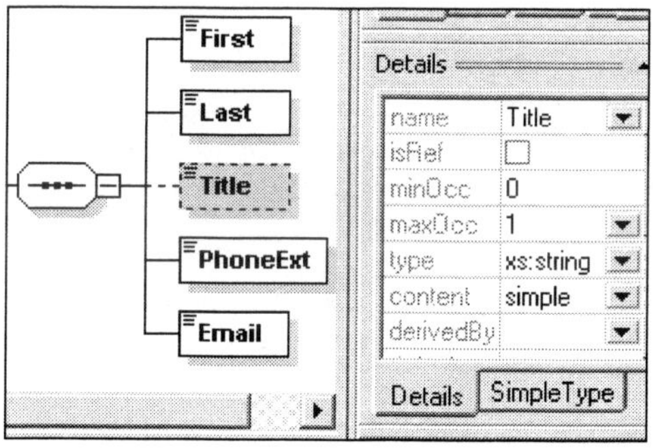

The "Details" fields have also been updated to **minOcc=0** and **maxOcc=1**.

To limit the content of an element (Facets):

1. Click the **type** combo box of the PhoneExt **element**, and select (or enter) the **xs:integer** entry from the drop down list.

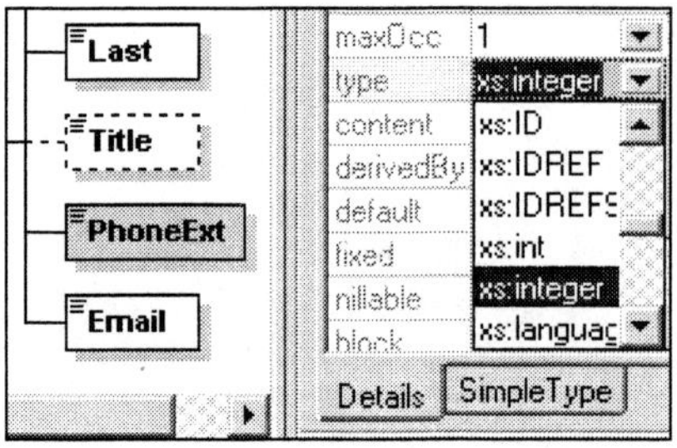

The items in the Facets tab (in the lowest entry helper) change at this point.

2. Double click in the "**maxIncl**" field of the Facets tab (in the lowest entry helper) and enter **99**, confirm with Enter.

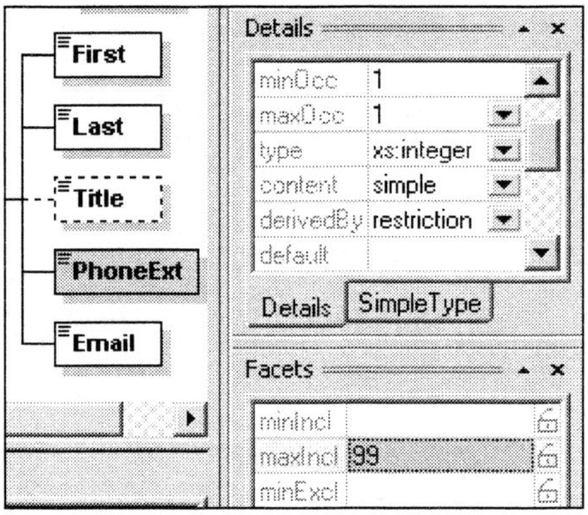

This defines that all phone extensions up to, and including 99, are valid.

3. Select the menu option **File | Save** to save the changes to the schema.

Please note:

- Selecting a predefined simple type "text" (i.e. xs:string, xs:date etc.) for an element, automatically changes the content model to: content = simple, in the Details entry helper.
- Adding a compositor to an element (selection, choice or all), automatically changes the content model to: content = complex, in the Details entry helper.

  This schema is available as '**AddressFirst**' in the ..\Tutorial folder.

Making schema components reusable

Goal of this section:
To create generic **schema** components which can be reused by other elements.

This will be achieved by:

- Creating a global **AddressType** component, which will be the basis for specific country addresses (a complex type)
- Creating two specific address templates for UK-, and US Addresses by **extending** the global address element (extend the complex type)
- Creating a global US-State element, by **restriction** (simpleType)
- Creating a global person element by **reference**
- Defining person **attributes** that supply information about the persons position in the company
- **Limiting** the **attribute contents** to a predefined set of attribute values (enumeration)

Functions (and their icons) in this section:

Schema design | Display all globals takes you back to the schema overview.

Append icon allows you to append an element, attribute or enumeration to a schema.

Schema design | Display diagram, the component icon displays the content model of the active global component in the schema overview.

Globals, extending simple and complex types

Having defined an element, you may then realize that you want to reuse it somewhere else in your schema. In STYLEVISION 2004 this is achieved by creating a **global component**.

To create a global component:

1. Right click the Address element, and select **Make Global | Complex type**.
   The Address elements appear in a yellow box.

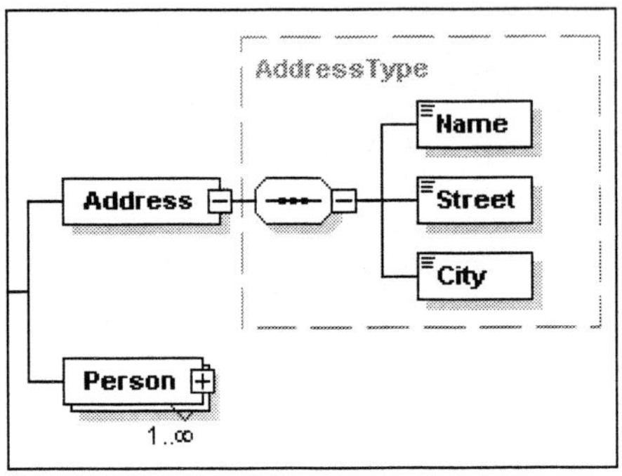

2. Click on the "Display all Globals" icon.
   The schema overview now displays two global components: the Company element and the complexType "AddressType".

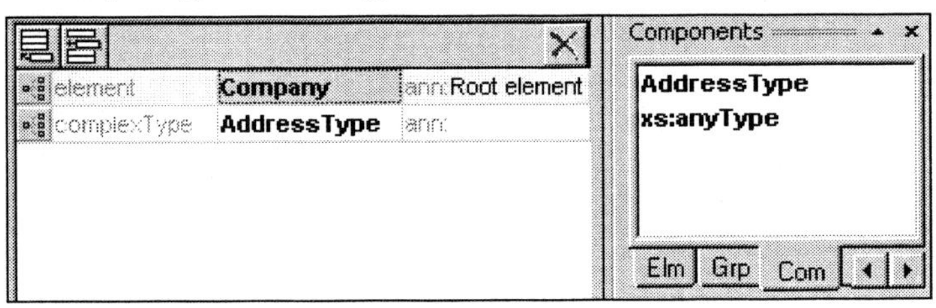

   Click on the **Com**(plex) tab of the **Component Navigator** to see that AddressType is also visible there.

3. Click on the AddressType component icon, to see the content model.

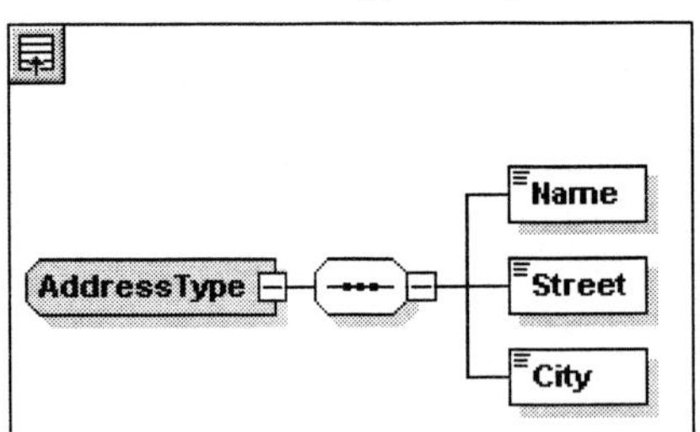

4. Click the "Display all Globals" icon to return to the schema overview.

Extending a "complex type" definition

We now want to use the global AddressType component, to create two kinds of country specific addresses. For this purpose we will define a **new** complex type **based** on the

AddressType component.

To extend a "complex type" definition:

1. Switch to the schema overview, if not already visible (Display all globals).
2. Click the **Append** icon, at the top left of the component window.
3. Select **ComplexType** from the context menu.

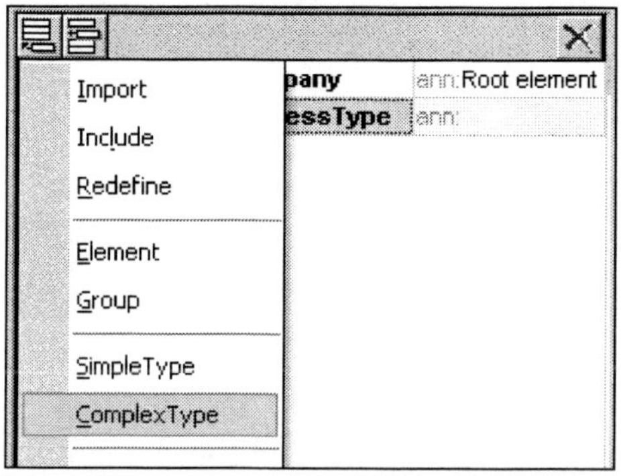

A new line appears in the component list, and the cursor is set for you to enter the component name.

4. Enter "US-Address" and confirm with Enter. (If you forget to enter the hyphen character "-" and enter a space, the element name will appear in **red,** signalling an illegal character.)

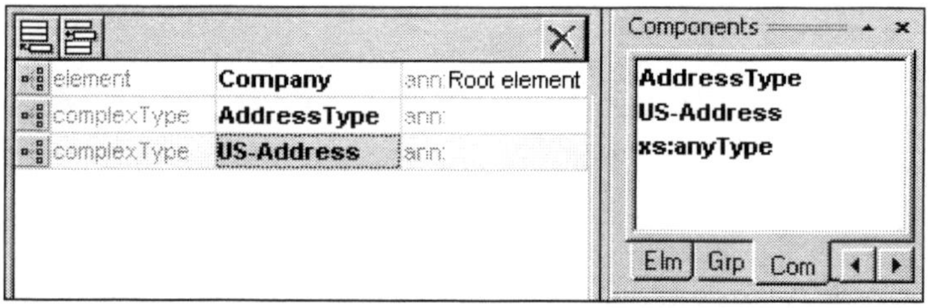

5. Click the **US-Address** component icon to see the content model.
6. Click the "**base**" combo box in the Details entry helper, and select the "AddressType" entry.

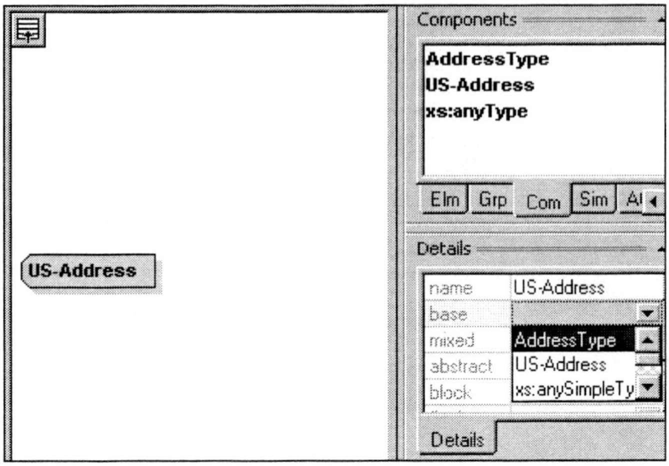

The content model view changes immediately and displays the previously defined generic address.

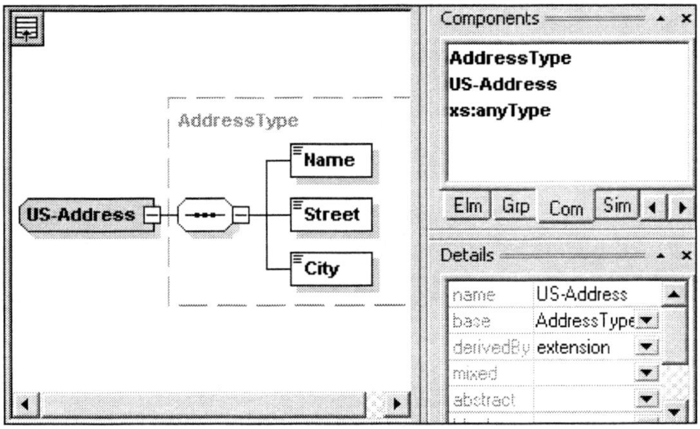

7. Right click the US-Address **element**, and select **Add Child | Sequence**.
   A new sequence compositor is displayed **outside** of the AddressType box. This is a visual indication that this is an **extension** to the element.

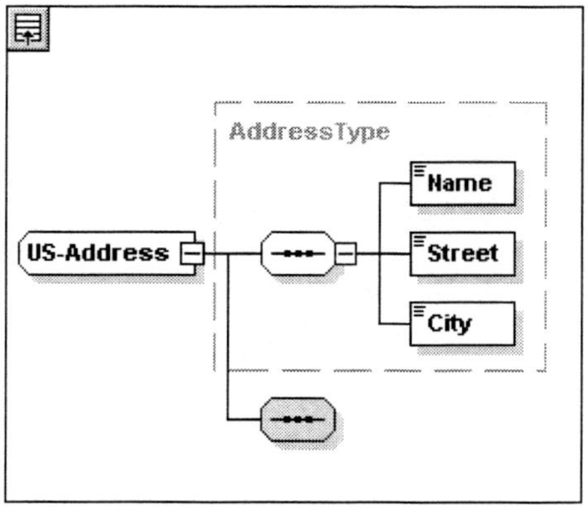

8. Right click the new **sequence** compositor, and select **Add Child | Element**.
9. Name the element "Zip", and hit Enter.
10. Select (or enter) **xs:positiveInteger** from the "type" combo box (in the Details entry helper), and confirm with Enter.

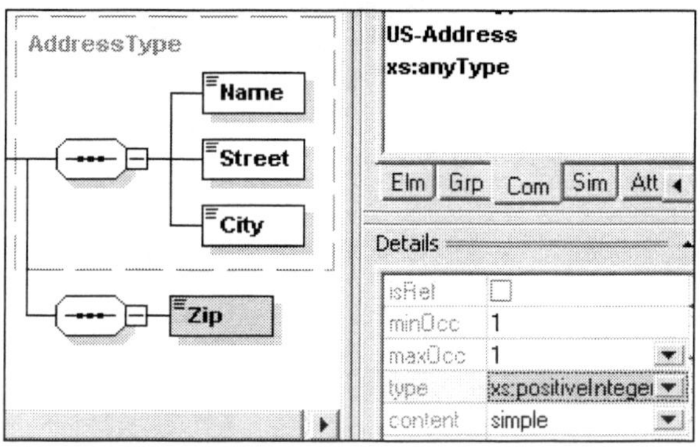

Creating reusable "simple type" elements
Simple type elements can also be made generic. In this case we want to make the State element reusable, so that an abbreviated version could also be included in address labels at a later time (GA for Georgia, for example).

To create reusable "simple type" elements:

1. Switch to the Schema overview (Display all Globals).
2. Click the **append** icon, select SimpleType, and enter "US-State" as the element name (Enter to confirm).
3. Select **xs:string** in the "**restr.**" value field of the Details entry helper.
   This completes the definition. This element can now be used in the US-Address definition.

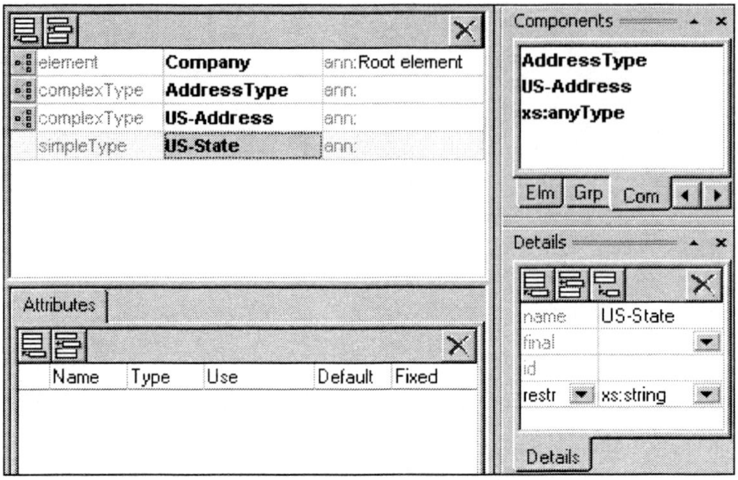

4. Click the US-Address component icon, then right click the lower sequence compositor and select **Add Child | Element**.
5. Enter "State" for the element name, and hit Enter.
6. Select (or enter) "US-State" from the "type" combo box, and hit Enter to confirm.

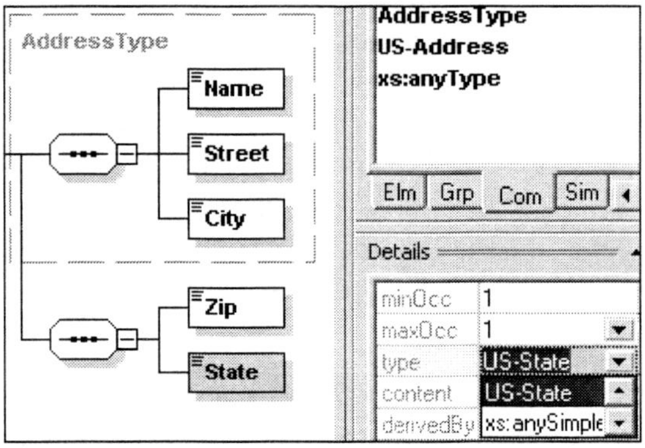

Please note:
Global simple types can only be created from the schema overview.

Creating the second Address template
Using the method described above, define the global complex type "**UK-Address**".

1. Create the global **complex type** "UK-Address", with the **base**="AddressType"
2. Add a new Postcode element to the content model of UK-Address.

Your UK-Address content model should finally look like this:

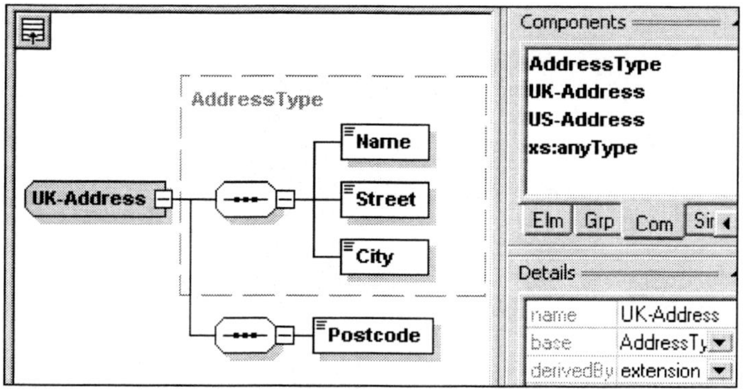

Please note:

Global definitions (global elements, complex types, etc.) can be moved or copied to other schemas visible in the schema overview, using drag and drop. You can of course, reposition definitions in the currently open schema. Right clicking a definition opens the context menu in which you can select the standard cut, copy, paste commands, to achieve the same thing.

The drag and drop method also allows you to move or copy **attributes** as well as **Identity constraints** between schemas.

References, attributes and enumerations

To finish off the schema definition we will make the Person element global, define specific element attributes, and limit the attribute selection.

To create a reference:

1. Switch to the Schema overview (Display all Globals).
2. Click the component icon of the **Company** element.
3. Right click the Person element, and select **Make Global | Element**.
   A small "link" icon appears in the Person element, showing that this element now references the globally declared "Person" element. The "**isRef**" check box in the Details entry helper is now active.

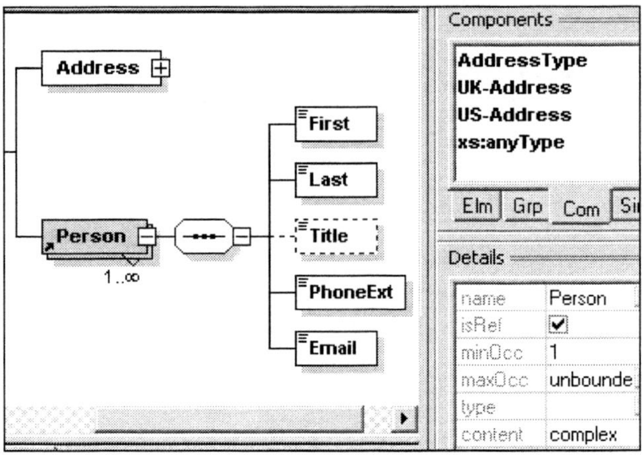

4. Click the "Display all Globals" icon to return to the schema overview.
   The Person element is now also visible in the component list, as well as in the "**Elm**" tab of the Component navigator. Click the Elm tab to see the global elements.

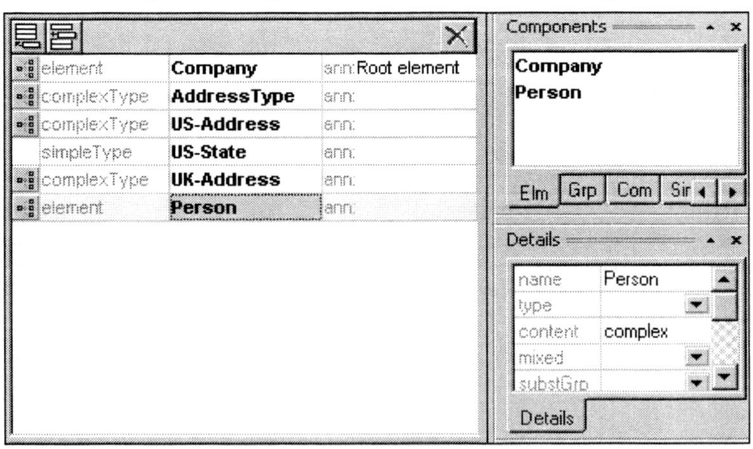

Please note:

Global declarations do not describe where an element is to be used in an XML document, they only describe what it contains. Global definitions have to be referenced from within a complex type, or another element, to determine their position in the XML document.

To define Element attributes:

1. Click the Person element to make it active.
2. Click the Append icon, in the top left of the **attributes** tab (the lower window of the schema overview), and select the "Attribute" entry.

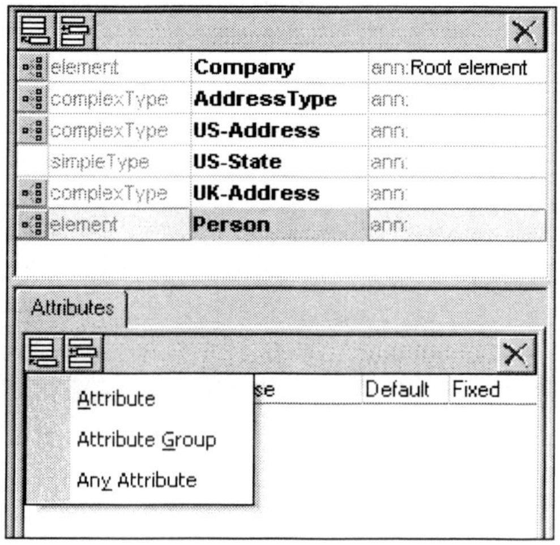

3. Enter "**Manager**" as the attribute name in Name field.
4. Use the **Type** combo box to select "xs:boolean".
5. Use the **Use** combo box to select "required".

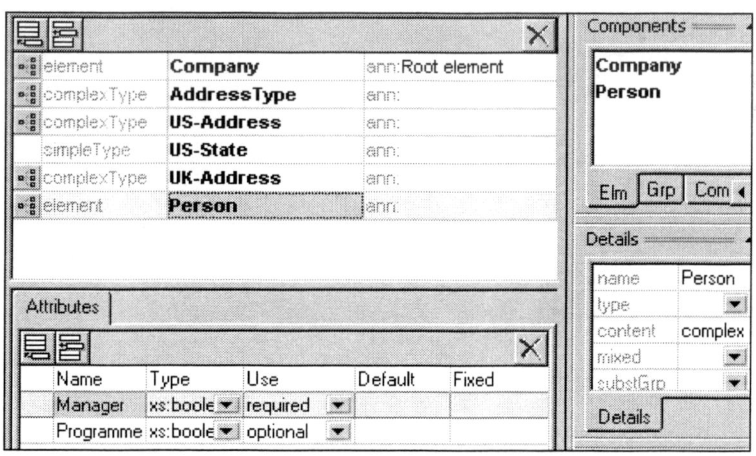

6. Use the same method to:
   Add a "Programmer" attribute in the Name field (type="xs:boolean"), and set its Use to "optional".

To limit the contents of an attribute (Enumerations):

1. Click the **Append** icon in the top left of the attribute window, and select the "**attribute**" entry.
2. Enter "**Degree**" as the attribute name, and select "xs:string" as the attribute type.
3. Click the **Enumerations** tab of the Facets entry helper.

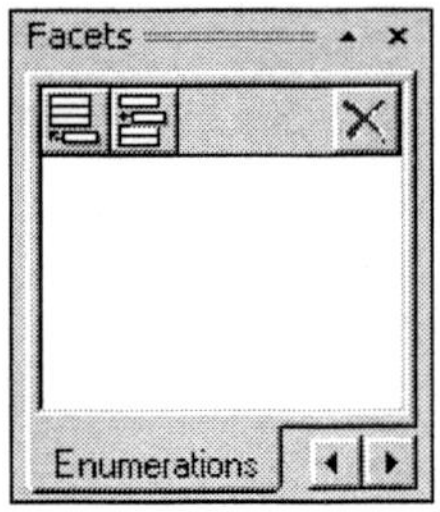

4. Click the Append icon  of the Enumerations tab and enter "BA", confirm with Enter.
5. Use the same method to add two more items to the enumerations list ("MA" and "Ph.D").

The finished schema should look like this:

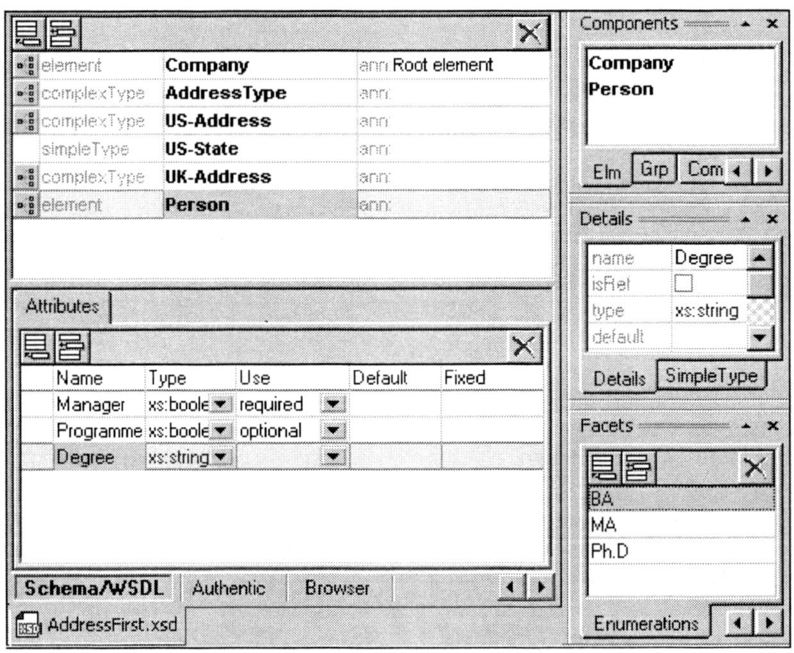

6. Select the menu command **File | Save as**, and save the file as **AddressLast.xsd**.

Please note:
Enumerations and patterns can be moved and copied between open schemas using drag and drop. This schema is available as '**AddressLast.xsd**' in the Tutorial folder.

Navigation shortcuts in schema documents

This section is designed to show you how you can navigate the Schema view efficiently.

Displaying the content model of any element:

- Select the **element type** you want to see by clicking the specific Component navigator **tab** e.g. Com(plex).

  Elm=global elements, Grp=element group, Com=Complex type, Sim=Simple type, Att=Attribute, AGrp=Attribute group. The Component navigator entries are independent of the content model currently visible in the main window.

- **Double click** the element name in the Com tab e.g. **UK-Address**.

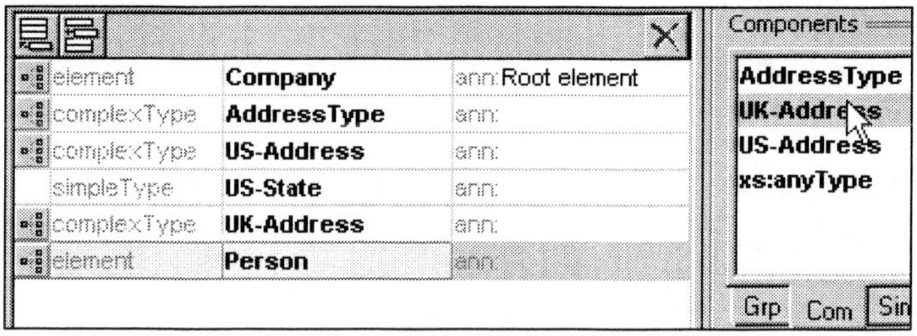

The content model of the UK-Address element is displayed. The specific settings are shown in the Details tab.

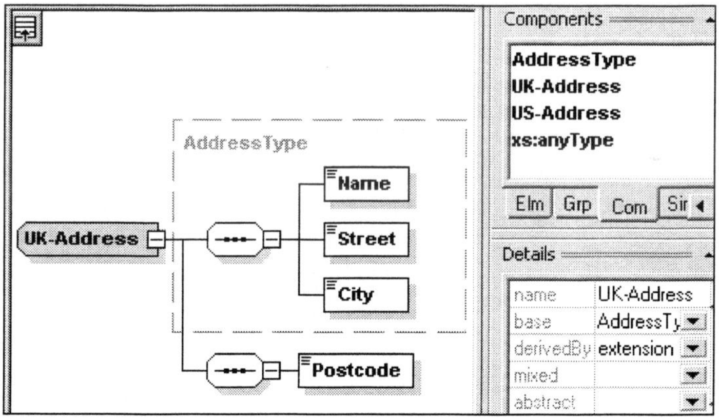

Go to "ElementType" definition:

E.g. While viewing the **Company** content model:

- Double clicking the *AddressType* **text** in the yellow box, takes you to the AddressType definition.

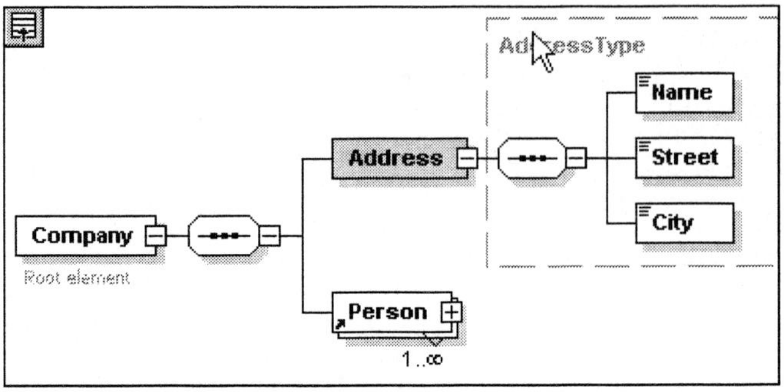

The AddressType definition:

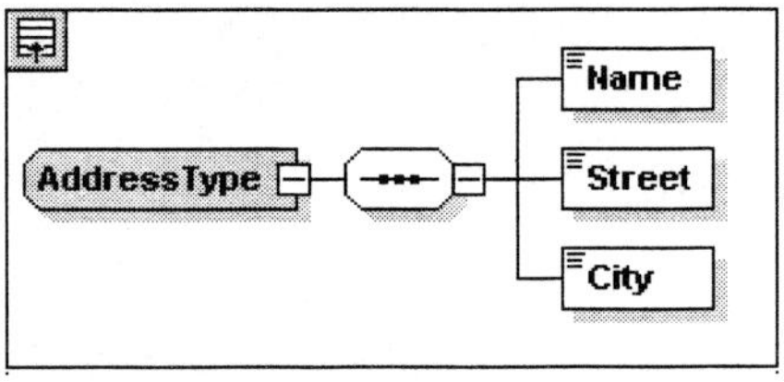

Go to element definition:

E.g. While viewing the **Company** content model:

- Press and hold down the **CTRL** keyboard key, and
- **Double click** on any element definition you want to see (here, the element **Last**).

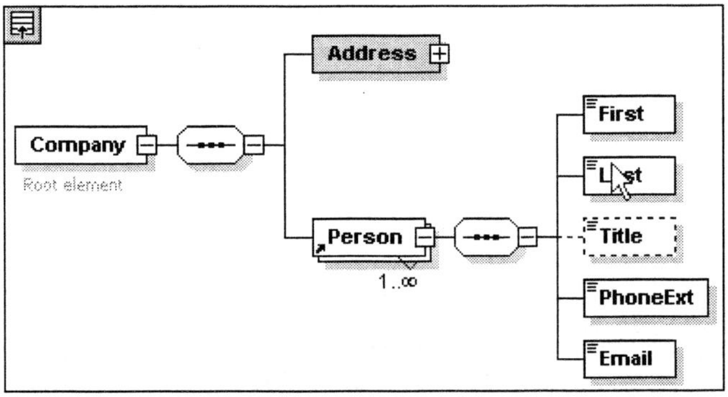

The element Last, which is a sub-element of the Person element, is displayed. The specific settings are shown in the Details tab.

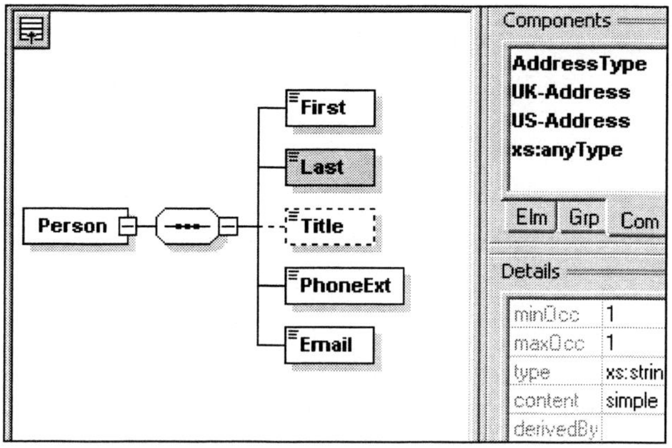
Components
AddressType
UK-Address
US-Address
xs:anyType
Elm
Grp
Com
Person
First
Last
Title
PhoneExt
Email
Details
minOcc
1
maxOcc
1
type
xs:strin
content
simple
derivedBy

Creating an XML document

Goal of this section:
To create a new XML document and use the various STYLEVISION 2004 views and intelligent editing capabilities, to rapidly enter and validate data.

This will be achieved by:

- Creating a new XML document based on the **AddressLast** schema
- Making **elementType** definitions available to an XML document
- Adding elements using **intelligent entry helpers** in the Text and Grid view
- Copying **XML data to Excel**, adding new data there, and pasting it back to STYLEVISION 2004 (Enhanced Grid-, and Database/Table view)
- **Sorting** table data by Last name in the **Database/Table** view
- **Validating** the XML document
- **Updating** the **schema definition** to allow for three digit phone extensions

Functions (and their icons) in this section:

File | New, creates a new type of XML file.

View | Text View, switches to the text view.

View | Enhanced Grid view, switches to the Enhanced Grid view.

XML | Table | Display as Table, displays recurring elements and attributes in table form. Switches between the Table and Enhanced Grid view.

Expand displays sub elements, in the Enhanced Grid view.

Checks for well-formedness. Hotkey: **F7**.

Validate the XML file against the associated DTD or Schema. Hotkey **F8**.

Opens the associated DTD or Schema file.

Creating and completing a new XML file

To create a new XML document:

1. Select the menu option **File | New**, and select the **.xml XML Document** entry from the dialog, then confirm with OK.

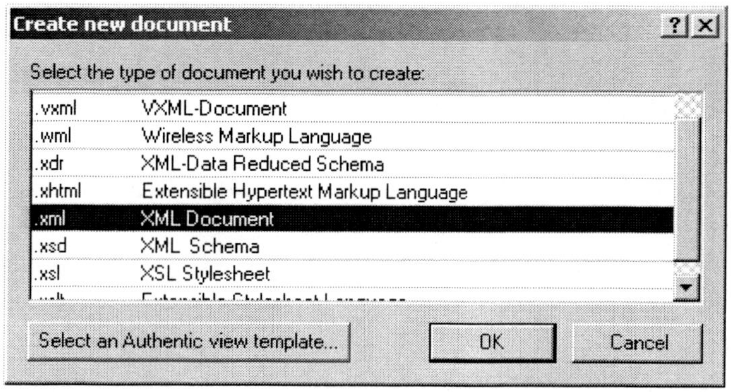

A prompt appears, asking if you want to base the XML document on a DTD or Schema.

2. Click the **Schema** radio button, and confirm with OK.

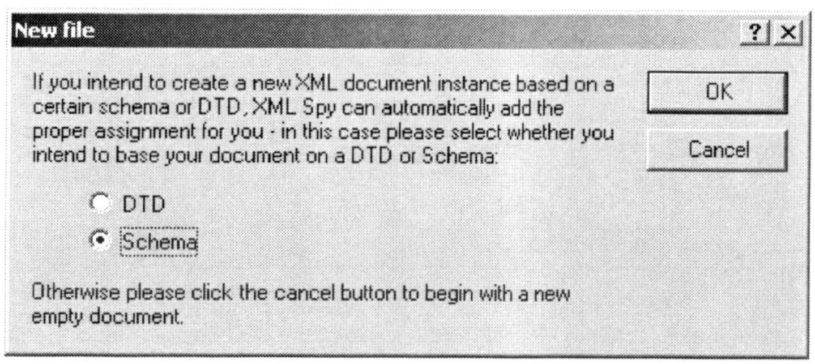

A further dialog appears, asking you to select the schema file your XML document is to be based on.

3. Use the Browse or Window buttons to find the schema file, in our case the **AddressLast** schema, and confirm the selection with OK.

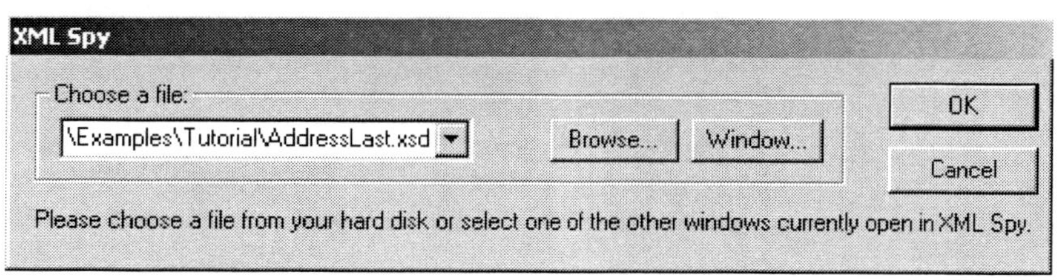

An XML document containing the main elements defined by the schema, opens in the main window. XML documents are automatically opened in the Grid View.

Please note:

STYLEVISION 2004 tries to find the root element of a schema automatically. The

"Select a root element" dialog box is opened, if it is unclear which is the root element. You can then select the root element manually.

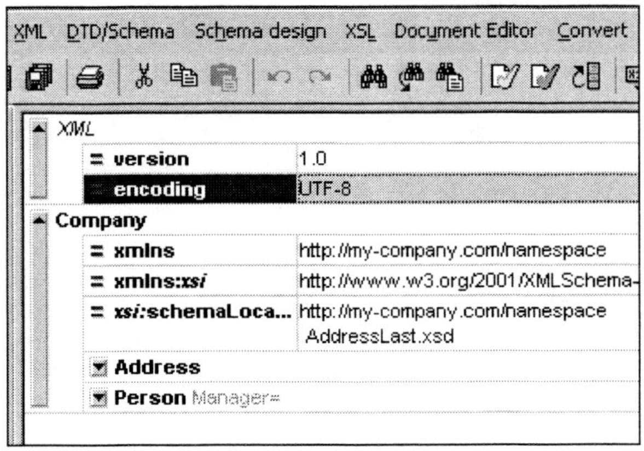

4. Click on any element to deselect the data.
5. Click on the icon next to Address, to view the Address sub-elements.

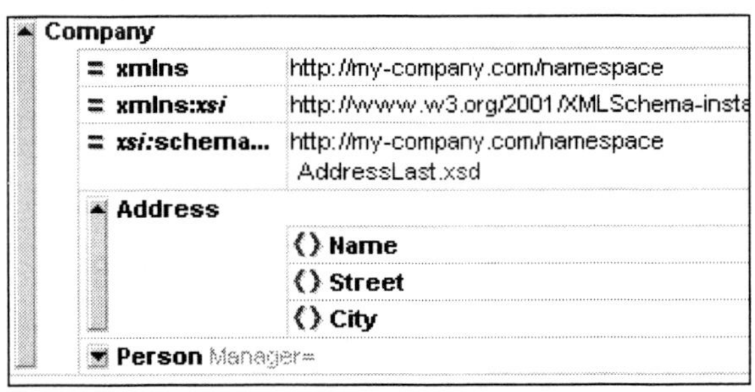

Making elementType definitions available in XML documents

The Address elements we see in the grid view are those that were defined by the global complex type "AddressType". We would, however, like to access the specific AddressTypes we defined: UK- and US-Address.

1. Right click the **Name** element, and select **Insert | Attribute** from the context menu. An attribute field is added to the Address element, and a popup containing **xsi:type** automatically opens.

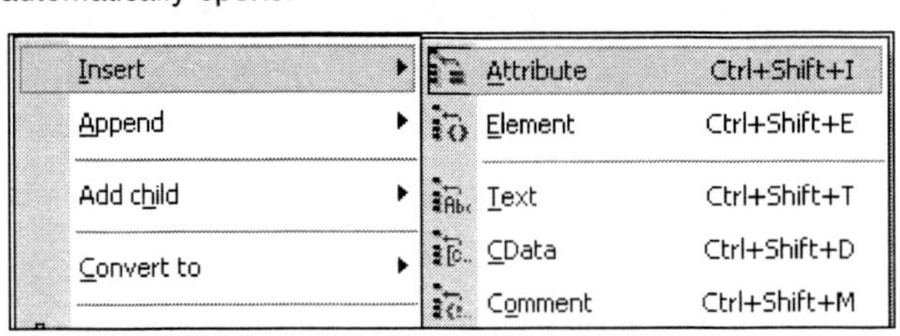

2. Hit the "Tab" key to move into the next field.
3. Select **US-Address** from the drop-down list, and confirm with Enter.

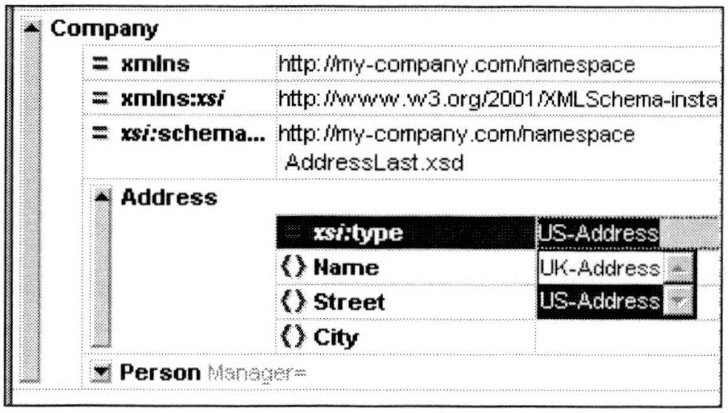

Please note:

The ***xsi*** prefix allows you to use special XML Schema related commands in your XML document instance. Please see the W3C website at http://www.w3.org/TR/2001/REC-xmlschema-0-20010502 for more information.

Entering (and deleting) data

1. Double click in the **Name** value field (or use the arrow keys) and enter "US dependency", confirm with Enter.

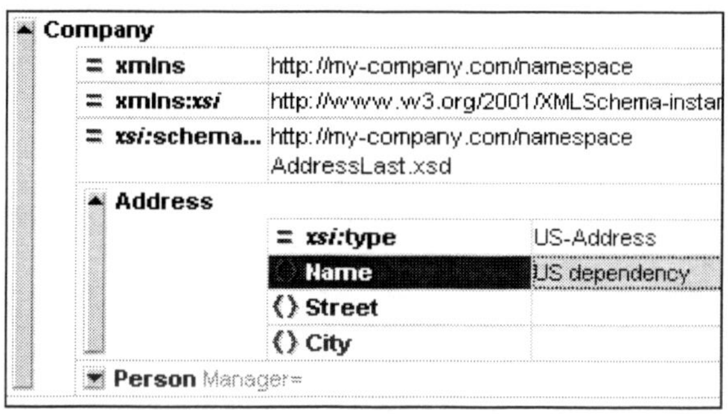

2. Use the same method to enter a **Street** and **City** name (e.g. Noble Ave. and Dallas).
3. Click the **Person** element, and hit the "**Del**" key to delete it (we will add it again in a few moments in the Text view!).
4. Click on any Address element to deselect the elements.
   Your XML document should look like this:

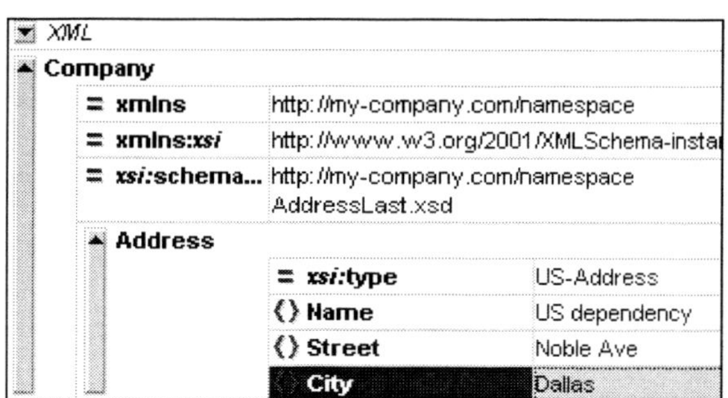

Editing in Text- and Grid view

STYLEVISION 2004 Text view

When it comes down to low-level work, the Text view of STYLEVISION 2004 is most suitable for editing any type of XML files in textual or source code form, and provides **intelligent editing** capabilities if you are working with an XML document based on a DTD or XML Schema.

Viewing and entering data in the Text view

1. Select the menu item **View | Text view**, or click on the Text tab.
   You now see the XML document in its raw text form (with syntax coloring).

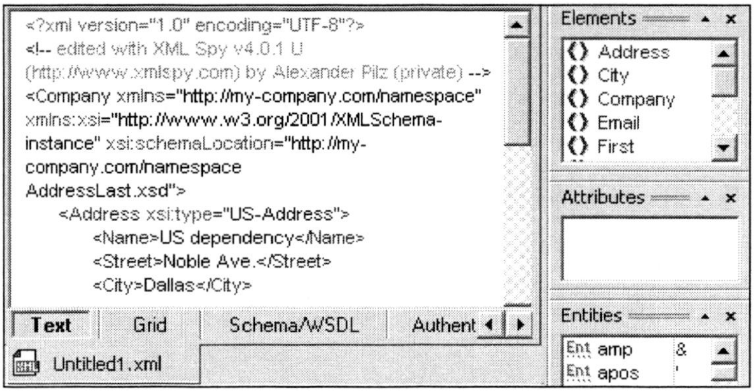

2. Place the text cursor after the </Address> | **end tag**, and hit Enter to add a new line.
3. Enter the "less than" angle bracket < at this position.

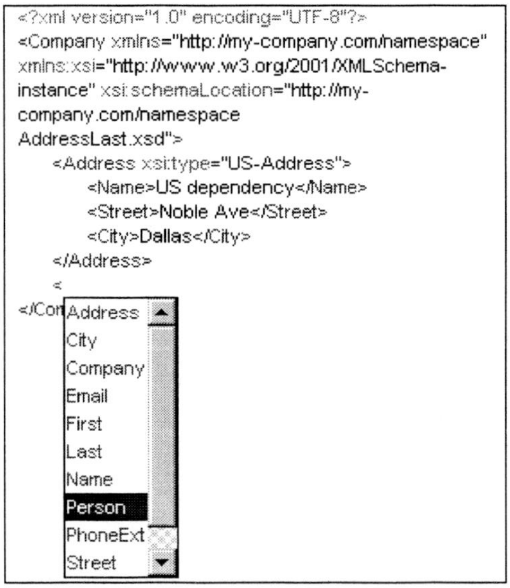

4. A drop-down list appears; select the **Person** entry (Note: this list contains all the predefined elements).
   The element name "Person" as well as the attribute "Manager", are inserted.

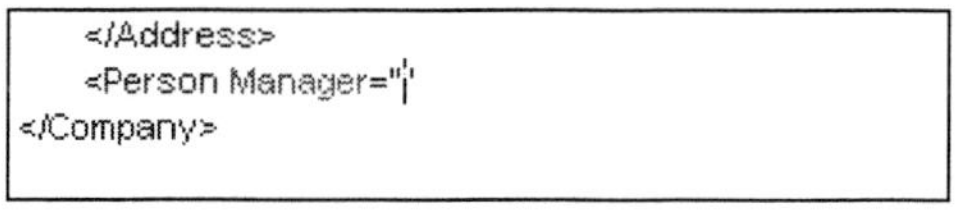

5. Enter the letter "**t**" and hit Enter.

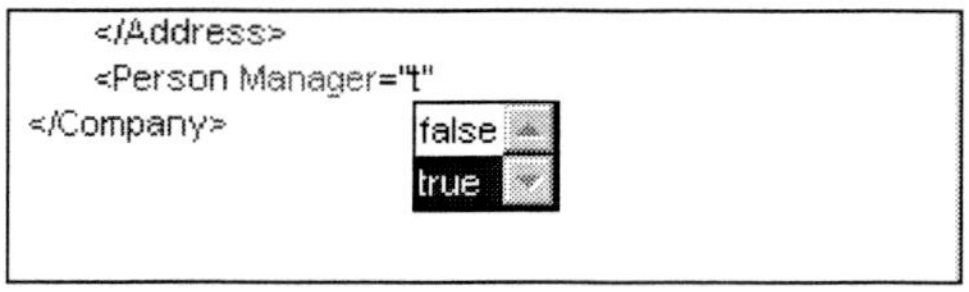

This opens a drop down list where "true" is highlighted. Enter, inserts the value (true) at the cursor position.

6. Move the cursor to the end of the line (End key), and hit the space bar.
This opens the drop-down list again. There are now fewer entries available in the list; "Manager" is grayed out in the Attribute entry helper.

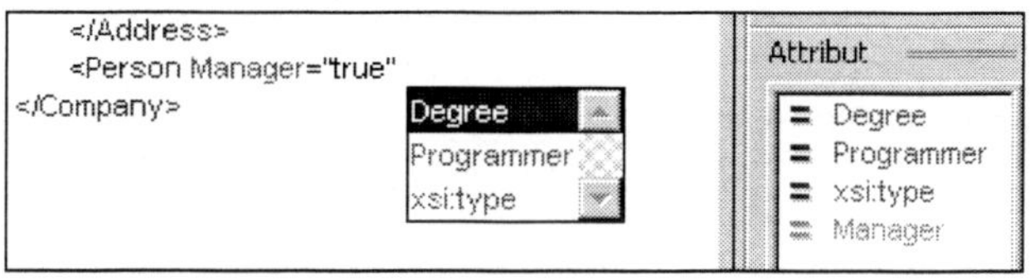

7. Select "Degree" with the Down arrow key, and hit Enter.
This opens another list box from which you can select one of the predefined enumerations (BA, MA or Ph.D).

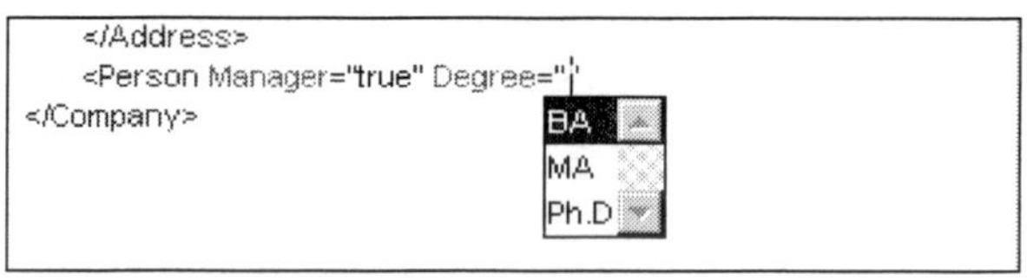

8. Select "BA" with the Down arrow key (confirm with Enter), move the cursor to the end of the line (End key), and hit the space bar. Manager and Degree are now grayed out in the Attribute entry helper.

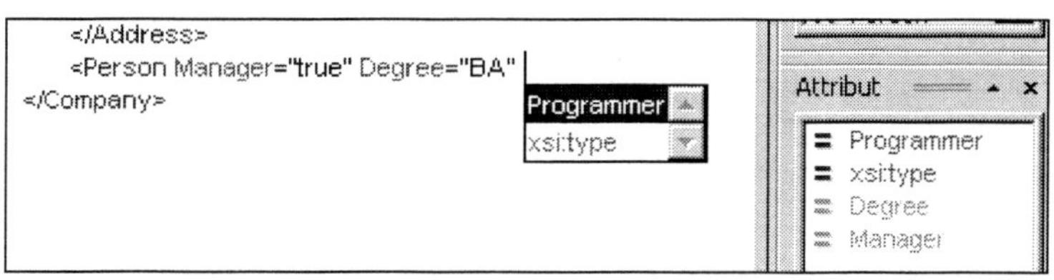

9. Select "Programmer" with the Down arrow key, and hit Enter.

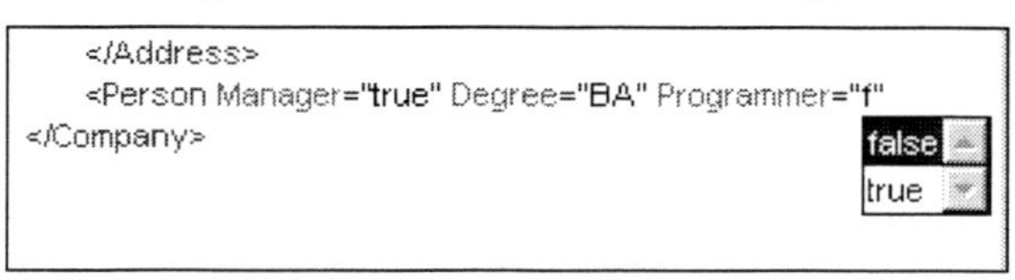

10. Enter a "**f**" character and hit Enter.

11. Move the cursor to the end of the line (End key), and enter the "greater than" angle bracket >.

```
<?xml version="1.0" encoding="UTF-8"?>
<Company xmlns="http://my-company.com/namespace"
xmlns:xsi="http://www.w3.org/2001/XMLSchema-instance"
xsi:schemaLocation="http://my-company.com/namespace
AddressLast.xsd">
    <Address xsi:type="US-Address">
        <Name>US dependency</Name>
        <Street>Noble Ave</Street>
        <City>Dallas</City>
    </Address>
    <Person Manager="true" Degree="BA" Programmer="false">
        <First></First>
        <Last></Last>
        <PhoneExt></PhoneExt>
        <Email></Email>
    </Person>
</Company>
```

STYLEVISION 2004 automatically inserts all the Person element tags. Each element is supplied with start and end tags.

You could now enter the Person data here in the Text view, but why do so? The Enhanced Grid view is a lot more comfortable, and contains a special view enabling recurring data to be presented in tabular form: the Database/Table view.

Enhanced Grid view

- Select the menu item **View | Enhanced Grid View,** or click the Grid tab. The Person attributes (and data) entered in the Text view, are also visible in the Enhanced Grid view.

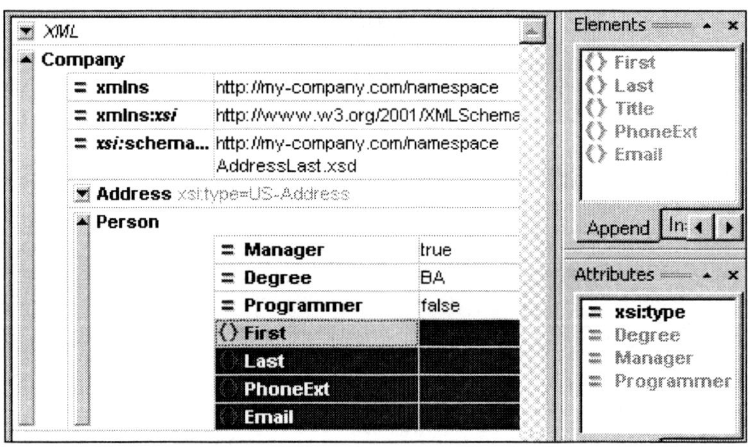

Validating and entering data

At this point let's check if the document is well-formed and valid, there might still be work to do.

To check for well-formedness:

1. Select the menu option **XML | Check well-formedness** or hit the **F7** key.
   A message appears at the bottom of the main window declaring that the document is well formed. Click OK to confirm and close the message.

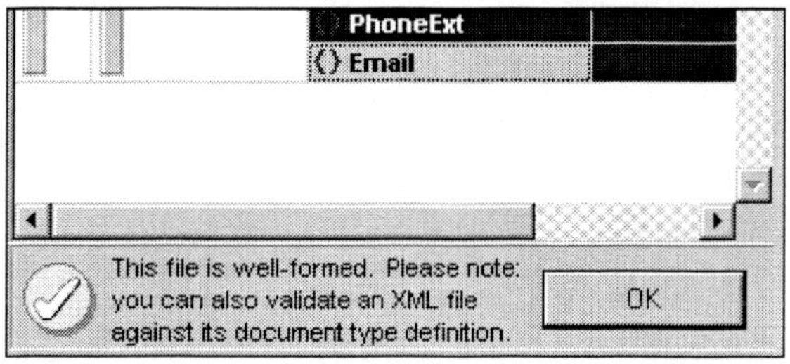

Being well-formed, means that the XML document **syntax** is correct (i.e. there is a root element, each start tag has a corresponding end tag, all elements are nested correctly etc.).

This check does not check against a schema file (or any other external file). Element sequence or element content are not checked either.

To check for validity:

1. Select the menu option **XML | Validate** or hit the **F8** key.
   An **error message** appears: "This file is not valid: Mandatory elements expected after 'City' (Zip, State).
   The error message describes in detail what is currently wrong with our XML document.

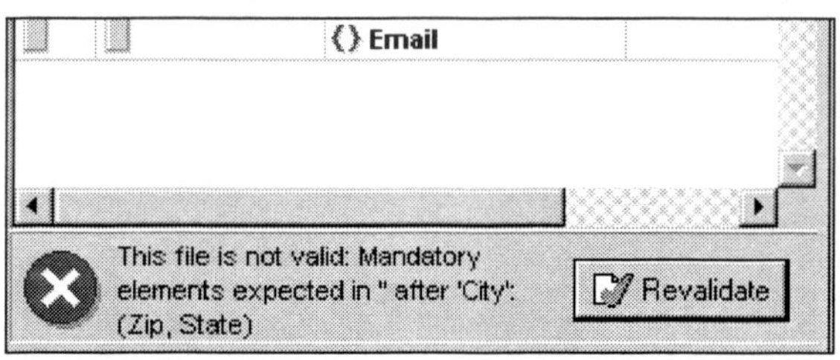

Fixing the invalid document (intelligent help):
At this point the element which is the "cause" of the error message is highlighted (City). Take note of the **Element entry helper** (top right). The Zip element is prefixed by an exclamation mark. This is the symbol for a **mandatory** element, and means that the US-Address element must contain the Zip sub-element.

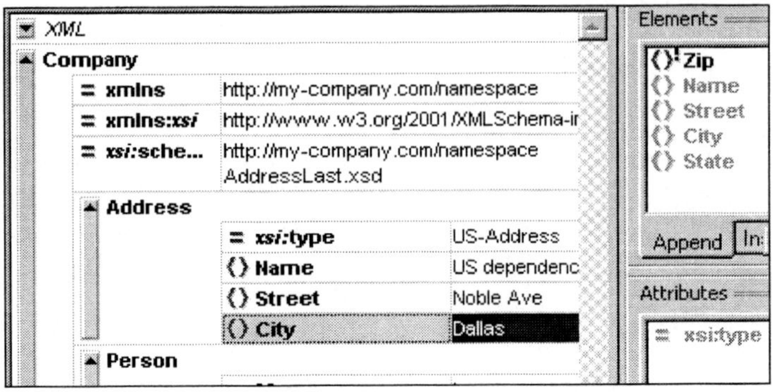

1. Double click the **!Zip** element in the **Element entry helper**.
   This inserts the Zip element under the City element (Append tab is active by default).
2. Hit the **Tab** key, enter the Zip Code of the State (04812), and confirm with Enter.
   The Element entry helper now contains the **!State** entry, which is also a mandatory element and must also appear with the Zip element.

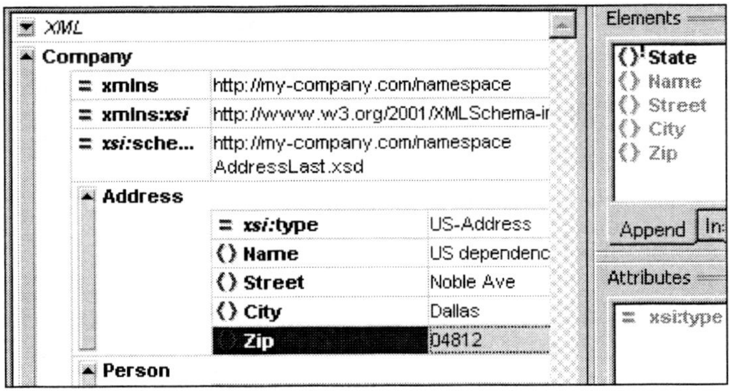

3. Double click the **!State** element, hit the Tab key and enter the name of the state (e.g. Texas), confirm with Enter.
   The Element entry helper now contains only grayed-out elements. This shows that all the required Address sub-elements have been inserted.

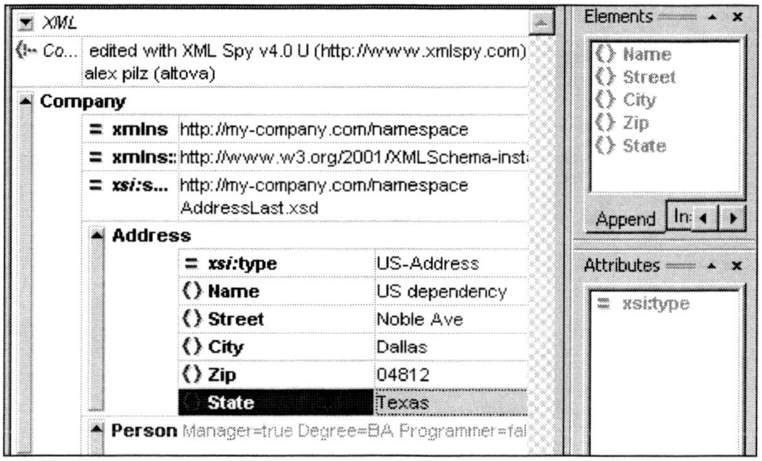

Filling in the rest of the XML document data & revalidating

1. Click the empty element content field (right of element name) of the element **First**, enter the persons first name (e.g. Fred), and hit the Enter key.

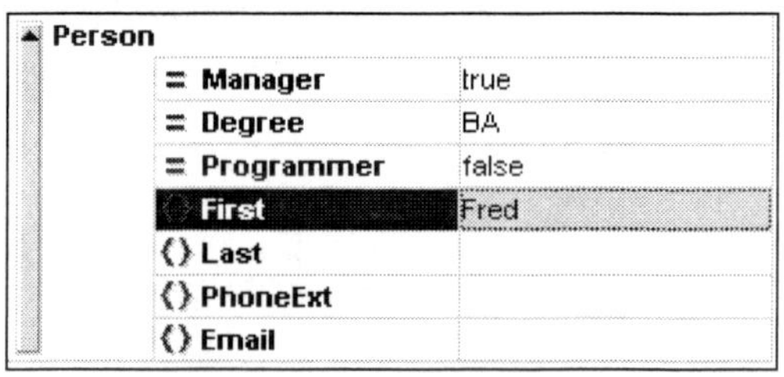

2. Hit the Down arrow key, and fill in the next field, **Last** (e.g. Smith)
3. Use the same method to enter PhoneExt (e.g. 22) and the persons e-mail address (e.g. smith@work.com). Your XML document should look like this:

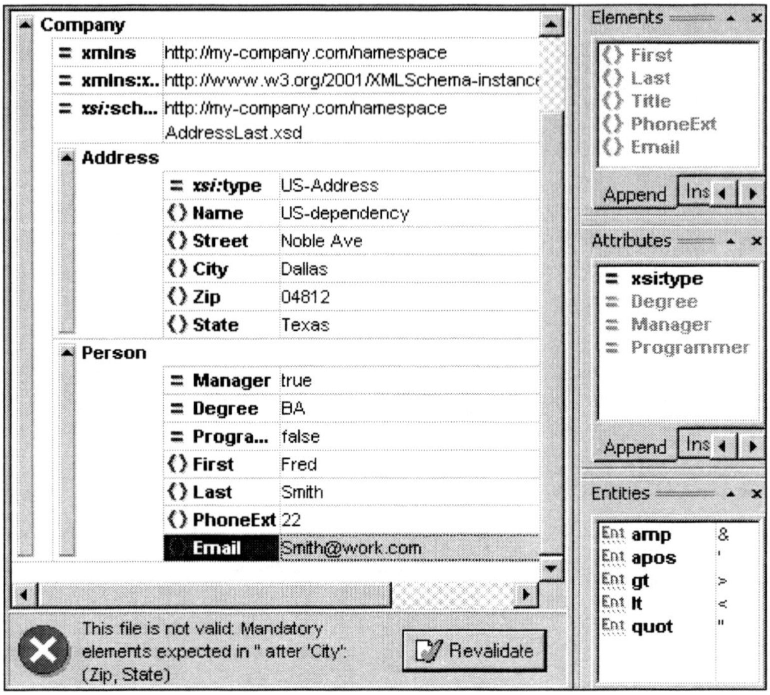

4. Click the **Revalidate** button to check if the document is valid.
   The "This file is valid" message appears. The XML document is now valid against its schema. Click OK to confirm and close the message.

   Being valid, means that the XML document adheres to the assigned schema i.e. the elements and the sequence they appear in is correct, as well as the element "contents" and their attributes.

5. Select the menu option **File | Save** and name the XML document (e.g. **CompanyFirst.xml**)

This XML document is available as 'CompanyFirst.xml' in the Tutorial folder.

Please note:
An XML document does not have to be valid in order to save it. Saving an invalid document causes a prompt to appear which then allows you to select "**Save anyway**", the document is then saved in its current state.

Manipulating data - Entry helpers

At this point we want to enter more person data in our XML document. STYLEVISION 2004 incorporates a special view (within the Enhanced Grid view), which allows you to enter data in tabular form - the **Database/Table view**.

Inserting elements and attributes (intelligent entry help):
We now want to add a new Person element to the document, as well as define specific person attributes.

1. Click the gray **side bar** to the left of the Address element, to collapse the Address elements.
2. Click on or below, the "**Person**" element text in the grid view.
   This marks the Person and all its sub-elements. Notice that **!Person** is now available in the Element entry helper.

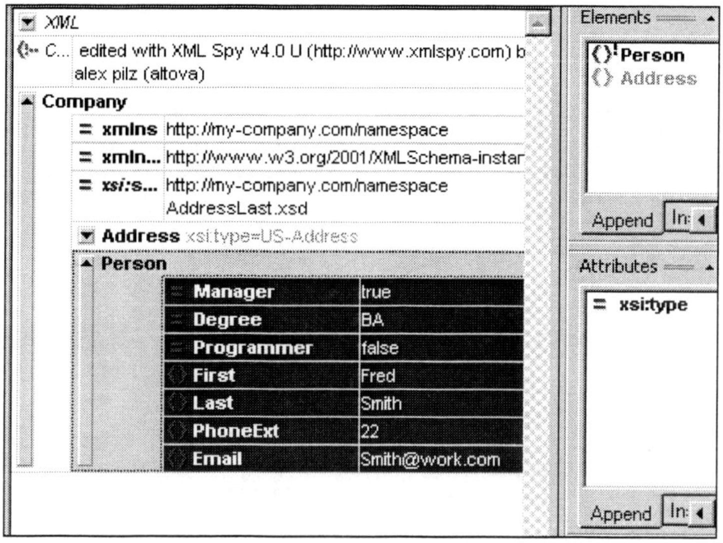

3. Double click the **!Person** element in the Element entry helper (Append tab active).
   A new Person element with all **required** sub-elements is appended.
4. Click on the **Manager** attribute of the new Person element. Notice the attributes available in the **Attribute entry helper**.

   The underlying schema document delivers information to the Entry helpers, specifically the elements or attributes that can be inserted at specific points in the XML document.

   Clicking the Update Entry Helpers icon, refreshes the Entry helper contents.

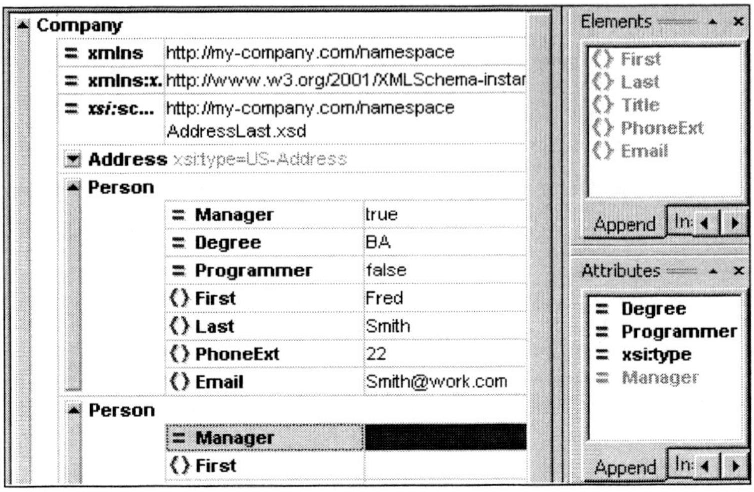

The "Manager" attribute has been **grayed out**, as it already exists in the Person element. Looking in the **Info** window, you can see all the Manager attribute information: Datatype=boolean, Occurrence=required (which means mandatory).

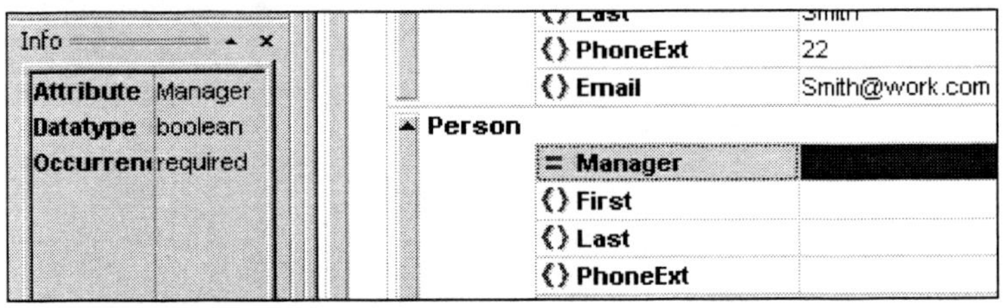

5. Double click the **Programmer** attribute in the Attribute entry helper.
   This inserts an empty **Programmer attribute** after the Manager attribute (append tab is active).

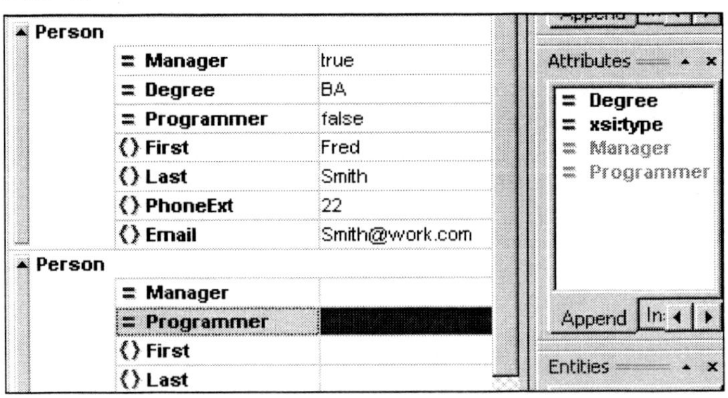

The Programmer attribute is now grayed out in the Attribute entry helper.
We could continue entering data here, but let's be more efficient and activate the Database/Table view.

Database/Table view

Database/Table view:

The Database/Table view is available wherever the Enhanced Grid view can be activated, and can be used when editing any type of XML file - XML, XSD, XSL etc.

Advantages:

- Drag and drop column headers
- Sort column (table) data using the menu command **XML | Table | Ascending Sort**
- Append (or insert) rows using the menu command **XML | Table | Insert Row**.
- Copy and paste **structured data** to and from third party products
- Intelligent entry help

Activating the Database/Table view:

1. Click on or near, Person element text in the grid view (this marks the person element).

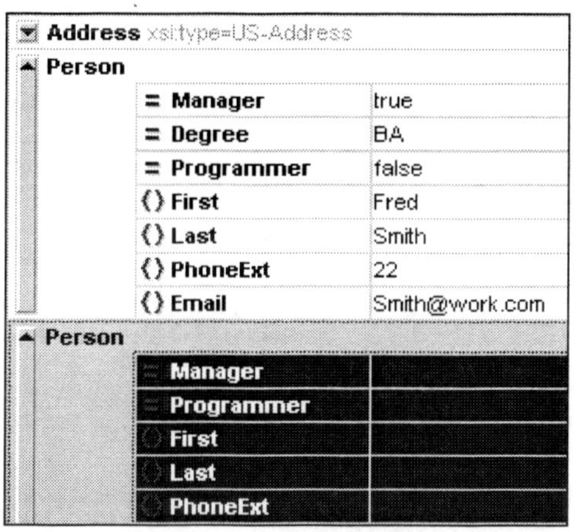

2. Select the menu option **XML | Table | Display as table**, or click the Display as table icon.
   The Person elements have now been combined into a single table. The Element and Attribute names are now the column headers, and the element contents (values) are now the rows of the table.
3. Select the menu option **View | Optimal widths**, or click the Optimal widths icon, to optimize the table view.

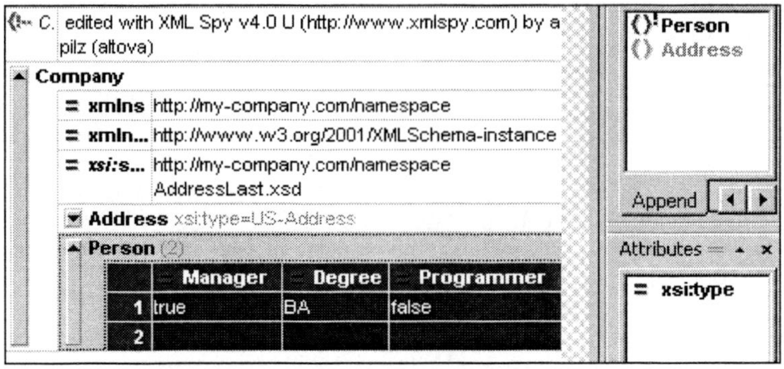

Please note:

The element and attribute entry helpers also function in the Database/Table view. The element entry helper now displays the mandatory **!Person** element; double clicking it would add a new row to the table.

4. Double click in the "Manager" cell of row 2, and select "false". Use the Tab key to get to the next cells, and select the following data: Degree=MA, Programmer=true, First=Alfred, Last=Aldrich, PhoneExt=33 and EMail=Aldrich@work.com

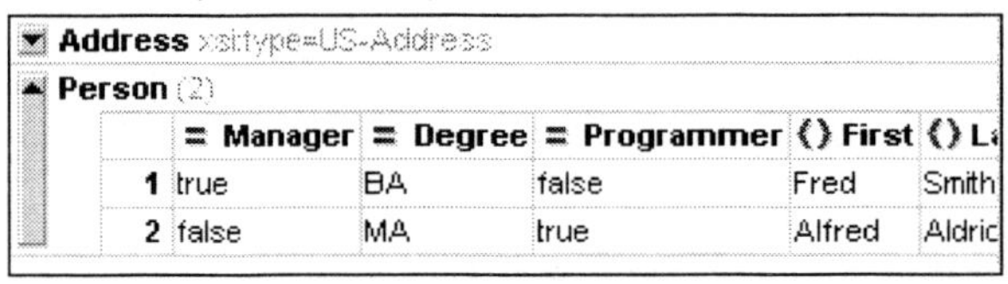

Copying XML data to and from third party products

STYLEVISION 2004 allows you to easily copy data to and from third party products. The copied data can be used within STYLEVISION 2004 as well as third-party products, enabling you to transfer XML data to spreadsheet-like applications (e.g. Microsoft Excel).

Copying XML data to and from Excel:

1. Click on the row label 1, hold down the CTRL key and click on row label 2. This marks both rows of the table.

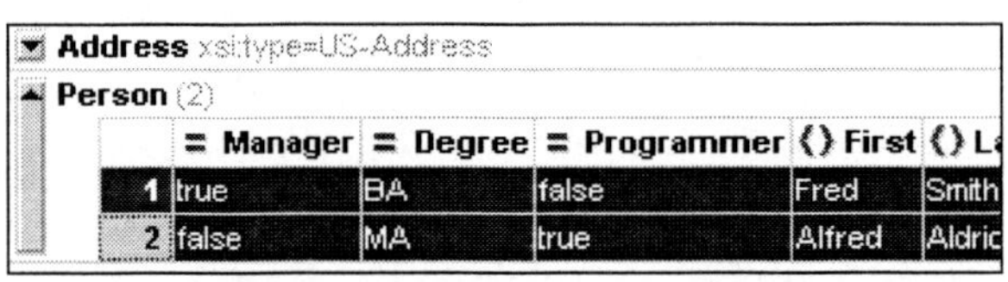

2. Select the menu option **Edit | Copy as Structured text.**
   The "Copy as Structured Text" command, copies elements to the clipboard as they appear on screen.
3. Switch to Excel and **paste** the XML data in an Excel worksheet.

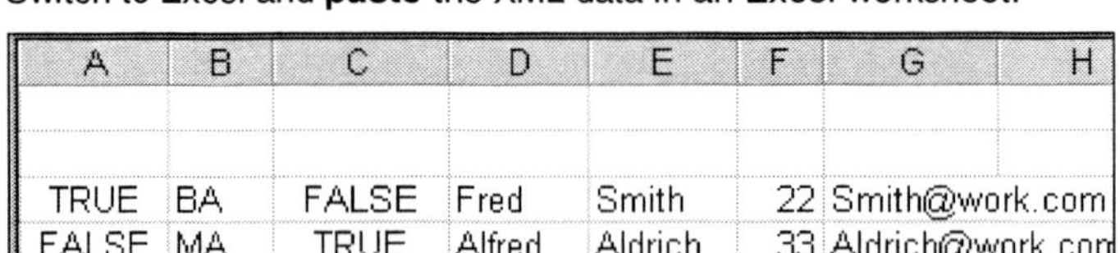

4. Enter a new row of data in Excel. Make sure that you enter a three digit number for the PhoneExt element (e.g. 444).

A	B	C	D	E	F	G	H
TRUE	BA	FALSE	Fred	Smith	22	Smith@work.com	
FALSE	MA	TRUE	Alfred	Aldrich	33	Aldrich@work.com	
TRUE	Ph.D	FALSE	Colin	Coletti	444	Coletti@work.com	

5. Mark the table data in Excel, select **Edit | Copy**, and switch back to STYLEVISION 2004.
6. Click in the top left cell of the table data in STYLEVISION 2004, and select **Edit | Paste**.

Address xsi:type=US-Address
Person (3)

	= Manager	= Degree	= Programmer	() First	() Last	() Pho
1	TRUE	BA	FALSE	Fred	Smith	22
2	FALSE	MA	TRUE	Alfred	Aldrich	33
3	TRUE	Ph.D	FALSE	Colin	Coletti	444

The updated table data is now visible in the table.

7. Change the uppercase boolean values, "TRUE/FALSE", to lowercase "true/false" using the menu option **Edit | Replace** (Hotkey CTRL+H).

Sorting data in the Database/Table view

The Database/Table view allows you to sort your XML table data by any column you wish. In this case we want to sort our table by last names.

1. Click on the **Last** column header. This marks the whole column.

Address xsi:type=US-Address
Person (3)

	= Manager	= Degree	= Programmer	() First	() Last	() Phone
1	true	BA	false	Fred	Smith	22
2	false	MA	true	Alfred	Aldrich	33
3	true	Ph.D	false	Colin	Coletti	444

2. Select the menu option **XML | Table | Ascending sort,** or click on the "Ascending sort" icon.
The column and **whole table** are now been sorted alphabetically (the column remains marked).

Address xsi:type=US-Address
Person (3)

	= Manager	= Degree	= Programmer	() First	() Last	() Phone
1	false	MA	true	Alfred	Aldrich	33
2	true	Ph.D	false	Colin	Coletti	444
3	true	BA	false	Fred	Smith	22

This sorting procedure affects your data at source level. (Click the Text tab if you want to see the changes there.)

3. Select the menu option **XML | Validate**, or hit the **F8** key.
   An **error message** appears: "This file is not valid: Value does not match facet **maxInclusive="99"** in element **'PhoneExt'**.

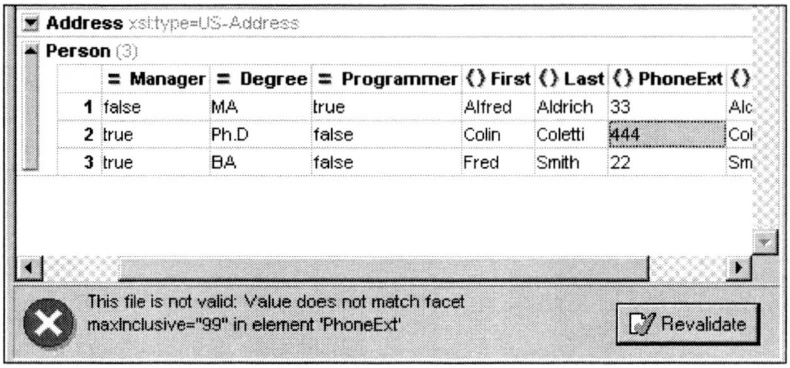

   The offending element is automatically marked in the Database/table view. We need more telephone extensions!

Updating a schema definition

At this point that we realize that two digit phone extensions are definitely not enough, and that we would like to allow for three digits. To do this we have to make a change to the underlying schema document.

1. Select the menu option **DTD/Schema | Go to definition** or click the "Go to definition" icon.
   The associated schema document, in this case **AddressLast.xsd**, is opened in the Schema overview.

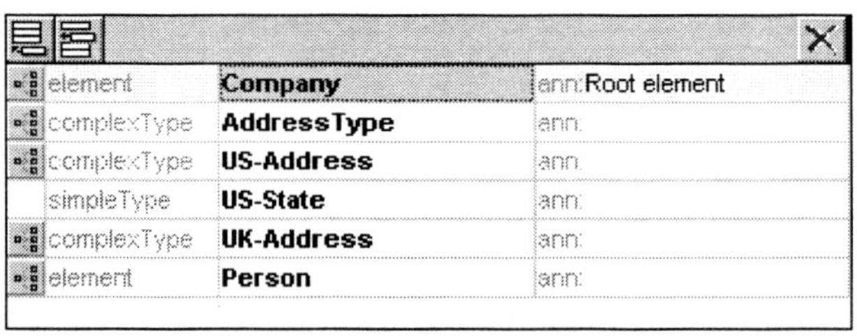

2. Click the "component" icon of the global **Person** element, and then click the PhoneExt element. You can now see the facet data in the facets tab.

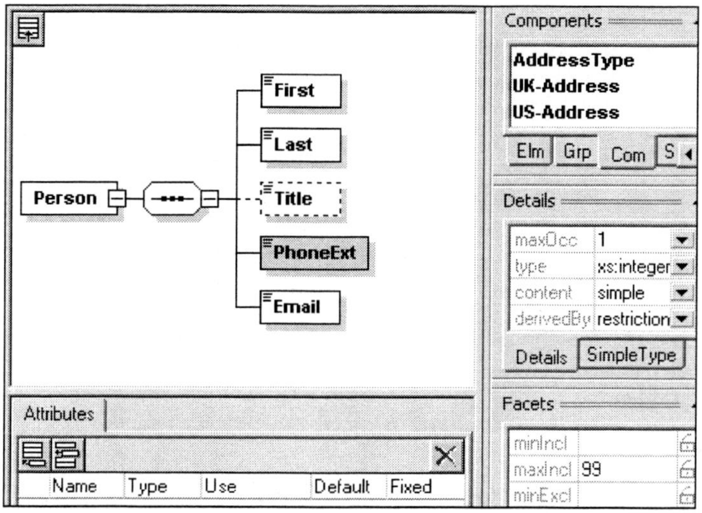

3. Click the "**maxIncl**" cell containing the facet data, enter **999**, and confirm with Enter.

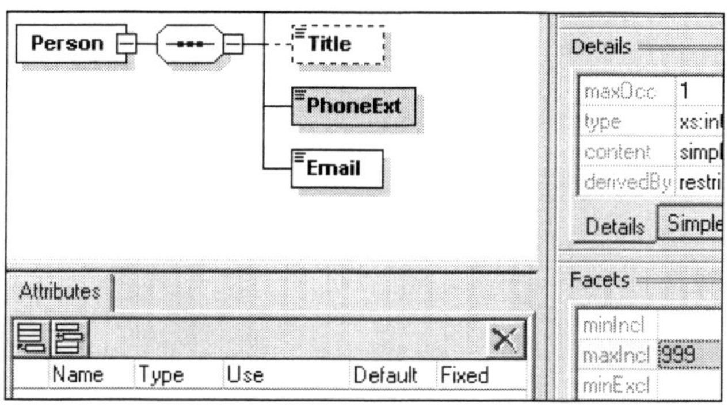

4. Hit CTRL+TAB to switch back to the XML document.
5. Click the "**Revalidate**" button to revalidate the XML document.

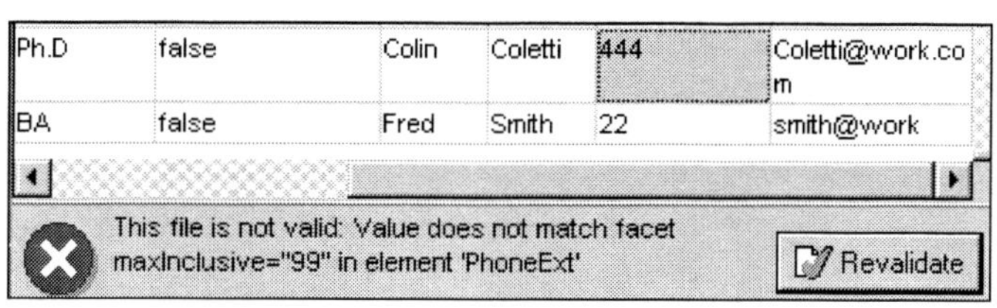

The "This file is valid" message appears. The XML document now conforms to the changed schema definition!

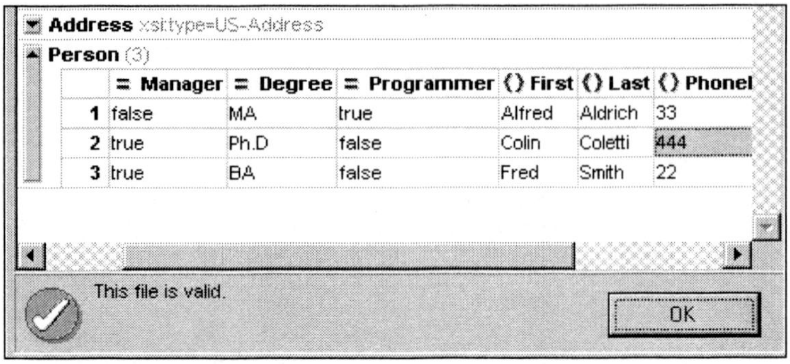

6. Select the menu option **File | Save As...** and name the XML document (e.g. **CompanyLast.xml**).
7. Hit CTRL+TAB to switch back to the schema document, and save the schema document.

   The XML document is available as 'CompanyLast.xml' in the Tutorial folder.

XSL Transformation

Goal of this section:
To generate a Company HTML document which can then be posted on the corporate website.

This will be achieved by:

- **Assigning** a predefined Company.**xsl** file to the XML document
- Using the XSL file to **transform** the XML file into an HTML document

Functions (and their icons) in this section:

XSL | Assign XSL, assigns an XSL file to an XML document.
XSL | Go to XSL, opens the XSL file referenced by the XML document.

XSL | XSL Transformation, transforms the XML document(s) into the files specified by the XSL Transformation document, in this case into an HTML file.
Hotkey: **F10**.

Please note:
If you encounter a problem while generating the HTML file, you only see the table header and no XML data, please download and install the **Microsoft XML Core Services (MSXML 4.0)** (649 KB) from the component download center on our website.

Transforming XML to HTML

To assign an XSL file to the CompanyLast XML file:

1. Click the **CompanyLast.xml** tab on the main window, to make it the active document.
2. Select the menu option **XSL | Assign XSL**.
3. Click the Browse button, select the **Company.xsl** file, and confirm with Open.

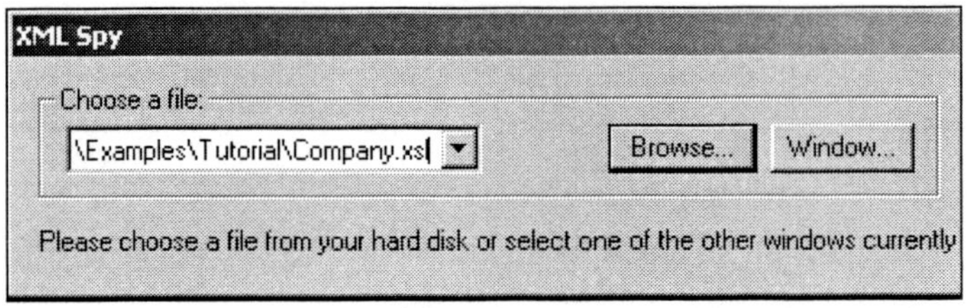

4. Click the OK button to assign the XSL file to the XML document.

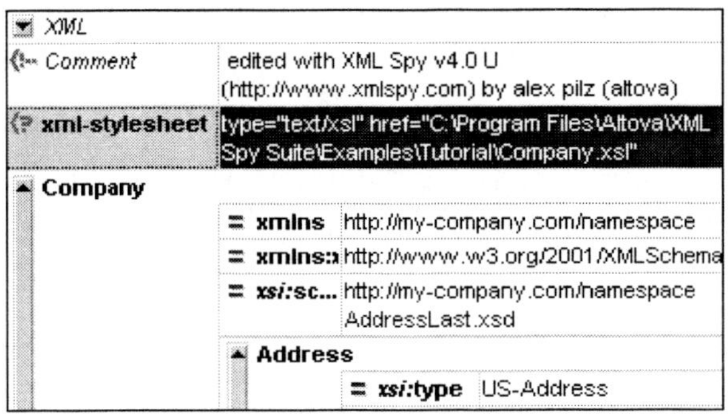

A XML-stylesheet reference is placed in the XML document.

To transform the XML document into HTML:

1. Select the menu option **XSL | XSL Transformation** or click the icon (Hotkey: **F10**)
   This creates a new document in the **Browser view** with the name **XSL Output.html**. It shows the Company data in one block down the left, and the Person data in tabular form below.

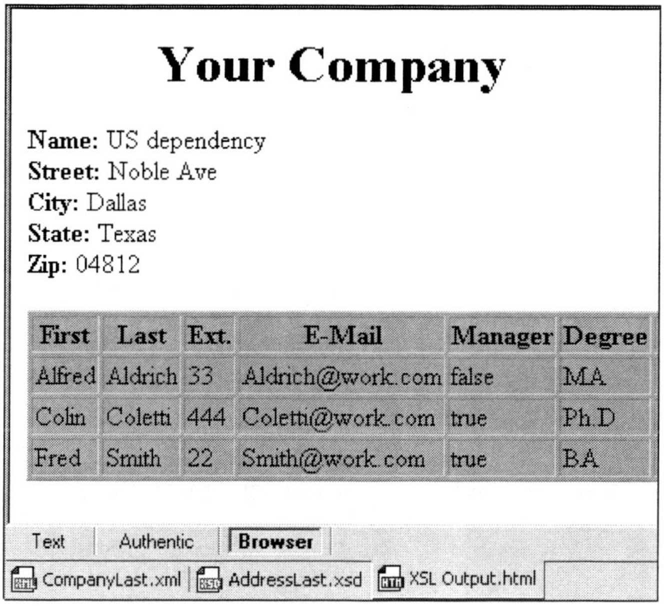

Changing the output of the HTML file:
You can change the appearance/output of the HTML file by editing the underlying XSL file. In this case, we want to change the table background color from lime to yellow.

1. Click the **CompanyLast.xml** tab to make it the active document.
2. Select the menu option **XSL | Go to XSL**.

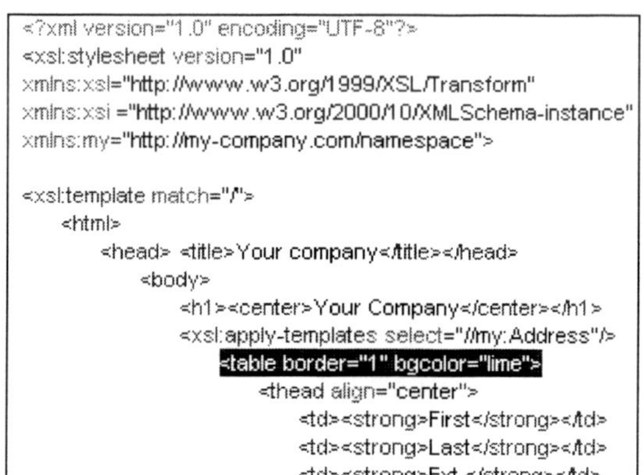

```
<?xml version="1.0" encoding="UTF-8"?>
<xsl:stylesheet version="1.0"
xmlns:xsl="http://www.w3.org/1999/XSL/Transform"
xmlns:xsi ="http://www.w3.org/2000/10/XMLSchema-instance"
xmlns:my="http://my-company.com/namespace">

<xsl:template match="/">
    <html>
        <head> <title>Your company</title></head>
            <body>
                <h1><center>Your Company</center></h1>
                <xsl:apply-templates select="//my:Address"/>
                    <table border="1" bgcolor="lime">
                        <thead align="center">
                            <td><strong>First</strong></td>
                            <td><strong>Last</strong></td>
                            <td><strong>Ext.</strong></td>
```

The command opens the Company.XSL file referenced in the XML document.

3. Find the line <table border="1" bgcolor="lime">, and change the entry bgcolor="**lime**" to bgcolor="**yellow**".

```
<h1><center>Your Company</center></h1>
<xsl:apply-templates select="//my:Address"/>
    <table border="1" bgcolor="yellow">
        <thead align="center">
            <td><strong>First</strong></td>
            <td><strong>Last</strong></td>
```

4. Select the menu option **File | Save** to retain the changes made to the XSL file.
5. Click the **CompanyLast.xml** tab to make the XML file active, and select **XSL | XSL Transformation,** or hit the **F10** key.

Your Company

Name: US dependency
Street: Noble Ave
City: Dallas
State: Texas
Zip: 04812

First	Last	Ext.	E-Mail	Manager	Degree
Alfred	Aldrich	33	Aldrich@work.com	false	MA
Colin	Coletti	444	Coletti@work.com	true	Ph.D
Fred	Smith	22	Smith@work.com	true	BA

A **new** XSL Output.html file appears in the Browser view. The table background now appears in yellow.

6. Select the menu option **File | Save**, and save the document as **Company.html**.

STYLEVISION 2004 and Stylesheet Designer

XMLSPY 2004 includes XSLT Designer which automates the generation of XSLT stylesheets for XML to HTML transformation. Please see the Stylesheet Designer documentation for more information on Stylesheet Designer. The documentation also includes a tutorial on how to generate a XSLT stylesheet.

Creating a project

Goal of this section:
To create an STYLEVISION 2004 project that includes all the files currently open in the main window.

This will be achieved by:

- using the menu option **Project** to create a project folder
- using the specific Project commands to add files to the project

Functions in this section:

Project | New Project
Project | Add active and related files to project
Project | Add active file to project

Advantages of Projects:

- Files and URLs can be grouped into folders by common extension or any other criteria
- Batch processing can be applied to specific folders, or the project as a whole
- DTD / Schemas can be assigned to specific folders, allowing immediate validation
- XSL transformations can be assigned to specific folders, allowing immediate transformations
- The destination folders of XSL transformation files can be specified

  These settings can all be defined by using the menu option **Project | Project Properties....**

- XML files can be placed under Source control using the menu option **Project | Source control | Add to source control...** (Please see the Source Control section in the online help for more information).
- Personal, network and web folders can be added to projects, allowing batch validation.

Adding files to a project

Creating and adding files to a Project:

There are now many different files open in the main window. You can access these files as a unit by grouping them into an STYLEVISION 2004 project.

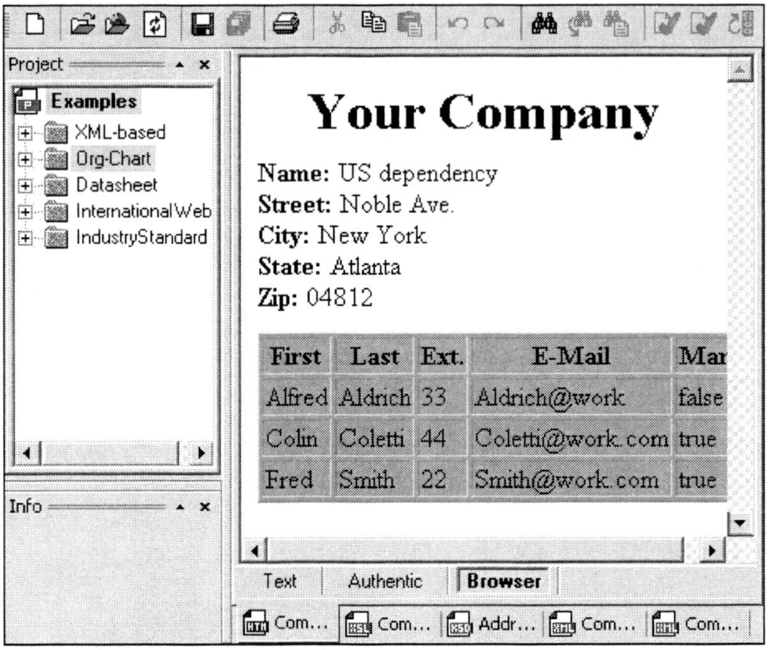

1. Select the menu option **Project | New Project**.

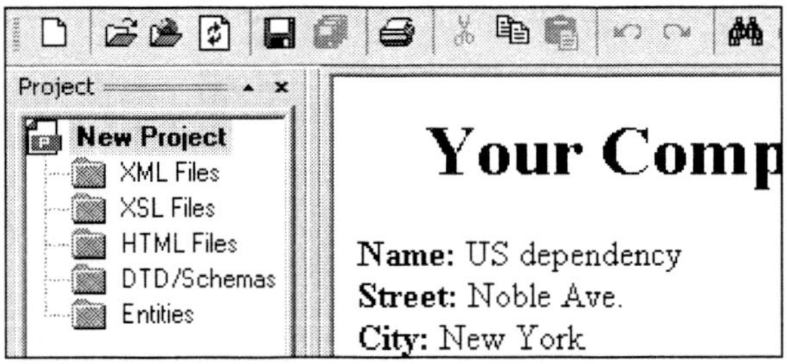

   The project window now contains several folders under the New Project folder.
2. Click the **CompanyLast.xml** tab, to make it the active file in the main window.
3. Select the menu option **Project | Add active and related files to project.**

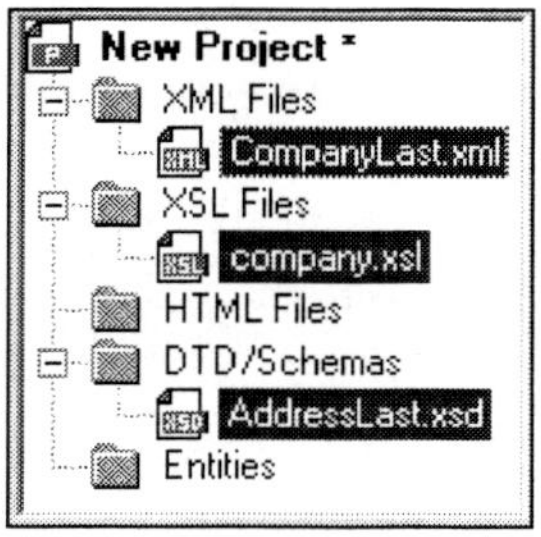

Three files have been added to the New Project folder: CompanyLast.xml, Company.xsl and AddressLast.xsd.

4. Click the **Company.html** tab, and then select the menu option **Project | Add active file to project**.
5. Select the menu option **Project | Save Project** and enter "Tutorial" as the project name.
   The project should look like the diagram below.

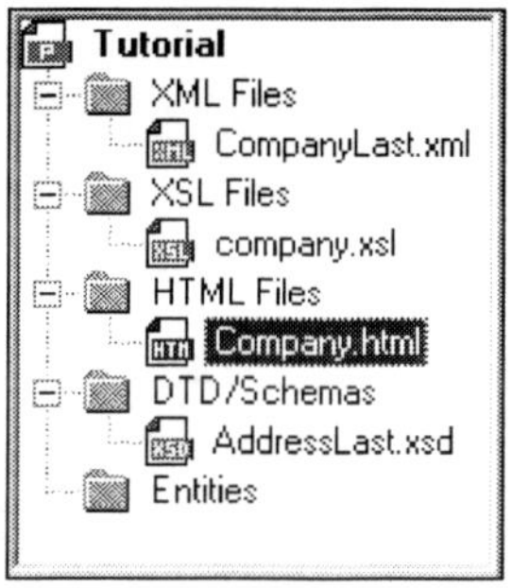

To delete files from a project:

1. Click on the file you want to delete in the project window, and hit the **Delete** key.

To add new folders to a project:

1. Select the menu option **Project | Add Project folder to Project**, and fill in the Properties dialog.

To add a file to a specific folder:

1. Click the file to make it active in the main window.
2. **Right click** the **folder** you want to place the active file into (in the Project window), and select the menu option "**Add active file**".
   This method allows you to add a file to any folder in the current project.

That's it!

If you have come this far congratulations, and thank you!

We hope that this tutorial has been helpful in introducing you to the basics of STYLEVISION 2004. If you need more information please use the context-sensitive online help system, or print out the Tutorial.PDF file that accompanied your version of STYLEVISION 2004.

Part IV

4 User Reference

The reference section contains a complete description of all STYLEVISION 2004 windows and menu commands and explains their use in general.

We've tried to make this user manual as comprehensive as possible. If you have questions which are not covered by this documentation and you are a registered user, please don't hesitate to contact us through the Support Center on the Altova web site.

Windows

The STYLEVISION 2004 user interface provides several windows that show both your document, project and intelligent editing "entry-helper" windows, that can be freely arranged to suit your personal working style.

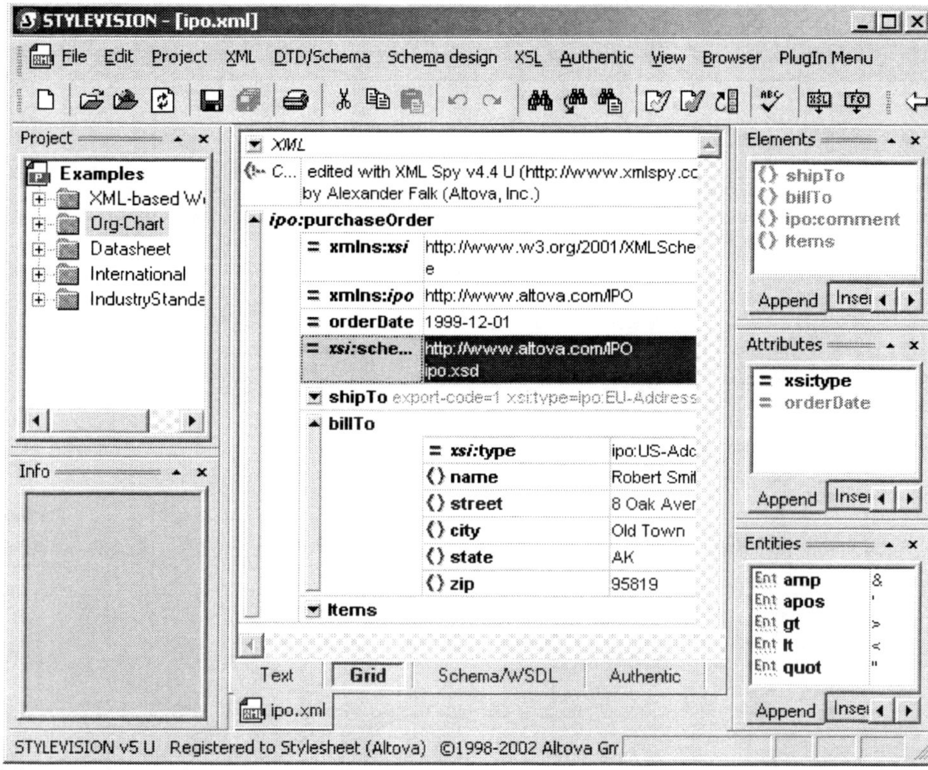

The central area shows the main window, where you edit (and view) your XML, XML Schema, or XSL documents in the Enhanced Grid view, Schema view, Text view, Authentic View, embedded Database/table view, or Browser view.

The left area contains the project and info windows; the right area contains the entry helpers for intelligent editing of elements, attributes, and entities. Please note: The Project window is not available in the Home Edition.

Main Window

The Main Window is where you view and edit all documents in STYLEVISION 2004. STYLEVISION 2004 allows you to open any number of XML documents simultaneously. To switch between them click the part of the window you want to bring to the front.

You can also use the commands on the Window menu to organize your windows. If your windows are maximized, STYLEVISION 2004 also provides tabs, letting you switch between all open windows. Keyboard equivalents are: CTRL+TAB and CTRL+F6.

Right click on a tab, opens the context-menu enabling you to perform various functions on that XML document. (e.g. print, close, mail etc.).

STYLEVISION 2004 provides advanced views on your documents:

- An Enhanced Grid View for structured editing
- An embedded Database/Table view, available from within the Enhanced Grid view, that shows repeated elements in a tabular fashion
- A Schema/WSDL view for viewing and editing XML Schemas
- A Text View with syntax-coloring for source-level work,
- An Authentic View allowing you to edit XML documents based on templates created in Stylesheet Designer , and
- An integrated Browser View that supports both CSS and XSL style-sheets.

To switch any main window between the different views, use the commands on the View menu or the corresponding toolbar buttons.

Please note:
You can set your personal default viewing preferences on a per-file-type basis in the File Types tab on the Tools | Options dialog. Select the menu option **Tools | Options** to open this dialog box.

Enhanced Grid View

Click the Grid tab to open this view.

The Enhanced Grid View is the core presentation and editing view of STYLEVISION 2004. It shows the hierarchical structure of any XML-compliant document through a set of nested containers, that can be easily expanded and collapsed to get a clear picture of the document's structure.

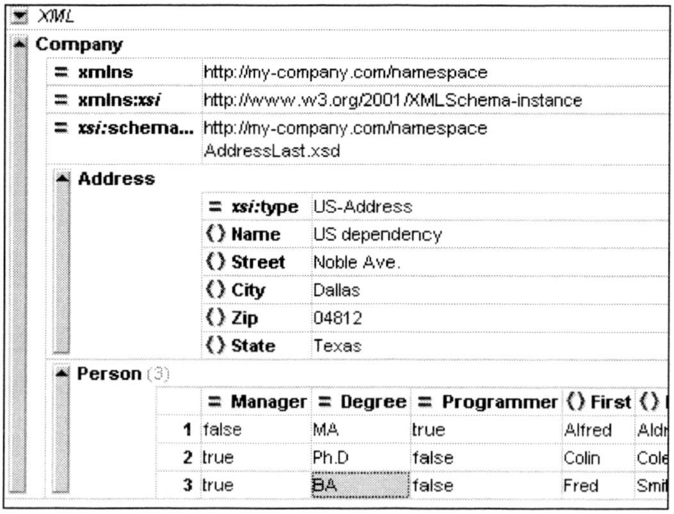

All items contained in an XML document are displayed in a structured way that allows for easy manipulation of contents and structure at the same time.

An hierarchical item (such as the XML declaration, document type declaration, or any element that contains child elements) is represented with a gray side bar and a tiny arrow. Clicking the side bar expands or collapses the item.

Please note:

An element is denoted with the icon, e.g. **header**
An attribute is denoted with the icon, e.g. style

Display & Navigating
The contents of an hierarchical item depend on its kind and – in the case of elements – mostly consists of attributes, character data, comments and child elements.

Element and Attribute order
To emphasize the strong coupling between attributes and the respective parent element, **attributes are always listed first** and cannot be preceded by comments, character data or child elements. The order of the individual attributes is, however, preserved from the input file and can be modified if necessary.

Following the attributes, the remaining items within an element appear exactly in the order found in the source file, and can be rearranged without restriction using drag & drop.

Elements and character data
If an element contains only character data, the data will be shown in the same line as the element and the element will not be considered hierarchical by nature. The character data for any other element will be shown indented with the attributes and potential child elements and will be labeled as "Text".

If an element is collapsed, its attributes can be shown in the same line in a different color. This attribute preview is especially helpful, when editing XML documents that contain a huge number of elements of the same kind that only differ by their contents and attributes (e.g. database-like applications).

Customizing the grid view
The grid view can easily be customized using the mouse to adjust column widths.

To resize a column to the width of its largest entry:
1. Double-click on the grid line to the right of that column.

To adjust the column widths to display all content:
1. Select the menu item View | Optimal widths command, or click on the Optimal widths icon .

The heights of the cells are generally determined by their contents and can only be adjusted by the user using the menu option **Tools | Options| View** tab **| Enhanced Grid view,** "Limit cell height to xx lines".

You can also use the keyboard to navigate an XML document in the Enhanced Grid View.

- The arrow keys move the selection bar in the tree and grid views
- the + and – keys on the numeric keypad allow you to expand and collapse items.

Please note:
You can activate the Text view at any time, to see marked data in the source file for example.

Embedded Database/Table view
STYLEVISION 2004 allows you to display recurring elements in a Database/Table view. This function is available wherever the Enhanced Grid view can be activated, and can be used when editing any type of XML file - XML, XSD, XSL etc.

Intelligent editing
When editing an XML document based on a DTD or Schema, the Enhanced Grid View provides many Intelligent Editing features based on the information gathered from the Schema or DTD.

Whenever editing the **name** of an element or attribute, a popup menu opens. The options available depend on the position of the element and the content model defined by the Schema or DTD. A similar popup is displayed, if the contents of an element or attribute are restricted by an enumeration or choice of some sort.

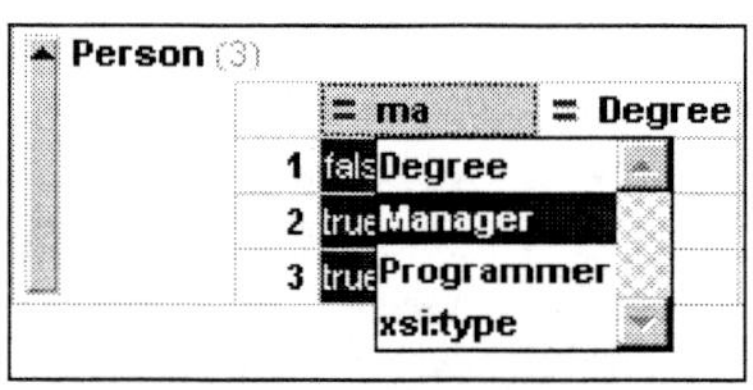

To edit an element or attribute name:
1. Double click on the element name.
2. Edit the name (STYLEVISION 2004 chooses the best match from the menu).
3. Accept the selection by hitting the Return key (Esc. abandons the change).

To insert or append elements or attribute names:
1. Click on the respective icon in the Attr. & Element toolbar, or

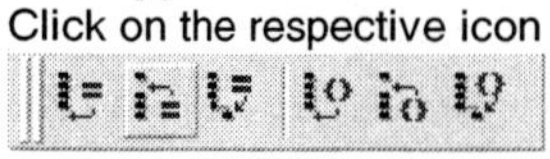

2. Double click on an element or attribute name in one of the Entry Helpers.

Select the menu option **Tools | Options**, and select the **Attr.& Elem**. entry in the Toolbars tab, if these icons are not visible.

You will notice that the various Entry Helpers are constantly updated depending on the current selection in the Enhanced Grid View. The Info Window constantly shows important information regarding the selected element or attribute.

Enhanced Grid View context menu
In addition to the commands available through menus and toolbars, the Enhanced Grid View also provides a context-menu, activated by the right mouse-button. It contains the most useful commands in one convenient place:

Enhanced Grid View context menu:

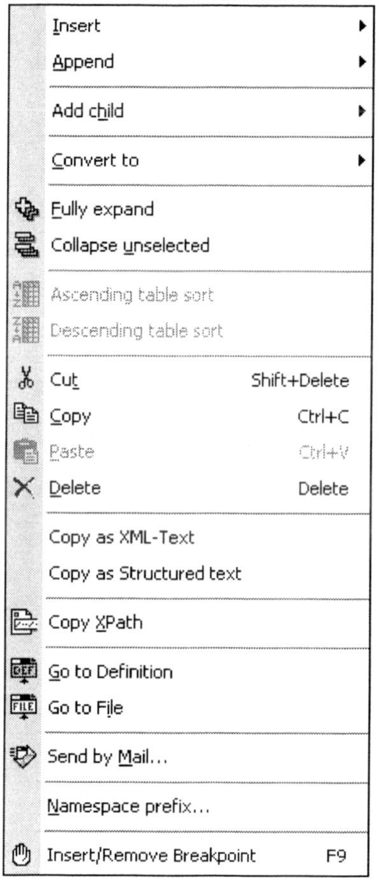

Database/Table View

Having clicked the Grid tab, click on the "Display as Table" icon .

The Database/Table View is integrated into the Enhanced Grid View, and allows you to view recurring elements in grid or compressed into table form. The Database /Table view is available wherever the Enhanced Grid view can be activated, and can be used when editing any type of XML file - XML, XSD, XSL etc.

You can switch between both views, grid and table, by clicking the "Display as Table" icon.

Editing in the table view supports drag&drop and intelligent editing functions. You can also use table-specific commands to sort elements or insert new rows.

XML documents often contain sequences of repeating elements of the same kind. STYLEVISION 2004 automatically detects such sequences and rearranges the presentation to show these elements in a tabular fashion - common to database- or spreadsheet-like applications.

STYLEVISION 2004 achieves this database/table view by taking the respective attributes and sub-elements of the repeating element, and showing them as columns of the table.

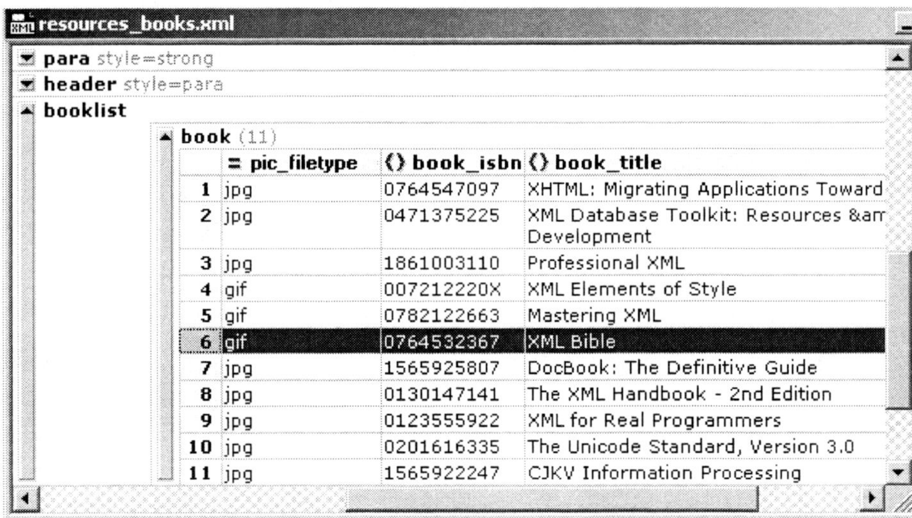

To display recurring elements in a table view:

1. Click on the recurring element in the Enhanced Grid View (flag, in this example). The "Display as table" icon is now active.

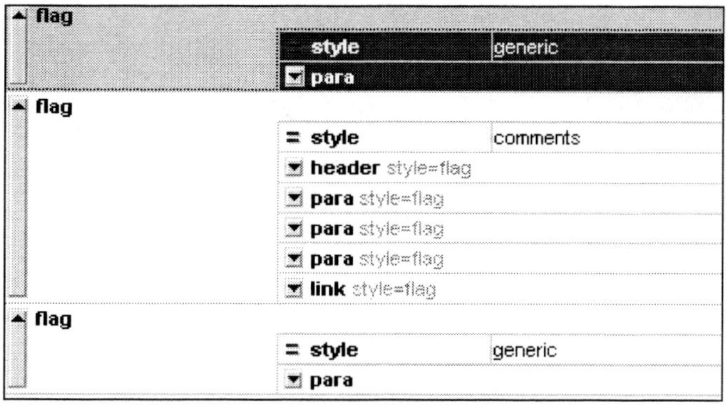

2. Click the "Display as table" icon to activate the Table View, or select the menu option **XML | Table | Display as Table**.

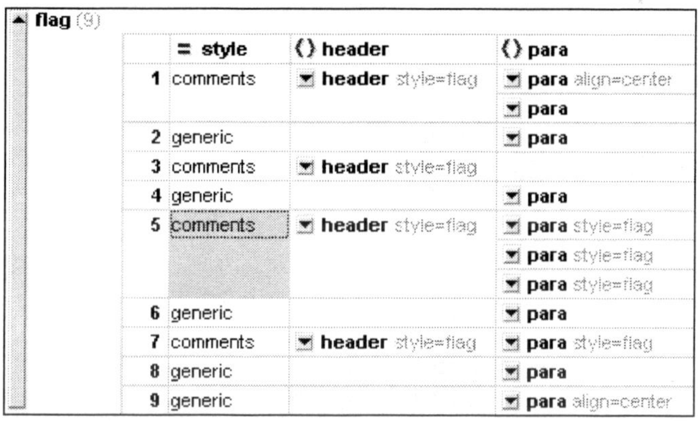

The nine "flag" elements are displayed in table form. Click in a cell to demark the table.

To return to the grid view, from the table view:

1. Click on the table "name" (flag (9) in this e.g.). This selects the whole table.
2. Click the "Display as Table" icon, to deactivate the Table view and return to the Grid view.

Manipulating table data:

- Drag and drop column headers to move columns
- Sort column data using the menu command **XML | Table | Ascending Sort**
- Append (or insert) rows using the menu command **XML | Table | Insert Row**.

Exchanging data from the Database/Table view

To exchange with other applications, select elements in this table and use the copy as structured text option to copy/paste them directly into Excel for example. Data exchange works in both ways. You can therefore copy data from any spreadsheet-like application and insert it directly into STYLEVISION 2004.

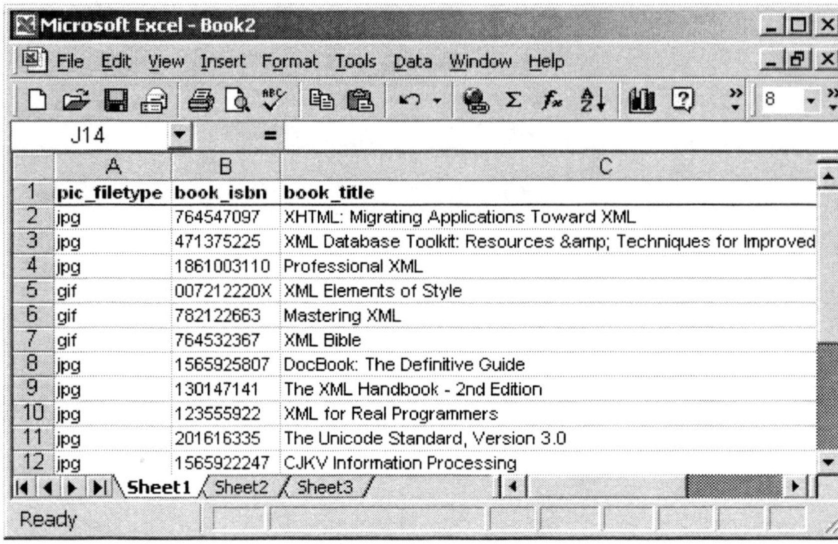

	A	B	C
1	pic_filetype	book_isbn	book_title
2	jpg	764547097	XHTML: Migrating Applications Toward XML
3	jpg	471375225	XML Database Toolkit: Resources & Techniques for Improved
4	jpg	1861003110	Professional XML
5	gif	007212220X	XML Elements of Style
6	gif	782122663	Mastering XML
7	gif	764532367	XML Bible
8	jpg	1565925807	DocBook: The Definitive Guide
9	jpg	130147141	The XML Handbook - 2nd Edition
10	jpg	123555922	XML for Real Programmers
11	jpg	201616335	The Unicode Standard, Version 3.0
12	jpg	1565922247	CJKV Information Processing

For more complex data exchange tasks, STYLEVISION 2004 also offers a set of unique conversion functions that let you directly import or export XML data from any text file, Word document or database.

Schema/WSDL Design View

This is the default view when you double click an .XSD file.

Click the Schema/WSDL tab to display W3C conformant schemas.

A Schema is a model describing the structure of information. A Schema in XML, describes the possible arrangement of tags and text in a valid document. The purpose of a schema is to allow machine validation of document structure, to enable large volume XML transactions over the web.

Schemas are defined in terms of constraints:

- The **content model** constraint, describes order and sequence of elements
- The **datatype** constraint, defines the valid units of data in the content model

Instead of using the syntax of XML 1.0 DTD declarations, schema definitions use XML element syntax. A correct XML schema definition is, therefore, a well-formed XML document.

STYLEVISION 2004 features:

- Supports the Final XML Schema Recommendation of May 2nd 2001, and the ability to convert schemas from the April 7th 2000 Working Draft, or Oct. 24th Candidate Recommendation to the Final Recommendation.
- Generation of DTD/Schema from an XML document
- Conversion of DTD/Schema to different Schema flavors (DTD, DCD, XML-Data, BizTalk, W3C-Schema)
- Generation of XML Schema documentation in Word or HTML format

Viewing and editing XML Schema documents
STYLEVISION 2004 Schema editor allows you to view and edit schemas in two different ways:

- As a Schema overview, in list form
- In a graphical view of specific schema components

Schema overview
Open an XSD document in the DTD/Schemas folder of the project window, or double click on an XSD document in Explorer. The main window then displays the Schema overview.

The top window displays all Global "definitions" (elements, complex types etc.) in list form. The bottom window displays the corresponding attributes of the currently selected component (eg. Mgr., Prg., etc.).

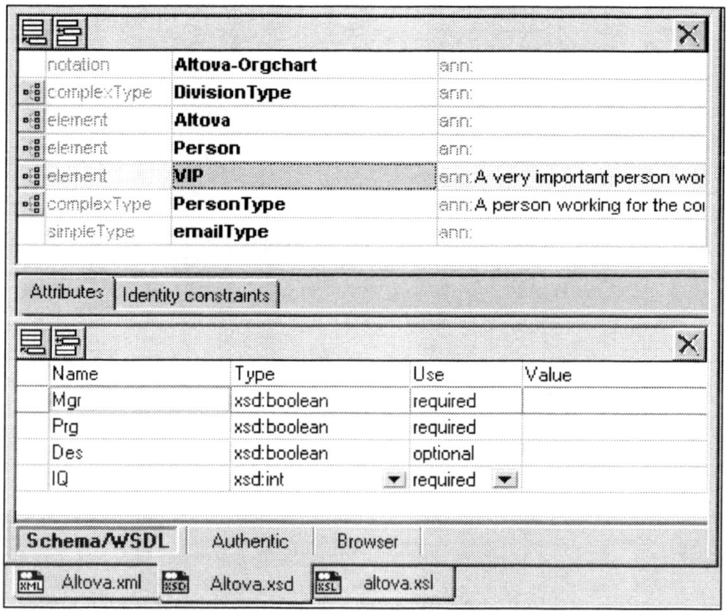

Global definitions (global elements, complex types, etc.) can be moved or copied to other schemas visible in the schema overview, using drag and drop. You can of course, reposition definitions in the currently open schema. Right clicking a definition opens the context menu in which you can select the standard cut, copy, paste commands, to achieve the same thing.

The drag and drop method also allows you to move or copy **attributes** as well as **Identity constraints** between schemas.

To see graphical representation (Content model) of a component:

- Click on the icon next to the component you want to display, or
- Select the menu option **Schema design | Display Diagram,** or
- Double click on a component name in the "Component Navigator" (Top right entry helper).

The *content model* for that component appears in a tree view.

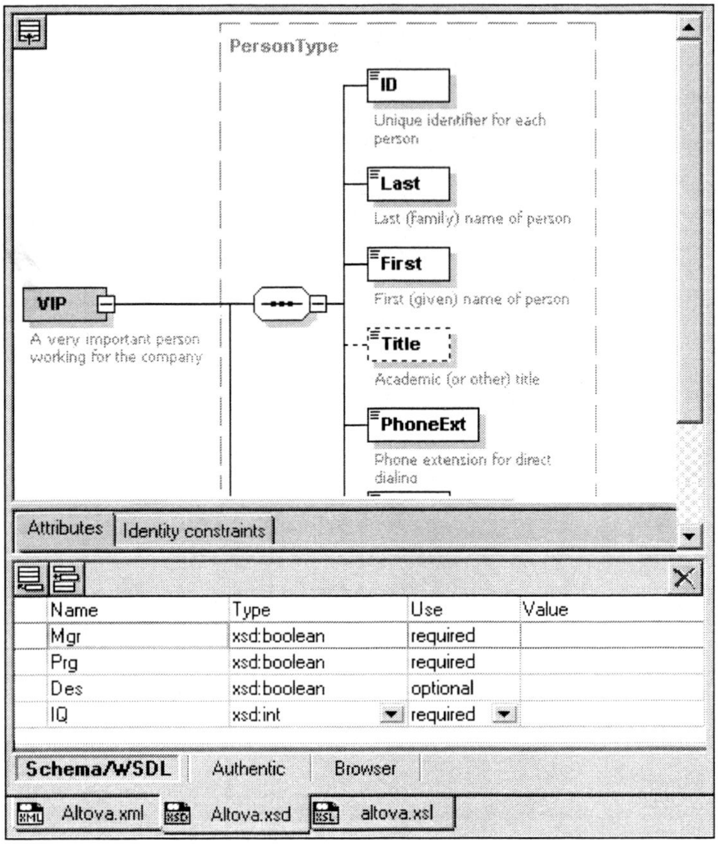

To return to the Schema overview:

- Click the "Show Globals" icon to return to the Schema Overview.
- Select the menu option **Schema design | Display All Globals**.

To append or insert Components:

1. Click the Append or Insert icon at the top left of the component window.
2. Select the component you want to append/insert from the popup.

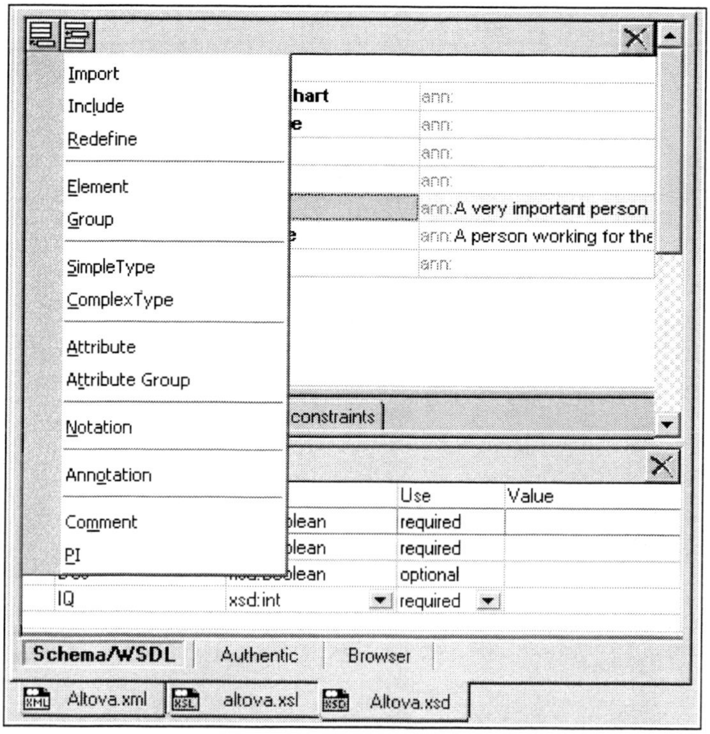

To append or insert Attributes to a component:

1. Click the Append or Insert icon at the top left of the attribute window.
2. Select the attribute you want to append/insert from the popup.

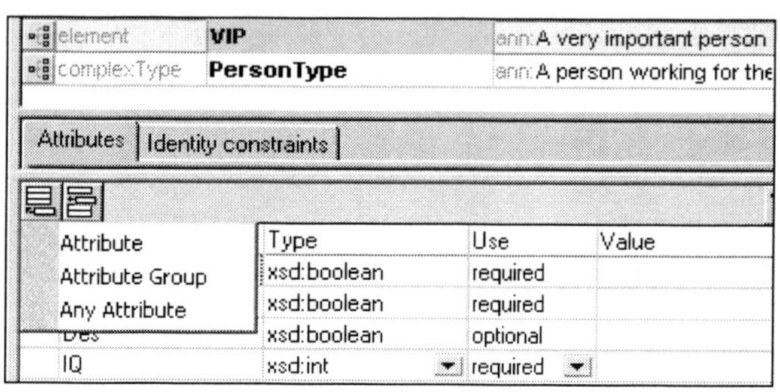

Schema design content model

The content model view enables you to directly manipulate the symbols depicting your schema. You can insert or append elements, as well as change their parameters directly.

Element Symbols

Mandatory single element. Details: MinOcc=1, MaxOcc=1

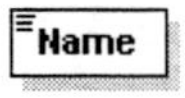

Mandatory single element, containing Parsed Character Data (#PC-Data).
The content may be simple content or mixed complex content.
Details: MinOcc=1, MaxOcc=1, type=xsd:string, content=simple.

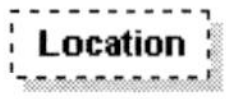

Single optional element. Details: MinOcc=0, MaxOcc=1
The context menu option **Optional,** converts a mandatory element into an optional one.

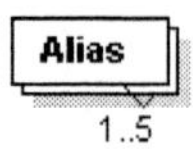

Mandatory multiple element. Details MinOcc=1, MaxOcc=5.

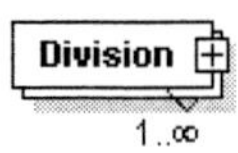

Mandatory multiple element containing child elements.
Details: MinOcc=1, MaxOcc=unbounded, type=DivisionType, content=complex.
The context menu option **Unbounded,** changes the max. occurrence of an element to unbounded.

Clicking on the + character of the element expands the tree view and shows the child elements.

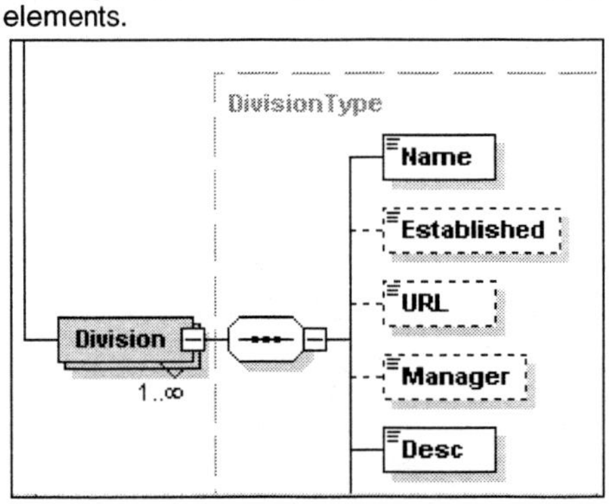

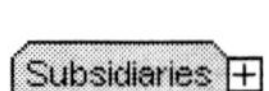

Group element. Details: name=Subsidiaries.
A named collection of elements to allow reuse in the construction of different complex types.

"Any" can be a placeholder for any element from a certain namespace.

Please note:
To display the definition of any element, hold down the CTRL key, and double click on the element you want to see the definition of.

To add / insert / append, elements or child elements:

1. Click right on the element (or "model type" symbol), to open the context menu.
2. Select the operation you want to carry out from the menu.

Please note:
Only those operations that are possible with the element appear in the context menu. Invalid operations are grayed out in the context menu and cannot be selected.

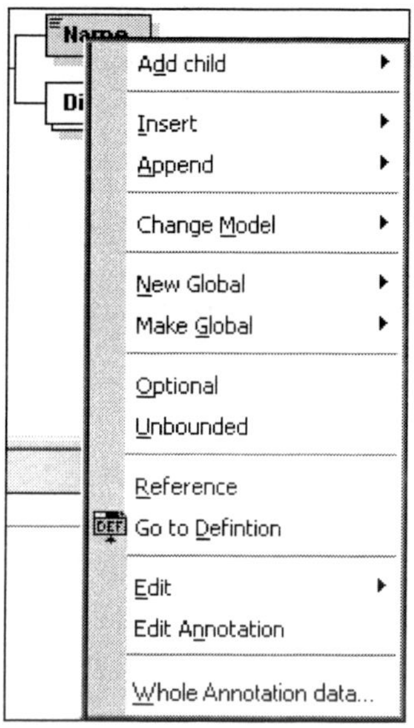

Simple types:
A "simple type" element is defined as a datatype that only contains values and no element or attributes. The element type is usually prefixed by the namespace prefix **xsd: string**, indicating that it is a predefined XML Schema datatype.

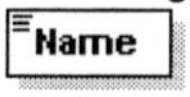

Details: name=Name, type=xsd:string, content=simple.

Complex types:
"Complex type" is a datatype which may contain attributes, elements and text.
Adding sub elements to an element, automatically defines the element with the content model as complex (Details entry helper content=complex.). Click on the "Com" tab of the component navigator, to see the complex types.

STYLEVISION 2004 displays references to "external" complex types with a yellow background. In the example below, the Person element references the PersonType complex element.

To view the referenced complex type element:

1. Double click the complex type name in the yellow box (here, PersonType), or
2. Click on the "Com" tab of the Component Navigator, and double click on the

PersonType entry.

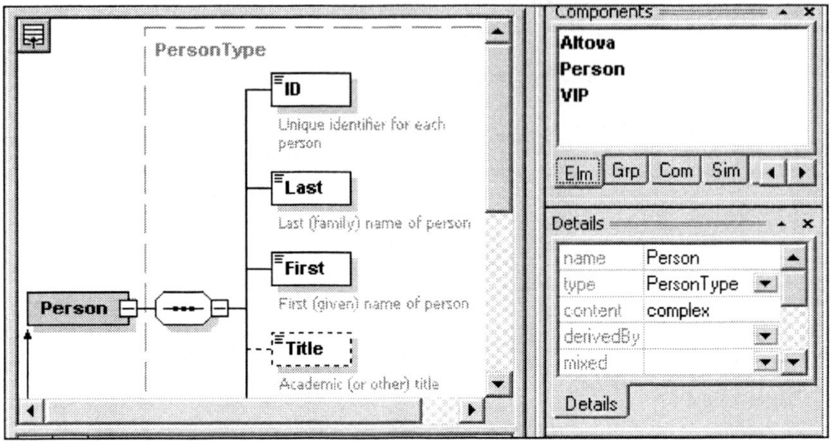

The PersonType element definition appears in the main window.

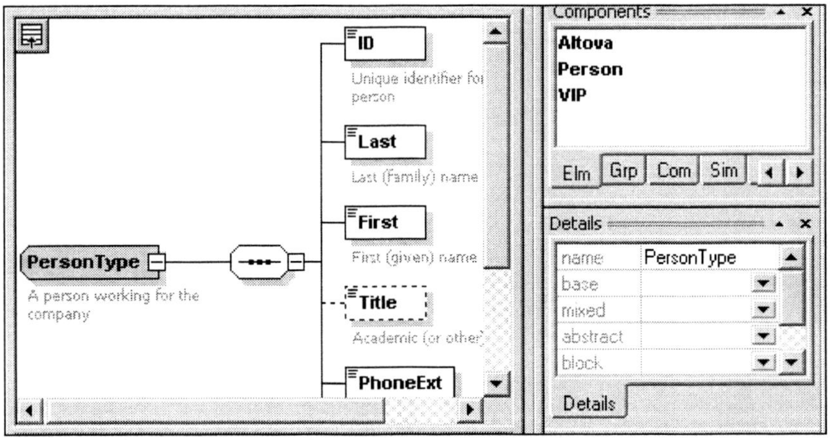

Schema, Content model

STYLEVISION 2004 enables you to define your content model with a few mouse clicks. All element types and methods of combining them can be defined in the content model.

Compositors
A "Compositor" defines an ordered sequence of sub elements (child elements).

To insert a compositor:

1. Click right on the element you want to add sub elements to.
2. Select **Add Child | Sequence** (Choice or All).
3. Click right on the compositor symbol and select **Add Child | Element**, to add further sub elements.

Sequence:

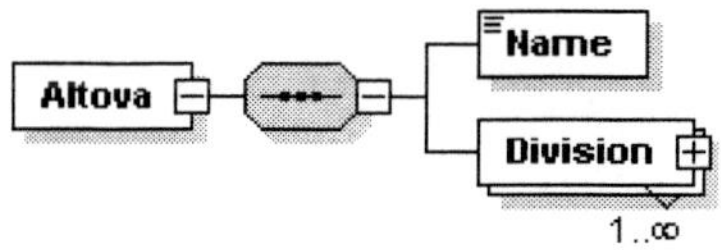

Choice:

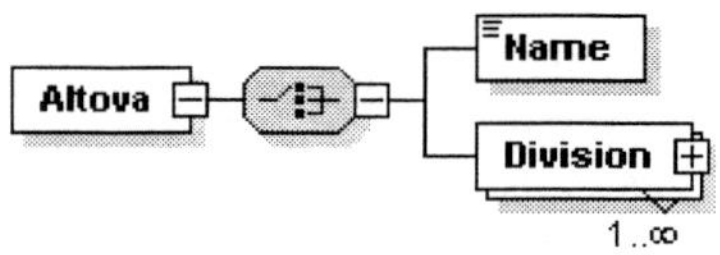

All:

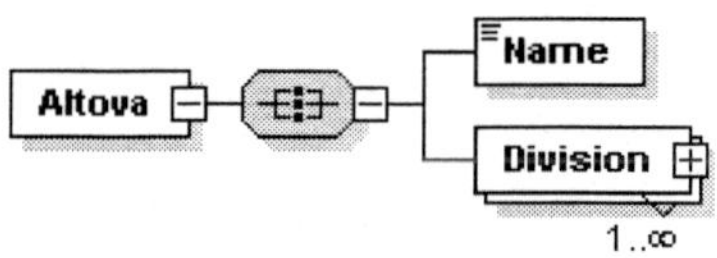

To change the compositor (model)

1. Click right on the compositor.
2. Select **Change Model | Sequence** (Choice or All).

Global components

There are two methods of defining global components: creating a new component from scratch, or changing an existing element into global component.

To create a global component from scratch:

1. Click the Insert / Append icon in the **Schema Overview**, and select the type of component you want (Element, Group, SimpleType, ComplexType etc.)
2. Enter the name of the component in the global list, and confirm with OK.

The global component appears in the respective tab (Elm, Grp, Com, Sim etc.) of the Component navigator. Double clicking on the component, displays the tree view of that component in the main window.

Please note:
You can create a global element while viewing a component in the content model. Click right in the main window, and select the option **New Global | Element**.

To delete a global component:

1. Switch to the Schema global overview, select the component and hit the delete key, or
2. Click the Delete icon  of the component window.

To change an element into a global component:

1. Click right on the element and select **Make Global | Element.**

If the element is a complex type, then the option **Make Global | Complex type** becomes available.

References to global components

A reference to a global component can be created in two ways:

- You add a component to a schema which has the same name as an existing global component. This causes a dialog box to appear, prompting you if you want to reference the element to it. Confirming with OK, references the component to the component definition.

- You right click an element and select the option **Reference** from the context menu.

In both cases, a link icon appears at the bottom left of the element symbol  and check box "**isRef**" is set active in the Details entry helper.

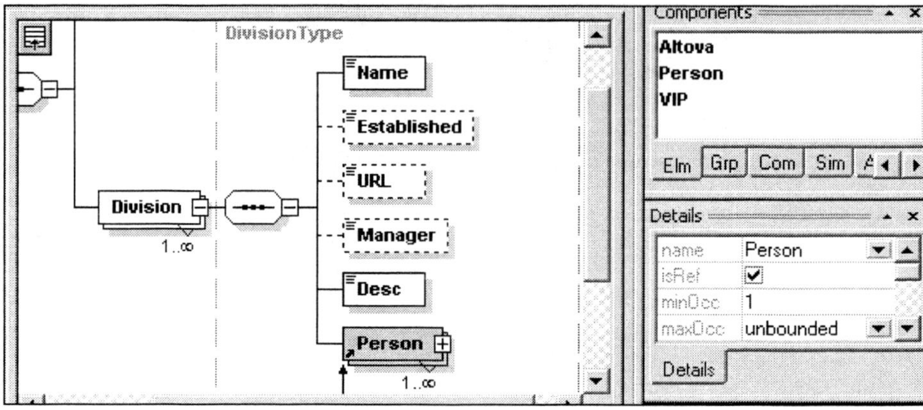

Please note:

If you create a reference to a component that does not exist, the element name appears in red as a warning that there is no definition to refer to.

To view the definition of a referenced element:

- Use the Hotkey **CTRL+Double click** on an element.
  The element definition appears, along with the corresponding info in the details window, or
- Right click the element and select **Go to Definition** from the context menu.

To edit the name of an element:

1. Right click the element
2. Select the context menu option **Edit | Name** and edit the name. (Double clicking the element name, also enables you to edit the name.)

Schema Annotation

There are two types of schema annotation, both of which are sub elements of the annotation element:

- **documentation**: allows you to add comments to the schema for readability / documentation purposes, and
- **appinfo**: which allows you to insert script or other program code, which can be processed by another application, an XSLT stylesheet or some other type of tool.

To edit (or create) element documentation:

1. Right click the element.

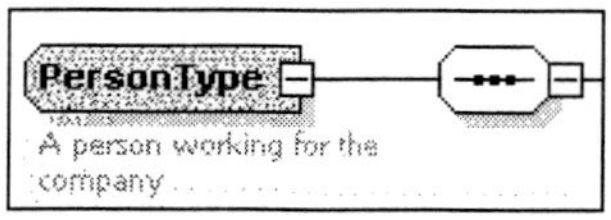

2. Select the context menu option **Edit Annotation**. (Double clicking the element annotation, if one exists, allows you to edit the annotation directly.)

```
<xsd:complexType name="PersonType">
    <xsd:annotation>
        <xsd:documentation>A person working for the company</xsd:documentation>
    </xsd:annotation>
```

This creates the annotation element with the sub element, documentation, containing the annotation text.

To edit (or create) appinfo for an element:

1. Right click the element.
2. Select the context menu option **Whole Annotation Data**.

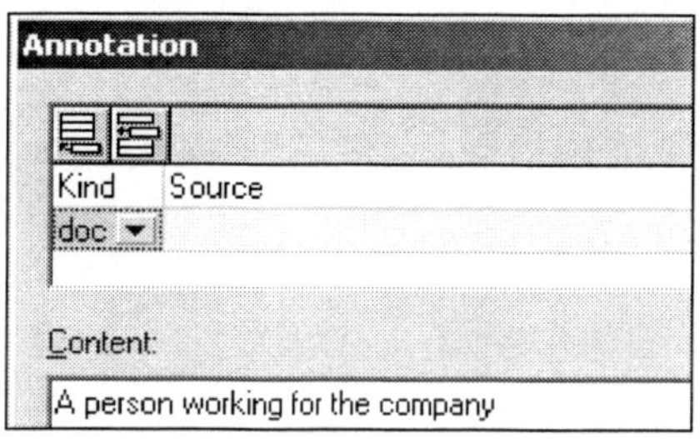

This opens the Annotation dialog box. If an element contains annotation text, then a row is visible when the dialog box is opened. The annotation type "doc", is displayed in the Kind column and the annotation text is visible in the Content text box.

3. Click the append or insert icon at the top left, to insert a new line. This automatically inserts a new "doc" line.
4. Click the drop down arrow next to the new doc line, and select "app".

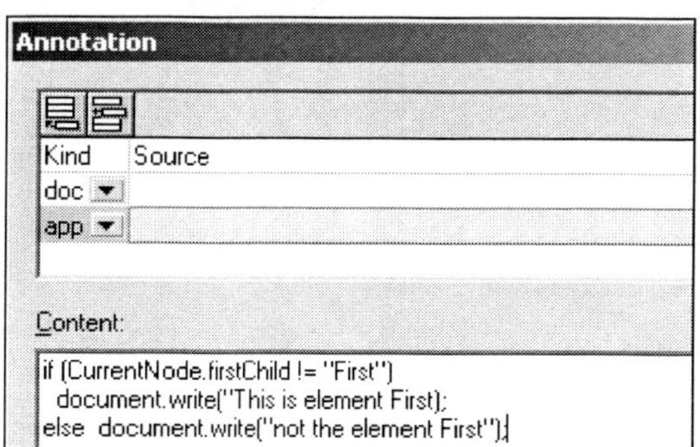

5. Enter the appinfo script/code in the Content text box.

```
    <xsd:element name="Person" type="PersonType"/>
    <xsd:complexType name="PersonType">
        <xsd:annotation>
            <xsd:documentation>A person working for the company</xsd:documentation>
            <xsd:appinfo>if (CurrentNode.firstChild != "First")
  document.write("This is element First);
else
  document.write("not the element First");</xsd:appinfo>
```

Please note:

The **Source** column allows you to enter a URI, where the parser can obtain the appinfo content for further processing. It is not mandatory that you enter a URI into the Source column.

Changing element parameters/values directly in the content model

- Double click the cell of the element (table) you want to edit and start entering data. If a selection is possible, a drop down list appears if not, enter the parameter or value and confirm the entry with the Return key.

  The entry helpers will be updated at this point, reflecting the data you entered.

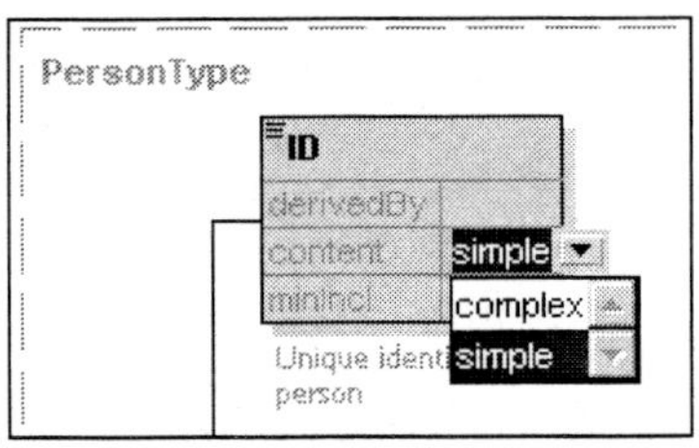

Documenting the content model

- Select the menu command **Schema design | Generate documentation**.

This command **generates** detailed documentation about your schema. Documentation is generated for each element using the settings you define in the dialog box. Related elements (child elements, complex types etc.) are hyperlinked, enabling you to navigate from element to element.

Text View

Click the Text tab, to open this view.

When it comes down to low-level work, the text view is ideally suited for XML editing in its textual or source form.

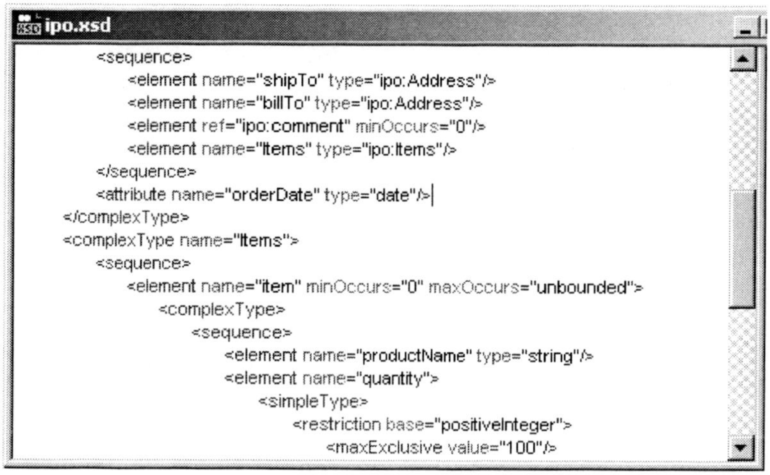

The text view can be used to edit any kind of text file (even non-XML conforming documents) and offers customizable syntax-coloring (including the ability to highlight server-side VBScript or JScript code in ASP pages) as well as an automatic display of the current line and character position in the status bar.

You can use the Find and Replace commands to quickly locate or change any information, and STYLEVISION 2004 offers unlimited levels of Undo and Redo for all your editing operations.

Intelligent Editing
If you are working with an XML document based on a DTD or XML Schema, STYLEVISION 2004 provides you with various intelligent editing capabilities.

1. Type the "<" less-than character at the position you want to insert an XML element, attribute, or attribute value.
   This opens a popup list.
2. Enter the first few characters of the item you want to insert.
   An item containing those characters is highlighted.

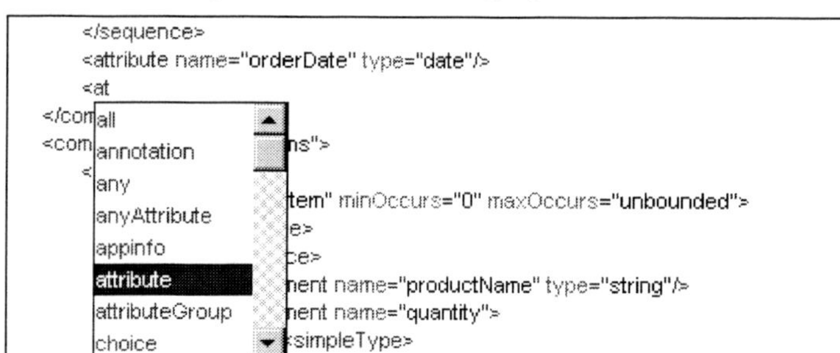

3. Click on the entry with the mouse pointer, or
   Use the arrow keys to highlight your selection and
4. Hit the Return or Space key to accept the selected choice and close the popup window.

Please note:
The popup window also appears when you edit elements or attributes in Text view. If a

specific attribute is defined to follow an element, a popup window containing all valid attributes will also appear.

Eg.

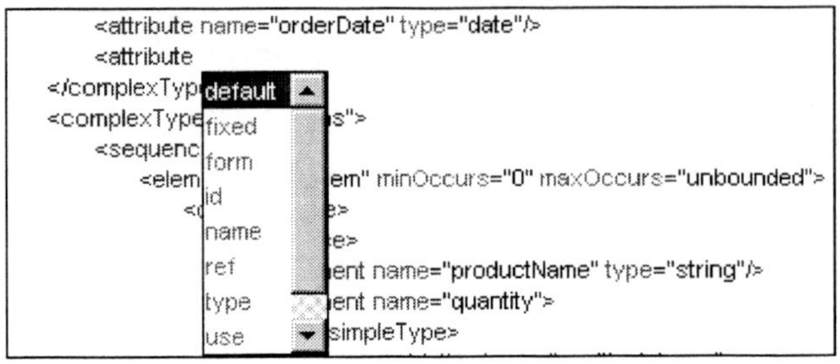

Auto-completion

Editing in the text view can easily result in unbalanced brackets, elements that are not closed properly, or other violations of the well-formedness principle.

STYLEVISION 2004 automatically completes elements as well as inserting all required attributes as soon as you finish entering the element name on your keyboard. The cursor is automatically positioned between the start and end tags of the element, so that you can immediately continue to add child elements or contents:

```
<img src="" alt=""></img>
```

Use the Check well-formedness command at any time to ensure that the document meets the XML 1.0 Specification criteria for well-formedness. This check is also automatically performed every time you open or save a document.

Mouse & Context-Menu

You can also use the mouse during editing in the Text View. If you select text, you can either use drag&drop to move the text block to a new location, or you can use the context-menu on the right mouse button, to directly access frequently used editing commands - such as Cut, Copy, Paste, Delete, Send by Mail, and Go to line/char:

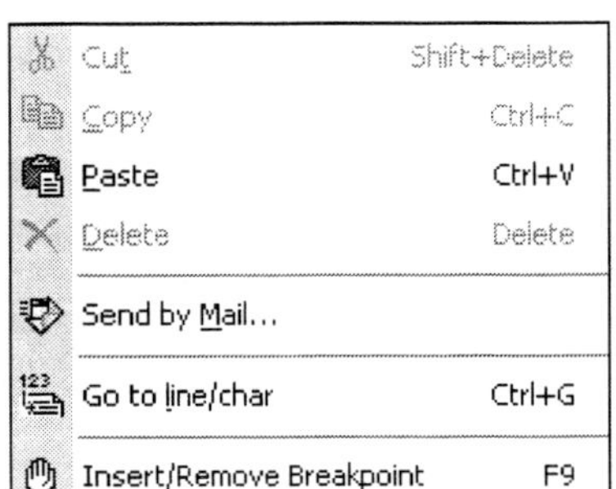

While most customers prefer the Enhanced Grid or Database/Table view for every-day work on XML data files, the text view can occasionally be very handy when editing XSL files or if you are using Active Server Pages (ASP) or any other non-XML files for your web application.

Authentic View

Click the Authentic View tab to open this view.

Authentic View enables you to edit XML documents **based on templates created in Stylesheet Designer!** The templates in Stylesheet Designer are saved as ***.sps** files, and supply all the necessary information needed by Authentic View.

Templates are **opened** by selecting the **File | New** command and then clicking the "Select a Authentic View template..." button. Please see the Authentic View documentation for further information.

Authentic View features:

- Free-flow WYSIWYG text editing
- Form-based data input
- Presentation and editing of repeating XML elements as tables
- Real-time validation, and consistency checking using XML Schema
- Support for CALS and HTML tables

Authentic View is available in several versions: as an integrated view within STYLEVISION 2004 or as a Browser Plug-In for Internet Explorer.

Authentic View has two main areas: the main window, and the entry helpers at right. The graphic below shows the OrgChart template with all the markup info hidden.

- The **main window** allows you to display the document in several different views: the Authentic View which is the default view for this type of document template, the Enhanced Grid view or Text view. The Enhanced Grid view incorporates a special view, called the Database/Table view, which collapses recurring XML data into table form.

- The **right area** contains three Entry helper windows, which allow you to insert specific elements (or attributes) depending on the current cursor position in the document.

Example of a partially filled in **Orgchart** template document.

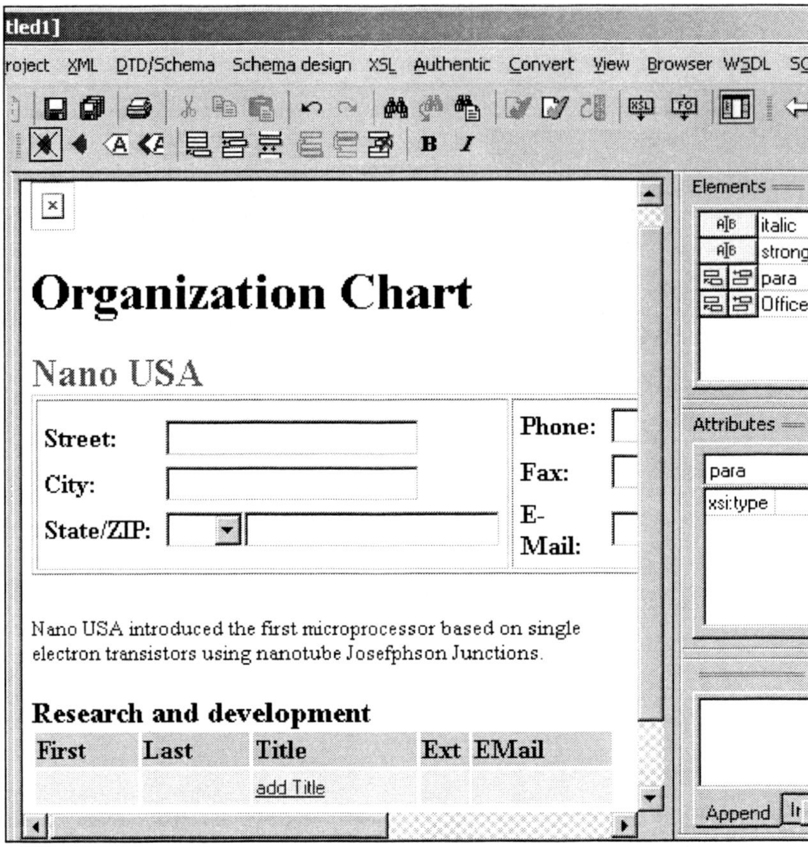

Browser View

Click the Browser tab, to open this view.

The Browser view requires Microsoft Internet Explorer 5, and we highly recommend you to also download the MSXML4 if you intend to work with XSLT in STYLEVISION 2004, as MSXML4 already supports most of the W3C XSLT Recommendation. Please see our Download Center for more details.

Use the integrated browser view to preview any XML file with an XSL stylesheet, or view the output from an XSLT transformation to HTML.

Displaying source code and Browser views:
If you are using STYLEVISION 2004 for XHTML editing or if you have an XSL stylesheet associated with your XML document, you can display the browser view in a separate window.

This allows you to take a look at the document source in the Enhanced Grid or Text views and have the browser preview side-by-side, so that it can easily be refreshed directly from the editing view (just hit F5 in the editing view and the browser view is automatically updated).

The browser view also supports find and printing functions for when you want to document XML files that use CSS or XSL style-sheets, and offers the typical browser commands from both the Browser menu and toolbar: Back, Forward, Stop, Refresh.

Project Window

STYLEVISION 2004 uses the familiar tree view to manage multiple files or URLs in XML projects. Files and URLs can be grouped into folders by common extension or any arbitrary criteria to allow easy structuring and batch manipulation.

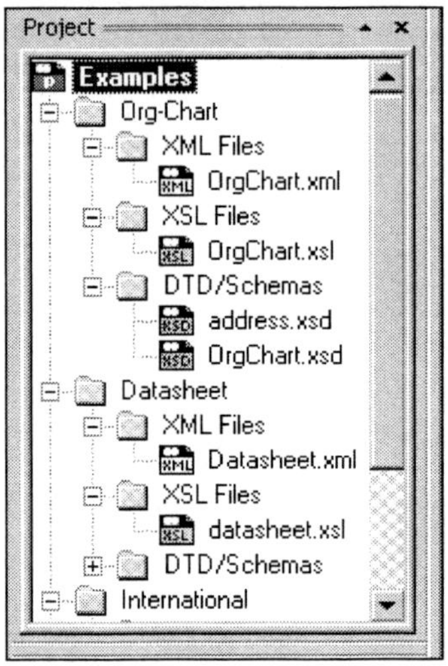

Folders can correspond to physical directories on your file system, or you can define file-type extensions for each folder to keep common files in one convenient place.

Project folders are "semantic" folders, that represent a logical grouping of files and do **not** necessarily need to correspond to any hierarchical organization of the files on your hard disk into several directories.

Assigning XSL transformations to project folders
You can assign different XSL transformation parameters to each folder and even have the same physical file present in more than one project folder - this is especially useful when you want to keep your data in one XML file and use different XSL stylesheets to produce different output (e.g. separate HTML and WML presentations).

The menu option **XSL | Assign XSL**, can only be selected when you are in the Enhanced Grid view.

Assigning DTDs / Schemas to project folders
You can assign different DTDs or Schemas to different folders. This allows you to validate a file against both a DTD and an XML Schema without changing the file itself, which is useful when you are in the process of making the transition from DTDs to Schemas.

The menu option **DTD/Schema | Assign DTD (Assign Schema)**, can only be selected when you are in the Enhanced Grid view.

Use the commands on the Project menu to manage your projects.

Entry Helper Windows

STYLEVISION 2004 helps you create valid XML documents by providing three palette-like windows that we call "entry helpers".

When you are working on an XML document based on a DTD or Schema, the built-in Intelligent Editing module constantly displays information on elements, attributes, and entities that can be inserted at the current cursor position, based on the information gathered from the Schema or DTD content model.

The entry helper windows have a STYLEVISION 2004 prefix in Visual Studio .NET.

Element Entry-Helper

The **element** entry helper, allows you to insert a new element into your document by showing what elements are permissible at the current location.

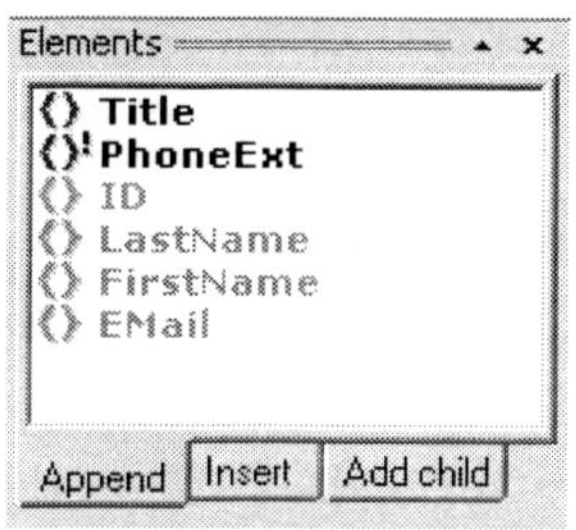

You can choose to **append** an element, **insert** it before the selected element or **add** a **child**-element to the currently selected element. Depending on this context, the entry helper will automatically adjust its list of available choices.

Mandatory elements are automatically highlighted by an exclamation mark "**!**"

Elements that are allowed within the current parent element, but not at the position of the current selection, are shown in **gray**.

Please note:
When editing in the **Text** view, **all** elements are displayed in the element entry helper, element dependencies are ignored while in this view. Switching to the Grid view displays the correct dependencies allowed by the associated schema/DTD.

To insert an element:

- Double-click on the desired item.
  The corresponding element is inserted into the XML document, and the entry helper is automatically updated to reflect your new options.

Should you create a sequence of elements that violate the content model specified by your schema or DTD, the built-in incremental validating parser automatically detects this violation and displays its error message directly in the entry helper window.

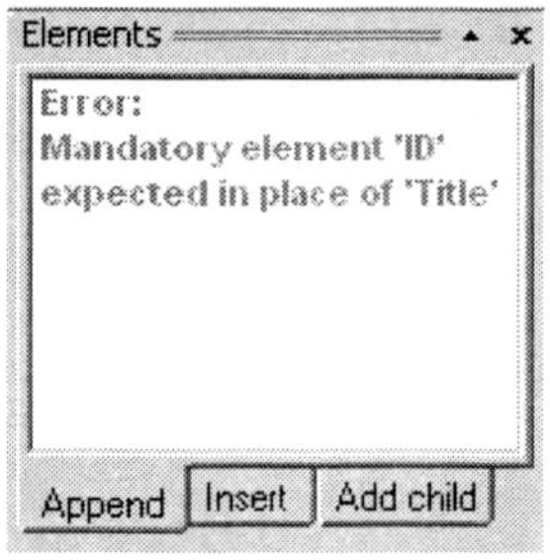

In the **Schema/WSDL Design View**, this window is called the **Component Navigator**, and displays information on **Global Components**: elements, groups, complex types, simple types, attributes and attribute groups.

To display the content model of a component:

- Click the component type tab (Elm., Grp., etc.), and
- Double click on the desired component, in the respective tab.

The content model appears in the main window as a graphic.

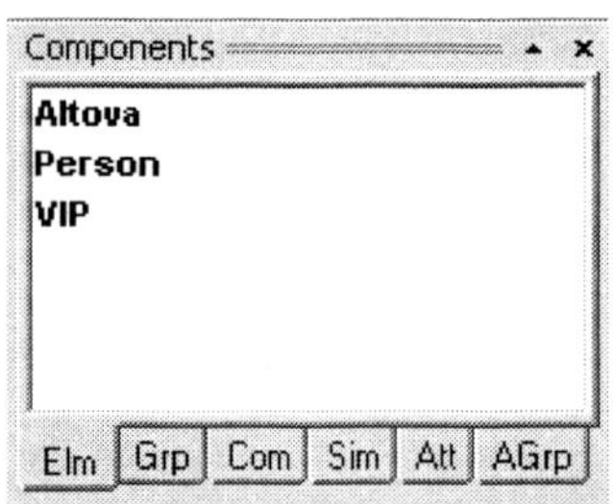

Attribute Entry-Helper

A list of available attributes for the element you are currently editing, are shown in the second palette-window and offer the same functionality as the element entry helper. The attributes displayed in the entry helper are identical in both the Grid and Text view.

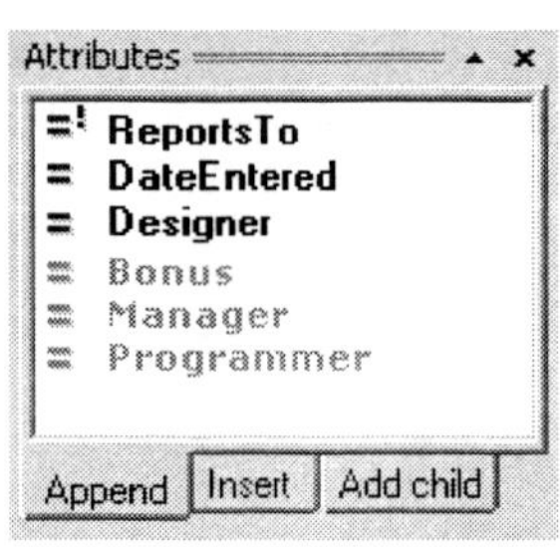

Mandatory attributes are automatically highlighted by an exclamation mark "**!**"

Existing attributes that cannot be added to the current element a second time - are shown in **gray**.

In the **Schema/WSDL Design View**, this window is called **Details**, and displays information on the currently selected element of the content model. A further tab may be visible if you are editing a schema file which contains database extensions. Currently supported databases are: Oracle, SQL Server or Tamino.

To change content model parameters:

1. Use the combo boxes to select different parameters, or
2. Double click into the respective row, and edit/enter text directly.

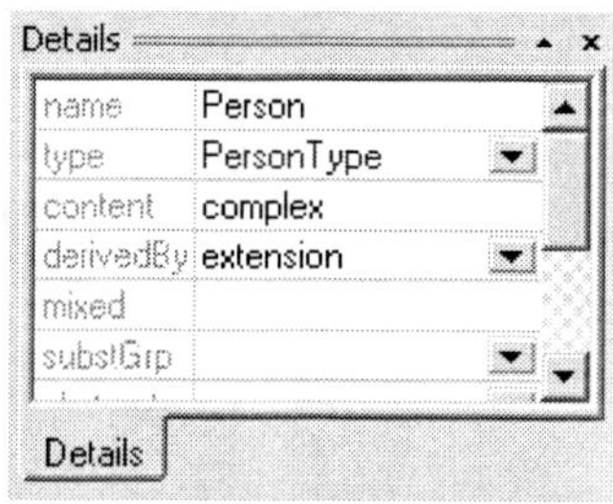

Entity Entry-Helper

The **entity entry helper** presents a list of defined entities or parameter entities that you can insert within your document.

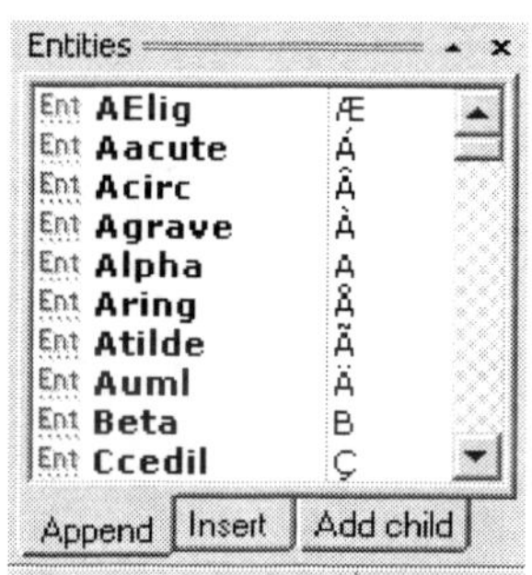

In the **Schema/WSDL Design View**, this window is called **Facets** and displays further information on the currently selected element of the content model.

To add enumerations or facets please see the relevant sections in the tutorial.

Facets, Patterns and Enumerations - drag and drop:

- Drag and Drop of enumerations or patterns in the current window repositions them.
- Holding the CTRL key and dragging, copies the item(s).
- Items can be moved or copied to other open schemas in the main window.
- The cut, copy and paste shortcuts (CTRL+X, CTRL+C, CTRL+V) can also be used on any of these items.
- Note that copying a **facet** item using the shortcut keys, copies the whole **element!**

To change these content model parameters:

1. Use the combo boxes to select different parameters, or
2. Double click into the respective row, and edit/enter text directly.

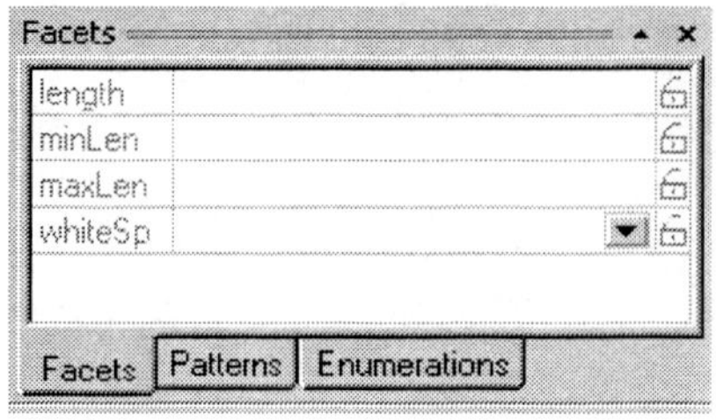
Facets
length
minLen
maxLen
whiteSp
Facets
Patterns
Enumerations

Info Window

In addition to the entry helper windows, STYLEVISION 2004 provides a handy information window that shows the detailed information about the attribute or element that you are working on.

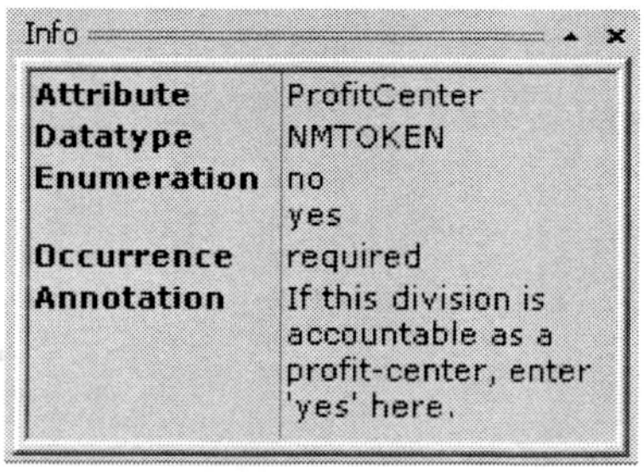

This information is available in all three editing views and can be a tremendous help in conjunction with the xsd:annotation feature of the new XML Schema draft, which allows a schema author to include comments or documentation on the use of each individual element or attribute into the schema itself.

Menus

STYLEVISION 2004 supports all standard Windows commands on the File and Edit menus to enable the user to quickly exploit all capabilities of the program.

Wherever appropriate, additional commands have been added to support special XML- or Internet-related features (e.g. such as opening documents directly from an URL).

In addition to the standard menus, STYLEVISION 2004 contains many XML-specific menus that cover the different aspects of XML editing tasks.

File Menu

The File menu contains all commands relevant to manipulating files, in the order common to most Windows software products.

In addition to the standard New, Open, Save, Print, Print Setup, and Exit commands, STYLEVISION 2004 offers special commands:

- open a document directly from a URL
- reload a file that may have changed
- switch the character-set encoding used by a file, and
- send a file by e-mail (only available, if a MAPI-compliant mail system, such as Microsoft Outlook, is installed).
- save file to URL

New...

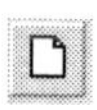

The "New..." command is used to create a new document.

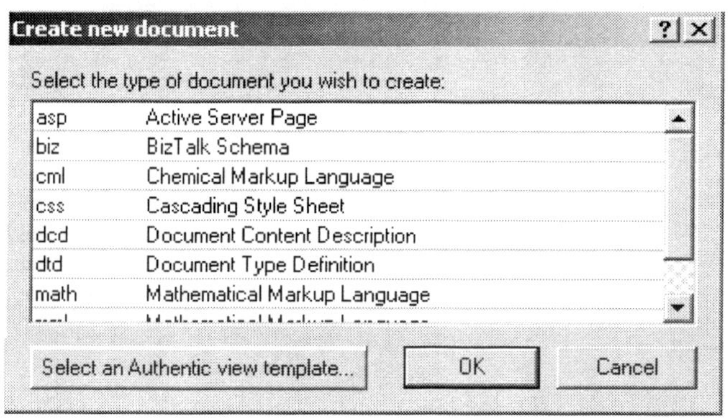

Since XML is such a versatile and universal concept, there are many different kinds of XML documents that you can create and edit with STYLEVISION 2004.

Creating files not available in the "Create new document" dialog box
If the document you want to create is not listed, simply select ".xml" and change the file extension when you save the file. You can also add new file types to this list using the Tools | Options | File types tab.

Creating new templates
You can create your own templates which will then appear in the "Create new document" dialog box when you select the **File | New** command.

1. Use MS Explorer or any other text editor to open one of the **new.xxx** template files in the **...\Template folder**. This file will act as the basis for your new XML template.
2. Make the necessary changes, declarations etc., to the new template file.
3. Use **Save as...** option to save the file using the convention, **Anyname.XXX**
   Anyname is the name of your personal template (e.g **my-xml**).
   .XXX is the extension it should appear under in the dialog box (e.g. **.XML**). You can

enter any type of XML extension here (.vml, .math etc.!)

4. Select **File | New** to select your new XML template.

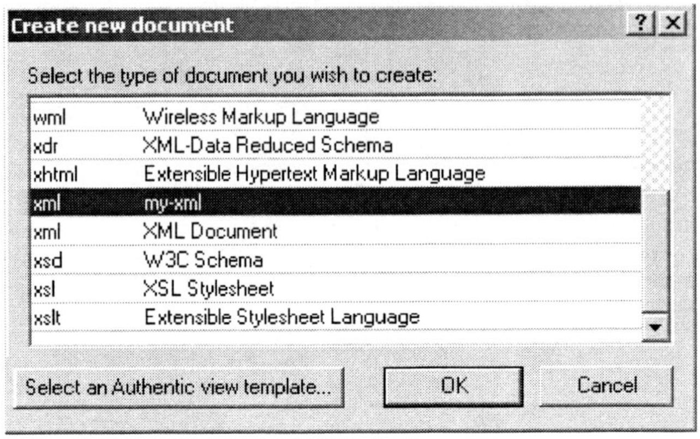

Please note:

To delete a template, delete the template file from the template folder.

Assigning a DTD / Schema to a new XML document

STYLEVISION 2004 contains built-in templates for most XML-based document types and automatically provides you with a meaningful starting point instead of a totally empty file (e.g. a ".xhtml" file automatically includes the correct DOCTYPE reference to the XHTML DTD as well as an empty <html> element to start with).

The predefined templates are placed in the \Template directory, automatically created one level below the installation directory. You can only assign a DTD/Schema to a document from within the Enhanced Grid view.

If you select the ".xml XML Document" entry, (typically a new XML instance document) in the above dialog box, STYLEVISION 2004 prompts you for a DTD or Schema for the new file to be based upon:

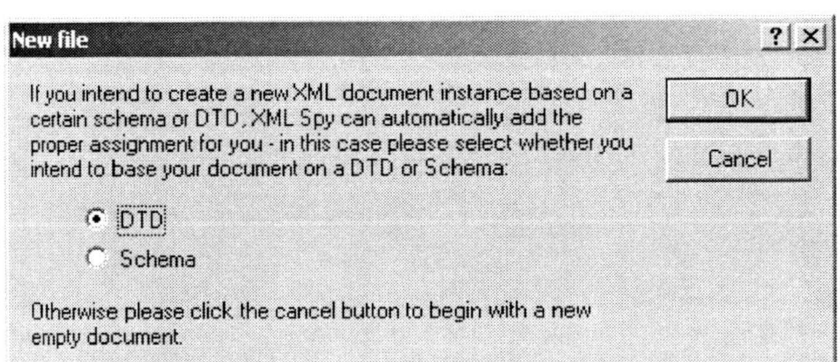

To create an empty XML document:

- Select the **File | New** menu entry, and
- Click the "**Cancel**" button in the New file dialog box, which prompts for a DTD/Schema.

Defining the root element

If you want to assign a DTD / Schema and the content model of the Schema or DTD contains more than one potential root element candidate, STYLEVISION 2004 asks you to select a root element from the list of possible candidates:

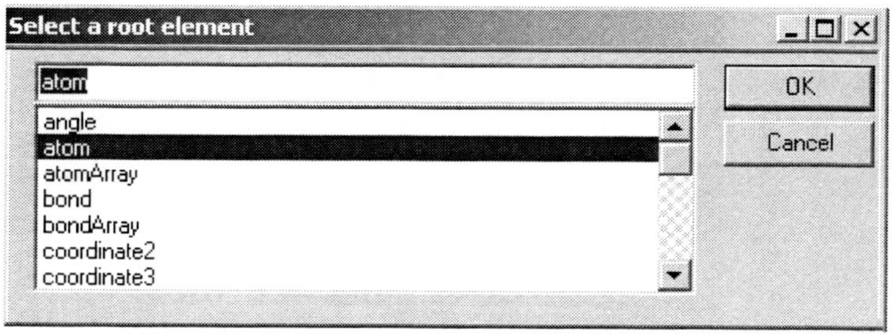

The new document is created with this element as its document root.

Open...

The "Open..." command opens any XML-related document or text file from your PC. The familiar Windows "Open" dialog box appears and allows you to select **one or more** files.

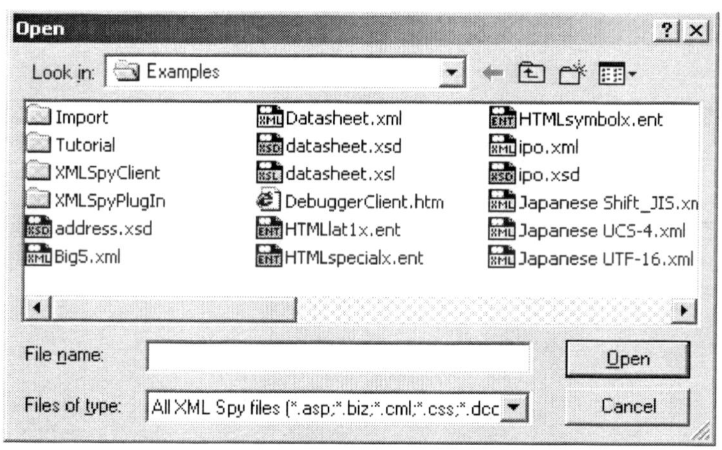

Use the "Files of type" combo box to select which kind of files you want to be displayed in the dialog box (the list of available file types can be configured through the File Types tab on the Tools | Options dialog).

After the file has been read into memory, the character-set encoding used within the file will be auto-detected and the file is decoded accordingly.
If the character-set used to encode the file, differs from the encoding-specification in the XML-declaration in the prolog, an error message is displayed and the file is automatically opened using the correct encoding.

Auto-checks on opening
You may get an error message if your file is either not well-formed or invalid, and you have selected to perform automatic validation upon opening.

In this case the document will be opened in the appropriate view, an error message popup will be displayed with the details about the error detected, and the offending item will be highlighted in the window.

In such a case simply fix the error and click on the Recheck or Revalidate button to continue opening the file.

Opening Unicode files
If you are using the Windows 98 version of STYLEVISION 2004 and have chosen to open a Unicode file, STYLEVISION 2004 converts the file to a Windows 98 code-page to be used for viewing and editing, as Windows 98 do not support Unicode on the operating system layer (for further information please see the Unicode chapter in the background information section). The conversion is done automatically according to the settings you provide in the "Encoding" tab of the Tools | Options dialog.

Open URL...

The "Open URL..." command allows you to open non-local files from a URL (uniform resource locator) using http and WebDAV.

To open an URL address:
1. Enter the URL you want to access, in the "Server URL" field.
2. Enter your User-ID in the User and Password fields, if the server is password protected.
3. Click the **Browse** button to view and navigate the directory structure of the server.

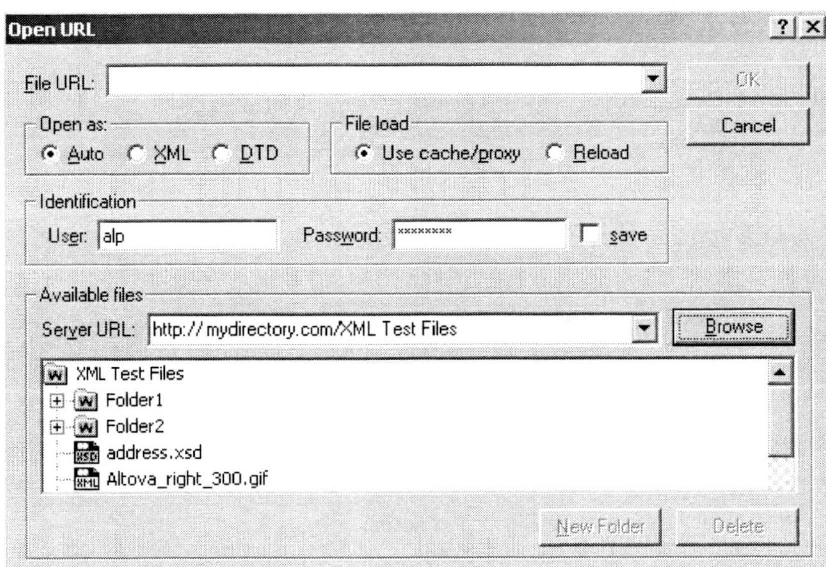

4. Click the file you want to load into STYLEVISION 2004.

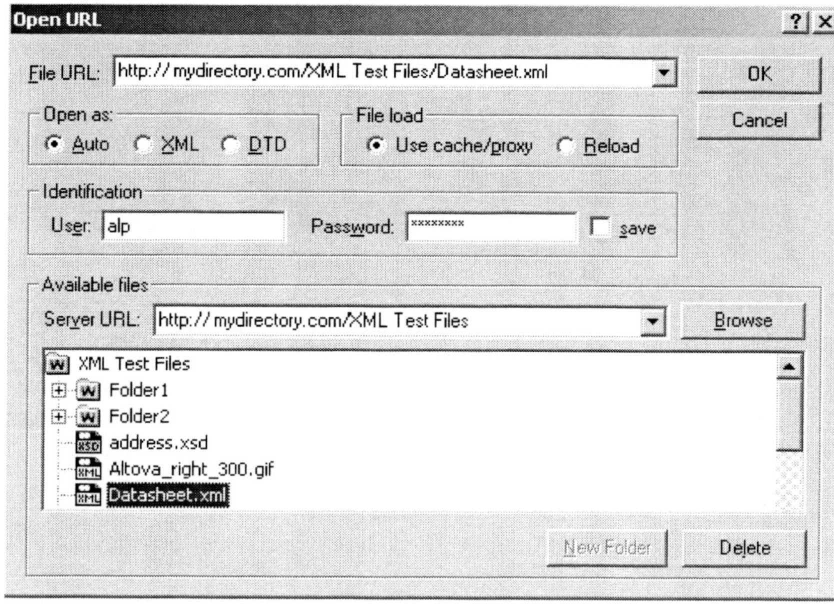

The file URL appears in the "File URL" field. The OK button only becomes active at this point.

5. Click the OK button to load the file.
   The file you open appears in the main window.

The **Browse** function is only available on servers which support the following protocols:

- FTP
- HTTP and HTTPS, if the server supports WebDAV
- or servers supporting WebDAV

File load:
To give you more control over the loading process, you can choose to load the file through the **local cache** or a **proxy** server (which considerably speeds up the process, if the file has been loaded before).

To reload the file anew in every case, select the **Reload** radio button - when you are working with an electronic publishing or database system for example, and wish to view the live output using STYLEVISION 2004.

Repositories
Repositories supported by STYLEVISION 2004 come in three flavors:

- Generic version control systems, such as Microsoft Visual Source-Safe (or compatible products)
- Generic web servers, such as FTP or WebDAV servers; and
- Specialized XML or schema repositories, such as Tamino, TEXTML Server, Virtuoso, or XML Canon.

STYLEVISION 2004 currently supports Source-Safe, FTP and WebDAV servers, as well as Virtuoso through WebDAV. Other repository interfaces will be available in future versions.

Reload

The Reload command allows you to reload documents from the URL.

STYLEVISION 2004 automatically monitors all open files (on the local network) for changes made by other programs (or people), and automatically prompts you to reload such a file, if you have checked the corresponding box on the File tab of the Tools | Options dialog.

This option is useful for documents that you open through a URL, which are dynamically created. This command is rarely used when working on documents that are accessed as files on your local hard disk or through a network file server.

Encoding...

The "Encoding..." command lets you view the current encoding of a file and select a different encoding when saving the current document the next time.

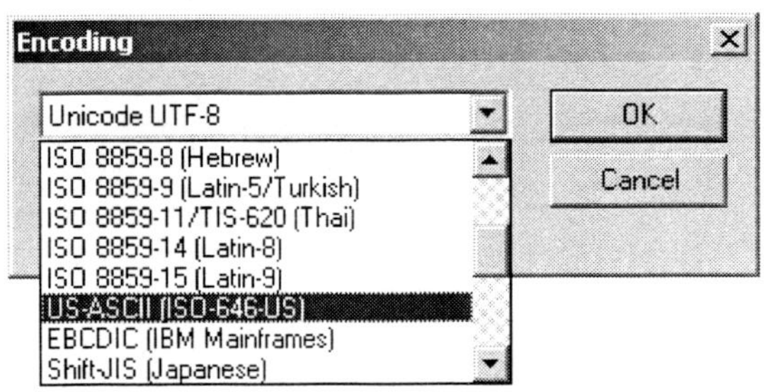

If you select a different encoding than the one in use before, the encoding-specification in the XML-declaration in the prolog will be adjusted accordingly. For 16-bit and 32-bit per character encodings (UTF-16, UCS-2, and UCS-4) you can also specify the byte-order to be used for the file.

You can also enter the new encoding into the encoding-specification of the XML-declaration. When saving a document, STYLEVISION 2004 automatically checks the encoding-specification and opens a dialog box if it cannot recognize the encoding name entered by the user.

If your document contains characters that cannot be represented in the selected encoding, you will get a warning message as soon as you save your file.

Close

The "Close" command closes the active document window. If the file was modified (the file name is appended with an asterisk "*" in the title bar), you will be asked if you wish to save the file first.

Close All

The "Close All" command closes all open document windows. If any document has been modified (asterisk "*" appended to the file name in the title bar), you will be asked if you wish to save the file first.

Save

The "Save" command saves the contents of the active document to the file it has been opened from.

When saving a document, the file is automatically checked for well-formedness. All XML documents must be well-formed – otherwise they could not be interpreted by any other XML application. The XML-Declaration is also checked for an encoding specification and it is applied to the document when the file is saved.

You can optionally have STYLEVISION 2004 automatically validate a document upon saving (this can be defined in the File tab on the Tools | Options dialog).

If a validation error occurs, STYLEVISION 2004 will bring up a popup message with a detailed error explanation and will highlight the offending item. You can then choose to fix the problem or save the document as is. In the latter case, you will be prompted to correct the error the next time you open the file with STYLEVISION 2004.

Save As...

The "Save As..." command shows the familiar Windows "Save as..." dialog box to prompt for the name and location of the file that is to be saved. The same checks and validations occur as for the "Save" command.

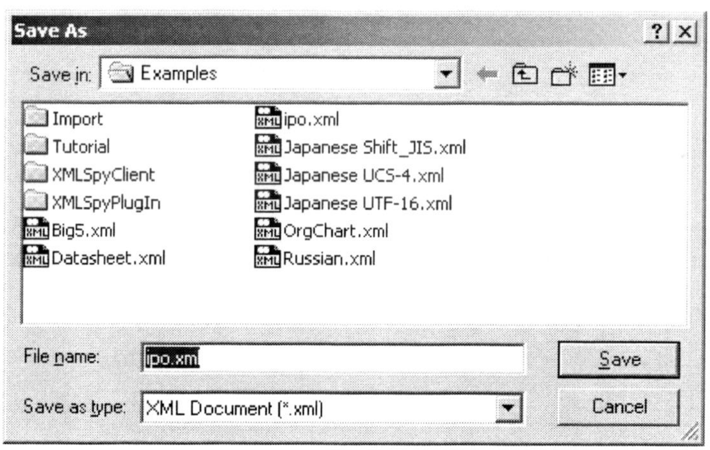

Save to URL...

The "Save to URL..." command allows you to save non-local files to a specified URL (uniform resource locator) address.

To save an XML document to a URL address:

1. Make sure the file you want to save is active in the main window.
2. Select the menu option **File | Save to URL**
3. Click the **Browse** button to see and navigate the directory structure of the server.

4. Enter the file name in the URL field, or mark the file in the "Available files" list box, if you want to overwrite it.

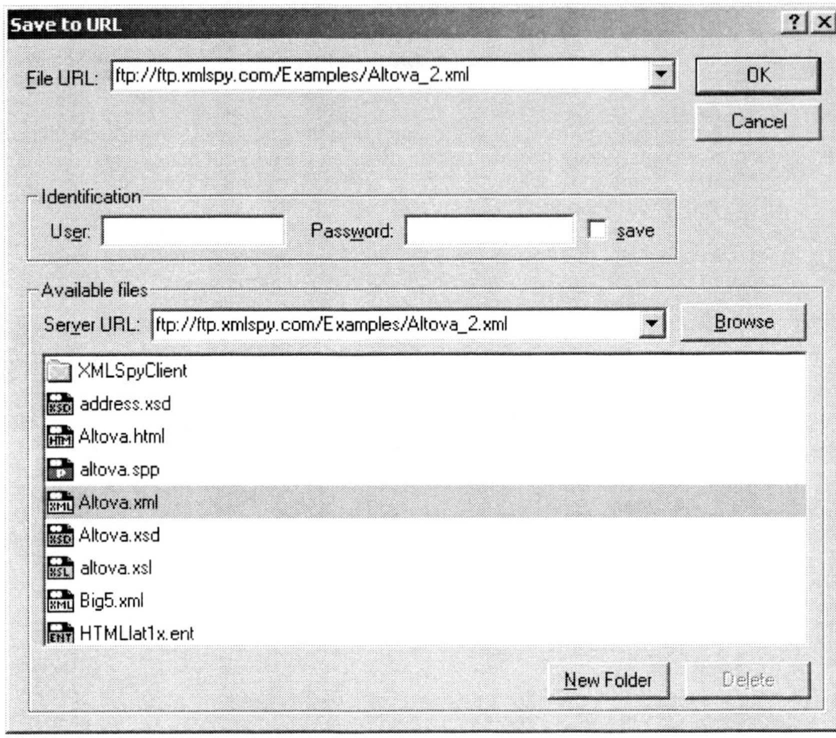

The **Browse** function is only available on servers which support the following protocols:

- FTP
- HTTP and HTTPS, if the server supports WebDAV
- or servers supporting WebDAV

Password protected servers
If the server you connect to is password protected, enter the required data and click the OK button to connect. You can also enter these data in the User and Password fields. The Save check box, supplies the password data for the logon attempt.

Save All

The "Save All" command saves all modifications that have been made to any open documents. The command is useful if you edit multiple documentations simultaneously.

If a document has never been saved (e.g. after using the New command), the Save as... dialog box is presented for that document.

Send by Mail...

The "Send by Mail" command lets you create mail messages from any XML file, group of files (in the Project window), or selection within a file. To use this function you must be using a MAPI compliant e-mail system.

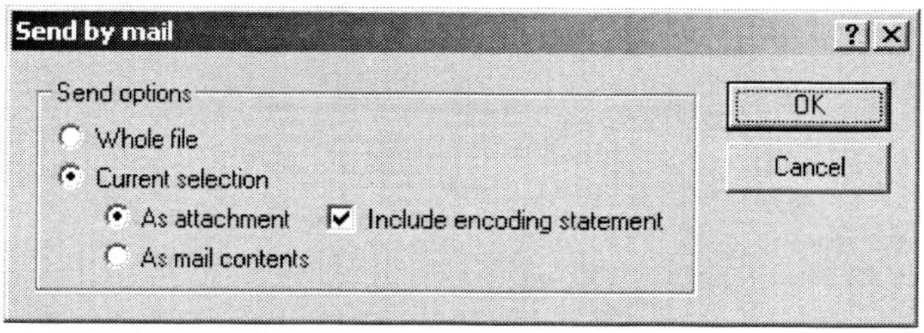

If you choose to send an entire file or group of files, they are always included as an attachment to the mail message:

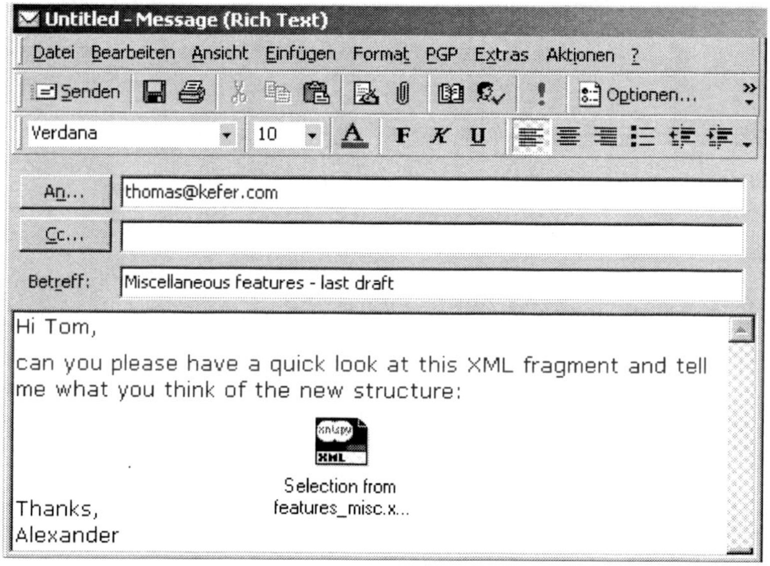

Sending fragments or portions of documents
When you want to send a fragment of an XML file, select the elements you wish to send in either Enhanced Grid View or Text View.

STYLEVISION 2004 gives you the choice of either creating an attachment file that contains only your current selection or simply sending the selection as XML text in the contents of the mail message.

Sending URLs by mail
When you send an URL (from the project window) you are prompted if you want to first retrieve the document referred to by the URL and then send the file as an attachment, or if you wish to just include the URL so that the recipient of your message can access the document through the URL:

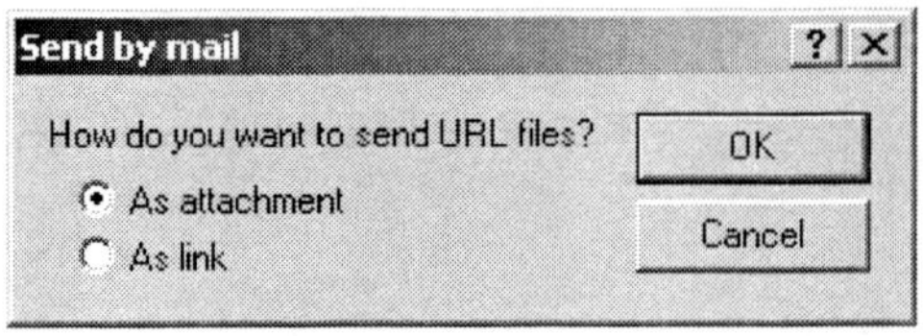

Print...

The "Print..." command opens the "Print" dialog box where you can control what appears on the printout. This dialog box contains different items, depending on the current view mode.

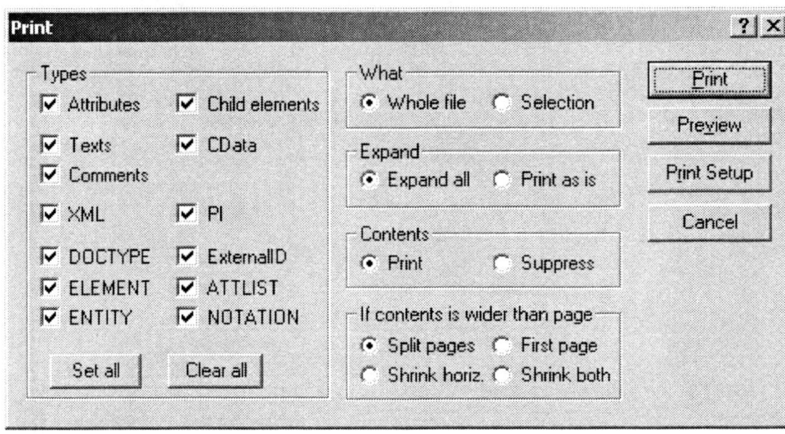

Enhanced Grid View options:

- The "**Types**" group box allows you to select the items you wish to appear in the output. You can hide comments as well as processing instructions or DTD items. For an explanation of the item types, please refer to the XML specification.
- The "**What**" group box allows you to print the entire file or just the current selection.
- The "**Expand**" group box allows you to print the document as is, or as a document with all child elements expanded fully.
- The "**Contents**" group box you can decide to print the contents of all elements in a document, or you may also print only those elements that form the hierarchical "tree" structure of the document.
  This should, however, not be confused with the optional tree view on the left side of each document window, which is only used as a navigation aid on the screen and cannot be printed.
- In the "**If contents are wider than page**" group box you can decide what to do if the document is larger than one page of paper.

- The "*Split pages*" option, prints the entire document in its regular size and splits the contents on as many pages (both horizontally and vertically) as are required. These pages can later be glued together to form a poster.
- The "*First page*" option, is useful if your page is slightly narrow and most of the important information is contained on the left side, anyway. This will result in output that is split into vertical pages (as necessary). Only the first page is printed horizontally - the

document is printed as one huge vertical strip.
- The "*Shrink horizontally*" option, reduces the size of the output, until it fits horizontally on the page. The output may, however, still span several pages vertically and is split accordingly.
- The "*Shrink both*" option, shrinks the document in both directions until it fits exactly on one sheet, thus making it useful for overviews.

- The "Print" button prints the document with the selected options.
- The "Preview" button opens a print preview window that lets you view the final output before committing it to paper.
- The "Print Setup" button opens the "Print Setup" dialog box and allows you to adjust the paper format, orientation, and other printer options for this print job only.

If you choose the Preview button, STYLEVISION 2004 will show a miniature image of the pages to be printed:

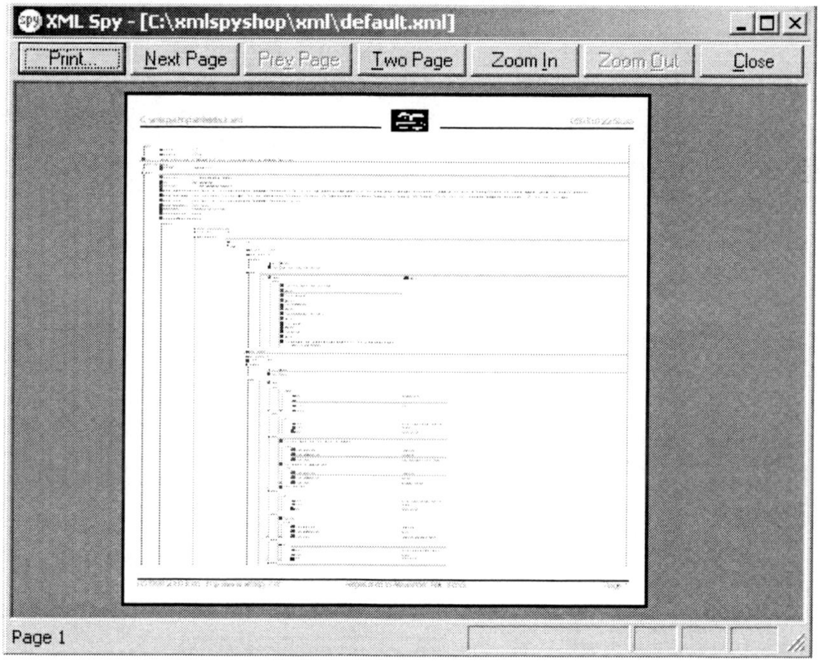

You can navigate within the preview mode using the "Next Page" and "Prev Page" buttons or "Zoom In" to take a close look at some details.

The "Print..." button lets you print the pages, whereas the "Close" button allows you to return to the previous dialog box without starting the print process.

Print Setup...

The "Print Setup..." command, displays the printer-specific "Print Setup" dialog box, enabling you to set the paper format, orientation, and other printer options for all **successive print jobs**.

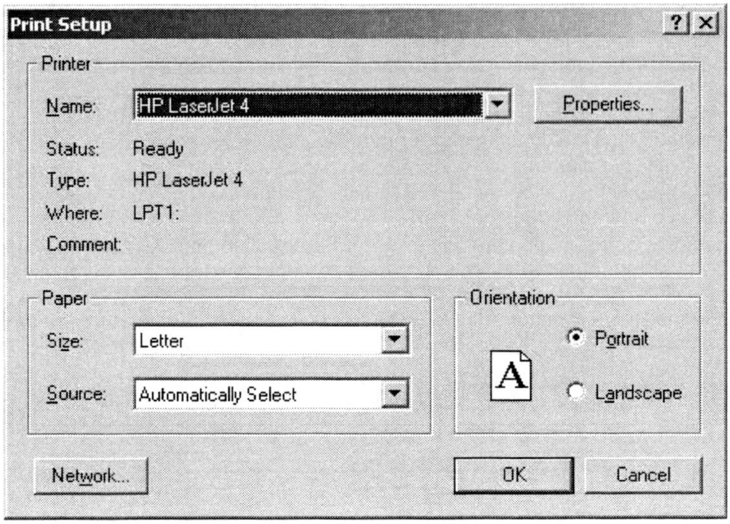

This is an example using an HP LaserJet 4 printer attached to the parallel port (LPT1:).

Most Recently Used Files

The list of most recently used files, shows the file name and path information for the nine most recently used files, which you can select with the mouse.

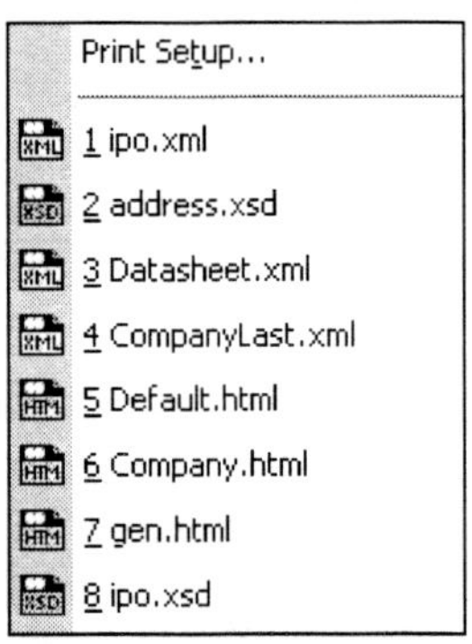

To access these files using the keyboard, press:
ALT+F to open the File menu, and hit the number of the file you want to open.

Exit

The exit command is used to quit STYLEVISION 2004 when you are finished working with your documents. If you have any open files with unsaved changes, STYLEVISION 2004 will automatically prompt you to save these changes.

STYLEVISION 2004 also saves modifications you have made to program settings, as well as information about the most recently used files and projects to the Registry, a message box appears during this process.

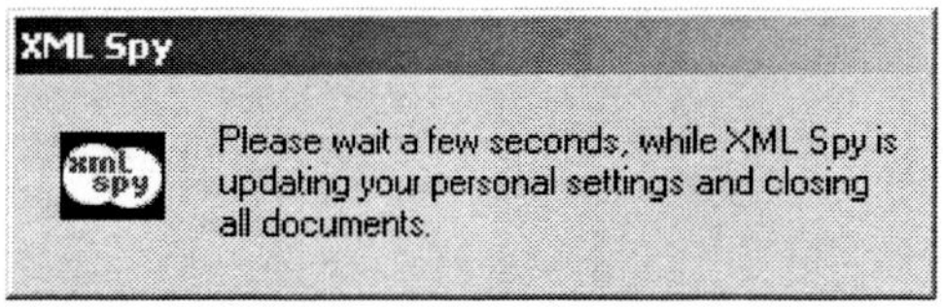
XML Spy
Please wait a few seconds, while XML Spy is updating your personal settings and closing all documents.

Edit Menu

The Edit menu contains all commands relevant to editing operations within STYLEVISION 2004 in the order common to most Windows software products.

In addition to the standard Undo, Redo, Cut, Copy, Paste, Delete, Select All, Find, Find next and Replace commands, STYLEVISION 2004 offers special commands to:

- copy the selection to the clipboard as XML-Text,
- copy as structured text, or
- copy an XPath selector to the selected item to the clipboard.

All commands can be applied while editing text, as well as while operating on whole items or even discontinuous selections of more than one item.

Undo

Hotkey: **CTRL + Z**

The "Undo" command contains support for unlimited levels of Undo! Every action can be undone and it is possible to undo one command after another. The Undo history is retained after using the "Save" command, enabling you go back to the state the document was in before you saved your changes.

Please note:

When you have turned on dynamic syntax coloring updates in the Text View and your operating system is using RichEdit 2.0 (i.e. earlier versions of Windows 98 and Windows NT 4.0), syntax coloring changes appear as undoable operations. If you want to avoid this, please update to RichEdit 3.0 or disable the dynamic syntax coloring update feature (for further information please see the background information on the RichEdit Component).

Redo

Hotkey: **CTRL + Y**

The "Redo" command allows you to redo previously undone commands – thereby giving you a complete history of the work you have completed. You can step back and forward through this history using the Undo and Redo commands.

Cut

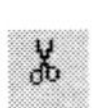

Hotkey: **Shift + Delete**, or **CTRL + X**

The Cut command copies the selected text or items to the clipboard and deletes them from their present location.

Copy

Hotkey: **CTRL + C**

The Copy command copies the selected text or items to the clipboard. This can be used to duplicate data within STYLEVISION 2004 or to move data to another application.

Please note:
There are two different commands for copying elements to the clipboard in a textual form: Copy as XML-Text and Copy as Structured Text.

You can use the Editing tab on the Tools | Options dialog, to choose which operation should be performed when you use the copy command on the Edit menu or the Ctrl-C shortcut.

Paste

Hotkey: **CTRL + V**

The Paste command inserts the contents of the clipboard at the current cursor position.

Delete

Keyboard: **Del.**

The Delete command deletes the currently selected text or items without placing them in the clipboard.

Copy as XML-Text

The "Copy as XML-Text" command lets you exchange data easily with other products that allow data manipulation on the XML source layer.

While editing your document in Enhanced Grid View, you may occasionally want to copy some elements to the clipboard in their XML-Text representation:

```
<row>
    <para align="left">
        <bold>Check the FAQ</bold>
    </para>
    <para>
        <link mode="internal">
            <link_section>support</link_section>
            <link_subsection>faq30</link_subsection>
            <link_text>XMLSPY 4.0 FAQ</link_text>
        </link>
        <link mode="internal">
            <link_section>support</link_section>
            <link_subsection>faq25</link_subsection>
            <link_text>XMLSPY 3.5 FAQ</link_text>
        </link>
    </para>
</row>
```

This command automatically formats text using the currently active settings for saving a file. These settings can be modified in the "Save File" section of the File tab of the Tools | Options dialog).

Copy as Structured Text

The " Copy as Structured Text" command copies elements to the clipboard as they appear on screen. This command is useful for copying table-like data from the Enhanced Grid View as well as the integrated Database/Table View.

The copied data can be used within STYLEVISION 2004 as well as third-party products, enabling you to transfer XML data to spreadsheet-like applications (e.g. Microsoft Excel).

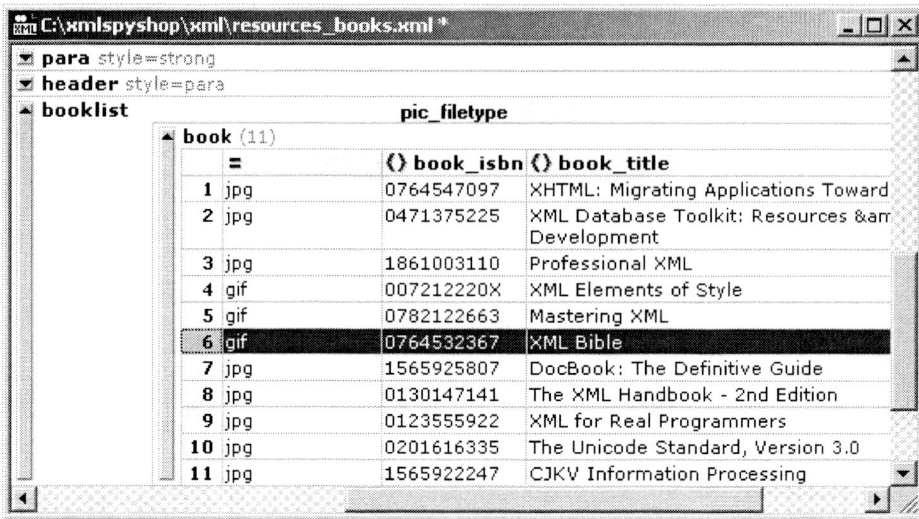

If you copy this table and paste it into Excel, the data will appear in the following way:

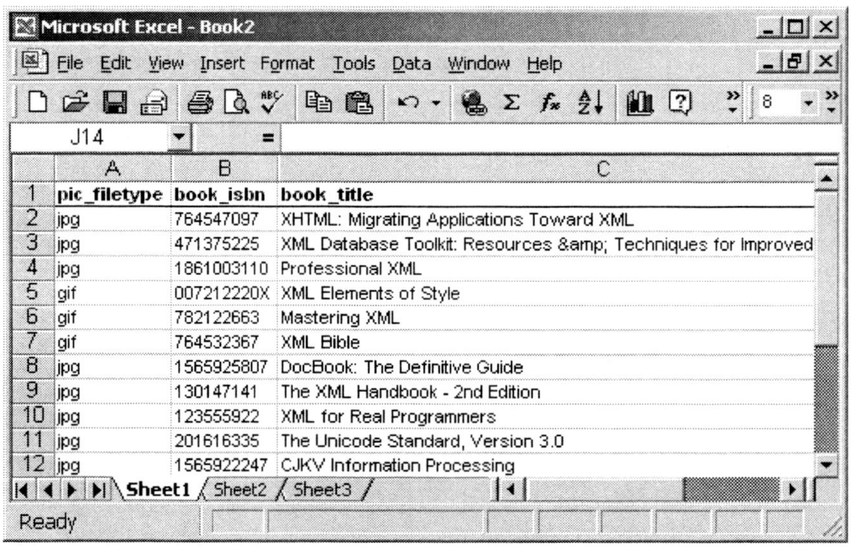

Please note:

The results of this command depend on the way the information is currently laid out on screen. Using the same XML data (that served as an example for the Copy as XML-Text command) in the Enhanced Grid view with the **Table view active**, would result in the following:

```
row
    para
        align    bold    link
        left     Check the FAQ
```

```
link
                   mode        link_section     link_subsection    link_text
                   internal    support          faq30              XMLSPY 3.5
FAQ
                   internal    support          faq25              XMLSPY 2.5
FAQ
```

The same data would be copied to the clipboard in the following format, with the **Table view deactivated** in the Enhanced Grid View.

```
row
    para
        align    left
        bold     Check the FAQ
    para
        link
            mode               internal
            link_section       support
            link_subsection    faq30
            link_text          XMLSPY 3.5 FAQ
        link
            mode               internal
            link_section       support
            link_subsection    faq25
            link_text          XMLSPY 2.5 FAQ
```

Copy XPath

The "Copy XPATH" command copies the corresponding XPath Selector to the clipboard enabling you to paste it into XSLT documents or any other file that uses XPath.

When using XSLT it is very often necessary to enter so-called Selector strings that help in selecting an element or attribute from within another XML document. Selector strings are built according to the XPath definition, and STYLEVISION 2004 helps you to create XPath Selectors, by selecting the item you wish to address and choosing Copy XPATH from the Edit menu.

```
/main/content/list/header/clipart/@style
```

Pretty-Print XML Text

The "Pretty-Print XML Text" command reformats your XML document in the text view, giving you a structured display. Note that the XML document must be well formed for this command to work.

Select All

Hotkey: **CTRL + A**

The "Select All" command selects all the text of an item or all the items in an XML document, enabling successive commands to operate on the entire text or document at once.

Find...

Hotkey: **CTRL + F**

The "Find" command allows you to search for any occurrence of a text string in your XML document. Depending on the view you are using, the Find command will have different options.

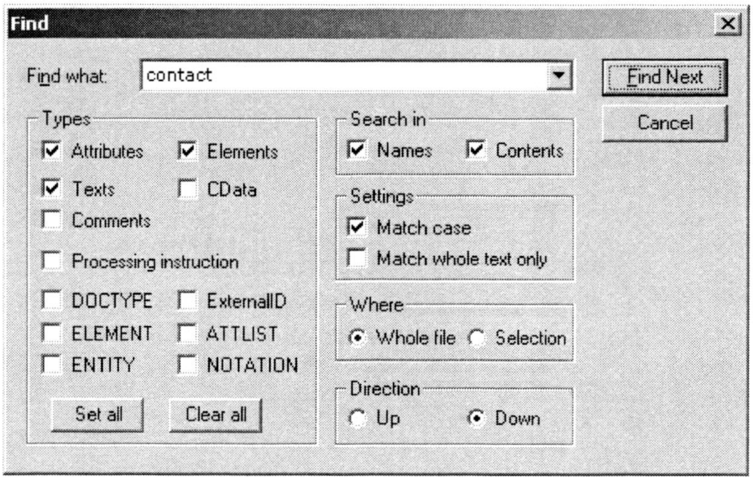

Enhanced Grid View find options:

- Enter the text string to be searched for in the "Find what" field, or use the combo box to select from one of the last 10 search criteria. The Find what field can be left empty, to search for elements, attributes etc.
- The "Types" group box, allows you to select what kind of items you wish to include in the search. This allows you to e.g. skip comments as well as processing instructions or DTD items. For an explanation of the item types, please refer to the XML specification.
- The "Search in" group box, allows you to define if you want to search for the specified text in the (element or attribute) names of items, in their contents, or in both.
- The "Settings" group box, allows you to define a case-sensitive and/or match string search.
- The "Where" group box, allows you to define your the scope of the search.
- The "Direction" group box, allows you to specify the search direction.
- The "Set all" button, activates all the check boxes in the Types group box, the "Clear all" deactivates them.

Find next

Hotkey: **F3**

The "Find next" command repeats the last Find command to search for the next occurrence of the requested text.

Replace...

 Hotkey: **CTRL + H**

The "Replace" command features the same options as the Find... command and allows you to replace the target text by any other text string of your choice.

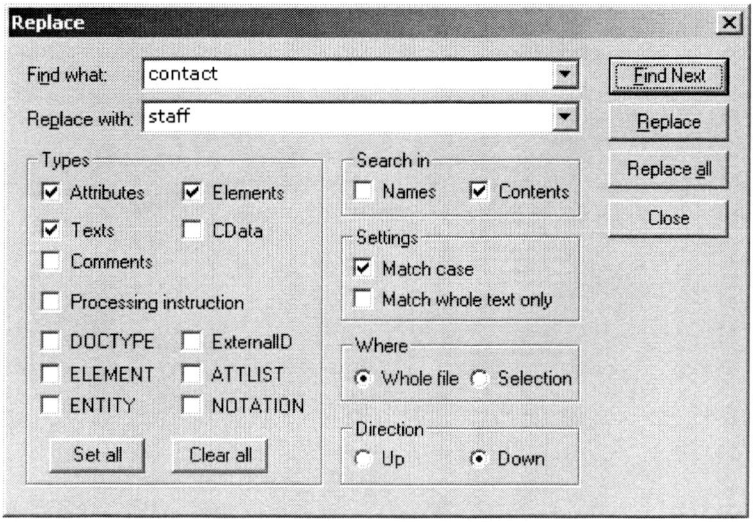

You can replace each item individually, or you can use the "Replace All" button to perform a global search and replace operation.

Please note:
As a security precaution, the "Replace all" command shows each individual replacement operation in the Enhanced Grid view. You can interrupt the operation by pressing the <ESC> key. Each replacement, is recorded as a single operation that can be undone individually.

Project Menu

STYLEVISION 2004 uses the familiar tree view to manage multiple files or URLs in XML projects. Files and URLs can be grouped into folders by common extension or any arbitrary criteria, allowing for easy structuring and batch manipulation.

Please see the description of the Project Window for a general introduction to the STYLEVISION 2004 project management.

Note: Most project-related commands are also available in the context-menu, which appears when you right-click any item in the project window.

Absolute and relative paths

Each project is saved as a project file, which has the `.spp` extension. In the project file, absolute paths are used for files/folders on the same level or higher, and relative paths for files/folders in the current folder or in sub-folders. For example, if your directory structure looks like this:

```
|-Folder1
|
|-Folder2-
|           |
|           |-Folder3
|
|-Folder4
```

...and your `.spp` file is located in `Folder2`, references to files in `Folder1` and `Folder4` will look something like this:

```
c:\Folder1\NameOfFile.ext
c:\Folder4\NameOfFile.ext
```

References to files in `Folder2` and `Folder3` will look something like this:

```
.\NameOfFile.ext
.\Folder3\NameOfFile.ext
```

If you wish to make all the paths relative, save the `.spp` files in the root directory of your working disk.

New Project

This command creates a **new** project in STYLEVISION 2004.

If you are currently working with another project, a prompt appears asking if you want to close all documents belonging to the current project.

Open Project...

This command **opens** an existing project in STYLEVISION 2004.

If you are currently working with another project, the previous project is closed first.

Reload Project

This command **reloads** the current project from disk.

If you are working in a multi-user environment, it can sometimes become necessary to reload the project from disk, as other users might have made changes to the project.

Please note:
STYLEVISION 2004 project (.spp) files are actually XML documents that you can edit like any regular XML File. This should only be attempted by advanced users!

Close Project

This command **closes** the active project.

If the project has been modified, you will be asked if you want to save the project first.

When a project, or XML file is modified, an asterisk "*" is automatically appended to the file name in the title bar.

Save Project

This command **saves** the current project.

Source control

STYLEVISION 2004 supports Microsoft Source-Safe and other compatible repositories.

Open source revision control systems:

- Concurrent Versions System (CVS).
  The Jalindi Igloo software must be downloaded for STYLEVISION 2004 to connect to CVS. Download this software component from the Altova components web site, or from the Jalindi.com site.

Commercial revision control systems:

- Microsoft Visual Source-Safe 6.0c
- PVCS Version Manager 6.7
- StarTeam 5.1

A source control project is, however, not the same as a STYLEVISION 2004 project. Source control projects are extremely directory dependent, whereas STYLEVISION 2004 projects are logical constructions without direct directory dependence.

The following text uses Microsoft Source-Safe as the Source Control provider.

Please note:

Microsoft has defined a Registry Entry, where all SCC compatible programs can register themselves. STYLEVISION 2004 only reads this entry.

HKEY_LOCAL_MACHINE\SOFTWARE\SourceCodeControlProvider\InstalledSCCProviders

Delta V
Extends the WebDAV protocol, where WebDAV is itself an extension of the HTTP 1.1 protocol. STYLEVISION 2004 now supports Delta V at the project, folder and single file level via the context menu (right click on the respective object). The Delta V protocol is supported by STYLEVISION 2004 but is only enabled, if the server capabilities on which the files under source control are placed, allow this.

Accessing files placed under source control on a Delta V enabled web server, automatically enable the Delta V versioning commands: check in/out, undo check out.

Delta V commands can be accessed by right clicking:

- the file tab of an open file in the main window
- a file in the Open URL browse window
- a file in an external web folder of a project

Delta V is the **versioning** part of the WebDAV standard and supports:

- Check out
- Undo check out
- Check in (plus comment)

WebDAV capabilities include:

- Overwrite protection: lock and unlock
- Properties: list, add and remove
- Namespace operations: move and copy
- Collections:hierarchy operations and mkcol.

For more in-depth information on Delta V please see www.webdav.org/deltav.

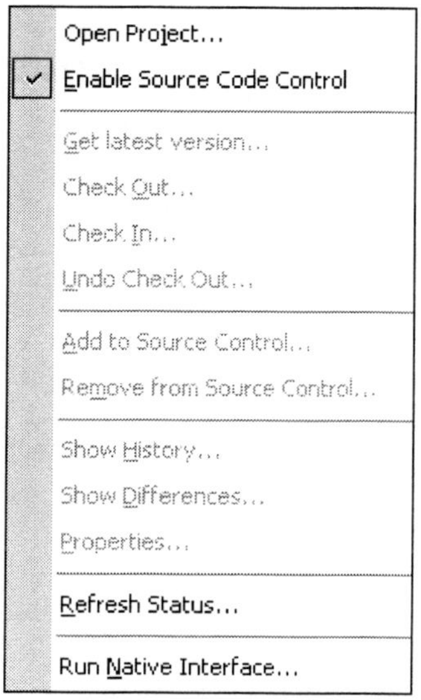

Open project

The Open Project command mirrors (or creates) an existing source control project locally. This command can only take effect if an STYLEVISION 2004 project has previously been added to source control provider using the menu option Add to Source Control.

1. Select a source control provider from the list of those installed on your PC, and confirm with the OK button.

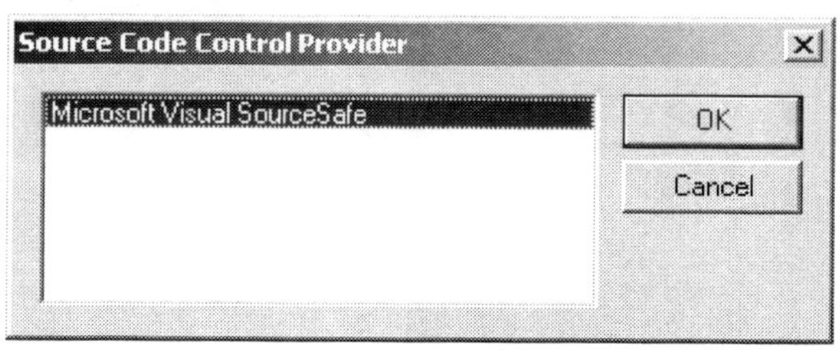

2. Enter your login data in the Source Control Login dialog box, and confirm with OK.

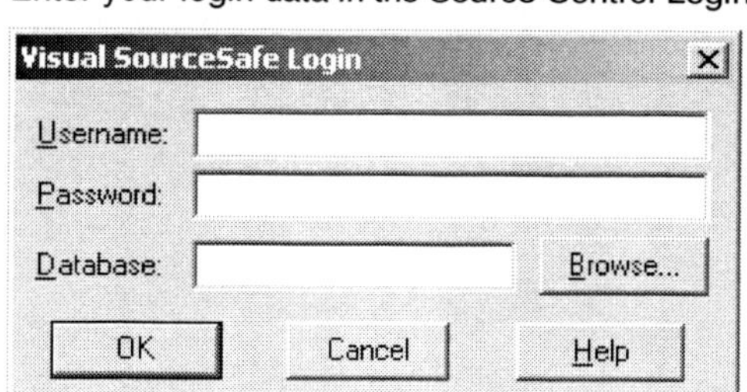

3. Define the directory to contain the local project.
4. Select the Source control project you want to download.
   If the folder you define does not exist at the location, a dialog box opens prompting you

to create it there. Click Yes to confirm the new directory.

5. Click the OK button to download the source control project.

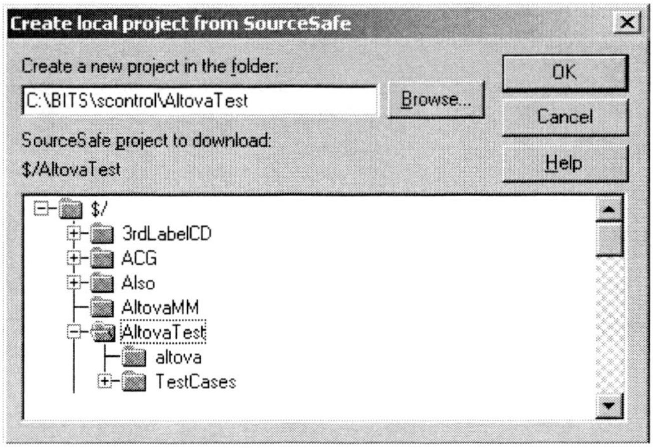

6. This displays the Open dialog box, and attempts to find the STYLEVISION 2004 project file (*.spp) in the local directory. Click the project file you want to create, if there are several to choose from.

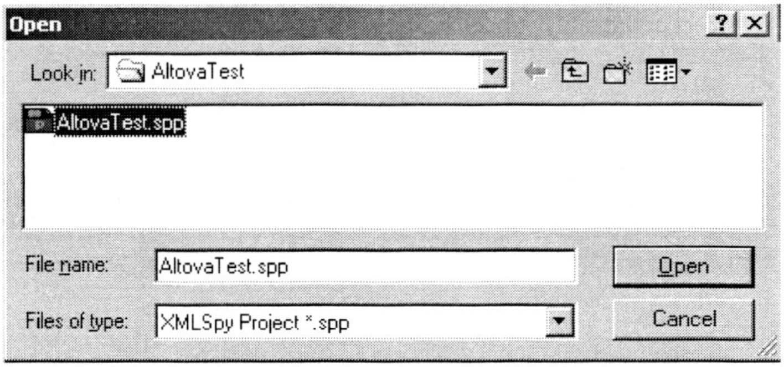

A message box might appear at this point stating that the directory is under source control, offering you the option of checking it out or not.

7. Click the OK, if you want source control to be enabled.
The Check out dialog box opens, allowing you to check out the *.spp file.
8. Add any comments to the file in the Comment text box and Click OK, to check out the STYLEVISION 2004 project file. Depending on your source control provider, the dialog box might contain extra command buttons. In this case the Advanced... button opens the Advanced Check Out Options dialog box.

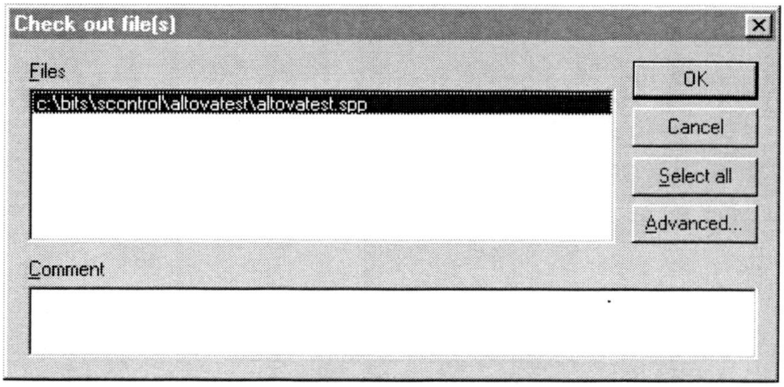

The *.spp file is checked out, and all the XML files contained in the STYLEVISION 2004 project, are copied to the local directory.

Result in STYLEVISION 2004:
The AltovaTest directory has been created locally, and all files included in the STYLEVISION 2004 project are made available in the project window. You can now work with these files as you normally do.

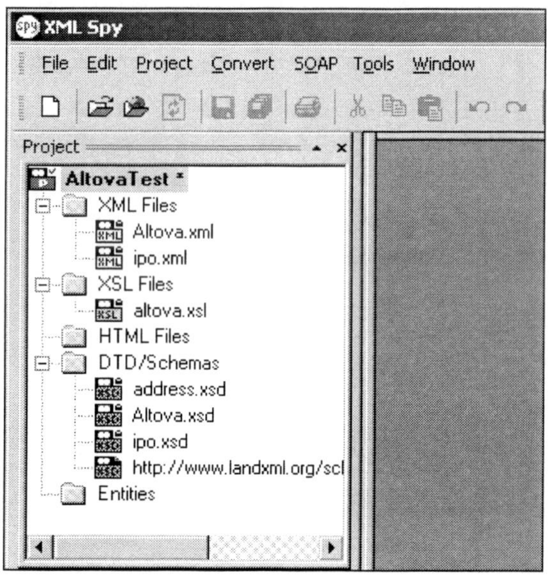

Source control symbols:

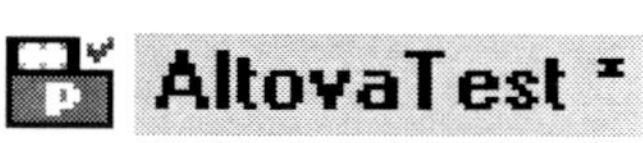

The **red check mark** denotes **checked out**, i.e. the AltovaTest project file has been checked out.
The asterisk denotes that changes have been made to the file, and you will be prompted to save it when you exit.

The lock symbol, at the top right corner the XML symbol, denotes that the file is **under source control**, but is currently not checked out.

This URL document is part of the AltovaTest project but is **not under source control**. Documents opened via URL, cannot be placed under source control.

Enable Source code control

This command allows you to enable or disable source control for a project.

To disable source control for a project:

1. Click on the project file or any other file in the project window.
2. Select the menu option **Project | Source control** and deactivate the **Enable Source Code Control** check box.

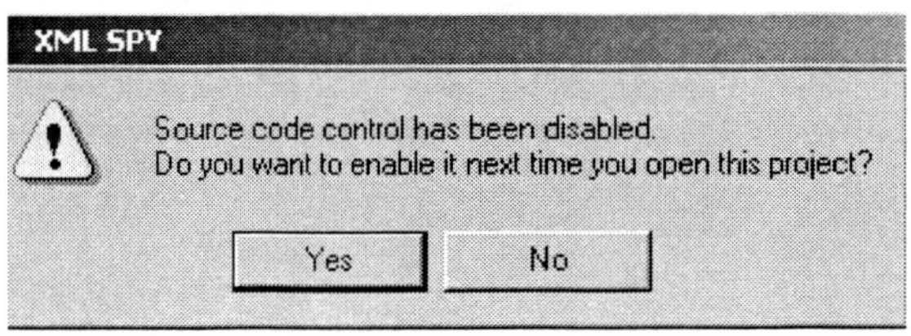

To **provisionally** disable source control for the project select YES.

To **permanently** disable source control for the project select NO.

Get Latest Version

This command **gets** the latest source control version of file you select.

The file is a copy of the source control file and is placed in your local working directory.

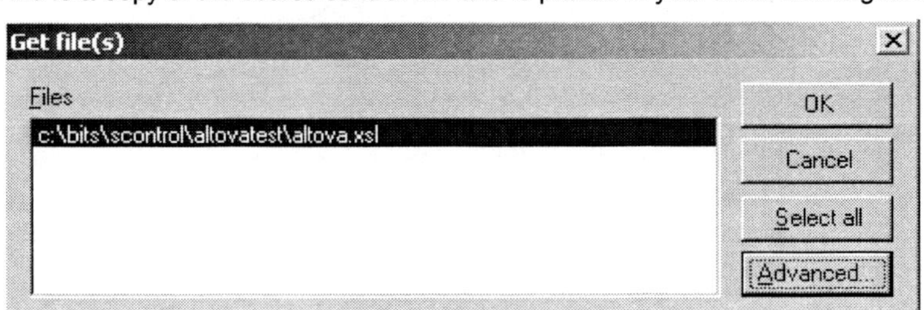

Check Out

This command **checks out** the latest source control version of file(s) you select, and flags it as "checked out" for all other users.

Shortcut: Right click an item in the project window, and select "Check out" from the context menu.

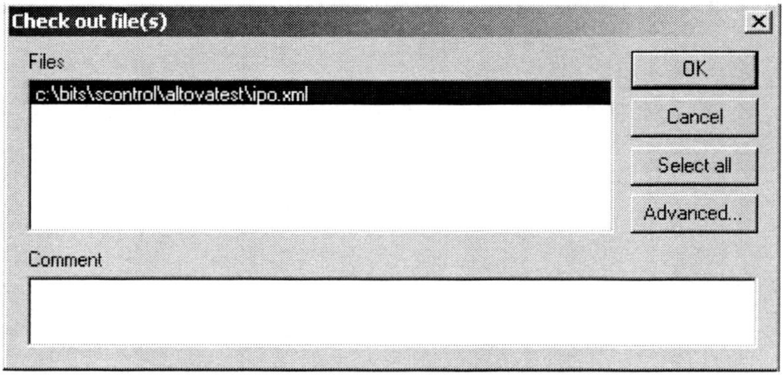

The following items can be checked out:

- Single files, click on the respective files (CTRL + click, for several)
- STYLEVISION 2004 project folders, click on the folders (CTRL + click, for several)
- STYLEVISION 2004 project, click on the project file icon.

The red check mark denotes that the file has been checked out.

Check In

This command **checks in** the previously checked out files, i.e. your locally updated files, and places them in the source control project.

Shortcut: Right click a checked out item in the project window, and select "Check in" from the Context menu.

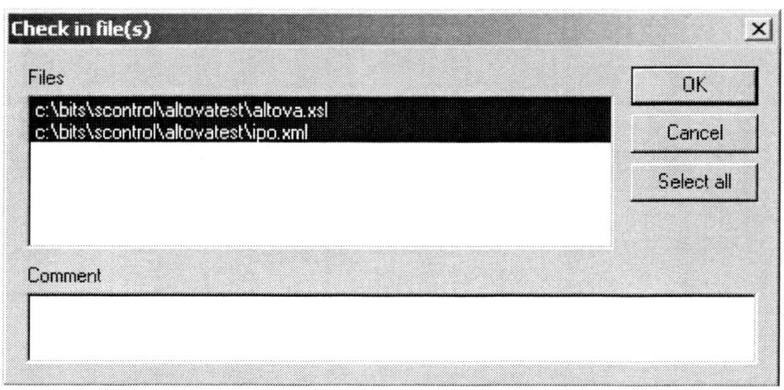

The following items can be checked in:

- Single files, click on the respective files (CTRL + click, for several)
- STYLEVISION 2004 project folders, click on the folders (CTRL + click, for several)
- A complete STYLEVISION 2004 project, click on the project file icon.

The lock symbol denotes that the file is **under source control**, but is currently not checked out.

Undo Check Out...

This command **rejects changes** made to previously checked out files, i.e. your locally updated files, and retains the old files in the source control project.

Shortcut: Right click a checked out item in the project window, and select "Undo Check out" from the Context menu.

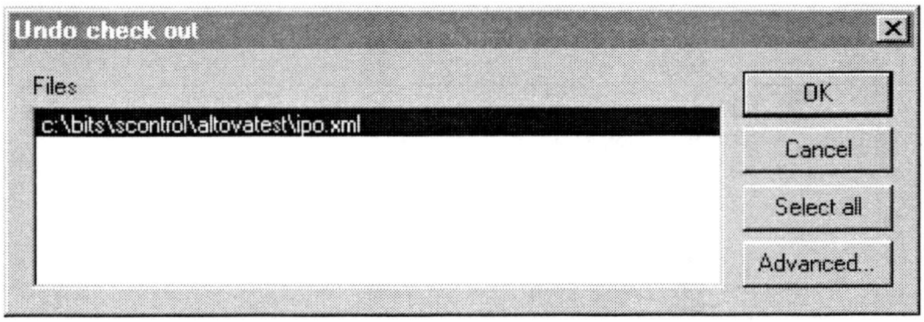

The Undo check out option can apply to the following items:

- Single files, click on the respective files (CTRL + click, for several)
- STYLEVISION 2004 project folders, click on the folders (CTRL + click, for several)
- STYLEVISION 2004 project, click on the project file icon.

Add to Source Control

This command **adds** an STYLEVISION 2004 project to your Source Control provider.

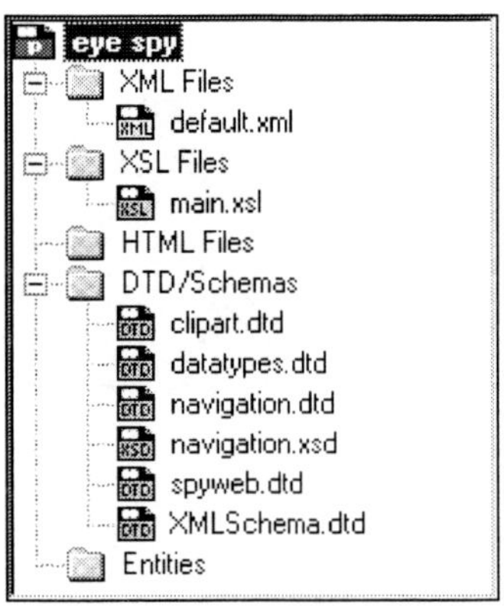

To add an XML project to the source control provider:

1. Click the STYLEVISION 2004 project icon and select the menu option **Project | Source control | Add to Source control.**
2. Select your source control provider from the list box.

3. Enter the source control login data.
4. Select the source control project (directory) to which your XML project should be added, and confirm with the OK button.

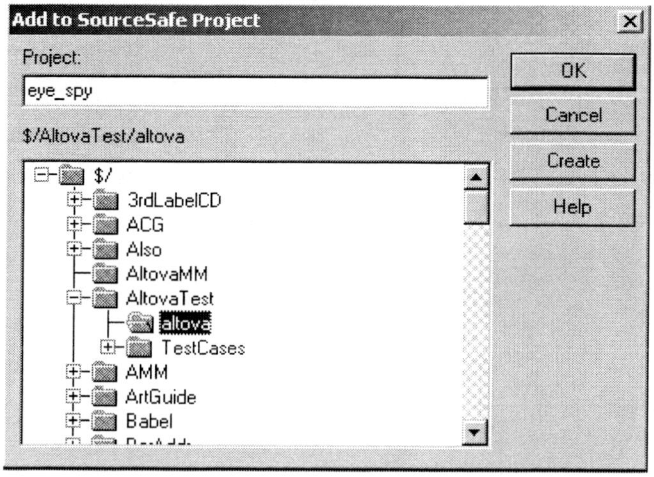

If the project does not exist, the following dialog box opens, prompting for more information.

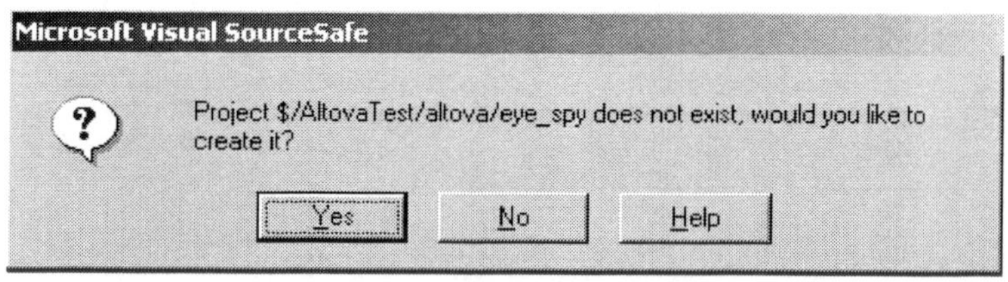

5. Select Yes to create the new project and NO to cancel.

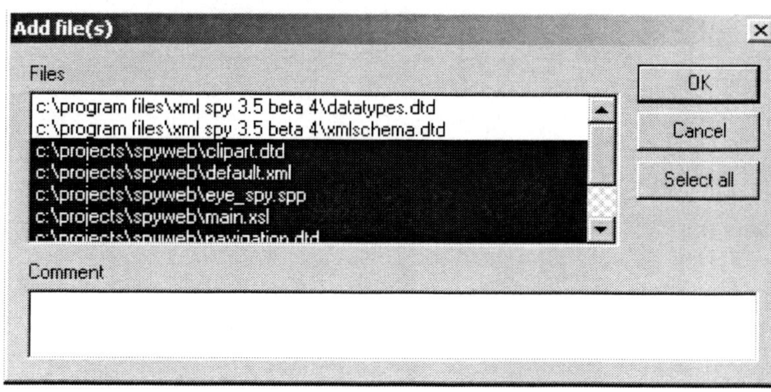

6. Select the STYLEVISION 2004 project files that you want to be placed under control of the source control provider, and confirm with OK.

The files are transferred to the source control provider and are now under source control. These files are marked with the "lock symbol" in the project window. The files you did not transfer do not have the lock symbol (datatypes.dtd and XMLschema.dtd in this example).

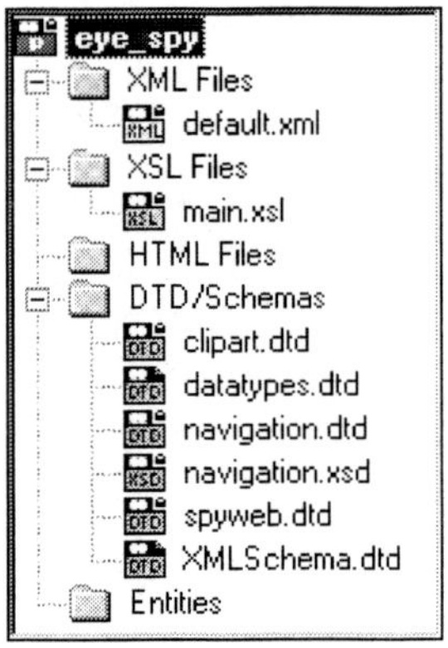

Remove from Source Control

This command **removes** previously added files, from the source control provider.

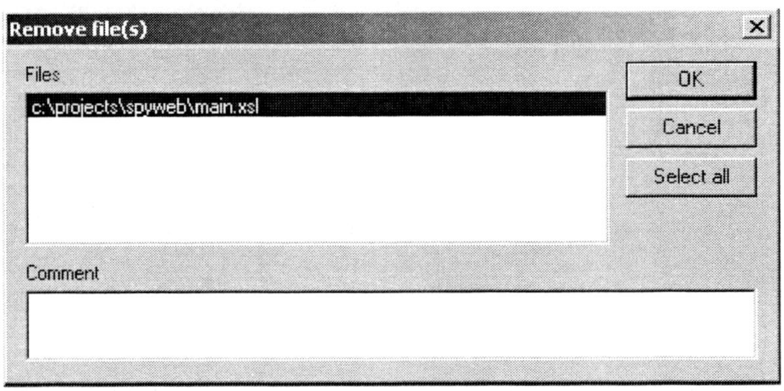

The following items can be removed from source control:

- Single files, click on the respective files (CTRL + click, for several)
- STYLEVISION 2004 project folders, click on the folders (CTRL + click, for several)
- A complete STYLEVISION 2004 project, click on the project file icon.

Show History

This command **displays** the history of a file, it can only be used on single files.

To show the history of a file:

1. Click on the file in the project window
2. Select the menu option **Project | Source control | Show history**.

   A dialog box prompting for more information may appear at this time (this example uses MS Source-Safe).

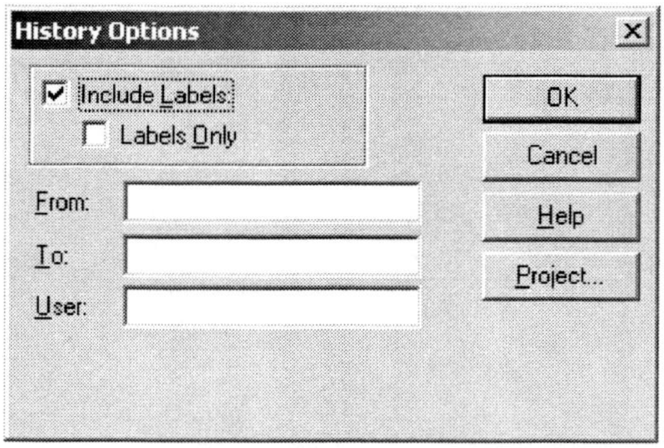

3. Select the appropriate entries and confirm with OK.

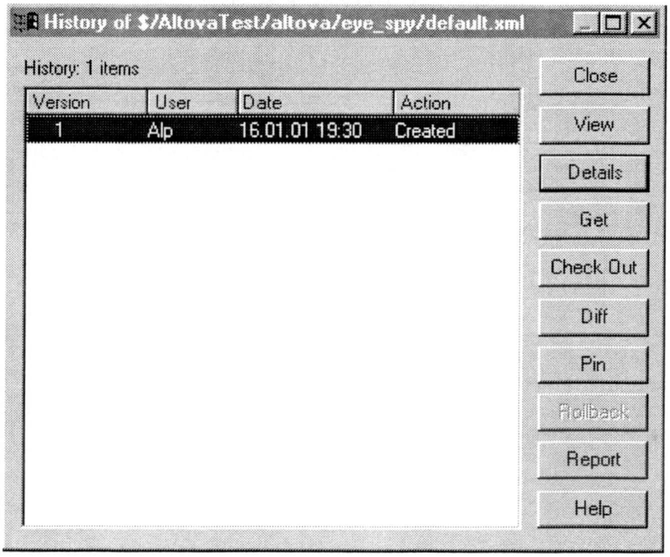

Show Differences

This command **displays** the differences between the file currently in the source control repository, and the file of the same name that you have checked out.

This command can only be used on single files.

To show the differences between two files:

Having checked out a file from your project,

1. Click on the file in the project window.
2. Select the menu option **Project | Source control | Show Differences**.
   A dialog box prompting for more information may appear at this time.

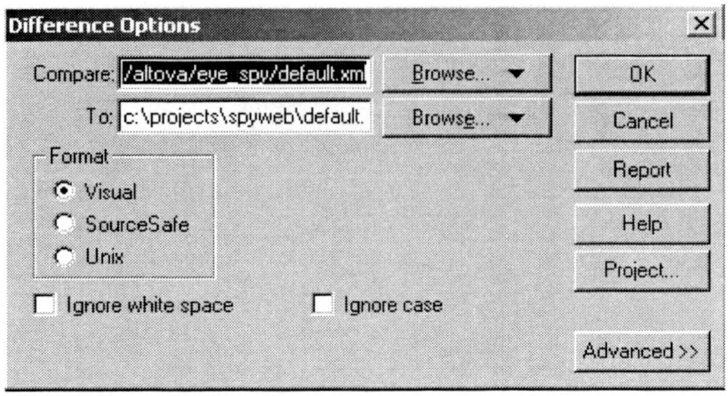

3. Select the appropriate entries and confirm with OK.

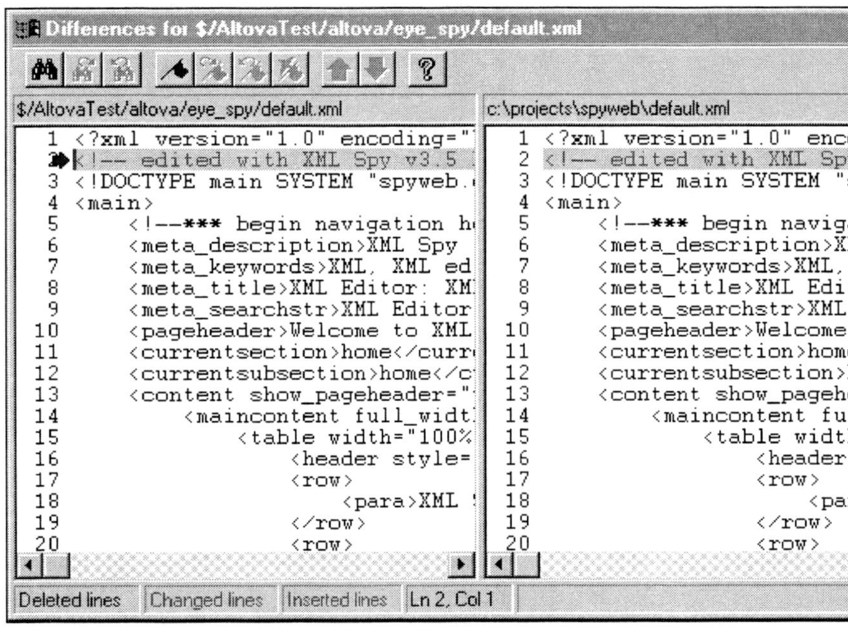

The differences between the two files are highlighted in both windows (this example uses MS Source-Safe).

Properties

This command **displays** the properties of the currently selected file, and is dependent on the source control provider you use.

This command can only be used on single files.

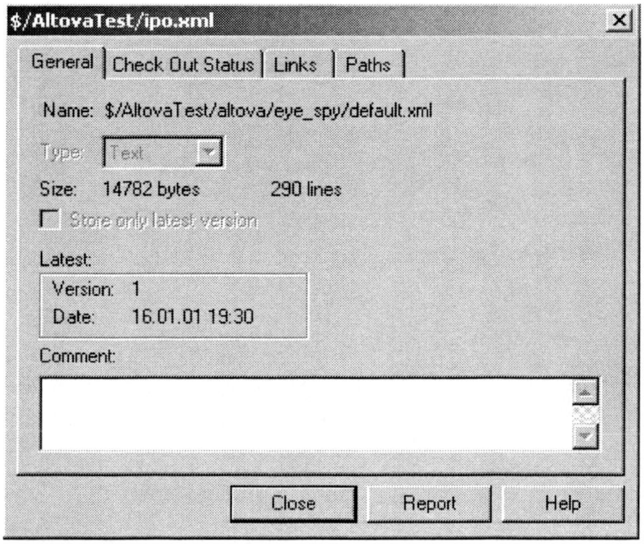

Refresh Status

This command **refreshes** the status of all project files independent of their current status.

Run Native Interface

This command **starts** your source control software with its usual user interface.

Add Files to Project...

This command **adds** files to the current project.

Use this command to add files to any folder in your project. You can either select a single file or any group of files (using CTRL + click) in the Open dialog box.

If you are adding files to the project, they will be distributed among the respective folders based on the File Type Extensions defined in the Project Properties dialog box.

Add URL to Project...

This command **adds** an URL to the current project.

STYLEVISION 2004 also allows you to add URLs to a project. Whenever a batch operation is performed on a URL or on a folder that contains a URL item, STYLEVISION 2004 will retrieve the document from the URL, and perform the requested operation.

Add Active File to Project

This command **adds** the active file to the current project.

If you have just opened a file from your hard disk or through an URL, you can add the file to the current project using this command.

Add Active And Related Files to Project

This command **adds** the currently active XML document and all related files to the project.

When working on an XML document that is based on a DTD or Schema, STYLEVISION 2004 also lets you add both the XML document and all related files (e.g. the DTD and all external parsed entities it refers to) to the current project.

Add Project Folder to Project...

This command **adds** a new folder to the current project.

Use this command to add a new folder to the current project. You can also access this command from the context-menu when you right-click on a folder in the project window.

Add External Folder to Project...

This command **adds** a new **external folder** to the current project.

Use this command to add a **local** or **network** folder to the current project. You can also access this command from the context-menu when you right-click a folder in the project window.

To add an external folder to the project

1. Select the menu option **Project | Add External Folder to project**.
2. Select the folder you want to include from the "Browse for Folder" dialog box, and click OK to confirm.

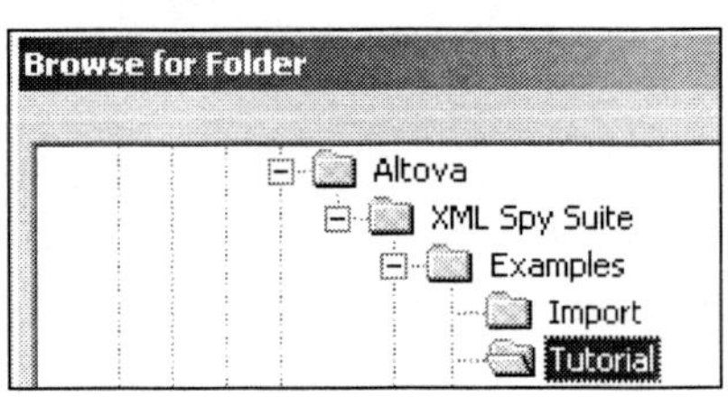

The selected folder now appears in the project window.

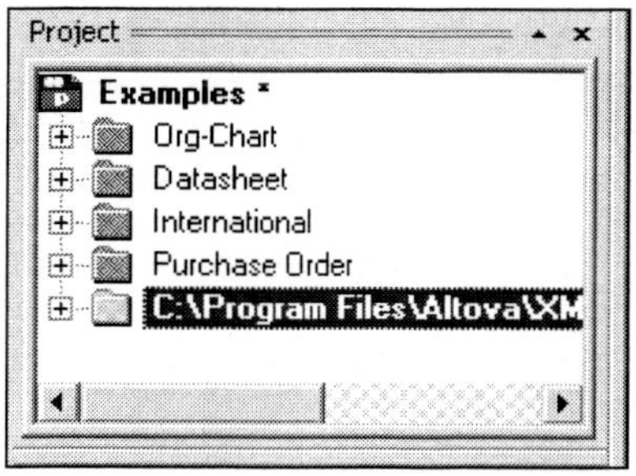

3. Click the plus icon to view the folder contents.

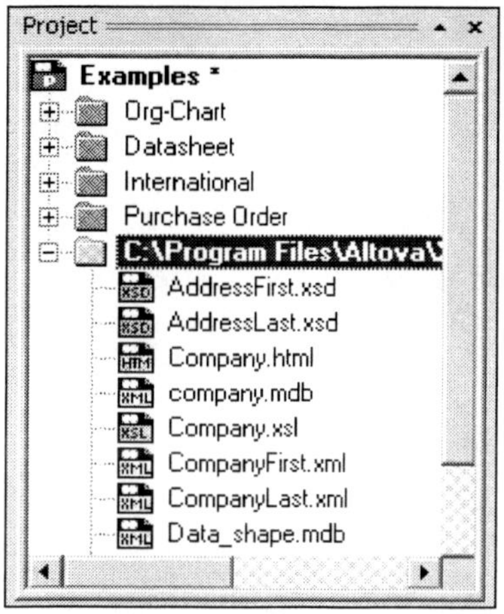

To filter the folder contents:

1. **Right click** the local folder, and select the popup menu option **Properties**. This opens the Properties dialog box.

2. Click in the **File extensions** field and enter the file extensions of the file types you want to see. You can separate each file type with a **semicolon** to define multiple types (XML and Schema XSDs in this example).
3. Click OK to confirm the selection.

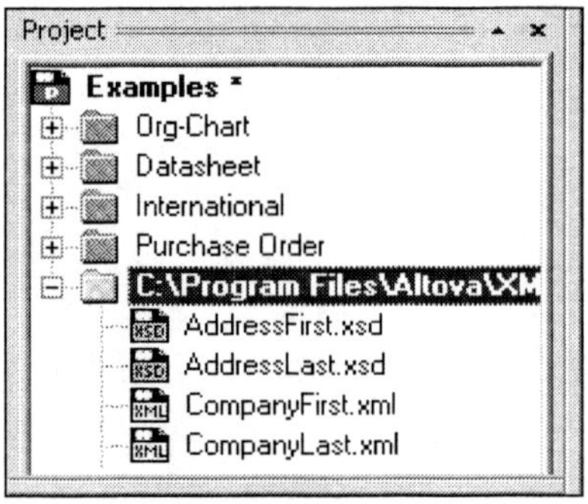

The Project window now only shows the XML and XSD files of the tutorial folder.

Validating and checking a folder for well-formedness:
Having selected the file types you want to see or check, from the external folder,

1. Click the folder and click the "Check well-formedness" or "Validate" icon, (hotkeys F7 or F8).
   All the files visible under the folder are checked.

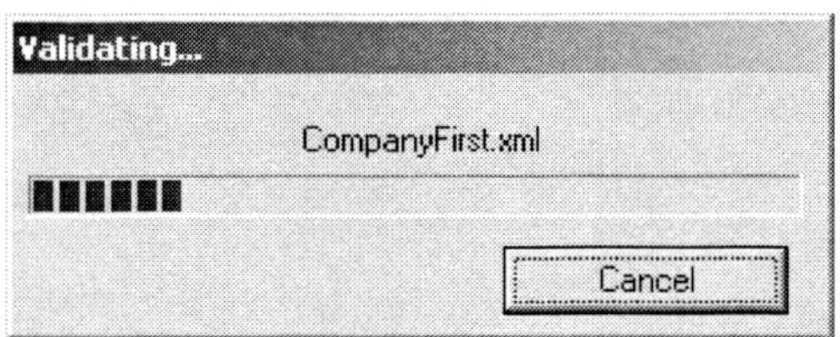

If a file is malformed or invalid, then this file is opened in the main window, allowing you to edit it. In this case the CompanyLast file is opened because the PhoneExt value does not match the facet defined in the underlying schema file. This schema only allows only two digit numbers.

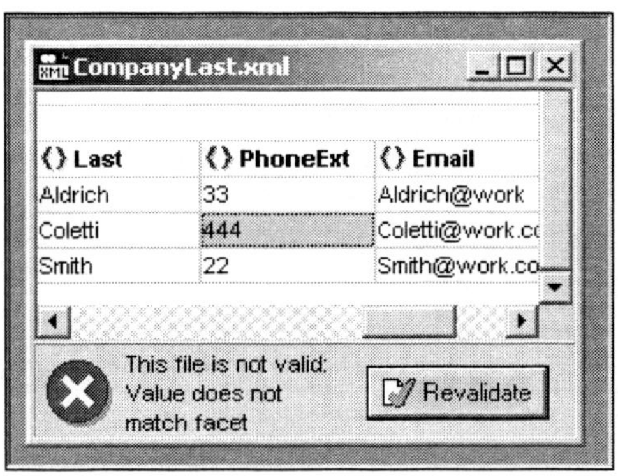

2. Correct the error and restart the process to recheck the rest of the folder.

Please note
You can select discontinuous files in the folder, by holding down CTRL and clicking the files singly. Only these files are then checked when you click F7 or F8.

To update the project folder contents:

You might add or delete files in the local or network directory at any time. To update the folder view,

- Right click the external folder, and select the popup menu option **Refresh external folder**.

Deleting files or folders:

- Right click a **folder** and hit the **Del.** key, to delete the folder from the Project window. This only deletes the folder from the Project view, and does not delete anything on your hard disk or network.
- Right clicking a **single file** and hitting Del. **does not delete** a file from the Project window. You have to delete it physically and then Refresh the external folder contents.

Add External Web Folder to Project...

This command **adds** a new **external web folder** to the current project.

Use this command to add a web folder to the current project. You can also access this command from the context-menu when you right-click a folder in the project window.

To add an external web folder to the project

1. Select the menu option **Project | Add External Web Folder to project**. This opens the "Add Web folder to project" dialog box.

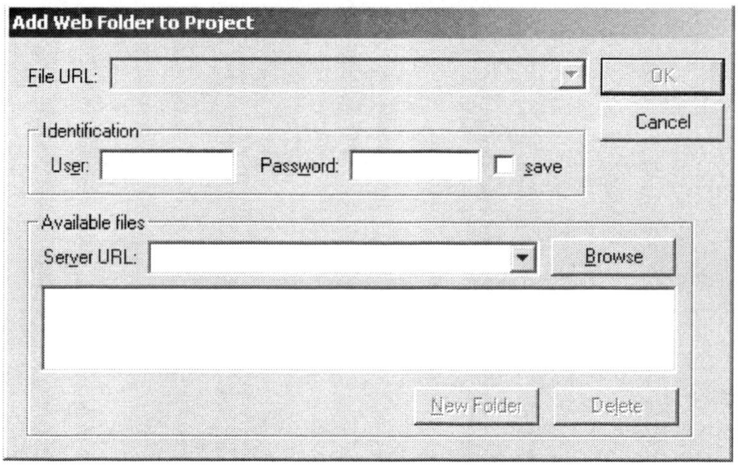

2. Click in the Server URL field to enter the server URL, and enter the login ID in the User and Password fields.
3. Click the Browse button to connect to the server and view the files available there.

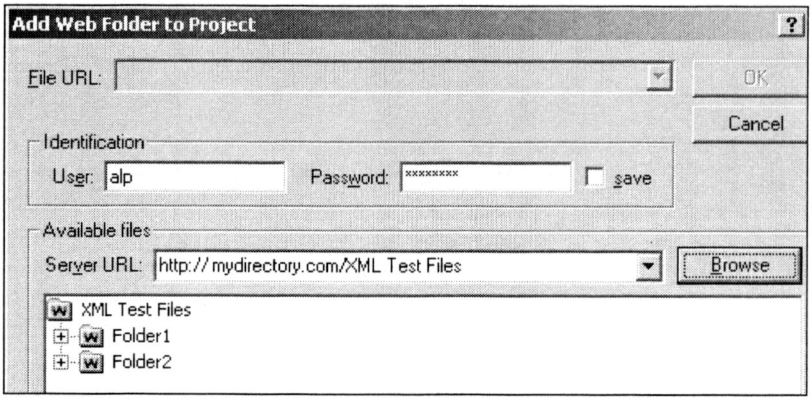

4. Click the **folder** you want to add to the project view. The OK button only becomes active once you do this. The Folder name and http: server address now appear in the File URL field.
5. Click OK to add the folder to the project.

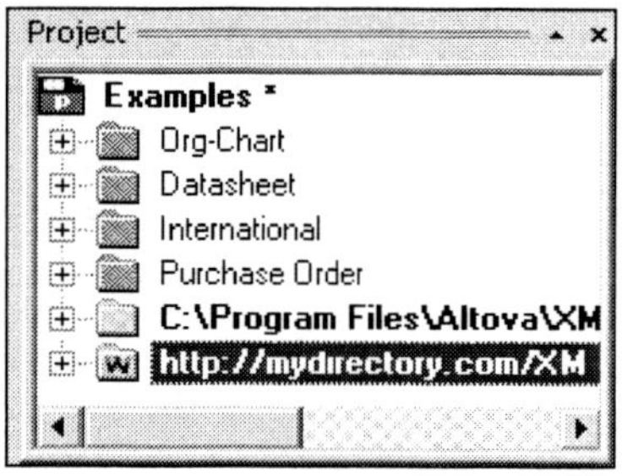

6. Click the plus icon to view the folder contents.

To filter the folder contents:

1. **Right click** the web folder, and select the popup menu option **Properties**. This opens the Properties dialog box.
2. Click in the **File extensions** field and enter the file extensions of the file types you want to see. You can separate each file type with a **semicolon** to define multiple types

(XML and Schema XSDs for example).
3. Click OK to confirm the selection.
The Project window now only shows the XML and XSD files of the web folder.

Validating and checking a folder for well-formedness:

1. Click the folder and click the "Check well-formedness" or "Validate" icon, (hotkeys F7 or F8).
All the files visible under the folder are checked.

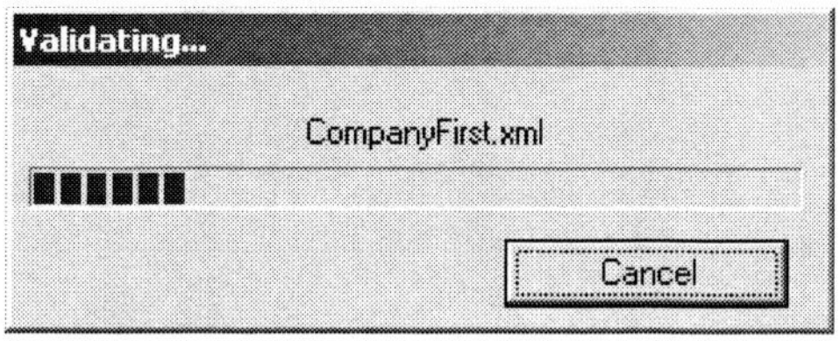

If a file is malformed or invalid, then this file is opened in the main window, allowing you to edit it.
2. Correct the error and restart the process to recheck the rest of the folder.

Please note
You can select discontinuous files in the folder, by holding down CTRL and clicking the files singly. Only these files are then checked when you click F7 or F8.

To update the project folder contents:
Files may be added or deleted from the web folder at any time. To update the folder view,

- Right click the external folder, and select the popup menu option **Refresh external folder**.

Deleting files or folders:

- Right click a **folder** and hit the **Del.** key, to delete the **folder** from the Project window. This only deletes the folder from the Project view, and does not delete anything on the web server.
- Right clicking a **single file** and hitting Del. **does not delete** a file from the Project window. You have to delete it physically and then Refresh the external folder contents.

Project Properties...

The Properties command lets you define important settings for any of the specific folders in your project.

The files specified in the "Use this xxx" entry, will take precedence over any local assignment directly within the XML file. Eg. The OrgChart.xsl file (in the "Use this XSL" entry), will always be used when transforming any of the XML files in the **XML Files** folder.

To define the Project Properties for a folder:

1. Right click on the folder you want to define the properties for, and
2. Select the **Properties...** command from the context menu.

Please note:
if your project file is under source control, a prompt appears asking if you want to check out the project file (*.spp). Click OK, if you want to edit settings and be able to save them.

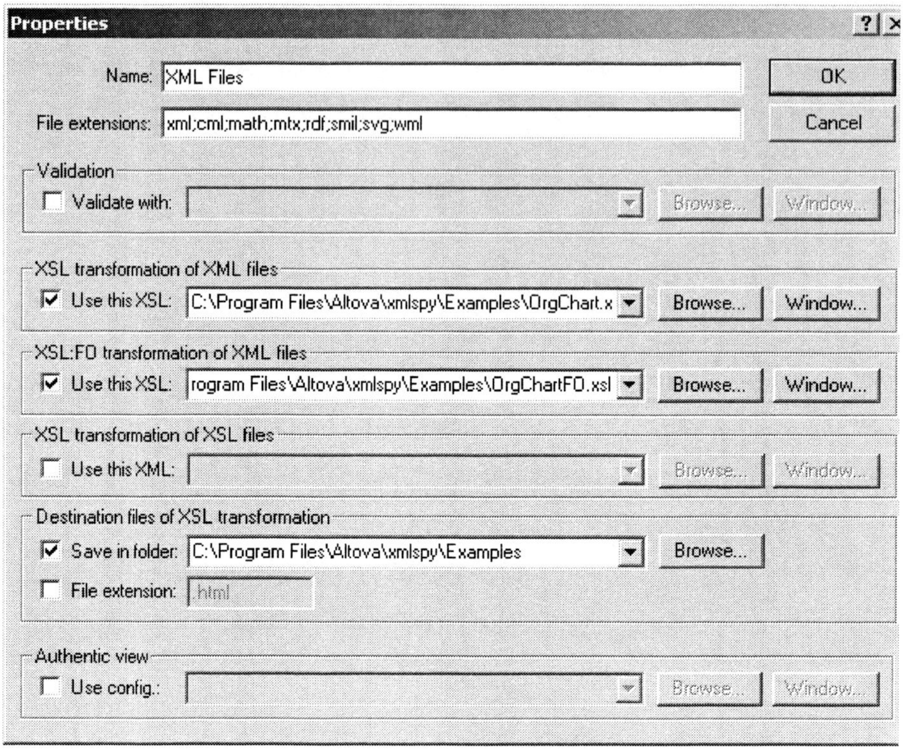

File extensions
The File extensions help to determine the automatic file-to-folder distribution that occurs when you add new files to the project (as opposed as to one particular folder).

Validate
Define the DTD or Schema document that should be used to validate all files in the current folder (Main Pages in this example).

XSL transformation of XML files
You can define the XSL Stylesheet to be used for XSL Transformation of all files in the folder.

If you are developing XSL Stylesheets yourself, you can also assign an example XML document to be used to preview the XSL Stylesheet in response to an XSL Transformation command issued from the stylesheet document, instead of the XML instance document.

XSL:FO transformation of XML files
You can define the XSL Stylesheet, containing XSL:FO markup, to be used for XSL:FO Transformation of all files in the folder.

Destination files of XSL transformation
For batch XSL Transformations, you can define the destination directory the transformed files should be placed in.

If you have added one file or URL to more than one folder in your project, you can use the properties command to set the default folder, whose settings should be used when you choose to validate or transform the file in non-batch mode.

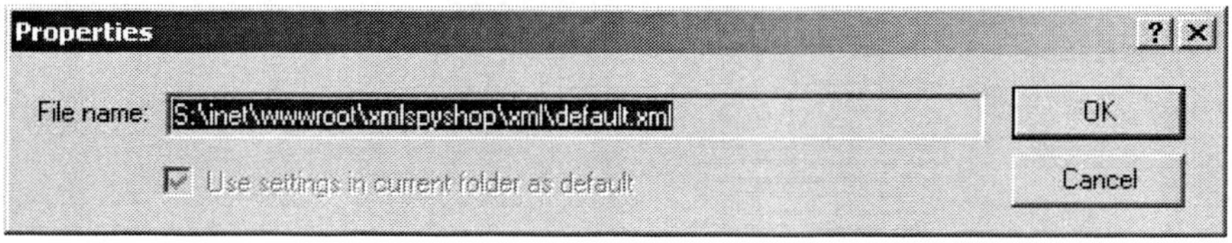

Authentic View
The "Use config." option allows you to select an SPS file when editing XML files using Authentic View, in the current folder. Please see the Authentic View manual for more information.

Most Recently Used Projects

This command displays the file name and path for the nine most recently used projects, allowing quick access to these files.

Also note, that STYLEVISION 2004 can automatically open the last project that you used, whenever you start STYLEVISION 2004. (**Tools | Options| File** tab, Project | Open last project on program start)

XML Menu

The XML menu contains all commands necessary for manipulating XML documents. You will find commands to insert or append elements, modify the element hierarchy, and set a namespace prefix for items.

You can also check documents for well-formedness or validate them against any Schema or DTD.

Insert

The Insert command inserts a new item directly before the currently selected one. In case of an attribute, it may appear a few lines before the current item, as all attributes must immediately follow their parent element.

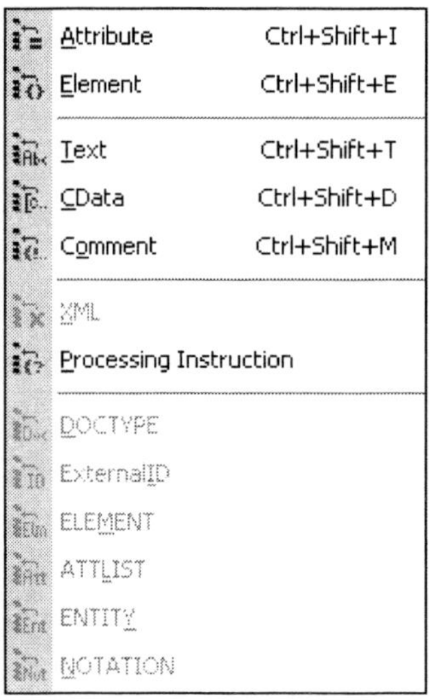

Insert Attribute

Hotkey: **CTRL+SHIFT+I**

This command **inserts** a new **attribute** before the selected item.

If the current selection is any element other than the first element, the attribute is inserted before the first element to satisfy the well-formedness constraints of XML.

Insert Element

Hotkey: **CTRL+SHIFT+E**

This command **inserts** a new **element** before the selected item.

If the current selection is an attribute, the new element is inserted before the first element to satisfy the well-formedness constraints of XML.

Insert Text

 Hotkey: **CTRL+SHIFT+T**

This command **inserts** new **text content** before the selected item.

If the current selection is an attribute, the text is inserted before the first element to satisfy the well-formedness constraints of XML.

Insert CDATA

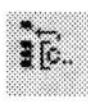 Hotkey: **CTRL+SHIFT+D**

This command **inserts** a new **CDATA block** before the selected item.

If the current selection is an attribute, the CDATA is inserted before the first element to satisfy the well-formedness constraints of XML.

Insert Comment

 Hotkey: **CTRL+SHIFT+M**

This command **inserts** a new **comment** before the selected item.

If the current selection is an attribute, the Comment is inserted before the first element to satisfy the well-formedness constraints of XML.

Insert XML

This command **inserts** new **XML declaration** `<?xml version="1.0" encoding="UTF-8"?>` before the selected item.

Please note:
Each XML document may only contain one XML declaration and it must appear at the very top of the file.

Insert Processing Instruction

This command **inserts** a new **Processing Instruction** (PI) before the selected item.

If the current selection is an attribute, the PI is inserted before the first element to satisfy the well-formedness constraints of XML.

Insert DOCTYPE

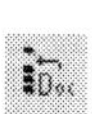

This command **inserts** a Document Type Declaration - or more precisely, the **DOCTYPE block** for the internal subset of a Document Type Declaration (DTD) - before the selected item.

Please note:
The DOCTYPE block may only appear at the top of an XML instance document between the XML Declaration and the root element of the XML document.

You could also use the Assign DTD command instead, which lets you create a DOCTYPE statement that refers to an external DTD document.

Insert ExternalID

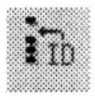

This command **inserts** an **external ID** (SYSTEM or PUBLIC) into a DOCTYPE declaration, before the selected item.

Insert ELEMENT

This command **inserts** an **element declaration** into a DOCTYPE declaration or into an external Document Type Definition (DTD), before the selected item.

Insert ATTLIST

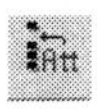

This command **inserts** an **attribute list declaration** into a DOCTYPE declaration or into an external Document Type Definition (DTD), before the selected item.

Insert ENTITY

This command **inserts** an **entity declaration** into a DOCTYPE declaration or into an external Document Type Definition (DTD) before the selected item.

Insert NOTATION

This command inserts a **notation declaration** into a DOCTYPE declaration or into an external Document Type Definition (DTD) before the selected item.

Append

The Append command appends an item as the last item **inside the parent** of the currently selected item. This is useful whenever you want to add more than one item in sequence.

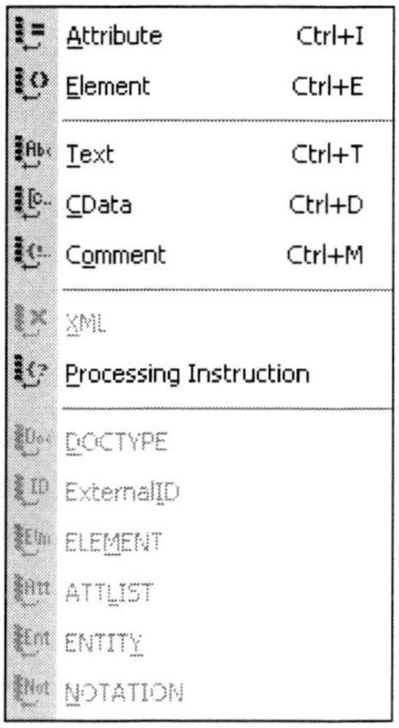

Append Attribute

 Hotkey: **CTRL+I**

This command **appends** a **new attribute** after the last element within the same parent.

Append Element

 Hotkey: **CTRL+E**

This command **appends** a **new element** after the last element within the same parent.

Append Text

 Hotkey: **CTRL+T**

This command **appends** a new **text content block** after the last element within the same parent.

Append CDATA

 Hotkey: **CTRL+D**

This command **appends** a new **CDATA block** after the last element within the same parent.

Append Comment

 hotkey: **CTRL+M**

This command appends a **new comment** after the last element within the same parent.

Append XML

This command **inserts** a new **XML declaration** `<?xml version="1.0" encoding="UTF-8"?>` as the first item in a document.

Please note:
Each XML document may only contain one XML declaration and it must appear at the very top of the file.

Append Processing Instruction

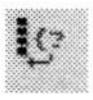

This command **appends** a new **Processing Instruction** (PI) after the last element within the same
parent.

Append DOCTYPE

This command **appends** a new Document Type Declaration - or more precisely, the **DOCTYPE block** for the internal subset of a Document Type Declaration (DTD) - after the last element within the same parent.

Please note:
A DOCTYPE block may only appear at the top of an XML instance document between the XML Declaration and the root element of the XML document.

Append ExternalID

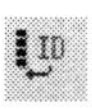

This command **appends** an **external ID** (SYSTEM or PUBLIC) in a DOCTYPE declaration after the last element of the same parent.

Append ELEMENT

This command **appends** an **element declaration** in a DOCTYPE declaration or in an external Document Type Definition (DTD).

Append ATTLIST

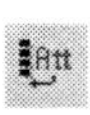

This command **appends** an **attribute list declaration** in a DOCTYPE declaration or in an external Document Type Definition (DTD).

Append ENTITY

This command **appends** an **entity declaration** in a DOCTYPE declaration or in an external Document Type Definition (DTD).

Append NOTATION

This command **appends** a **notation declaration** in a DOCTYPE declaration or in an external Document Type Definition (DTD).

Add Child

The Add Child command adds a child item to the currently selected element. This is useful for adding attributes to an item, or creating child elements.

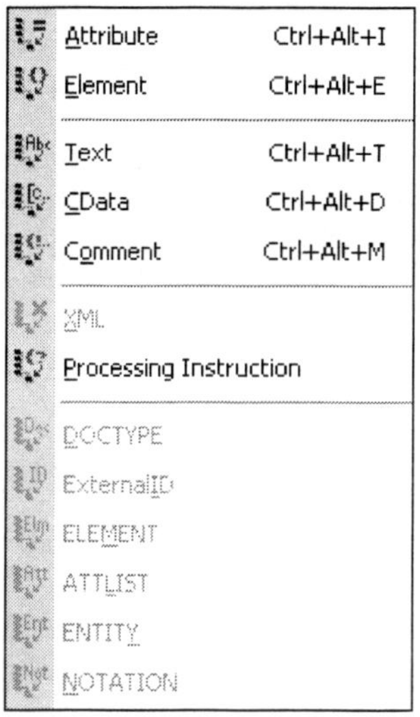

Add Child Attribute

Hotkey: **CTRL+ALT+I**

This command **inserts** a **new attribute** as a child of the selected item.

Add Child Element

Hotkey: **CTRL+ALT+E**

This command **inserts** a **new element** as a child of the selected item.

Add Child Text

Hotkey: **CTRL+ALT+T**

This command **inserts** new **text content** as a child of the selected item.

Add Child CDATA

Hotkey: **CTRL+ALT+D**

This command **inserts** a new **CDATA block** as a child of the selected item.

Add Child Comment

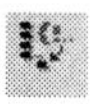

Hotkey: **CTRL+ALT+M**

This command **inserts** new **Comment** as a child of the selected item.

Add Child XML

This command is only available, when you are looking at a totally empty file...

This command **inserts** a new **XML declaration**
<?xml version="1.0" encoding="UTF-8"?> as a child of the selected item.

Add Child Processing Instruction

This command **inserts** a new **Processing Instruction** (PI) as a child of the selected item.

Add Child DOCTYPE

This command is only available, if you are looking at a total empty file.

This command **inserts** a **Document Type Declaration** - or more precisely, the DOCTYPE block for the internal subset of a Document Type Declaration (DTD) - as a child of the selected item.

Please note:
A DOCTYPE block may only appear at the top of an XML instance document between the XML Declaration and the root element of the XML document.

Add Child ExternalID

This command **inserts** an **external ID** (SYSTEM or PUBLIC) into a DOCTYPE **declaration** as a child of the selected item.

Add Child ELEMENT

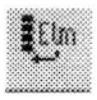

This command **inserts** an **element declaration** into a DOCTYPE declaration or into an external Document Type Definition (DTD) as a child of the selected item.

Add Child ATTLIST

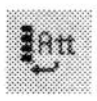

This command **inserts** an **attribute list declaration** into a DOCTYPE declaration or into an external Document Type Definition (DTD) as a child of the selected item.

Add Child ENTITY

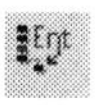

This command **inserts** an **entity declaration** into a DOCTYPE declaration or into an external Document Type Definition (DTD) as a child of the selected item.

Add Child NOTATION

This command **inserts** a **notation declaration** into a DOCTYPE declaration or into an external Document Type Definition (DTD) as a child of the selected item.

Convert To

The convert to command converts an item to a different item type. Depending on the location of the item (not on its current kind), some or all options on the item type submenu may or may not be available. This operation can only be performed on one individual item, not on an element that contains any child elements.

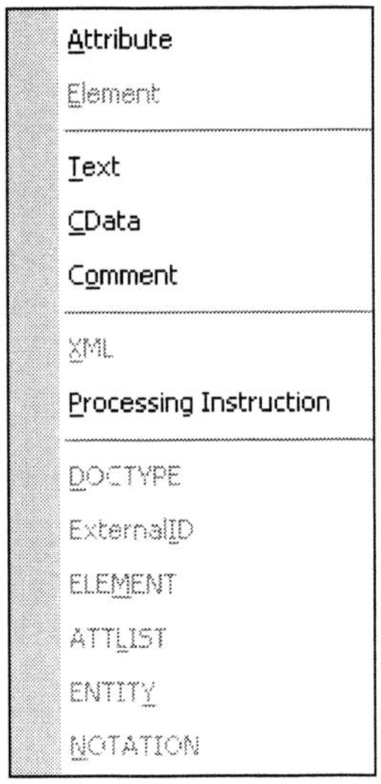

If the operation would result in the loss of data (e.g. converting an attribute to a comment looses the attribute name), a brief warning dialog box will appear.

Convert To Attribute

This command **converts** the selected item into a new **attribute**.

Convert To Element

This command **converts** the selected item into an **element**.

Convert To Text

This command **converts** the selected item into **text content**.

Convert To CDATA

This command **converts** the selected item into a **CDATA block**.

Convert To Comment

This command **converts** the selected item into a **comment**.

Convert To XML

This command **converts** the selected item to an XML declaration
<?xml version="1.0" encoding="UTF-8"?>.

Please note:
Each XML document may only contain one XML declaration and it must appear at the very top of the file.

Convert To Processing Instruction

This command **converts** the selected item to a new **Processing Instruction** (PI)

Convert To DOCTYPE

This command **converts** the selected item to a Document Type **Declaration** - or more precisely, the **DOCTYPE block** for the internal subset of a Document Type Declaration (DTD).

Please note:
A DOCTYPE block may only appear at the top of an XML instance document between the XML Declaration and the root element of the XML document.

Convert To ExternalID

This command **converts** the selected item to an **external ID** (SYSTEM or PUBLIC) in a DOCTYPE **declaration**.

Convert To ELEMENT

This command **converts** the selected item to an **element declaration** in a DOCTYPE declaration or in an external Document Type **Definition** (DTD).

Convert To ATTLIST

This command **converts** the selected item to an **attribute list** declaration in a DOCTYPE declaration or in an external Document Type **Definition** (DTD).

Convert To ENTITY

This command **converts** the selected item to an **entity declaration** in a DOCTYPE declaration or in an external Document Type **Definition** (DTD).

Convert To NOTATION

This command **converts** the selected item to a **notation declaration** in a DOCTYPE declaration or in an external Document Type **Definition** (DTD).

Table

The Table menu command contains all commands relevant to the Database/Table View in STYLEVISION 2004.

The **Database/Table** commands can only be selected if the **Enhanced Grid view** is active!

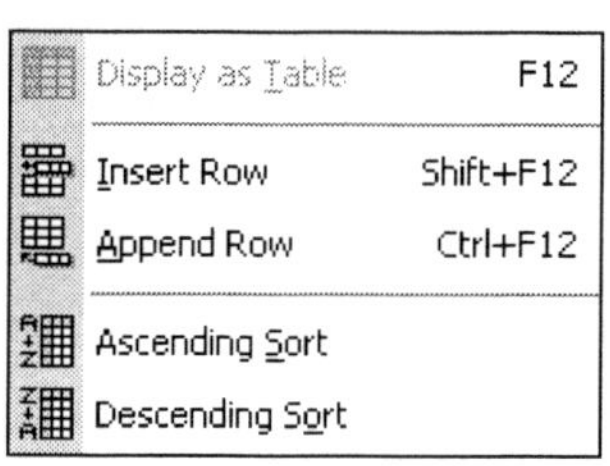

Display as Table

This command allows you **switch** between two views of repeated elements in the **Enhanced Grid view**. The Grid view (default view, in the Enhanced Grid view) and the Database/Table view.

1. Select one of the repeated elements in the grid view.
   The Displays as Table icon is only made active when you make the correct selection.

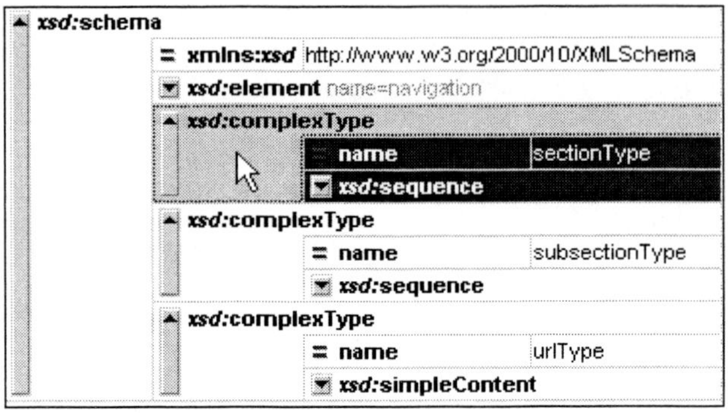

2. Click the Display as table icon.

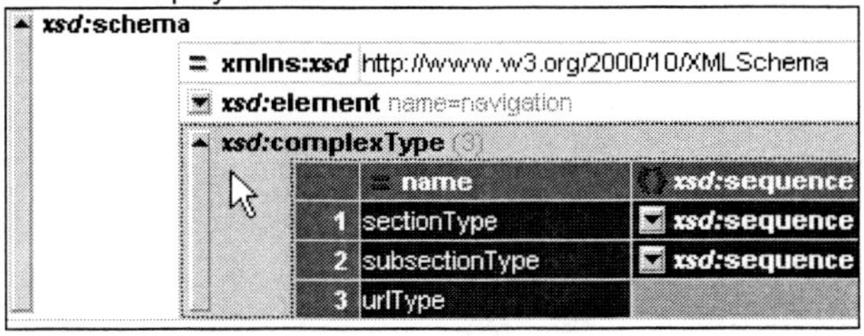

This effectively breaks out all attributes and sub-elements, and show them as columns similar to any spreadsheet- or database-like application.

Insert Row

This command **inserts** new **rows** to the table in the Database/Table View:

1. Click a row number in the table (or one of the cells), and
2. Select the menu option **XML | Table | Insert row.**

This inserts a new row (i.e. a new element) before the currently selected row.

Append Row

This command **appends** new rows to the table in the Database/Table View

1. Click a row number in the table (or one of the cells), and
2. Select the menu option **XML | Table | Insert row**.

This appends a new row (i.e. a new element) to the end of the table.

Ascending Sort

This command **sorts** column elements in ascending order (in the table) in the Database/Table View:

1. Click a column header in the table, and
2. Select the menu option **XML | Table | Ascending sort** (or clicking on the A-Z icon)

STYLEVISION 2004 will automatically try to determine what kind of data you are using in the selected column, and choose an alphabetic or numeric sort method accordingly.

If STYLEVISION 2004 is not sure which sort order to use, it opens this dialog box to prompt for help:

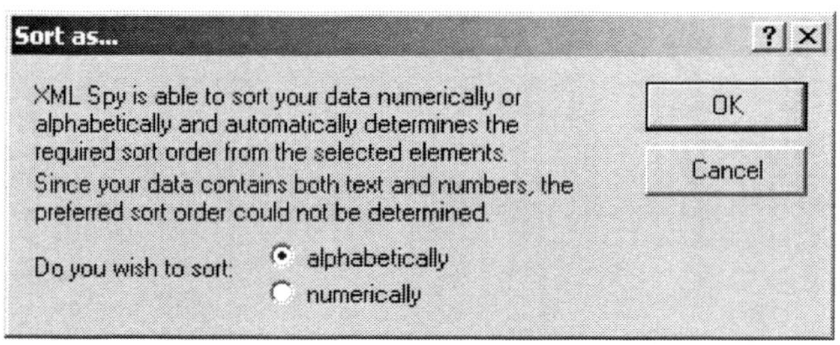

Descending Sort

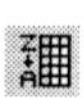

This command **sorts** column elements in descending order (in the table) in the Database/Table View

1. Click a column header in the table, and
2. Select the menu option **XML | Table | Descending sort** (or clicking on the Z-A icon)

STYLEVISION 2004 will automatically try to determine what kind of data you are using in the selected column, and choose an alphabetic or numeric sort method accordingly.

If STYLEVISION 2004 is not sure which sort order to use, it opens a dialog box to prompt for help.

Move Left

 Hotkey: **CTRL+L**

This command **moves** the current element to the left by one level, thereby changing a child element into a sibling of its parent. This is also often referred to as the "**Promote**" command.

Move Right

 Hotkey: **CTRL+R**

This command **moves** the current element to the right by one level, thereby turning it into a child element of the element directly above. This is also often referred to as the "**Demote**" command.

Enclose in Element

When editing textual data, it is often convenient to insert a new sub-element that contains some text, which is already present in the document.

The Enclose in Element command lets you accomplish this with any text selection within another element. Once you select this command from the menu or toolbar, the **currently selected text** is cut from its parent element and **inserted** into a newly created **child element**.

If you are editing a document based on a Schema or DTD, you will automatically be presented with a list of valid choices for the kind of element you are allowed to insert in this position.

Evaluate XPath

STYLEVISION 2004 includes an **XPath Visualizer** that enables you to evaluate an XPath expression. You enter an expression in the XPath field, and the nodes in the nodeset returned by the XPath expression is listed in the result window. Attribute-value pairs, as well as text content if the node has text content only, are displayed for each node in the result list. Clicking a node displays that node in the XML Document. The XPath expression is also automatically checked to see if it is valid when you enter it.

Note: You can use an XPath 1.0 or XPath 2.0 expression. The XPath 2.0 feature, however, is Beta software and subject to Section 4 of the Software License Agreement. It is provided on an "as-is" basis, and Altova disclaims liability or warranty obligation of any kind, whether express or implied.

The XPath Visualizer is available in the **Enhanced Grid** and **Text view**.

Please see the XPath specifications at http://www.w3.org/TR/xpath for more information.

XPath uses in STYLEVISION 2004

- When creating Identity Constraints
- Setting breakpoints using the SOAP debugger
- Checking XSLT code

To evaluate an XPath expression:

1. Open an XML document in STYLEVISION 2004 (e.g. CompanyLast).
2. Select the menu option **XML | Evaluate XPath** or click the Evaluate XPath  icon.
3. Type an XPath expression in the XPath field (e.g. //Name).

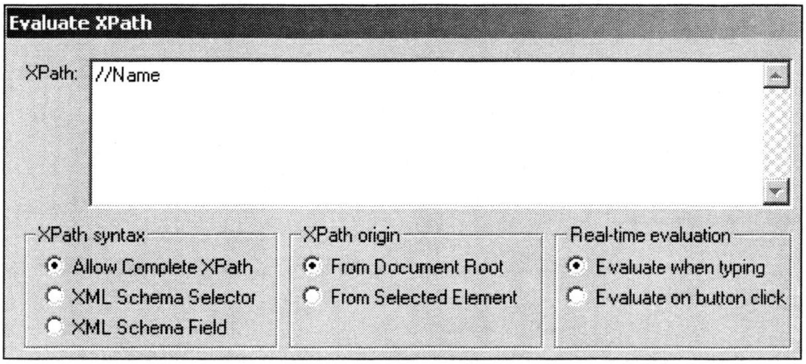

The resultant node set, all "Name" elements under the Document Root, appears in the node set window.

name	value / attributes
() Name	Organization Chart
() Name	Nanonull, Inc.
() Name	Administration
() Name	Marketing
() Name	Engineering
() Name	IT & Technical Support
() Name	Nanonull Europe, AG
() Name	Administration
() Name	IT & Technical Support
() Name	Research & Development

4. Click one of the "Name" elements in the node set window.
5. The corresponding element in the XML document is highlighted.

XPath Visualizer options

XPath syntax
This option group allows you to select which syntax you want to use when evaluating an XPath. When entering an XPath, the expression is constantly monitored for adherence to these syntax rules. An invalid expression automatically appears in red. As soon as the expression becomes valid the expression changes from red into black.

Allow Complete XPath:
This is the default option and checks against the complete XPath syntax.

XML Schema Selector:
This option checks the XPath against the XML Schema Selector syntax.

XML Schema Field:
This option checks the XPath against the XML Schema Field syntax.

XPath origin
This option group lets you define **from where** in the XML document you want to start your search. The option you select here remains active the next time you search for an XPath.

From Document Root:
This is the default option, and starts the search from the beginning of the XML document.

From Selected Element:
Select this option if you want to start your search from the currently selected element, attribute etc. in the XML document. Note that the current element position does not change if you click one of the node set results in the node set window.

Real-time evaluation
Evaluate when typing:
This is the default option, and presents results in the node set window while you are typing in the expression.

Evaluate on button click:
This option defers the XPath evaluation until you click the Evaluate button.

Node set window
This window displays the results of the evaluated XPath expression. The XPath results in this window can appear as nodes, numbers, boolean expressions, or error messages.

XPath examples

A few examples of XPath expressions and their results are shown below. These examples use the **CompanyLast.xml** file available in the **..\Examples\Tutorial** folder supplied with STYLEVISION 2004.

Find all the child elements of the first Person child element of any element.

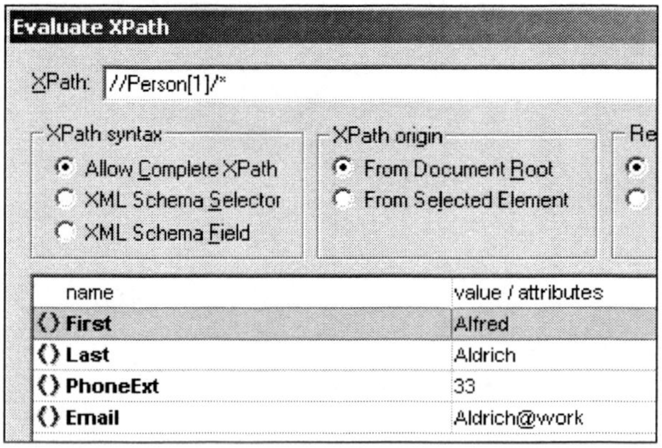

Find all the person elements, where the Manager attribute value is true.

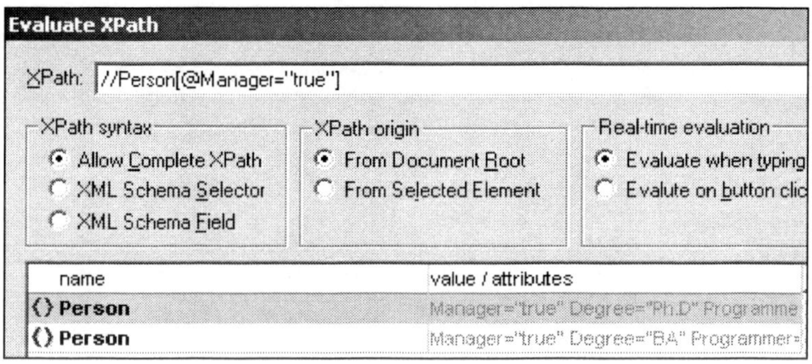

Find the total value of all the PhoneExt elements.

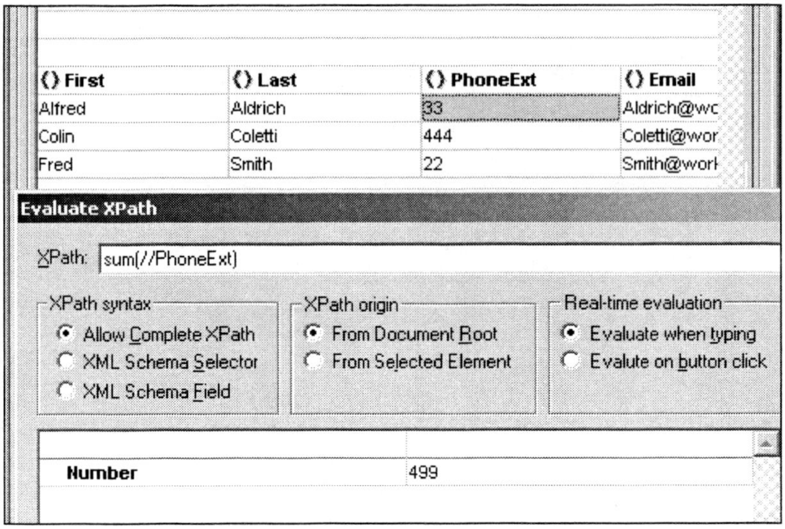

Entering the SUM-Function in CAPS displays an error message in the node set window. All XPath expressions are case sensitive, this includes function names as well as node names.

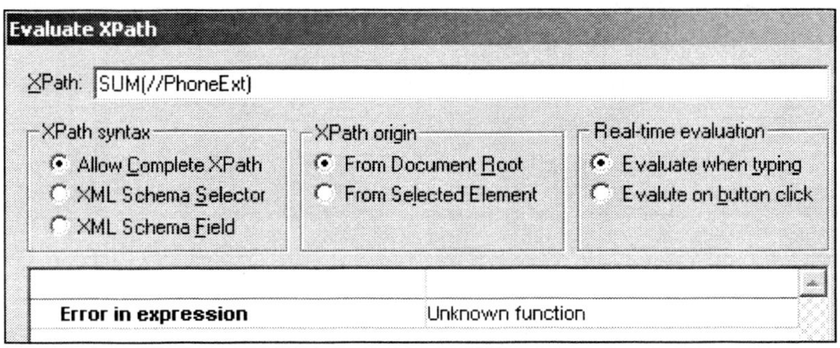

Check Well-Formedness

This command **checks** the document for well-formedness by the definitions of the XML 1.0 specification.

Every XML document must be well-formed and therefore STYLEVISION 2004 automatically checks for well-formedness whenever a document is opened, saved, or the view mode is switched from Text to any other view.

If the well-formedness check succeeds, a brief message is displayed at the bottom of the main window:

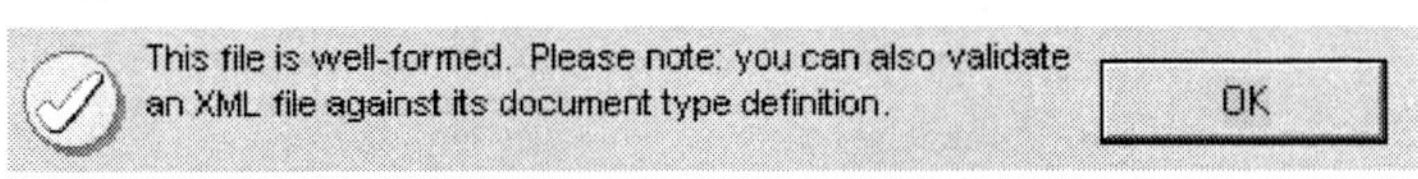

If any error is encountered during the well-formedness check, the source of the problem is highlighted and a corresponding error message is shown:

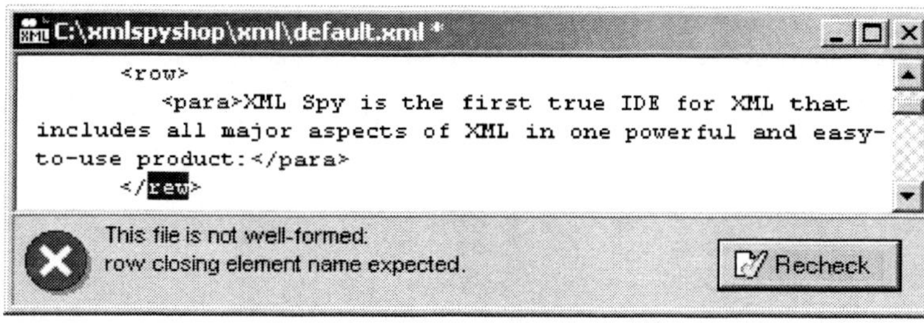

It is generally not permitted to save a malformed XML document, but STYLEVISION 2004 gives you a "Save anyway" option when the automatic well-formedness check upon saving fails. This is useful, when you want to suspend your work temporarily and resume it later, without being able to make the intermediate version of the file well-formed.

The Check well-formedness command normally operates on the active main window.

Validate

This command validates an XML document against the rules set forth in its Schema or Document Type Definition (DTD) or it can validate any XML Schema or DTD against the rules set forth in the corresponding specification.

STYLEVISION 2004 uses its built-in incremental validating parser that supports all major Schema dialects, such as DTD, DCD, XDR, XML-Data, BizTalk, and the new W3C XML Schema Definition Language (XSD) .

If the validation succeeds, a brief message is displayed at the bottom of the main window:

If an error is encountered during the validation, the source of the problem is highlighted and a corresponding error message is shown:

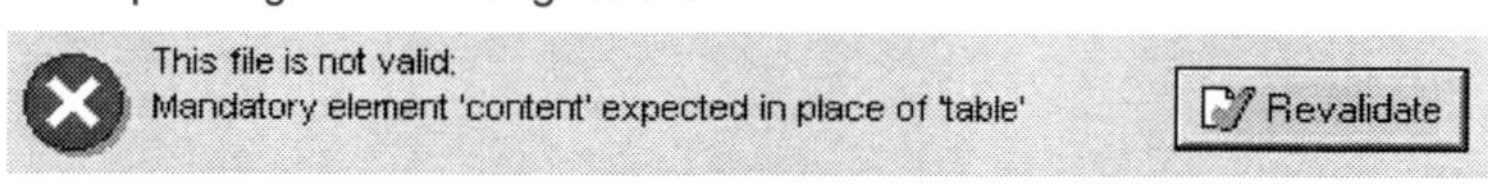

The Validate command also automatically includes a well-formedness check, so there is no need to first use the Check well-formedness command manually before validating a file.

Please note that you can use this command to validate XML instance documents and for validating XML schemas or DTDs.

This command normally operates on the active main window, but you can also use the Validate command on any file, folder, or group of files in the active project window, where you can also define the Schema or DTD to validate with on a per-folder basis in the project properties. Click on the respective folder, and then on the "Validate" icon.

Validate XML

When you validate an XML document, STYLEVISION 2004 first tries to locate any reference to a supported schema dialect within the document. It then loads the corresponding schema or DTD into memory, and uses its definitions to validate your XML instance document.

Once the Schema or DTD has been loaded into memory, STYLEVISION 2004 also provides you with intelligent editing functions in the Info Window and Entry-Helpers.

As long as the XML instance document is open, STYLEVISION 2004 will also keep the Schema or DTD in memory (see the Flush Memory Cache command on the DTD/Schema menu).

Validate Schema

STYLEVISION 2004 supports all major Schema dialects, such as DTD, DCD, XDR, XML-Data, BizTalk, and the new W3C XML Schema Definition Language (XSDL).

Validate these **schemas** against their specification by clicking on the Validate button. You can then be sure that they can be used to create, edit, and validate XML instance documents that are based on these schemata.

STYLEVISION 2004 now supports a subset of OASIS XML catalogs. These catalogs allow STYLEVISION 2004 to retrieve the most commonly used Schemas, Stylesheets and other files, which are available on the web, from users local folders. This increases the overall processing speed, and eliminates the need to be connected to Internet, which is helpful when you are on the road with your laptop.

The catalog is controlled via two files: **MainCatalog.xml**, which contains predefined entries to Schema and other files, installed with STYLEVISION 2004, and **CustomCatalog.xml** which allows you to make your own catalog extensions. Schemas, Stylesheets and other files are installed in specific subfolders of the STYLEVISION 2004 installation folder.

Please note:
Although the April 7th. 1999 and Oct. 2000 Schema for Schemas DTD are included in the main catalog, you cannot validate your instance files against either of these schemas. The purpose of these two DTDs is to provide entry helper info for editing purposes, should you wish to create files according to these older recommendations.

Please see the following link for more information:
<http://xml.coverpages.org/OASIS-EntityResolution-spec-2001-07-16.html>

Update Entry-Helpers

This command **updates** the Entry-Helper windows, by reloading the underlying DTD or Schema.

If you have modified the Schema or DTD that an open XML document is based upon, it is advisable to reload that Schema or DTD to update the intelligent editing information (such as the Entry-Helper and Info windows) presented in the XML document, to reflect your changes.

Namespace Prefix...

This command lets you set the namespace prefix (identifier) for a group of selected elements (including their child elements).

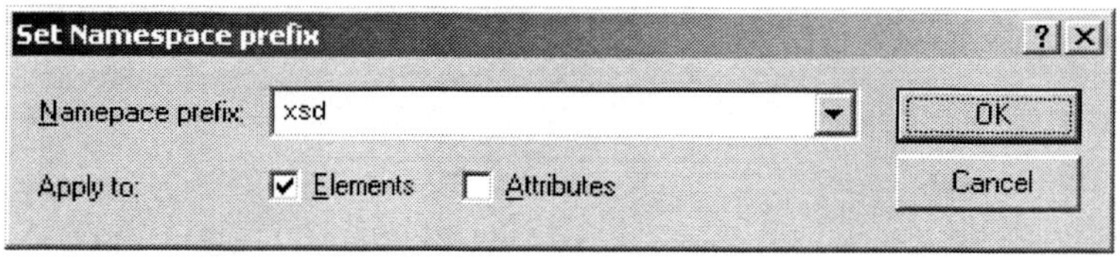

You can choose to set the namespace prefix on either elements, attributes, or both.

Please note:
Attributes don't need to have the same prefix as their parent elements, since attributes always inherit the element's namespace, if no prefix is given.

DTD/Schema Menu

STYLEVISION 2004 contains many commands that let you operate with Schemas and Document Type Definitions (DTDs) efficiently.

You can:

- Assign DTDs or Schemas to be used for validation with any XML instance document
- Go to the definition of any element or attribute in the corresponding schema while editing your XML documents.

Assign DTD...

This command **assigns** a Document Type Definition (**DTD**) to an XML document to enable Validation and Intelligent editing.

The command opens the Assign File dialog to let you specify the DTD file you wish to assign, and inserts the required DOCTYPE statement into your XML document:

```
<!DOCTYPE main SYSTEM "http://link.xmlspy.com/spyweb.dtd">
```

Assign Schema...

This command **assigns** a Schema to an XML document to enable Validation and Intelligent editing.

The command opens the Assign File dialog to let you specify the XSD, XDR, or BizTalk schema file you wish to assign, inserts the required namespace declaration attributes into your XML document:

```
xmlns="http://www.xmlspy.com/schemas/icon/orgchart"
xmlns:xsi="http://www.w3.org/1999/XMLSchema-instance"
xsi:schemaLocation="http://www.xmlspy.com/schemas/icon/orgchart
http://schema.xmlspy.com/schemas/icon/orgchart.xsd"
```

The declarations generated by STYLEVISION 2004 depend on the Schema kind and - in case of the new W3C XML Schemas - also on the potential use of a targetNamespace in the Schema document.

Include another DTD...

This command allows you to include another Document Type Definition (DTD) or external parsed entity into the internal subset of a document type definition, or in any DTD document. This is done by defining a corresponding external parsed entity declaration and using that entity in the following line:

```
<!ENTITY % navigation.dtd SYSTEM "S:\xml\navigation.dtd">
%navigation.dtd;
```

The command opens the Assign File dialog to let you specify the DTD file you want to include in your DTD.

Go to DTD

This command **opens** the Document Type Definition document (**DTD**) on which the current XML document is based.

Go to Schema

This command **opens** the Schema document (**XSD**) on which the current XML document is based.

Go to Definition

.

This command **displays** the exact definition of an element or attribute in the corresponding Document Type Definition or Schema document.

To see the item definition in Enhanced Grid view:

1. Click left on the item.
2. Select the menu item **DTD/Schema | Go to Definition,** or click on the icon.

To see the item definition in Schema/WSDL design view:

1. Use CTRL + Double click on the item you want to see the definition of, or
2. Click the item and select menu option **DTD/Schema | Go to Definition,** or click on the icon.

   In both cases, the corresponding DTD or Schema file is opened, and the item definition is highlighted.

Flush Memory Cache

This command **flushes** all cached Schema and DTD documents from memory.

To speed up validation and intelligent editing, STYLEVISION 2004 caches all recently used DTD, external parsed entity, and Schema documents in memory. Information from these documents is also displayed, when you are using the Go to Definition command.

Use this command if memory is tight on your system, or if you have been using many different documents based on different schemas recently.

Schema design Menu

The Schema design menu allows you to:

- Define your schema settings
- Define zoom settings
- Display the schema diagram of global elements

Schema settings

This command lets you define the **global schema settings**.

You set the **Default Element Form** to Qualified or Unqualified. The same can be defined for the Default Attribute form. These defaults can be changed for each element or form in the Details entry helper.

Enter the Block and Final defaults in the respective text boxes, and enter the schema version number in the Version field.

Click on the "Target namespace" radio button, and enter the namespace if you want to include it.

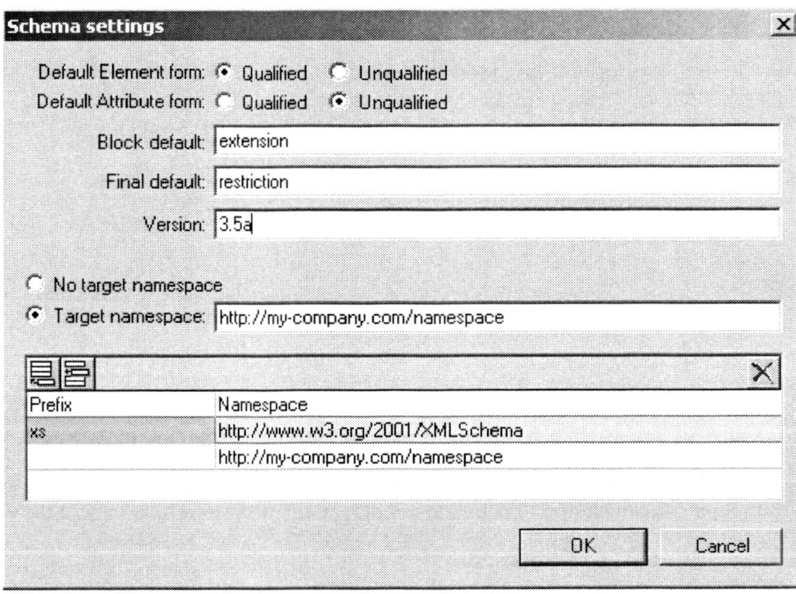

You can see these settings if you switch to the Text view of STYLEVISION 2004.

```
<?xml version="1.0" encoding="UTF-8"?>
<xsd:schema
targetNamespace="http://www.xmlspy.com/schemas/Altova/orgc
hart" xmlns="http://www.xmlspy.com/schemas/Altova/orgchart"
xmlns:xsd="http://www.w3.org/2000/10/XMLSchema"
elementFormDefault="unqualified"
attributeFormDefault="unqualified" blockDefault="extension"
finalDefault="restriction" version="3.5a">
    <xsd:notation name="Altova-Orgchart"
public="http://www.xmlspy.com/schemas/Altova/orgchart"/>
    <xsd:complexType name="DivisionType">
        <xsd:sequence>
            <xsd:element name="Name" type="xsd:string">
                <xsd:annotation>
                    <xsd:documentation>Division Name
```

Zoom

This command controls the zoom factor of the content model view.

Drag the slider to see to change the zoom factor directly, or click in the entry box and enter the numeric value.

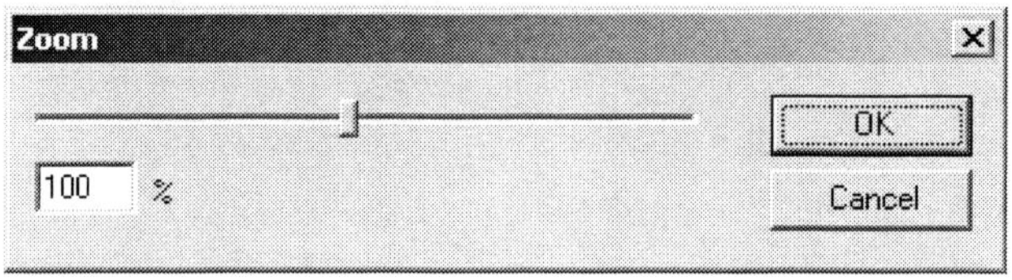

Display all Globals

This command displays the global components in the Schema overview, and is only available when you are viewing the content model of a component.

Alternatively:

- Click the "Show Globals" icon to return to the Schema Overview.

Display Diagram

This command **displays** the **content model** of the currently selected **component**.

To see the content model of a component:

- Click on the icon next to the component you want to display, or
- Select the menu option **Schema design | Display Diagram,** or
- Double click on a component name in the "Component Navigator" (Top right entry helper).

XSL Menu

The eXtensible Stylesheet Language (XSL) and in particular the XSL Transformation (XSLT), lets you specify how an XML document should be converted into other XML documents or text files, such a HTML, XHTML, or WML pages.

STYLEVISION 2004 supports XSL and XSLT through both its Intelligent editing features in the Text and Enhanced Grid Views, as well as through a set of commands that lets you perform common XSL-related operations.

This menu allows you to:

- Perform an XSL transformation of any type of XML document
-
- Assign an XSL Stylesheet to an XML document
- Assign an XSL:FO stylesheet to an XML document
- Assign a sample XML file to an XSL file
- Go to the underlying XSL stylesheet

Please see the technical background information on XSLT Processors for further details.

XSL Transformation

Hotkey: **F10**

This command performs an **XSL Transformation** of any XML document.

STYLEVISION 2004 can either use the Microsoft-supplied MSXML module or you can specify an external XSLT processor in the XSL tab on the Tools | Options dialog. You can also download other XSLT processors using the **Help | Components Download** menu option.

If your XML document contains a reference to an XSL stylesheet, which can be assigned using the Assign XSL command, then it is automatically used by the XSLT transformation command. Alternatively, you can also define the XSLT stylesheet to transform from, on a per-folder basis in the project properties (Select **Project | Project Properties** to open this dialog).

This command generally operates on the currently active main window, but you can also use the XSL Transformation command in batch-processing mode on any file, folder, or group of files in the active project window.

Please see the technical background information on XSLT Processors for further details.

Assign XSL...

This command **assigns** an **XSL stylesheet** to an XML document, enabling XSL Transformation or rendering by an XML-compatible browser.

The command opens the Assign File dialog to let you specify the XSL or XSLT file you want to assign, and inserts the required processing instruction into your XML document:

<**?xml-stylesheet type**="text/xsl" href="http://link.xmlspy.com/main.xsl"?>

Assign XSL:FO...

This command **assigns** an **XSL stylesheet**, containing **Formatting Object** markup, to an XML document enabling transformation of XML files to PDF and other formats.

The command opens the Assign File dialog to let you specify the XSL or XSLT file you want to assign, and inserts the required processing instruction into your XML document:

<?**xmlspyxslfo** C:\Program Files\Altova\xmlspy\Examples\OrgChartFO.xsl?>

An XML document may have two XSL files associated to it: a standard XSL transformation file, as well as one containing XSL:FO markup.

Assign sample XML file

This command **assigns** an **XML file** to an XSL document, enabling XSL Transformation or rendering by an XML-compatible browser.

Go to XSL

This command **opens** the corresponding XSL or **XSLT document**, if your XML document contains a reference to an XSL stylesheet.

Authentic Menu

Authentic View enables you to edit XML documents **based on templates created in Stylesheet Designer!** The templates in Stylesheet Designer are saved as ***.sps** files, and supply all the necessary information needed by Authentic View.

Templates are **opened** by selecting the **File | New** command and then clicking the "Select a Authentic View template..." button. Please see the Authentic View documentation for further information.

Authentic View is available in several versions:

- Integrated as a view within STYLEVISION 2004, or
- As a Browser Plug-In for Internet Explorer.

Assign an Authentic Stylesheet...

This command assigns a Spy Structure file (SPS) to an **XML document** to enable viewing and editing in the Authentic View.

The command opens a dialog box enabling you to specify the SPS file you wish to assign, and inserts the required SPS statement into your XML document.

Hide markup

This command hides markup symbols in the Authentic View.

Show small markup

This command shows small markup symbols in the Authentic View.

Show large markup

This command shows large markup symbols in the Authentic View.

Show mixed markup

This command shows mixed markup symbols in the Authentic View.

Append row

This command appends a row to the current table in the Authentic View.

Insert row

This command inserts a row into the current table in the Authentic View.

Duplicate row

This command duplicates the current table row in the Authentic View.

Move row up

This command moves current row up by one row in the Authentic View.

Move row down

This command moves the current row down by one row in the Authentic View.

Delete row

This command deletes the currently active row in the Authentic View.

View Menu

The View menu controls the display of the active Main window and allows you to change the way STYLEVISION 2004 displays your XML documents.

Enhanced Grid View

This command **switches** the current document into Enhanced Grid View.

This view includes an (optional) tree and structured grid display and is the preferred view for editing XML documents. If the previous view was the Text View, the document is automatically checked for well-formedness.

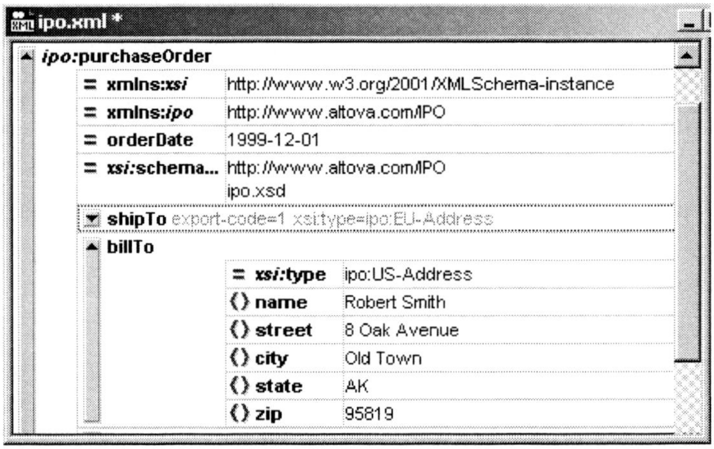

Embedded Database/Table view
STYLEVISION 2004 allows you to display recurring elements in a Database/Table view from within the Enhanced Grid view. This function is available wherever the Enhanced Grid view can be activated, and can be used when editing any type of XML file - XML, XSD, XSL etc.

For further information on this view, please see the detailed description of the various views in the Main Window section.

Schema/WSDL Design View

This command **switches** the current document into Schema/WSDL Design view.

STYLEVISION 2004 Schema editor allows you to view and edit schemas in two different ways:

- As a Schema overview, in list form
- In a graphical view of specific schema components

Schema overview
Open an XSD document in the DTD/Schemas folder of the project window, or double click on an XSD document in Explorer. The main window then displays the Schema overview.

The **top window** displays **all Global** "components" (elements, complex types etc.) in list form.

The bottom window displays the corresponding attributes of the currently selected component (eg. VIP Mgr. Prg etc.).

Schema overview:

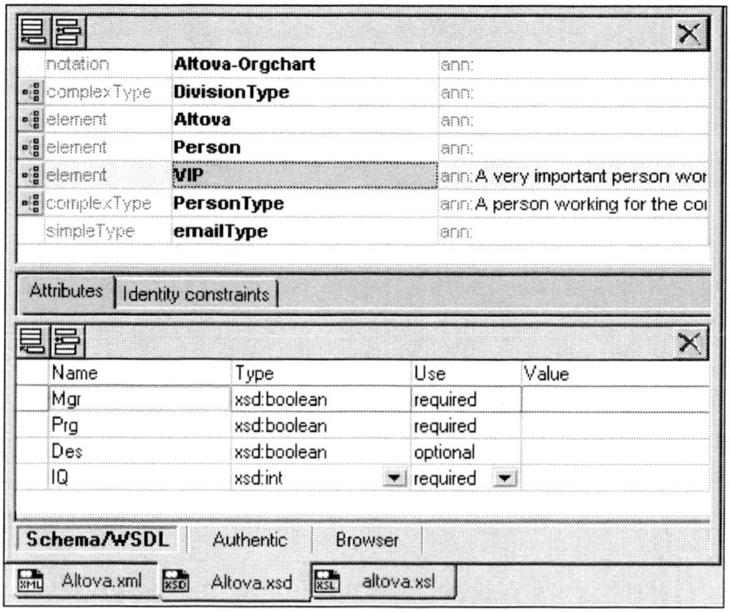

To see graphical representation (Content model) of a component:

- Click on the icon next to the component you want to display, or
- Select the menu option **Schema design | Display Diagram,** or
- Double click on a component name in the "Component Navigator" (Top right entry helper).

The *content model* for that component, appears in a tree view.

Graphical content model view

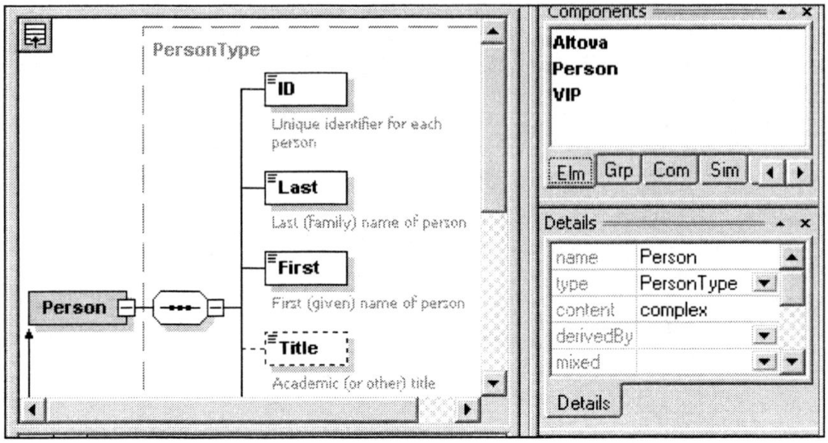

Text View

This command **switches** the current document into Text View.

This view allows you to edit the XML source in a source-code fashion and includes syntax-coloring.

If the previous view was the Enhanced Grid View, the document is automatically formatted according to the settings defined when saving a file (these can be modified in the "Save File" section of the File tab of the Options dialog). Use the menu command **Tools | Options** to open this dialog.

For further information on this view, see the detailed description of the various views in the Main Window section.

Authentic View

This command **switches** the current document into the Authentic View.

Authentic View enables you to edit XML documents **based on templates created in Stylesheet Designer!** The templates in Stylesheet Designer are saved as ***.sps** files, and supply all the necessary information needed by Authentic View.

Templates are **opened** by Selecting the **File | New** command and then clicking the "Select a Authentic View template..." button. Please see the Authentic View documentation for further information.

Browser View

This command **switches** the current document into Browser View.

This view uses an XML-enabled browser (preferably Internet Explorer 5) to render the XML document using information from potential CSS or XSL style-sheets.

When switching to browser view, the document is first checked for validity, if you have selected Validate upon saving in the File tab of the I Options dialog. Use the menu command **Tools | Options** to open this dialog.

For further information on this view, please see the detailed description of the various views in the Main Window section.

Synchronize

This command **synchronizes** the **Enhanced Grid view** and **Tree view** in the main window.

To see the Tree view, you must activate the "Show Tree" check box in the File tab of the Options dialog). Use the menu command **Tools | Options** to open this dialog box.

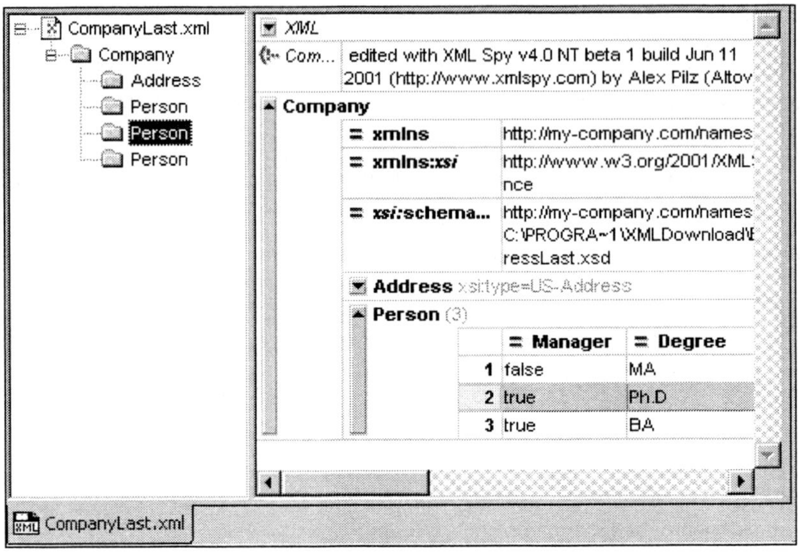

Click an item in the Tree or Grid view, and select the menu option **View | Synchronize.** The view in the other window is opened to the same level, and the item is highlighted.

You can also double-click on an element in the tree view, to navigate to that item in the grid.

Expand

Hotkey: **Num +**

This command **expands** the selected element by one level.

The command can be used in the Tree and Enhanced Grid views. The keyboard shortcut is the + key on the **numeric keypad**.

In the Enhanced Grid view, the element and all its children remain selected after expansion. This allows you to expand a large element by pressing the + key repeatedly.

You can expand and collapse any element by clicking on the gray bar to the left of each element.

Collapse

Hotkey: **Num -**

This command **collapses** the selected element by one level.

The command can be used in the Tree and Enhanced Grid views. The keyboard shortcut is the - key on the **numeric keypad**.

You can expand and collapse any element by clicking on the gray bar to the left of each element.

Expand fully

 Hotkey: **Num ***

This command **expands** all child items of the **selected element**, down to the last level of nesting.

The command can be used in the Tree and Enhanced Grid views. The keyboard shortcut is the * key on the **numeric keypad**.

Collapse unselected

Hotkey: **CTRL Num -**

This command allows you to focus on one element and its children, and ignore all the other surrounding elements.

The command can be used in the Tree and Enhanced Grid views. The keyboard shortcut is the **CTRL** and - key on the **numeric keypad**.

Simply select the item that you want to work with and choose this command to collapse all other (unselected) elements.

Optimal widths

This command **adjusts** the widths of all columns so that the text of the entire document fit into the designated columns.

If you expand and collapse several elements, select the "Optimal widths" command, as only visible items are taken into account when calculating the optimum column widths.

Word wrap

This command enables or disables word wrapping in the **Text view**.

Go to line/char...

 Hotkey: **CTRL+G**

This command goes to a **specific line number** and/or character position in an XML document in the Text view.

If you are working with an external XSLT processor (see the XSL page on the Tools | Options dialog for details) you may often get error messages by line number and character position. STYLEVISION 2004 lets you quickly navigate to that spot, using this command:

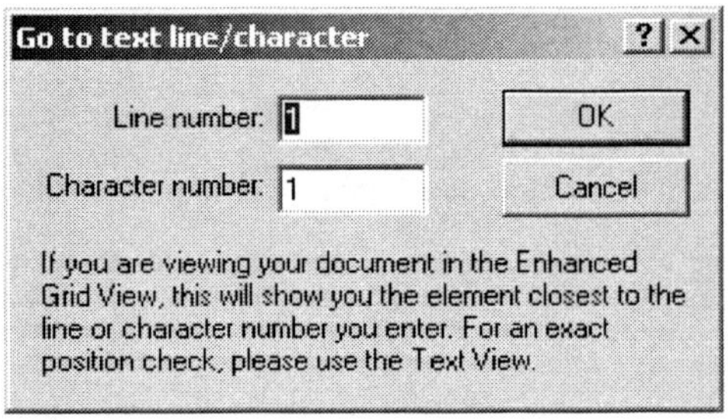

This command works in both the Text View and Enhanced Grid View, but will only be able to show an approximate position in the grid view by highlighting the element closest to the character position specified.

Go to File

This command **opens** a document that is being **referred** to, from within the file you are currently editing.

Select the file name, path name, or URL you are interested in, and choose this command from the View menu.

You can select:

- An entire element or attribute in the Enhanced Grid View
- Some characters from within any item in the Text or Enhanced Grid Views.
- An enclosed string. If you text cursor is between quotes, STYLEVISION 2004 will automatically use the entire string that is enclosed in the quotes.

Browser Menu

This menu contains commands that are only available when the Browser View has been activated.

Back

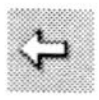 Hotkey: **Backspace**

This command displays a previously viewed page. You can also use the keyboard Backspace key to achieve the same effect.

This can be useful if you click a link in your XML document and want to return to it.

Forward

This command is only available once you have used the Back command, and moves you forward through previously viewed pages.

Stop

This command instructs the browser to stop loading your document.

This is useful if large external files or graphics would be loaded over a slow Internet connection.

Refresh

 Hotkey: **F5**

This command updates the Browser View by reloading the XML document and potential external CSS or XSL style-sheets as well as DTDs. You can also use the F5 key to trigger this command.

Fonts

This command allows you to select the default font site for rendering the text of your XML document. It is similar to the Font-Size command in most browsers.

Separate Window

This command opens the browser view in a separate window, so that side-by-side viewing is possible. (eg. text or enhanced grid) view.

If you have separated the browser view, press F5 in the editing view to automatically refresh the corresponding browser view.

Tools

The tools menu allows you to:

- Check the spelling of your XML documents.
- View the currently assigned macros
-
- Compare any two files to check for differences
- Compare any two folders to check for differences
- Customize your version: define your own toolbars, keyboard shortcuts, menus, and macros
- Define the global program settings

Spelling...

STYLEVISION 2004 now includes a built-in spelling checker.

The spelling checker can be used in the following views: Enhanced grid, Text and Authentic View as well as in Stylesheet Designer. Please note that you can check any type of XML file. The view you select influences the spelling checker options that are made available. A schema file (*.xsd) can be checked in the Text and Enhanced grid view, but not in the Schema/WSDL Design view.

Spell checking in the **Text** and **Enhanced grid** view presents you with the most options, you can additionally check the spelling of:

- Element content
- Attribute content
- CDATA content
- Comment text

  You can also define which specific element or attribute content to check or ignore. These selections are defined in the "Spelling context" dialog box.

The **Tools | Spelling...** command (hotkey Shift+F7) opens the Spelling dialog box, and automatically starts checking the currently active XML document (in this case the OrgChart.xml document in the Authentic View).

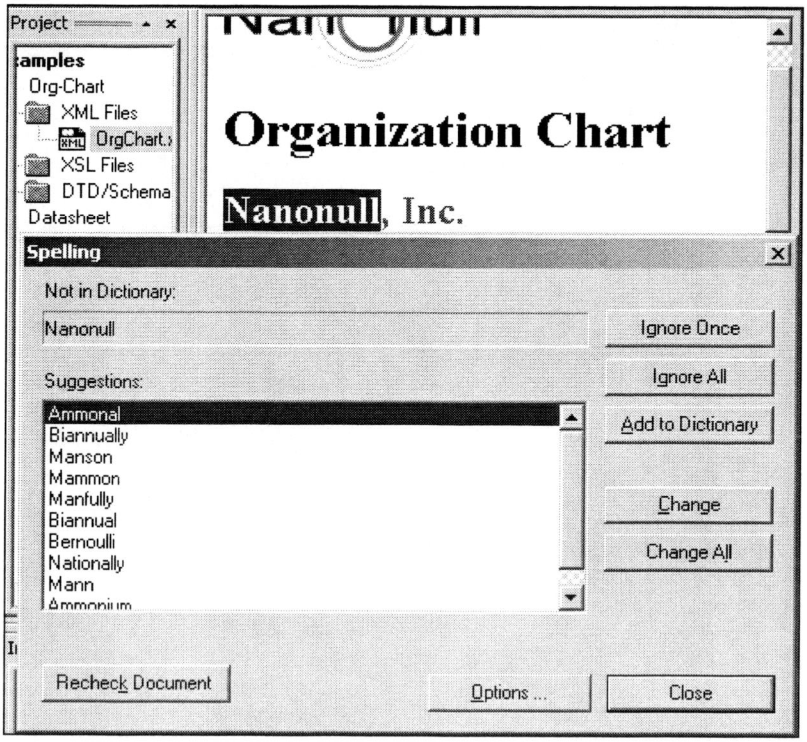

Not in Dictionary
This text box contains the word that cannot be found in any of the existing dictionaries (default and custom dictionaries). You can also edit the text here. The word is also highlighted in the XML document. The command buttons become active at this point and allow you to decide which action to take.

Suggestions
This list box displays a list of words that resemble the unknown word (supplied from all dictionaries). Double clicking a word in this list automatically inserts it in the document and continues the spell checking process.

Ignore once
This command allows you to continue checking the document while ignoring the first occurrence of the unknown word. The same word will be flagged again if it appears in the document.

Ignore all
This command ignores all instances of the unknown word in the whole document.

Add to dictionary
This command adds the unknown word to the currently active **custom dictionary**. This is the dictionary containing the check mark in the Custom Dictionaries dialog box (custom.tlx).

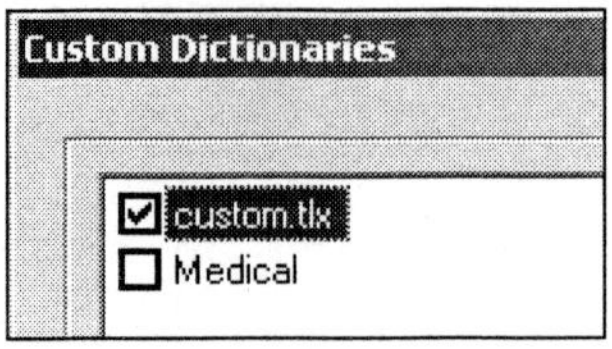

Change
This command replaces the currently highlighted word in the XML document, with the selected word in the Suggestions list box.

Change all
This command replaces all occurrences of the currently highlighted word in the XML document, with the selected word in the Suggestions list box.

Recheck
The Recheck button restarts the check from the beginning of the document.

Close
This command closes the Spelling dialog box.

Options...
This command opens a dialog box depending on the current view.

- If opened from Authentic View, the Options dialog box is opened.
- If opened from the Text or Enhanced Grid view, the Spelling context dialog box is opened.

Spelling options...

This command opens either the **Options** or **Spelling context** dialog box, depending on the view you are using to display your XML document.

Options - **Authentic View** and **Stylesheet Designer**
When viewing an XML document in Authentic View, this command opens the Options dialog box. Use this dialog box to define the global spelling checker options.

Always suggest corrections:
Activating this option causes suggestions (from all of the dictionaries) to be displayed in the Suggestions list box. Disabling this option causes no suggestions to be shown.

Make corrections only from main dictionary:
Activating this option causes only the default dictionary to be used, none of the custom dictionaries are scanned for suggestions. It also disables the Custom Dictionaries button, preventing any editing of the custom dictionaries.

Ignore words in UPPER case:
Activating this option causes all upper case words to be ignored.

Ignore words with numbers:
Activating this number causes all words containing numbers to be ignored.

Dictionary Language
Use this combo box to select the dictionary language for the spelling checking. The default installation allows you to select English. Other language dictionaries will be made available on the Altova download web site.

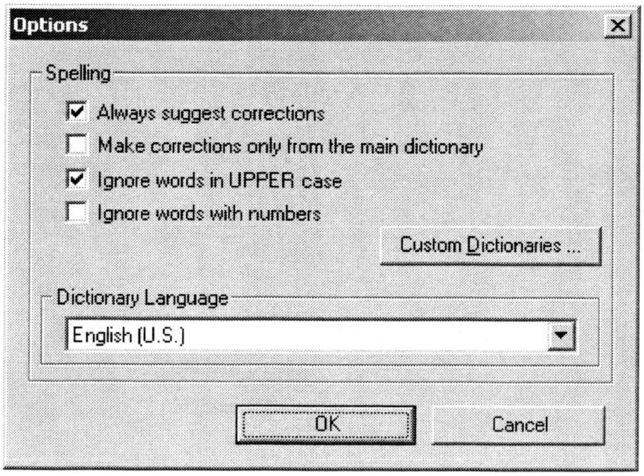

Custom dictionaries

The Custom Dictionaries... button allows you to:

- modify an existing dictionary (add or delete dictionary entries)
- create a totally new dictionary
- add an existing dictionary
- remove an existing dictionary

When you start the spell checking process, all dictionaries listed in the Custom Dictionaries list box are searched. If you want to limit the search to specific dictionaries, use the Remove command to delete those you do not want searched.

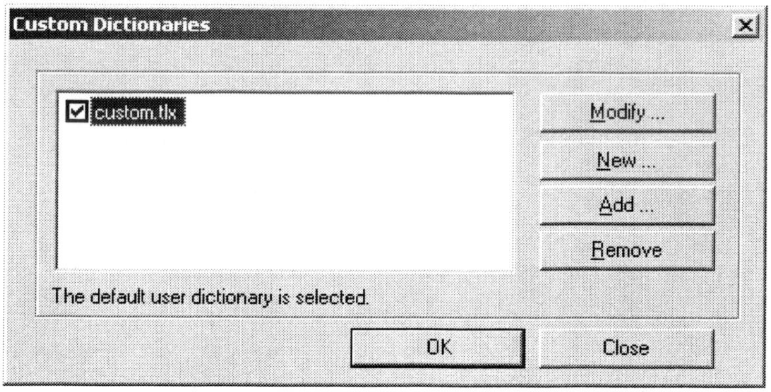

To modify dictionary entries:

1. Click the custom dictionary name whose entries you want to change, and click Modify...
   This opens the dictionary highlighted in the list box (custom.tlx in this case). A prompt appears if none of the dictionaries has been selected.

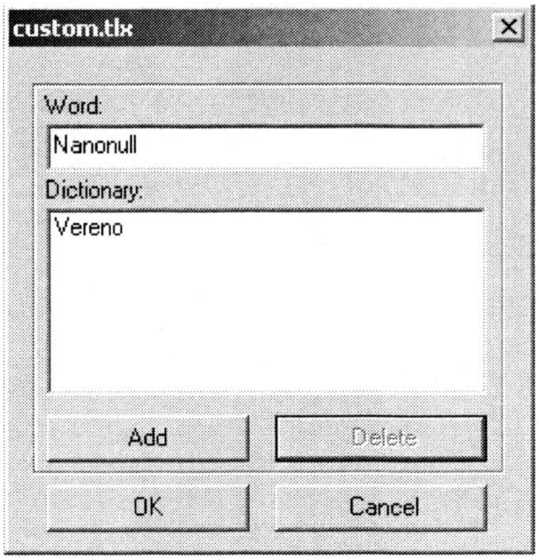

2. Click in the Word: field and enter the new dictionary entry (this automatically activates the Add button).
3. Click Add to add it to the dictionary.

To delete an entry from the dictionary:

1. Click the word in the Dictionary list box to highlight it, and click Delete.
2. Click OK to confirm the changes made in this dialog box.

To add a new dictionary:

1. Click New, and enter the name of the new **custom dictionary** in the File name... field.
2. Click Save to save the dictionary.
3. You can now add entries to the dictionary using the Add button, or the Add to Dictionary button while performing a spell check.

To add an existing dictionary:

Use this option to add previously removed (or third party dictionaries).

1. Click Add and select a dictionary from the list box. Dictionaries have a *.**tlx** extension.
2. Click Open to add the dictionary to the Custom dictionary list.

Please note:

It is not mandatory for a dictionary to have a *.tlx extension. It can have any, or no extension at all, and still be added to the dictionary list box.

To remove a dictionary:

- Click the dictionary name in the list and click Remove. This removes the dictionary from the list, it does not physically delete it from your hard disk.

Spelling context - **Text** and **Enhanced Grid** view

When viewing an XML document in the Text or Enhanced Grid view, this command opens the "Spelling context" dialog box. Starting the spelling checking in the **Text** and **Enhanced grid** view presents you with the most options, you can define the specific content which is to be checked:

- Element content
- Attribute content
- CDATA content
- Comment text

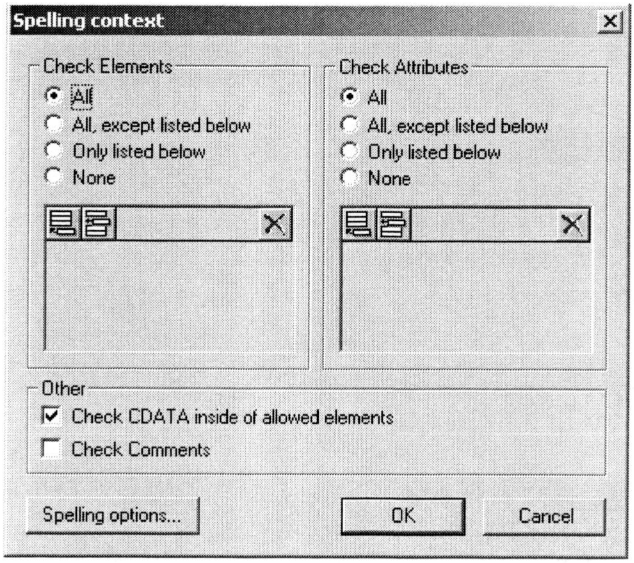

The Spelling options.. button opens the Options dialog box, which allows you to define the global spelling checker options.

To define specific element or attribute "content" you want to check:

1. Click the "All, except listed below", or "Only listed below" radio button.
2. Click the Append element/attribute icon , and enter the tag name containing the text you want checked (e.g. para). Hit return to confirm.

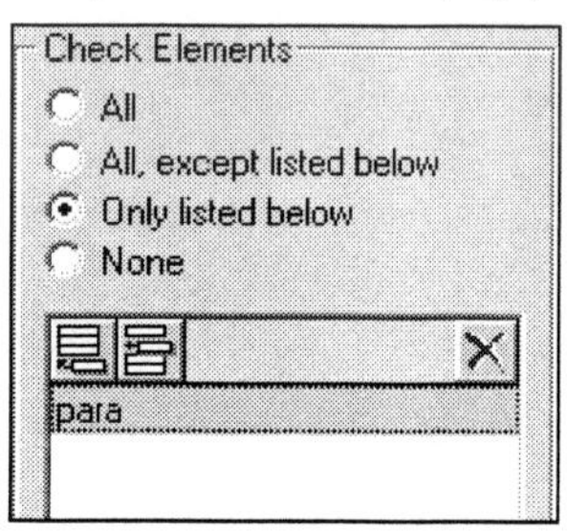

3. Click the OK button to confirm these settings, and click it again in the Spelling dialog box to start the spelling checker with these new settings.
   The only **element content** to be checked will be the text between the **para** tags, attribute content will also be checked.

To delete a tag name:

- Select the tag name, and hit the Delete or Backspace key.

Compare open file with...

This command allows you to compare the open file with another file. The comparison shows both files tiled vertically in the main window with the differences between them highlighted in each file in green.

To compare the open file with another file, do the following:

1. With the file active in the Main Window (only one open file can be active in the Main Window at a given time), click **Tools | Compare open file with...**. The following dialog appears:

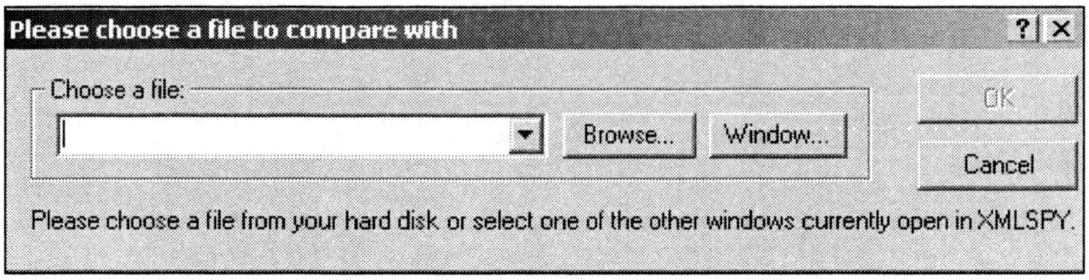

2. Browse for the file you wish to compare the open file with, and select it. Alternatively, if the file you wish to select is open (but not active) in the Main Window, or if the file is in a project, click the **Window...** button, and select the file.
3. Click OK. The second file is opened, and the Settings dialog appears:

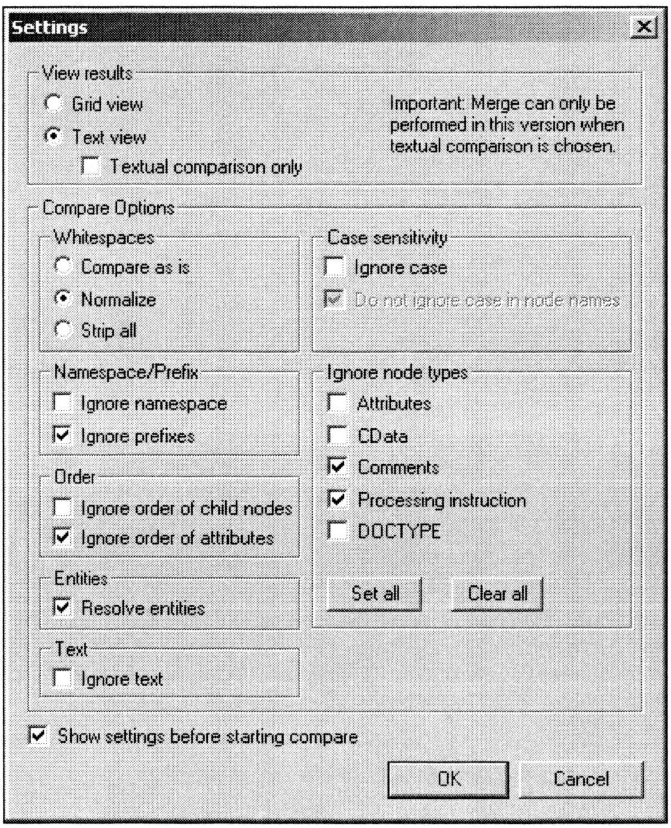

These settings are described under Compare options. If you do not wish to have this dialog appear each time you start a compare session, uncheck "Show settings before starting compare", which is at the bottom of the dialog.

4. Select the required settings, then click OK. The two files now appear in the Main Window. Lines that are different are highlighted in green.

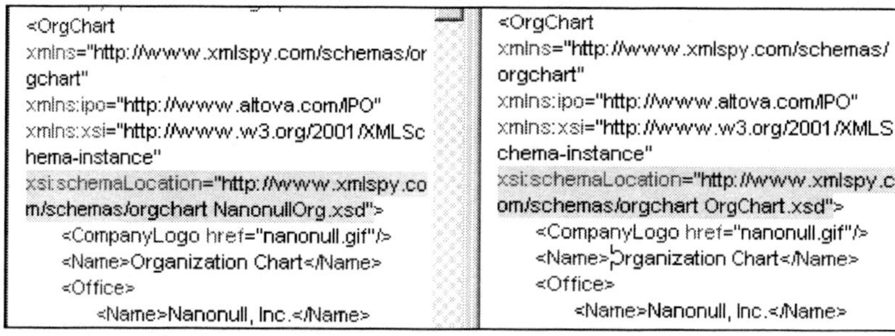

A Compare Files control window also appears:

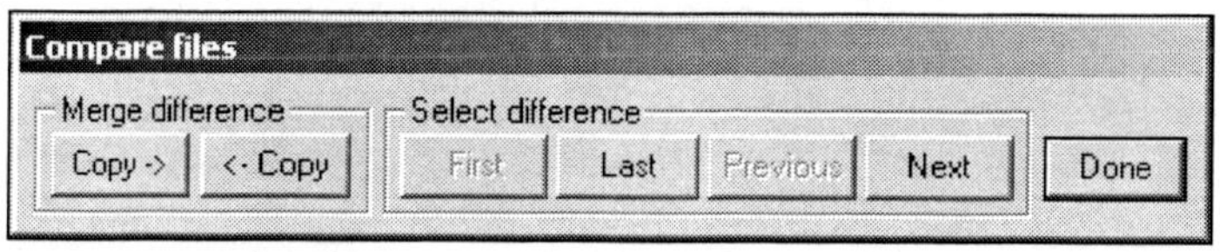

The "Merge difference" pane appears only if you have set the compare (in the Settings dialog) for textual comparison. You can navigate up and down through the differences by clicking the appropriate button in the "Select difference" pane. The currently selected difference is displayed in the Main Window as a darker green. If you wish to have the line/s from one file replace the corresponding line/s in the other file, click the appropriate button in the Merge difference pane.

5. When you are done with reviewing the differences and merging differences, click Done.

Note:

- The Merge difference feature is available for textual comparisons only, and not for XML differences.
- While the Compare session is active, no editing or change of views is allowed. Any attempt to edit or change the view of either file will pop up a message warning that the Compare session will be ended.
- Compare settings can be changed during a Compare session, but will only take effect from the next Compare session onward; the new settings will not affect the current session.

Compare directories

The Compare directories command allows you to compare two directories, with or without their sub-directories. Directories are compared to indicate missing files, and whether files of the same name are different or not.

To compare two directories, do the following:

1. Click **Tools | Compare directories**. The following dialog appears.

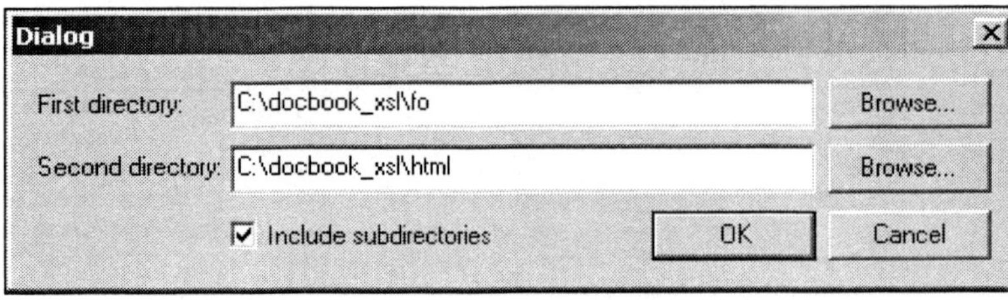

2. Browse for the directories to compare, and check the Include subdirectories check box if you wish to include subdirectories in the Compare.
3. Click OK. The Compare File Settings dialog (described in Compare options) appears.
4. Select the required settings for comparing files.
5. Click OK. A dialog will appear indicating the progress of the Compare.

The result will appear in a window, and will look like this:

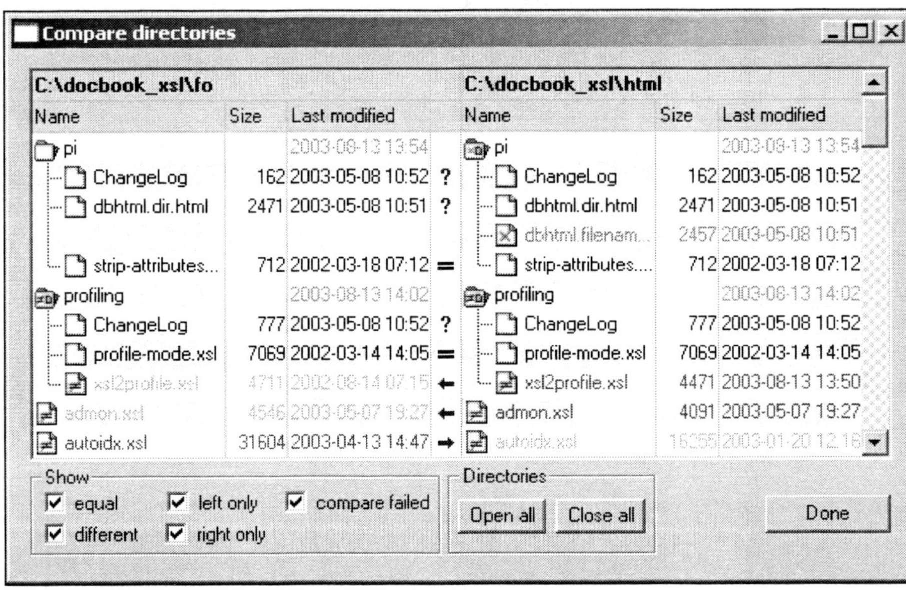

Directory symbols
All directory names are given in black.

This directory contains files, all of which either cannot be compared or are not different from the corresponding file in the compared directory.

This directory contains one or more files that do not exist in the compared directory.

This directory contains one or more files that are different from the corresponding file in the compared directory.

Note: If a directory contains both a file that does not exist in the compared directory as well as a file that is different from the corresponding file in the compared directory, then the directory will be shown with the icon 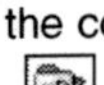.

File symbols
The colors in which file names appear depend on their compare status. These colors are noted below.

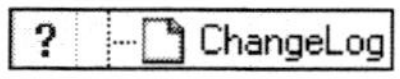

This file cannot be compared (with the corresponding file in the compared directory). A question mark appears in the middle column. The file name appears in black.

This file is not different from the corresponding file in the compared directory. An equals-to sign appears in the middle column. The file name appears in black.

This file does not exist in the compared directory. The middle column is empty. The file name appears in blue.

This file is different from the corresponding file in the compared directory, and the last modification to this file is more recent than the last modification to the corresponding file. An arrow pointing towards the older file appears in the middle column. The file name appears in dark red.

This file is different from the corresponding file in the compared directory, and the last modification to this file is older than the last modification to the corresponding file in the compared directory. An arrow pointing towards this (the older) file appears in the middle column. The file name appears in light red.

Viewing options

- Select what files to show by checking or unchecking the options in the Show pane at the bottom of the Result window.
- Open or close all subdirectories by clicking the appropriate button in the Directories pane.
- Expand or collapse subdirectories by double-clicking the folder icon.
- The Size and Last Modified can be toggled on and off by right-clicking on either file titlebar and clicking Size and Last Modified.

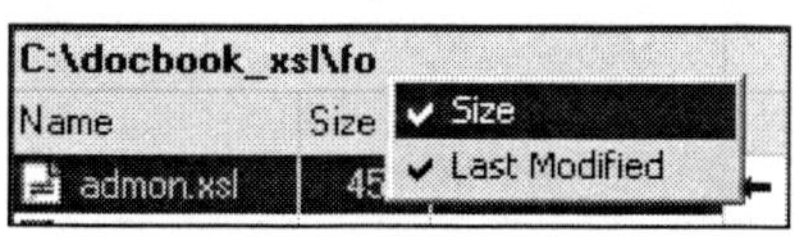

- Change column widths by dragging columns.
- The Result window can be maximized, minimized, and resized.

Comparing and merging files
Double-clicking on a line opens both files on that line in the Main Window, and directly starts a File Compare for the two files. You can then continue as in a regular Compare session (see Compare open file with...).

Compare options

Clicking **Compare options** pops up the Settings dialog shown below. In it you make the settings for your Compare sessions. The settings that are current when a Compare session is started are the settings that are applied to that Compare session.

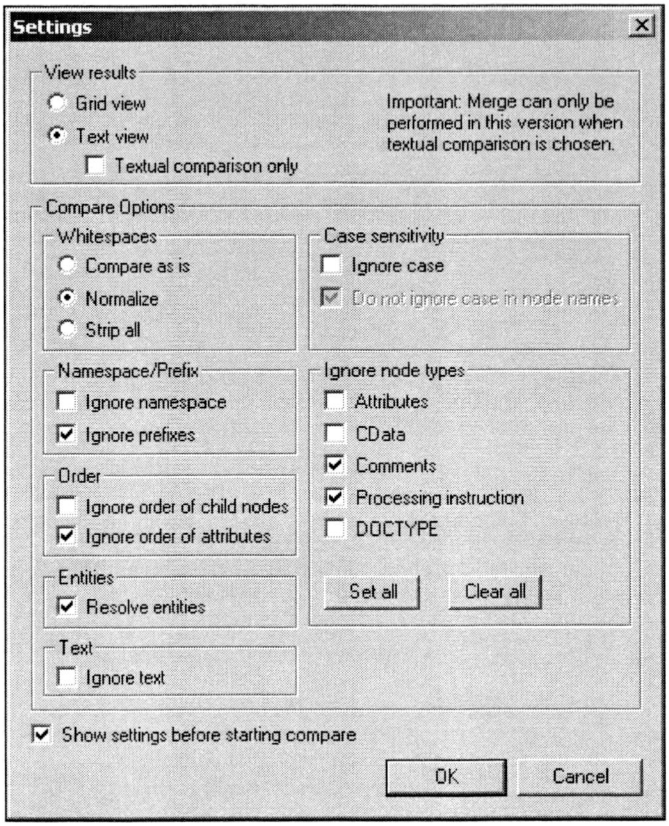

View results
Selects the view in which results are shown. If either Text View (with the "Textual comparison only" check-box unchecked) or the Grid View is selected the documents are treated as XML documents, and XML Compare Options are enabled. If Text View (with the "Textual comparison only" check-box checked) is selected, the documents are treated as text documents, and XML Compare Options are disabled.

Note: Merging differences is allowed only when textual comparison is chosen.

Whitespaces
Whitespace characters in XML are space, tab, carriage return, and line feed. The three options here compare files with whitespace unchanged; with whitespace normalized (i.e. all consecutive whitespace characters are reduced to one whitespace character); and with all whitespace stripped.

Case sensitivity
If the "Ignore case" check box is checked, then you have the option of ignoring or not ignoring case in node names.

Namespace/Prefix
These are options for ignoring namespaces and prefixes when searching for differences.

Order
If "Ignore order of child nodes" is selected, then, as long as the set of corresponding child nodes are present in both files, the position of child nodes relative to each other does not matter. This option is also available for the attributes of elements.

Entities
If "Resolve entities" is selected, then all entities in the document are resolved. Otherwise the files are compared with the entities as is.

Text
If "Ignore text" is selected, then differences in corresponding text nodes are not reported.

Ignore node types
Check the node types to be ignored in the comparison. Node types that may be ignored are Attributes, CDATA, Comments, Processing Instructions, and DOCTYPE statements.

Show settings before starting compare
Checking this option causes this dialog to appear whenever the **Compare open file with** and **Redo last comparison** commands are clicked. Having the Settings dialog appear before each comparison allows you to check and modify the settings for each comparison.

If this command is unchecked, then the Compare session will start directly when a comparison is invoked.

Customize...

The customize command lets you customize STYLEVISION 2004 to suit your personal needs.

Commands

The Commands tab allows you customize your menus or toolbars.

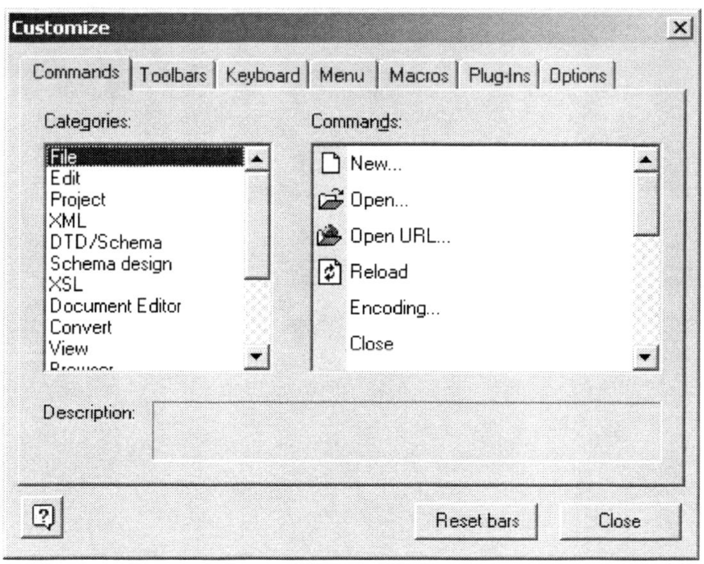

To add a command to a toolbar or menu:

1. Open this dialog box using **Tools | Customize.**
2. Select the command category in the Categories list box. The commands available appear in the Commands list box.
3. Click on a command in the commands list box and drag "it" to an to an existing menu or toolbar.
4. An **I**-beam appears when you place the cursor over a valid position to drop the command.
5. Release the mouse button at the position you want to insert the command.

- A small button appears at the tip of mouse pointer when you drag a command. The check mark below the pointer means that the command cannot be dropped at the current cursor position.
- The check mark disappears whenever you can drop the command (over a tool bar or menu).
- Placing the cursor over a menu when dragging, opens it, allowing you to insert the command anywhere in the menu.
- Commands can be placed in menus or tool bars. If you created you own toolbar you can populate it with your own commands/icons.

Please note:
You can also edit the commands in the **context menus** (right click anywhere opens the context menu), using the same method. Click the Menu tab and then select the specific context menu available in the Context Menus combo box.

To delete a command or menu:

1. Open this dialog box using **Tools | Customize.**
2. Click on the menu entry or icon you want to delete, and drag with the mouse.
3. Release the mouse button whenever the check mark icon appears below the mouse pointer.
   The command, or menu item is deleted from the menu or tool bar.

Toolbars

The Toolbars tab allows you to activate or deactivate specific toolbars, as well as create your own specialized ones.

STYLEVISION 2004 toolbars contain symbols for the most frequently used menu commands. For each symbol you get a brief "tool tip" explanation when the mouse cursor is directly over the item and the status bar shows a more detailed description of the command.

You can drag the toolbars from their standard position to any location on the screen, where they appear as a floating window. Alternatively you can also dock them to the left or right edge of the main window.

- Toolbar settings defined in the Grid, Schema/WSDL design and Text view are valid in those views. The Browser view toolbars are independent of all the other views.

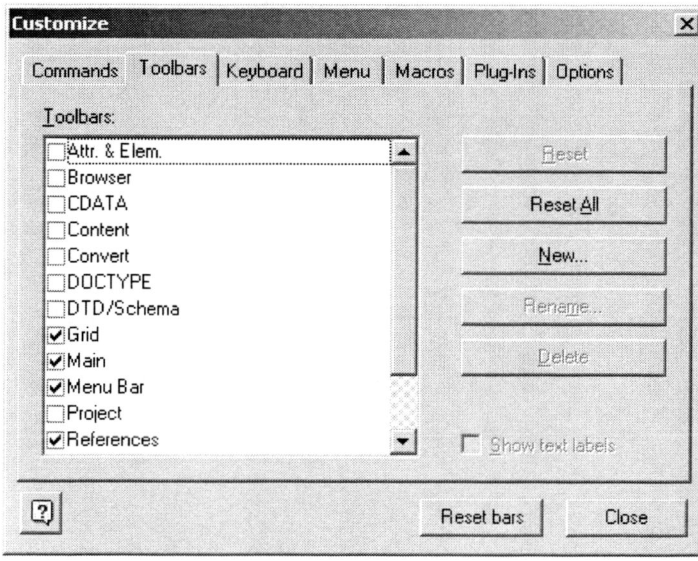

To activate or deactivate a toolbar:

1. Click the check box to activate (or deactivate) the specific toolbar.

To create a new toolbar:

1. Click the **New...** button, and give the toolbar a name in the Toolbar name dialog box.
2. Add commands to the toolbar using the Commands tab of the Customize dialog box.

To reset the Menu Bar

- Click the Menu Bar entry and
- Click the **Reset** button, to reset the menu commands to the state they were in when STYLEVISION 2004 was installed.

To reset all toolbar and menu commands

- Click the **Reset All** button, to reset all the toolbar commands to the state they were when the program was installed. A prompt appears stating that all toolbars and menus will be reset.
- Click Yes to confirm the reset.

To change a toolbar name:

- Click the **Rename**... button to edit the name of the toolbar.

To delete a toolbar:

- Click the **Delete** button to delete the currently highlighted toolbar in the Toolbars list box.
- A prompt appears, asking if you really want to delete the toolbar. Click Yes to confirm the deletion.
- or, click right on the menu or icon bar, and select the Delete entry in the popup menu.

Show text labels:

This option places explanatory text below toolbar icons when activated.

Keyboard

The Keyboard tab allows you to define (or change) keyboard shortcuts for any STYLEVISION 2004 command.

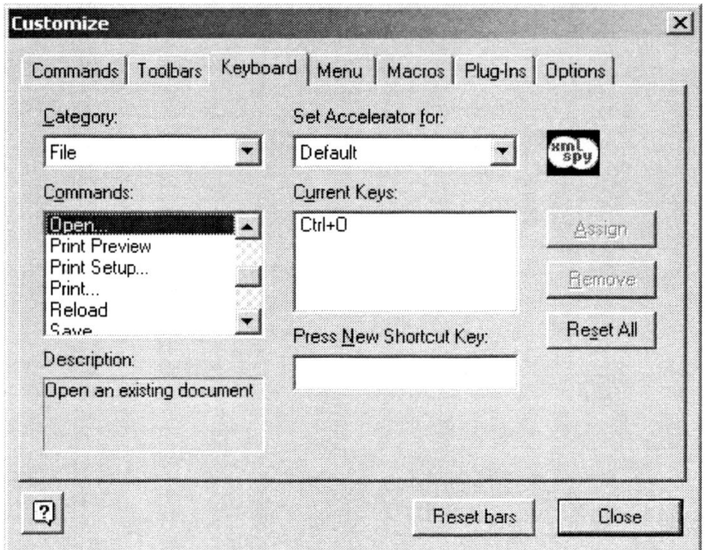

To assign a new Shortcut to a command:

1. Select the commands category using the **Category** combo box.
2. Select the **command** you want to assign a new shortcut to, in the Commands list box
3. Click in the "**Press New Shortcut Key**:" text box, and press the shortcut keys that are to activate the command.
   The shortcuts appear immediately in the text box. If the shortcut was assigned previously, then that function is displayed below the text box.
4. Click the **Assign** button to permanently assign the shortcut.
   The shortcut now appears in the Current Keys list box.
   (To **clear** this text box, press any of the control keys, CTRL, ALT or SHIFT).

To de-assign (or delete a shortcut):

1. Click the shortcut you want to delete in the Current Keys list box, and
2. Click the **Remove** button (which has now become active).
3. Click the Close button to confirm all the changes made in the Customize dialog box.

Set accelerator for:

Currently no function.

Currently assigned keyboard shortcuts:

Hotkeys by key

F1	Help Menu
F3	Find Next
F5	Refresh
F7	Check well-formedness
F8	Validate
F9	Insert/Remove breakpoint
CTRL+F9	Enable/Disable breakpoint
F10	XSL Transformation
CTRL+F10	XSL:FO Transformation
F11	Step into
CTRL+F11	Step Over
Shift + F11	Step Out
Alt+F11	Start Debugger/Go
Num +	Expand
Num -	Collapse
Num *	Expand fully
CTRL+Num-	Collapse unselected
CTRL + G	Goto line/char
CTRL+TAB	and
CTRL+F6	Cycle through open windows
Arrow keys	
(up / down)	Move selection bar
Esc.	Abandon edits/close dialog box
Return/Space bar	confirms a selection
Alt + F4	Closes STYLEVISION 2004
CTRL + F4	Closes active window
Alt + F, 1	Open last file

CTRL + Double click an element (Schema view)	Display element definition
CTRL + N	File New
CTRL + O	File Open
CTRL + S	File Save
CTRL + P	File Print
CTRL + A	Select All
Shift + Del	Cut (or CTRL + X)
CTRL + C	Copy
CTRL + V	Paste
CTRL + Z	Undo
CTRL + Y	Redo
Del	Delete (Delete item in Schema/Enhanced Grid view)
CTRL + F	Find
F3	Find Next
CTRL + H	Replace
CTRL + I	Append Attribute
CTRL + E	Append Element
CTRL + T	Append Text
CTRL + D	Append CDATA
CTRL + M	Append Comment
CTRL + SHIFT + I	Insert Attribute
CTRL + SHIFT + E	Insert Element
CTRL + SHIFT + T	Insert Text content
CTRL + SHIFT + D	Insert CDATA
CTRL + SHIFT + M	Insert Comment
CTRL + ALT + I	Add Child Attribute
CTRL + ALT + E	Add Child Element
CTRL + ALT + T	Add Child Text
CTRL + ALT + D	Add Child CDATA
CTRL + ALT + M	Add Child Comment

Currently assigned keyboard shortcuts:

Hotkeys by function

Abandon edits	Esc.
Add Child Attribute	CTRL + ALT + I
Add Child CDATA	CTRL + ALT + D
Add Child Comment	CTRL + ALT + M
Add Child Element	CTRL + ALT + E
Add Child Text	CTRL + ALT + T
Append Attribute	CTRL + I
Append CDATA	CTRL + D
Append Comment	CTRL + M
Append Element	CTRL + E
Append Text	CTRL + T
Check well-formedness	F7
Closes active window	CTRL + F4
Close STYLEVISION 2004	Alt + F4
Collapse	Num -
Collapse unselected	CTRL + Num-
Confirms a selection	Return / Space bar
Copy	CTRL + C
Cut	SHIFT + Del (or CTRL + X)
Cycle through windows	CTRL + TAB and CTRL + F6
Delete item	Del
Enable/Disable breakpoint	CTRL + F9
Expand	Num +
Expand fully	Num *
File New	CTRL + N
File Open	CTRL + O
File Print	CTRL + P
File Save	CTRL + S

Find	CTRL + F
Find Next	F3
Goto line/char	CTRL + G
Help Menu	F1
Insert Attribute	CTRL + SHIFT + I
Insert CDATA	CTRL + SHIFT + D
Insert Comment	CTRL + SHIFT + M
Insert Element	CTRL + SHIFT + E
Insert/Remove breakpoint	F9
Insert Text content	CTRL + SHIFT + T
Move selection bar	Arrow keys (up / down)
Open last file	Alt + F, 1
Paste	CTRL + V
Redo	CTRL + Y
Refresh	F5
Replace	CTRL + H
Select All	CTRL + A
Start Debugger/Go	Alt + F11
Step Into	F11
Step Out	Shift + F11
Step Over	CTRL + F11
To view an element definition	CTRL + Double click on an element.
Undo	CTRL + Z
Validate	F8
XSL Transformation	F10
XSL:FO Transformation	CTRL + F10

Menu

The Menu tab allows you to customize the main menu bars as well as the (popup - right click) context menus.

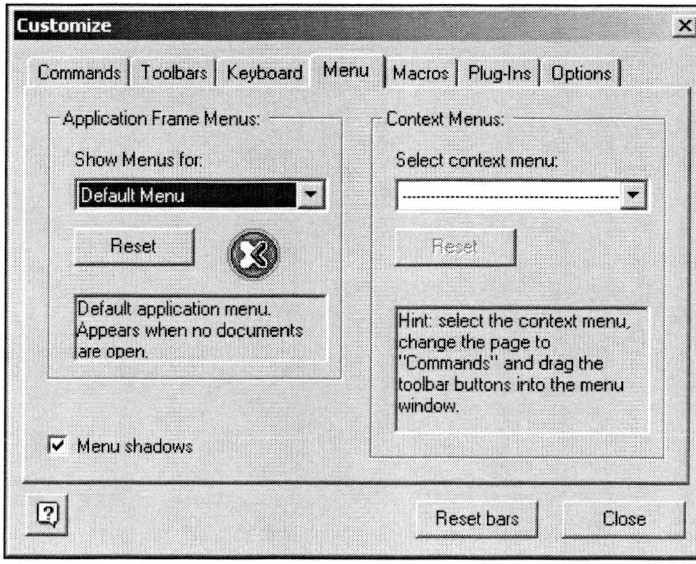

You can customize both the Default and STYLEVISION 2004 menu bars.

The **Default** menu is the one visible when no XML documents of any type are open in STYLEVISION 2004.

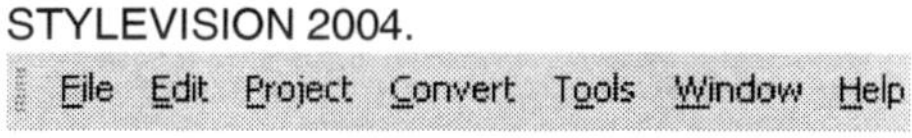

The STYLEVISION 2004 menu is the menu bar visible when at least one XML document has been opened.

To customize a menu:

1. Select the menu bar you want to customize from the "Show Menus for:" combo box
2. Click the **Commands** tab, and drag the commands to the menu bar of your choice.

To delete commands from a menu:

1. Click right on the command, or icon representing the command, and
2. Select the **Delete** option from the popup menu,

   or,

1. Select **Tools | Customize** to open the Customize dialog box, and
2. Drag the command away from the menu, and drop it as soon as the check mark icon appears below the mouse pointer.

To reset either of the menu bars:

1. Select either the Default or STYLEVISION 2004 entry in the combo box, and
2. Click the **Reset** button just below the menu name.
   A prompt appears asking if you are sure you want to reset the menu bar.

To customize any of the Context menus (right click menus):

1. Select the context menu from the combo box.
2. Click the **Commands** tab, and drag the commands to context menu that is now open.

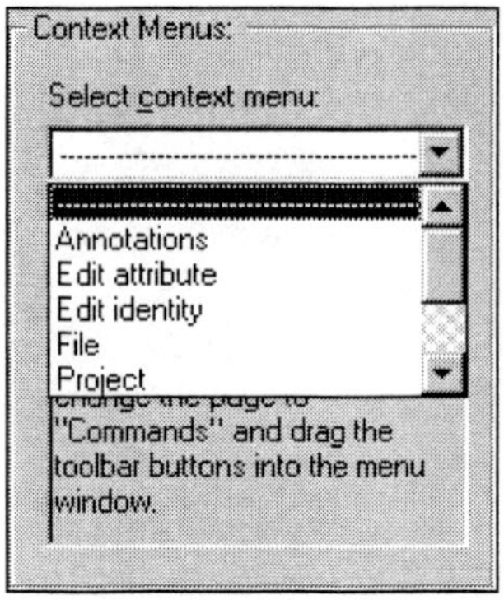

To delete commands from a context menu:

1. Click right on the command, or icon representing the command, and
2. Select the **Delete** option from the popup menu

or,

1. Select **Tools | Customize** to open the Customize dialog box, and
2. Drag the command away from the context menu, and drop it as soon as the check mark icon appears below the mouse pointer.

To reset any of the context menus:

1. Select the context menu from the combo box, and
2. Click the **Reset** button just below the context menu name.
   A prompt appears asking if you are sure you want to reset the context menu.

To close an context menu window:

1. Click on the **Close icon** at the top right of the title bar, or
2. Click the Close button of the Customize dialog box.

Menu animations (only prior to Windows 2000)

- Select one of the menu animations from the combo box, if you want animated menus. Please note that the combo box is only visible in Windows versions prior to Windows 20000. For Windows 2000 and later, these settings have to be changed in the Effects tab of the Display properties dialog box. Double click the Display icon in the Control Panel to open the dialog box.

Menu shadows

- Click the Menu shadows check box, if you want all your menus to have shadows.

Options

The Options tab allows you to set general environment settings.

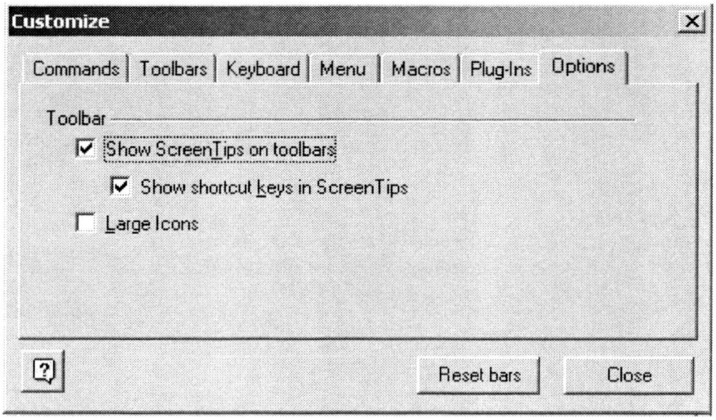

Toolbar
When active, the **Show Tooltips on toolbars** check box displays a popup when the mouse pointer is placed over an icon in any of the icon bars. The popup contains a short description of the icon function, as well as the associated keyboard shortcut, if one has been assigned.

The **Show shortcut keys in Tooltips** check box, allows you to decide if you want to have the shortcut displayed in the tooltip.

When active, the **Large icons** check box switches between the standard size icons, and larger versions of the icons.

Customize context menu

The Customize context menu allows you to further customize icons and menu items.

To open the customize context menu:
1. First open the Customize menu by selecting **Tools | Customize**.
2. Then place the mouse pointer over an icon (or menu) and **click right** to open the context menu.

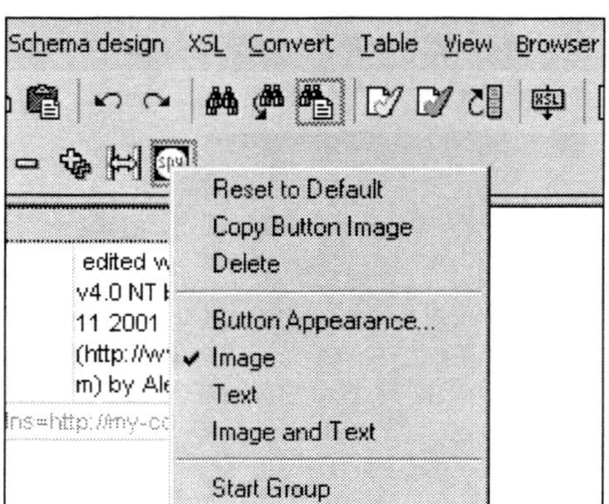

Reset to default
Currently no function.

Copy Button image
This option copies the icon you right click, to the clipboard.

Delete
This option deletes the icon or menu you right click. Deleting a menu, deletes all menu options contained in it!

To restore a deleted menu:

- Select the Menu tab
- Select the menu you want to restore (STYLEVISION 2004 or Default).
- Click the Reset button below the menu selection combo box.

Button Appearance...
This option allows you to edit the button image as well as the button text. Currently only the macro icons can be edited (default STYLEVISION 2004 icon).

The Image only, Text only and Image and text radio buttons, let you define what you want to edit. Click the Select User-defined Image radio button and click one of the icons.

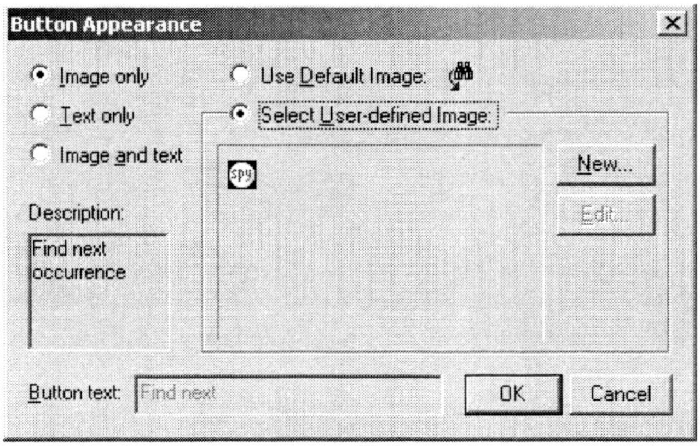

Click the Edit... button, to open the Edit button image dialog box. The Button text can be edited if you select either Text only or Image and text options.

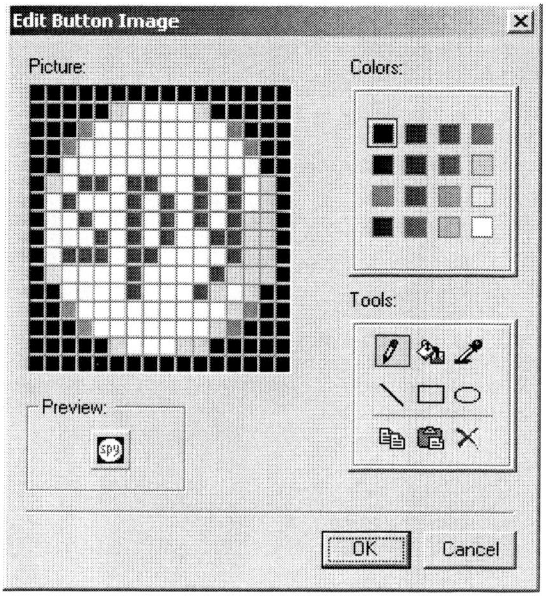

Image
This option changes the graphical display of an icon to the text representing it.

Text
This option changes the textual description of a function to the graphical image (icon) representing that function.

Image and Text
This option enables the simultaneous display of an icon and its text.

Start group
This option inserts a vertical divider to the left of the icon you right clicked.

Options

The "Options" command allows you to define the global program settings in a tabbed dialog box. These settings are saved in the registry, and apply to all current and future document windows.

The Apply button displays the changes in the currently open documents, and fixes the current settings. The changes are seen immediately in the background windows.

File

The "File" tab defines the way STYLEVISION 2004 opens and saves XML documents. You can also find related settings in the Encoding tab.

Open/New file in Grid view
You can choose to open an existing file or create a new file either in the Enhanced Grid View or in the text view. If you select the grid view, you can optionally show the tree structure, and

automatically expand all lines at the same time.

Automatic reload of changed files
If you are working in a multi-user environment, or if you are working on files that are dynamically generated on a server, you can watch for changes to the files that you are currently editing. STYLEVISION 2004 will then prompt you to reload the file, whenever a change is detected.

Validation
If you are using document type definitions (DTDs) or schemas to define the structure of your XML documents, you can automatically check the document for validity whenever it is opened or saved.

STYLEVISION 2004 can also cache these files in memory to save any unnecessary reloading (e.g. when the Schema being referred to, is accessed through a URL).

Project
When you start STYLEVISION 2004, you can open the last-used project automatically.

Save File
TAB-characters (0x09) are used to indent the individual elements forming the structure of the XML document. In certain situations this may be undesirable. Deactivate the "Indent elements using tabs" check box, if this is the case.

No formatting output for
You can selectively turn off output formatting for certain elements, by entering them in the list box (e.g. necessary for xsl:attribute when you are editing XSL Stylesheets).

When saving an XML document, STYLEVISION 2004 includes a short comment <!-- Edited with STYLEVISION 2004 http://www.altova.com --> near the top of the file. This option can only be deactivated by licensed users.

When saving a content model diagram (using the menu option Schema design | Generate Documentation), STYLEVISION 2004 includes a comment <!-- Generated with STYLEVISION 2004 Schema Editor - http://www.altova.com -->) at the bottom of the diagram. This option can only be deactivated by licensed users.

Line breaks
Line-breaks in the document file can be preserved so that the same characters will be used that were found when opening the file. You can choose to encode line breaks in any of the three possible forms (CR&LF for PCs, CR for the MacOS, or LF for Unix).

File types

The "File types" tab allows you to customize the behavior of STYLEVISION 2004 on a per-file-type basis.

Choose a file type from the "File types" list box, to customize the functions for that particular file type:

Windows Explorer settings
You can modify the file type description and MIME-compliant content type used by Windows Explorer, and you can define if STYLEVISION 2004 is to be the default editor for this file type.

XML Conformance

STYLEVISION 2004 lets you edit XML files as well as non-XML files. You must define the XML-Conformance settings for each new file type you add. Since XML allows for special grammar rules when dealing with external Document Type Definitions (DTDs) and external parsed entities, the exact grammar to be used can also be set here.

Do not modify these settings unless you are adding a new file type and are sure of what you are doing.

Default view
This group lets you define the default view to be used for each file type.

Grid view
This check box lets you define if the Enhanced Grid View should automatically build tables.

Text view
This text box lets you set syntax-coloring for particular file types.

Disable automatic validation
If you are using partial XML-documents that are included in another file and cannot be validated individually, you can turn off automatic validation per file type.

Save empty elements in short <E/> format
Some XML tools may have problems understanding the short <Element/> form for empty elements defined in the XML 1.0 Specification. You can instruct STYLEVISION 2004 to save elements in the longer (but nonetheless also valid) <Element></Element> form.

Add new file extension button
Adds a new file type to the File types list. Define the settings for this new file type using the options in this dialog box.

Delete selected file extension button
Deletes the currently selected file type and all associated settings.

Editing

The "Editing" tab defines the behavior of the Enhanced Grid View, when exchanging data using the clipboard and moving items with drag & drop.

Intelligent editing
While editing documents, STYLEVISION 2004 provides Intelligent Editing based on these settings. You can also customize various aspects of the behavior of these Entry helpers here.

Default copy to clipboard in grid view as
You can choose the format in which data will be exported to foreign applications using the clipboard. If you select XML-Text, the contents of the clipboard will be formatted and tagged just like the resulting XML file itself.

The structured text mode attempts to format the clipboard contents as a table, for use in a spreadsheet or database application. This option does not affect the internal clipboard format that STYLEVISION 2004 uses for copying and pasting.

Table view
You can also control, how STYLEVISION 2004 decides when to display repeating elements in the Table View.

View

The "View" tab allows you customize the XML documents presentation.

Enhanced Grid view
Collapsed elements in the Enhanced Grid View can be displayed in preview form. This displays the attributes and their values in gray in the same line as the element.

You can automatically apply the Optimal Widths command while editing, and limit the maximum cell width and height.

Text view
The Text View supports syntax-coloring, which can be updated dynamically while typing or be disabled entirely.

Program logo
You can turn off the splash screen upon program startup, to speed up the application.

Window title
The window title for each document window can contain only file name, or the full path name.

Authentic View
XML files based on a document template (*.sps), are automatically opened in the Authentic View when this option is active.

Browser view
You can choose to see the browser view in a separate window, enabling side-by-side placement of the edit and browser views.

Grid fonts

The "Grid fonts" tab allows you to customize the appearance of text in the Enhanced Grid view.

Font face and script
You can select the font face and size to be used for displaying the various items in the Enhanced Grid View. The same fonts are also used for printing and consequently only TrueType fonts can be selected.

Size
If you want to use the same font size for all items, click on the "Use same for all" check box.

Styles
The style and color can be set using the combo boxes. The current settings are immediately reflected in the list, so that you can preview the way your document is going to look.

In the Windows 98 version of STYLEVISION 2004, it is possible to select a "Script" for some fonts. This is especially necessary when editing documents with a non-Roman writing systems. The script selected in the font settings dialog box, needs to match the character set code-page selected when opening a document (i.e. when editing a Cyrillic ISO-8859-5 document, the code-page being used to edit the file should be set to 1251 and the font script needs to be set to "Cyrillic").

Schema fonts

The "Schema fonts" tab allows you to customize the appearance of text in the Text view.

Font face and script
You can select the font face and size to be used for displaying the various items in the Schema/WSDL Design view. The same fonts are used when printing and creating schema documentation, consequently only TrueType fonts can be selected.

The "Doc." Schema and Element headers, are the fonts that are used when creating schema documentation.

Size
If you want to use the same font size for all items, click on the "Use same for all" check box.

Styles
The style and color can be set using the combo boxes. The current settings are immediately reflected in the list, so that you can preview the way your document is going to look.

In the Windows 98 version of STYLEVISION 2004, it is possible to select a "Script" for some fonts. This is especially necessary when editing documents with a non-Roman writing systems. The script selected in the font settings dialog box, needs to match the character set code-page selected when opening a document (i.e. when editing a Cyrillic ISO-8859-5 document, the code-page being used to edit the file should be set to 1251 and the font script needs to be set to "Cyrillic").

Text fonts

The "Text fonts" tab allows you to customize the appearance of text in the Text view.

Again you can choose the font face, style and size, but this time the same font, style and size is always being used for all elements. Only the color can be adjusted individually to provide full customization of the syntax coloring option.

Setting the background color is only supported when RichEdit 3.0 is available on your system.

Colors

The "Colors" tab allows you to customize the colors used in the **Enhanced Grid view**, when viewing elements in the Database/Table view.

Example:

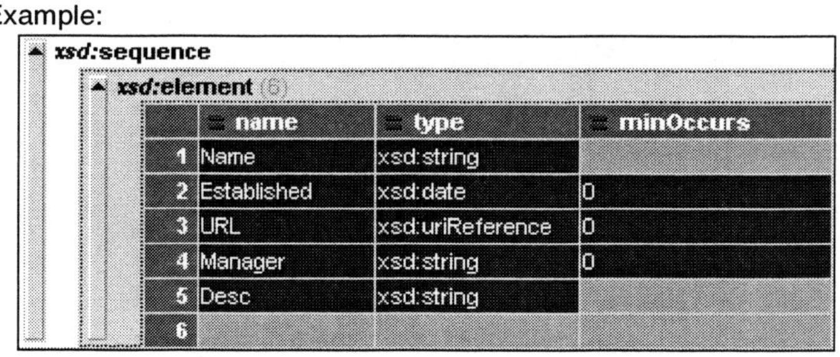

Header unselected

This option defines the color of the table header when deselected.

Header selected
This option defines the color of the table header when selected.

Non-existing elements unselected
This option defines the color of the empty elements when deselected.

Non-existing elements selected
This option defines the color of the empty elements when selected.

In addition to the colors you define here, STYLEVISION 2004 uses the regular selection and menu color preferences set in the Display Settings on the Control Panel of your Windows installation.

Encoding

The "Encoding" tab specifies the kind of character-set encoding to be used when creating new files, as well as the encoding to be assumed, when opening files that lack an encoding declaration.

Default encoding for new files
The default encoding for new files can be pre-determined in the Settings dialog box so that each new document is automatically created with a proper XML-declaration and includes the encoding-specification that you most commonly need.

The encoding for existing files will, of course, always be remembered independently of this setting and can only be changed by the "Encoding" command on the "File" menu.
If a two- or four-byte encoding is selected as the default encoding (i.e. UTF-16, UCS-2, or UCS-4) you can also choose between little-endian and big-endian byte-ordering for the XML files.

Open/save files with unknown encoding as
You can choose how an XML file is to be interpreted if the encoding-specification is missing, and the encoding cannot be auto-detected. In most cases this will very likely be UTF-8 or ISO-8895-1, even though the XML specification theoretically only allows UTF-8 files to lack an encoding-specification.

Open/save non-XML files in
Sometimes is can be convenient to also use STYLEVISION 2004 for editing non-XML files (such as Active Server Pages (ASP) or similar web-related documents. Since these files do not contain any encoding statements, you must specify a default Windows Code Page to be used for access these files.

XSL

The "XSL" tab allows you to define which program to use for XSL Transformations.

The built-in XSLT engine is automatically enabled, and is always used when using the XSLT Debugger. Selecting any other engine, uses that version when transforming XML files.

STYLEVISION 2004 includes full support for XSL Transformations, and can either use the MSXML 3.0 or 4.0 parser (which is pre-installed) or any external XSLT processor for this purpose. The "Choose version automatically" option is active per default. STYLEVISION 2004 first tries to use version 4.0 and if not available version 3.0. You can however, manually choose either version by clicking the respective radio button.

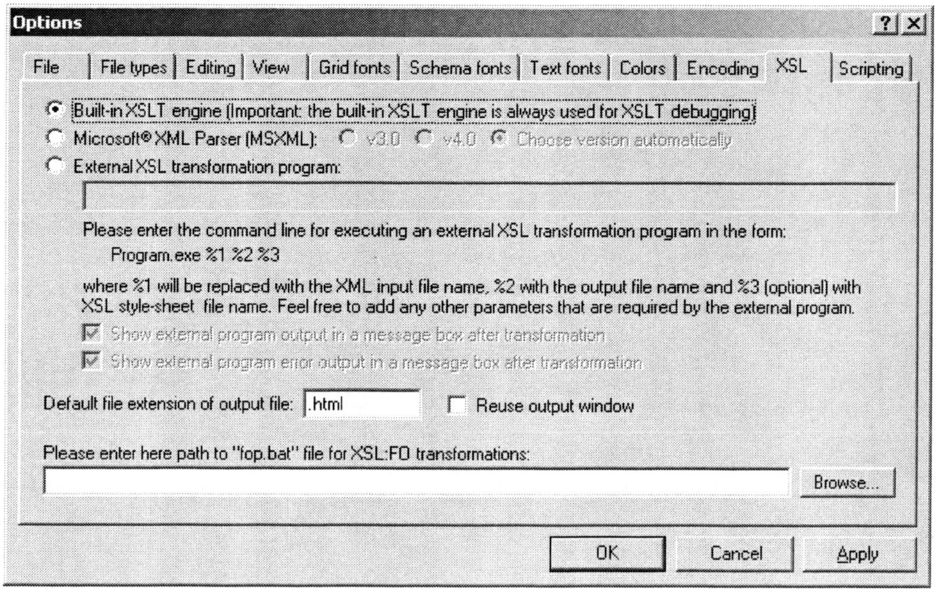

Use Microsoft XML Parser (MSXML) 3.0 or 4.0
If you are using Internet Explorer 5 or above (i.e. the MSXML module) for XSLT processing, you must specify if the resulting output is to be transformed as an XML-compliant document (such as XHTML or WML), or non-XML compliant text files.

Installing other XML Parsers
The Component Download Center, accessible through the menu option **Help | Components Download**, allows you to download and use different XSL processors.

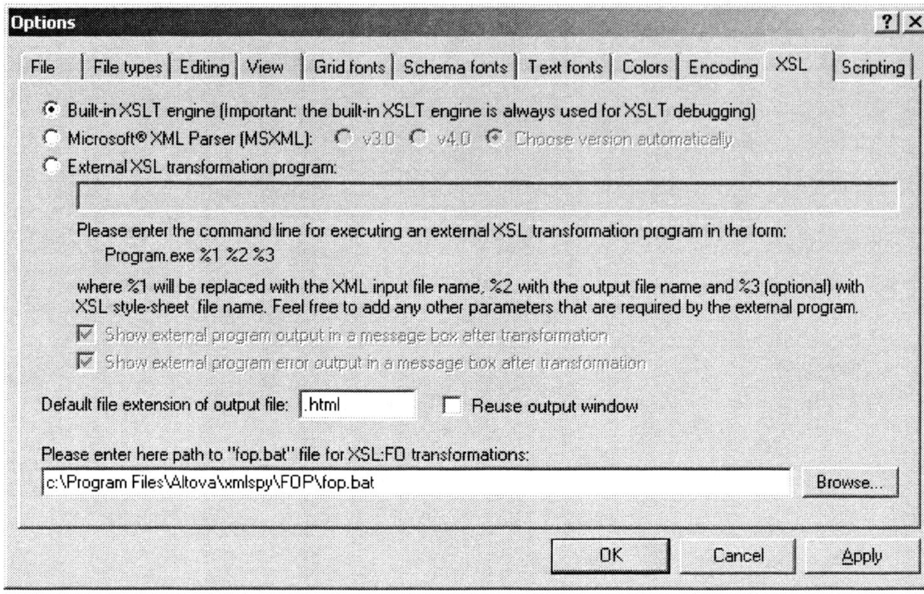

External XSL transformation program
If you are using an external XSL processor, you must specify a command-line string that is to be executed by STYLEVISION 2004 in order to initiate the XSL Transformation. In this case, use the following variables to build your command-line string:

%1	the XML instance document that is to be processed
%2	the output file that is to be generated
%3	the XSL Stylesheet to be used (optional, if the document contains an <?xsl-stylesheet ...?> reference

You can also choose to show the result of the external XSLT processor directly within STYLEVISION 2004 in a message box.

Please see the technical background information on XSLT Processors for further details.

Reuse output window:
When disabled, the reuse output window option, only takes effect when you **also** disable the "Save in folder" output file path in the folder properties of the respective XML file in a STYLEVISION 2004 project.

Folder properties window:

Scripting

The "Scripting" tab allows you to select the scripting environment and other scripting specific parameters.

Activation:
Define if the scripting environment is to be active when STYLEVISION 2004 starts. Click the Browse... button to select the scripting project file.

Standard script language:
Select the scripting language you want to use, JavaScript or VBScript.

Automatic script processing:
This section defines if auto-macros have the right to run, and if event processing is to be enabled.

Window Menu

To organize the individual document windows in an STYLEVISION 2004 session, the Window menu contains standard commands common to most Windows applications.

You can cascade the open document windows, tile them, or arrange document icons once you have minimized them. You can also switch the various Entry Helper windows on or off (such as Project, Info, or Entry-Helpers) or switch to each open document window directly from the menu.

Cascade

This command rearranges all open document windows so that they are all cascaded (i.e. staggered) on top of each other.

Tile horizontally

This command rearranges all open document windows as **horizontal tiles**, making them all visible at the same time.

Tile vertically

This command rearranges all open document windows as **vertical tiles**, making them all visible at the same time.

Project Window

This command lets you switch the Project Window on or off.

This is a dockable window. Dragging on its title bar detaches it from its current position and makes it a floating window. Click right on the title bar, to allow docking or hide the window.

Info Window

This command lets you switch the Info Window on or off.

This is a dockable window. Dragging on its title bar detaches it from its current position and makes it a floating window. Click right on the title bar, to allow docking or hide the window.

Entry Helpers

This command lets you switch all three Entry-Helper Windows on or off.

All three Entry helpers are dockable windows. Dragging on a title bar detaches it from its current position and makes it a floating window. Click right on the title bar, to allow docking or hide the window.

All on/off

This command lets you switch all dockable windows on, or off:

- the Project Window
- the Info Window
- the three Entry-Helper Windows

This is useful if you want to hide all non-document windows quickly, to get the maximum viewing area for the document you are working on.

Currently open window list

This list shows all currently open windows, and lets you quickly switch between them.

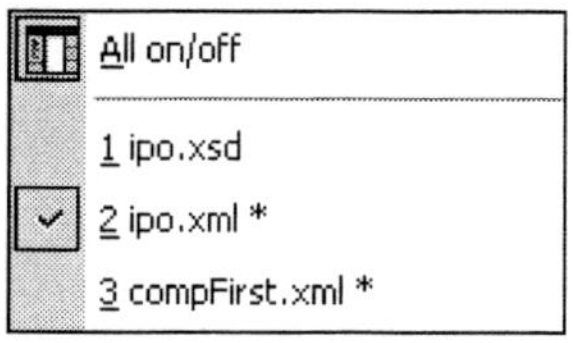

You can also use the Ctrl-TAB or CTRL F6 keyboard shortcuts to cycle through the open windows.

Help Menu

The Help menu contains all commands required to get help or more information on STYLEVISION 2004, as well as links to information and support pages on our web server.

The Help menu also contains the Registration dialog, which lets you enter your license key-code, once you have purchased the product.

Table of contents...

This command displays a **hierarchical representation** of all chapters and topics contained in the online help system. Use this command to jump to the table of contents directly from within STYLEVISION 2004.

Once the help window is open, use the three tabs to toggle between the table of contents, index, and search panes. The Favorites tab lets you bookmark certain pages within the help system.

Index...

This command accesses the **keyword index** of the Online Help. You can also use the Index tab in the left pane of the online help system.

The index, lists all relevant keywords and lets you navigate to a topic by double-clicking the respective keyword. If more than one topic matches the selected keyword, you are presented a list of available topics to choose from.

Search...

The Search command performs a **full-text search** in the entire online help system.

- Once you enter your search term into the query field and hit the Return key.
  The online help system displays a list of available topics that contain the search term you've entered.
- Double-click on any item in the list to display the corresponding topic.

Registration...

When you start STYLEVISION 2004 for the first time, you are automatically presented with the Registration dialog box, which lets you register your software product in order to be eligible for technical support and activate your license, which is done by entering a unique key-code to unlock the software.

FREE Evaluation Version

If you have downloaded the STYLEVISION 2004 from our web server and would like to activate your **FREE** 30-day evaluation version, please enter your name, company, and e-mail address and click on the "Request FREE evaluation key..." button. STYLEVISION 2004 then uses your Internet connection to transmit the information you have just entered to our web server, where a personal unique evaluation license will be generated for you. The license key-code, which is necessary to unlock your software, will then be sent to the e-mail address you have entered - it is therefore important, that you enter your **real e-mail address** in the registration dialog box!

Once you have clicked the request button, please go to your favorite mail software and retrieve the license key-code from our e-mail message, which you should be receiving in a matter of a few minutes (depending on transient Internet conditions).

If you requested a key-code and it didn't arrive in a short space of time, the process may have failed due to Firewall restrictions in your network. If this is the case, please send a short message with your information via e-mail to our website and our support staff will generate a key-code for you manually.

When you have received your evaluation key-code, please enter it into the key-code field in the registration dialog box and click on OK to start working with STYLEVISION 2004.

Whenever you want to place an order for a licensed version of STYLEVISION 2004, you can also use the "Order license key..." button in the registration dialog box or the Order form menu command to proceed to the Secure Online Shop on the Internet.

Licensed Version

If you have purchased a *single-user* license for STYLEVISION 2004, you will receive an e-mail message from us that contains your license-data and includes your name, company and key-code. Please make sure that you enter **all fields** from your license e-mail into the registration dialog box. The key-code will only be able to unlock your software installation, if the entries in the name and company fields match the name and company entered into our order form.

If your company has purchased a *multi-user* license for STYLEVISION 2004, you will receive an e-mail message from us that contains your license-data and includes your company name and key-code.

Please make sure that you enter the company name and key-code from your license e-mail into the registration dialog box and also enter your personal name into the name field. The key-code will only be able to unlock your software installation, if the value in the company field match the company name entered into our order form.

Please note that the STYLEVISION 2004 License-Agreement does not allow you to install more than the licensed number of copies of STYLEVISION 2004 on the computers in your organization (per-seat license).

Order form...

When you want to place an order for a licensed version of STYLEVISION 2004, use this command or the "Order license key..." button in the registration dialog to proceed to the Secure Online Shop on the Internet, where you can choose between different single- and multi-user license packs.

Once you have placed your order, you can choose to pay by credit card, send a check by mail, or use a bank wire transfer.

Support Center...

If you have any questions regarding our product, please feel free to use this command to query to our support center on the Internet at any time. This is the place where you'll find links to the FAQ, support form, and e-mail addresses for contacting our support staff directly.

FAQ on the web

To help you in getting the best support possible, we are providing a list of Frequently Asked Questions (FAQ) on the Internet, that is constantly updated as our support staff encounters new issues that are raised by our customers.

Please make sure to check the FAQ before contacting our technical support team. This will allow you to get help more quickly.

We regret that we are not able to offer technical support by phone at this time, but our support staff will typically answer your e-mail incidents within one business day.

If you would like to make a feature suggestion for a future version of STYLEVISION 2004 or if you wish to send us any other general feedback, please use the questionnaire form.

Components download

The Components download option, currently lets you to download the latest Microsoft XML Parser, as well as an alternate XSLT Transformation System, and will be expanded in the future.

Altova on the Internet...

This command takes you directly to the Altova web-server http://www.altova.com where you can find out about news, product updates and additional offers from the Altova team.

Training

This command takes you directly to the Altova web-server http://www.altova.com where you can find out about our authorized Training Partners who provide courses on using STYLEVISION 2004 and Advanced XML Application Development (AXAD).

Japanese distributor...

If you are located in Japan, you may prefer to contact our Japanese distributor on the Internet by using this menu command.

About...

This command shows the STYLEVISION 2004 splash screen and copyright information dialog box, which includes the STYLEVISION 2004 logo.

Please note that this dialog box shows the version number - to find the number of the actual build you are using, please look at the status bar, which always includes the full version and build number.

Dialogs

Most dialog boxes in STYLEVISION 2004 are shown in response to a certain menu command or click on a toolbar button and are, therefore, explained in the individual chapters that describe the respective commands.

This section describes standard dialog boxes, that are used by more than one command.

Assign File
The Assign File dialog box is opened by the Assign DTD, Assign Schema, or Assign XSL commands and prompts you for a file or path name to be used for the requested process:

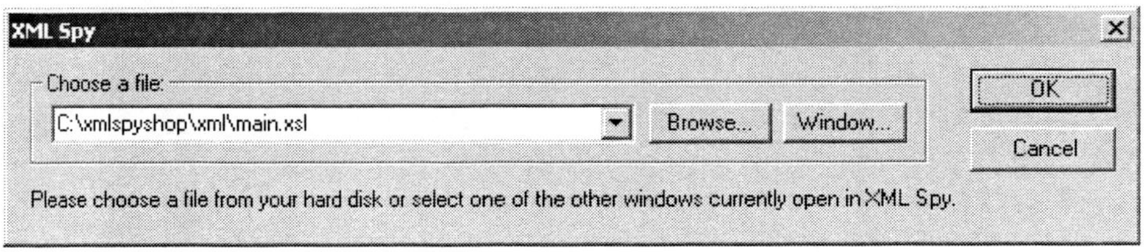

You can either:

- enter a path name into the text box
- select from a list of most recently used filenames using the drop-down list
- browse for a file on your computer (using the common Open dialog box), or
- use the Window button to select any currently open window or any file that is part of the current project.

Select file
The Select File dialog box lets you choose any currently open window or any file from your current project, as a convenient way to locate a file to be used for the various Assign commands.

Double clicking an entry in either window, places the file name in the Assign File dialog box.

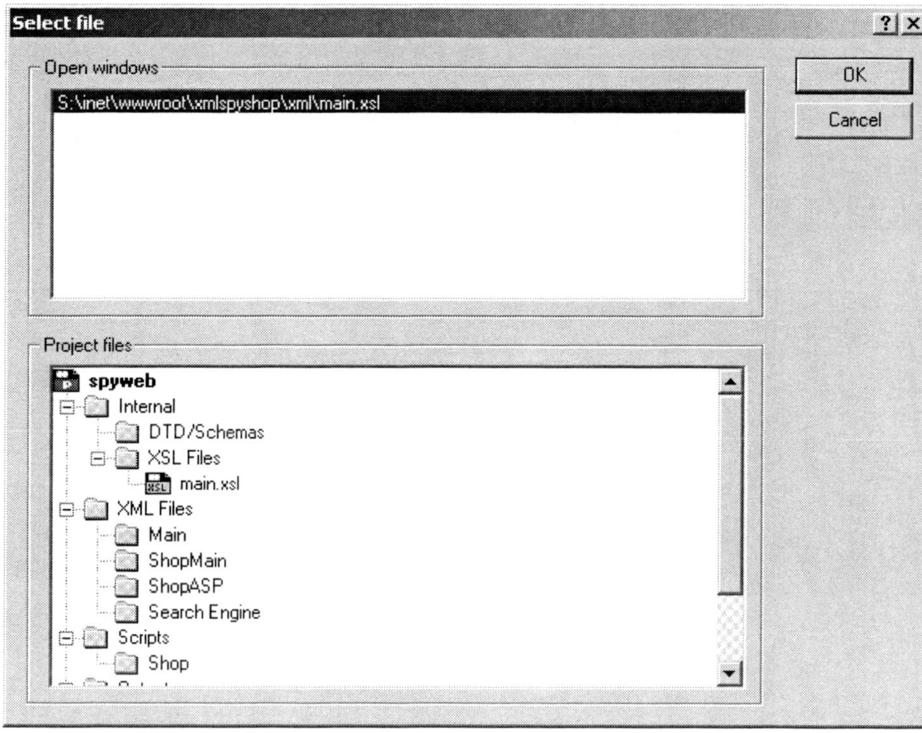

Both windows show the available files based on their extensions depending on which command was selected: Assign DTD, Assign Schema, or Assign XSL.

Part V

5 HTML to XML Conversion

STYLEVISION 2004 enables a web designer to convert an HTML file to XML by using a drag-and-drop mechanism available in Stylesheet Designer.

The conversion process consists of the following steps:

1. Save the Web page as an HTML file.
2. Import the HTML file into Stylesheet Designer.
3. Create an XML document tree by dragging elements from the HTML document.
4. Once the XML tree has been built, generate and save:
   - an XML file containing the corresponding data from the HTML file;
   - a schema (DTD or XML Schema) corresponding to the XML tree you have created;
   - an XSLT stylesheet for your XML file based on the XML tree and the design in the main window;
   - an Authentic Stylesheet (`.sps` file) based on the XML tree and the design in the main window.

The HTML-to-XML conversion is done with Stylesheet Designer.

Description of the Interface

Stylesheet Designer, which is used for the conversion of HTML to XML, has four main areas: the three panes on the left, and the main window at right (shown below). The screenshot below shows the Stylesheet Designer interface directly after an HTML file has been imported.

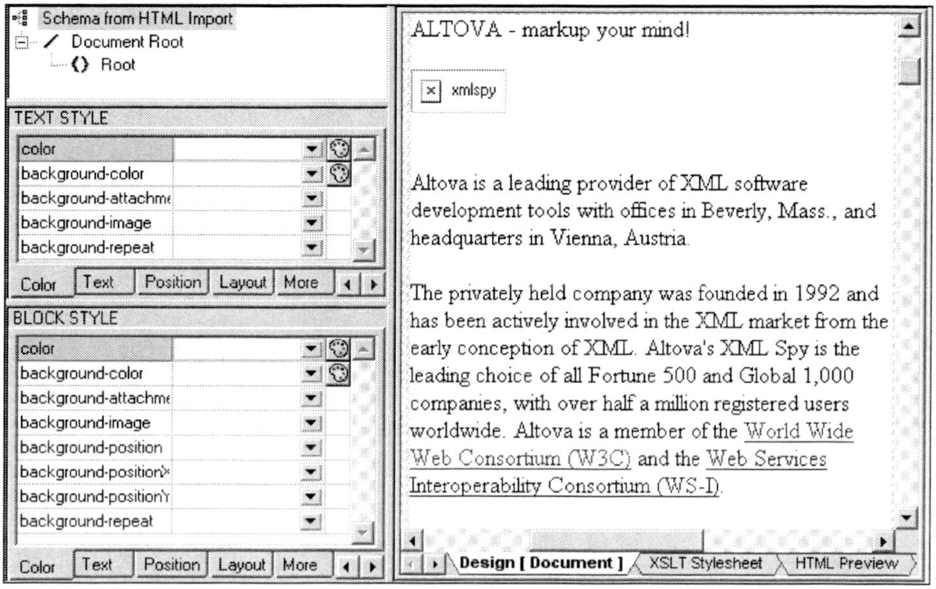

- The main window is where the **imported HTML content** appears. The HTML markup is hidden. When an HTML element has been converted to XML, the XML markup is displayed in both the XML document tree as well as the main window.
- The top left pane displays the **XML document tree** (hereafter also called XML tree). The tree shows the structure of the XML document at a glance. Nodes in the tree can be expanded and collapsed so as to provide a better view of the structure. The figure above shows the rudimentary tree that is created directly after an HTML document has been imported. To convert HTML content to XML, HTML content from the main window is dragged to the required location in the XML tree and dropped as an XML node.
- The **Text Style** pane consists of five tabs, each containing a set of text formatting properties. Using these properties, text formatting can be applied to the selected element. The formatting you assign is contained in a dynamically generated XSLT.
- The **Block Style** pane also consists of five tabs, each containing a set of block formatting properties that you can apply to the selected element. As with the text formatting, the block formatting is contained in a dynamically generated XSLT.

HTML to XML Tutorial

In this tutorial, you will learn how to convert an HTML page into an XML document. Specifically, you will convert some of the data on the Internet page **http://www.altova.com/company.html** into an XML document.

The tutorial consists of the following steps:

1. Saving the Web page **http://www.altova.com/company.html** as the HTML file **altova.html** using XMLSPY 2004.
2. Importing `altova.html` into Stylesheet Designer for conversion to XML.
3. Building the XML document tree.
4. Generating and saving:
   - an XML file containing the corresponding data from the HTML file: **altova.xml**;
   - an XML Schema corresponding to the XML tree you have created: **altova.xsd**;
   - an XSLT stylesheet for your XML file: **altova.xslt**;
   - an Authentic Stylesheet: **altova.sps.**

If you need more details about Stylesheet Designer features, please see the Stylesheet Designer tutorial and reference section.

Saving an Internet page locally using XMLSPY 2004

Using XMLSPY 2004, you can save an Internet page locally as an HTML file. You would do this as follows:

1. View the page in XMLSPY 2004 by either
   - Exporting the page from the browser to XMLSPY 2004; or
   - Importing the page into XMLSPY 2004.
2. In XMLSPY 2004, use the **File | Save as...** command to save the page as an HTML file.

Exporting an Internet page from a browser to XMLSPY 2004
To export the Internet page **http://www.xmlspy.com/company.html** from a browser to XMLSPY 2004, do the following:

1. Open your Internet browser, and in the Address field type in: **http://www.xmlspy.com/company.html**.
2. Click the **Edit with STYLEVISION 2004** icon in the browser's toolbar.

   STYLEVISION 2004 opens, and the file `www.altova.com/company.html` is displayed in the main window of STYLEVISION 2004. A part of this view is shown below.

   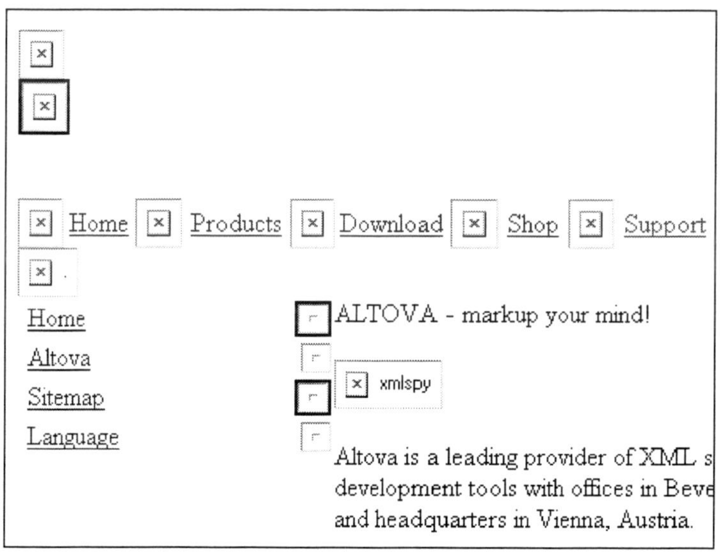

   Images and animations in the original Web page are indicated with the 'Not Available' icon.

   In some cases, images or animations display the *alt* text tag instead of the image.
3. Click **File | Save as...** and save the file in the Examples folder as `altova.html`.

Importing an Internet page into XMLSPY 2004
You can also import the Internet page into XMLSPY 2004 from within XMLSPY 2004. Use this

method if your Internet browser toolbar does not show the Edit with STYLEVISION 2004 button. To import the page, do the following:

1. In the Address field of your browser, highlight the URL `http://www.xmlspy.com/company.html`, and copy it (Ctrl + C).
2. Open STYLEVISION 2004, and select **File | Open URL**.

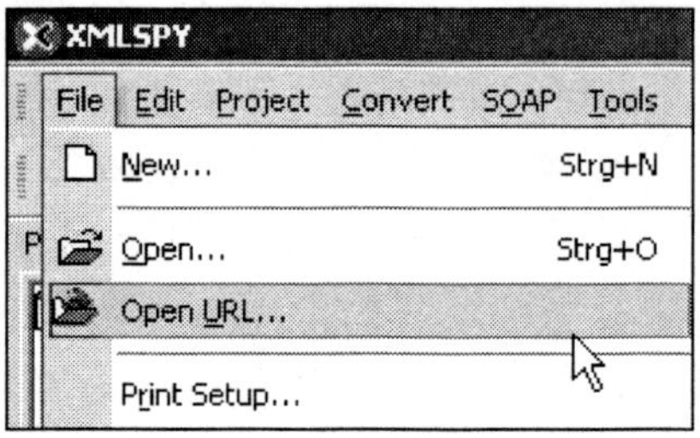

3. Paste the URL into the Address field (shortcut CTRL + V). Click **OK**.

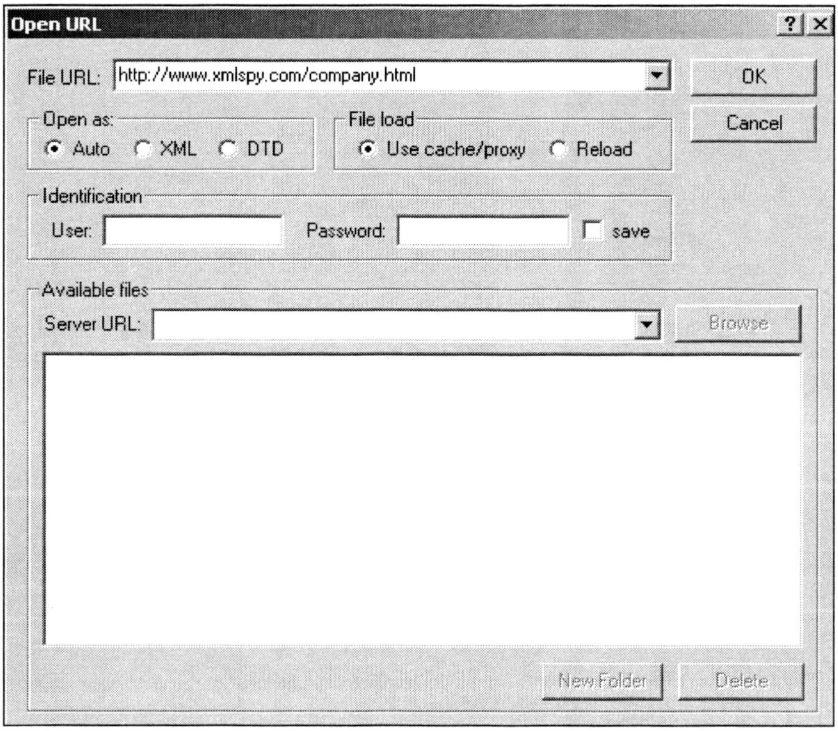

The page `www.altova.com/company.html` is imported and shown in the main window.

4. Click **File | Save as...** and save the file in the Examples folder as `altova.html`.

Saving a Web page with viewable images and animations

Alternatively, if you wish to save a Web page so that its images and animations can be viewed in XMLSPY 2004, then save it directly from the browser as follows:

1. Open Internet Explorer, and type the URL into the Address field, and press Enter.
2. Click **File | Save as...** and save the file to your Examples folder as `altova.html`.

The HTML document is now saved locally and ready for conversion into XML.

Importing an HTML file into Stylesheet Designer

Stylesheet DesignerThe conversion from HTML to XML is done with Stylesheet Designer. You must therefore import the HTML file `altova.html` into Stylesheet Designer. Do this as follows:

1. Start Stylesheet Designer by double clicking the Stylesheet Designer icon.

   Stylesheet Designer is launched.
2. Select **HTML Import | Open HTML file...**

   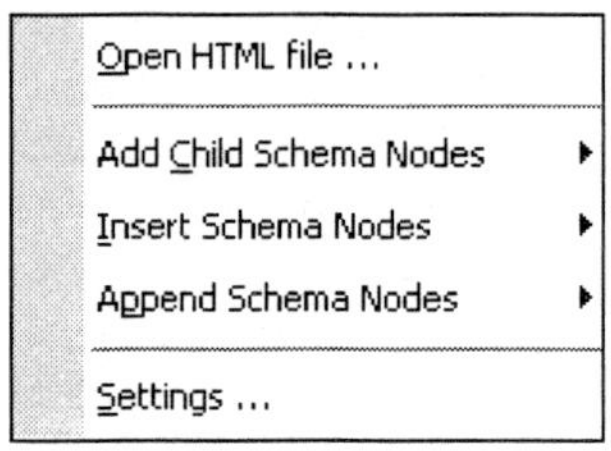

3. Open the file `Altova.html` which you saved in the Examples folder. The Stylesheet Designer interface should now look like this:

   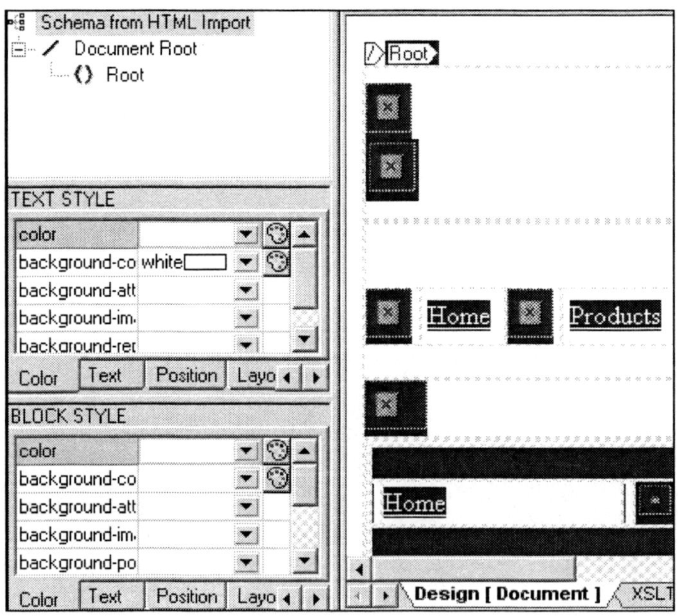

You are now ready to build the XML document tree.

Building the XML document tree

The imported HTML file in Stylesheet Designer

The HTML file `altova.html` is displayed in the main window of Stylesheet Designer. Note the following:

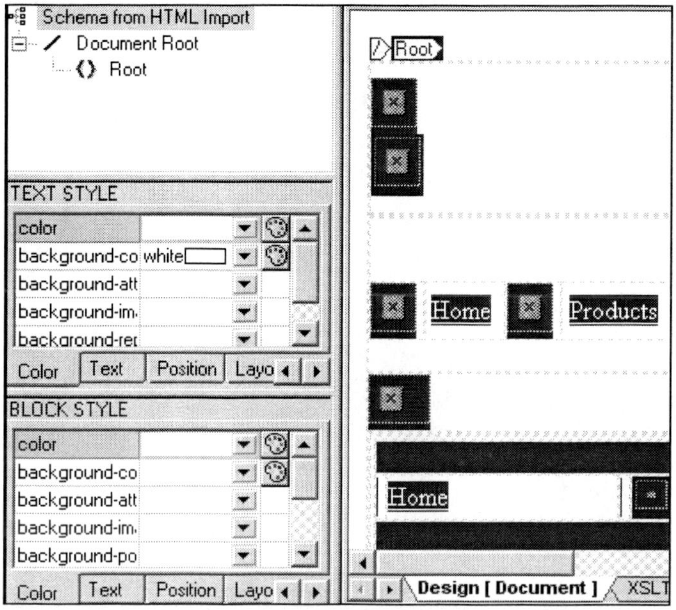

- The HTML markup tags are not displayed; only the content is.
- A rudimentary XML document tree has been created in the top left pane (called the XML window in this tutorial);
- In the main window, a `Root` element tag encloses the entire content. This is the Root element of the XML file that will be created; the `Root` element is also present in the XML document tree.

Building the XML document tree: general procedure

The general procedure for building the XML document tree is as follows:

1. Drag the required HTML content into the top left pane.
2. Drop it at the required location in the XML document tree.
3. Specify what XML element the dragged-and-dropped content is to be created as.

The XML document tree is built element by element. As new elements are added, tags for these elements appear in the main window.

Building the XML document tree: tutorial steps

Now build an XML document tree by carrying out the following steps:

1. In the HTML document, highlight the <u>HOME</u> entry.
2. Drag the <u>HOME</u> entry into the XML window and to the Root element till the Root element is highlighted and a right-and-down arrow appears.

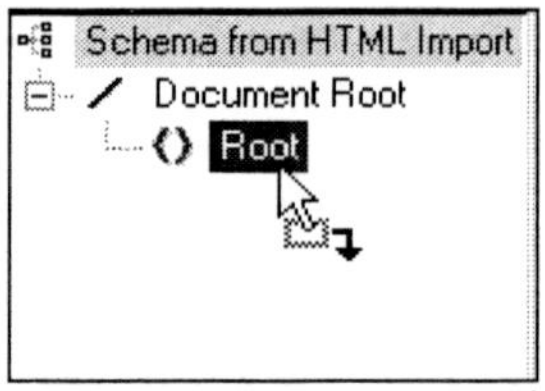

The right-and-down arrow inserts a **child** element or attribute.

(In other situations, a down arrow appears, which indicates that an **element** will be appended as a sibling or as an **attribute** of the parent element.)

3. Now release the mouse button. This opens a pop-up window.

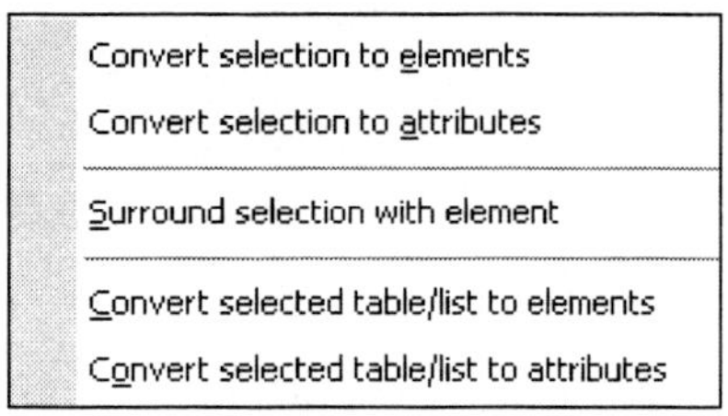

Since the HOME object is part of a table, click **Convert selected table/list to elements** to convert the whole table at once.

4. At this point a new window opens:

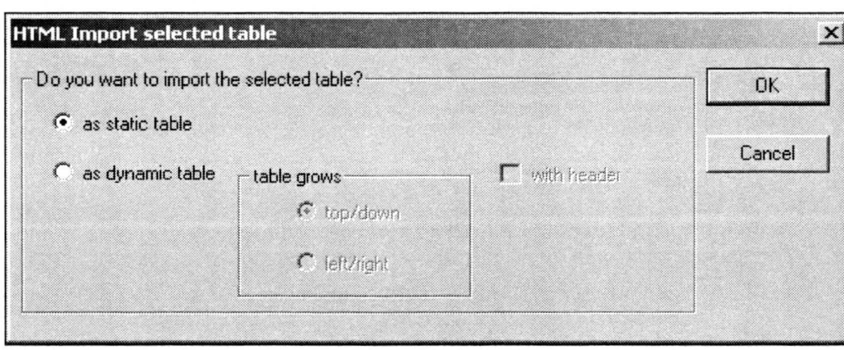

Select 'as static table' to import all fields in the HTML table, and click OK. Two things now happen:

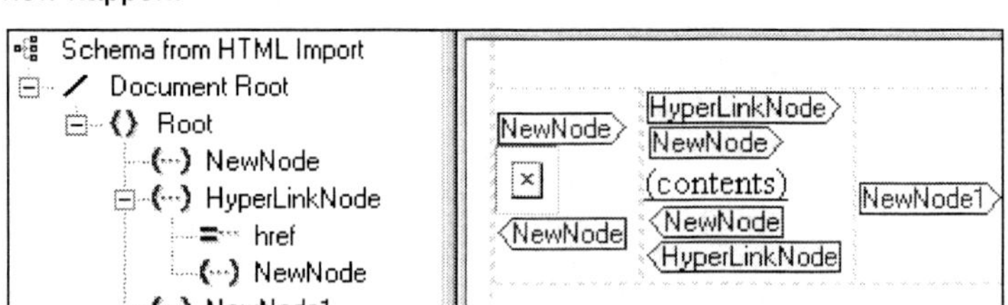

- In the XML window, a tree fragment is added to the `root` element. The structure of this tree fragmet is that of the HTML table of which the HOME object is a part.
- Element start and end tags corresponding to the newly created XML elements are displayed in the main window .

5. Right click on Root and select Rename.

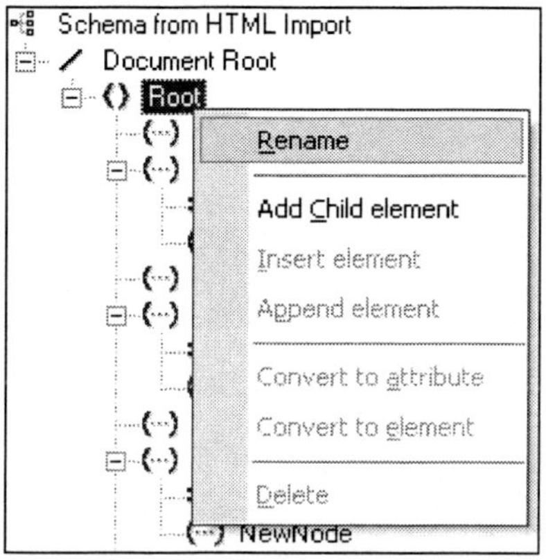

Rename `Root` to `Links`. Then rename the `HyperLinkNode` elements according to the list below and the NewNode child elements of the HyperLinkNode elements to LinkText. The list of nodes to be renamed is given below, together with the new names of each node.

`/Root` to `Links`
`//HyperLinkNode` to `Home`
`//HyperLinkNode1` to `Products`
`//HyperLinkNode2` to `Download`
`//HyperLinkNode3` to `Shop`
`//HyperLinkNode4` to `Support`
`//HyperLinkNode5` to `Developers`
`//HyperLinkNodeX/NewNode` to `LinkText`

6. After renaming the elements, the XML document tree should look like this:

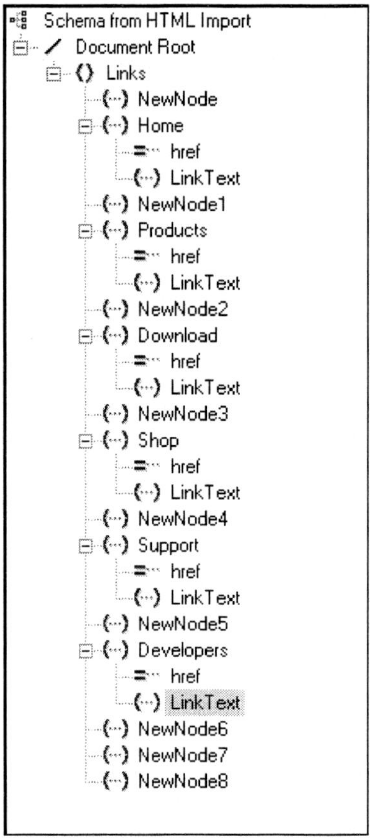

You have created a `Links` element which contains several child elements, including six nodes containing links. The renamed items in the main window should now look like this:

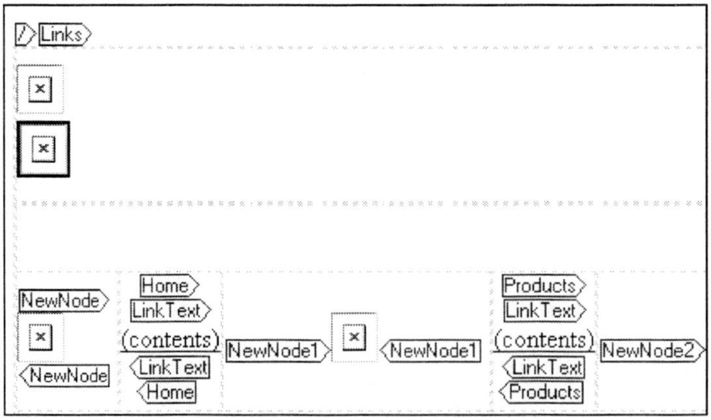

7. Notice that the `Links` element has child elements called `NewNode, NewNode1...`

`NewNode8`, which represent the spacer graphics in the original HTML page. In the XML tree, delete these elements by right-clicking each and selecting Delete. Your XML tree will now look like this:

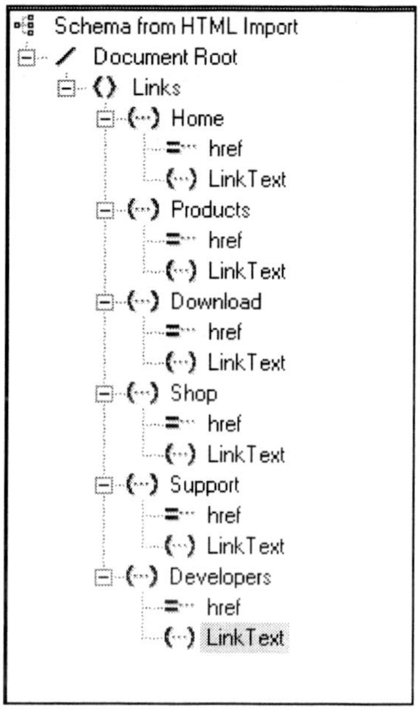

The main window will look like this:

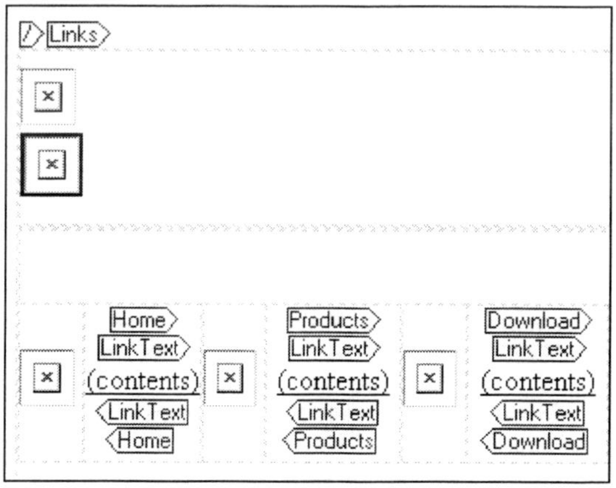

8. Notice that although the nodes have been deleted from the XML tree, the columns of the Links table and their graphic content have not been deleted in the main window. If a stylesheet or Authentic Stylesheet (`.sps` file) is saved now, such columns will be included in these files. Delete each column in the Links table by placing the cursor in a column and clicking **Table | Delete column** or its icon in the toolbar.

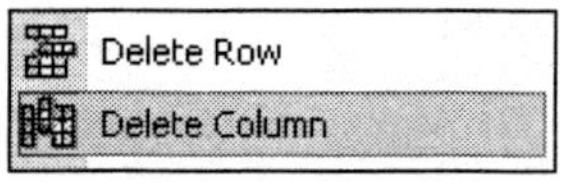

The Links table in the main window will now look like this:

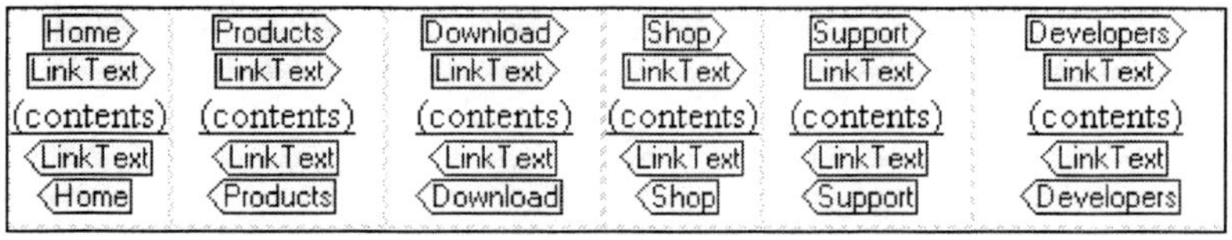

9. Now use the **Table | Delete Row** and **Table | Delete column** commands to clear the remaining content from the main window. The bottom part of your main window should finally look like this:

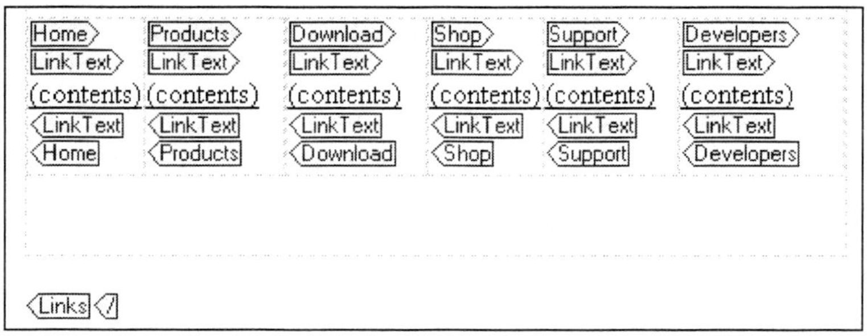

It is important to delete the unrequired elements from the main window so as to not clutter up the stylesheet with processing rules for elements that you do not need.

10. If you wish to add any formatting to your document, you should do it now using normal Stylesheet Designer methods. Please see the Stylesheet Designer tutorial and reference section for details.

Generating the XML, DTD or XML Schema, and XSLT files

After you have created the XML tree in the XML window and have completed the document design in the main window, you are ready to save your project. You can save not only the XML file, but also the schema (DTD or XML Schema), XSLT file, and Authentic Stylesheet (`.sps` file) for the XML tree you have created.

The **XML file** and **schema (DTD or XML Schema)** are derived from the XML tree you have created. The data for the XML file is the data contained in the elements imported from the original HTML file.

The formatting rules for the **XSLT** and **Authentic Stylesheet (.sps file)** are derived from the document design you have created in the main window. Note that the XSLT and Authentic Stylesheet will contain formatting rules for all elements present in the main window—even if these elements are not present in the XML tree. So if you want an XSLT and Authentic Stylesheet to contain formatting rules for only those elements present in the XML tree, then make sure you delete any non-required element from the main window.

Save the files of the project as follows.

1. Select **File | Save as**. The following dialog opens:

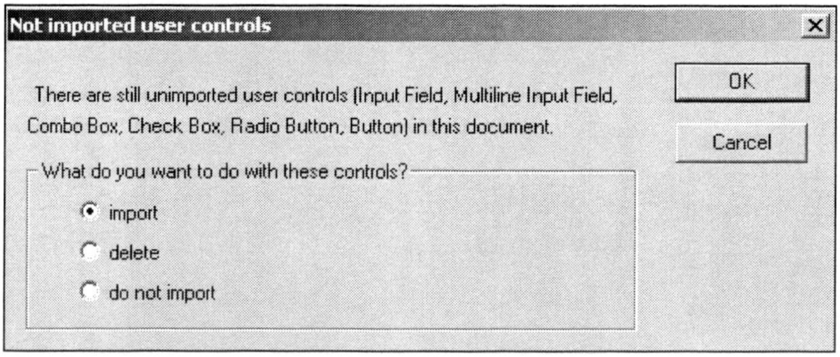

User controls are features such as the Search input field. Select **do not import** and click OK. This causes the following dialog to be displayed.

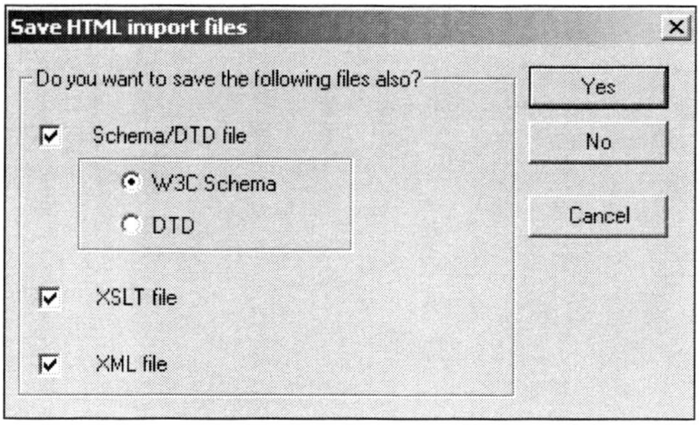

Click **Yes** to save all files.

3. Select a name for the XML Schema file. Type 'altova'.

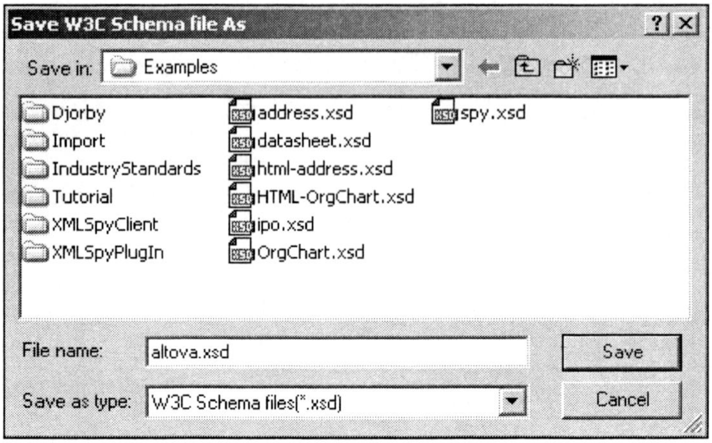

The file is saved as **altova.xsd**.

4. Select a name for the XSLT file. Type 'altova'

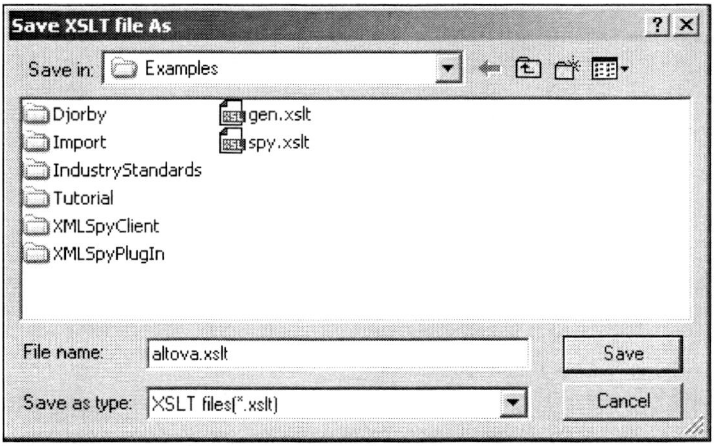

The file is saved as **altova.xslt**.

5. Select a name for the XML file. Type 'altova'

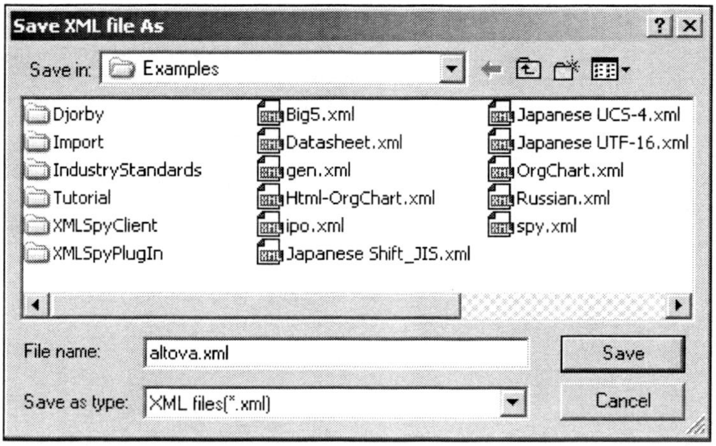

The file is saved as **Altova.xml**.

6. Select a name for the Authentic Stylesheet (.sps file). Type 'altova'.

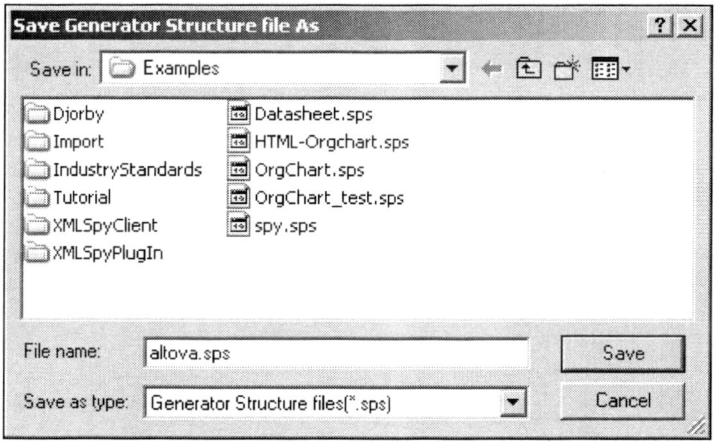

The file is saved as **altova.sps**.

All your files have now been saved and are ready for editing.

HTML to XML Conversion Reference

This Reference section covers those commands in STYLEVISION 2004 and Stylesheet Designer that are used for the conversion of an HTML file to an XML file.

It consists of six sections. The first section describes STYLEVISION 2004 commands used to open an Internet page in the application and save it locally. The remaining five sections describe Stylesheet Designer commands.

- Save HTML file wth STYLEVISION 2004
- Import HTML into Stylesheet Designer
- Build the XML document tree: pop-up menu
- Build the XML document tree: **HTML Import** menu
- Context menus
- Help menu

For a description of all Stylesheet Designer windows and menu commands, please see the Stylesheet Designer Reference section.

Save HTML file with XMLSPY 2004

If you wish to convert some data from an Internet page to XML, you would need to save the Internet page locally as an HTML page. You can do this conveniently with STYLEVISION 2004 as follows:

1. Open your Internet browser and type in the URL of the page you want to edit.
2. If the **Edit with STYLEVISION 2004** button

   is available in the Internet browser toolbar, then click it.

   If the **Edit with STYLEVISION 2004** button is not available:
   - Open STYLEVISION 2004 and select **File | Open URL**. Type the URL of the document to import.
   - Click OK.

3. Select **File | Save as...** and save the file with a `.html` extension.

Import HTML file into Stylesheet Designer

The HTML to XML conversion is done with Stylesheet Designer, so the first thing you need to do is import the HTML file into Stylesheet Designer. You do this with the **HTML Import** menu of Stylesheet Designer.

1. Open Stylesheet Designer and click **HTML Import** in the menu bar. This opens the menu shown below.

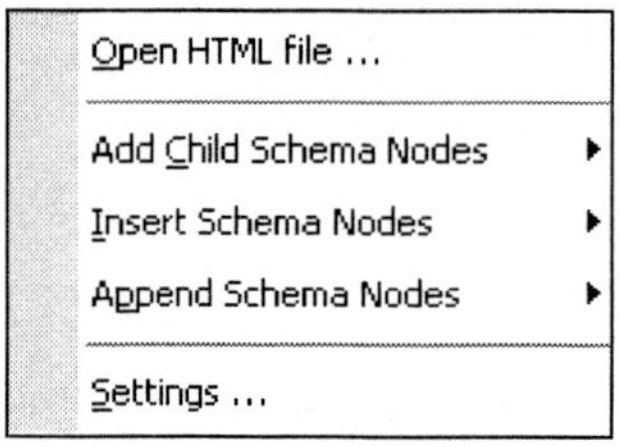

2. Select **Open HTML file...** and choose the HTML file you want to import. Then click **Open**.

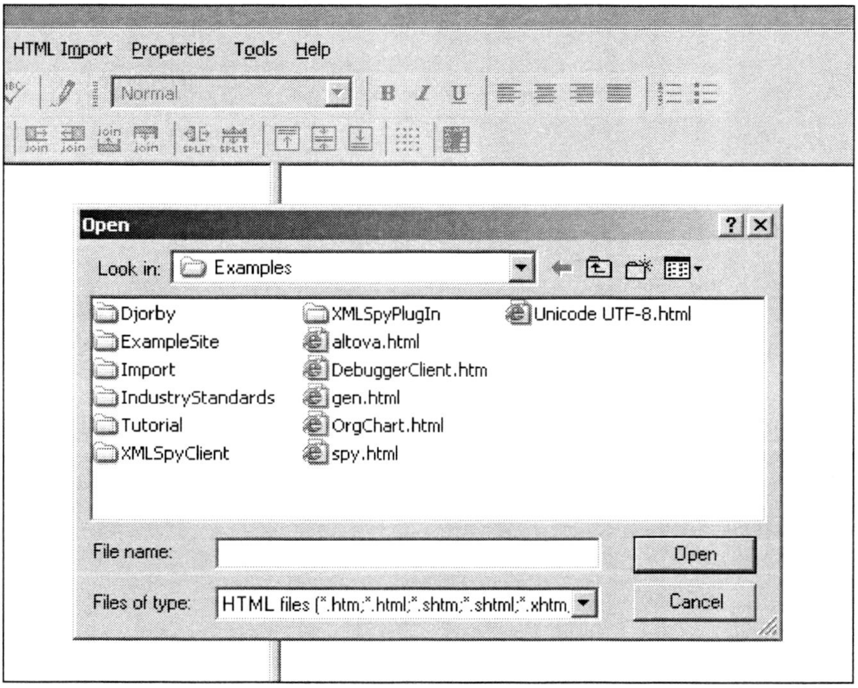

3. The selected file will be inserted into the main window of Stylesheet Designer.

Building the XML tree: pop-up menu

To add a node to the XML document tree, you mark some HTML content in the main window (we call such content an object) and drag it to the required location in the XML window. When you release the mouse button in order to drop the object and create the node, the pop-up menu shown below appears.

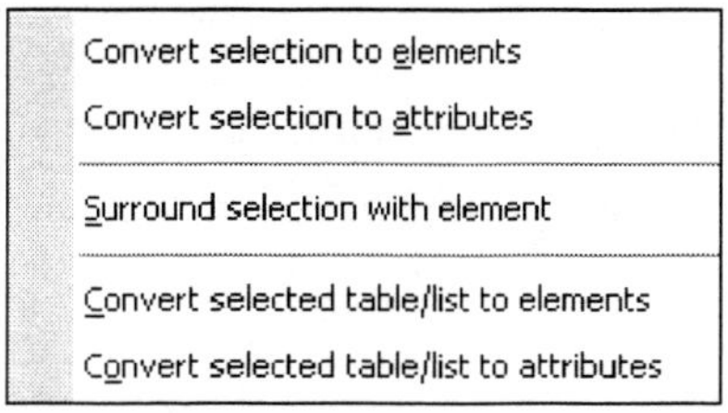

This pop-up menu is divided into three parts corresponding to the three broad ways in which the node will be created:

- As standalone node or nodes in the XML document tree.
- As a single node in the XML document tree, the content of which can be used as static XSLT and Authentic Stylesheet content.
- As part of a structure corresponding to an original HTML table or list structure.

The different commands are described below.

Convert selection to elements
The object is inserted as an element or elements into the tree. How many elements are created depends on the structure of the object.

Convert selection to attributes
The object is inserted as an attribute or attributes into the tree.

Surround selection with element
The object is inserted as the content of an element. It can now be used as a template for the generated XSLT and Authentic Stylesheet. You will, however, still need to format this template, for which see the Stylesheet Designer Reference.

Convert selected table/list to elements
The whole HTML table or list of which the object is a part will be imported as elements into the XML tree.

Convert selected table/list to attributes
The whole HTML table or list of which the object is a part will be imported as attributes into the XML tree.

When you select either **Convert selected table/list to elements** or **Convert selected table/list to attributes**, the following dialog box appears:

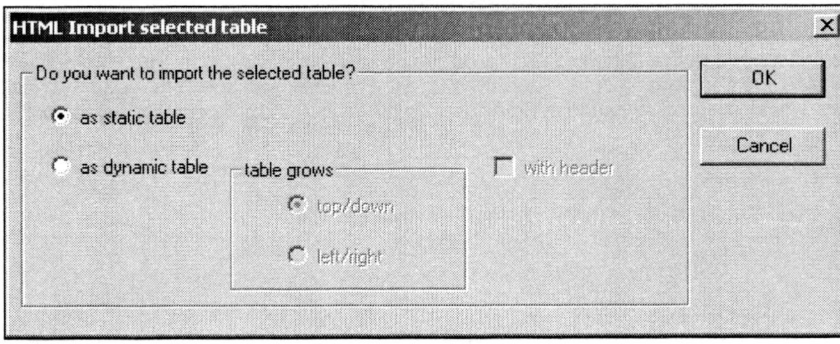

Creating the node as part of a table element is useful if the object is, say, a table cell and you wish to create an XML structure corresponding to the HTML table structure. See the Stylesheet Designer Reference Section for details about static and dynamic tables.

Location in XML tree where new nodes are created

When you drag an object from the main window into the XML tree, you must highlight a node in the XML tree as the location relative to which the new node/s wil be created. When a node in the XML tree is highlighted, one of the following icons appears:

 indicates that the object will be created as a **child element or child attribute** of the highlighted node.

 indicates that the object will be appended as a **sibling element** of the highlighted node or as an **attribute of the parent element** of the highlighted node.

Building the XML tree: HTML Import menu

The following commands are available under the **HTML Import** menu (shown below), which is opened from the menu bar in **Stylesheet Designer**.

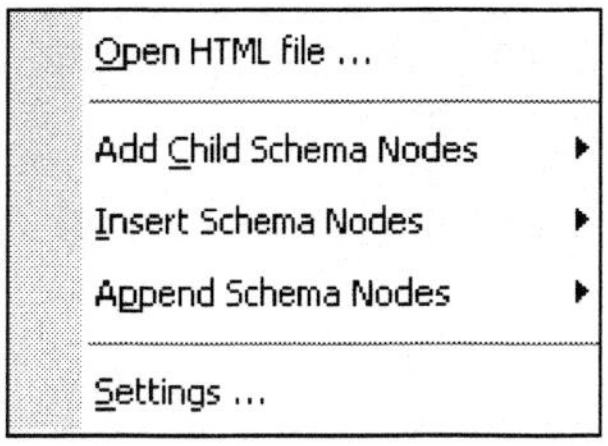

Open HTML file...

Use this command to import an HTML file into Stylesheet Designer. Browse your computer to locate the HTML file to import.

Add to Parent...

When you click **HTML Import | Add to Parent**, the following submenu appears:

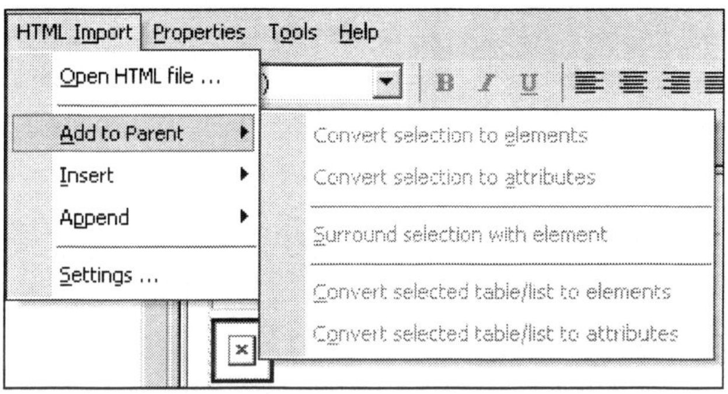

Select this option and then the appropriate submenu item to **add the selection to the parent** as any of the following:

- an element or attribute
- to surround the selection with an element, or
- if the selection is a table/list, to convert it to elements or attributes.

Insert

Select this option to **insert** the selection as:

- an element or attribute
- to surround the selection with an element, or
- if the selection is a table/list, to convert it to elements or attributes.

Append

Select this option to **append** the selection as:

- element or attribute
- to surround the selection with an element, or
- if the selection is a table/list, to convert it to elements or attributes.

Settings...

Opens the HTML Import settings window:

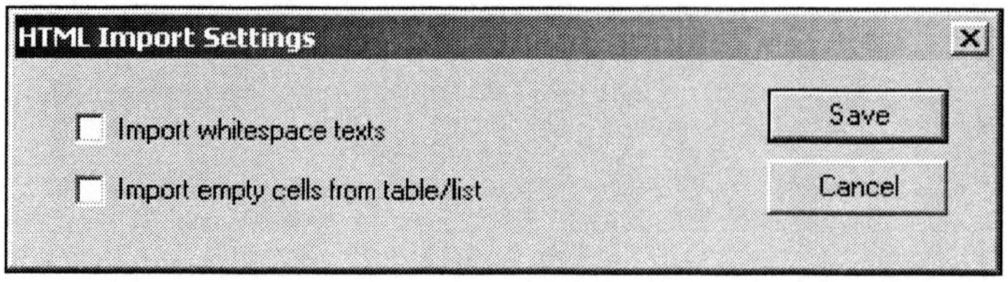

These settings allow you to import whitespace texts from the HTML document, and to import empty cells from tables and lists in the HTML document.

Context menus

Two different context menus are available in two different contexts:

- After dragging-and-dropping an object into the XML tree, right-clicking the created node opens the **XML Tree context menu.**
- In the main window, right-clicking a selection pops up a **Formatting context menu**, which allows you to edit the formatting of the selection.

Formatting context menu

In the main window, when you highlight some content and right-click, the Formatting context menu appears. One possible context menu is shown below. (What items are listed in the menu depends on the type of selection that has been right-clicked.) The commands in the Formatting context menu allow you to format the selection.

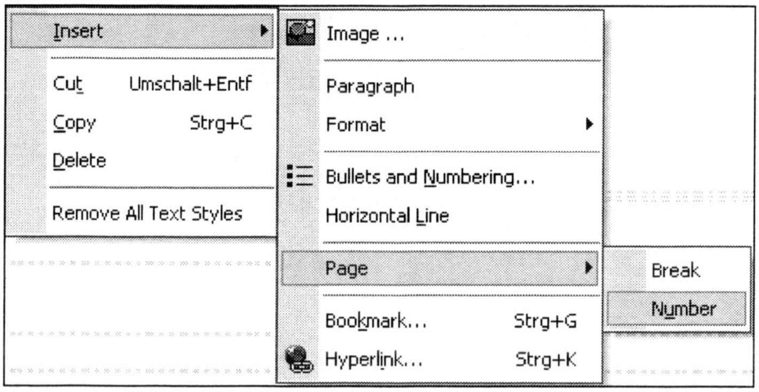

The formatting that you apply to objects in this window is the formatting that will be used for these objects in the XSLT and Authentic Stylesheet that are generated from your conversion project.

The commands in the Formatting context menu are described in detail in the Stylesheet Designer Reference.

XML Tree context menu

In the XML window, when you right-click a node in the XML tree, the XML Tree context menu appears (shown below). If an action in the menu is not allowed for the selected node, the menu item is grayed out. To select an action, click the menu item.

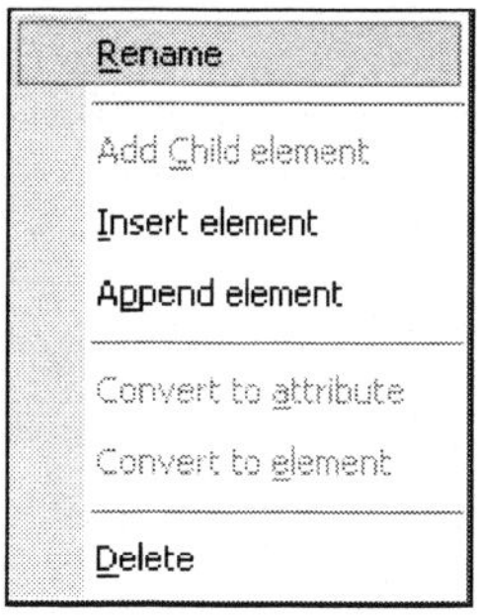

The actions in this menu allow you to rename nodes and edit the structure of the XML tree.

They are described below.

Rename
Renames a node in the XML tree.

Add Child element
Adds a child element to the selected node.

Insert element
Inserts a sibling element before the selected node.

Append element
Appends a sibling element to the selected node.

Convert to attribute
Converts the selected node from an element to attribute. (Will be grayed out if the selected node is an attribute.)

Convert to element
Converts the selected node from attribute to element. (Will be grayed out if the selected node is an element.)

Delete
Deletes the selected element and all sub-elements.

Help

The Help menu makes available the Online Help for Stylesheet Designer. This Online Help contains:

- the tutorial for the HTML to XML conversion;
- the HTML to XML Conversion Reference; and
- the complete Stylesheet Designer Reference.

Part VI

6 Authentic View

Authentic View in Altova products
Authentic View is available in the following Altova products:

- Integrated as a separate view within XMLSPY 2004
- Integrated as a separate view within STYLEVISION 2004
- Integrated as a separate view within AUTHENTIC 2004 Desktop Edition
- As a Browser Plug-In for Internet Explorer: AUTHENTIC 2004 Browser Edition. This interface is different than the three above, and is explained separately in the documentation for the AUTHENTIC 2004 Browser Edition.

The Authentic View interface available in XMLSPY 2004, STYLEVISION 2004, and AUTHENTIC 2004 Desktop Edition is basically the same, and it is described in this documentation. The Authentic View interface of AUTHENTIC 2004 Browser Edition is described in the documentation for the AUTHENTIC 2004 Browser Edition.

Authentic View documentation
The Authentic View documentation consists of the following sections:

- An introduction, which describes Authentic View in relation to Authentic Stylesheets, highlights the advantages of Authentic View, and explains the concepts behind the working of Authentic View: Introduction
- A description of the Authentic View interface: Authentic View interface
- A tutorial to get you started using Authentic View: Authentic View Tutorial
- A how-to section for commonly used Authentic View features: Authentic View: How To ...

Related documentation

- If you wish to create an Authentic Stylesheet, or get to know how an Authentic Stylesheet is created, please see the Stylesheet Designer documentation.

Introduction

Authentic View enables you to create and edit an XML document that is based on an **Authentic Stylesheet**. It is a flexible and easy-to-use interface that features WYSIWYG capabilities and familiar data-entry devices. This enables even users unfamiliar with XML to easily create and edit an XML document.

The Authentic Stylesheet to which an XML document is linked is created in Stylesheet Designer by the person who designs the document—and not by you, the user of Authentic View.

Benefits of using Authentic View
The key benefit of using Authentic View is that it provides users unfamiliar to XML with an **easy-to-use interface** that allows them to create **valid XML documents**.

Ease-of-use
The ease-of-use aspect of Authentic View is due to the presence of familiar interface devices and mechanisms. These include menus and toolbar icons; a WYSIWYG view of the document (which hides the XML markup and enables visualization of the output document); and data-entry devices such as entry fields, check-boxes, radio buttons, etc., for quick and accurate data-entry.

The figure below shows a WYSIWYG view of an XML document (without the menu bar, toolbar, entry helpers, etc.).

In Authentic View, the familiarity of interface components and the interactive editing help (such as entry helpers and inline prompts) give the user not only confidence but also an intuitive feeling for the way in which the XML document is to be built.

Valid XML

An XML document must not only be well-formed, but also valid, both as XML and according to the schema it is based on. This means that the document must conform strictly to the rules of XML and the associated schema. The Authentic Stylesheet to which the XML document is linked controls the display in Authentic View, and together with Authentic View, automatically ensures that the document is built as a valid XML document. Users of Authentic View, therefore, do not have to worry about the correctness of the XML; all they need to do is enter the document content.

Authentic View and Authentic Stylesheets

Creating an XML document in Authentic View is the second (content editing) part of the larger document creation process. This process consists of two separate parts: **document design** and **content editing**. The Authentic Stylesheet that is created in the document design stage is linked to the XML document in Authentic View and controls the way the XML document is displayed.

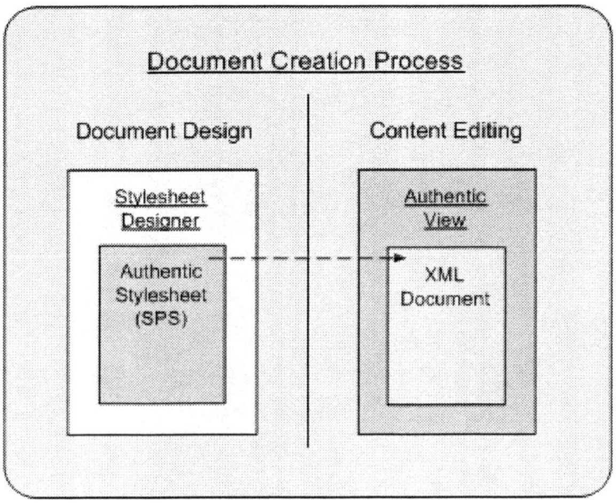

Document design with Stylesheet Designer
In the document design process, a developer—typically an XML-knowledgable person—uses Altova's Stylesheet Designer to create an Authentic Stylesheet. An Authentic Stylesheet controls the way an XML document is displayed in Authentic View, determines the degree of interaction with the user of Authentic View, and specifies how data is entered as XML document content.

An Authentic Stylesheet is based on a given schema. It specifies the outline of the XML document that will be displayed in Authentic View in terms of the schema's elements and attributes. It also specifies how content entered in Authentic View is to be translated into XML document content.

To view an XML document in Authentic View, the document must be linked to an Authentic Stylesheet.

For information about creating an Authentic Stylesheet with Stylesheet Designer, see the Stylesheet Designer documentation.

Content editing with Authentic View
Authentic View is an interface for editing an XML document that is linked to an Authentic Stylesheet. When a new XML document is created, it can be assigned an Authentic Stylesheet, and the document can then be edited in Authentic View. Existing XML documents can be assigned an Authentic Stylesheet (that is based on the same schema) at any time, and can be edited subsequently in Authentic View.

The user of Authentic View is not expected to be knowledgable about either XML or the schema being used for the document. The document display in Authentic View should make content editing as easy and non-technical as possible. (It is the task of the person who has designed the Authentic Stylesheet to produce a user-friendly Authentic View display.) The user of Authentic View must be free to concentrate on content editing. The rest of this documentation describes how the Authentic View interface is to be used.

Authentic View terminology

The following concepts and terminology are important for an understanding of how Authentic View and Authentic Stylesheets work.

- An **Authentic Stylesheet** is a **.sps file** created with **Stylesheet Designer**; it basically uses the XSLT programming language
- An Authentic Stylesheet is based on a particular **schema** (DTD or XML Schema)
- An **XML Document** that is linked to a given Authentic Stylesheet must conform with the schema on which that Authentic Stylesheet is based
- An Authentic Stylesheet can—but does not need to—have a **Template XML file** associated with it. A Template XML file is an XML file that provides the starting data of the XML Document. It must be valid according to the schema on which the Authentic Stylesheet is based. A Template XML file is assigned to an Authentic Stylesheet in Stylesheet Designer
- Any XML file can be assigned an Authentic Stylesheet at any time in XMLSPY 2004. Once an Authentic Stylesheet has been assigned, the XML document can be opened in Authentic View and edited
- An XML document created or edited with Authentic View is an XML document like any other

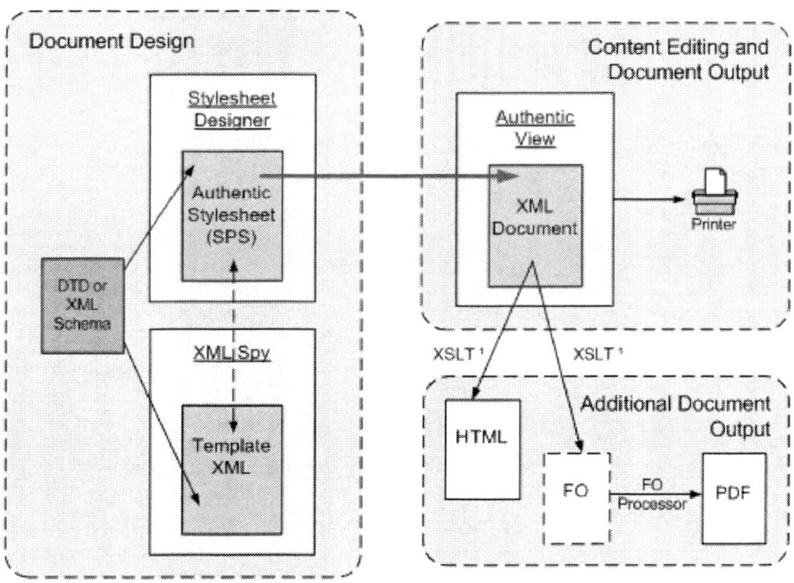

¹ An XML Document created in Authentic View can be processed outside Authentic View with XSLT stylesheets to obtain additional HTML and PDF output.

Authentic View features

This section describes the main features of Authentic View.

Free-flowing WYSIWYG text editing
Authentic View can hide the markup of the XML file to a degree determined by the user. When all markup is hidden, the XML document is displayed as free-flowing text. This text can also contain user-friendly data-entry devices, such as combo boxes and radio buttons. Since the formatting displayed in Authentic View is sent unchanged to the printer, the Authentic View display is a proper WYSIWYG display.

The advantages of Authentic View's WYSIWYG view are that it:

- hides XML markup, and so looks less formidable to users not familiar with XML;
- is easier to read and faster to navigate;
- accommodates data-entry devices to facilitate data input;
- produces printer output that looks exactly like the display in Authentic View, as well as similar HTML and PDF output.

Form-based data input
The document designer (the person who designs the Authentic Stylesheet) can specify that data entered by the user in Authentic View be accepted via data-entry devices. This has the following advantages:

- Data-entry devices are familiar to computer users from HTML Forms and GUI dialogs, so most users are comfortable using them.
- The accuracy of data entered is improved because users must either select from a list of options or (in the case of input fields) be more specific than they otherwise might be.
- When input options are specified in a list, the validity of the input data is guaranteed.
- Data entry is easier, and therefore more efficient.

Real-time validation and dynamic display
Authentic View provides dynamic validation of the XML document. All data entered can therefore be checked for validity against the underlying schema and the user notified accordingly. Under normal circumstances, Authentic View will not allow any modification that

will cause a validation error.

Data that is entered by the user is not only validated. It is also immediately processed according to rules in the Authentic Stylesheet, and the results are dynamically displayed. For example, if the Authentic View user enters the number of articles purchased, this number can be multiplied by the price of the article and te result displayed in a column for purchase value.

Conditional structures
When the value of entered data determines the structure of the XML document, Authentic View can dynamically modify the structure. For example, a data structure for an address in the US would require different fields than that for an address in Europe. So, as soon as US or a country in Europe is specified, the appropriate data structure can be displayed.

Tables for multiple element occurrences
A repetitive data structure can be represented as a table in Authentic View. This kind of presentation makes the data structure easier to understand, and, therefore, makes data entry simpler.

Tables at user's discretion
If data needs to be presented as a table (for easier comprehension), the Authentic View user can insert an HTML or CALS type table, define the table's dimensions, format it, and enter content in it.

Authentic Stylesheets for standard industry schemas
Altova's Authentic View package includes Authentic Stylesheets for a number of standard industry schemas. Users can therefore immediately create an XML document based on a standard schema in Authentic View. The figure below shows a partial Authentic View of the NCA Invoice.

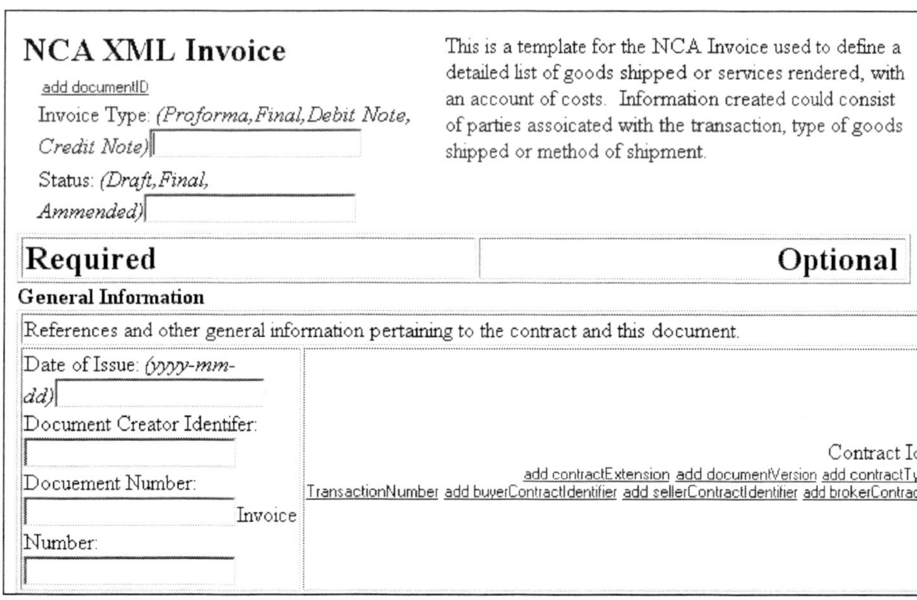

If any of these Authentic Stylesheets needs to be customized, this can be done easily with Stylesheet Designer.

Authentic View interface

The Authentic View interface is one view of your XML document. There are alternative views, the number of which depends upon the product you are using. For example, XMLSPY 2004 has the Enhanced Grid View; Schema/WSDL Design View; Text View; and Browser View as alternative views. Each view is suited to a particular set of purposes and provides a different set of mechanisms and tools for the user.

The Authentic View is intended for XML content creation and editing by a user not necessarily familiar with XML. This section describes the Authentic View interface.

It provides:

- an overview of the interface
- a description of the toolbar icons specific to Authentic View
- a description of viewing modes available in the main window
- a description of the Entry Helpers and how they are to be used

The menu commands available in Authentic View are described in the User Reference section of your product documentation. The use of special Authentic View features is described in the How To section of this documentation (Authentic View: How To ...).

Overview of the GUI

Authentic View has a menu bar and toolbar running across the top of the window, and three areas that cover the rest of the interface: the Project Window, Main Window, and Entry Helpers Window. These areas are shown below.

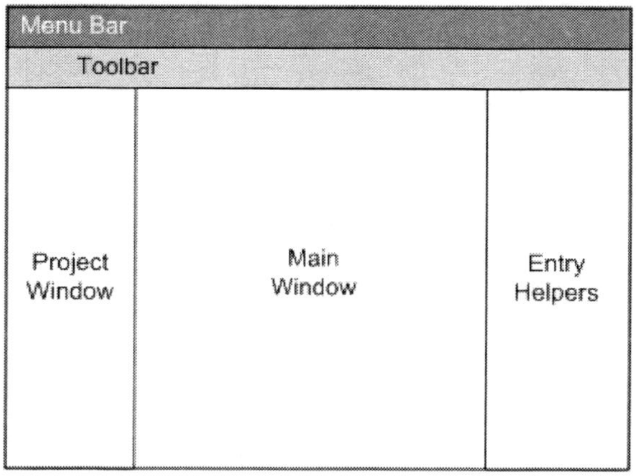

Menu bar

The menus available in the menu bar are described in detail in the User Reference section of your product documentation.

Toolbar

The symbols and icons displayed in the toolbar are described in the section, Authentic View toolbar icons.

Project window

You can group XML, XSL, HTML schema, and Entity files together in a project. To create and modify the list of project files, use the comands in the Project menu (described in the User Reference section of your product documentation). The list of project files is displayed in the Project window. A file in the Project window can be accessed by double-clicking it.

Main window

This is the window in which the XML document is displayed and edited. It is described in the section, Authentic View main window.

Entry helpers

There are three entry helper windows in this area: Elements, Attributes, and Entities. What entries appear in these windows (Elements and Attributes Entry Helpers) are context-sensitive, i.e. it depends on where in the document the cursor is. You can enter an element or entity into the document by double-clicking its entry helper. The value of an attribute is entered into the value field of that attribute in the Attributes Entry Helper. See the section Authentic View entry helpers for details.

Authentic View toolbar icons

Icons in the Authentic View toolbar are command shortcuts. Some icons will be familiar to you already (from other Windows applications and your Altova product), others might be new to you. This section describes icons specific to Authentic View.

In the description below, related icons are grouped together.

Switching to Authentic View

If the document **is linked** to an Authentic Stylesheet, switches to Authentic View from another view.
If the document **is not linked** to an Authentic Stylesheet, displays a dialog that asks you to link the document to an Authentic Stylesheet.

Show/hide XML markup
In Authentic View, the tags for all, some, or none of the XML elements or attributes can be displayed, either with their names (large markup) or without names(small markup). The four markup icons appear in the toolbar, and the corresponding commands are available in the **Authentic** menu.

Hide markup. All XML tags are hidden.

Show small markup. XML element/attribute tags are shown without names.

Show large markup. XML element/attribute tags are shown with names.

Show mixed markup. In the Authentic Stylesheet, each XML element or attribute can be specified to display (as either large or small markup), or not display at all, in mixed markup mode. In mixed markup mode, therefore, the Authentic View user sees a customized markup. Note, however, that this customization is created by the person who has designed the Authentic Stylesheet.

Editing dynamic table structures
Rows in a **dynamic SPS table** are repetitions of a data structure. Each row represents an occurrence of a single element. Each row, therefore, has the same XML substructure as the next.

The dynamic table editing commands manipulate the rows of a dynamic SPS table. That is, you can modify the number and order of the element occurrences. You cannot, however, edit the columns of a dynamic SPS table, since this would entail changing the substructure of individual element occurrences.

The icons for dynamic table editing commands appear in the toolbar, and are also available in the **Authentic** menu.

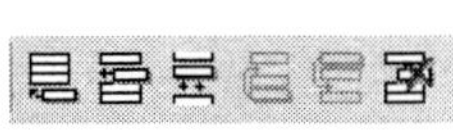

Append row to table

 Insert row in table

 Duplicate current table row (i.e. cell contents are duplicated)

 Move current row up by one row

 Move current row down by one row

 Deletes the current row

Note: These commands apply only to **dynamic SPS tables**. The various types of tables used in Authentic View are described in the Using tables in Authentic View section of this documentation.

Creating and editing XML tables
You can insert your own tables should you want to present your data as a table. Such tables are inserted as XML tables. You can modify the structure of an XML table, and format the table. The icons for creating and editing XML tables are available in the toolbar, and are shown below. They are described in the section XML table editing icons.

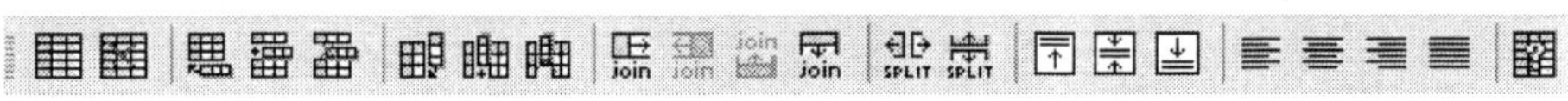

The commands corresponding to these icons are **not available as menu items**. Note also that for you to be able to use XML tables, this function must be enabled and suitably configured in the Authentic Stylesheet.

A detailed description of the types of tables used in Authentic View and of how XML tables are to be created and edited is given in the Using tables in Authentic View section of the documentation.

Text formatting icons
Text in Authentic View is formatted by applying to it an XML element or attribute that has the required formatting. If such formatting has been defined, the designer of the Authentic Stylesheet can provide icons in the Authentic View toolbar to apply the formatting.

To apply text formatting using a text formatting icon, highlight the text you want to format, and click the appropriate icon.

Authentic View main window

There are four viewing modes in Authentic View: large markup; small markup; mixed markup; and hide all markup. These modes enable you to view the document with varying levels of markup information.

To switch between modes, use the commands in the Authentic menu or the icons in the toolbar (see the previous section, Authentic View toolbar icons).

Large markup
This shows the start and end tags of elements and attributes with the element/attribute names in the tags:

The element `Name` in the figure above is **expanded**, i.e. the start and end tags, as well as the content of the element, are shown. An element/attribute can be **contracted** by double-clicking either its start or end tag:

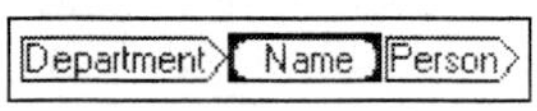

To expand the contracted element/attribute, double-click the contracted tag.

In large markup, attributes are recognized by the symbol @ in the start and end tags of the attribute:

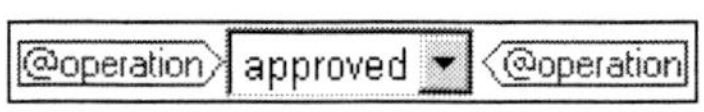

Small markup
This shows the start and end tags of elements/attributes without names:

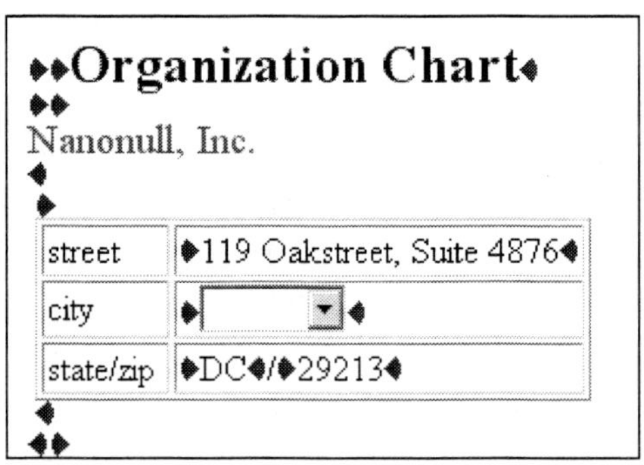

To contract and expand an element/attribute, double-click the appropriate tag. The example below shows two contracted elements in the table:

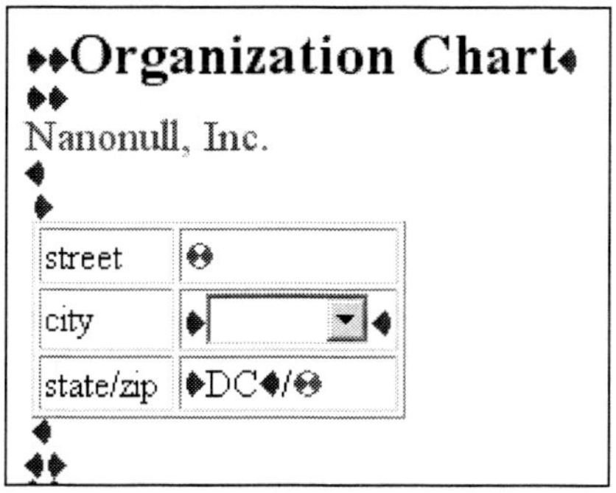

Mixed markup
Mixed markup shows a customized level of markup. The person who has designed the Authentic Stylesheet can specify either large markup, small markup, or no markup for individual elements/attributes in the document. The Authentic View user see this customized markup in mixed markup viewing mode.

Hide all markup
All XML markup is hidden. Since the formatting seen in Authentic View is the formatting of the printed document, this viewing mode is a WYSIWYG view of the document.

Content display
Content is displayed in two broad categories:

- Plain text. You type in the text, and this text becomes the content of the element or the value of the attribute.

- Data-entry devices. The display contains either an input field (text box), a multiline input field, combo box, check box, radio button, or button. In the case of input fields and multiline input fields, the text you enter in the field becomes the XML content of the element or the value of the attribute.

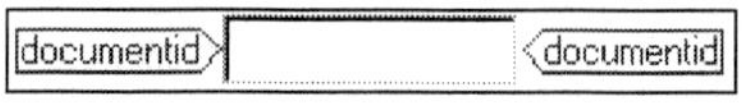

In the case of the other data-entry devices, your selection produces a corresponding XML value, which is specified in the Authentic Stylesheet. Thus the selection "approved" in the display example below could map to an XML value of "1", or to "approved", or anything else; while "not approved" in the display could map to "0", or "not approved", or anything else.

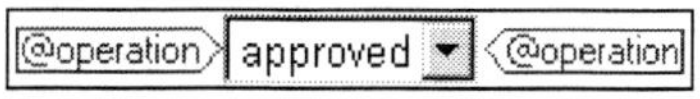

Optional nodes
When an element or attribute is **optional** (according to the referenced schema), a prompt of type "add [*element/attribute*]" is displayed:

Clicking the prompt, adds the element, and places the cursor for data entry.

Authentic View entry helpers

There are three entry helpers in Authentic View: for Elements, Attributes, and Entities. They are displayed as windows down the right side of the Authentic View interface.

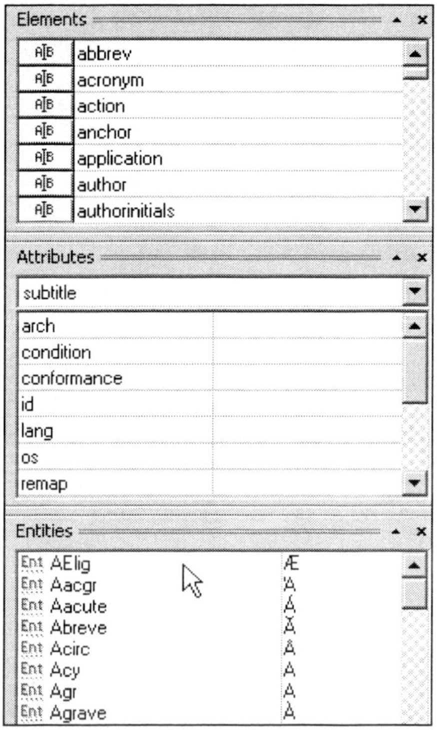

The Elements and Attributes Entry Helpers are context-sensitive, i.e. what appears in the entry helper depends on where the cursor is in the document. The entities displayed in the Entities Entry Helper are not context-sensitive; all entities allowed for the document are displayed no matter where the cursor is.

Each of the entry helpers is described separately below.

Elements Entry Helper
The Elements Entry Helper lists the elements that can be appended after, inserted before, inserted within, applied to (i.e. replace), the selected element or text range in Authentic View. What you can do with an element listed in the Entry Helper is indicated by the icon to the left of the element name in the Entry Helper. The icons that occur in the Elements Entry Helper are listed below, together with an explanation of what they mean.

To use an element from the Entry Helper, click its icon.

Append After Element
The element in the Entry Helper is appended after the selected element. Note that it is appended at the correct hierarchic level. For example, if your cursor is inside a `//sect1/para` element, and you append a `sect1` element, then the new `sect1` element will be appended not as a following sibling of

`//sect1/para` but as a following sibling of the `sect1` element that is the parent of that `para` element.

Insert Before Element
The element in the Entry Helper is inserted before the selected element. Note that, just as with the Append After Element command, the element is inserted at the correct hierarchic level.

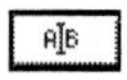

Insert Element
An element from the Entry Helper can also be inserted **within an element**. When the cursor is placed within an element, then the allowed child elements of that element can be inserted. Note that allowed child elements can be part of an elements-only content model as well as a mixed content model (text plus child elements).

An allowed child element can be inserted either when a text range is selected or when the cursor is placed as an insertion point within the text.

- When a text range is selected and an element inserted, the text range becomes the content of the inserted element.
- When an element is inserted at an insertion point, the element is inserted at that point.

After an element has been inserted, it can be cleared by clicking either of the two Clear Element icons that appear (in the Elements Entry Helper) for these inline elements. Which of the two icons appears depends on whether you select a text range or place the cursor in the text as an insertion point (see below).

Apply Element
If you select an element in your document (by clicking either its start or end tag in the Show large markup view), this icon indicates that the element in the Entry Helper can be applied to the selected (original) element. The applied element *replaces* the original element.

- If the applied element has a **child element with the same name** as a child of the original element and an instance of this child element exists in the original element, then the child element of the original is retained in the new element's content.
- If the applied element has **no child element with the same name** as that of an instantiated child of the original element, then the instantiated child of the original element is appended as a sibling of any child element or elements that the new element may have.
- If the applied element has **a child element for which no equivalent exists** in the original element's content model, then this child element is not created directly but Authentic View offers you the option of inserting it.

If a text range is selected rather than an element, applying an element to the selection will create the applied element at that location with the selected text range as its content. Applying an element when the cursor is an insertion point is not allowed.

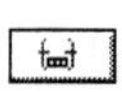

Clear Element (when range selected)
This icon appears to the left of the inline element within which the selected text range is. Clicking the icon clears that inline element but not the selected text

range.

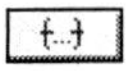

Clear Element (when insertion point selected)
This icon appears to the left of the inline element within which the cursor is. Clicking the icon clears that inline element but not its contents.

Attributes Entry Helper
The Attributes Entry Helper consists of a drop-down combo box and a list of attributes. The element that you have selected (you can click the start or end tag, or place the cursor anywhere in the element content to select it) appears in the combo box.

The Attributes Entry Helper shown in the figures below has a `para` element in the combo box. Clicking the arrow in the combo box drops down a list of all the `para` element's **ancestors up to the document's root element**, which in this case is `article`.

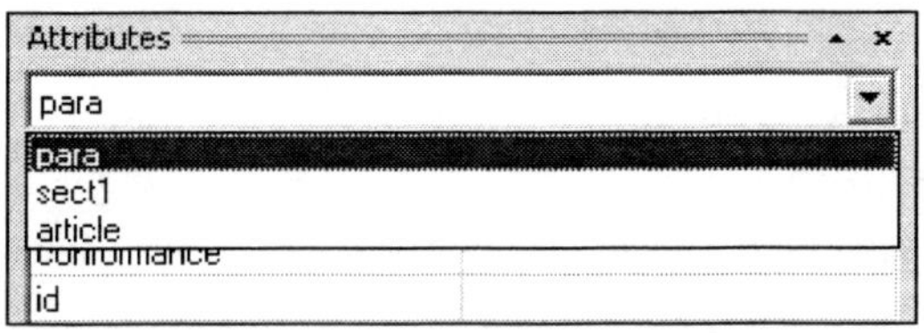

Below the combo box, a list of valid attributes for that element is displayed, in this case for `para`. If an attribute is mandatory on a given element, then it appears in bold. (In the example below, there are no mandatory attributes; they are all optional.)

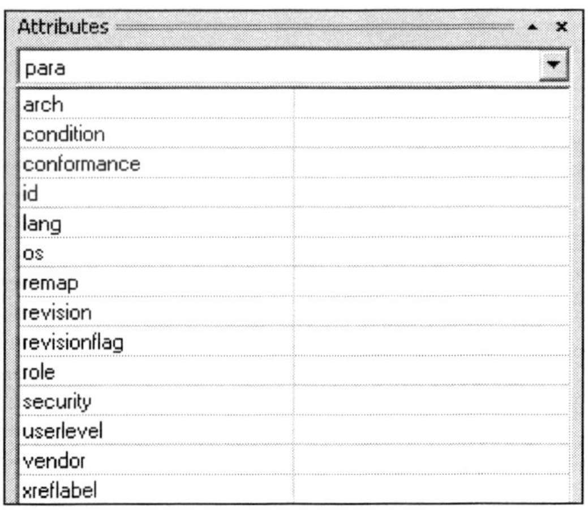

To enter a value for an attribute, click in the value field of the attribute and enter the value. This creates the attribute and its value in the XML document.

Note: Entering a value for an attribute will have an effect in the Authentic View display only if such an effect has been specified in the Authentic Stylesheet.

Entities Entry Helper
The Entities Entry Helper allows you to insert an entity in your document. Entities can be used to insert special characters or text fragments that occur often in a document (such as the name

of a company).

To insert an entity, place the cursor at the point in the text where you want to have the entity inserted, then double-click the entity in the Entities Entry Helper.

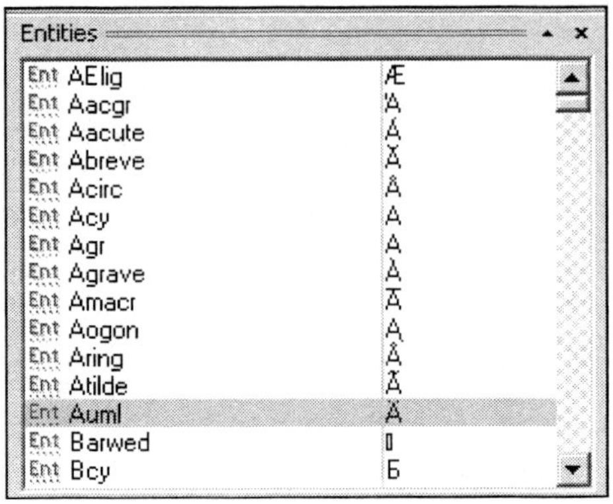

Note: An internal entity is one that has its value defined within the DTD. An external entity is one that has its value contained in an external source, e.g. another XML file. Both internal and external entities are listed in the Entities Entry Helper. When you insert an entity, whether internal or external, the entity—not its value—is inserted into the XML text. If the entity is an internal entity, Authentic View displays **the value of the entity**. If the entity is an external entity, Authentic View displays the entity—and not its value. This means, for example, that an XML file that is an external entity will be shown in the Authentic View display as an entity; its content does not replace the entity in the Authentic View display.

Context Menu
All of the above commands are available in the context menu that appears when you right-click within the XML Document. The context menu that appears depends on where in the document the cursor is. The context menu for all selections is shown below. The figure below also shows part of the Insert submenu, which is a list of all elements that can be inserted at that point. Note that the **Insert submenu** shows the elements that can be **inserted within the current element** (above the rule), and the elements that can be **inserted before the current element** (below the rule). In the figure below, the current element is the `para` element. The `italic` and `strong` elements can be inserted within the current `para` element. The `para` and `Office` elements can be inserted before the current `para` element.

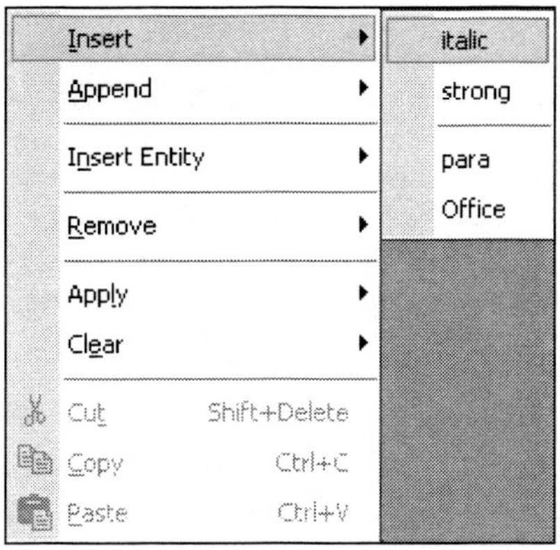

Pointing over the **Remove** command pops up a menu list consisting of the selected element and all its ancestors up to the document element. Click the element to be removed. This is a quick way to delete an element or any of its ancestors. Note that clicking an ancestor element will remove all its descendants, including the selected element.

Authentic View Tutorial

The aim of this tutorial is to make you familiar with the Authentic View interface. In Authentic View, you will open an existing XML file that contains data and is linked to an Authentic Stylesheet. You then modify the file using the various Authentic View features. The tutorial consists of three broad parts:

- Opening an existing XML file
- Editing data (adding new document components as well as content); this section forms the bulk of the tutorial
- Printing out the document

Remember that this tutorial is intended to get you started, and is intentionally simple. You will find additional reference material and feature descriptions in the Authentic View interface and Authentic View: How To ... sections. For additional tutorials, see the start page of the Authentic View documentation.

Tutorial requirements
All **the files** you need for the tutorial are in the `Examples` folder of your Altova application folder. These files are :

- `NanonullOrg.xml` (the XML document you will open)
- `NanonullOrg.sps` (the Authentic Stylesheet to which the XML document is linked)
- `NanonullOrg.xsd` (the XML Schema on which the XML document and Authentic Stylesheet are based, and to which they are linked)
- `nanonull.gif` and `Altova_right_300.gif` (two image files used in the tutorial)

Note: At some points in the tutorial, we ask you to look at the XML text of the XML document (as opposed to the Authentic View of the document). If the Altova product edition you are using does not include a Text View (as in the case of the free AUTHENTIC 2004), then use a plain **text editor** like Wordpad or Notepad to view the text of the XML document.

Caution: We recommend that you use a copy of `NanonullOrg.xml` for the tutorial, so that you can always retrieve the original should the need arise.

Opening an XML document in Authentic View

The file `NanonullOrg.xml` is in the `Examples` folder in the folder where you have installed the application. Typically, the path to the file would be:
`c:\Program\Files\Altova\STYLEVISION 2004\Examples\NanonullOrg.xml`

You can open `NanonullOrg.xml` in one of two ways:

- Click **File | Open** in your Altova product, then browse for `NanonullOrg.xml` in the dialog that appears, and click Open.
- Use Windows Explorer to locate the file, right-click, and select your Altova product.

The file `NanonullOrg.xml` opens directly in Authentic View. This is because the file already has an Authentic Stylesheet assigned to it. If this were not the case, you would be prompted to assign an Authentic Stylesheet whenever you try to switch to Authentic View.

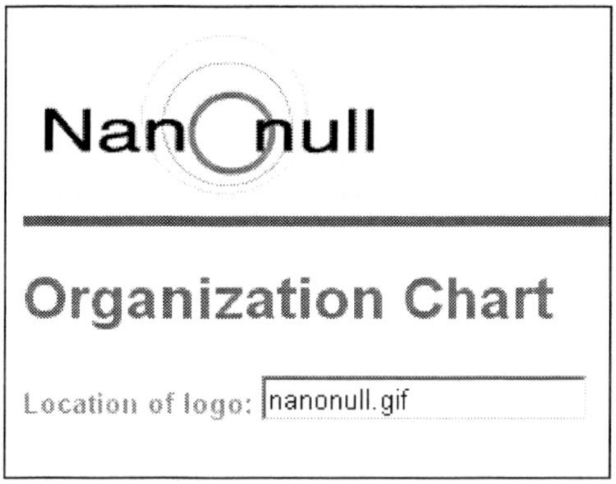

Remember: It is the Authentic Stylesheet that defines and controls how an XML document is displayed in Authentic View. Without an Authentic Stylesheet, there can be no Authentic View of the document.

Entering data in Authentic View

Entering data in Authentic View can be as simple as the associated Authentic Stylesheet makes it.

In the **simplest user scenario**, you will enter content as free-flowing text or into data-input fields, or you will make a selection from a list of user options. In short, you focus on entering content; user-side structural modification (adding elements, tables, etc) and document formatting is kept to a minimum. These restrictions help ensure the validity of the document and the accuracy of data. They also keep you focused on the content.

In most cases, however, you will be given the **option of adding a few elements**. These additions can be implicit, as when you press Enter to add a new paragraph element or click an icon to mark text bold. Or they can be explicit, as when you append an element via the Elements Entry Helper. In such scenarios, you would require a working knowledge of how the document is structured.

At the other extreme, users may be given complete freedom to structure the document. To do this, however, you would require a good knowledge of the schema on which the document is based.

In Authentic View, you can enter or edit the following types of data and data structures:

- Element content (can be entered as a text entry or via a data-entry device)
- Attribute values (can be entered as a text entry or via a data-entry device, or as a value in the Attributes Entry Helper)
- Entities (can be inserted via the Entities Entry Helper)
- Elements (can be added, changed to other elements, and deleted)
- XML tables (can be inserted, and its structure, formatting, and content specified)

This tutorial shows you how to manipulate elements and enter content in Authentic View. XML tables are discussed in detail in the Using tables in Authentic View section.

Adding document content and elements

Adding text content

You can enter element content and attribute values directly as text. To insert content, place the cursor at the location where you want to insert the text, and type. You can also edit such content by highlighting the text, and typing in the replacement text or deleting the highlighted text.

To change the name of the company from Nanonull, Inc to Nanonull USA, Inc, place the cursor after Nanonull, and type in the text to be inserted.

If text is editable, you will be able to place your cursor in it and highlight it, otherwise you will not be able to. Try changing any of the field names, "Street", "City", "State/Zip" (in the address block). You are not able to place the cursor in this text because such text is not XML content; it is derived from the Authentic Stylesheet.

Note: In Hide markup mode, an empty element can easily be overlooked. To make sure that you are not overlooking an empty element, switch to Show large markup or Show small markup mode.

Adding content via a data-entry device

In the content editing you have learned above, content is added by directly typing in text as element content. There is one other way that **element content** (or attribute values) can be entered in Authentic View: via data-entry devices.

Given below is a list of data-entry devices in Authentic View, together with an explanation of how data is entered in the XML file for each device.

Data-Entry Device	Data in XML File
Input Field (Text Box)	Text entered by user
Multiline Input Field	Text entered by user
Combo box	User selection mapped to value
Check box	User selection mapped to value
Radio button	User selection mapped to value
Button	User selection mapped to value

In the static table containing the address fields (shown below), there are two data-entry devices: an input field for the Zip field and a combo-box for the State field. The values that you enter in the text fields are entered directly as the XML content of the respective elements. For other data-entry devices, your selection is mapped to a value.

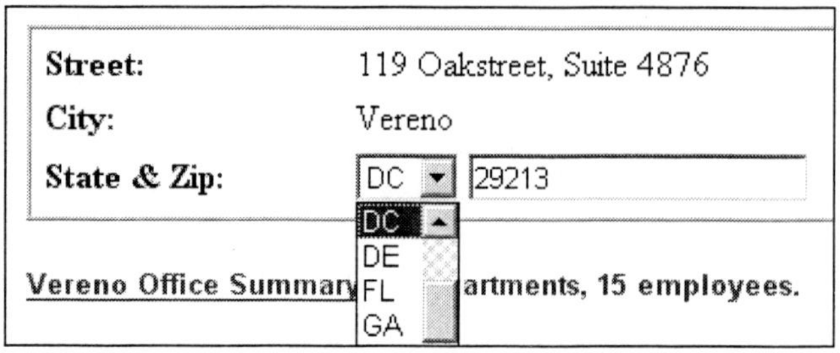

For the Authentic View shown above, here is the corresponding XML text:

```
<Address>
  <ipo:street>119 Oakstreet, Suite 4876</ipo:street>
  <ipo:city>Vereno</ipo:city>
  <ipo:state>DC</ipo:state>
  <ipo:zip>29213</ipo:zip>
</Address>
```

Notice that the combo-box selection "DC" is mapped to a value of "DC". The value of the Zip field is entered directly as content of the `ipo:zip` element.

Adding elements = inserting before or appending
You can add an element by **inserting it before** or **appending it** to the **current element** (the element in which the cursor is).

Add another paragraph to the description of the company. This involves appending the paragraph element (`para`, in this case) and entering content for the element. Do this as follows:

1. Place the cursor in the last paragraph of the description text.
2. Click the (Insert Before Element) icon that is located to the left of the `para` element in the Elements Entry Helper. This **inserts** a `para` **before** the current `para`—which is not where you want the new `para` element.
3. Click the (Append Element) icon that is located to the left of the `para` element in the Elements Entry Helper. This **appends** a `para` element, which is what we want.
4. Type in the content of `para` at the blinking cursor.

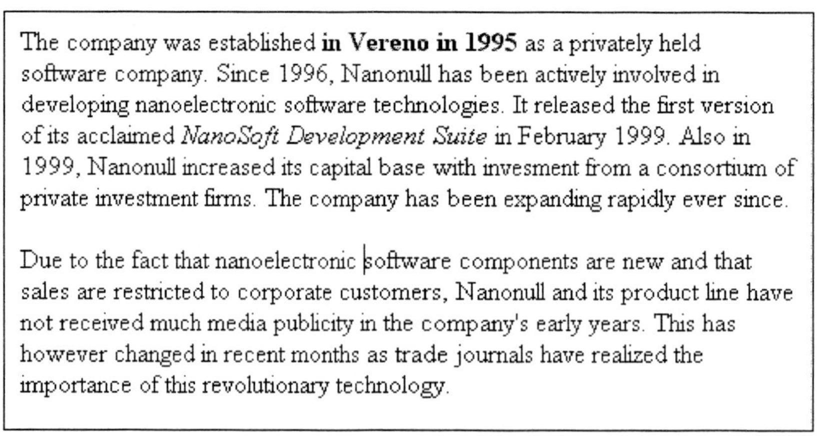
The company was established **in Vereno in 1995** as a privately held software company. Since 1996, Nanonull has been actively involved in developing nanoelectronic software technologies. It released the first version of its acclaimed *NanoSoft Development Suite* in February 1999. Also in 1999, Nanonull increased its capital base with invesment from a consortium of private investment firms. The company has been expanding rapidly ever since.

Due to the fact that nanoelectronic software components are new and that sales are restricted to corporate customers, Nanonull and its product line have not received much media publicity in the company's early years. This has however changed in recent months as trade journals have realized the importance of this revolutionary technology.

Alternatively, to append a `para` (or any paragraph-type) element, press **Enter** at the point where you want to append the new element.

Note: You can also use the Enter key to insert and append list items in numbered lists and itemized (bulleted) lists.

Adding elements in the document
It is important to remember that **only same- or higher-level elements** can be inserted before or appended after the current element.

Same-level elements are siblings. Siblings of a paragraph element would be other paragraph elements, but could also be lists, a table, an image, etc. Siblings could occur before or after an element.

Higher-level elements are ancestor elements and siblings of ancestors. For a paragraph element, ancestor elements could be a section, chapter, article, etc. A paragraph in a valid XML would already have ancestors. Therefore, adding a higher-level element in Authentic View, creates it as a sibling of the relevant ancestor. For example, if a section element is appended to a paragraph, it is created as a sibling of the section that contains the current paragraph element, and it is created as the last sibling section.

At any given location in the document, the elements you can insert before or append are shown in the Elements Entry Helper with the icons to their left.

Inserting an element

You can **insert** an element **as a child** of the **current element** (the element in which the cursor is).

In `NanonullOrg.xml`, the `para` element can contain the elements `italic` and `bold`. Now experiment with inserting these elements, as follows:

1. Place the cursor at a location in the `para` element where you want to insert the child element. Notice that in the Elements Entry Helper, the `italic` and `bold` elements are listed with (Insert Element) icons next to the listing.
2. Click the icon next to the `italic` element. This inserts the `italic` element with a placeholder, "Text", which is highlighted. Switch to Show large markup mode to see the element tags.

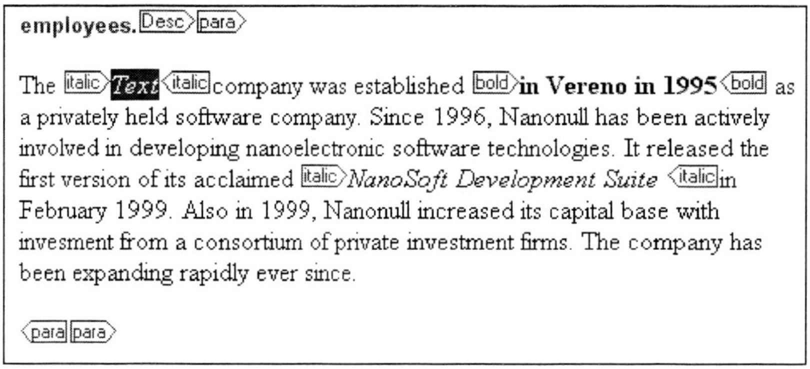

3. Type in the content of the element.

When the cursor is within an element, any element which can be inserted as a child is shown in the Elements Entry Helper with the Insert Element icon next to it.

Now place the cursor inside the `italic` element, and look at the Elements Entry Helper.

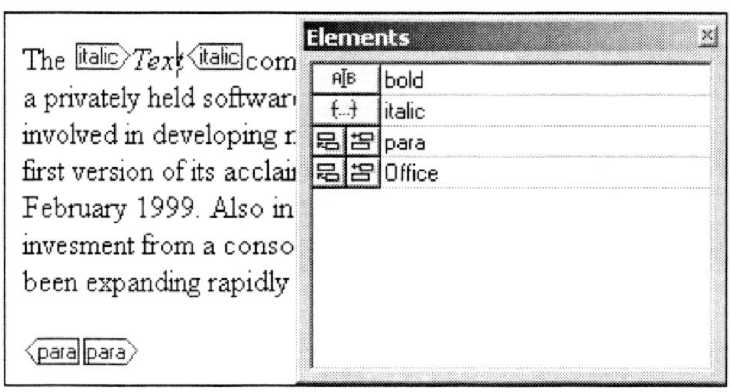

The Elements Entry Helper shows that the `bold` element can be inserted as a child of `italic`. Click the Insert Element icon for the `bold` element, and see what happens.

Applying and clearing elements

Applying (replacing) an element

The Apply Element icon allows you to replace the selected element with another element allowed at that location.

To apply the `bold` element to the `italic` element you have just created, do the following:

1. Switch to Show large markup mode. It is easier to select an entire element in this mode.
2. Select the `italic` element by clicking either its start or end tag. The `bold` element in the Elements Entry Helper is displayed with the (Apply Element) icon next to it.
3. Click the icon. The `italic` element in the main window changes to a `bold` element.

When the entire element is selected, elements which can be applied to the selected element are shown in the Elements Entry Helper with the (Apply Element) icon next to it.

Note: It is important to select the entire element, and not just its contents. Selecting the content activates the Clear Element context of the selected element.

Clearing an element

When you clear an element, you remove its markup without modifying its content.

To clear the `italic` element, do the following:

1. Switch to Show large markup mode.
2. Place the cursor as an insertion point within the `italic` element. The `italic` element is shown in the Elements Entry Helper with the icon next to it.
3. Click the icon. In the main window, the `italic` element markup is removed, and the italic formatting is removed.

You can also select a text fragment within the `italic` element (instead of placing the cursor as an insertion point), and clear the `italic` element. The only difference is that the `italic` element in the Elements Entry Helper will be shown with a second variant of the Clear Element icon next to it: . This icon does the same thing as the icon.

Note: It is important to place the cursor within the element content and not to select the entire element. Selecting the entire element causes the Apply Element context to be activated instead, which allows you to replace the selected element with another element.

Entering attribute values

An attribute is a property of an element, and an element can have any number of attributes. Attributes have values. You may sometimes be required to enter XML data as an attribute value. In Authentic View, you enter attribute values in two ways:

- As content in the main window if the Attribute has been created to accept its value in this way
- In the Attributes Entry Helper

Attribute values in the main window
Attribute values can be entered as free-flowing text or as text in an input field, or as a user selection that will be mapped to an XML value. They are entered in the same way that element content is entered: see Adding document content and elements.

In such cases, the distinction between element content and attribute value is made by the Authentic Stylesheet and the data is handled appropriately.

Attribute values in the Attributes Entry Helper
If you wish to enter or change an attribute value, you can also do this in the Attributes Entry Helper.

The location of the logo that is used in `NanonullOrg.xml` is stored as the value of the `href` attribute of the `CompanyLogo` element. You can change the logo to be used by doing the following:

1. Select the `CompanyLogo` element by either selecting the element or clicking the Nanonull logo. The attributes of the `CompanyLogo` element are displayed in the Attributes Entry Helper.
2. In the Attributes Entry Helper, change the value of the `href` attribute from `nanonull.gif` to `Altova_right_300.gif` (an image in the `Examples` folder).

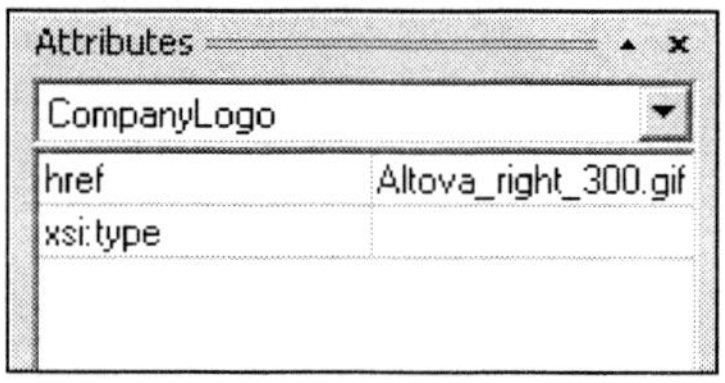

This causes the Nanonull logo to be replaced by the Altova logo.

Note: If you are required to enter the value of an attribute, the designer of the Authentic Stylesheet will, typically, include an input mechanism for this data in Authentic View.

Adding entities

An entity in Authentic View is typically XML data (but not necessarily), such as a single character; a text string; and even a fragment of an XML document. An entity can also be a binary file, such as an image file.

All the entities available to you are displayed in the Entities Entry Helper. To insert an entity, double-click it.

In `NanonullOrg.xml`, change the title of Joe Martin (in Marketing) to Marketing Manager Europe & Asia.

The ampersand character (&) has special significance in XML (as have the apostrophe, less than and greater than symbols, and the double quote). To insert these characters, entities are used so that they are not confused with XML-significant characters. In `NanonullOrg.xml`, entities have been declared for these characters, and are therefore displayed in the Entities Entry Helper.

To insert the ampersand entity in the title, "Marketing Manager Europe & Asia", do the following:

1. Place the cursor where the ampersand is to be inserted.
2. Double click the entity listed as "amp".

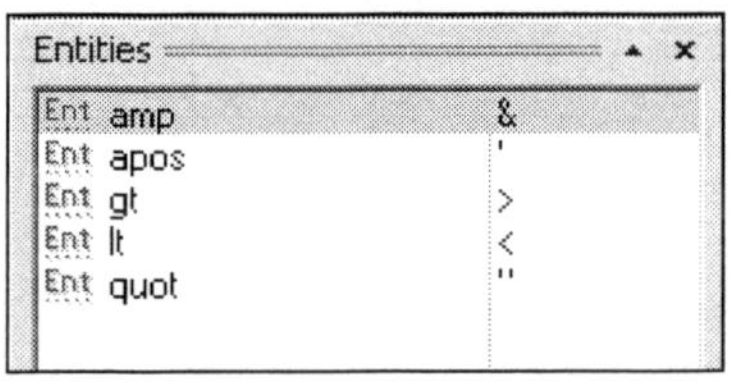

This inserts an ampersand.

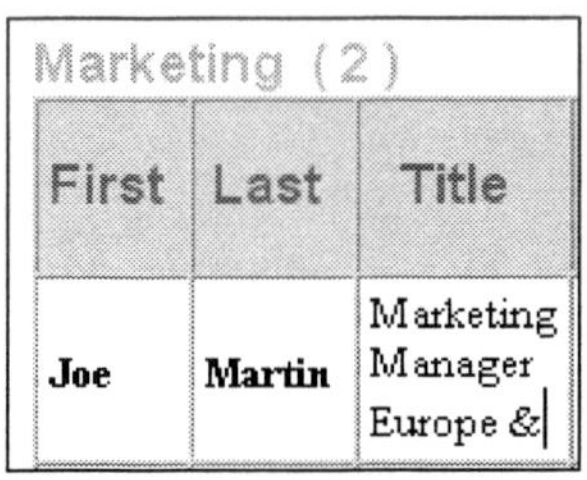

Note: The Entities Entry Helper is not context-sensitive. All available entities are displayed no matter where the cursor is positioned. This does not mean that an entity can be inserted at all locations in the document. If you are not sure, then validate the document after inserting the entity: **XML | Validate** (**F8**).

Also see: Attributes Entry Helper under Authentic View entry helpers.

Printing the document

A printout from Authentic View of an XML document preserves the formatting seen in Authentic View.

To print `NanonullOrg.xml`, do the following:

1. Switch to Hide Markup mode if you are not already in it. You must do this if you do not want markup to be printed.
2. Select **File | Print Preview** to see a preview of all pages. Shown below is part of a print preview page, reduced by 50%.

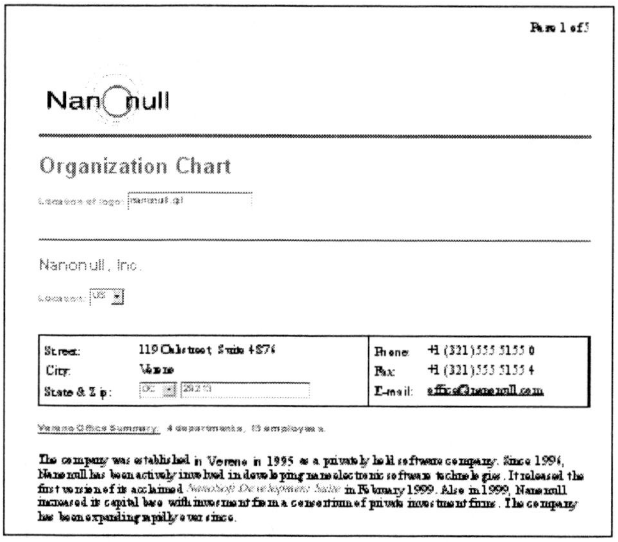

   Notice that the formatting of the page is the same as that in Authentic View.
3. To print the file, click **File | Print**.

Note that you can also print a version of the document that displays (small) markup. To do this, switch Authentic View to Show small markup mode or Show large markup mode, and then print. Both modes produce a printout that displays small markup.

Authentic View: How To ...

This section describes important features of Authentic View in detail. Features have been included in this section either because they are commonly used or require an explanation of the mechanisms or concepts involved.

The section explains the following :

- There are three distinct types of tables used in Authentic View. The section Using tables in Authentic View explains the three types of tables, and when and how to use them. This is a detailed reference that starts with the broad, conceptual picture and moves to the details of usage.
- The context menus provide a fast way to access Authentic View's document editing commands. The section Using context menus describes how they are to be used.

Using tables in Authentic View

There are two types of tables in Authentic View: SPS tables and XML tables.

SPS tables have been pre-designed by the designer of the Authentic Stylesheet to which your XML document is linked. SPS tables are displayed directly in Authentic View. You yourself cannot insert an SPS table into the XML document, but you can enter data into table fields and edit the rows of dynamic SPS tables. The section on SPS tables below explains these features in detail.

XML tables are inserted by you, the user of Authentic View. This is useful because it gives you the freedom to insert tables at any allowed location in the document. The editing features of XML tables and the XML table editing icons are described below.

SPS tables

Two types of SPS tables are used in Authentic View: static tables and dynamic tables.

Static tables are fixed in their structure and in the content-type of cells; you, as the user of Authentic View, cannot change them. You might be required to enter data into some (or all) cells of the table, and this data is entered in your XML document. You enter data either by typing in text, or by selecting from options presented in the form of check-box or radio button alternatives or as a list in a combo-box. After you enter data, you can edit it. But you **cannot** edit any part of the table structure (i.e. add rows or columns, etc) or change the content-type of a cell.

Nanonull, Inc.

Street:	119 Oakstreet, Suite 4876	**Phone:**	+1 (321) 555 5155
City:	Vereno	**Fax:**	+1 (321) 555 5155 - 9
State & Zip:	DC 29213	**E-mail:**	office@nanonull.com

Dynamic tables have rows that represent a repeating data structure, i.e. each row has an identical data structure (not the case with static tables). Therefore, you can perform row operations: append row, insert row, move row up, move row down, and delete row. These commands are available as icons and under the **Authentic** menu. To use these commands, place the cursor anywhere in the appropriate row, and then select the required command.

Administration

First	Last	Title	Ext	EMail	Shares	Leave		
						Total	Used	Left
Vernon	**Callaby**	Office Manager	581	v.callaby@nanonull.com	1500	25	4	21
Frank	Further	Accounts Receivable	471	f.further@nanonull.com	0	22	2	20
Loby	Matise	Accounting Manager	963	l.matise@nanonull.com	add Shares	25	7	18
Employees: 3 (20% of Office, 9% of Company)					**Shares: 1500 (13% of Office, 6% of Company)**			
Non-Shareholders: Frank Further, Loby Matise.								

To move among cells in the table, use the Up, Down, Left, and Right arrow keys. To move forward from one cell to the next, use the Tab key. Pressing the Tab key in the last cell of a row creates a new row.

XML tables

XML tables can be inserted by you, the user of Authentic View. They enable you to insert tables anywhere in the XML document where they are allowed, which is useful if you need to insert tabular information in your document. These tables will be printed out as tables when you print out directly from Authentic View. If you are also generating output with XSLT stylesheets, discuss the required output with the designer of the Authentic Stylesheet.

Note that you can insert XML tables only at allowed locations. These locations are specified in the schema (DTD or XML Schema). If you wish to insert a table at additional locations, discuss this with the person designing the Authentic Stylesheet.

Working with XML tables
There are three steps involved when working with XML tables: inserting the table; formatting it; and entering data. The commands for working with XML tables are available as icons in the toolbar (see XML table editing icons).

Inserting tables

To insert an XML table place your cursor where you wish to insert the table, and click the icon. (Note that where you can insert tables is determined by the schema.) This pops up the Insert Table dialog (shown below).

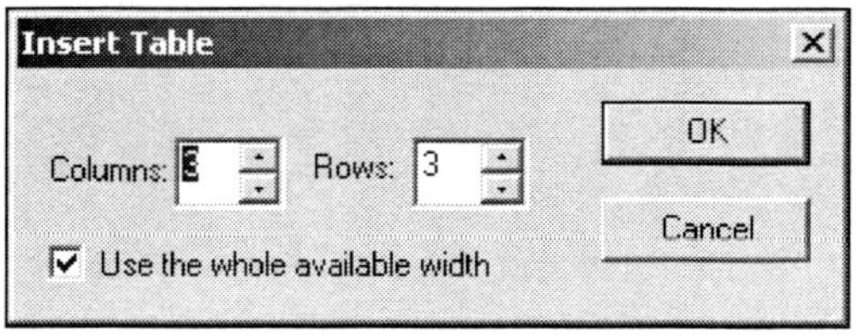

Select the number of columns and rows, and specify whether you wish the table to extend the entire available width. For the specifications given in the dialog box shown above, the following table is created.

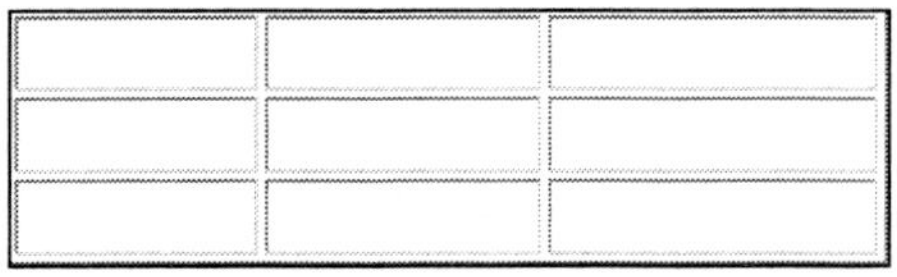

You can add and delete columns, create row and column joins later. So create the broad structure first.

Formatting tables and entering data

To format your table, place the cursor anywhere in the table and click the (Table Properties) icon. This pops up the Table Properties dialog (shown below), where you specify formatting for the table, or for a row, column, or cell.

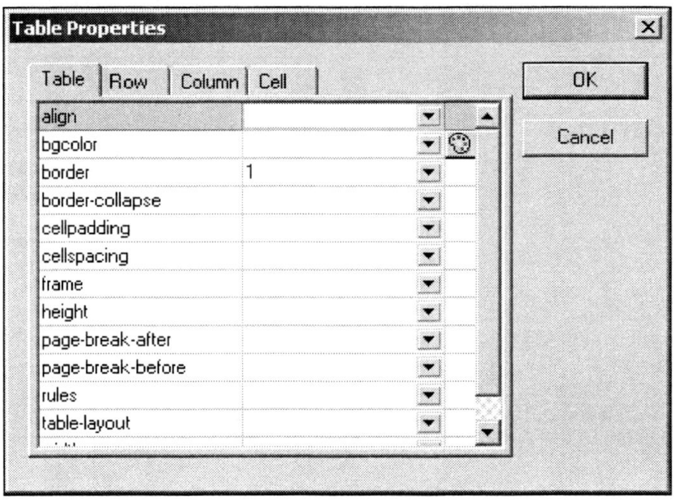

Set the cellspacing and cellpadding properties to "0". Your table will now look like this:

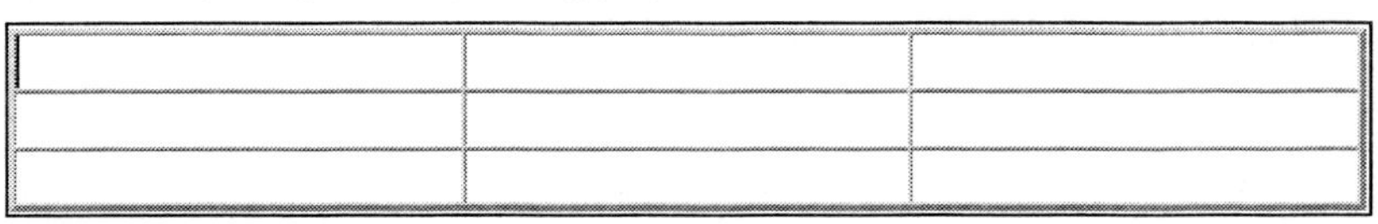

Now place the cursor in the first row to format it, and click the (Table Properties) icon. Click the Row tab.

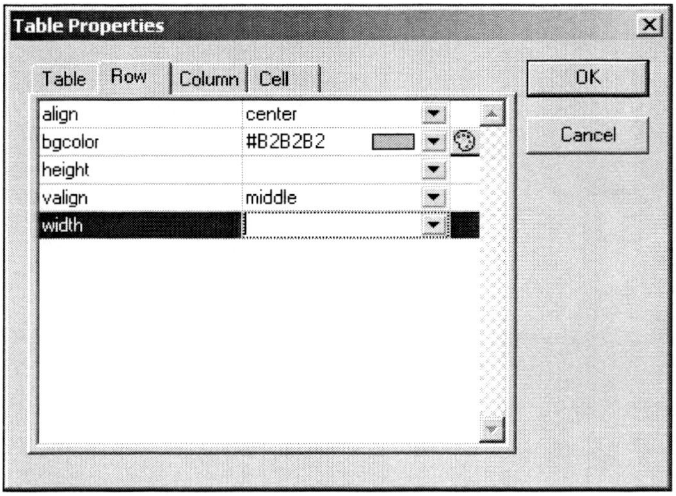

Since the first row will be the header row, set a background color to differentiate this row from the other rows. Note the Row properties that have been set in the figure above. Then enter the column header text. Your table will now look like this:

Name	Telephone	Email

Notice that the alignment is centered as specified. Now, say you want to divide the "Telephone" column into the sub-columns "Office" and "Home", you would need to join cells.

Place the cursor in the "Telephone" cell, and click the (Split vertically) icon. Your table will look like this:

Name	Telephone	Email

Now place the cursor in the cell below the cell containing "Telephone", and click the (Split horizontally) icon. Then type in the column headers "Office" and "Home". Your table will now look like this:

Name	Telephone		Email
	Office	Home	

Now you will have to vertically split each cell in the "Telephone" column.

You can also add and delete columns and rows, and vertically align cell content, using the table-editing icons. The XML table editing icons are described in the User Reference, in the section titled "XML Table Icons".

Moving among cells in the table
To move among cells in the XML table, use the Up, Down, Right, and Left arrow keys.

Entering data in a cell
To enter data in a cell, place the cursor in the cell, and type in the data.

Formatting text
Text in an XML table, as with other text in the XML document, must be formatted using XML elements or attributes. To add an element, highlight the text and double-click the required element in the Elements Entry Helper. To specify an attribute value, place the cursor within the text fragment and enter the required attribute value in the Attributes Entry Helper. After formatting the header text bold, your table will look like this.

Name	**Telephone**		**Email**
	Office	**Home**	

The text above was formatted by highlighting the text, and double-clicking the element `strong`, for which a global template exists that specifies bold as the font-weight. The text formatting becomes immediately visible.

Please note: For text formatting to be displayed in Authentic View, a global template with the required text formatting must have been created in Stylesheet Designer for the element in question.

XML table editing icons

The commands required to edit XML tables are available as icons in the toolbar, and are listed below. Note that no corresponding menu commands exist for these icons.

For a full description of when and how XML tables are to be used, see XML tables.

Insert table

The "Insert Table" command inserts a **CALS / HTML table** at the current cursor position.

Delete table

The "Delete table" command deletes the currently active table.

Append row

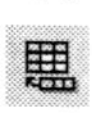
The "Append row" command appends a row to the end of the currently active table.

Append column

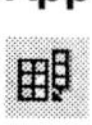
The "Append column" command appends a column to the end of the currently active table.

Insert row

The "Insert row" command inserts a row above the current cursor position in the currently active table.

Insert column

The "Insert column" command inserts a column to the left of the current cursor position in the currently active table.

Join cell left

The "Join cell left" command joins the current cell (current cursor position) with the cell to the left. The tags of both cells remain in the new cell, the column headers remain unchanged.

Join cell right

The "Join cell right" command joins the current cell (current cursor position) with the cell to the right. The tags of both cells remain in the new cell, the column headers remain unchanged.

Join cell below

The "Join cell below" command joins the current cell (current cursor position) with the cell below. The tags of both cells remain in the new cell, the column headers remain unchanged.

Join cell above

The "Join cell above" command joins the current cell (current cursor position) with the cell above. The tags of both cells remain in the new cell, the column headers remain unchanged.

Split cell horizontally

The "Split cell Horizontally" command creates a new cell to the right of the currently active cell. The size of both cells, is now the same as the original cell.

Split cell vertically

The "Split cell Vertically" command creates a new cell below the currently active cell.

Align top

This command aligns the cell contents to the top of the cell.

Center vertically

This command centers the cell contents.

Align bottom

This command aligns the cell contents to the bottom of the cell.

Table properties

The "Table properties" command opens the Table Properties dialog box. This icon is only made active for HTML tables, it cannot be clicked for CALS tables.

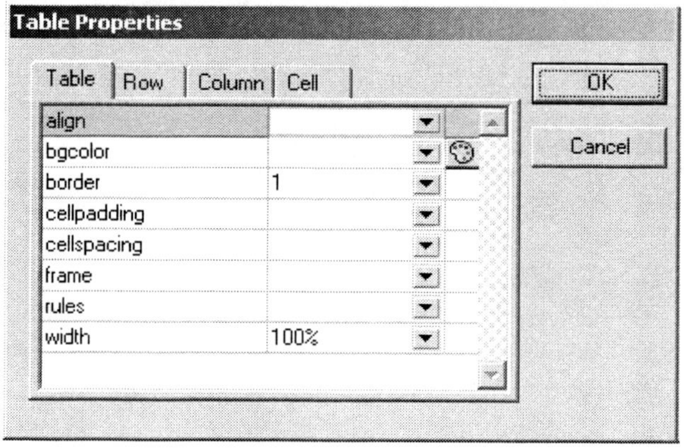

Using context menus

When the cursor is placed within the document, or when some part of the document is selected, right-clicking opens a context menu. Context menus contain all available commands for that location or selection. For example, if the cursor is placed within an element, the context menu will display items for inserting elements before, after, and within the current element; applying, clearing, and removing elements; and so on.

The figure below shows a complete context menu and part of the Insert submenu, which is a list of elements that can be inserted before and within the current element.

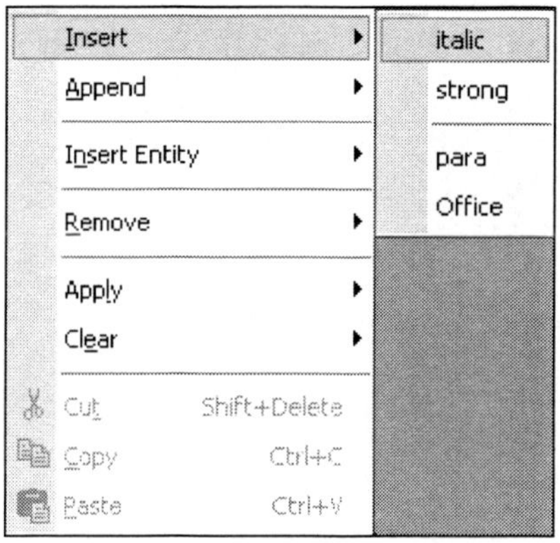

Most of the commands available in the context menu are explained in Authentic View entry helpers and Authentic View Tutorial.

Remove element command

Pointing over the **Remove** command pops up a menu list consisting of the selected element and all its ancestors **up to** the document element. Click the element to be removed. This is a quick way to delete an element or any of its ancestors. Note that clicking an ancestor element will remove all its descendants, including the current element.

Using the Date Picker

The Date Picker is a graphical calendar used to enter dates in a standard format into the XML document. Having a standard format is important for the processing of data in the document. The Date Picker icon appears near the date field it modifies; it is shown below.

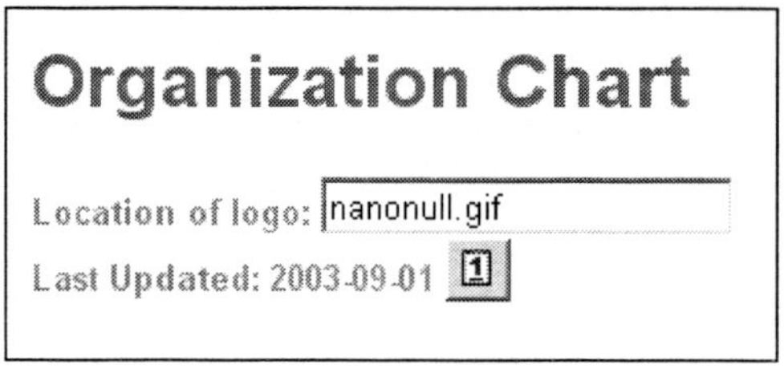

To display the Date Picker (shown below), click the Date Picker icon.

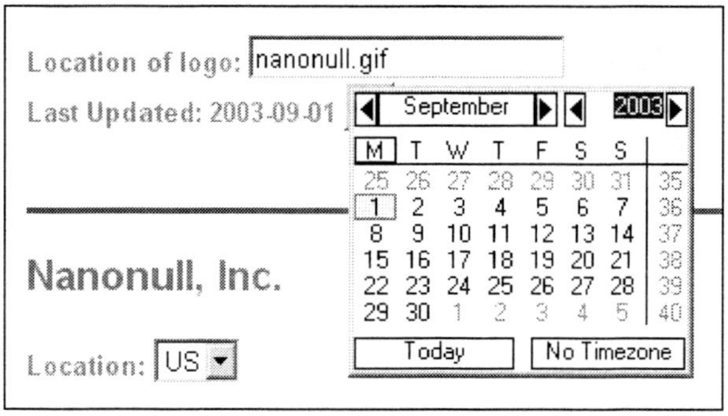

To select a date, click on the desired date, month, or year. The date is enterd in the XML document, and the date in the display is modified accordingly. You can also enter a timezone if this is required.

Part VII

7 Stylesheet Designer

Stylesheet Designer enables you to write stylesheets using a graphical interface. Stylesheets produced with Stylesheet Designer are in the XSLT programming language. A stylesheet created with Stylesheet Designer can be used to:

- display an XML document in Authentic View, a user-friendly view of XML documents that is available in Altova products (see below)
- generate HTML documents from your XML documents
- generate PDF documents from your XML documents

Stylesheet Designer also enables you to convert an HTML file to an XML file.

Stylesheet Designer in Altova products
Stylesheet Designer is available as a component in the following Altova products:

- XMLSPY 2004: All Stylesheet Designer features are available in the Enterprise edition. If you have the Professional edition, check (at the Altova Website) what Stylesheet Designer features are available. Stylesheet Designer is not included in the Home edition.
- STYLEVISION 2004: All Stylesheet Designer features are available.

If Stylesheet Designer is included as a component in your product, the Stylesheet Designer icon  will appear in your **Start | Programs | [Altova Product]** menu. The icon is red for XMLSPY 2004, green for STYLEVISION 2004.

Stylesheet Designer documentation
The Stylesheet Designer documentation consists of the following sections:

- An introduction, which shows the relationship between Authentic Stylesheets and Authentic View; describes the benefits of using Authentic View; and explains the concepts behind the working of Authentic Stylesheets and Authentic View: Introduction.
- A description of how to set up Stylesheet Designer, and an explanation of the Stylesheet Designer interface, and of the symbols and icons in the interface: Getting Started.
- A tutorial to get you started using Stylesheet Designer: Stylesheet Designer Tutorial.
- A how-to-use section for commonly used Stylesheet Designer features: Stylesheet Designer How To Use
- A user reference containing a description of the various menu commands: Stylesheet Designer User Reference.

Related documentation

- Authentic View documentation: The Altova documentation on how to use Authentic View. It contains a description of Authentic View, a tutorial, and a user reference.

Introduction

XSLT stylesheets are used by XSLT engines to transform one XML document into another XML (or HTML) document. In the transformation process, according to instructions in the XSLT, the XSLT engine selects content from the XML source, and places it in the output document. The selected content is usually placed as element content or as an attribute value. If the output document is intended for rendition on some output medium, or is part of a processing chain that produces a document to be rendered, then the stylesheet can also be used to add presentation properties to the output document. The instructions for content selection, processing, placement, and formatting are all contained in the stylesheet.

Stylesheet Designer enables you to create a special type of XSLT-based stylesheet, called an **Authentic Stylesheet**. You do not need to know XSLT in order to create an Authentic Stylesheet. Most of the XSLT constructs are created by the use of mechanisms in the Stylesheet Designer interface, and you will be able to construct simple Authentic Stylesheets after learning to use these mechanisms. However, in order to build stylesheets that use conditions and mathematical operations, it is helpful to have a basic knowledge of XPath.

This introduction gives you the overall picture of how Stylesheet Designer and Authentic Stylesheets fit into an XML document creation process. It covers:

- The purpose of Authentic Stylesheets
- The relationship between Authentic Stylesheets and Authentic View
- The relationship between an Authentic Stylesheet and XSLT stylesheets for HTML and PDF output
- The concepts involved in the creation of an Authentic Stylesheet, and the terminology used in the Stylesheet Designer interface and this documentation

Uses of Authentic Stylesheets

The stylesheet you create with Stylesheet Designer is saved as an **Authentic Stylesheet**, or **SPS file** (so called because of its `.sps` file extension). An Authentic Stylesheet can be used for the following purposes:

- To display an XML file in Authentic View. Authentic View is a graphical user interface that allows users unfamiliar with XML to enter content in the XML document. If your Authentic Stylesheet is being constructed for this purpose, it should aim to make the Authentic View display of the XML document as user-friendly as possible. The WYSIWYG Authentic View of an XML document can also be printed directly to the printer. If this is a requirement, then attention should also be paid to the formatting of the document.
- To generate an XSLT stylesheet to obtain HTML output from the source XML.
- To generate an XSLT stylesheet to obtain XSL-FO output. XSL-FO, typically, would be further processed to obtain PDF output.

The illustration below shows how the output generated from the Design Document (created in Stylesheet Designer) can be used in an XML environment.

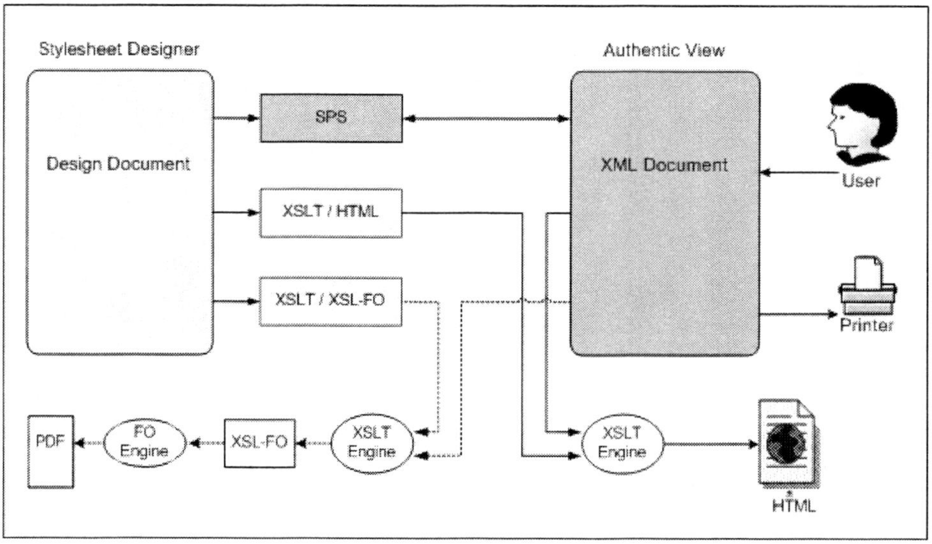

Note: Since all editions of XMLSPY 2004 and STYLEVISION 2004 have an inbuilt XSLT processor (or engine), XML documents can be processed with a Stylesheet Designer-generated XSLT stylesheet using the internal XSLT processor of these Altova products. Additionally, XMLSPY 2004 (Enterprise and Professional editions) and STYLEVISION 2004 also include support for external XSLT processors and FO processors. This means that you can process your XML documents to obtain HTML and PDF output directly from within these product interfaces, using an XSLT processor of your choice.

Stylesheet Designer and Authentic View

The Authentic Stylesheet you create with Stylesheet Designer is used to control the display of an XML document in Authentic View (a document view available in Altova products). With Authentic View, users who are unfamiliar with XML can easily enter XML document content without needing to learn XML.

A document creation process that involves Authentic View consists of two separate stages: **document design** and **content editing**. The Authentic Stylesheet that is created (with Stylesheet Designer) in the document design stage is linked to the XML document in Authentic View and controls the way the XML document is processed and displayed.

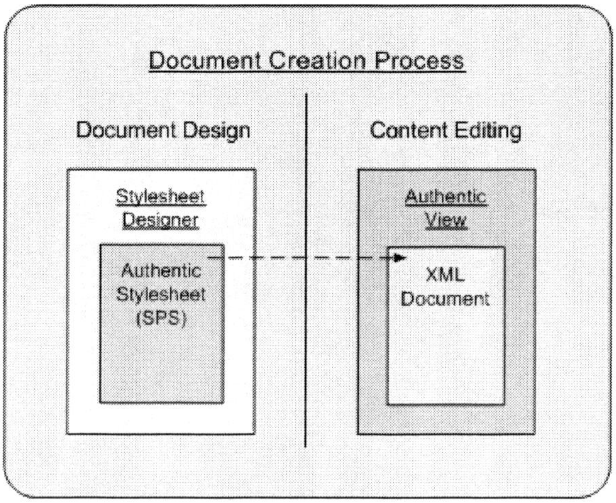

Document design with Stylesheet Designer
In the document design stage, a developer—typically an XML-knowledgable person—uses Altova's Stylesheet Designer to create an Authentic Stylesheet.

The Authentic Stylesheet basically processes the XML document to produce a display of the XML document. Most importantly, however, and unlike typical XSLT stylesheets, which are used to process **finished XML documents**, the Authentic Stylesheet also provides mechanisms for the Authentic View user to **input data into the XML file**. Authentic View therefore provides users the opportunity to input XML data and to instantaneously see the output of the XML document.

The Authentic Stylesheet, therefore, controls the data input as well as defines how the data should be processed and output.

The broad mechanism used is as follows. An Authentic Stylesheet is based on a given schema. It specifies the outline of the XML document that will be displayed in Authentic View in terms of the schema's elements and attributes. It specifies how content entered in Authentic View is to be translated into XML document content. Further, it specifies how each of the schema components is to be processed and output. These processing definitions are used to produce the end-outputs: the Authentic View display, and HTML and PDF files.

Content editing with Authentic View
Authentic View is an interface for editing an XML document that is linked to an Authentic Stylesheet. When a new XML document is created, it can be assigned an Authentic Stylesheet,

and the document can then be edited in Authentic View. Existing XML documents can be assigned an Authentic Stylesheet (that is based on the same schema) at any time, and can be edited subsequently in Authentic View.

The user of Authentic View is not expected to be knowledgable about either XML or the schema being used for the document. The document display in Authentic View should make content editing as easy and non-technical as possible. It is, therefore, the task of the person who designs the Authentic Stylesheet to produce a user-friendly Authentic View display.

For information about using Authentic View, see the Authentic View documentation.

Stylesheet Designer and HTML / PDF output

In Stylesheet Designer, you can generate XSLT stylesheets for output to HTML and XSL-FO from your Authentic Stylesheet. See figure in Uses of Authentic Stylesheets.

All presentation properties (formatting, layout, hyperlinking, etc) in the Authentic Stylesheet are translated into the corresponding HTML and XSL-FO markup. Therefore, all three outputs, Authentic View, HTML, and PDF, will closely resemble each other. You can see previews of the HTML and PDF outputs in Stylesheet Designer.

XSLT for HTML output

For HTML output obtained by using an Authentic Stylesheet-generated XSLT, the following points should be noted:

- The formatting and layout of the HTML will be identical to the HTML Preview of Stylesheet Designer and near-identical to the Authentic View of the XML document.
- Data-input devices in the HTML do not allow input. These data-input devices are intended for XML data input in Authentic View, and are translated unchanged into the HTML.

XSLT for XSL-FO output

XSL-FO is a markup language used for producing PDF. The XSL-FO file has to be processed with an FO engine to obtain the PDF.

The following points should be noted:

- In general, the translation of Authentic Stylesheet formatting and layout properties to the XSL-FO syntax is a straightforward correspondence. However, to render a document to paged media requires specifications for left/right pagination, the location and composition of headers and footers, the design of a cover page, etc. In Stylesheet Designer, you can specify these additional properties, and these are included in the XSLT stylesheet for XSL-FO.
- If data-input devices have been used in the Authentic Stylesheet, then, where possible, these are rendered as graphics on the PDF page. When a data-entry device cannot easily be simulated as a graphic (e.g. check boxes), a substitute presentation is used.

Stylesheet Designer concepts and terminology

The following concepts and terminology are important for an understanding of how Authentic Stylesheets and Authentic View work.

- An **Authentic Stylesheet** is a **.sps file** created with **Stylesheet Designer**; it basically uses the XSLT programming language
- An Authentic Stylesheet is based on a particular **schema** (DTD or XML Schema)
- An Authentic Stylesheet can—but does not need to—have a **Template XML file** associated with it. A Template XML file is an XML file that provides the starting data of the XML Document. It must be conformant with the schema on which the Authentic Stylesheet is based. A Template XML file is assigned to an Authentic Stylesheet in Stylesheet Designer
- An Authentic Stylesheet can—but does not need to—have a **Working XML file** associated with it. A Working XML file is used to preview the Authentic View of an XML document in Stylesheet Designer. A Working XML file is assigned to an Authentic Stylesheet in Stylesheet Designer
- An **XML Document** that is linked to a given Authentic Stylesheet must conform with the schema on which that Authentic Stylesheet is based
- When an XML document that is associated with an Authentic Stylesheet is opened in Authentic View, it can be edited and re-saved
- Any XML file can be assigned an Authentic Stylesheet at any time in XMLSPY 2004. Once an Authentic Stylesheet has been assigned, the XML document can be opened in Authentic View and edited
- An XML document created or edited with Authentic View is an XML document like any other

The diagram below illustrates the concepts noted above.

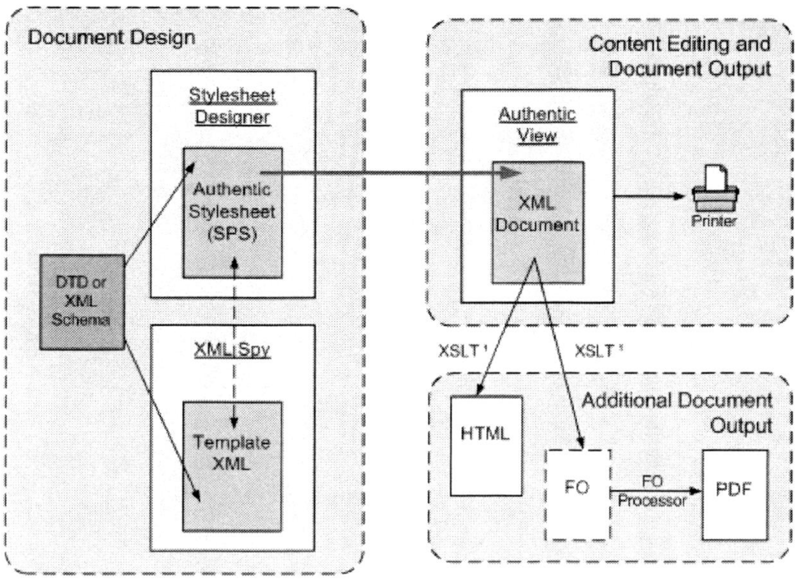

[1] An XML Document created in Authentic View can be processed outside Authentic View with XSLT stylesheets to obtain additional HTML and PDF output.

Getting Started

This section discusses issues related to starting work with Stylesheet Designer. It covers the following:

- A discussion about installing Stylesheet Designer and setting up related components.
- A high-level description of the Stylesheet Designer interface.
- A discussion of the document design process.

Setting up Stylesheet Designer

Stylesheet Designer is packaged as a component of XMLSPY 2004 and STYLEVISION 2004 (see Stylesheet Designer). It is installed as part of either of these products; you do not have to install it separately. In order to preview HTML and PDF outputs in Stylesheet Designer, you need an XSLT processor and FO processor.

XSLT processor
Your Altova product has an internal XSLT processor, which is installed with the product. No additional installation or setting is required.

Alternatively, you could use an external XSLT processor if this feature is supported in your product. To set the external processor as your default, in the interface of your product(XMLSPY 2004 or STYLEVISION 2004), go to **Tools | Options | XSL**, and make the required settings.

FO processor
In order to obtain the PDF preview, you need to install an FO processor. The FO processor processes the XSL-FO generated by the XSLT, and produces the PDF.

After installing an FO processor, you need to make the required settings for it. To do this, in Stylesheet Designer, click **Tools | XSL-FO Options....** This opens the following dialog:

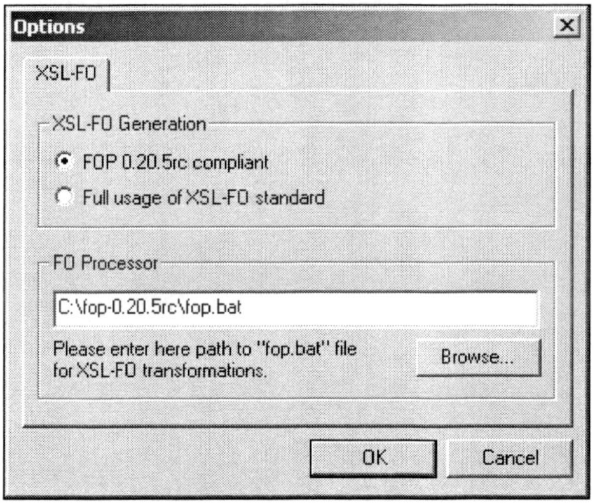

Location of FO processor executable
Set the path to the executable of the FO processor.

Compliance level for XSL-FO to PDF conversion
The FO file that is generated by the XSLT transformation of the XML will typically be in compliance with the complete XSL-FO specification. This means that it makes use of the full range of properties and values available in the complete compliance level of the XSL-FO specification. Currently available FO processors, however, may not implement all these properties and values. Such a processor may generate an error when required to process an unimplemented property or value, and cause the conversion to stop.

If you set the compliance level to basic (the supported FOP compliance level), then only properties and values in the basic level of the specification are processed, and others are filtered out. This allows the processing to be completed successfully, even though some properties/values are not processed.

If you set the compliance level to complete (full usage), then the processor may report a fatal error if it encounters a property or value for which no processing action has been implemented.

FOP from the Apache XML Project
FOP is a popular FO processor that is available free of charge. You can download and install FOP from the Altova Website. This package downloads, installs, and configures FOP for use within your product interface. Alternatively, you could download FOP from the Apache Website.

Note that FOP requires a Java Runtime Environment, downloadable free of charge from Sun's Java Site.

After you have installed FOP, make sure that Stylesheet Designer knows where to find the FOP executable. To do this, click **Tools | XSL-FO Options...** in Stylesheet Designer, and enter the path to the `fop.bat` file (see figure above).

Note: Since conformance levels between any two FO processors can differ widely, and since the XSL-FO specification may be interpreted differently from processor to processor, the PDF produced by different processors from a single FO file could be different.

Stylesheet Designer interface

The graphical user interface of Stylesheet Designer is made up of two broad parts:

- the Main Window, which displays the design of the document; and
- the schema tree and styling windows, in which content is selected in terms of schema elements and attributes (Schema Window), and in which items selected in the Design Document can be formatted (Text Style Window and Block Style Window).

The functions of individual parts of the interface are described below.

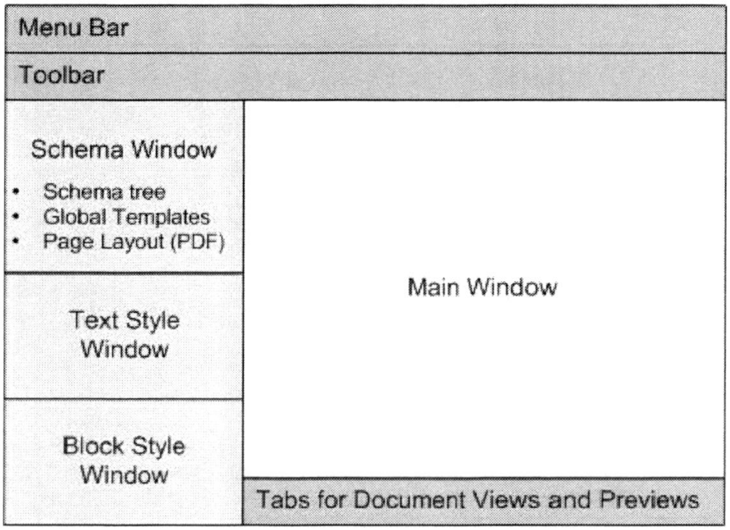

Menu Bar
The Menu Bar contains the Stylesheet Designer menus.

Toolbar
The Toolbar contains icons for common commands. Some icons will be familiar from other Windows applications. Others are for specialized Stylesheet Designer actions. Note that the bottom row of the toolbar contains icons for the creation of static SPS tables and the editing of both static and dynamic SPS tables; these icons correspond to commands in the Table menu.

Main Window
The Main Window has five tabs. The most important tab is the Design Document tab, which displays the document you are designing and its formatting. Dynamic components (content that comes from the XML document) are displayed in terms of schema elements and attributes. Static components (such as images, non-XML text, etc) are actually displayed. All components of the Design Document are displayed with their formatting and layout properties.

Additional views in the Main Window are: the XSLT and XSL-FO views, which show the text of the XSLT for HTML and the XSLT for PDF files, respectively. You are not allowed to edit the code displayed in these views.

Additionally, there are the HTML and PDF Preview tabs. Clicking these tabs starts the respective transformation processes, and displays the previews. In the HTML preview, although data-entry devices for XML data are displayed, you cannot enter XML data in the

HTML Preview.

Schema Window
The Schema Window displays the following:

- A **tree representation of the schema** (DTD or XML Schema) in terms of its elements and attributes. Elements and attributes are dragged from the Schema Window and placed at the required location in the Design Document.
- A list of all elements and attributes for which **global templates** are possible. When you select an element or attribute from this list, a global template is created. The formatting that you specify in a global template, is applied to all occurrences of that element in the document.
- A list of **page layout components for PDF** output (such as a cover page design, and headers and footers). These components are specific to paged media, and need to be defined additionally.

Text Style Window
The Text Style Window has tabs, each with different groups of text formatting properties (such as font-weight and font-style). When text or an element containing text is selected in the Design Document, text formatting properties are applied **to the text** via the properties in the Text Style Window. Some text style properties are also available as icons in the toolbar.

Block Style Window
The Block Style Window has tabs, each with different groups of block formatting properties (such as spacing before and after a block). When a block component is selected in the Design Document, block formatting properties are applied **to the block** via the properties in the Block Style Window. If the selected Design Document component is not a block, the Block Style Window is disabled (grayed out).

Note: Only one Authentic Stylesheet can be open at a time in Stylesheet Designer. The Stylesheet Designer title bar and the Authentic Stylesheet title bar are one and the same. Clicking the Close button in the title bar therefore closes both the Authentic Stylesheet as well as Stylesheet Designer.

Document design process

The document you create with Stylesheet Designer is an Authentic Stylesheet. The Authentic Stylesheet is created in the Design Document tab of the Main Window, and it defines how an XML document based on a given schema is to be processed and output. The process of creating an Authentic Stylesheet with Stylesheet Designer can be divided into the following general parts:

Selection of dynamic content and its placement in document

- **Schema:** A schema (DTD or XML Schema) is used as the starting point. The schema, which provides the structural outline of the XML document in terms of its elements and attributes, is loaded into Stylesheet Designer. It is displayed as a **tree** in the Schema Window.
- **Content to be selected:** XML content is selected by dragging an element or attribute from the schema tree.
- **Location in output document:** The dragged element/attribute is placed in the **design document**. Where it is dropped determines the **location** of that particular element/attribute in the design document. Since the actual content comes from the XML document and could vary depending on the XML content of the element/attribute, this kind of content is known as dynamic content and its containing component is known as a dynamic component.

Authentic Stylesheet Components

Authentic Stylesheet components can be categorized in terms of:

- Type (static or dynamic), and
- Form (e.g. contents, data-entry device, table, image, etc).

Type of component
Static components are those with static content, that is, content entered in the Authentic Stylesheet; static content does not come from the XML document. The most common examples of static content are text and images. Static text is text that is entered directly in the Authentic Stylesheet. Static images are those that have their URLs specified in the Authentic Stylesheet. Dynamic components are those components which have content that comes from the XML document, specifically from nodes in the XML document.

Form of component
This refers to the form the component takes, which could be text, or a table, image, hyperlink, etc. Two forms that require explanation are the `(contents)` placeholder and data-entry devices. The `(contents)` placeholder is used with dynamic components, specifically an element or attribute, and serves to output the contents of the node. Data-entry devices are described in the section Data-entry devices.

Inserting static components

- **Static components:** Additional components that are external to the XML source can be added to the design document. These components could be text, images, table structures, hyperlinks, etc. They are considered static because they are non-XML, and do not change after being added to the design document.

Processing of dynamic content

- **Basic processing:** When an element/attribute is dropped into the design document, you must decide in what form its content is to be displayed. Some possibilities are as follows. If the content model of the selected node is text, you might want to create the content as a paragraph. If the content model of the selected node is other elements, you might want to create the selected element as a table, with the child elements forming the columns of the table. If the selected node is an attribute, you might want to create the attribute as an image, with the value of the attribute being the location of the image. Or yet again, you may wish to create the selected node as a data-entry device to accept XML input in Authentic View.

- **Advanced processing:** You can build conditional templates to process a node in alternative ways depending on the value of any node in the XML document. You can also use XPath expressions to (i) generate XML values from other XML content, and (ii) perform additional validation of nodes.

Formatting of content

- Precise formatting can be applied to any static or dynamic component in the design document. Formatting properties include text and block styling, as well as those for complex table layouts.

The above provides a broad outline of how an Authentic Stylesheet is designed. The more detailed aspects are explained in subsequent sections.

Stylesheet Designer Tutorial

The aim of this tutorial is to create an Authentic Stylesheet for a company with offices in the US and EU. After the Authentic Stylesheet has been created, it can be used to edit an XML document in Authentic View. To do this, the XML document must be linked to the Authentic Stylesheet. The following general points apply to this tutorial.

Previewing the outputs and checking for differences among them
While you create the Authentic Stylesheet in Stylesheet Designer, you can preview the HTML and PDF outputs. To do this you must assign a Working XML file to the Authentic Stylesheet. There are small differences in the way different components are rendered in these two outputs. For the most part the differences are subtle, and do not need your special attention. One component that needs to be checked is the table. Since table and column widths for tables in PDF must be explicitly specified, it is important to check the PDF Preview when you create or modify a table. Note also that the PDF Previews described in this tutorial have been generated using FOP as the FO processor. If you use another processor, the PDF output may be rendered differently than shown in this tutorial.

You should also check the Authentic View of the Working XML file, which is different than the HTML Preview. This is because in Authentic View, the Working XML file can be edited, as a result of which dynamic changes are immediately visible. In the HTML Preview you cannot edit the XML file, so you will not be able to see dynamic changes. Use Authentic View when you wish to test dynamic changes. To use the latest version of your Authentic Stylesheet in Authentic View, first save the Authentic Stylesheet in Stylesheet Designer, then refresh the Authentic View of your Working XML file by changing to another view and then changing back to Authentic View.

Remember that the previews you see in Stylesheet Designer are of the Working XML file you have assigned to your Authentic Stylesheet. If you have modified and re-saved your Working XML file subsequent to opening your Authentic Stylesheet, you must close and reopen your Authentic Stylesheet in order to see previews of the revised XML document.

Text View of Working XML file
Occasionally, you might want to see the text of your Working XML file. You can see the text by viewing the Working XML file in the Text View of your Altova product, or by opening the file in a text editor.

Tutorial files
The following files are used in this tutorial. They are in the `Examples` folder of your application:

- Authentic Stylesheet: `NanonullOrg.sps`
- XML Schemas: `NanonullOrg.xsd`
- Working XML file: `NanonullOrg.xml`. Assign this file to the Authentic Stylesheet as the Working XML file. Use this file also in Authentic View.

You will create your Authentic Stylesheet from scratch. When you have completed it, it should be similar to the finished Authentic Stylesheet `NanonullOrg.sps`. Before you start work on the tutorial, rename the supplied `NanonullOrg.sps` to something else, such as `NanonullOrg_original.sps`. It is also a good idea to make a copy of the XML file `NanonullOrg.xml` before you start editing it.

Note: Stylesheet Designer supports **unlimited undo**; you can always go back and retrace your steps.

Setting up the Authentic Stylesheet

Setting up an Authentic Stylesheet entails the following:

- Opening a schema in Stylesheet Designer
- Assigning a Working XML file
- Creating a rudimentary document outline
- Saving the Authentic Stylesheet with a name

Starting Stylesheet Designer and opening a schema

1. Start Stylesheet Designer by double clicking the Stylesheet Designer icon on your Desktop or by clicking **Start | Programs | [Your Altova Product] | Stylesheet Designer**.

Stylesheet Designer starts. The Schema Window and the Design Document window are empty.

2. Select the menu option **File | Open** and open the `NanonullOrg.xsd` schema file supplied with your Altova product. This file is in the `Examples` folder of your product installation folder.

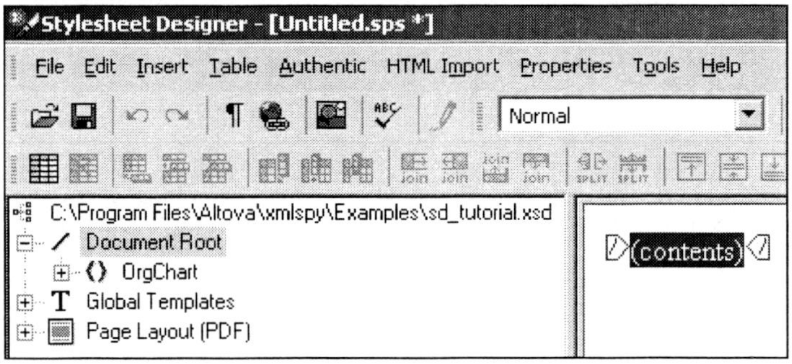

This creates a tree of the OrgChart schema in the Schema Window, as well as entries for Global Templates and Page Layout features immediately below the schema tree. A `(contents)` placeholder for the root element is also created in the Design Document window.

Note: We use the word schema (not capitalized) to denote the superset that contains DTDs and XML Schemas (capitalized). While this tutorial uses an XML Schema (`NanonullOrg.xsd`), note that you can also use DTDs in Stylesheet Designer.

Assigning the Working XML file

The Working XML file is used to preview how an XML file based on the selected schema will be processed by your Authentic Stylesheet. Stylesheet Designer provides HTML and PDF previews of the Working XML file so you can quickly see how your Authentic Stylesheet will process the XML.

To assign a Working XML file, select **File | Assign Working XML file...**. Then browse and select `NanonullOrg.xml`, which is in the `Examples` folder. Before assigning the Working XML file, you should save a copy of the original `NanonullOrg.xml` with some other name.

The Working XML file, including the path to it, now appears in the title bar.

Creating the document outline in the Design view

1. In the Schema Window, expand the `OrgChart` element.
2. Select the `/OrgChart/Name` element and drag it into the Design window. Position it just after the `(contents)` placeholder. A blinking cursor appears after the `(contents)` placeholder, and the dragged element becomes an arrow. When you release the mouse button, a popup menu appears:

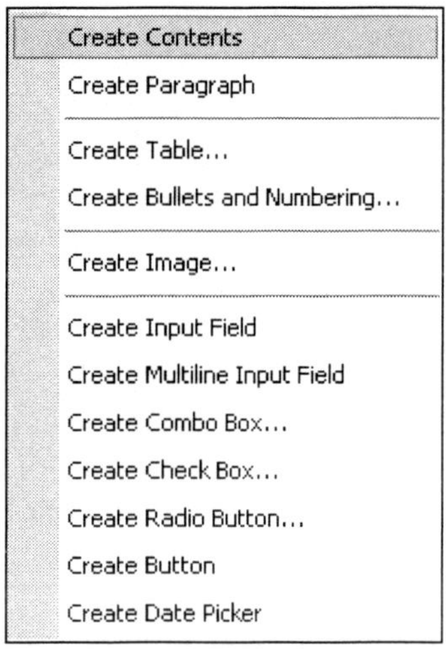

3. Click the **Create Contents** option in the popup. The Design Document now looks like this:

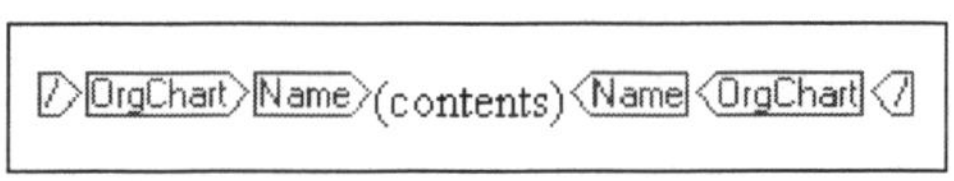

The `Name` element with a `(contents)` placeholder is inserted. The `(contents)` placeholder represents the content of the `Name` element. When the XML file is processed with this Authentic Stylesheet (for Authentic View, HTML, and PDF output), the XML content of the `Name` element will be displayed.

Previewing the XML file

There are two preview tabs in the Main Window of Stylesheet Designer.

- HTML Preview provides an accurate preview of HTML output (shown below) and a near-accurate preview of the Authentic View output.

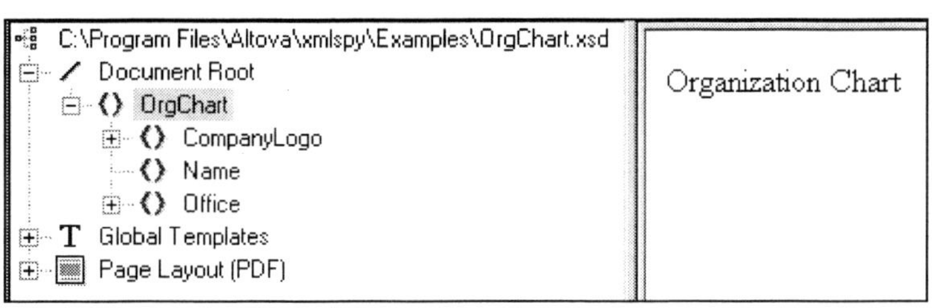

If you look in the Text View of your Working XML file, you will see that the contents of the `/OrgChart/Name` element is "Organization Chart", which is what appears in the HTML Preview. Note that HTML Preview is a browser preview; it does not provide a view of the HTML source.

- PDF Preview provides a preview of the PDF output. For instructions about setting up Stylesheet Designer for PDF preview, see the section, Setting up Stylesheet Designer

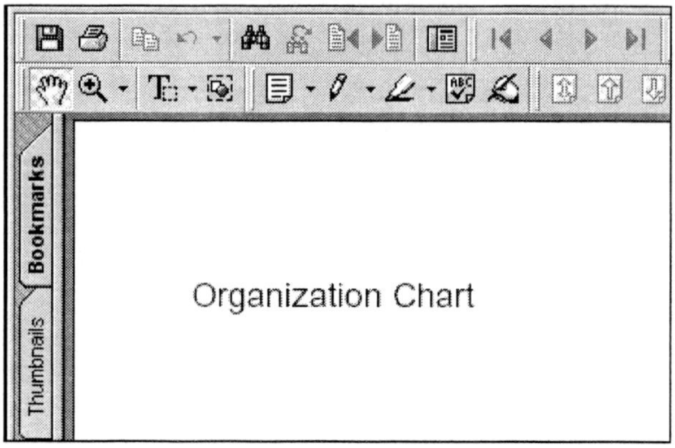

The PDF page layout you see is a default layout. How to customize the page layout is described in PDF processing and page layout in the How To section of this documentation.

Viewing the XSLT stylesheets

To view the XSLT stylesheet (for Authentic View and HTML), click the XSLT Stylesheet tab at the bottom of the Main Window. This is what it will look like:

```
<?xml version="1.0" encoding="UTF-8"?>
<xsl:stylesheet version="1.0"
  xmlns:xsl="http://www.w3.org/1999/XSL/Transform"
  xmlns:n1="http://www.xmlspy.com/schemas/orgchart"
  xmlns:ipo="http://www.altova.com/IPO"
  xmlns:xsi="http://www.w3.org/2001/XMLSchema-instance">
  <xsl:template match="/">
    <html>
      <head />
      <body>
        <xsl:for-each select="n1:OrgChart">
          <xsl:for-each select="n1:Name">
            <xsl:apply-templates />
          </xsl:for-each>
        </xsl:for-each>
      </body>
    </html>
  </xsl:template>
</xsl:stylesheet>
```

To view the stylesheet for XSL-FO output, click the XSL-FO tab at the bottom of the Main Window. This is what it will look like:

```
<?xml version="1.0" encoding="UTF-8"?>
<xsl:stylesheet version="1.0"
  xmlns:xsl="http://www.w3.org/1999/XSL/Transform"
  xmlns:fo="http://www.w3.org/1999/XSL/Format"
  xmlns:n1="http://www.xmlspy.com/schemas/orgchart"
  xmlns:ipo="http://www.altova.com/IPO"
  xmlns:xsi="http://www.w3.org/2001/XMLSchema-instance">
  <xsl:variable name="fo:layout-master-set">
    <fo:layout-master-set>
```

```
<fo:simple-page-master master-name="default-page"
        page-height="11in" page-width="8.5in"
        margin-left="0.6in" margin-right="0.6in">
        <fo:region-body margin-top="0.79in" margin-bottom="0.79in" />
      </fo:simple-page-master>
    </fo:layout-master-set>
  </xsl:variable>
  <xsl:template match="/">
    <fo:root>
      <xsl:copy-of select="$fo:layout-master-set" />
      <fo:page-sequence master-reference="default-page"
        initial-page-number="1" format="1">
        <fo:flow flow-name="xsl-region-body">
          <fo:block>
            <xsl:for-each select="n1:OrgChart">
              <xsl:for-each select="n1:Name">
                <xsl:apply-templates />
              </xsl:for-each>
            </xsl:for-each>
          </fo:block>
        </fo:flow>
      </fo:page-sequence>
    </fo:root>
  </xsl:template>
</xsl:stylesheet>
```

You are not allowed to edit the XSLT code. If you wish to modify these XSLT files, you can save them as a generated XSLT or XSL-FO file, and then edit the generated files in XMLSPY 2004 or STYLEVISION 2004. If you do this, however, note that the modified file will be different from the Authentic Stylesheet, which you can modify only in the Design view of Stylesheet Designer.

The generated XSLT stylesheets can be saved by selecting the menu command **File | Save Generated XSLT file....**

Saving the Authentic Stylesheet

The Authentic Stylesheet is saved as an SPS (`.sps`) file; it controls the display and processing of the Authentic View of an XML document. The SPS file also contains information about related files, such as the underlying schema, Working XML file, and Template XML file.

To save the Authentic Stylesheet, click **File | Save**, and enter `NanonullOrg.sps` as the name of the file. (Be sure to save a copy of the original (supplied) `NanonullOrg.sps` file under another name.) The name you enter appears in the title bar.

Processing attribute values for output

The Design Document defines how the XML document is to be processed. XML content is included as follows. First, the required XML content (element or attribute) is dragged from the schema tree. It is dropped into the Design Document as one of several types of Authentic Stylesheet components (such as contents, data-entry device, table, etc). Then, further XSLT/XPath processing can be specified for it. Finally the required formatting is applied.

In this section you will learn how to include attribute values in your output.

Including an attribute as a data-entry device

In the schema tree, you will see that the element `CompanyLogo` has an `href` attribute, the value of which gives the location of the logo image. Now let us say we want the user of Authentic View to specify what image should be used as the logo. We can create the `href` attribute as an input field, and the user can enter the location of the image here. This is how:

1. In the Design window, place the cursor between the start tags of `OrgChart` and `Name`. Press Enter to put the `Name` element on the next line.
2. Drag the `href` attribute from the Schema Window into the Design Document. Drop it just after the `OrgChart` start tag.
3. In the pop-up menu that appears, select "Create Input Field". Your Design Document will now look like this:

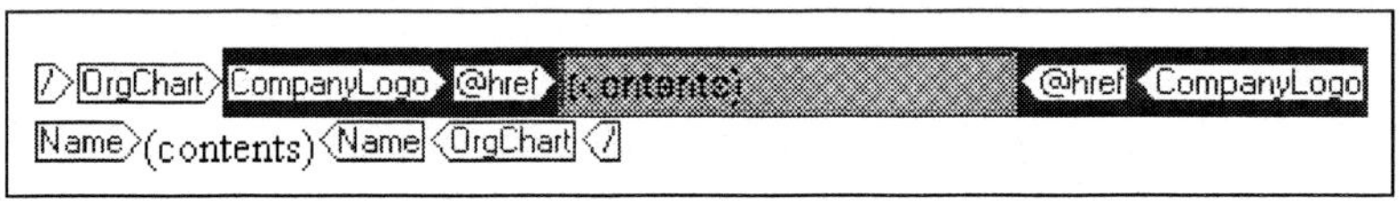

The HTML Preview will look like this (the data comes from the Working XML file):

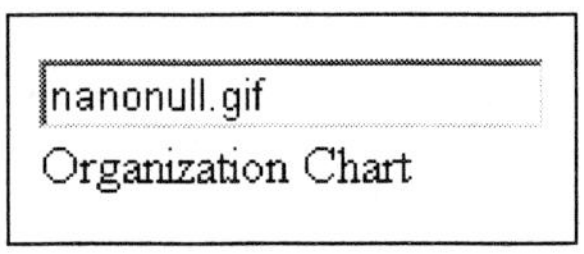

Note that the `href` attribute has been created as an input field, while the `Name` element was created as `(contents)`. The Authentic View user will be able to edit both types of display. The input field, however, indicates more clearly to the user that data in this field can be modified.

Adding non-XML XSLT text

In order to indicate what data is contained in the input field, text can be added before the input field. This text is part of the Authentic Stylesheet; it does not come from the XML document.

To add text to the XSLT document, type it into the Design Document at the required location. In your Authentic Stylesheet, do the following:

1. Place the cursor before the start tag of the `CompanyLogo` element and press Enter. This adds a line break.
2. Type "Location of logo: " before the opening tag of the `href` attribute. The Design Document now looks like this:

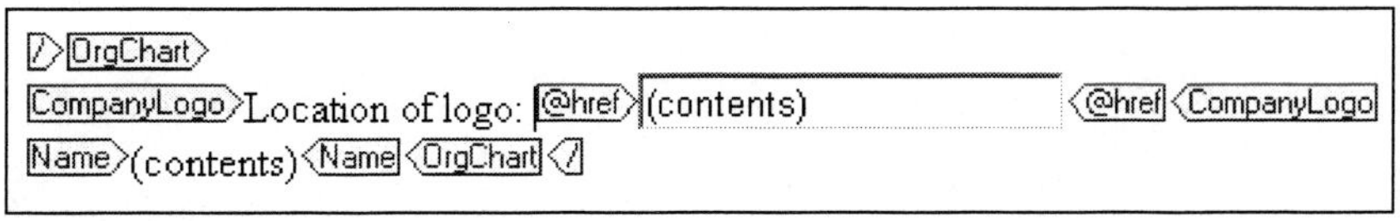

The HTML Preview will look like this:

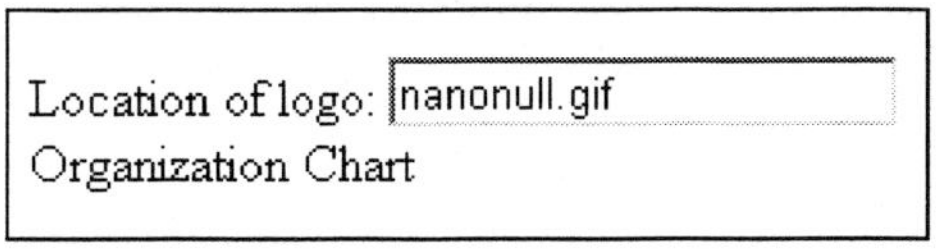

A note on data-entry devices
Data-entry devices are used by the **Authentic View user** to enter **XML data into the XML document**. In an HTML or PDF file that has been created with an XSLT generated from an Authentic Stylesheet, a data-entry device cannot be used for data-entry purposes. Data-entry devices in these outputs **only display** the relevant XML data.

Shown below is the PDF preview of your document:

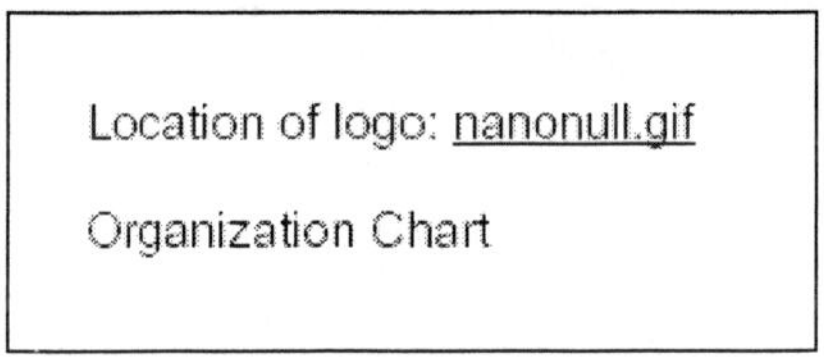

Notice that the input field is rendered as underlined text, and that the content of the input field is the content of the component—in this case the value of the `href` attribute.

Including an image

An image can be included in the output of the XML document by including a link to it in the Authentic Stylesheet. If the link is explicitly specified in the Authentic Stylesheet, the included image is referred to as a static image—because its address does not, and cannot, be changed in the XML document. If, on the other hand, the Authentic Stylesheet specifies, instead of the image address, a location in the XML document where the address is to be found, then the image is dynamic; it changes when the corresponding XML content changes.

Inserting a dynamic image

In the previous section, we created an input field for the value of the `href` attribute. This value provides the address of the logo image, and it can be specified by the Authentic View user. Now we will create a display for the image specified in the `href` attribute value. Do the following:

1. Drag the `href` attribute from the schema tree, and drop it immediately after the start tag of the `CompanyLogo` element.
2. In the pop-up menu that appears, select Create Image.
3. In the Insert Image dialog (shown below), switch to the Dynamic tab.

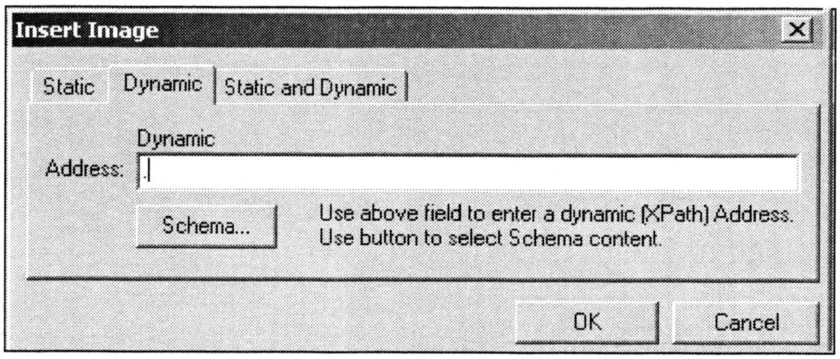

4. In the Insert Image dialog, check that the Address field contains a period. This is the XPath expression for the current node, which is the `href` attribute (this is the node that was dragged from the schema tree). If there is no period, then type in one.
5. Click OK.
6. Save your changes.

The Design Document will now look like this:

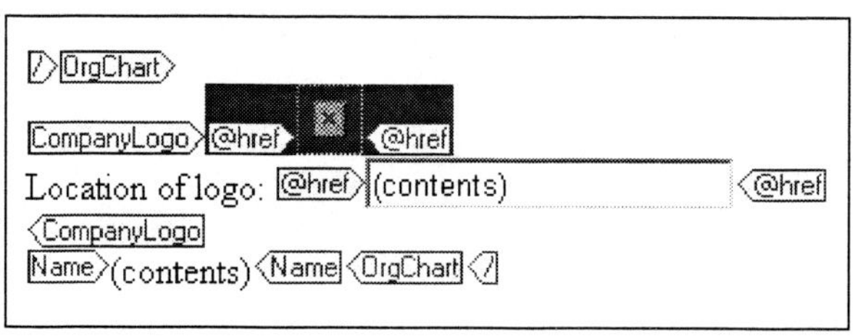

Notice that the `href` attribute attribute appears twice in the Authentic Stylesheet: first as an image, then as an input field.

The HTML preview will look like this:

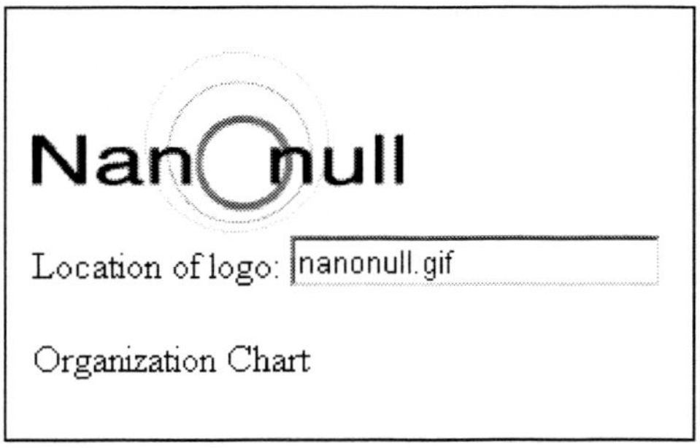

If you have the file `NanonullOrg.xml` open in Authentic View, refresh the Authentic View by changing to another view and then switching back to Authentic View. Otherwise open `NanonullOrg.xml` in Authentic View.

Now, in Authentic View, change the value of the `href` attribute and see the dynamic effect on the logo display. Do it this way:

1. In Authentic View, place your cursor in the "Location of logo" input field.
2. Replace `nanonull.gif` with `altova.gif` (or any other image in any folder); use a relative path to specify the logo's location. Your Authentic View will look like this.

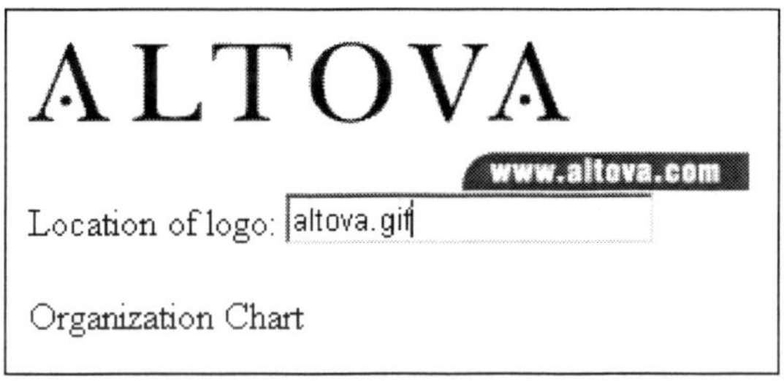

3. Now change the logo back to `nanonull.gif`.

Note: You cannot change XML values in the HTML Preview of Stylesheet Designer since this is **an output** of the XML document. Authentic View, on the other hand, is **a view** of the XML document.

Processing element content for output

The processing of element content is defined in the Design Document in the same way as the processing of attribute values is: drag the element from the schema tree, drop it into the Design Document as an Authentic Stylesheet component, specify further XSLT/XPath processing, and apply the required formatting.

In this section you will add element content to the Design Document. The objective is to create the contents of the `//Office/Name` element on one line, and the contents of the `//Desc/para` elements below it. This is how you will do it.

Inserting the `//Office/Name` element

1. Place the cursor before the end tag of the `OrgChart` element and press Enter to insert a line break.
2. Expand the `Office` element in the schema tree.
3. Drag the `//Office/Name` element to the location before the `OrgChart` end tag, and create the element as contents. Your Design Document will look like this.

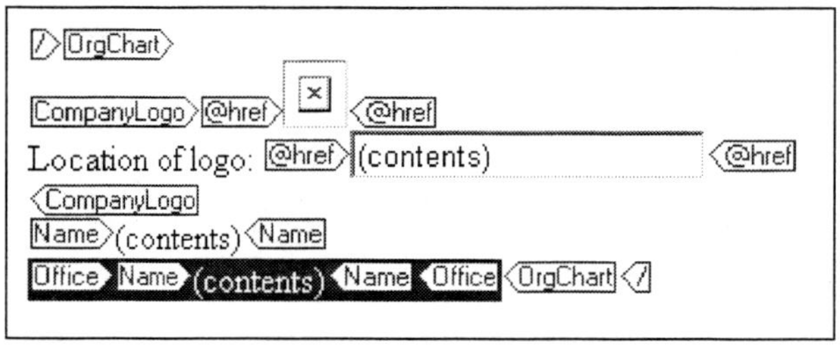

Notice that tags are created for all levels of the hierarchy between the `//Office/Name` element and the containing `OrgChart` element.

The HTML Preview will look like this:

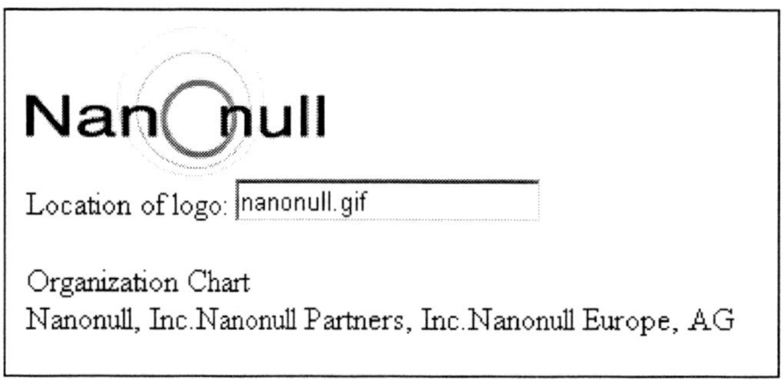

The Working XML file has three `//Office/Name` elements. Notice that the contents of all three are output (without any whitespace between elements).

Create the `//Office/Desc/para` element

1. Put a line break before the `OrgChart` end tag.
2. Drag the `//Office/Desc/para` element to the location before the `OrgChart` end tag, and create the element as contents. Your Design Document will look like this.

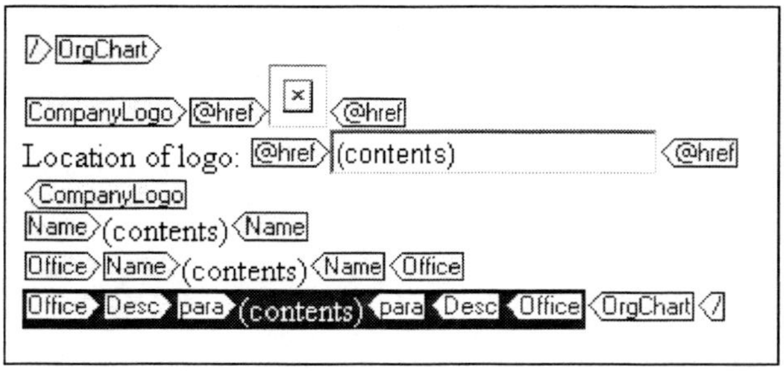

Notice that tags for all ancestors of `para` are created up to but excluding the containing ancestor (which is `OrgChart`).

Now look at the HTML preview.

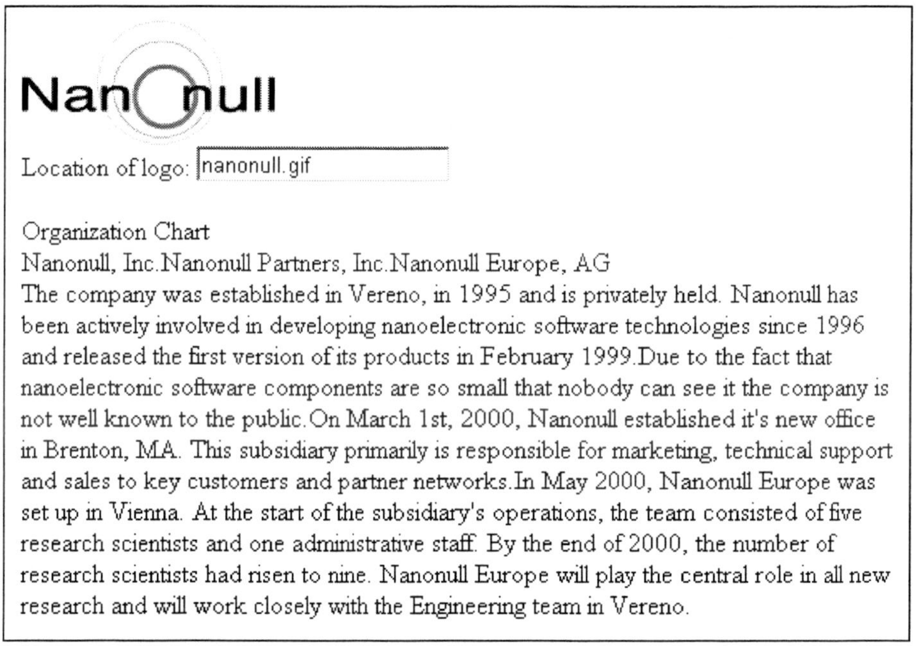

All three `//Office/Name` elements are displayed before the `//Office/Desc/para` elements. This is not the desired result. What we want is the content of the first `//Office/Name` element followed by the content of the `Desc/para` elements for that office, and then the content of the second `//Office/Name` element followed by the contents of the `Desc/para` elements for that office; and so on.

If you look at your Design Document, you will see that all the `//Office/Name` elements are processed first, and then all the `//Office/Desc/para` elements. In order to process the `Name` child element of an `Office` element followed immediately by the `Desc/para` elements of that `Office` element, you need to change the location of the `//Office/Desc/para` element so that it is included in a single `Office` element loop and follows the `Name` element directly.

Changing the location of the `//Office/Desc/para` element

1. Select the `//Office/Desc/para` element by clicking the start tag of its `Office` element.
2. Drag the selected element and drop it before the end tag of the `Office` element on the line above. Your Design Window will display the error message shown below.

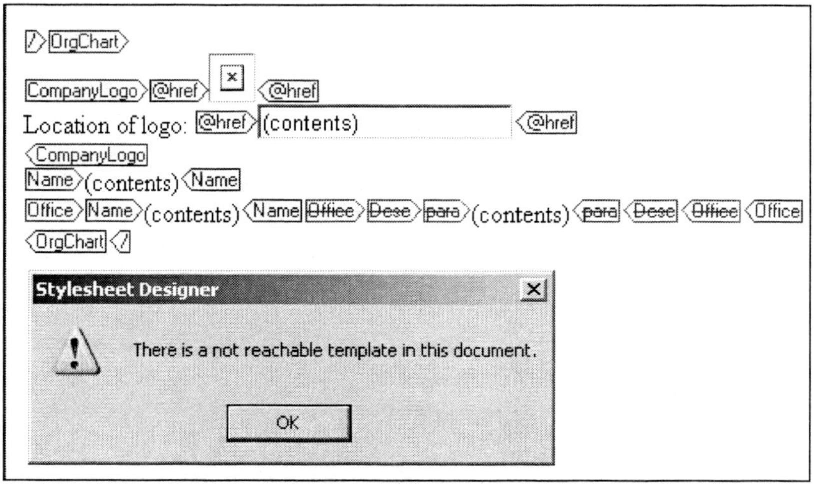

Notice that the tags of the unreachable template have a red strikethrough. The template is unreachable because the XPath `Office/Desc/para` within the containing `Office` element is wrong because the XPath in context then is: `//Office/Office/Desc/para`; that's one `Office` element too many. The correct XPath in the context of the `Office` element is `Desc/para`, not `Office/Desc/para`.

3. In the error dialog, click OK, then press Ctrl + Z to undo the move.
4. Select the `Desc/para` element by clicking the start `Desc` tag.
5. Drag the `Desc/para` element and drop it before the end tag of the `Office` element on the line above. Your Design Window will now look like this.

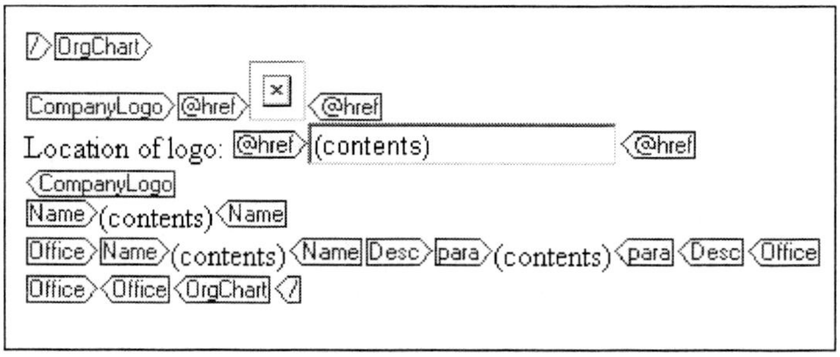

6. Delete the `Office` start and end tags on the last line, and put a line break after the `//Office/Name` element and after the `//Office/Desc` element. Your Design Window should now look like this.

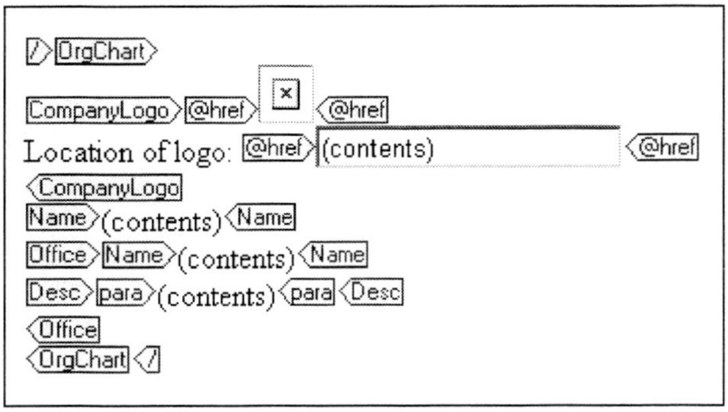

The HTML Preview will look like this:

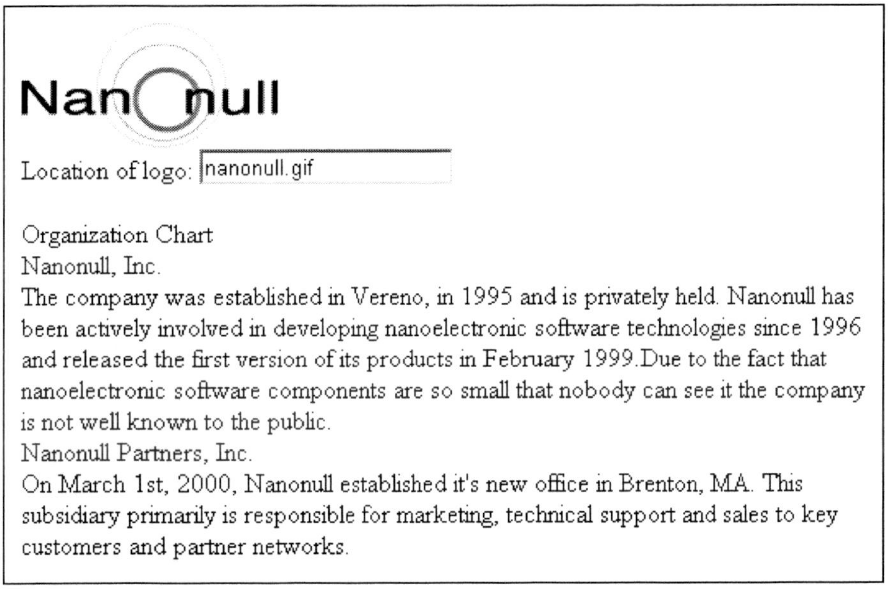

The PDF Preview will look like this:

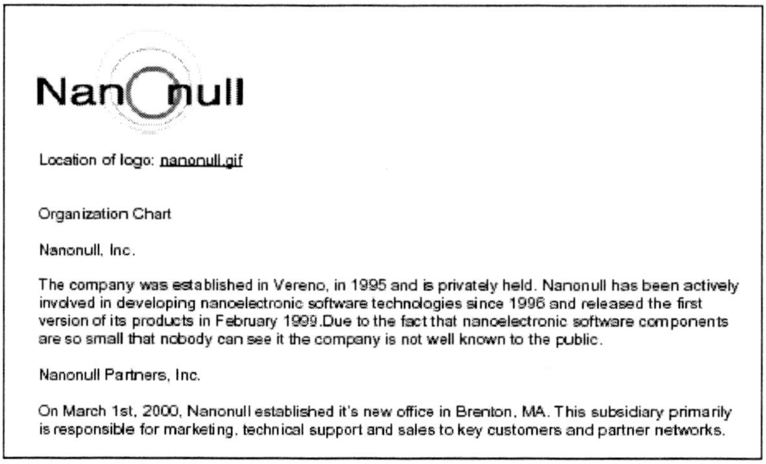

Nanonull

Location of logo: nanonull.gif

Organization Chart

Nanonull, Inc.

The company was established in Vereno, in 1995 and is privately held. Nanonull has been actively involved in developing nanoelectronic software technologies since 1996 and released the first version of its products in February 1999.Due to the fact that nanoelectronic software components are so small that nobody can see it the company is not well known to the public.

Nanonull Partners, Inc.

On March 1st, 2000, Nanonull established it's new office in Brenton, MA. This subsidiary primarily is responsible for marketing, technical support and sales to key customers and partner networks.

Notice that although the formatting in both previews is generally similar, there are small differences. These are because the two outputs have different defaults for their formatting properties. You can override these defaults by explicitly specifying the formatting you want.

Formatting the components

The formatting that can be applied to an Authentic Stylesheet component is of two types: text formatting and block formatting. Text formatting is applied to text, and includes font sizes, font weights, and font colors. Block formatting can be applied to components that have been explicitly defined as blocks, and include background colors for the block, spacing around the block, and borders for the block. A component can be explicitly defined as a block by assigning it a pre-defined format.

To apply formatting to a component, the following three mechanisms are used, either alone or in combination:

- Applying a pre-defined format (a pre-defined format includes text and block formatting, and is also used to define a component as a block)
- Applying Text Style properties (in the Text Style Window or using toolbar icons)
- Applying Block Style properties (in the Block Style Window; additional properties are available with toolbar icons)

In this section, you will learn to apply formatting using all three mechanisms.

Applying a pre-defined format to para

1. Select the `//Desc/para` element by clicking the start tag of the `para` element.
2. Right-click, and select **Change to | Paragraph**.

This creates the pre-defined paragraph formatting **for each** para element child of `Desc`. The Design Document now looks like this:

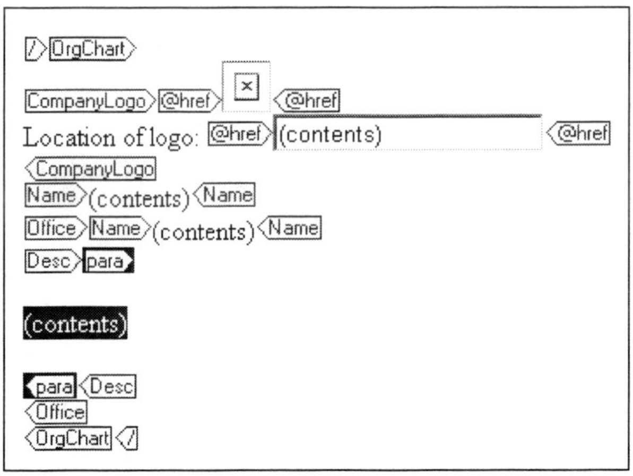

Alternatively, select the `(contents)` placeholder of the `//Desc/para` element (by clicking the placeholder), and in the drop-down Pre-defined Format menu in the toolbar (shown below) select **Paragraph (p)**.

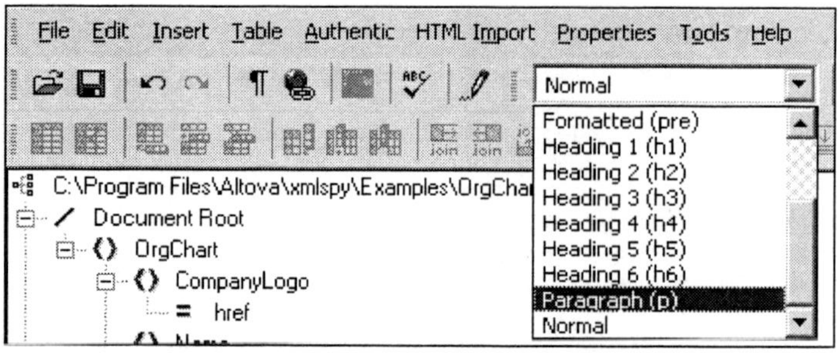

This applies the same formatting as above. Note that in the first case, the **`para` element was selected** and its processing was changed from normal to paragraph; in the second case the **`(contents)` placeholder was selected** and a pre-defined paragraph format was applied. In both cases, each `para` child element of `Desc` is created as a paragraph.

Note: If you select the `para` element—and not the `(contents)` placeholder—and then apply the pre-defined paragraph format (from the Drop-down Format menu in the toolbar), the contents of all `para` elements in that `Desc` element will run on and be displayed as a single paragraph, i.e. the entire selection is formatted as a single paragraph.

Specifying Text Style properties

1. Select the `(contents)` placeholder of the `/OrgChart/Name` element. Notice that the Text Style Window is enabled, but the Block Style Window is disabled (grayed-out). This is because the selected component is not a block. It gives the appearance of being a block because it is on a line by itself. This effect, however, was created by a line-break—which by itself **does not** make the component a block.
2. In the Text Style Window, select the Text tab, and set the font to Arial, 18pt, bold.

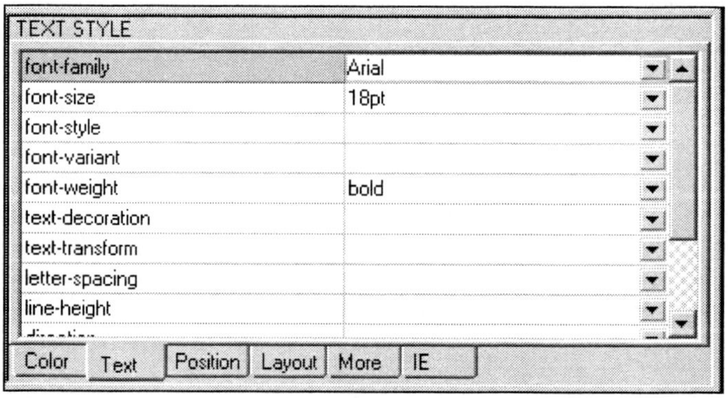

3. Now select the color tab, and specify a color for the text. The component in the Design Window displays the specified formatting.
4. Check the HTML Preview, and make changes if required.
5. In the Design Window, select the `(contents)` placeholder of the `//Office/Name` element, set the font to Arial, 15pt, bold, and give it a color.
6. Insert a line break before the `Office` element.
7. Check the HTML and PDF Previews, and take a look at the XSLT and XSL-FO code.

Your HTML Preview should look something like this:

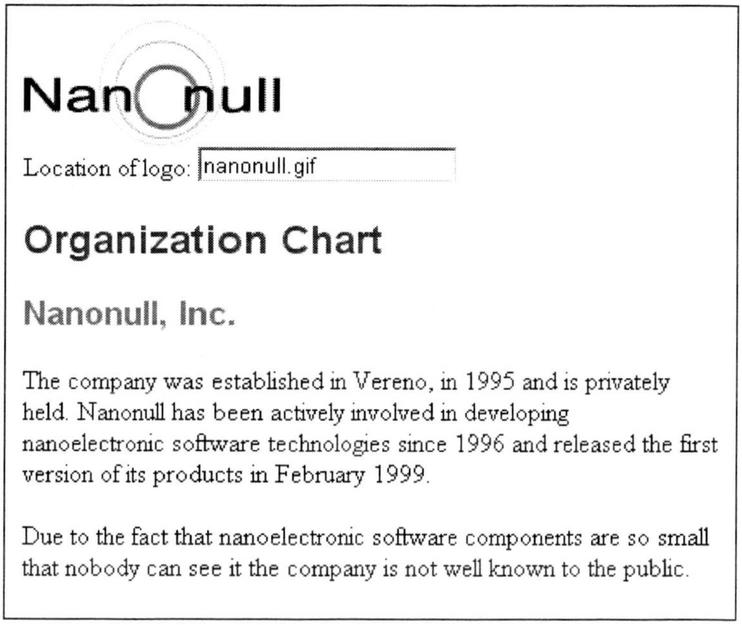

Note: To control vertical spacing for text components, use the line-break feature in the Design Window and/or the properties in the Position tab of the Text Style window.

Text formatting icons: You can also make text bold, italic, or underlined by highlighting the text and then clicking the appropriate icon in the toolbar. These icons are shortcuts to creating the required values in the Text Style Window.

Specifying Block Style properties

Block Style properties are applied to blocks via the Block Style Window. In order for this window to be enabled, the selected component must be a block. A component is specified as a block by assigning it a pre-defined format.

1. Select the `href` element that has been created as an image (not the one created as an Input Field) by clicking its start tag.
2. From the drop-down Pre-defined Format menu in the toolbar, select Block (div). This makes the image display as a block, and enables the Block Style Window.
3. Place the cursor before the `CompanyLogo` start tag and press Backspace to remove the line break.
4. In the Block Style Window, select the Layout tab (shown below), and specify `border-bottom-style=solid`; `border-bottom-width=medium`; and any color for `border-bottom-color`.

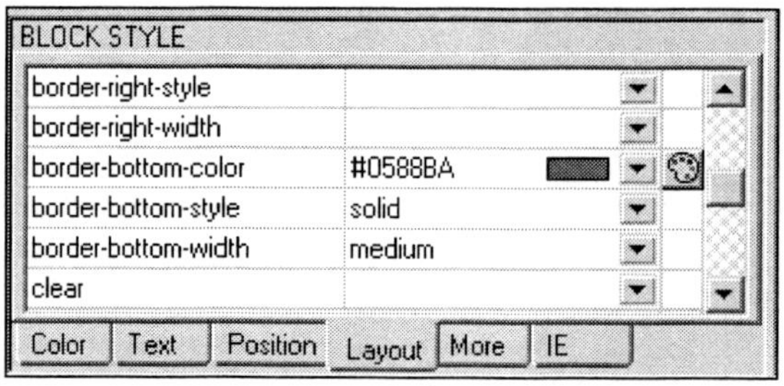

5. Check the HTML Preview, which should look like this:

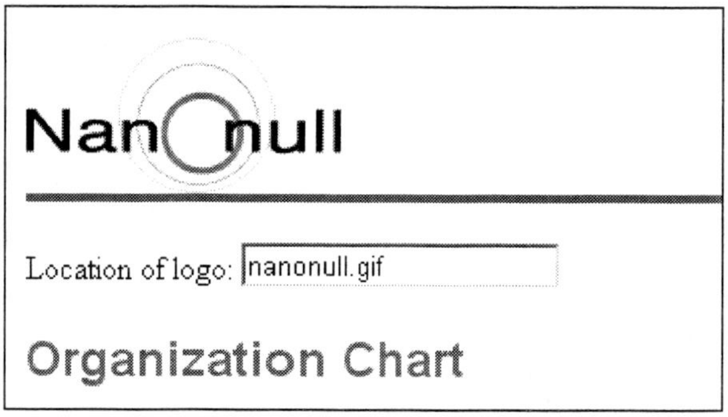

The logo is flush with the left margin of the page and with the bottom border. Some padding would improve the display.

6. In the Design Window, select the `href` element again, and in the Layout tab of the Block Style Window set the `padding-left` and `padding-bottom` properties to 10px. The HTML Preview will now look like this:

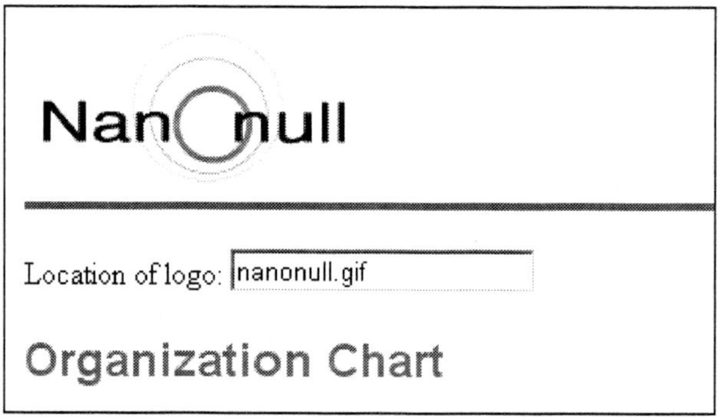

The PDF Preview will look like this:

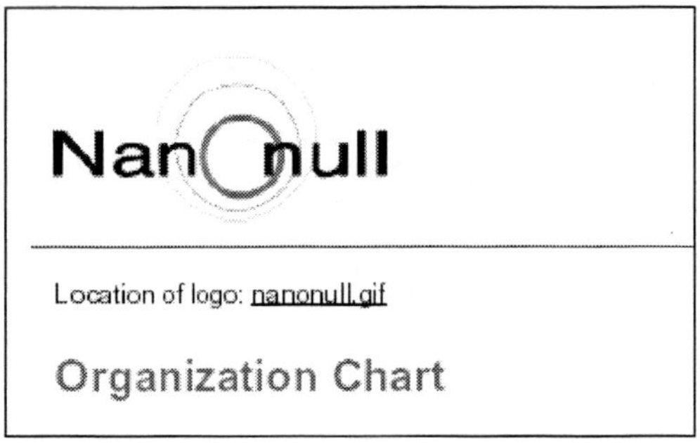

Now format the components currently in the Design Document as you wish using the pre-defined formats and the Text Style and Block Style Windows.

Inserting a dynamic SPS table

A dynamic SPS table (hereafter called dynamic table) organizes the child nodes (elements and attributes) of a given element into a table. The table can have headers and footers which can have static or dynamic content, and structures, that can be modified. One dimension of the table (say the columns) consists of the child elements; the other (the rows) would then consist of the occurrences of the selected element. Dynamic tables are ideal for presenting the content of repeating data structures.

The structure and formatting of a dynamic table are defined by you, the designer of the Authentic Stylesheet. The Authentic View user is not allowed to modify the formatting of the table, but can insert, append, or delete occurrences of the element that has been created as the table, i.e. modify one dimension of the table structure. The Authentic View user can also edit the XML content (dynamic content) of the table (excepting for Auto-Calculation nodes and nodes that you specify as non-editable).

Inserting the `Person` element as a dynamic SPS table

The `Department` element has two child elements: `Name` and `Person`. The `Person` element has several child elements: `First`, `Last`, `Title`, etc. Since there are a number of people in a given department, the `Person` element will occur several times. The `Person` element is a repeating data structure.

In this part of the tutorial, you will first insert the department's name and, below it, a table containing the names and other details of the persons in that department. Do the following:

1. Drag the `//Department/Name` element from the schema tree, and drop it just after the end tag of the Desc element. Create it as contents, and give it suitable text formatting.
2. Drag the `//Department/Person` element from the schema tree, and drop it just after the end tag of the `//Department/Name` element.
3. In the pop-up menu that appears, select Create as Table. The Create dynamic table dialog appears:

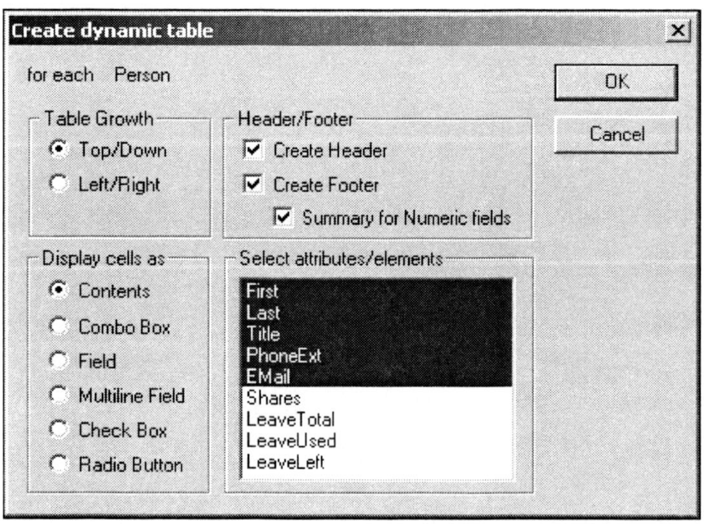

4. All the child element fields are highlighted by default, and will be created as columns. Deselect `Shares`, `LeaveTotal`, `LeaveUsed`, and `LeaveLeft`. The default setting

creates a header row for the table, in which the header for each column is the name of the respective child element. If the table grows fom top to bottom, you can also create a footer with or without sums of numeric columns. Check the Create Footer and Summary for Numeric Fields checkboxes. Click OK to create the table.

5. To adjust the vertical spacing, put a line break before the `//Department/Name` element and after the `//Department/Person` element. This part of the Design Document will look like this:

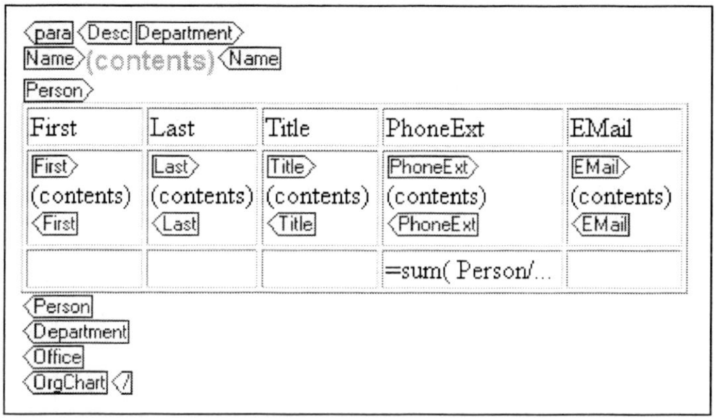

Notice that the column headers are the names of the child elements of the `Person` element, and that a footer has been created with a sum of the numeric column for telephone extensions.

In the HTML Preview, the corresponding output for the first department will look like this:

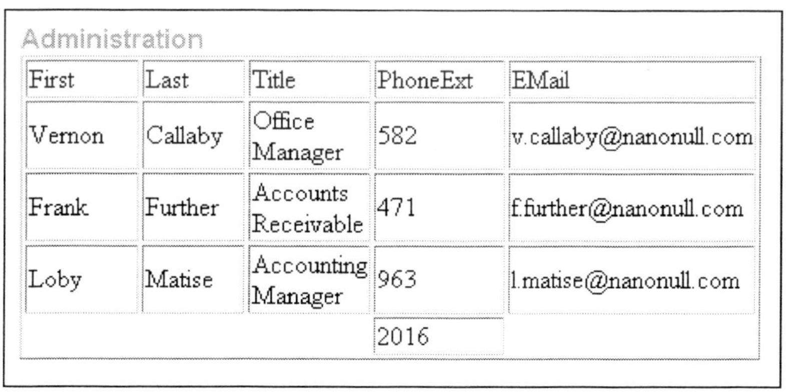

Administration

First	Last	Title	PhoneExt	EMail
Vernon	Callaby	Office Manager	582	v.callaby@nanonull.com
Frank	Further	Accounts Receivable	471	f.further@nanonull.com
Loby	Matise	Accounting Manager	963	l.matise@nanonull.com
			2016	

The PDF Preview will look like this:

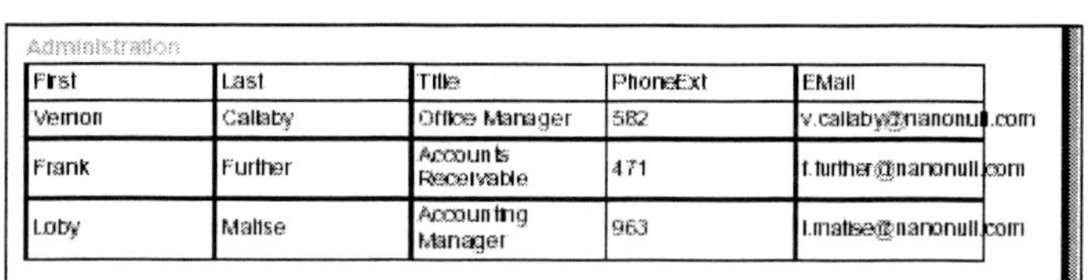

Administration

First	Last	Title	PhoneExt	EMail
Vernon	Callaby	Office Manager	582	v.callaby@nanonull.com
Frank	Further	Accounts Receivable	471	f.further@nanonull.com
Loby	Matise	Accounting Manager	963	l.matise@nanonull.com

Notice that the contents of the EMail column flow over the cell and table boundary. This is because the email address is a single non-breaking string for which hyphenation is not possible. If you look closely, you will also notice that all the column widths are equal. This is the default for XSL-FO output. In Stylesheet Designer, however, you can modify column widths and other table properties.

Modifying table properties

To modify the table properties, place the cursor anywhere in the table, and click  or **Table | Table Properties**. The following dialog pops up:

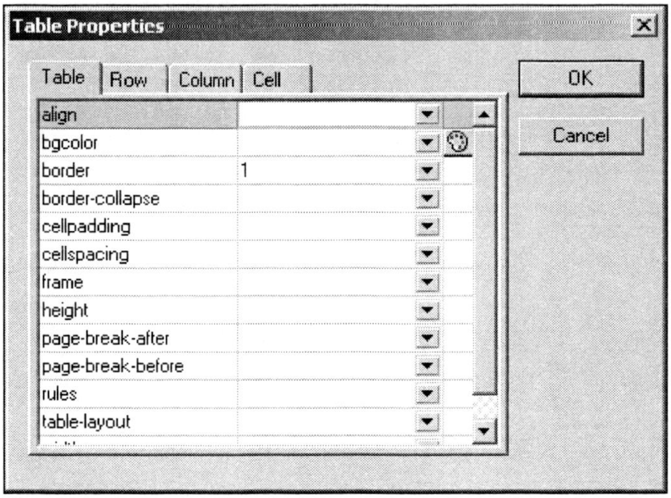

Make the following modifications:

1. For the entire table, in the Table tab, set border to 1, cellpadding to 3, cellspacing to 0, and width to 100%.
2. To give the header row a background color, place the cursor in the header row, click **Table | Table Properties**, and, in the Row tab, specify a bgcolor.
3. Now give the footer row a background color using the same method.
4. To modify the column widths, place the cursor in the first column, click **Table | Table Properties**, and, in the Column tab, specify a width of 15%. Repeat the steps for each column, using the following widths: second column=15%, third column=25%, fourth column=15%, fifth column=30%.
5. If you wish to assign the column headers some text formatting, mark each header, and assign properties in the Text Style Window. You can also set text alignment properties.

   The HTML Preview should look something like this:

Administration

First	Last	Title	Ext	Email
Vernon	Callaby	Office Manager	582	v.callaby@nanonull.com
Frank	Further	Accounts Receivable	471	f.further@nanonull.com
Loby	Matise	Accounting Manager	963	l.matise@nanonull.com
			2016	

The PDF Preview will look like this:

Administration (3)

First	Last	Title	Ext	EMail
Vernon	Callaby	Office Manager	582	v.callaby@nanonull.com
Frank	Further	Accounts Receivable	471	f.further@nanonull.com
Loby	Matise	Accounting Manager	963	l.matise@nanonull.com
			2016	

Advanced table formatting
Later in the tutorial, we will increase the complexity of this dynamic table, at which stage you will learn advanced table formatting. In the Using Auto-Calculation section, you will append columns to the dynamic table and split the header into two rows. In Creating the Table Footer, you will add content to the footer and format it.

Note:

1. Footers must be created when the table is first created. **You cannot append a row and treat it as a footer** because every appended row will repeat after each occurrence of the element that was created as the table. We will format the footer in the Creating the Table Footer section later in the tutorial.
2. When you set column widths as percentages, they must add up to 100%.
3. You can also modify column widths by dragging column borders. However, it is advisable not to mix different measurement formats (pecentages and absolute values) or different measurement units (px and mm).

Inserting a static SPS table

A static SPS table is an Authentic Stylesheet component that you use for improved visual presentation. The cells of a static SPS table can be filled with various types of components: dynamic content (from the XML document) as well as static content (from other sources; such content could be text in the Authentic Stylesheet, images, etc.).

The structure and formatting of a static SPS table are defined by you, the designer of the Authentic Stylesheet; the Authentic View user is not allowed to modify either the structure or formatting. The Authentic View user can edit the XML content (dynamic content) of the table (excepting for Auto-Calculation nodes and nodes that you specify as non-editable).

Inserting a static table with miscellaneous content

The objective is to create a table that presents the contact details of each office in a visually attractive way. Let us put the address in the first column of a two-column table, and the telephone and fax numbers and the e-mail address in the second column. We start with a table of three columns and one row, and edit it as we go along.

To create the static SPS table, do the following:

1. In the Design Window, place the cursor after the end tag of the `//Office/Name` element (by clicking the element's end tag and pressing Cursor Right). You get a blinking cursor after the end tag of `//Office/Name`.
2. Click the table icon, or select **Table | Insert Table**. This causes a static SPS table to be inserted at the cursor location. The Insert Table dialog (shown below) appears.

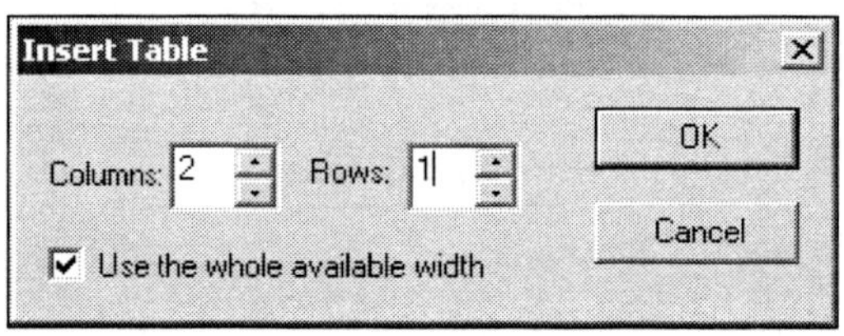

3. In the Insert Table dialog, specify a table of 2 columns and 1 row, and click OK. A 2x1 table is inserted in the Design Document (shown below).

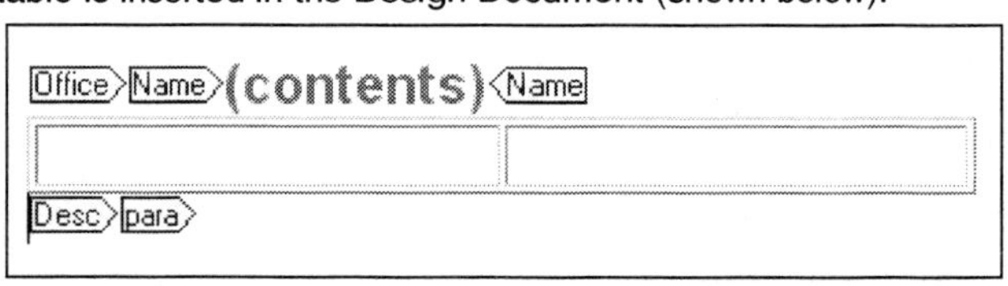

4. Drag the `Address` element from the schema tree and drop it into the first cell of the table.
5. Select Create Table from the popup. This opens the "Create dynamic table" dialog box.

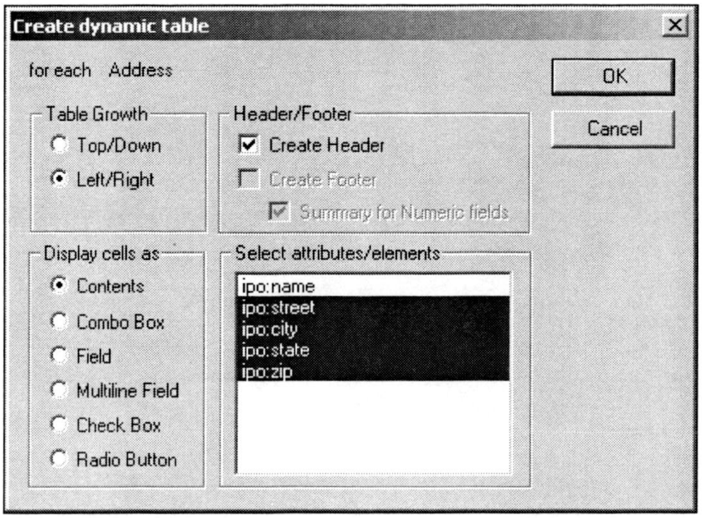

6. Click the "ipo:name" entry (in the Select attributes/elements box) to deselect it.
7. In the Table Growth option, select the Left/Right radio button. Notice that the option for creating a Footer is automatically disabled; it is enabled only when the dynamic table grows top-down. Click OK. This inserts a dynamic SPS table in the first cell of the static SPS table you just created.
8. Set the cellspacing for the outer static table to 0 and the border for the inner dynamic table to 0 (in the Table Properties for each). Then format the field names as shown below. Your Design Document will now look like this:

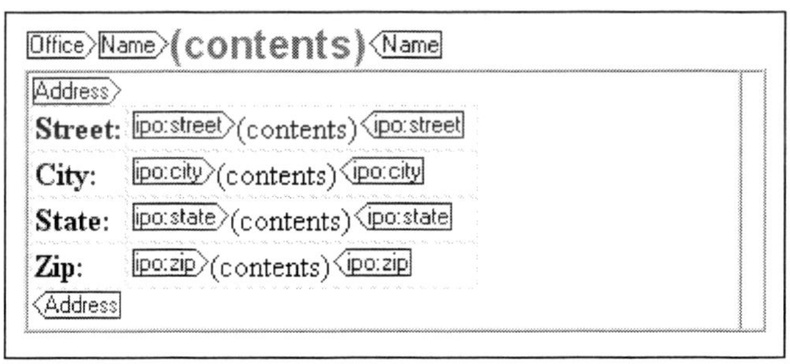

9. Place the cursor in the second column of the outer static table, and click  or select **Table | Insert Table**. In the Insert Table dialog, define the table as having 2 columns and 3 rows. This creates a nested static table in the second column of the outer static table.
10. Click in the first column of the new static table, and enter Phone, Fax, and E-mail in each row as shown below, and make the font bold. In the Table Properties dialog, set the table border to 0.

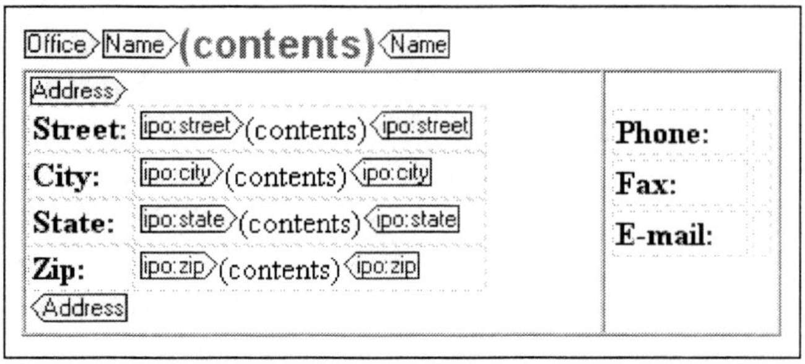

11. Drag the `Phone` element from the schema tree, and drop it in the cell adjacent to that with "Phone" in it. Select Create Contents from the popup.
12. Do the same for the `Fax` and `Email` elements: drop these elements into the appropriate cells, selecting "Create Contents" in both cases.

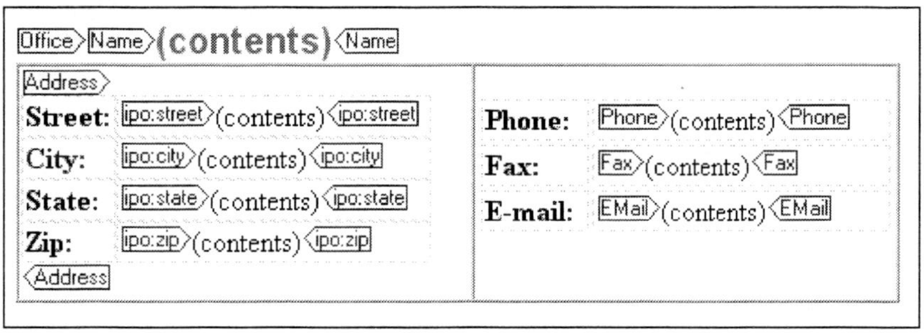

Check the HTML Preview. The static SPS table in the HTML Preview should look like this:

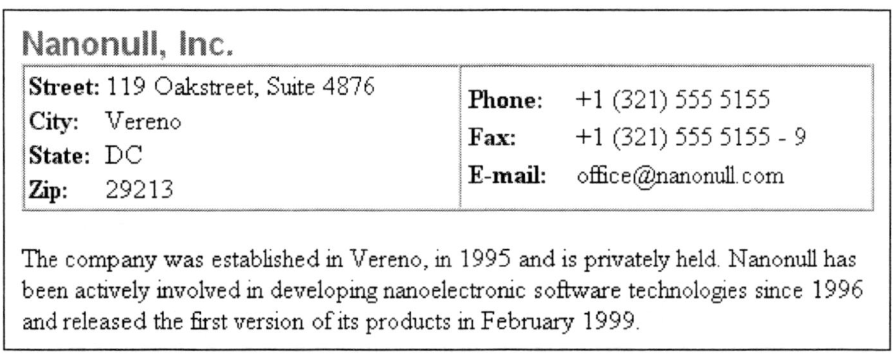

Adjusting the vertical alignment

In the HTML Preview, notice that the text in the two columns are not vertically aligned. You can ensure alignment by vertically aligning both columns of the outer static table, and specifying the same cellspacing value for both nested tables.

1. Place the cursor anywhere in the first column of the static table, taking care not to place it in the nested table in that column.
2. Click 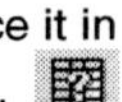 or **Table | Table Properties**, and select the Column tab.
3. For the `valign` property, select the value `top`.

4. Repeat the above three steps for the second column of the outer static table.
5. Specify cellspacing of 4px for both nested tables (in the Table tab of the Table Properties dialog for each table).
6. Check the HTML Preview to see the effect of your changes. The text in both columns should now be aligned.

Joining cells

The objective is to have the State and Zip fields apper in a single row (so that both columns have three-row tables). Do the following:

1. Place the cursor in the cell containing the text "Zip:".
2. Click or **Table | Join cell above**.
3. Change the text to "State & Zip:".
4. Place the cursor in the cell containing the contents of the `ipo:state` element.
5. Click or **Table | Join cell below**.
6. Put a space between the two `(contents)` placeholders in the cell.

The nested dynamic table in the Design Document will now look like this:

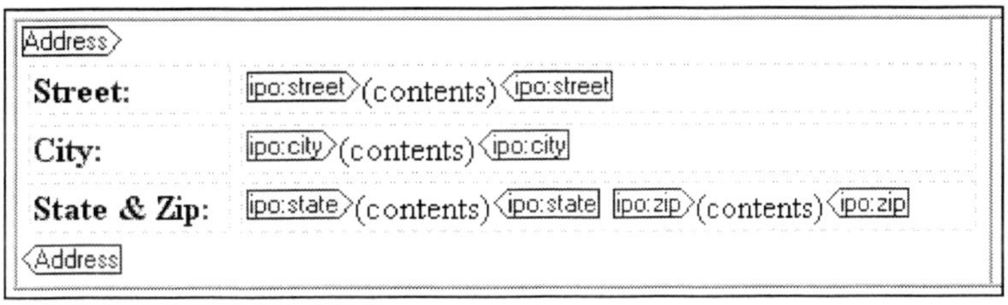

Specifying the widths of columns

Check the HTML and PDF Previews so you can judge the optimal column widths to use. After checking the previews, do the following:

1. Place the cursor anywhere in the first column of the outer static table, but not in the nested dynamic table, and click or **Table | Table Properties**.
2. In the Table tab, set (table) `width` to 100%.
3. In the Column tab, set (column) `width` to 60%.
4. Place the cursor in the second column of the outer static table, but not in the nested static table, and click or **Table | Table Properties**.
5. In the Column tab, set (column) `width` to 40%.
6. For the nested dynamic table, set the table width to 100%, width of first column to 30%, and width of second column to 70%.
7. For the nested static table, set table width to 100%, width of first column to 25%, and width of second column to 75%.

The HTML Preview of the static SPS table should look like this:

Nanonull, Inc.

Street:	119 Oakstreet, Suite 4876	**Phone:**	+1 (321) 555 5155
City:	Vereno	**Fax:**	+1 (321) 555 5155 - 9
State & Zip:	DC 29213	**E-mail:**	office@nanonull.com

The PDF Preview of the static SPS table should look like this:

Nanonull, Inc.

Street:	119 Oakstreet, Suite 4876	**Phone:**	+1 (321) 555 5155 0
City:	Vereno	**Fax:**	+1 (321) 555 5155 4
State & Zip:	DC 29213	**E-mail:**	office@nanonull.com

Inserting bookmarks and hyperlinks

You can create bookmarks (anchors) and hyperlinks in the output documents (HTML, PDF, and Authentic View; in Authentic View, hyperlinking is restricted to linking within the document). In the Authentic Stylesheet, you can insert a bookmark at any location in the Design Document. You can then insert a hyperlink to a bookmark in the document or to any URL.

In this section you will:

- Create a bookmark at the top of your document.
- Create a hyperlink at the bottom of the document which links back to the bookmark.
- Create a hyperlink to a Website.
- Create a hyperlink to a pre-addressed e-mail.

Creating a bookmark at the top of your document

1. Place the cursor just after the start tag of the `OrgChart` element, and right-click.
2. From the popup menu that appears, select **Insert | Bookmark**. The following dialog appears:

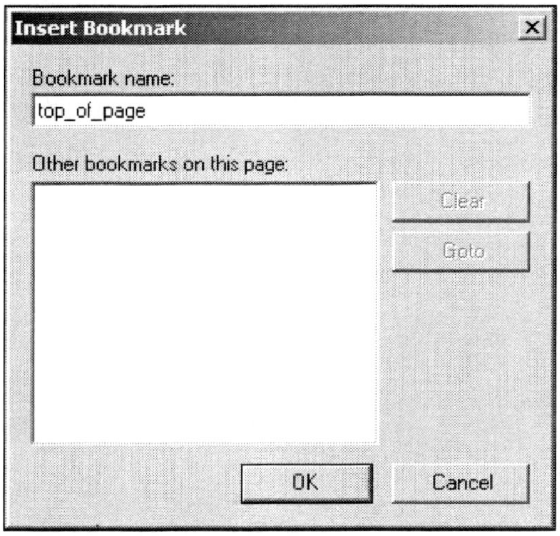

3. Give your bookmark a name, such as `top_of_page`, and click OK. The bookmark is created and is indicated by a flag.

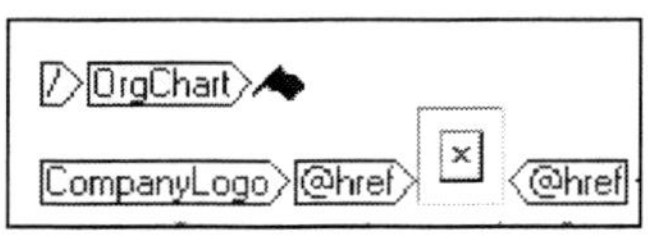

Inserting a hyperlink to a bookmark

1. Place the cursor just before the end tag of the `OrgChart` element, and type in "Go to top".
2. Format this text in the Text Style Window, and modify the line breaks at the bottom of the document to your satisfaction.
3. Highlight the text and right-click.
4. From the popup menu that appears, select **Insert | Hyperlink**. The Insert Hyperlink dialog appears:

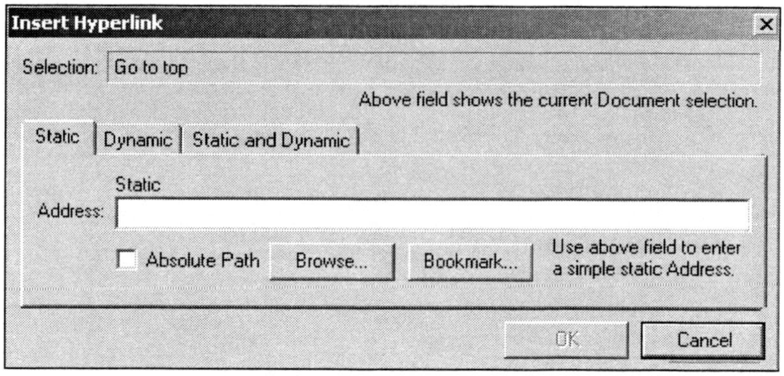

5. Since you want to link to a bookmark, click the Bookmark button. The following dialog appears with all the bookmarks in the document listed.

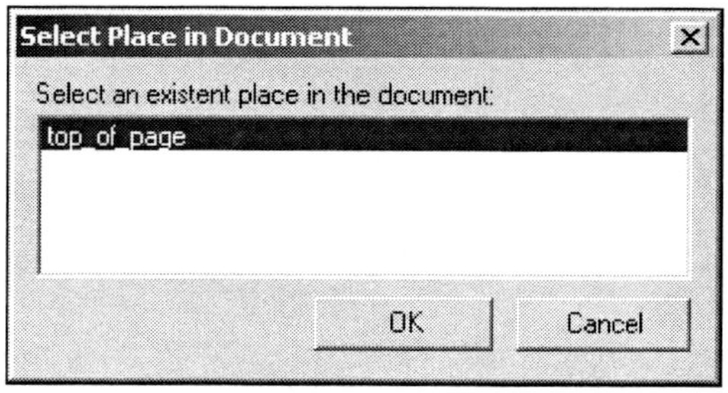

6. Select the bookmark you want, and click OK. The bookmark appears as the static address of the hyperlink in the Insert Hyperlink dialog, i.e. the hyperlink is explicitly specified in the Authentic Stylesheet and is not contained in the XML document.
7. Click OK. The hyperlink is created.
8. In the HTML and PDF Previews, go to the end of the document, and click the hyperlink "Go to top". The view will change to the top of the document.

Inserting a hyperlink to a Website

1. Right-click the logo image, and in the popup menu that appears select **Insert | Hyperlink**.
2. In the Insert Hyperlink dialog that appears, enter `http://www.nanonull.com/` as the static address of the hyperlink target.
3. Click OK. The hyperlink is created.
4. In the HTML and PDF documents, click the logo image. The `www.nanonull.com` Web page appears in the view.

Inserting a hyperlink to a pre-addressed e-mail
The objective is to create a link to an e-mail that has in its address field the correct office or employee address.

1. In the Design Document, right-click the `/OrgChart/Office/EMail` element (or its `(contents)` placeholder), and in the popup menu that appears select **Insert | Hyperlink**.
2. In the Insert Hyperlink dialog, click the **Static and Dynamic** tab.
3. The address consists of a static part and a dynamic part. Fill these in as shown in the

figure below. (Don't miss the period in the dynamic part of the address; this specifies that the content of the current node (shown in the Selection field) is to be processed.)

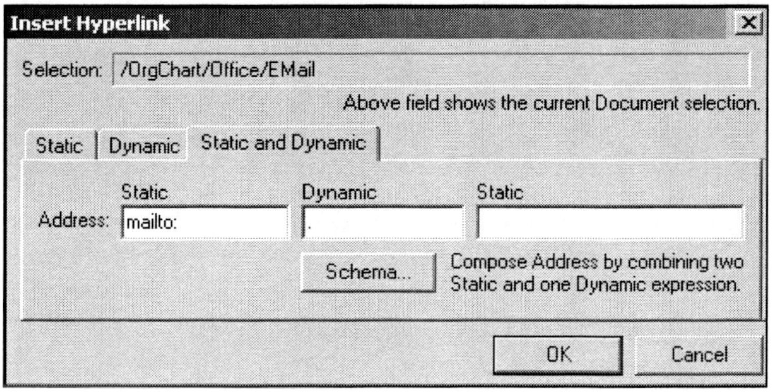

4. Click OK. The hyperlink is created. The static `mailto:` part of the address is the protocol part of the URL. The dynamic part of the address is the content of the `//Office/EMail` element, which is the e-mail address of each office, respectively.
5. Right-click the `//Person/EMail` element (or its `(contents)` placeholder), and follow the same steps as for the previous (office) e-mail address. Each person's e-mail address is now a hyperlink, which, on being clicked, generates an e-mail with that person's e-mail address in the Address field of the e-mail.
6. In the HTML and PDF outputs, click a few e-mail addresses for various offices and persons. For each, a new e-mail with the correct address will be opened.

The HTML Preview is shown below:

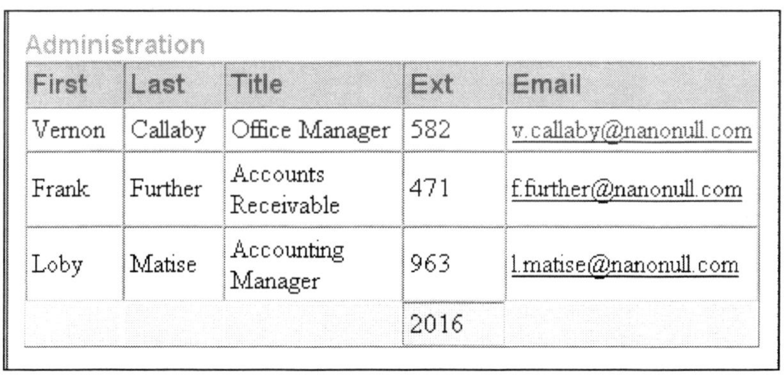

Administration

First	Last	Title	Ext	Email
Vernon	Callaby	Office Manager	582	v.callaby@nanonull.com
Frank	Further	Accounts Receivable	471	f.further@nanonull.com
Loby	Matise	Accounting Manager	963	l.matise@nanonull.com
			2016	

Note: In Authentic View, hyperlinking is restricted to linking **within** the document.

Using Auto-Calculation

Stylesheet Designer includes an Auto-Calculation function, which enables you to display the result of a calculation in Authentic View, HTML, and PDF output. The result is calculated using an XPath expression. It changes dynamically when the value of a node used in the XPath expression changes.

In this tutorial, you will use the Auto-Calculation feature to add the following information to your Authentic Stylesheet:

- The number of employees in each department
- The number of departments and employees in each office
- The leave available to each employee, which is the total leave allowed each employee minus the leave used up.

Auto-calculating employees in each department

1. Place the cursor after the end tag of the `//Department/Name` element.
2. Right-click, and from the popup menu select **Insert | Auto-Calculation | Value**. The Auto-Calculation dialog appears:

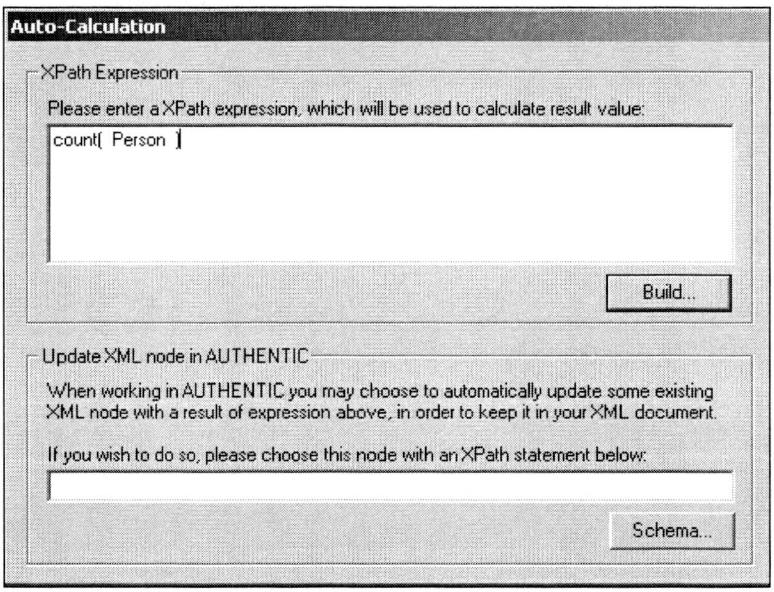

3. Build the XPath expression by clicking the **Build...** button. Notice that the context node is `Department`, indicated by its being highlighted in gray. Now build the XPath expression: `count(Person)` (by double-clicking the required node and XPath operators and functions). Alternatively, you can type the XPath expression directly into the XPath expression field.
4. Click OK. The Auto-Calculation placeholder is inserted.
5. Format the placeholder as desired using the Text Style Window. This part of the Design Document will look something like this:

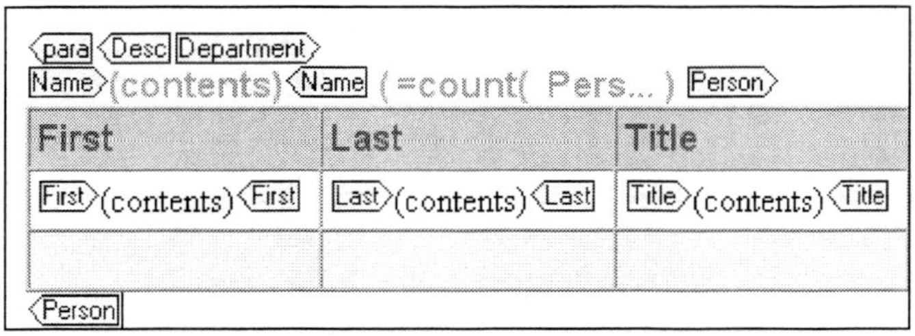

Note that the parentheses in the figure above have been inserted as a design item; they are not placeholder delimiters.

6. Check the HTML and PDF Previews. The HTML Preview of the Auto-Calculation result for the first department is shown below:

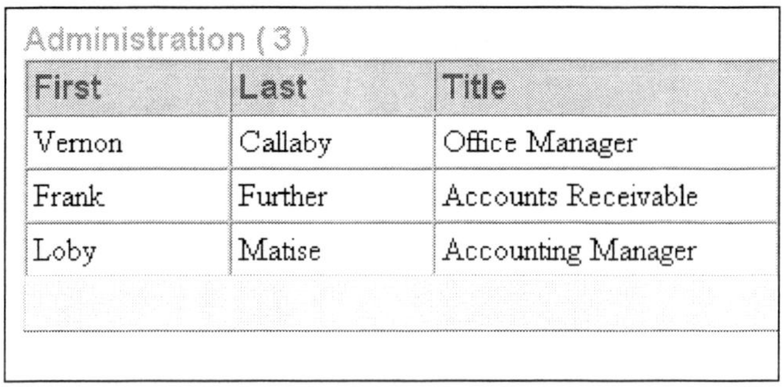

Auto-calculating departments and employees in each office

1. Place the cursor in front of the start tag of the `//Office/Desc` element. (Note that the context node will therefore be `Office`.)
2. Use the method above to create Auto-Calculation values for the number of departments (`count(Department)`) and the number of employees in the department (`count(Department/Person)`).
3. Add the word "departments" after the auto-calculation for the number of departments, and "employees" after the auto-calculation for the number of employees.
4. Format the line as required.

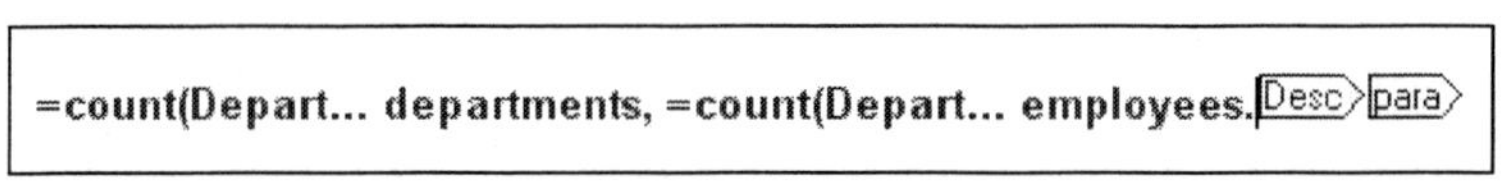

5. Insert the `//Address/ipo:city` element as contents before the Auto-Calculation placeholders, and append the words "Office Summary" so that the line in the Authentic Stylesheet now looks similar to this.

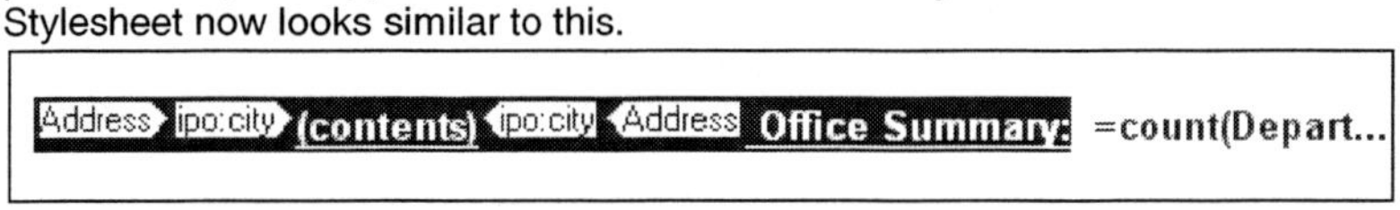

6. Format the inserted components as required. The corresponding line in the HTML Preview should look something like this:

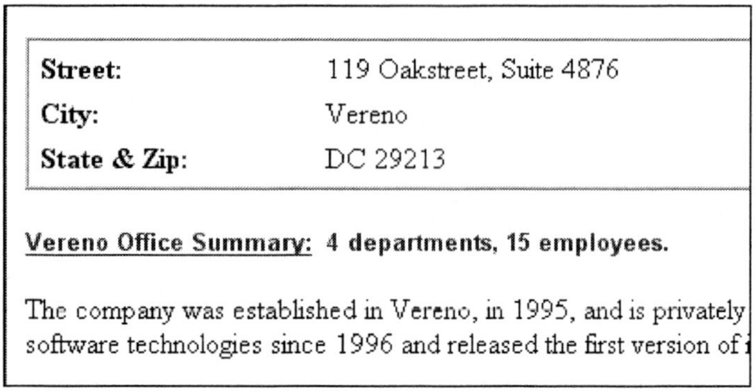

Including the leave details

The objective is to allow the Authentic View user to edit the `LeaveTotal` and `LeaveUsed` entry for each employee. The `LeaveLeft` is auto-calculated (`LeaveTotal` minus `LeaveUsed`), and displayed.

Appending the LeaveTotal, LeaveUsed, and LeaveLeft columns

1. Place the cursor anywhere in the dynamic table for the `Person` element and click **Table | Append Column** or the icon thrice to create three new columns.
2. Type in "Leave Total", "Leave Used" and "Leave Left" as the headers of the three appended columns, respectively.
3. Format the headers appropriately.
4. Drag the `LeaveTotal` and `LeaveUsed` elements from the schema tree into the Leave Total and Leave Used columns respectively, and create them as contents.
5. In the Leave Left column, create an Auto-Calculation (`LeaveTotal-LeaveUsed`). See figure below.

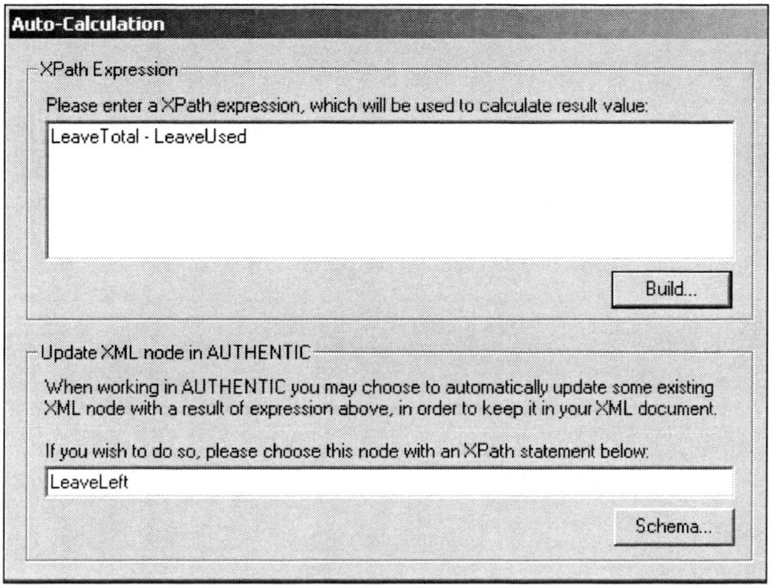

6. Set `LeaveLeft` as the node to be updated. This updates the XML value of `LeaveLeft` whenever the Authentic View user edits the `LeaveTotal` or `LeaveUsed` value.
7. To accommodate the new column, change the font size of all the element contents in the cell to 10pt.
8. Change the table properties as follows: Place the cursor by turn in each of the three new columns, and for each column, in the Table Properties dialog (Column tab), set `align` to center. Reset all the column widths as follows: First = 10%; Last = 13%; Title = 20%; Ext = 7%; EMail = 26%; Leave Total = 8%; Leave Used = 8%, Leave Left = 8%.

The HTML Preview will look like this:

Administration (3)

First	Last	Title	Ext	EMail	Leave Total	Leave Used	Leave Left
Vernon	Callaby	Office Manager	582	v.callaby@nanonull.com	25	4	21
Frank	Further	Accounts Receivable	471	f.further@nanonull.com	22	2	20
Loby	Matise	Accounting Manager	963	l.matise@nanonull.com	25	7	18
			2016				

Notice that although the Leave fields are numeric fields, no summary has been created for these columns in the footer. This is because the Leave columns were appended to the table after the table was created. (If you wish to add a summary for a numeric field after the footer has been created, insert an auto-calculation for that column in the footer.)

The PDF Preview will look like this:

Administration (3)

First	Last	Title	Ext	EMail	Leave Total	Leave Used	Leave Left
Vernon	Callaby	Office Manager	582	v.callaby@nanonull.com	25	4	21
Frank	Further	Accounts Receivable	471	f.further@nanonull.com	22	2	20
Loby	Matise	Accounting Manager	963	l.matise@nanonull.com	25	7	18
			2016				

Note: In the PDF output, if a table overflows onto a new page, the footer (with the full table summary) is inserted before the page-break and the header is created again at the top of the new page.

Restructuring the table header
The header can be restructured by splitting and joining cells. Content of header cells can also be modified, and can include both static and dynamic content. Restructure as follows:

1. Place the cursor in the header cell "Leave Total", and click or **Table | Split Cell Vertically**.
2. Do the same for the Leave Used and Leave Left headers.
3. Place the cursor in the cell containing the text "Leave Left", and click or **Table | Join Cell Left.**
4. Click or **Table | Join Cell Left** once more.
5. Now edit the text in these header cells according to the HTML Preview shown below.

Administration (3)

First	Last	Title	Ext	EMail	Leave		
					Total	Used	Left
Vernon	Callaby	Office Manager	582	v.callaby@nanonull.com	25	4	21
Frank	Further	Accounts Receivable	471	f.further@nanonull.com	22	2	20
Loby	Matise	Accounting Manager	963	l.matise@nanonull.com	25	7	18
			2016				

Now look at the PDF Preview.

Administration (3)

First	Last	Title	Ext	EMail	Leave		
					Total	Used	Left
Vernon	Callaby	Office Manager	582	v.callaby@nanonull.com	25	4	21
Frank	Further	Accounts Receivable	471	f.further@nanonull.com	22	2	20
Loby	Matise	Accounting Manager	963	l.matise@nanonull.com	25	7	18
			2016				

The background-color of the second row of the header is painted over the first row, covering the bottom part of text in header columns that have not been horizontally split. This is because of the way FOP currently renders tables. The workaround is to remove the background-color from the second row (and, if you wish, from the first row as well), and then apply background-color to each cell of the header. Do this as follows

1. Place the cursor in the cell with the text "Total".
2. In the Table Properties dialog (**Table | Table Properties**), go to the Row tab, and delete the entry for `bgcolor`.
3. Place the cursor in the header cell with the text "First", and in the Table Properties dialog, go to the Cell tab, and enter the value for `bgcolor`.
4. Repeat Step 3 above for each header cell of the table. The header in the PDF will now look like this:

Administration (3)

First	Last	Title	Ext	EMail	Leave		
					Total	Used	Left
Vernon	Callaby	Office Manager	582	v.callaby@nanonull.com	25	4	21
Frank	Further	Accounts Receivable	471	f.further@nanonull.com	22	2	20
Loby	Matise	Accounting Manager	963	l.matise@nanonull.com	25	7	18
			2016				

General Note:

- Auto-Calculation can also be created as an Input Field, but the node is non-editable in Authentic View—as is the case with all Auto-Calculations. The Input Field in this case is intended only as a presentational device.
- When an existing XML file is opened in Authentic View, Auto-Calculations are carried out, and the correct Auto-Calculation value is displayed in Authentic View. However, no value in the XML document will be modified. It is only when the user edits a node that is used in the XPath expression of an Auto-Calculation that XML values affected by such an Auto-Calculation are changed.
- When the Authentic View user appends a new `Person` element, all mandatory children are created with empty content. This is because adding mandatory children is the default setting for the `Person` node; it can be changed in the Authentic Node Settings dialog for the `Person` node (select the `Person` element in the Design Window and click **Authentic | Node settings...**). Any non-mandatory child of the `Person` element is indicated with the prompt `Add` *`element-name`*.

Using Conditional Templates

A conditional template defines how a component is to be processed in the event that a specified condition is fulfilled. Multiple conditions can be specified for a component, thus allowing you to provide alternative ways to process a component for a range of conditions. In this section of the tutorial, you will create conditional templates for the following situations:

- Depending on whether an office is located in the US or Europe, the address field will be structured differently.
- In the Office Summary statement, a condition will be used to select the correct city element dependng on whether the US or EU address model is used.
- If an employee is a shareholder, the employee's name will be displayed in bold.

Setting up alternative address content models based on a condition
The objective is to display the appropriate address content model depending on whether the office is located in the US or European Union (EU). You will first create a combo box to accept input for the `Location` element (US or EU), and then create two conditional templates. One conditional template defines that, if the `Location` element has a value of US, the address content model for US locations is used. The other conditional template causes the address content model for EU locations to be used if the value of `Location` is EU.

Include the `Location` element in the Authentic Stylesheet as follows:

1. Put a line above the `//Office/Name` element by making it a block (**Insert | Format | Block (div)**) and by assigning, in the Layout tab of the Block Style Window, suitable values for the following properties: `border-top-color`, `border-top-style`, and `border-top-width`.
2. Insert a line-break after the `//Office/Name` element, and type in "Location: ".
3. Drag the `Location` element from the schema tree, drop it immediately after the text "Location: ", and create it as a combo box. The following dialog appears:

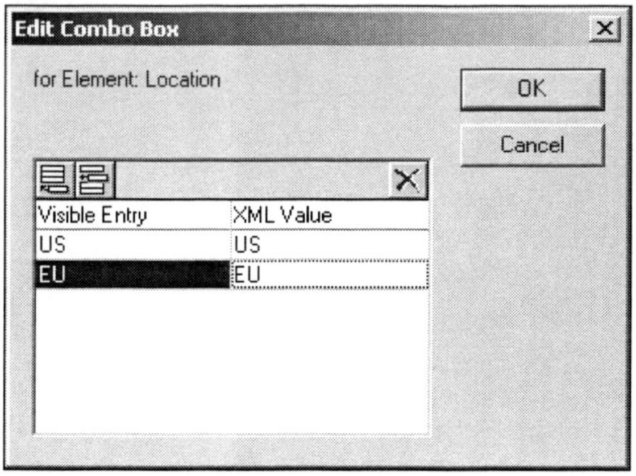

4. Click the Append Row icon twice to append two rows in the dialog box. Enter the two values for US and EU as shown in the figure above. The Visible Entry is the entry that will be visible in the combo box and available for selection. The XML Value is the corresponding value that will be entered in the XML file when a Visible Entry is selected.
5. Click OK when done. The Design Document will now look something like this:

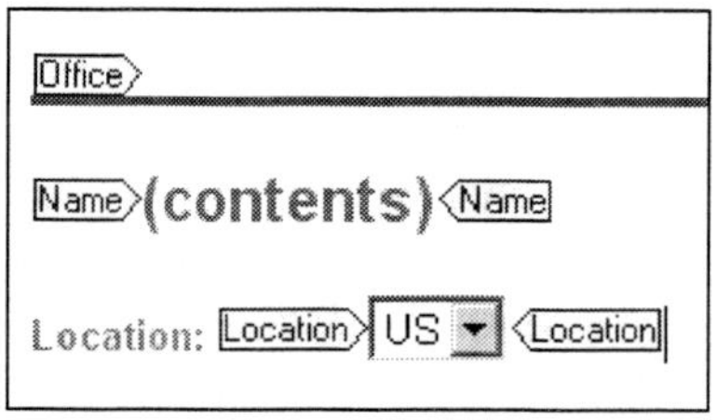

The corresponding output in Authentic View will look like this:

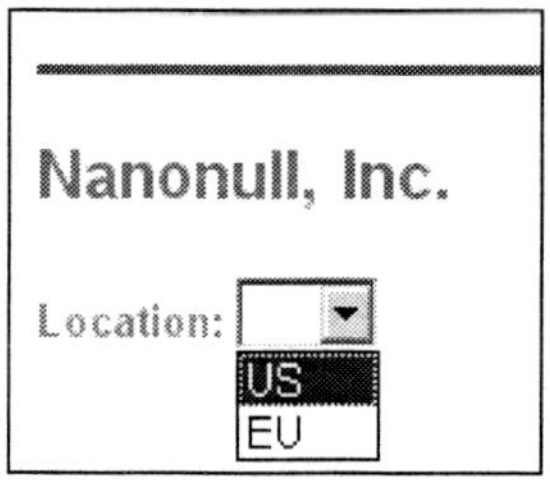

Now specify the conditions that determine the selection of the appropriate address content model. Do the following:

1. Right-click the `Address` element in the static table, and select **Insert | Condition...** to insert a condition for the entire `Address` component in the Authentic Stylesheet. The Edit XPath expression dialog appears:

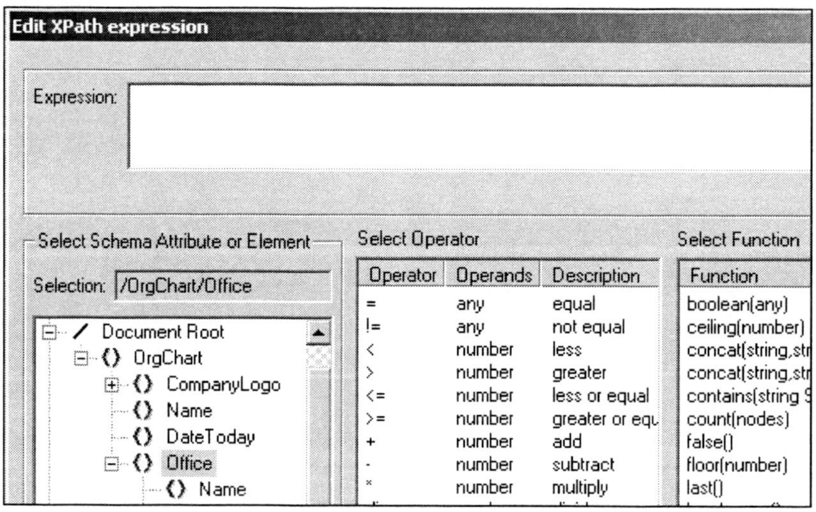

Notice that, in the Select Schema Attribute or Element pane, the `Office` element is highlighted in gray. This indicates that `Office` is the context node, and that the XPath expression will be created relative to it. You can build the XPath expression by double-clicking the required elements/attributes, operators, and functions. Alternatively, you can type the correct XPath expression directly into the Expression field.

2. Build the expression by double-clicking the `Location` element in the Select Schema Attribute or Element pane. This causes `Location` to be entered into the Expression

field. Then click the = operator, and enter "US". The XPath should read: `Location = "US"`.

3. Click OK. The start and end of the conditional template are indicated by cyan tags with a question mark: ? Location = "... ?. The conditional template in the Design Document will look like this:

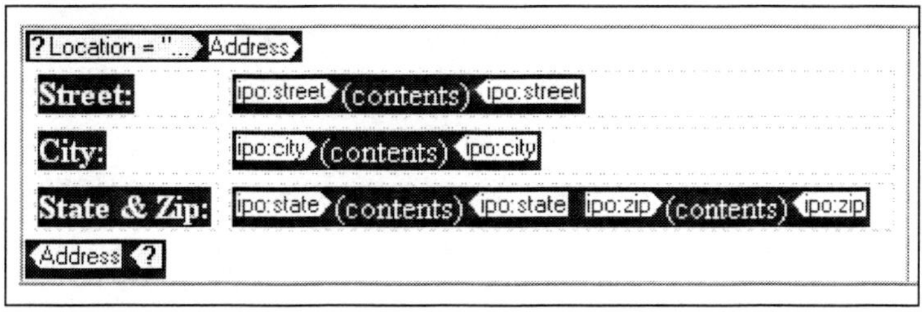

   Notice that the entire dynamic table contained by the `Address` element is contained by the tags of the conditional template. This is because you have inserted the condition around the `Address` element.
4. Since the content model of the `Address` element already in the table is that for the US, do not alter it.

This conditional template defines that its contents will be processed and displayed as specified when the `Location` element has content with a value of US.

Now create a conditional template for displaying the content model for European addresses whenever the value of the `Location` element is EU. Do the following:

1. Right-click either of the condition tags of the conditional template you have just created, and select **Condition | Add Copy**.
2. In the Edit XPath expression dialog that apears, enter or build the XPath: `Location = "EU"`.
3. Click OK. You have now created a second conditional template. Only one conditional template is shown at a time. To see which conditional template is currently displayed, right-click, and select **Condition**. The following context menu appears:

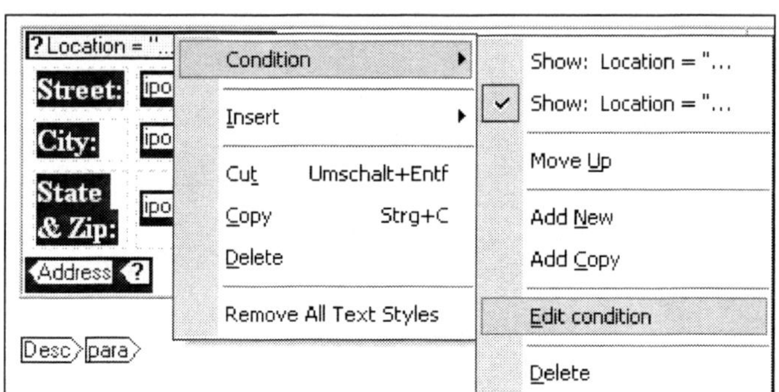

   Which conditional template is currently displayed is indicated with a check mark next to it. (If you wish to edit a condition, select **Edit condition**.)

The currently displayed conditional template specifies processing to be carried out when `Location` has a value of EU. The address content model within it, however, is that for the US (since this is a copy of the first conditional template). Change this as follows:

1. Delete the entire `Address` element (by clicking either its start or end tag, and pressing Delete).
2. From the schema tree drag the element `Address_EU` into the static table, drop it between the conditional template tags, and create it as a table. The following dialog appears:

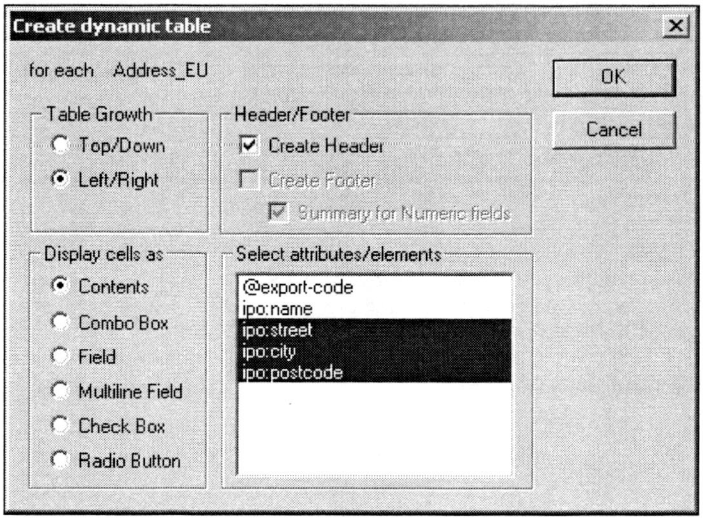

3. Deselect `@export-code` and `ipo:name`. Select Create Header; Table Growth Left/Right; and Display cells as Field.
4. Click OK. The table is created.
5. Format the headers in bold (by highlighting the text and clicking the Bold icon or setting `font-weight` to bold);
6. Set the following table properties: `border` to 0; `cellspacing` to 4px; `table-width` to 100%.

The Design Document looks like this:

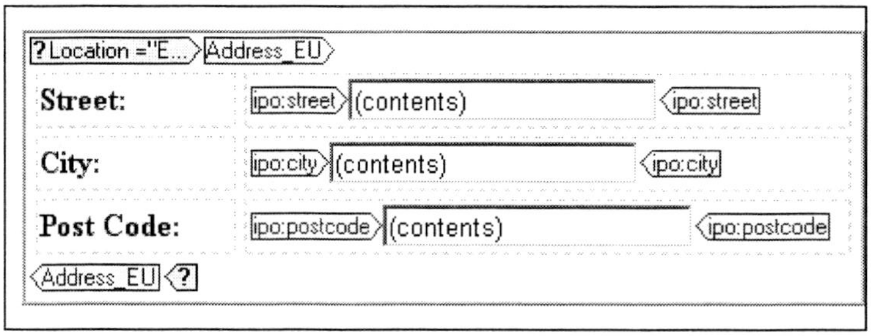

Note that the EU address components have Input Fields; the US address components are created as normal text. However, both types of display can be edited in Authentic View.

The Authentic View output looks like this:

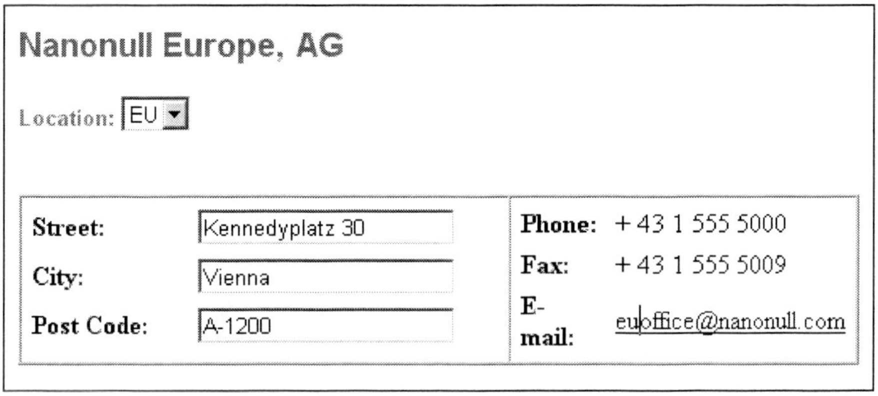

Creating a condition to select the correct city element
In the Office Summary line for each office the city is selected using an Auto-Calculation. Since the city element is a different element in each of the address content models (US and EU address content models), a condition must be created to select the correct city element. Do this as follows:

1. Right-click the `Address` element in the Office Summary line, and select **Insert | Condition...**.
2. In the Edit XPath expression dialog, the context node is `Office`. Enter the XPath: `Address`, and click OK. This creates a conditional template in which the condition tests for the presence of an an `Address` child element. The Design Window will look like this:

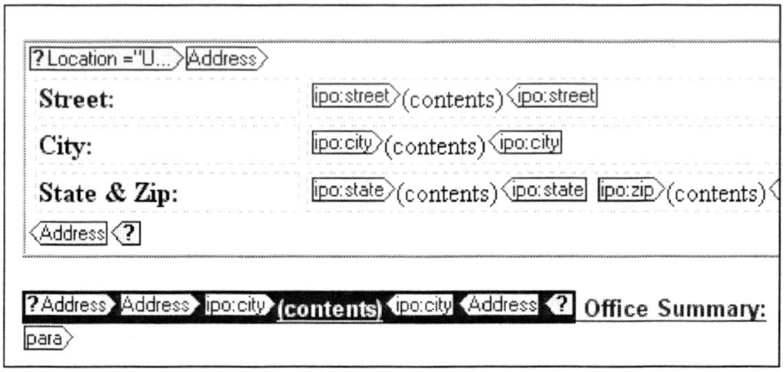

3. The `//Address/ipo:city` element is the correct child of the `Address` element, so do not alter the content of this conditional template. The result is that when the address element is `Address`, the content of the `//Address/ipo:city` element will be selected.
4. Right-click the conditional template tag, and select **Insert | Condition... | Add New**.
5. In the Edit XPath expression dialog, enter the XPath: `Address_EU`, and click OK.
6. Drag the `//Address_EU/ipo:city` element into the Design Window, and create it as contents of the new conditional template. The Design Window will look like this:

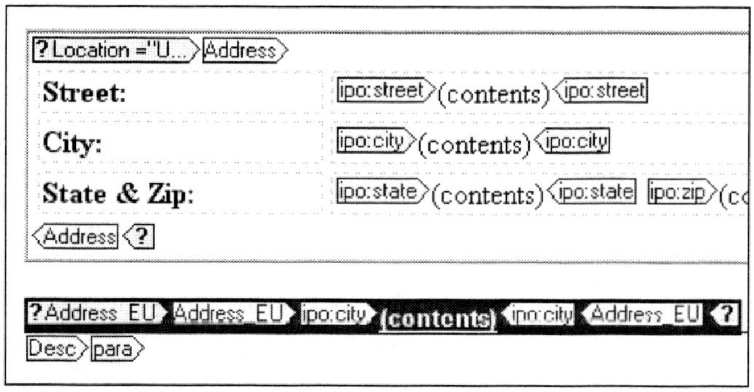

The result is a condition that selects the content of the `//Address_EU/ipo:city` element when the address element is `Address_EU`.

Creating a condition to make sharehoders' names bold
In the dynamic table for the `Person` element, you will first create a column for the number of shares each employee holds. Then create a conditional template around the `First` element to display the element's content in bold if the `Share` element is non-empty and greater than 0. Do the following.

1. Place the cursor in the Leave column, and click **Table | Insert Column** or the icon to insert a column before the Leave column.
2. Type in the column header Shares, join the two header cells of the column, and format the header text.
3. Drag the element `Shares` from the schema tree into the Shares column body. Create the element as content.
4. Set font-size of the `Shares` element content to 10pt. The column should look like this:

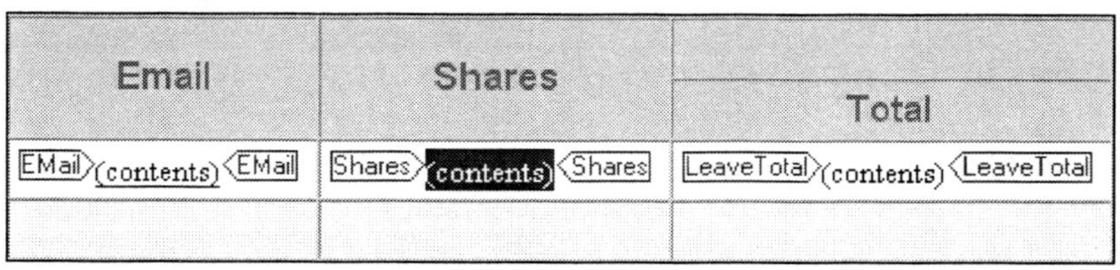

4. Check the the display of the Shares column in the HTML and PDF previews.
5. Now right-click the `(contents)` placeholder of the `First` element, and select **Insert | Condition....** This pops up the Edit XPath expression dialog:

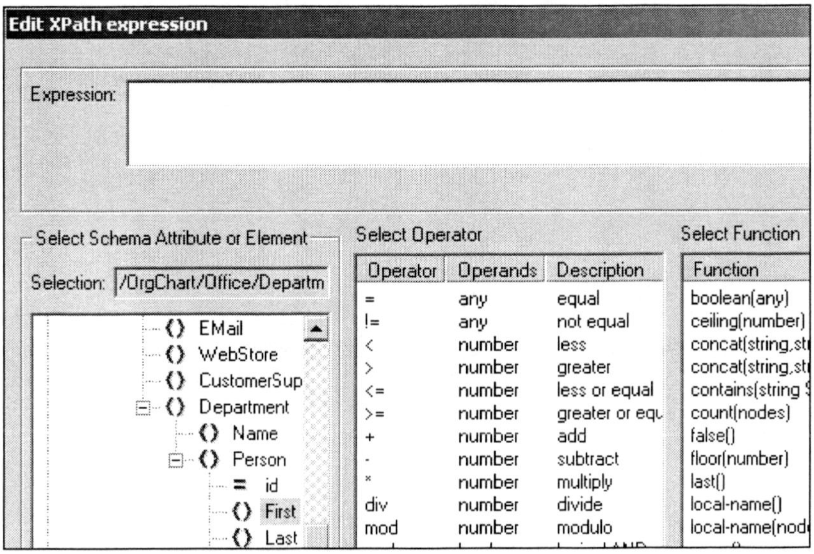

Notice that in the Select Schema Attribute or Element window, the `First` element is highlighted in gray. This indicates that for the XPath expression you are creating, the context node is the `First` element.

6. Double-click the `Shares` element to insert it into the Expression field. Then select the `>` operator, and type in the value 0. Your XPath expression should be: `../Shares > 0`. Click OK to create the condition.
7. Make the `(contents)` placeholder bold. This means that if the condition is evaluated as true (i.e. if the content of `Shares` (which is a numeric field) is a number greater than 0), then the content of `First` will be displayed in bold. The `First` element in the Design Document should now look like this:

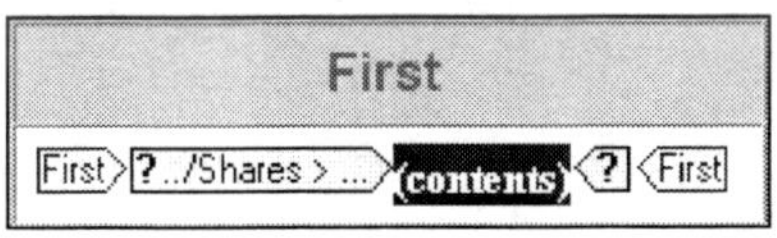

Check the HTML View. Notice that Frank Further has 0 shares, and his `First` name is not displayed in the table. This is because you have defined processing in the event that the condition is true, but no processing if the condition is false (as is the case with Frank Further since he has 0 shares). You therefore have to define a condition to process the element in the event that the condition is false.

8. To process the element's content when the above condition is false, you must define a condition that specifies the all other eventualities not defined in the above condition. Right-click the condition, and select **Condition | Add New**. The Edit Xpath expression dialog appears.

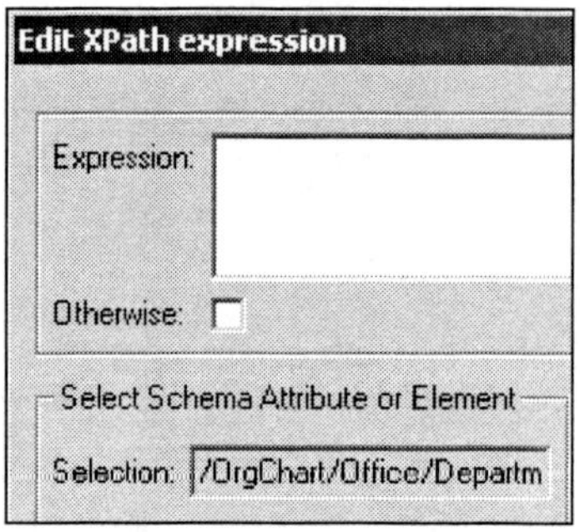

9. Check the Otherwise box. This condition covers all events not covered by the previously defined condition. The `First` element in the Design Document now looks like this:

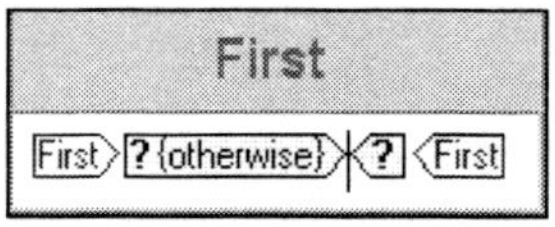

Notice that the conditional template is empty. This means that no processiing has been defined for it, and, as a result, nothing will be displayed in the output.

10. Place the cursor between the start and end tags of the condition, right-click, and select **Insert | Contents**. The `(contents)` placeholder is inserted.
11. Select the `(contents)` placeholder, and set font-size to 10pt.

The HTML Preview will look like this:

Administration (3)

First	Last	Title	Ext	EMail	Shares
Vernon	Callaby	Office Manager	582	v.callaby@nanonull.com	1500
Frank	Further	Accounts Receivable	471	f.further@nanonull.com	0
Loby	Matise	Accounting Manager	963	l.matise@nanonull.com	

The Authentic View display will look as below. To see the Authentic View using the updated Authentic Stylesheet, save the Authentic Stylesheet and open `NanonullOrg.xml` in Authentic View. If `NanonullOrg.xml` is already open in Authentic View, you need to change to another view and then change back to Authentic View in order to see the latest changes.

Administration (3)

First	Last	Title	Ext	EMail	Shares
Vernon	Callaby	Office Manager	582	v.callaby@nanonull.com	1500
Frank	Further	Accounts Receivable	471	f.further@nanonull.com	0
Loby	Matise	Accounting Manager	963	l.matise@nanonull.com	add Shares

Notice in both the above figures, that the `First` element is displayed in normal font if the content of `Shares` is 0 or if no `Shares` element exists for that employee.

Now create the same conditions for the `Last` element so that both `First` and `Last` appear in bold if the employee is a shareholder and in normal if not.

Formatting the table

Since another column has been added, you need to change the column widths again to ensure proper PDF output. First, check the PDF Preview. Now set column widths for each column (by placing the cursor in the respective column, clicking the Table Properties icon, and in the Column tab of the Table Properties dialog entering a value for `width`) as follows: `First`: 10%; `Last`: 12%; `Title`: 16%; `Ext`: 5%; `EMail`: 23%; `Shares`: 10%; `LeaveTotal`: 8%; `LeaveUsed`: 8%; `LeaveLeft`: 8%.

Creating the Table Footer

A table footer can contain both static and dynamic content, and can therefore be used to display summaries of data in the table. You can also insert, append and delete footer rows, as well as split and join cells, thus allowing you considerable flexibility in designing footers.

In this section, we will create the following summaries for the `//Department/Person` dynamic table:

- Number of employees in the department, and this number as a percentage of Office employees and Company employees.
- Number of shares held by Department members, and this number as a percentage of shares held by Office shareholders and Company shareholders.
- A list of all non-shareholders in the department.

Before starting, delete the summary auto-calculation in the footer of the Extensions column, which sums up the telephone extension numbers of employees. This summary was created when the table was created because you checked the Summary for Numeric Fields checkbox and because the `PhoneExt` element is defined as an integer datatype. To delete the summary auto-calculation, click it, and press Delete.

Note that, when the cursor is in the footer, the context node is `//Department`.

Summarizing the shares in departments

1. Place the cursor in the Shares column footer, and click 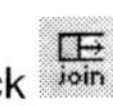 (or **Table | Join Cell Right**) thrice in order to combine these cells into one cell.
2. Type in "Shares: ".
3. Insert an Auto-Calculation to sum the number of shares held by department employees. The XPath expression will be: `sum(Person/Shares)`.
4. Insert an Auto-Calculation to sum the number of shares held by department employees as a percentage of shares held by all shareholders in that office. The XPath expression will be: `round((sum(Person/Shares)) div (sum(../Department/Person/Shares)) * 100)`. The `round()` function is used to round off the result of the Auto-Calculation.
5. Insert an Auto-Calculation to sum the number of shares held by department employees as a percentage of shares held by all shareholders in the whole company. The XPath expression will be: `round((sum(Person/Shares)) div (sum(../../Office/Department/Person/Shares)) * 100)`.
6. Insert text so that your output reads: `Shares: X ( Y% of Office; Z% of company )`, where `X`, `Y`, and `Z` are the Auto-Calculations you have created.
7. Format the entire footer text suitably. The Design Document will look like this:

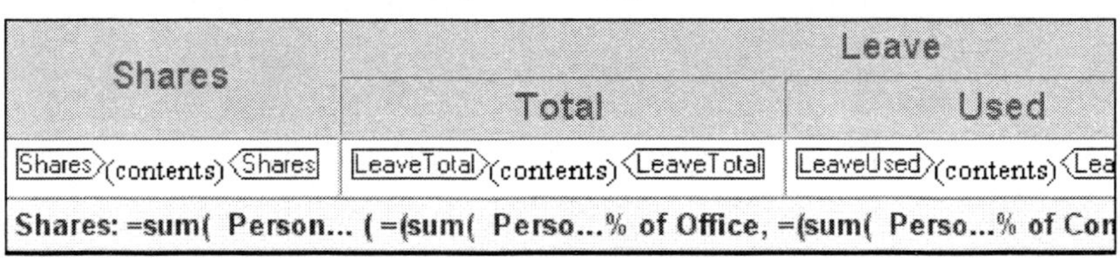

The HTML Preview will look like this:

Shares	Leave		
	Total	Used	Left
1500	25	4	21
0	22	2	20
	25	7	18
Shares: 1500 (30% of Office, 12% of Company)			

Summarizing the employees in departments

1. Place the cursor in the footer of the `First` column, and click Join (or **Table | Join Cell Right**) four times in order to combine these cells into one cell.
2. Type in "Employees: ".
3. Insert an Auto-Calculation to count the number of department employees. The XPath expression will be: `count(Person)`.
4. Insert an Auto-Calculation to count the number of department employees as a percentage of employees in that office. The XPath expression will be: `round((count(Person)) div (count(../Department/ Person)) * 100)`. The `round()` function is used to round off the result of the Auto-Calculation.
5. Insert an Auto-Calculation to count the number of department employees as a percentage of employees in the whole company. The XPath expression will be: `round((count(Person)) div (sum(../../Office/Department/ Person)) * 100)`.
6. Insert text so that your output reads: `Employees: X ( Y% of Office; Z% of company )`, where `X`, `Y`, and `Z` are the Auto-Calculations you have created.
7. Format the entire footer text suitably. The HTML Preview will look like this:

Administration

First	Last	Title
Vernon	**Callaby**	Office Manager
Frank	Further	Accounts Receivable
Loby	Matise	Accounting Manager
Employees: 3 (20% of Office, 8% of Company)		

Listing the non-shareholders by department

1. Place the cursor in the Employees column footer, and click (or **Table | Append Row**). The appended footer row has two cells just like the first row.
2. Place the cursor in the first cell, and click Join (or **Table | Join Cell Right**) to join the two cells.
3. Type in "Non-Shareholders: ".
4. Drag the `Person` element into the footer as shown below:

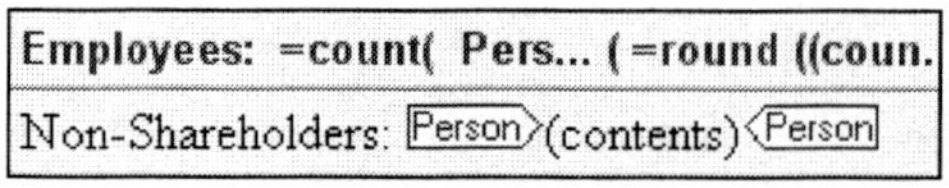

5. Insert a Condition after the start tag of the `Person` element. The XPath expression should select those `Person` elements (the current element) that have a `Share` value of less than or equal to 0, or no `Share` element. The XPath will be: `Shares <= 0 or not (Shares)`. This part of the footer in the Design Document will look like this:

6. Drag the `First` element into the Design Window, and drop it between the tags of the condition you created in the previous step, and create it as contents.
7. Do the same for the `Last` element. This part of this footer row will now look like this:

8. We now want to put commas after each non-shareholder except the last in the list. To do this, place the cursor after the end tag of the `Last` element, and insert a condition. The XPath should be: `following-sibling::Person[Shares<=0 or not(Shares)]`.
9. Insert a comma and a space. Then put a period after the `Person` end tag. The Design Window of this part of the footer will look like this:

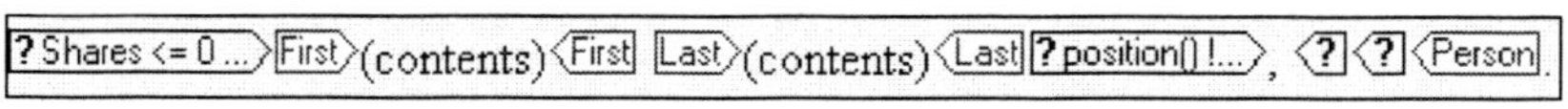

10. You still have to make allowance for the event that there are no non-shareholders in a department (i.e. all department employees are shareholders). To cover this eventuality, place the cursor before the period, and insert a condition. The XPath should be: `count(Person) = count(Person[Shares>0])`. Insert the text "None" between the tags of the condition, as shown below.

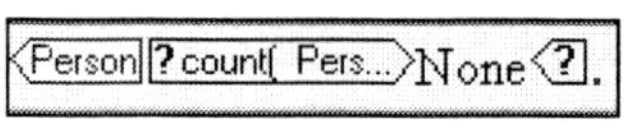

11. Format the entire footer row text suitably.
12. Save the Authentic Stylesheet, and refresh the Authentic View of the Working XML file.

The Authentic View of the dynamic table with the footer modifications will look like this:

Administration

First	Last	Title	Ext	EMail	Shares	Leave		
						Total	Used	Left
Vernon	**Callaby**	Office Manager	581	v.callaby@nanonull.com	1500	25	4	21
Frank	Further	Accounts Receivable	471	f.further@nanonull.com	0	22	2	20
Loby	Matise	Accounting Manager	963	l.matise@nanonull.com	add Shares	25	7	18
Employees: 3 (20% of Office, 9% of Company)					**Shares: 1500 (13% of Office, 6% of Company)**			
Non-Shareholders: Frank Further, Loby Matise.								

Text formatting with global templates and text state icons

The schema `NanonullOrg.xsd` contains two **elements** that are intended for applying text styling. These two elements are `bold` and `italic`; they are child elements of `para` and are recursive with respect to themselves and each other, i.e. they can occur multiple times within themselves and each other.

The `bold` and `italic` elements can occur at any location and at multiple locations within a `para` element. Since their location cannot be precisely fixed in the Design Document, the formatting for these two elements must be specified in a global template.

Creating a global template for the `bold` element

1. In the Schema Window, expand the Global Templates entry. A tree showing all the elements for which global templates are allowed is displayed.

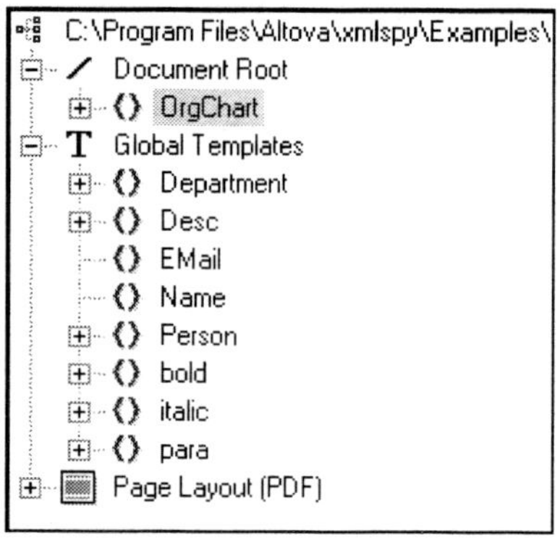

2. Select the `bold` element. The `bold` element in the Global Templates tree is marked with a "+" to indicate that a global template has been created. In the Design Window, the view changes to show the `bold` element, which has a `(contents)` placeholder (see below).

3. Note that the entire element is selected. Keeping the element selected, in the Text Style Window, select the Text tab, and set `font-weight` to bold. The global template is now created with bold formatting. Alternatively, you could select the `(contents)` placeholder and assign the bold formatting.

4. Now check the HTML Preview. All text in `para` elements that is marked up with the `bold` element is now displayed in bold. (Such text was earlier not displayed bold because there was no formatting defined for the `bold` element.)

Creating a Text State Icon

A Text State Icon is a toolbar icon in Authentic View that is used to add formatting to text in

Authentic View. A text state icon is created for **a particular element** in Stylesheet Designer. The formatting for that element must be defined as a global template, and it is this formatting that is applied when the Authentic View user clicks the text state icon.

Create a text state icon for the `bold` element as follows:

1. Click **Authentic | Text State Icons....** The Text State Icons dialog appears:

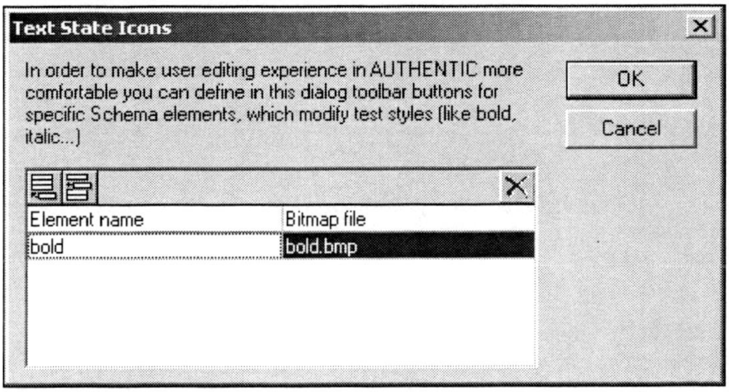

2. Enter `bold` as the element name for which the text state icon is being created.
3. Enter `bold.bmp` as the name of the bitmap file in the `sps\Picts` folder in your application folder. This bitmap will be used as the toolbar icon in Authentic View. It is already present in the `sps\Picts` folder, so you do not have to create the bitmap.
4. Now append a row, and add the `italic` element and `italic.bmp` as the bitmap file for the italic icon (also present in the `sps\Picts` folder).
5. Save the Authentic Stylesheet.
6. If you have `NanonullOrg.xml` open in Authentic View, close it, and open it again to see the toolbar icons for bold and italic that you have created.

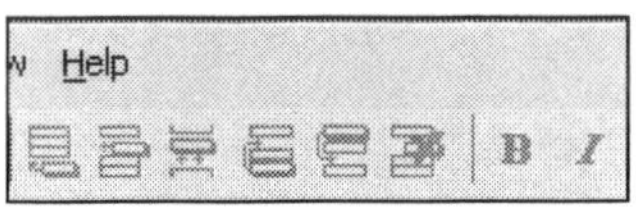

The text state icons are grayed out when you open the file. They will be enabled when you place the cursor inside a `para` element (because the `bold` and `italic` elements are child elements of `para`).

7. In Authentic View, now mark some text in a `para` element, and click the bold icon. The text turns bold.
8. Now mark some text, and click the italic icon. Nothing happens. This is because you have not yet defined a global template for the `italic` element in your Authentic Stylesheet.
9. In the Authentic Stylesheet, create a global template for the `italic` element, and assign it an italic style (in the Text Style Window).
10. Save the Authentic Stylesheet. In Authentic View, refresh the view by switching to another view before switching back again. All text that has been marked up as italic will now be displayed as italic.

Using Additional Validation

The Additional Validation feature allows you to check data on the basis of XPath expessions and to draw the attention of the Authentic View user to values that are outside the range of values specified by the XPath expression. When an invalid value is entered or becomes the result of an auto-calculation, then the user is informed about this in two ways:

- On validating the document, a validation error is reported.
- Optionally, the value can be displayed in red and an error message will be displayed in a mouseover.

This feature is useful if you wish to inform users that certain values are not allowed and that appropriate action is required. Additional validation is also useful when the validity check you wish to make is not specified in the schema.

Additional validation of Telephone Extensions
The objective is to validate the content of the `PhoneExt` element, which is an integer datatype. The validation should check whether the extension has three digits or not. If not, the user should be notified.

To build additional validation for the `PhoneExt` element, do the following:

1. Select the `(contents)` placeholder of the `PhoneExt` element.
   - Selecting the `(contents)` placeholder—and not the entire node—is the mechanism to be used in order to display invalid data in red and display an error message when the user mouses over the invalid data. On validation **(F8)** also, an error message will be generated.
   - Selecting the entitre node on the other hand only generates an error message on validation.

   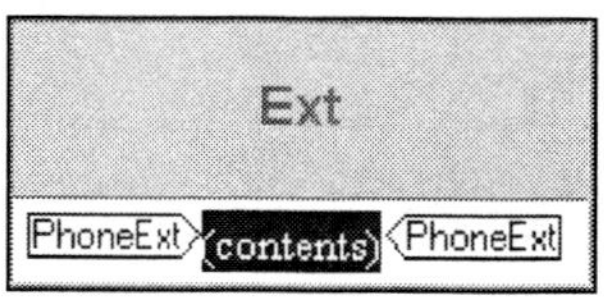

2. Select **Authentic | Node Settings...** The following dialog appears:

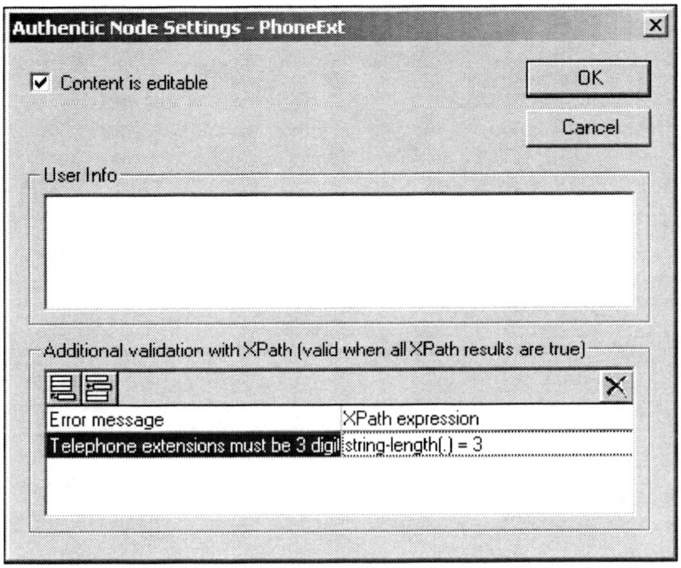

3. In the Additional Validation field, click the Append button.
4. Enter the XPath expression for valid values: `string-length(.)=3`. The . indicates the current node. When the number of characters in the current node (the `PhoneExt` node) is equal to 3, the XPath expression is true and the data is valid. The expression is false when the number of characters in the `PhoneExt` node is any other than 3. If this happens, the node content will be displayed red in Authentic View and a mouseover displays the error message that you key into the Error message box of the Additional Validation field.
5. Now enter the error message in the Error message box of the Additional Validation field, such as: "`Telephone extensions must be three digits long.`"
6. You can also key in text for the User Info. The text you key in here is displayed in Authentic View shortly after the cursor is placed over that node.

When the Authentic View user validates the XML document, any invalid data wil generate the error message for that node.

Completing the stylesheet

To complete the stylesheet, you should check the following:

- Whether Auto-Calculations, Conditional Templates, and Additional Validation statements are correct, especially whether all user situations are covered.
- Whether formatting and layout is as required.
- Whether the Authentic Node Settings for individual nodes are correctly set.

Checking Auto-Calculations, Conditional Templates, and Additional Validation

Two kinds of error are likely here: first, that the XPath expression is incorrect, either in syntax or because it selects the wrong node/nodeset or operates on the selected node/nodeset in an unintended way; second, that some data input scenario has not been covered. You should check all XPaths for correct syntax and correct processing, and then test your Authentic Stylesheet with different data (to check that various data input scenarios are covered).

Your Authentic Stylesheet is correct in the first respect, i.e. correctness of XPath expressions, if you have followed this tutorial exactly. There is, however, one significant data input scenario that has not been covered. This is as follows. Suppose the Authentic View user selects a value in the `Location` combo-box, say `US`, and then creates the `Address` element and enters data into the child elements of `Address`. Suppose now that the user (for whatever reason) changes the value in the `Location` combo-box to `EU`. The `add Address_EU` prompt appears, and the user does add the `Address_EU` element. The XML document now contains an `Address` element as well as an `Address_EU` element; this is invalid, since the schema specifies that either of the two, but not both, must be present.

To cover this data input scenario, you can take one of the following measures:

- Inform the Authentic View user about not adding a second address element in a pop-up message that appears on mousing over the `Location` combo-box. You can enter the message in the User Info field of the Authentic Node Settings for the `Location` node. This, however, does not prevent the user from going ahead and doing just what is not supposed to be done.
- Make the `Location` combo-box non-editable once an address element has been created for the Office, and explaining this to the user in a pop-up. This effectively rules out the possibility of two address elements occurring inside an `Office` element.

Additional specifications for how the `Location` combo-box is processed

The objective is to make the `Location` combo-box non-editable after the address element corresponding to the `Location` selection has been created. This prevents the possibility of a second address element being created. Do this as follows:

1. Select the `Location` element, and insert a condition around it with the XPath: `not(Address or Address_EU)`.

   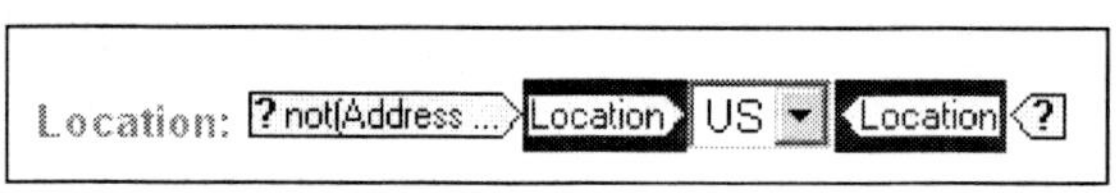

   This creates a conditional template for the scenario where neither an `Address` nor an `Address_EU` element exists for that `Office` element.
2. Right-click the `Location` node and select **Authentic Node Settings...** (or select **Authentic | Node Settings...**).

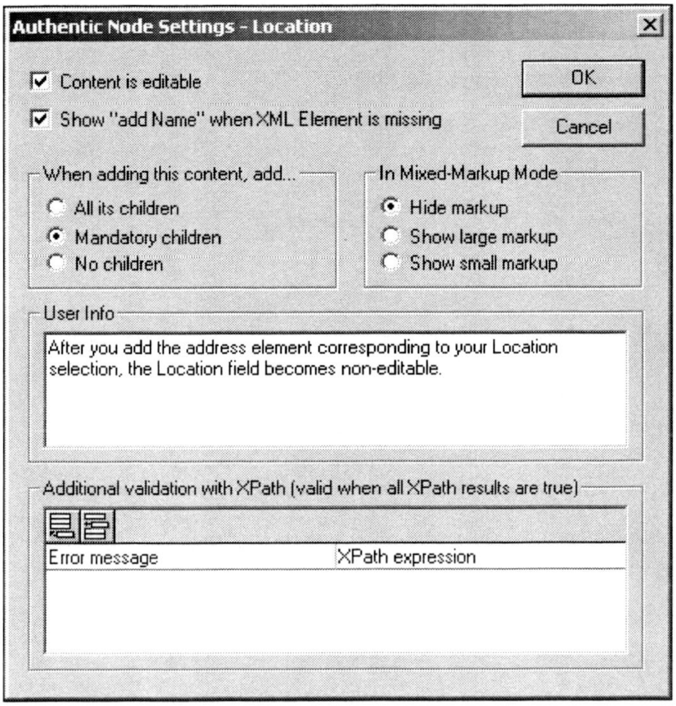

In the dialog, leave the default settings unchanged. The most important of these in this context is the "Content is editable" checkbox. Remember that these settings are for the condition where neither `Address` nor `Address_EU` element exist; you do want the user to be able to add content to the `Location` element.

3. Add text in the User Info field as shown in the figure above, and click OK.
4. Right-click the condition and select Add Copy.
5. For the new conditional template, change the XPath to: `Address`. This is the conditional template to execute when an `Address` element exists.
6. Select the `Location` node in this conditional template, and in the Node Settings dialog uncheck the "Content is editable" checkbox and enter a suitable text message in the User Info field, such as: "To edit this field, the `Address` element of this `Office` element will have to be deleted using a Text View of the document."
7. Repeat Steps 4, 5 and 6 to create a third conditional template for cases where an `Address_EU` element exists.

Checking the document formatting

Compare the Authentic View, and HTML and PDF Previews, and make any desired formatting changes, such as adding or deleting line breaks, changing text color and background color, and so on.

In the static table that contains the US address fields, the last row contains two elements: `ipo:state` and `ipo:zip`. In order to make the input areas for the two elements easily recognizable to the Authentic View user, change the `ipo:state` and `ipo:zip` nodes to a Combo box and an Input Field, respectively.

To change the `ipo:state` element to a combo box, do the following:

1. Right-click the element in the Design Document and select **Change to | Combo Box...**. The following dialog pops up:

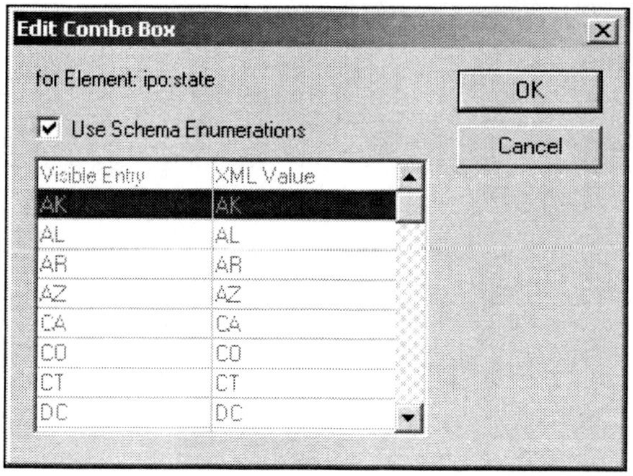

2. Check the Use Schema Enumerations option, so that the values enumerated in the schema become the options available in the combo box. The Visible Entries will be the same as the XML Values that have been enumerated in the schema.
3. Click OK to finish creating the combo box.

To change the `ipo:zip` element to an input field, right-click the `ipo:zip` element and select **Change to | Input Field**.

The Design Window, after these two changes have been made, should now look like this:

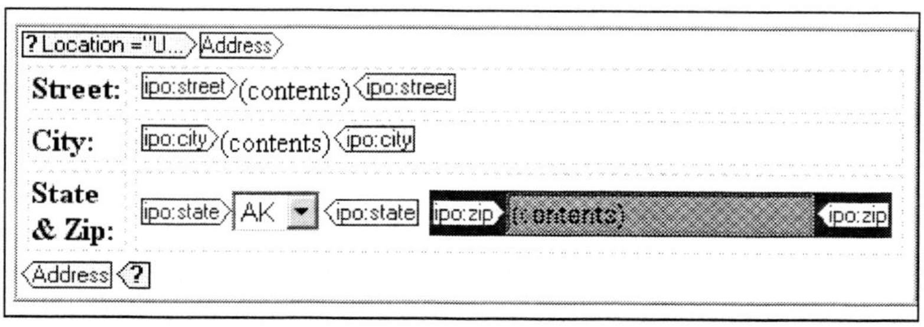

Checking the Node Settings

You can make detailed and specific settings for each node in your document (right-click the node and click **Authentic Node Settings...** (or select **Authentic | Node Settings...**)). For example, you might want to add User Info for some nodes; Authentic View users will see this information when they mouseover the node. The following screenshot shows how User Info is displayed in Authentic View.

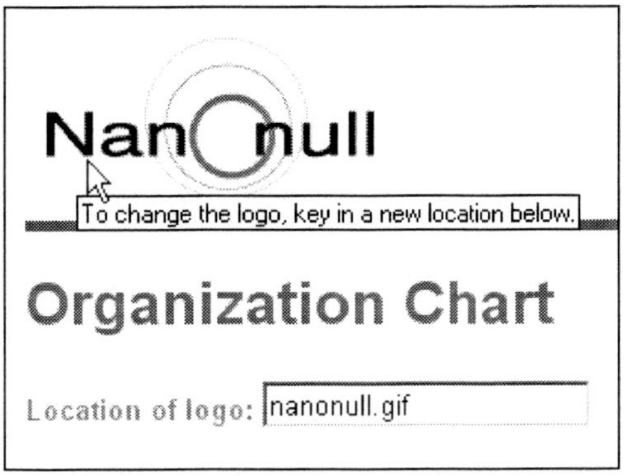

The pop-up message that appears on mousing over the logo is the text keyed in as the User Info for this node.

Additional modifications
Try the following modification yourself. In the Office Summary Line just below the address of each office, the number of departments and employees are listed, as shown here:

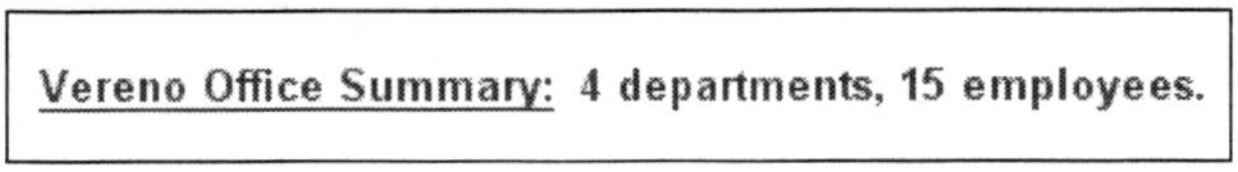

Modify the line so that the singular (department / employee) appears when the corresponding value is one, and the plural (departments / employees) appears when the corresponding value is zero or more than one. (This modification is included in `NanonullOrg.sps`, should you need to look it up.)

Stylesheet Designer How To Use

This section describes how to use the more complex features of Stylesheet Designer. For each of the features considered, there is an explanation of the feature's function followed by a description of its usage.

The following features are discussed:

- Global Templates
- Tables
- Conditional templates
- Date Picker
- Input Formatting
- PDF processing and page layout

Data-entry devices

Function
Stylesheet Designer enables you to add data-entry devices into an Authentic Stylesheet. In Authentic View, when data is entered into a data-entry device, it is inserted into the XML document as element content or as an attribute's value. Data-entry devices enable you to constrain the data that goes into the XML document, and are, therefore, a useful way of improving data integrity.

General mechanism
Given below is a list of data-entry devices you can use, together with an explanation of how data is entered in the XML file for each device.

Data-Entry Device	Data in XML File
Input Field (Text Box)	Text entered by user
Multiline Input Field	Text entered by user
Combo box	User selection mapped to value
Check box	User selection mapped to value
Radio button	User selection mapped to value
Button	User selection mapped to value

The values entered in the text input fields are entered directly as XML content.

For the other data-entry devices, the Authentic View user's selection is mapped to a value. Stylesheet Designer enables you to define the list of options the user will see and the XML value to which each option is mapped. Typically, you will define the options and their correspondig values in a dialog, like the one shown below.

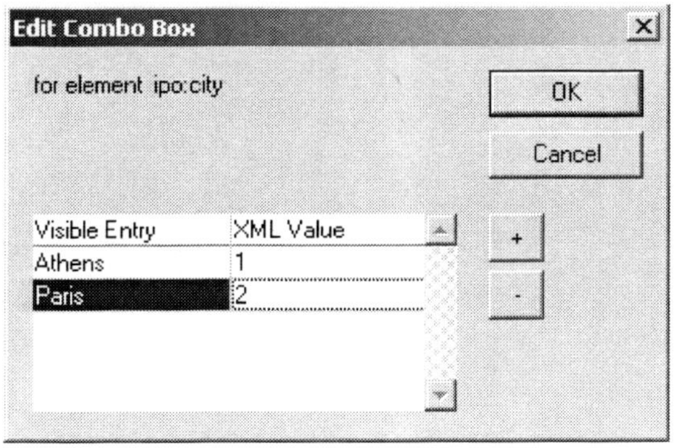

When the user makes a selection from the visible options, the corresponding XML value is entered in the XML value.

Usage
Data-entry devices can be created when an element or attribute is dragged from the Schema window into the Design Document window. When the node is dropped into the design

document, select the data-entry device you wish to create the node as, and, if required, complete the necessary dialog.

Data-entry devices can also be created by changing the current presentation of a node to a data-entry device.

Note:

- User input is allowed only in Authentic View. In the HTML and PDF output, the visible entry that has been selected by the user is displayed in the output; the text value cannot be changed—even if the visible entry is changed.
- In the case of some data-entry devices, such as check-boxes, where the device cannot correctly be rendered in print, an alternative rendition is implemented.

Lists

Function

If an element has multiple instances, to output its instances as the items of a list. A list can be bulletted or numbered.

General mechanism

- Any element can be created as a list.
- When an element is created as a list, the instances of that element are created as the items of the list. For example, if in a `department` element, there are several `person` elements (i.e. instances), and you wanted to create a list of all the persons in the department, then you must create the `person` element as the list.
- Once the list has been created for the element, you can modify the content of the list item.

Usage: Basic

1. Create the required element as a list. In the example below, the element `person` is created as the list.

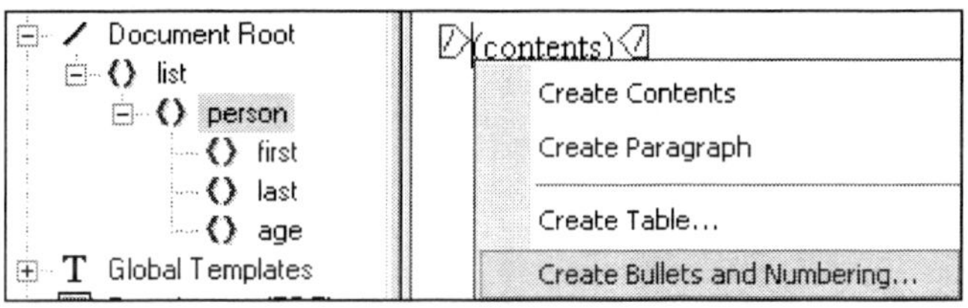

After you select the appropriate list formatting (bullets or numbering), this part of your Design Document will look like this:

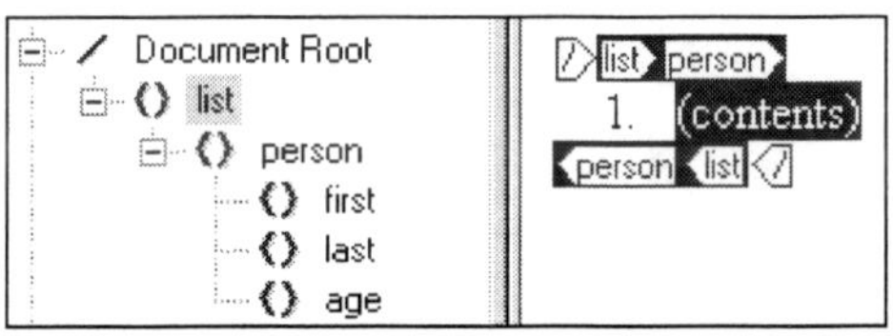

The HTML Preview will look like this:

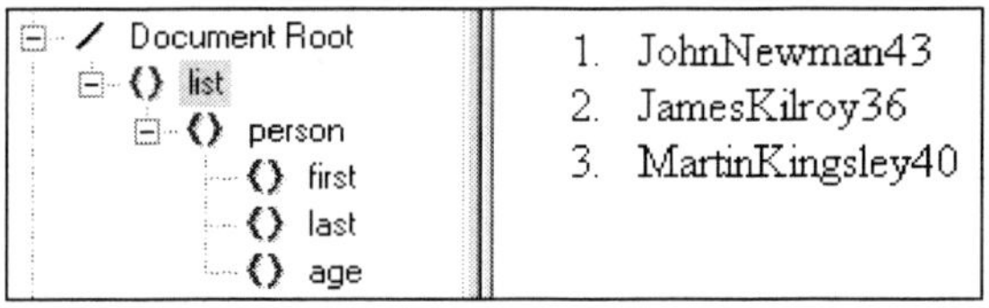

Notice that a list item has been created for each instance of the `person` element, and that the content of the **entire person element** (which includes content of all child elements) has been output.

2. To modify the content of a list item, add new content or text after the list item marker. For instance, to list only the last name of persons, in the Design Document, drop the `last` element from the schema tree as contents into the list item. The contents of `//person/last` replaces the contents of the `person` element in the list item.

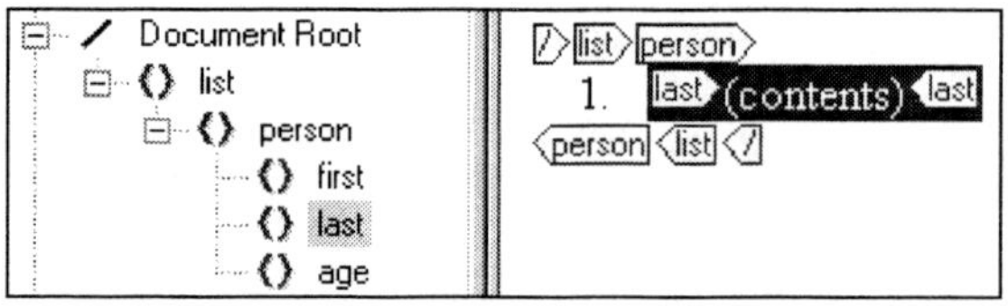

The HTML Preview looks like this:

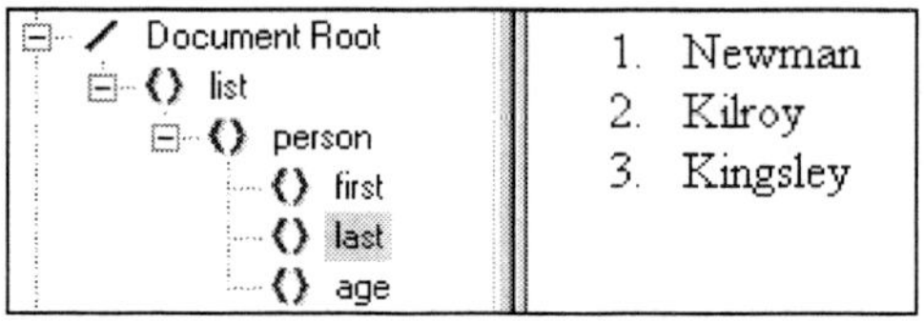

3. You could modify the list item further, as follows. Add the text shown in the illustration below. The equals to symbol indicates an Auto-Calculation; it returns the position of the current `person` element in the node-set.

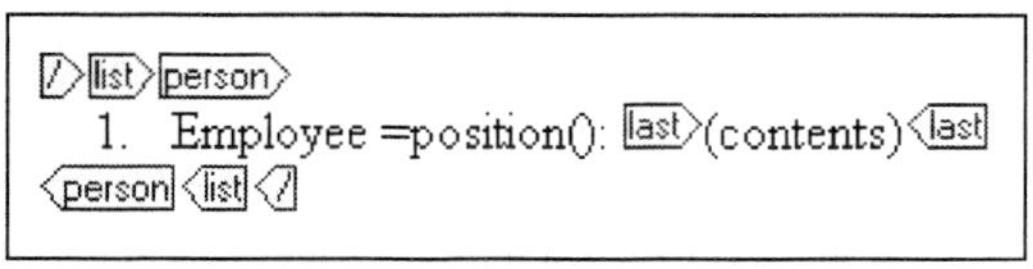

The HTML Preview looks like this:

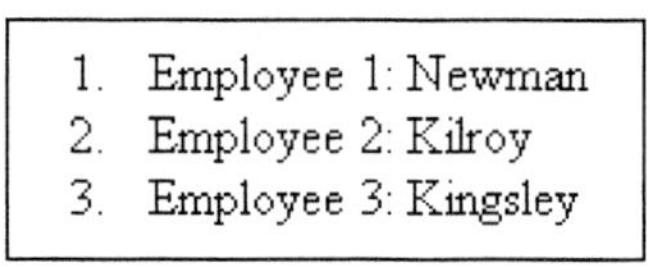

Usage: Advanced

The following issues, which are related to more complex list structures in schemas, are considered:

- Schemas often have separate elements for numbered lists and for bulleted lists. However, they usually have a common listitem-type element. An example is the HTML language, in which both the `ol` and `ul` elements have `li` as the listitem element. In this kind of scenario, it is best to define global templates for both the `ol` and `ul` elements, making sure to create the correct element as the list. Shown below is a view of the Design Document for the global template of an `ol`-type element.

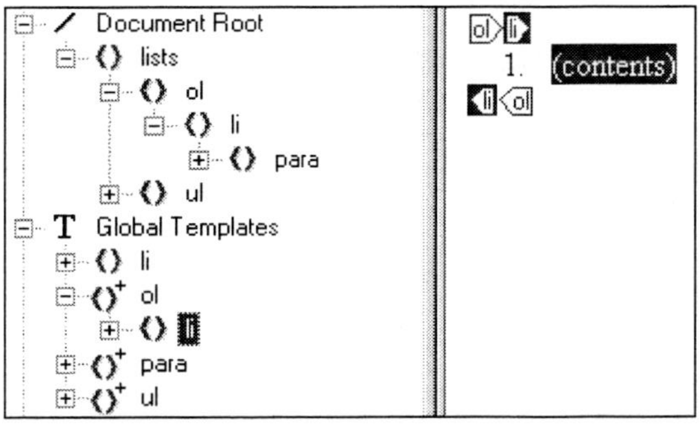

The `li` element was dragged from the content model of the `ol` element in the Global Templates list in the Schema Window, and was created as a numbered list. Similarly, create a global template for the `ul`-type element (but create the `li` element as a bulletteed list in this case).

- The schema might have a `para`-type element as a child of the `li`-type element, and an `li`-type element may have more than one `para`-type element within it. The best way to deal with this kind of situation is to first define the `para`-type element as a global element in the XML Schema (this step is not necessary for DTDs). Then create a global template for the `para`-type element, making sure to create it as a paragraph. Shown below is a view of the Design Document for the global template of a `para`-type element.

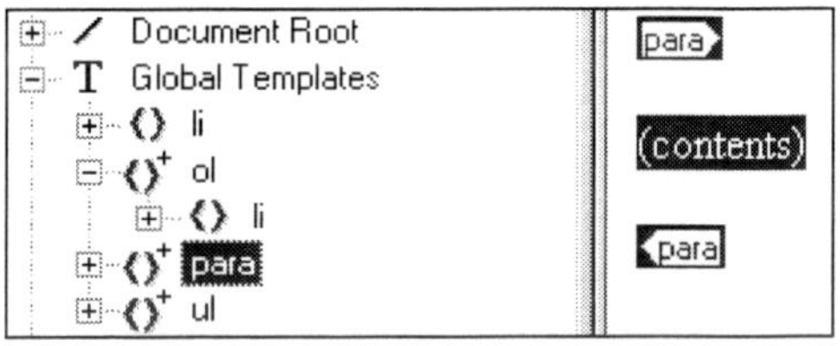

- If nested lists are allowed by the schema, you must define global templates for the list-type elements (`ol`, `ul`, etc), making sure to create the listitem-type element/s as lists. Given below is the HTML Preview of part of a list that includes nested lists.

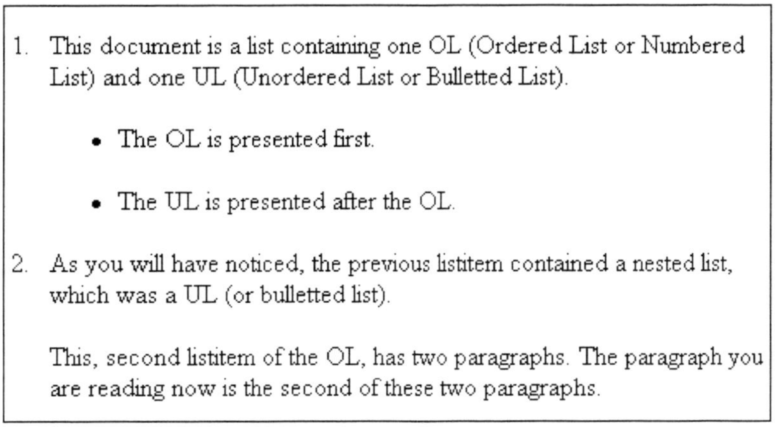

Limitations

- In the Show Large Markup and Show Small Markup modes of Authentic View, the tags for listitem-type elements are not shown for the individual list items; instead only one pair of start and end tags is shown at the beginning and end of the entire list.

  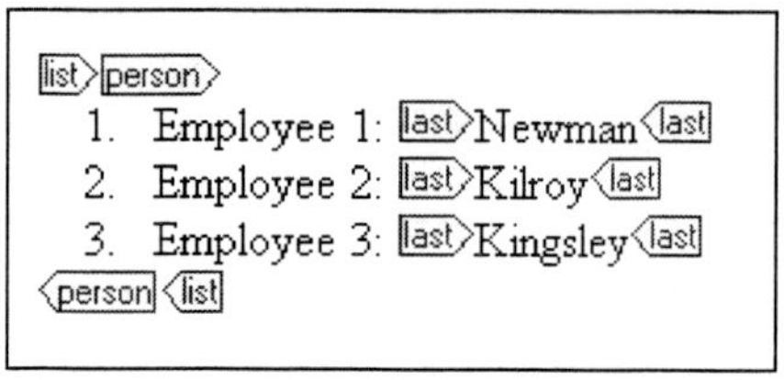

  In the figure above, only one pair of `person` tags occur—at the beginning and end of the list—when, in fact, there are three separate `person` elements (the list items in this list).
- If you are using a DTD with a complex list item content model, Authentic View may append elements after the list element instead of within a list item.

Tables

In an Authentic Stylesheet, two types of tables are used: **SPS tables** and **XML tables**. There are crucial differences between the two types, and it is important to understand these. A detailed description of SPS tables and XML tables, and instructions about how to use them, follows in the next sections. For now, we look at the broad picture.

The illustration below shows the relationship of SPS tables and XML tables to the Authentic Stylesheet and to the XML document.

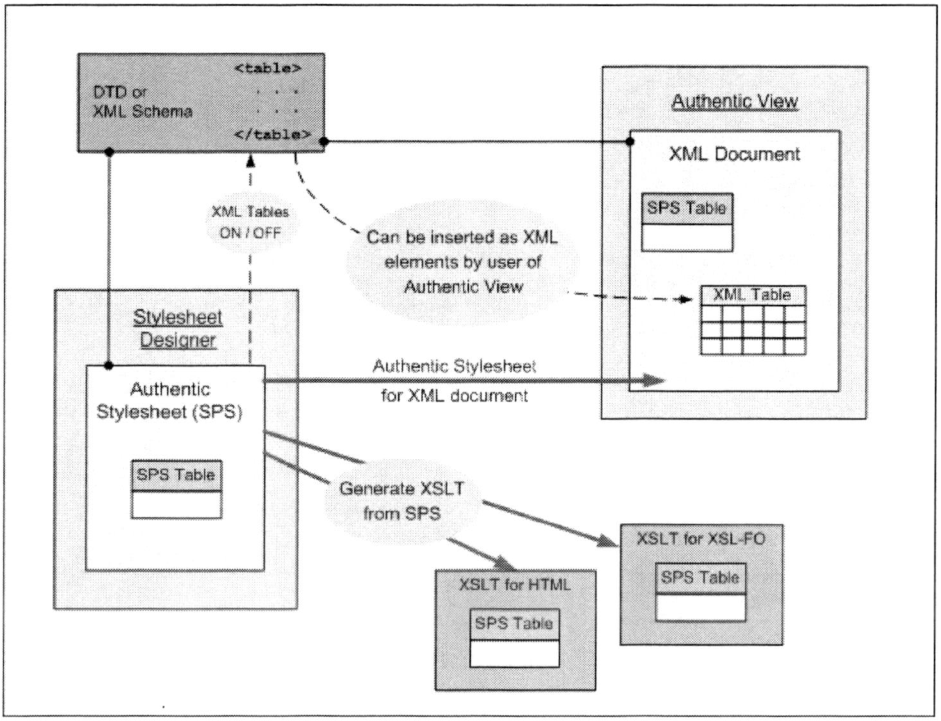

SPS tables

An **SPS table** is a component of an Authentic Stylesheet, and is created and formatted using Stylesheet Designer. If present in an Authentic Stylesheet, an SPS table appears in Authentic View as well as in the XSLT stylesheets you can generate with Stylesheet Designer.

An SPS table has no pre-determined structure. The structure is specified by the person who designs the Authentic Stylesheet. An SPS table can be created anywhere in an Authentic Stylesheet, and any number of SPS tables can be created.

The **structure** of an SPS table is **not represented as XML elements** in the XML document. SPS tables are entirely presentational devices. In whatever kind of document an SPS table is rendered, the table's structure is specified not in the markup vocabulary of the XML document but in the respective presentational vocabulary. SPS tables occur in three types of output:

- Rendered in Authentic View; a vocabulary specific to Authentic View is used to mark up SPS tables
- In Stylesheet Designer-generated XSLT stylesheets for HTML output, SPS tables are

marked up as HTML tables
- In Stylesheet Designer-generated XSLT stylesheets for XSL-FO output, SPS tables are marked up as XSL-FO tables

There are two types of SPS tables:

- **Static tables** are built up, step-by-step, by the person designing the Authentic Stylesheet. After the table structure is created, the content of each cell is defined separately. The content of cells can come from random locations in the schema tree and even can be of different types. It is important to realize that the rows of a static table are not intended to represent a repeating data structure. This is why the table is said to be static: it has a fixed structure that does not change with the XML content.
- **Dynamic tables** are intended for data structures that repeat, and they are based on schema elements that have a substructure (at least one child attribute or element). Any element with a substructure repeats if there is more than one instance of it. Each instance of the element would be a row in the dynamic table, and all or some of its child elements or attributes would be the columns. In Authentic View, a dynamic table's structure reflects the content of the XML file and changes dynamically with the content.

XML tables
An XML table is created by the **Authentic View user** as a data structure in the XML document. The purpose of XML tables is to give the Authentic View user the option of inserting a table-type data structure in the XML document. This XML data structure can then be transformed to the table markup of the output format.

The data structure for an XML table must correspond to either the HTML or CALS table model. This XML table element and its content model must exist in the schema. An XML table can be inserted at any point in the XML document where it is allowed according to the schema. An XML table is formatted after it is inserted in the XML document.

Shown below is the Authentic View of an XML table that corresponds to the HTML table model.

Name	Phone
John Merrimack	6517890
Joe Concord	6402387

Data that is entered into the table's cells is entered as content of the corresponding XML elements. For example, the text view of the XML table shown in the illustration above looks like this:

```
<table border="1" width="40%">
  <tbody>
    <tr>
      <td>Name</td>
      <td>Phone</td>
    </tr>
    <tr>
      <td>John Merrimack</td>
      <td>6517890</td>
    </tr>
    <tr>
      <td>Joe Concord</td>
      <td>6402387</td>
    </tr>
  </tbody>
</table>
```

Note that the structure of the table exists as XML elements. An element in the XML table hierarchy can have any name; it is only important that the table structure correspond to the

HTML or CALS table model. The elements of the XML table (from the example above) could as easily be:

```
<phonelist border="1" width="40%">
  <items>
    <person>
      <name>Name</name>
      <phone>Phone</phone>
    </person>
    <person>
      <name>John Merrimack</name>
      <phone>6517890</phone>
    </person>
    <person>
      <name>Joe Concord</name>
      <phone>6402387</phone>
    </person>
  </items>
</phonelist>
```

Also note the following:

- An XML table can be inserted at any location in the XML document where, according to the schema, a table is allowed.
- In Authentic View, data is entered directly into table cells. This data is stored as the content of the corresponding XML table element.
- The formatting properties of an XML table are assigned in Authentic View.

Note that XSLT stylesheets generated with Stylesheet Designer will not contain XML tables—because the XML tables are not included in the Authentic Stylesheet.

Summary for designer
From the document designer's perspective, the following points should be noted:

- An **SPS table** occurs in the XML document at a location determined by the designer of the document—not the user of Authentic View. The structure and formatting of SPS tables are specified by the designer of the Authentic Stylesheet in Stylesheet Designer.
- The location, structure, and formatting of **XML tables** are specified by the user of Authentic View. The user may insert an XML table wherever this is allowed by the schema (remember: the table element corresponds to an element in the schema).

Creating static tables

To insert a static table, click **Table | Insert table** or the  icon. The following dialog appears:

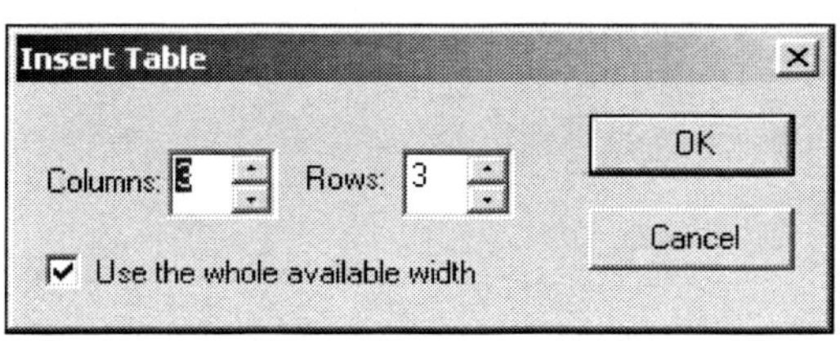

You can select the dimensions of the table and specify whether the table should occupy the whole available width. When you click OK, an empty table with the specified dimensions, as shown below, is created.

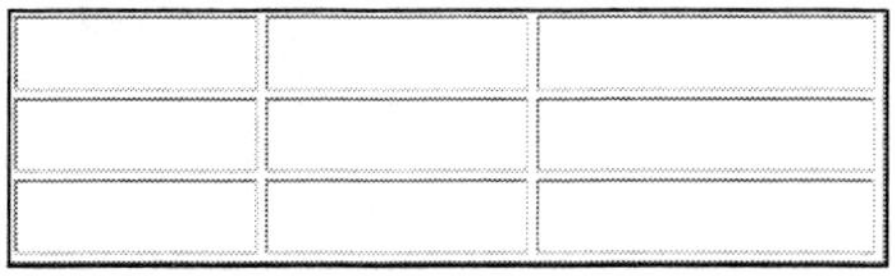

You can now enter content into table cells using regular Stylesheet Designer features. Cell content could be text, or elements dragged from the XML tree, or objects such as images and nested tables. The figure below shows a table containing nested tables.

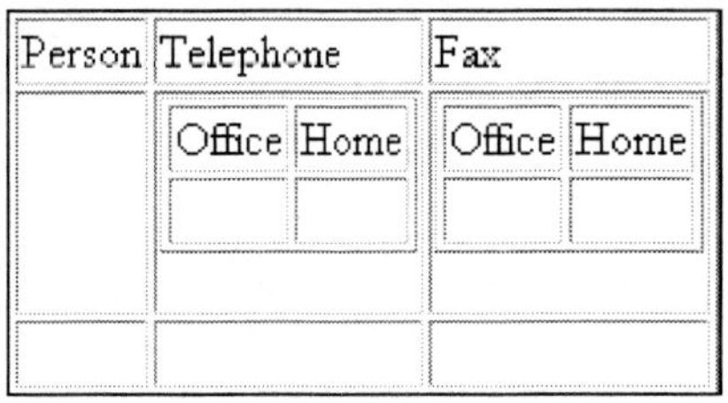

Static SPS tables are especially well-suited for organizing XML data that is randomly situated in the schema hierarchy.

Creating dynamic tables

Creating a dynamic SPS table
A dynamic SPS table is created by dragging an element from the XML tree into the Design window. On dropping the element into the desired location, the following context menu appears.

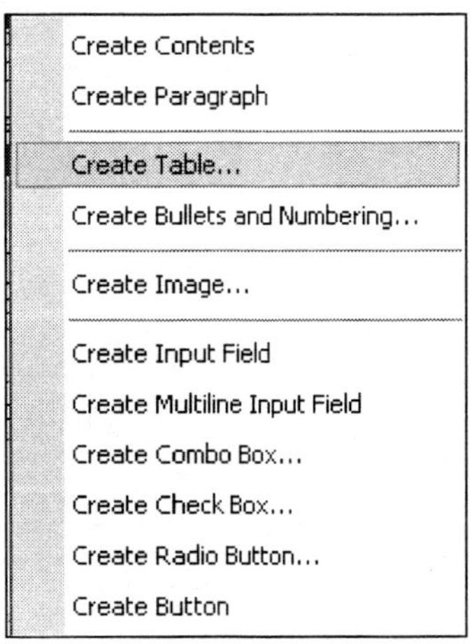

Click Create Table. This brings up the following dialog.

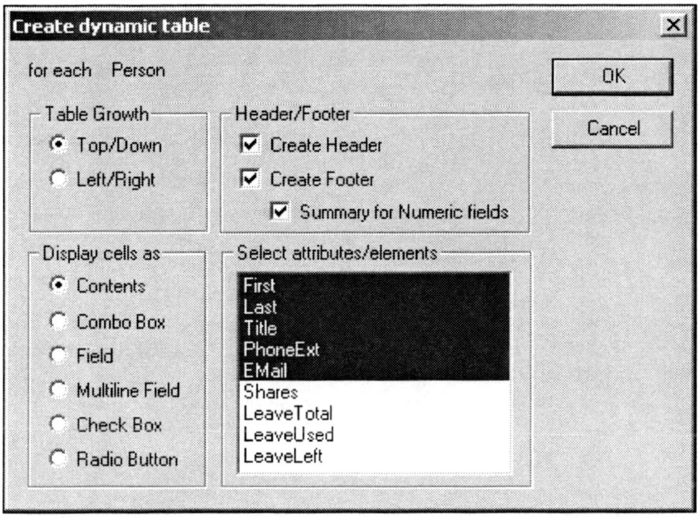

The child elements and attributes of the element that has been dragged into the Design window are displayed In the "Select attributes/element" list and can be created as columns of the table. Deselect the child nodes that you do not want and select any attribute you want to include as columns. (In the figure above, the elements `Shares`, `LeaveTotal`, `LeaveUsed` and `LeaveLeft` have been deselected.)

Note that columns are created only for child elements and attributes, but for no descendant on a lower level.

Table grows down or right
When a table grows top-down, this is what it would look like:

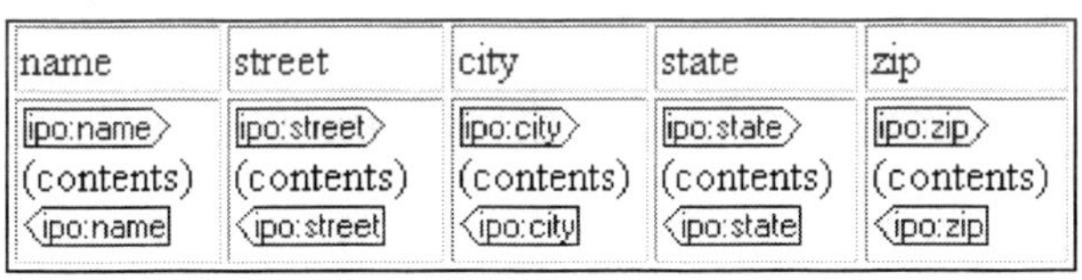

When a table grows left-right it looks like this:

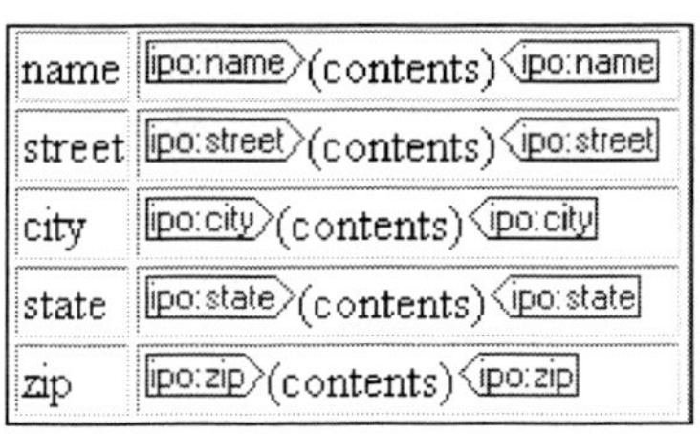

Headers and footers
Columns can be given headers, which will be the names of the column elements. To include headers, check the Create Header check-box. To include footers, check the Create Footer check-box. Footers can only be created for tables that grow top-down. The footer of numeric columns will also sum each of these columns if the Summary for Numeric Fields check box is

checked.

Header and footer cells can be joined and split, and rows can be inserted, appended, and deleted; this gives you considerable flexibility in structuring headers and footers. Additionally, headers and footers can contain any type of static or dynamic content, including conditional templates and auto-calculations.

Contents of table body cells
When you create a dynamic table, you can create the node content as any one of a number of Stylesheet Designer components. In the examples above, the table body cells were created as contents. They could also be created as a data-entry device. There are two points to note here:

- The setting you select is a global setting for all the table body cells. If you wish to have an individual cell appear differently, edit the cell after you have created the table: right-click in the cell and, in the context menu that appoears, select "Change to" and then the required cell content type.
- If you create cells as element contents, and if the element has descendant elements, then the content of the cell will be a concatenation of the text strings of the element and all its descendant elements.

Formatting static and dynamic tables

After they have been created, static and dynamic tables can be formatted to a high degree of detail and precision. The formatting mechanism is the same for both types of table. Formatting properties are available at the table, row, column, and cell levels. To assign formatting properties, place the cursor anywhere inside the table, row, column, or cell you wish to format, and click either **Table | Table Properties...** or **Properties | Table...** or the 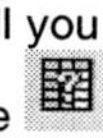 icon. The following dialog appears:

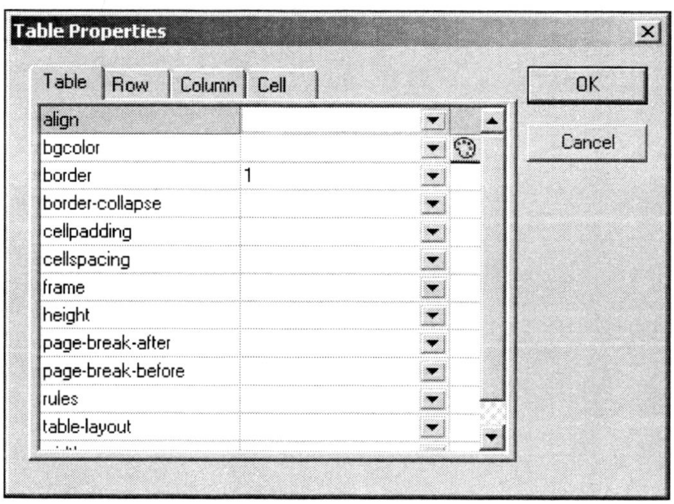

Click the required tab (Table, Row, Column, or Cell), enter a value for the formatting property you want to set, and click OK.

XML tables

In order for users of Authentic View to be able to insert XML tables the following two conditions must be fulfilled:

- An element must exist in the schema (DTD or XML Schema) with a content model corresponding either to the HTML or CALS table model
- XML tables must be enabled in the Authentic Stylesheet

Defining the table content model in the schema
The table element in the schema must have a content model corresponding to either the HTML or CALS table model. For example, a table model corresponding to the HTML table model would have a structure as shown in the XML fragment below.

```
<table>
  <tbody>
    <tr>
      <td/>
    </tr>
  </tbody>
</table>
```

The element names in the example above are the default names you will find in the Authentic Stylesheet. If the names of the table elements in the schema do not match these default names, you must map the names of the table elements in your schema to the default names in the Authentic Stylesheet. You can do this when you enable XML tables. If there is more than one element in the schema that has a valid table content model, then the mapping to the default names determines which element will be used as the table element.

Caution: If an element called `table` exists in the schema, it will be treated as the XML table element (because `table` is the deafult name for the table element in the Authentic Stylesheet). This could lead to errors if the element `table` is not intended to be used as a table element.

Enabling XML tables with Stylesheet Designer
In order for the user of Authentic View to be able to create XML tables in an XML document, XML tables must be enabled in the Authentic Stylesheet.

To enable XML tables, click **Authentic | CALS/HTML Tables...**. This pops up the CALS / HTML Table Properties dialog shown below.

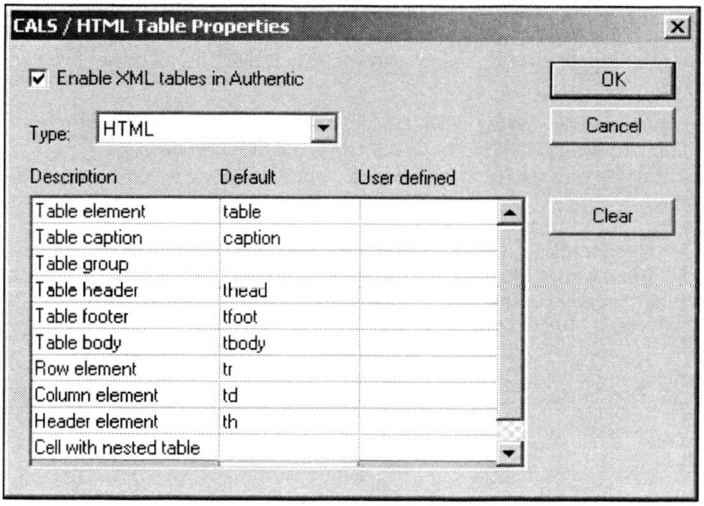

To enable XML tables in Authentic View, check the "Enable XML tables in Authentic" check-box.

Then select the table model type: either HTML or CALS. The screenshot above shows the default names for the HTML table model. If the default names match the table element names in the schema, then the default names are colored black, otherwise red. The screenshot above indicates the following about the schema:

- there is an element called `table` with a content model the same as the HTML table model (all default names appear black)
- all the default HTML elements exist in the content model of `table` (not one of the default names appears red)

Obviously the content model of the element `table` in this schema would not correspond exactly with the CALS table model, which is different than the HTML model. Given below is a screenshot of the CALS / HTML Table Properties dialog with the table model type set to CALS.

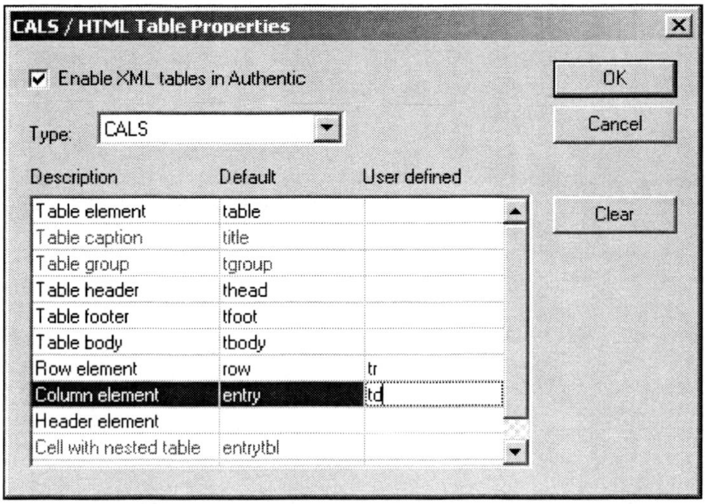

The default CALS table element names colored red do not exist in the schema. Notice that:

- these four elements are present in the existing schema (the default elements appear black)
- the default names of the row element and column element are `row` and `entry`, respectively; whereas in the schema these elements are named `tr` and `td`.

If you wish to use the CALS table model, you should alter the schema to properly include the missing elements. Once you have selected the appropriate table model, click OK. XML tables are now ready to be used in Authentic View. Note that they can only be inserted at locations where the schema allows the table element, and that they must be formatted in Authentic View.

Conditional templates

Function

To specify alternative outputs that vary according to the value of dynamic XML content.

General mechanism

- A conditional template can be inserted anywhere in the Design Document, at a cursor insertion point or around a highlighted node or static component. The node within which the conditional template is inserted is the **context node**.
- The condition to be tested is specified in an XPath expression.
- The **content** of the conditional template will be processed and output if the condition is evaluated as true. To specify an alternative output if the condition is evaluated false, a second conditional template—the "Otherwise" template—must be specified, with the alternative output as its content.
- If multiple outputs are required, each to match a different condition, then multiple conditional templates can be inserted for that node or static content. Each such conditional template specifies a condition and the corresponding output. The first conditional template to be evaluated as true (for that node or ststic content) is executed. With multiple templates, therefore, the sequence in which the templates are ordered is important. Multiple templates can also have a final Otherwise template for the eventuality that none of the preceding conditions are evaluated as true.

Usage

1. Place the cursor where the conditional output is required, or select the node or static content (or both) around which the condition is to be created.
2. Right-click, and select **Insert | Condition...**. The Edit XPath expression dialog appears. It looks like this:

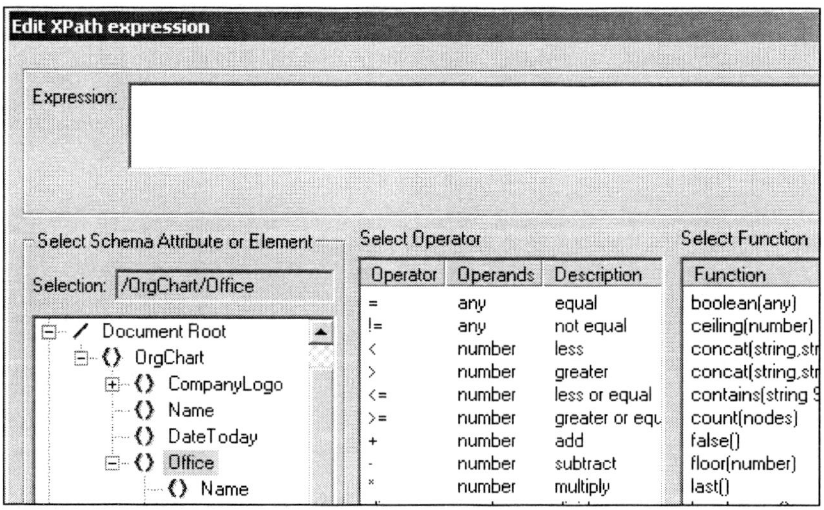

The context node is highlighted in gray.

3. Build the XPath expression by double-clicking schema nodes and XPath operators and functions. Alternatively, you can enter the XPath expression directly in the Expression field.
4. Click OK. The start and end of the conditional template are indicated by cyan tags with a question mark: ?Location = "..." ?.

5. Place the cursor within the conditional template tags, and add the content (static or dynamic) to be processed and output if the condition (specified in the XPath expression) is true. If a node or static content was selected in Step 1, the conditional template tags are placed around this document fragment, and that document fragment is the content of the conditional template.
6. To add an alternative condition, right-click either the start or end tag of the conditional template, and select **Condition | Add New** or **Condition | Add Copy**. In either case, the Edit XPath expression dialog appears, in which you enter the XPath exprseeion to test for the alternative condition.
7. Click OK. Another conditional template is added. If you selected **Condition | Add New**, the new conditional template is empty, and you have to add the content to process and display when this condition is evaluated as true. If you selected **Condition | Add Copy**, then the content of the newly created conditional template is a copy of the content of the selected conditional template; you can modify this content as required.
8. To create, an Otherwise template, follow Step 6 to create another conditional template. In the Edit XPath expression dialog, check the Otherwise check box (shown below). (The Otherwise check box appears if one conditional template already exists on that node, static content, or document fragment.)

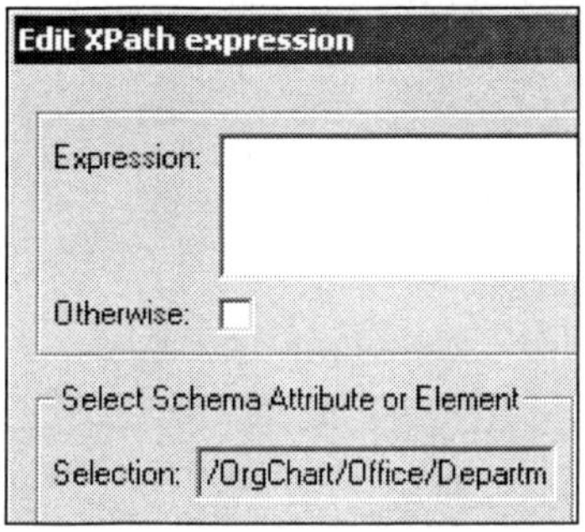

   The Expression field is grayed out.
9. Click OK to create the Otherwise template, and then add or modify content for the template.

Examples
The section Using Conditional Templates in the Stylesheet Designer tutorial has examples of conditional templates for:

- Setting up alternative data structures based on the value of a node
- Selecting and processing a node according to the value of another node
- Formatting text differently based on the numeric value of a node.

The section Creating the Table Footer in the Stylesheet Designer tutorial has examples of conditional templates for:

- Compiling a list based on the numeric value of a descendant node
- Inserting characters based on the position of a node in a nodeset.

Date Picker

Function

The Date Picker is a graphical calendar in Authentic View for entering dates in the ISO format (`YYYY-MM-DD`) in the XML document. The Date Picker can be enabled for any element of datatype `xs:date`. Including the Date Picker is useful since it provides a quick and easy way for the Authentic View user to enter a date in the fixed XML document. to have a known fixed format for dates as this enables easy manipulation of the data through XSLT transformations.

General mechanism

- The Date Picker must first be enabled for one or more XML schema elements of datatype of `xs:date` in the Authentic Stylesheet.
- In Authentic View, dates are entered via the Date Picker by clicking the required date.
- Dates entered via the Date Picker are stored in the standard XML Schema format `YYYY-MM-DD`.

Creating the Date Picker

In order to insert the Date Picker in your Authentic Stylesheet, you must toggle on the Auto-Addition of the Date Picker. You can do this by toggling the icon ON or toggling on **Authentic | Auto-add Date Picker**. When the Auto-Addition of the Date Picker is switched on, the Date Picker is inserted when any element of datatype `xs:date` is created as either contents or an Input Field, or changed to either of these two components.

To create an `xs:date` datatype element with an included Date Picker, do the following:

1. Ensure that the Auto-add Date Picker feature has been switched on.
2. Drag the `date` datatype element (called `Date` in the example below) from the schema tree and create it at the desired location in the Design Document as contents or an Input Field. The Design Document for such an element created as contents will look like this:

   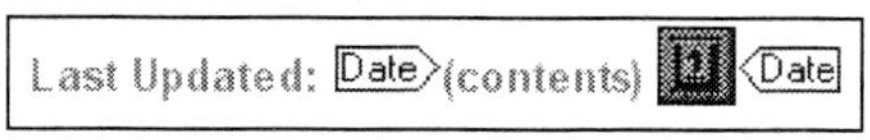

   The Date Picker is created.

Using this Authentic Stylesheet, the Authentic View will look like this:

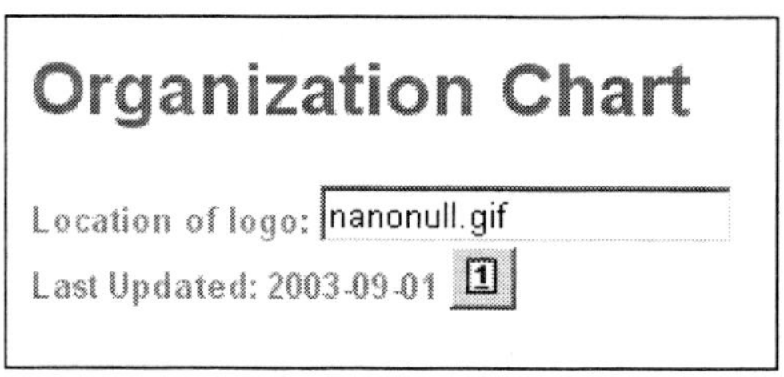

In Authentic View, the content of the Date element is displayed first (in the example above: `2003-09-01`), and after it the icon for the Date Picker. To modify the date, click the icon; this pops up the Date Picker (shown below):

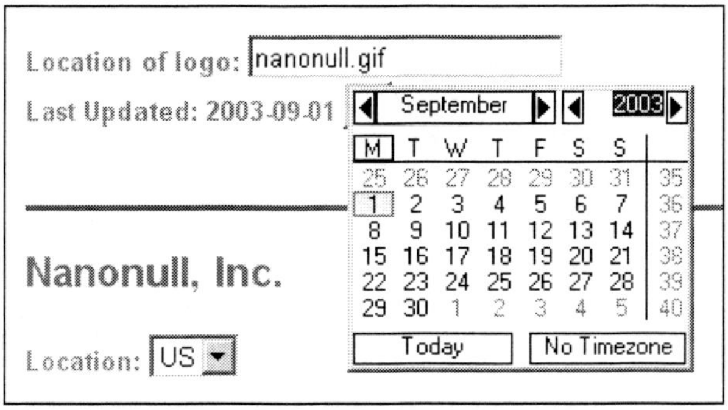

The Authentic View user can also enter the timezone by clicking the Timezone button, which is set to a default of No Timezone. The XML entries for the timezone are also in the standard XML Schema format for timezones, e.g. `2003-09-01+01:00`.

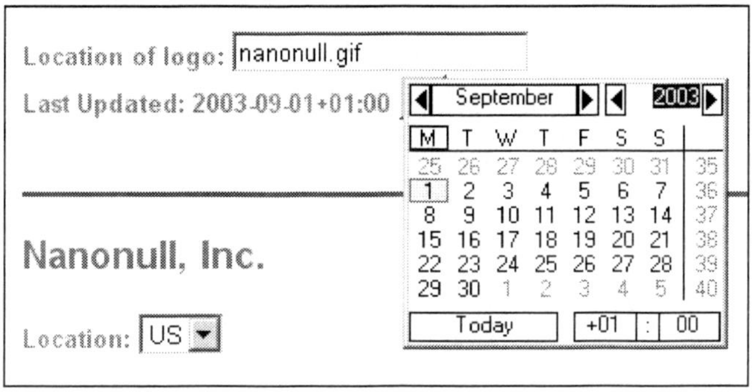

Note: If you have created the `xs:date` datatype element as contents or Input Field, but without the Date Picker, you can subsequently insert the Date Picker in your Authentic Stylesheet by placing the cursor at the desired location inside the element, and clicking **Insert | Date Picker**.

Input Formatting

Function

With Input Formatting, the contents of numeric XML Schema datatype elements can be formatted for Authentic View and/or HTML and PDF outputs as required. Input Formatting can also be used to format the result of an Auto-Calculation.

General mechanism

- The numeric XML Schema datatype element to be formatted must be present in the Design Document as contents or as an input field.
- Select the `(contents)` placeholder or input field, and apply the required formatting via the Input Formatting dialog. Formatting can also be applied to an Auto-Calculation field.
- The formatting applies to Authentic View, and optionally to HTML and PDF outputs. (The actual data in the XML file is stored in the standard format for that datatype.)

Applying input formatting

Input formatting can be applied to any numeric XML Schema datatype element, such as `xs:date`, which is present in the Design Document as contents or an input field. To format such an element, do the following:

1. In the Design Document, right-click the `(contents)` placeholder or input field of the element, and in the context menu that appears (shown below), click **Input Formatting...**.

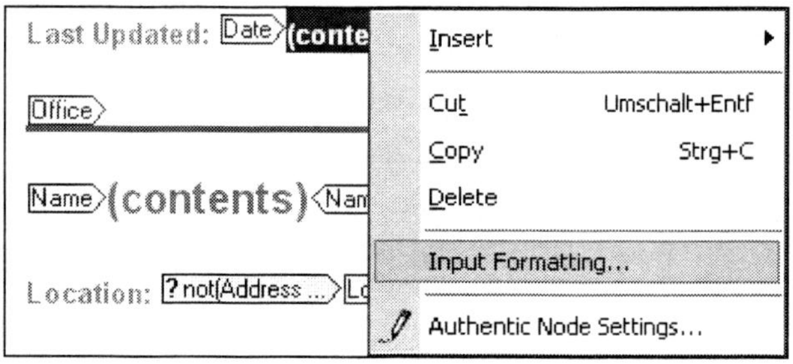

2. The Input Formatting dialog (shown below) appears. Note that the dialog below contains the line: "Formats for type 'date'" and that the standard format for the date datatype is given. This is because the datatype of the element selected in this case is `xs:date`. For another datatype, the information and options in the dialog would be correspondingly different.

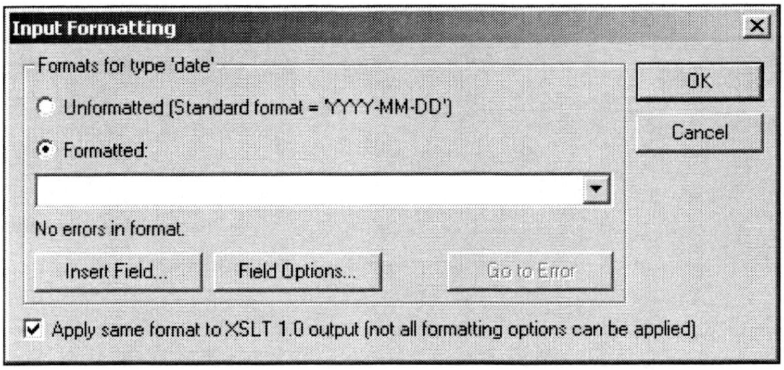
Input Formatting
Formats for type 'date'
Unformatted (Standard format = 'YYYY-MM-DD')
Formatted:
No errors in format.
Insert Field...
Field Options...
Go to Error
OK
Cancel
Apply same format to XSLT 1.0 output (not all formatting options can be applied)

You can specify that the element's content be unformatted (i.e. that it have the standard formatting for that datatype), or that it have a customized formatting. If you are formatting an Auto-Calculation field, the following dialog appears:

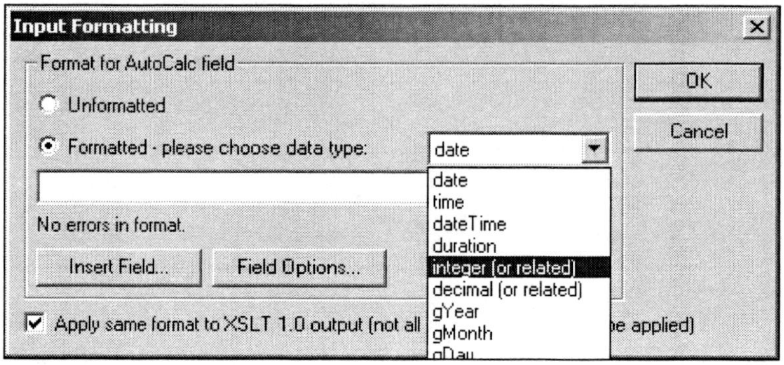

Since an Auto-Calculation field has no datatype assigned to it, you must select one from the drop-down menu shown in the figure above.

3. To specify a customized format, select the Formatted radio button, then enter a format in the input field. You can enter a format by selecting a pre-defined format from the drop down menu (shown below), by building one using the Insert Field and Field Options buttons, or by typing in the format. What pre-defined formats are available depends upon the datatype of the element or, in the case of an Auto-Calculation, the datatype you select.

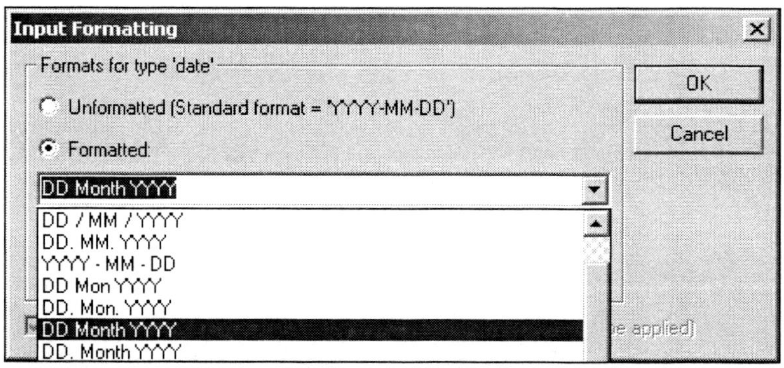

For details of syntax, see the section below.

4. The formatting that you enter will apply to the Authentic View of an XML document. By default, the check box "Apply same format to XSLT 1.0 output" is checked, which means that the formatting will also be applied to HTML and PDF outputs via the generated XSLT stylesheets. If you wish to not have the formatting apply to HTML and PDF outputs, uncheck this check box. In the event some part of the formatting you specify cannot be applied to the HTML and PDF outputs, the "Apply same format to XSLT 1.0..." option will be grayed out.
5. Click OK to apply the formatting.

Note:

- An error in syntax causes the OK button in the Input Formatting dialog to be disabled and the Go to Error button to be enabled. An error message is also displayed in the line below the combo box. Clicking the Go to Error button takes you the point in the format statement where the syntax error is.
- If the result of an Auto-Calculation does not match the fixed XML Schema format of that datatype, then the formatting will be undefined and the Auto-Calculation result will not be displayed correctly.

Insertion and Overwrite fields

Depending on the datatype, the Authentic View user will be able to insert or overwrite digits in the input field. Fields which do not have any semantic meaning beyond their numerical significance, such as integers and decimals, are insertion fields. Fields that do have some kind of semantic meaning, such as years and days, are overwrite fields.

Syntax for input formatting

The basic syntax is:

```
[prefix character/s]field[suffix character/s] [{field-option1,field-option2,...}]
```

where **`prefix character/s`** and **`suffix character/s`** are optional specifiers used to control alignment and the display of positive/negative symbols; **`field`** can be any datatype-specific formatting or text; and **`{field-option(s)}`** is an optional qualifier, that enables additional formatting options.

- Any number of fields can be specified, and any two fields can be separated by the following characters: space, hyphen, comma, colon, period, or by a text string in single or double quotes. Note, however, that fields do not need to be separated.
- One or more optional field-options are allowed per field. The field-option/s for each field must be contained in curly braces, and must follow the field without any intervening space. Multiple options are separated by "," (comma).

Example for an `xs:date` datatype element:

```
DD Month{uc,ro} YYYY
```

where `uc` and `ro` are field-options for making the `Month` field uppercase and read-only, respectively

An example of the output would be:

```
24 SEPTEMBER 2003
```

Example for an `xs:decimal` datatype element:

```
"$"(##0.00)
```

Examples of the output would be:

```
$ 25.00
$ 25.42
$267.56
```

Field types: You will find examples for the datatype-specific field types in the drop-down menu of the Input Formatting dialog. The following tables list the available field types.

Field Type	Explanation
#	Space if no digit at position
0	Zero if no digit at position
,	Digit separator
Y	Year
y	year (base = 1930); see Note below
M	Month
D	Day
W	Week number
d	Weekday number (1 to 7)
i	Day in the year (1 to 366)
h	Hour (0 to 23)
H	Hour (1 to 12)
m	Minute
s	Second
AM	AM or PM
am	am or pm
AD	AD or BC
ad	ad or bc
CE	CE or BCE
ce	ce or bce

Field Type	Explanation
Weekday	Weekday (Sunday, Monday...)
WEEKDAY	Weekday (SUNDAY, MONDAY...)
weekday	Weekday (sunday, monday...)
Wkd	Weekday (Sun, Mon...)
WKD	Weekday (SUN, MON...)
wkd	Weekday (sun, mon...)
Month	Month (January, February...)
MONTH	Month (JANUARY, FEBRUARY...)
month	Month (january, february...)
Mon	Month (Jan, Feb...)
MON	Month (JAN, FEB...)
mon	Month (jan, feb...)

Field length: The following points should be noted:

- When fields such as Y, M, and m are used, the exact length is output. When a field type is repeated, then the length is what is specified in the formatting. For example, if you specify YYYYYY, then the first two (redundant) spaces are filled with 0s. See also Base Year below.
- The Authentic View user is not allowed to add more digits than are specified in the format. If the length of a **pre-existing** value in the XML file exceeds the length specified in the format, the entire value is displayed; the user will, however, not be allowed to enter more digits.
- The * (asterisk) symbol is used to extend the length of a non-semantic numeric field (integers, decimals, etc). In the case of decimals, it can be used on either or both sides of the decimal point. For example, the input formatting *0.00* ensures that a number will have zeroes as specified in the formatting if these digit locations are empty, as well as any number of digits on both sides of the decimal point.

Prefix and suffix characters: Prefix and suffix characters are used to specify alignment and details of the positive/negative symbol. The following table lists the prefix and suffix characters.

Prefix	Suffix	Explanation
<		Left aligned; default for text
>		Right aligned; default for numbers
?		Minus symbol if negative; nothing otherwise; default
?>		Minus symbol flush left if negative; nothing otherwise
<?>		Minus symbol flush left if negative; nothing otherwise
-	-	Minus symbol if negative; space otherwise; located before (prefix), after (suffix)
->	>-	Minus symbol if negative; space otherwise; located flush left (prefix); fixed position (suffix)
<->		Minus symbol flush left if negative; space otherwise
+	+	Plus or minus sign always; located before (prefix), after (suffix)
+>	>+	Plus or minus sign always; flush left (prefix), fixed position (suffix)
<+>		Plus or minus sign always; located flush left
(	)	Parentheses if negative; space otherwise
(>	>)	Parentheses if negative; space otherwise; located flush left (prefix); fixed position (suffix)
<(>		Parentheses if negative; space otherwise; located flush left
[	]	Parentheses if negative; nothing otherwise
[>	>]	Parentheses if negative; nothing otherwise; located flush left (prefix); fixed position (suffix)
<[>		Parentheses if negative; nothing otherwise; located flush left
*	*	Extendable number of digits to left (prefix) or to right (suffix)
_	_	Space
^	^	Fill character (defined in options)
	th	Ordinality of number (st, nd, rd, or th)
	TH	Ordinality of number (ST, ND, RD, or TH)

Options: The following options are available:

Option	Explanation
uc	Make uppercase
lc	Make lowercase
left	Left aligned
right	Right aligned
ro	Read (XML) only; no editing allowed
edit	The field is editable (active by default)
dec=<char>	Specify a character for the decimal point (default is point)
fill=<char>	Specify fill character
base=<year>	Base year for year fields (see Note below)
pos	Show only positive numbers; input of negative numbers allowed

Note on Base Year: When using short year formats (for example, `DD-MM-YY{base=1940}`), the base year specifies a cut-off for a century. If the user enters a value that is equal to or greater than the last two digits (considered together as a number) of the base year, then the century is the same as that of the base year. If the user value is less than the last two digits, the century is the century of the base year plus one. For example if you set `base=1940`, then if the Authentic View user enters "50", the XML value for the year will be `1950`; if the user enters "23", the XML value will be `2023`. Although two digits are commonly used as the short year format, one-digit and three-digit short year formats can also be used with a base year. Note that if you use the `y` field type, the base year is taken to be 1930.

Global Templates

Function

Global templates can be created for individual elements. In the Design Document, for a given element you can specify whether the locally defined template or the global template (if this is defined) is to be used. In some cases, using a global template is the only way to process an element.

Global templates can—and, in some cases, must—be used in the following situations:

- For elements that can occur at multiple locations in various parts of the document, and where the locations cannot be known to you, the designer of the document, a global template must be used. An example of such an element is one marking up italic or bold text. (You cannot know where such elements will occur in the text; therefore, a global template for each such element must be used.)
- If an element can occur recursively, i.e. within itself or a descendant, then a global template is required. An example is a numbered list, an item of which may iteslf contain a numbered list.
- For an element type that occurs as a child of different parents (for example, `//office/email` and `//person/email`), using a global template ensures that both `//email` elements are processed in the same way—if, that is, you want to process them in the same way. The advantage of using a global template in this kind of scenario is that the processing for several elements of a single element type is defined in a single global template; a change in the global template will therefore apply to all the elements that use this global template.

General mechanism

- The Design Document is a single large template that defines the stucture of the output document. It consists of several **local templates**.
- A local templates defines the processing of a particular element in the Design Document.
- A global template defines the processing of a global element. For example, a global template can be created for the element `title`, which could then be used for any title element in the document (e.g. `//book/title`, `//chapter/title`, `//section/title`, etc).
- If an element used in the Design Document has a global template defined for it, either the local template or the global template can be used.
- If an element only has a global template defined, then, in order for the template to be processed and produce output, it must be "reached". It is reached if there are other (local or global) templates that specify processing for each element in the hierarchy, starting from the root element and reaching down to this element.

Elements for which Global Templates are allowed to be created

When a schema is loaded into Stylesheet Designer, a single Global Templates entry is created in the Schema Window. This entry contains all the elements for which global template rules are allowed.

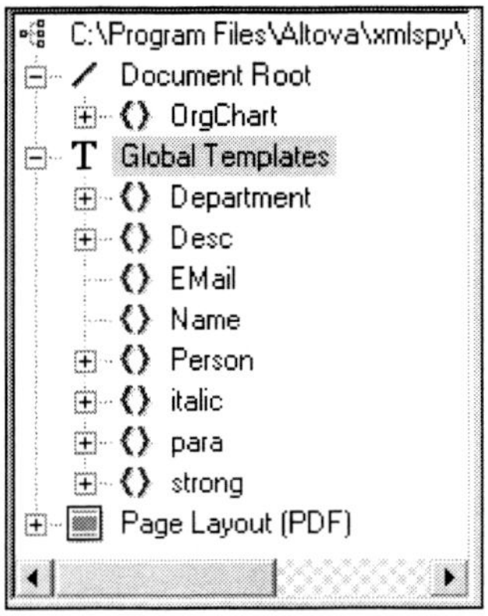

Elements that appear in the Global Templates list are:

- All elements named in element declarations in a DTD
- All elements declared as global elements in an XML Schema, i.e. elements declared as children of the `xs:schema` element.

Creating Global Templates
Global templates can be created in either of two ways.

1. By clicking an entry in the Global Templates list and defining properties for it. Clicking an element listed under Global Templates will create an *empty* global template for that element. An empty global template has only the `<apply-templates />` rule specified but no other template rule; that is, it will process child elements but not do anything else (such as format text).
2. By right-clicking an item in the Design window, and selecting Make Global Template. A global template is created for that element type *from the local template* (that is, the global template will be created with the properties of the local template); the local template is deleted; and the global template is used for that element. Note that the Make Global Template command is displayed in the context menu only for those elements that are listed in the Global Templates list.

Whenever a global template is created (empty or not), a "+" sign appears to the left of the element's name in the "Global Templates" list (see figure below). Note that a global template can be created only for the global element itself—not for the descendants that are displayed when the global element is expanded.

After a global template is created, it will not automatically be used for an element in the Design Document—unless it has been created from a local template. The use of the global template for an element in the Design Document must be explicitly specified. This is described in the section "Using Global Templates" below.

Defining properties for Global Templates
To add formatting properties to an empty global template, key in values for the required text properties in the Text Style and/or Block Style windows. In the example below, the global template for the `<italic>` element has been assigned a font-style value of "italic".

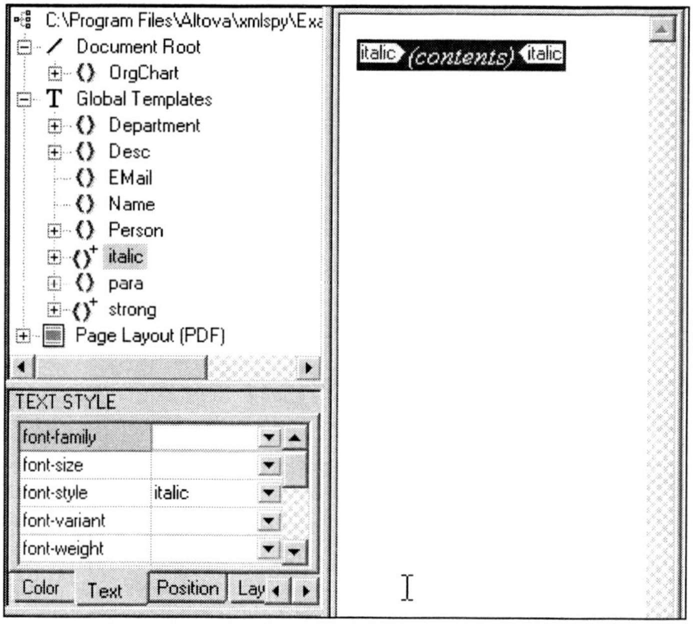

In the example above, note that only the font-style property has been assigned a value. Other properties, such as font-family, font-size, and font-weight have not been assigned any value. For these properties, the values are inherited from the respective parent of each *instance* of `<italic>`. So if the parent of one instance of `<italic>` were `<para>`, and `<para>` had a font-size value of "11pt", then this instance of `<italic>` would inherit the font-size value of "11pt". If the parent of another instance of `<italic>` were `<email>`, and `<email>` had a font-size value of "10pt", then this instance of `<italic>` would inherit the font-size value of "10pt". Defining the global template for `<italic>` as above has the advantage that the `<italic>` markup changes only the font style (to italic) while the rest of the formatting is exactly the same as the surrounding text, no matter what the surrounding text. For example, an `<italic>` element contained within a `<bold>` element would inherit the font-weight value of "bold", thus producing text in bold italic.

Using Global Templates

Global templates are *created* in either of the two ways described in the section "Creating Global Templates" above. If you wish to use a global template with any element occurrence after it has been created, you have to specify this explicitly.

By default each occurrence of an element uses the local template. So, for example, if from the three occurrences of an `<email>` element: `//company/address/email` and `//employee/office/email` and `//employee/home/email`, you wish to use the global template with the two occurrences: `//employee/office/email` and `//employee/home/email`, then you have to specify that these two occurrences should use the global template.

There are two ways to specify that a given element occurrence should use a Global Template:

1. If a global template exists for a given element name, and an element with that name is then dragged from the Schema window, then on dropping the element into the Design window a menu (shown below) pops up. In the figure below, the `<Desc>` element, for which a global template exists, has been dragged to a location just before the

Department tag (location shown by cursor). Since a global template exists for `<Desc>`, the Use Global Template command appears in the pop-up menu.

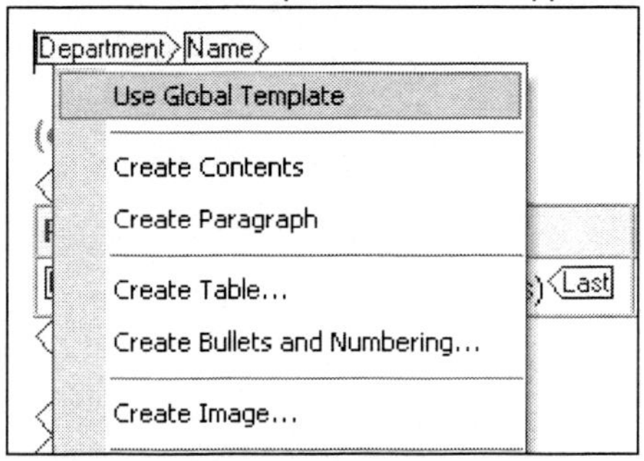

Clicking Use Global Template, creates this element occurrence (`<Desc>`, in the example above) at that location using the global template properties. The element tags will be gray, indicating that the element uses the global template.

2. If the element occurrence already exists, right-click the element in the Design window, and click "Use Global Template". In the figure below, the `<Desc>` element has been right-clicked. Since a global template exists for <Desc>, the Use Global Template command appears in the context menu.

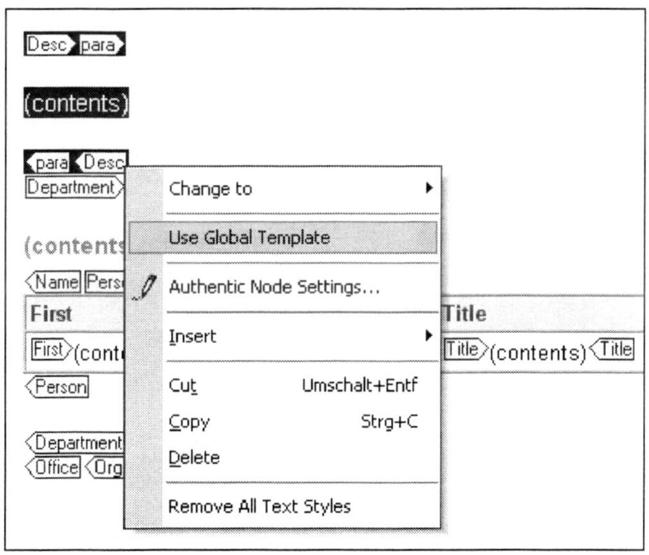

The local template will be deleted, and the global template will be used. The element tags turn gray, indicating that the element uses the global template.

Copying Global Template properties to a Local Template

When an element uses a global template, no local template exists. You can, however, create a local template from the global template. This is useful when you have a global template for an element and wish, for example, to change the formatting for a majority of element occurrences but retain the current global template properties for a few element occurrences. In such a case, you would copy the global template to local templates wherever required, and then make the change in the global template.

To copy a global template to a local template, in the Design window, right-click the element that uses the global template (the element tags will be gray), and click "Copy Global Template Locally". The global template is copied as the local template for the element, and the newly created local template is applied. The element tags turn from gray to beige, indicating that the local template is being used. The global template remains unchanged; it can be used for other occurrences of that element type.

Editing a Global Template
To change the formatting properties of a global template, do the following:

1. Select the Design window tab.
2. In the Schema Window, from the list of Global Templates, click the global template you wish to edit.
3. Enter the required values in the Text Style and/or Block Style windows.

The changes in the global template will be applied to all the element occurrences that use this particular global template.

Removing a Global Template
To remove a global template, do the following:

1. Select the Design window tab.
2. In the Schema Window, from the list of Global Templates, right-click the global template you wish to remove.
3. Select "Remove Global Template".

This removes the global template.

Caution: Use this command with care since it not only removes the global template but also removes *any element type occurrence that is currently using this global template*. If you wish to not have these element occurrences deleted, then ensure that you switch these occurrences to use a local template before you remove the global template.

PDF processing and page layout

Generating PDF output from an XML file is a two-stage process. In the first step, an XSLT transformation (or stylesheet) is used to transform the XML file into an XSL-FO file (FO file, for short). XSL-FO is a markup language, similar to CSS, that provides presentation information for a variety of media, including paged media. The FO file, therefore, contains the page sequencing and layout information (markup) that will be used to generate the PDF. In the second step, an FO processor uses the FO file as input to generate the PDF.

Stylesheet Designer produces an XSLT that will transform an XML file into an FO file. The document schema is loaded into Stylesheet Designer, and the required output document is designed entirely in terms of the graphical representation of the schema's components. This design describes the functionality, content, and appearance of the final document. From this design specification, Stylesheet Designer creates two XSLT stylesheets, one to create HTML output, the other to create FO output.

The markup in the HTML and FO files will produce functionality and presentation that match each other as closely as possible. However, there are limitations to the correspondence between the two formats. This is for two reasons. Firstly, some functionality available in one format might not be available in the other format, such as marquee text, which is a common HTML functionality but is not available in PDF. Secondly, available FO processors (that generate PDF from FO) do not as yet fully support the FO recommendations. As a result, some presentation aspects that will apppear in the HTML output and are provided for by the FO recommendation will not appear in the PDF output; this because the FO processor cannot generate the required presentation. Therefore, when using Stylesheet Designer's Design interface you should bear in mind that, although you will be able to generate sophisticated HTML documents with your design, the PDF output will be limited by what the PDF format can deal with and by what the FO processor you use can deliver.

Currently available FO processors implement the FO specification differently and to varying degrees of compliance. Stylesheet Designer currently offers two compliance options when it internally processes the FO file to generate a PDF preview:

1. compliance-level of the latest FOP version. With this option, you can use FOP ver 0.20.5rc. Any presentation properties in your design that are not supported by this version of FOP are filtered out.
2. complete compliance with the XSL-FO specification. Since full compliance is assumed, any property not supported by the processor in use could cause a processing error. You can select any processor of your choice with this option.

From the design you make, Stylesheet Designer creates an XSLT file that will generate the FO file. This XSLT file can be viewed in Stylesheet Designer and also be saved for use outside Stylesheet Designer. You can also generate a PDF preview within Stylesheet Designer. Using this feature, first the FO file is created using the internal XSLT processor, and then the temporary FO file is processed by an FO processor of your choice to generate the PDF preview. The FO and PDF files can also be saved.

FO Processing for PDF Preview

Stylesheet Designer provides an inbuilt PDF Preview option. Clicking the PDF Preview tab in the main window, does the following:

1. Takes you to the Preview window
2. Generates an FO file behind the scenes
3. Processes the FO file with the user-defined FO processor
4. Displays the PDF

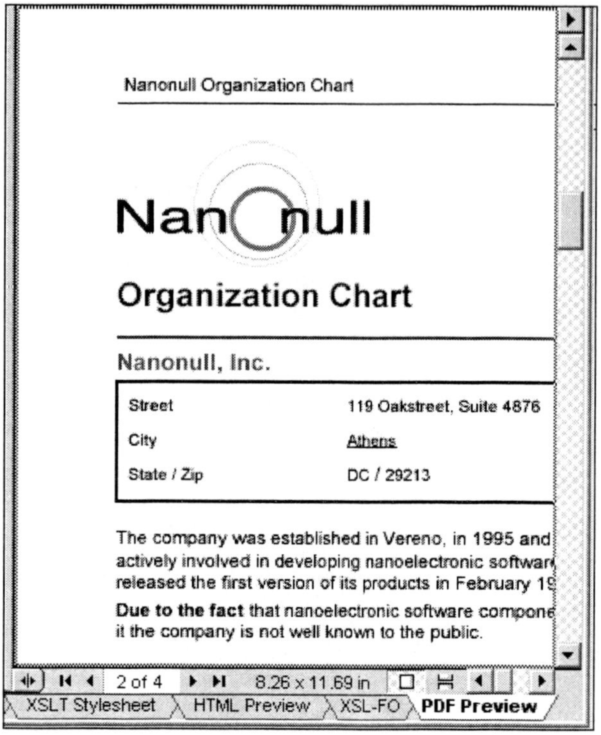

Software required to enable PDF Preview:
In order to enable PDF Preview in Stylesheet Designer, the following software must be installed:

- an FO processor to generate PDF from the FO file. The open-source FOP processor from the Apache XML Project and some commercial products are currently good options. Our Download Center (www.altova.com/components_processors.html) offers links to the download sites, as well as direct downloads, of some popular processors.
- Acrobat Reader to read the generated PDF within Stylesheet Designer .

Note that both the FOP and XEP processors resourced from our Download Center require a Java Virtual Machine, so one will have to be installed. For FOP, Sun's JDK/JRE 1.2 or later is required. For XEP, Sun's JDK/JRE 1.1.8 or later, or Microsoft's JVM 5.0 or later is required.

Setting up the FO processor
After installing the FO processor of your choice, you need to configure Stylesheet Designer to use it.

1. Select the menu option **Tools | XSL:FO**.

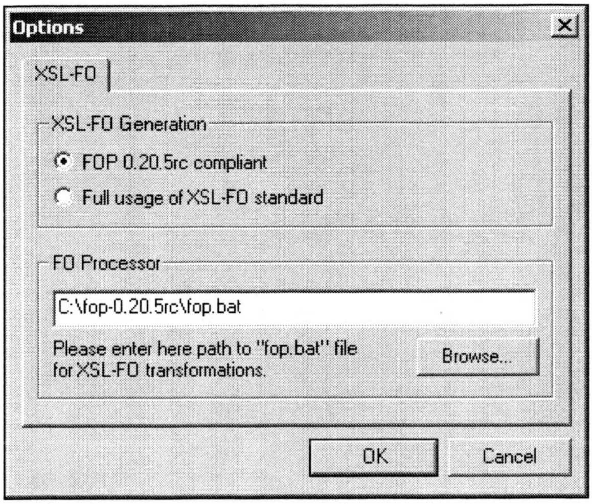

2. Click the Browse button and select the batch file that starts the FO processor. The batch file is available after you have installed the FO processor.
3. Select the compliance level. Two options are available: (i) FOP 0.20.5rc compliant (if you are using the latest version of FOP), and (ii) full compliance (any processor; note, however, that if the processor is not fully compliant it could generate a processing error.)

The **FOP 0.20.5rc** radio button is selected by default. This option causes any FO properties defined by you but not supported by FOP 0.20.5rc to be filtered out. A list of these properties is available at http://xml.apache.org/fop/compliance.html.

XSL-FO Object Support

The following is a summary of FOP's current support for the standard XSL-FO objects.

Object Name	Support			Comments
	Basic	Extended	Complete	
Declarations and Pagination and Layout Formatting Objects				
root	yes	.	.	.
declarations	no	.	.	.
color-profile	.	no	.	.
page-sequence	yes	.	.	.

Properties supported by FOP are marked with a YES in the compliance table (shown above). Properties that are not supported or incompletely supported could cause a processor error, as a result of which no PDF preview will be generated. Using the FOP 0.20.5rc filter ensures that only those properties suported by FOP 0.20.5rc will be used.

Selecting "**Full usage of XSL:FO standard**" will make available all properties of the complete XSL-FO specification. To ensure that you successfully obtain a PDF preview with this option, you must use an FO processor that supports the complete XSL-FO recommendation. However, even if you use an FO processor that does not support the full XSL-FO recommendation, an FO file that does not contain any property that is beyond the support of the FO processor will still successfully generate a PDF preview.

Stylesheet Designer automatically maps CSS2 and HTML properties to the equivalent FO properties, the aim being to obtain a PDF rendition that matches the HTML output as closely as possible. However, the level of correspondence between the HTML and PDF formats will vary according to: (a) whether both formats support a given functionality; (b) the level of compliance offered by the FO processor you use, and (c) the way in which the FO processor implements the formatting. As a result, certain Web page elements, such as radio buttons, check boxes, buttons, combo boxes, input fields and multiline input fields, cannot be displayed in the PDF because this support has not yet been implemented in FOP. Such elements are all displayed as underlined text when the FOP processor is used.

PDF page definition

For the PDF output, certain basic page properties can be defined. These include the size of the PDF page, the margins of the page, and certain page numbering options. All these settings are available in the **PDF Page Properties** dialog, which you open by selecting the menu option **Properties | PDF page**. The dialog is as shown below.

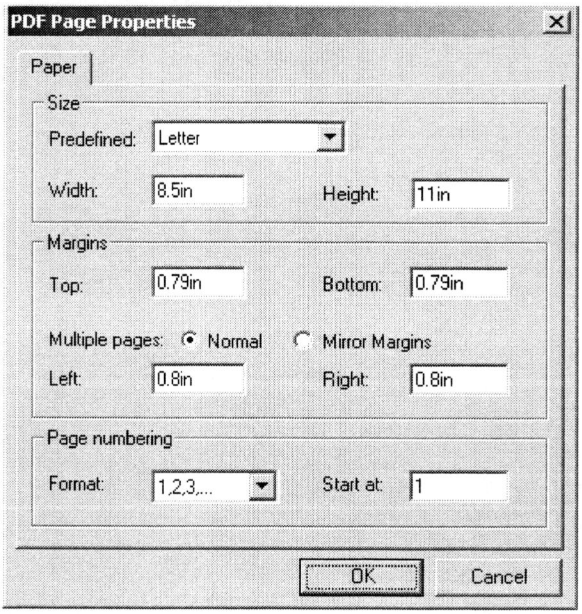

Page size
Set the page size by selecting one of the pre-defined options from the drop-down menu, or by selecting "**Custom size**" and then entering the desired width and height.

Page margins
Set the top, bottom, left and right margins by entering the required number followed by any of the XSL units: points (pt), picas (pc), centimeters (cm), millimeters (mm), and inches (in). Note

that (i) there must not be a space between the number and the unit; (ii) there is no default unit; (iii) a unit is mandatory.

If you set **Multiple pages** to "Normal", then all pages in the PDF will have the same value for the left margin and the same value for the right margin, that is, they will not be treated as facing pages. If on the other hand you set **Multiple pages** to "Mirror Margins", then the document pages are treated as facing pages. This means that for even-numbered pages (left-hand-side pages), the outer margin is the left margin while the inner margin is the right margin; for odd-numbered pages (right-hand-size pages), the outer margin is the right margin while the inner margin is the left margin.

Page numbering
Set the required page number format by selecting one of the pre-defined options from the drop-down menu. Set the page numbering to start with any positive integer. Page numbering starts with the first body page, that is, the first page after the cover page.

PDF layout elements

The following page layout elements for the document can be defined: the cover page, and headers and footers.

Defining the cover page
A simple template for the cover page is provided as a page layout template. To make a cover page, do the following:

1. With the Design window selected, go to the document tree view, expand the Page Layout (PDF) entry, and click the Cover Page icon to access the cover page.

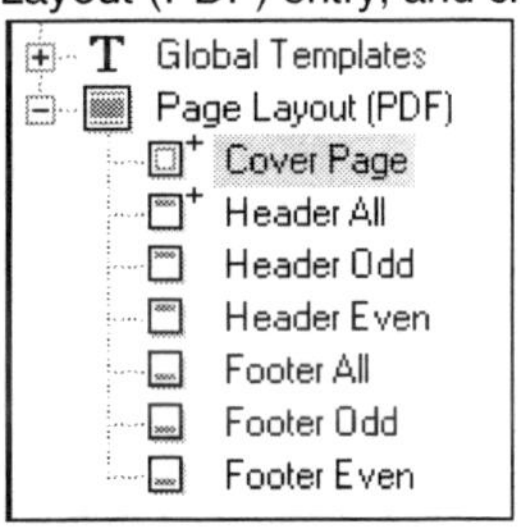

2. Edit the default text as required, or drag elements from the document tree into the cover page.
3. Drag the **OrgChart | Name** tags into the top line of the cover page.
4. Use the Text Style window to format the text. For example, change the font-size to Medium.

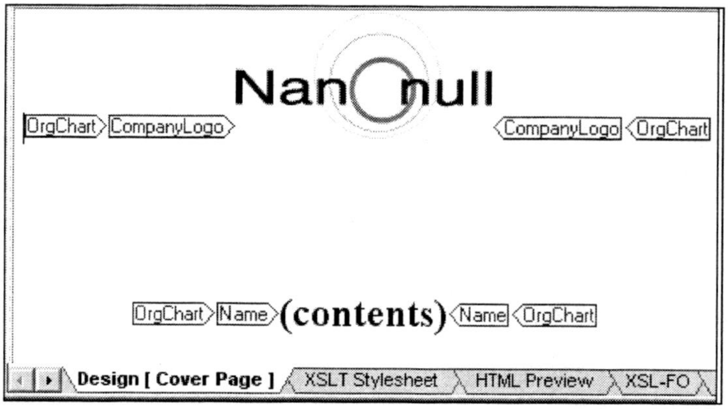

5. Click the PDF Preview tab to see the result in the Preview window.

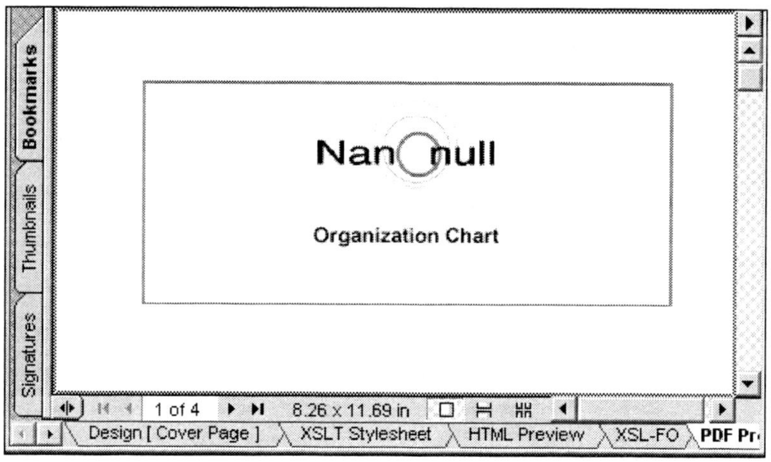

Note that a small plus symbol appears next to the text "Cover Page". This indicates that the template now contains user-defined content.

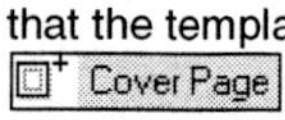

Defining headers and footers

Headers and footers are defined using the same method as for the cover page. A single header/footer can be defined for all pages by using the Header All / Footer All icons, or different headers/footers can be defined for odd and even pages, using the Header Odd / Footer Odd icons and Header Even / Footer Even icons.

1. Click the Header All icon to access the Header All definition window. The default header template shown below appears.

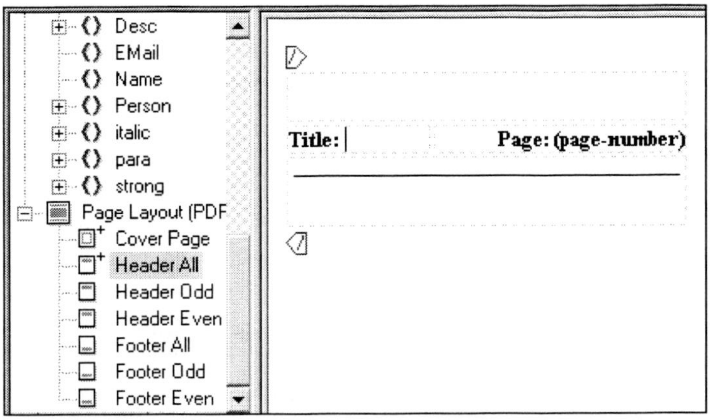

2. Change the header as required. to suit your needs, Tutorial in this case.
3. Drag elements from under the schema root into the window. In this case the **OrgChart | CompanyLogo** element was dragged into the top cell, and the option "Create image" was selected from the popup menu. The image was also made to align right using the Align Right icon in the icon bar.

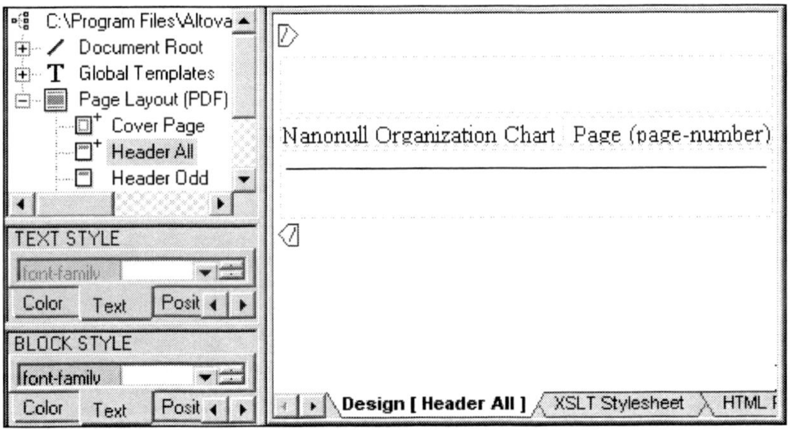

4. Click the PDF Preview tab to see the results in the Preview window. The illustration below shows Page 2 of the Organization Chart document, with the header as defined above.

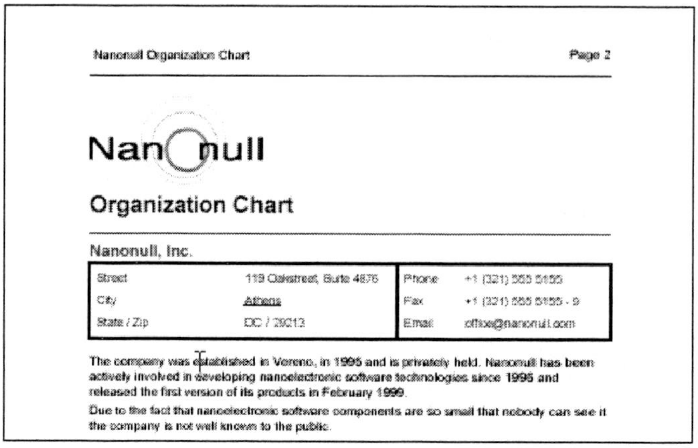
Nanonull Organization Chart Page 2

Nanonull

Organization Chart

Nanonull, Inc.

Street	119 Oakstreet, Suite 4876	Phone	+1 (321) 555 5155
City	Athens	Fax	+1 (321) 555 5155 - 9
State / Zip	DC / 29013	Email	office@nanonull.com

The company was established in Vereno, in 1995 and is privately held. Nanonull has been actively involved in developing nanoelectronic software technologies since 1995 and released the first version of its products in February 1999.

Due to the fact that nanoelectronic software components are so small that nobody can see it the company is not well known to the public.

Please note:

The Header All and Header Even / Header Odd definitions are mutully exclusive. If, after having defined Header All, you click either Header Odd or Header Even, a dialog box opens asking if you want to delete the Header All definition and define separate odd and even headers. This also happens in the opposite situation: if you have defined separate odd and even page headers and then click the Header All icon, you are asked if you want to delete the existing definitions and create a single header for odd and even pages instead.

Note also that the header must fit within the top margin defined for the PDF page (under **Properties | PDF Page**). The height of the header should therefore be lesser than the vertical extent of the top margin. If the header does not fit, then you can adjust either the header height or the top margin.

Footers are defined in the same way as headers are. You can set either Footer All or Footer Even / Footer Odd as described for headers above. Note that the height of footers must be lesser than the vertical extent of the bottom margin of the page.

Stylesheet Designer User Reference

The reference section contains a complete description of all Stylesheet Designer windows and menu commands.

Symbols and icons

Stylesheet Designer uses easily recognizable symbols to display the various schema elements in the tree view, and uses tag symbols for the XSLT elements in the Design view.

Format combo box

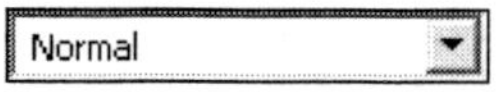

Selecting a format from this list box applies it to the currently marked element in the Design view. All tags dragged from the schema pane into the Design view, are automatically assigned the Normal format.

Tree view symbols and icons

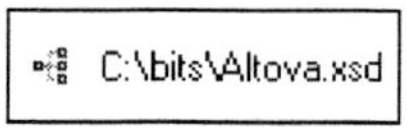

Schema name and folder

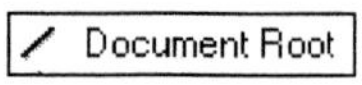

Document root.

All elements inserted from below the Document root (but not under the Global Templates) into the Design view, become **local elements**. The Design view tab contains the text **Design [Document]**. Local elements can be converted to global templates in the Design view. (??link here).

Global templates are defined using the elements under the Global Templates element.

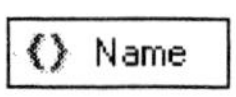

Element

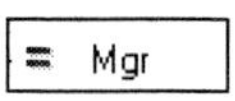

Attribute.

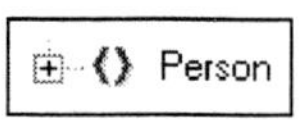

Element with child/sub elements.

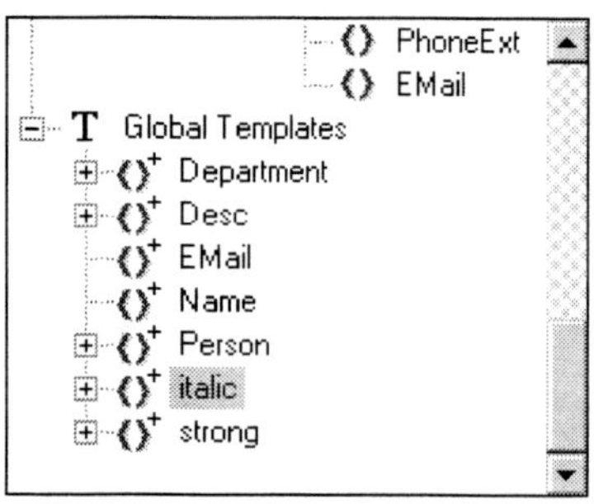

Global templates, these are equivalent to global elements in a schema.

Design view symbols and icons
Element and attribute symbols can be moved around using **drag and drop** in the Design window. The standard Cut, Copy and Paste commands can also be used to achieve the same thing.

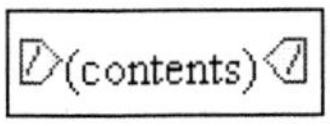

Root element tags.

The **(contents)** "text" between the two tags in the Design view, is the symbol for an XML data **placeholder**. The placeholder is filled with data when you switch to the HTML Preview tab. The data is supplied by the XML file assigned to the schema visible in the tree view. Use the menu option **File | Assign working XML file...** to assign the XML file to the schema.

To delete a placeholder:

1. Click the placeholder and press the keyboard Del. key.

   This deletes the placeholder in the Design tab, and causes the XML data to be suppressed in the HTML Preview.

To (re) insert a placeholder:

1. Click between the two tags where you want to insert the placeholder.
2. Click right (at the cursor position) to open the context menu, and select "Insert Contents".

   The placeholder is inserted at the cursor position.

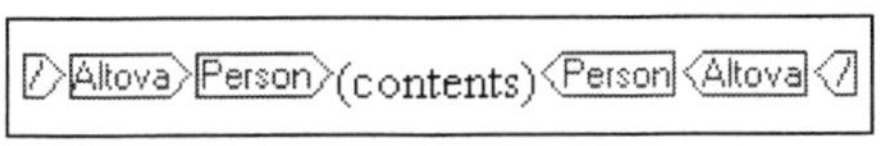

Start and end tags of the Person element, expanded. The parent tags of the Person element (Altova) are also included.

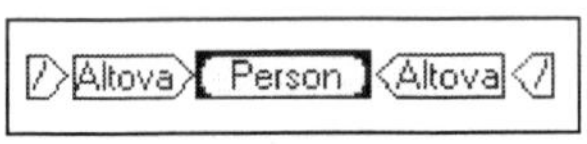

Person element tag, contracted. To expand or contract tags, double click the specific tag.

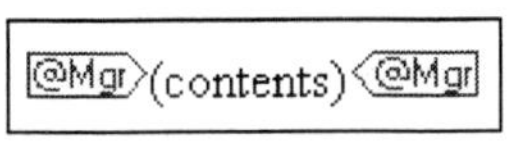

Manager attribute, start and end tag.

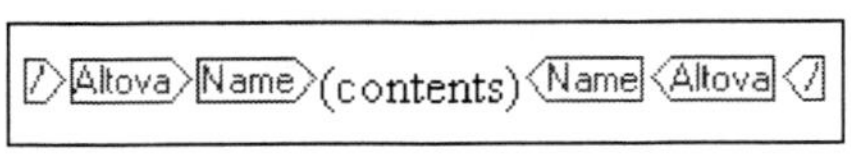

"Contents", placeholder for XML data.

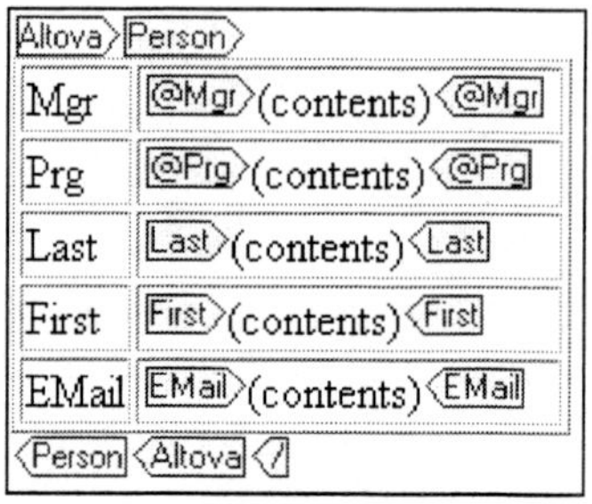

Person element inserted as a table containing both elements and attributes.

Email element "input field". Clicking right on the vertical border at the right allows you to directly change the size of this field by dragging with the mouse.

Text and Block Style Windows

Text Style Window

The Text Style window allows you to apply formatting to text and text components (such as the (contents) placeholder and data-entry devices). To apply text formatting, select the text component to be formatted and enter a value for the required property.

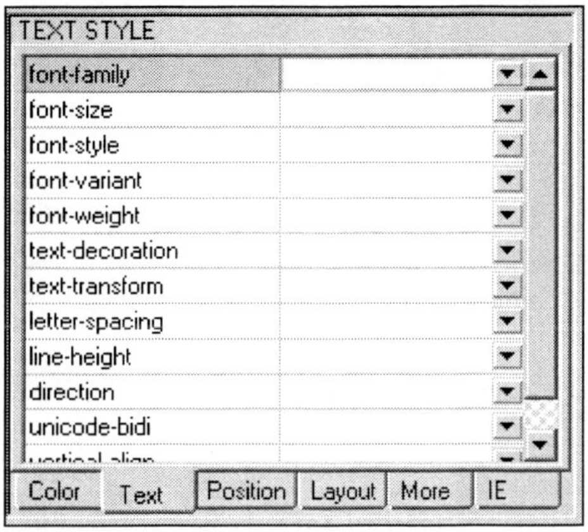

Block Style Window

The Block Style window allows you to apply formatting to block components. Block components include paragraphs, headings, tables, lists, etc. Any component that is not a block component (i.e. it is an inline component) can be made into a block component by assigning it a pre-defined format. When a block component is selected, the Block Style window is enabled; otherwise it is grayed out.

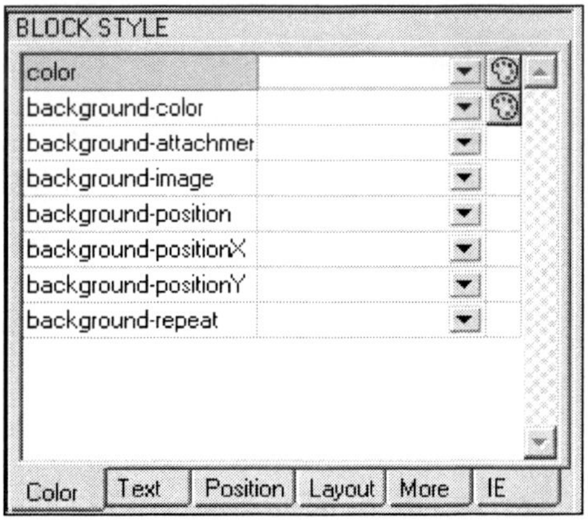

Note: When a property is assigned in the Block Style window, it applies to the entire block. For example, if a table is selected, and a text property is assigned in the Block Style window, then that text property applies to text in all the cells of the table. If you wish to have some property apply to the text of one particular cell only, you must select that text, and assign the required property in the Text Style window.

Formatting

Formatting can be applied to a selected component in one of, or a combination of any of, the following three ways:

- By selecting a pre-defined format
- By specifying values for Block Style properties
- By specifying values for Text Style properties

To assign formatting to a component, select it, and then use one or more of the three methods listed. Each method is explained below.

Pre-defined formats

Stylesheet Designer has a number of pre-defined formats, the properties of which you cannot change. When you apply a pre-defined format to a component, the formatting markup is created **around the selected component**. When an element or attribute is created in the Design Document, it is assigned the Normal format by default. Any pre-defined format must be explicitly assigned.

Pre-defined formats can be assigned by clicking **Insert | Format**, and then the required format, or by selecting the required format from the Format drop-down list in the Toolbar (shown below).

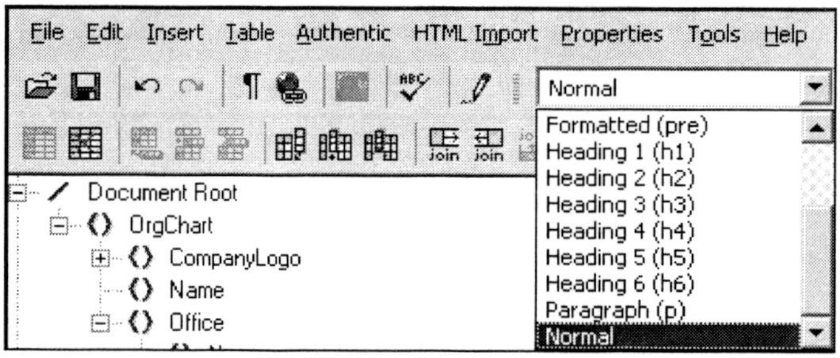

Note: Assigning a pre-defined format to a component makes that component a block component.

The pre-defined formats used in Stylesheet Designer have either one or both of the following two components:

- a text-formatting component
- a spacing component.

For example, the pre-defined `para (p)` format has a spacing component only; it puts vertical space before and after the selected component, and does not apply any text formatting. On the other hand, the pre-defined `Heading 1 (h1)` format has both a text-formatting component and a spacing component.

The following points about pre-defined formats should be noted:

- The spacing component of a pre-defined format applies for any type of component, but the text formatting only if it can be applied. For example, if you select an image, and apply a pre-defined format of `Heading 1 (h1)` to it, then the spacing component will take effect, but the text-formatting component will not.
- The text-formatting component of pre-defined formats does not apply to data-entry devices.

- Only one pre-defined format applies to a component at any given time.

Block Style properties
Block Style properties are assigned in the Block Style window. When an element/attribute is created, it is created with the default pre-defined format of `Normal` and is not a block. To make the element/attribute a block, assign it any pre-defined format other than `Normal`.

Caution: When applying block styles within a table cell, remember that the table cell is a block. It may be that the component in the table cell is also a block (you can find out by checking its pre-defined formatting). If the component is also a block, be sure to select the correct block (i.e. table-cell block or component block). Note that you can also apply table formatting through the Table Properties dialog.

Tip: You do not need to make a component a block in order to apply certain block styles (such as spacing) to it. You can apply such block styles in the Text Style window.

Text Style properties
Text Style properties are assigned in the Text Style window, and the properties are assigned as **inline** markup surrounding the component in the markup of the output. Text style properties, therefore, override block style properties and pre-defined formats if there is a conflict.

Formatting conflicts
If there is a formatting conflict, i.e. a formatting property is defined using more than one of the above methods, the conflict is resolved using the same principle used in Cascading Style Sheets: inline markup has priority over higher-level markup. The priority for the different methods is as follows:

1. Text Style (since this is inline markup)
2. Block Style (since this applied to the block)
3. Pre-defined format (the formatting is inherent in the element name, e.g. `h2` and `div`)

File

The File menu contains all commands relevant to manipulating files in the order common to most Windows software products.

Open

The "Open..." command allows you to open an **XML schema**, **DTD** or **.sps** file. The familiar Windows "Open" dialog is opened and allows you to select one of these file types.

You may get an error message if your file is either not well-formed or invalid, in this case switch to STYLEVISION 2004 and try to resolve the problem there.

Opening a .sps file displays the tags in the Design view, and automatically loads all the XML files associated with this file (Schema/DTD and XML document instance).

Save

The "Save" command saves the currently open Stylesheet Designer file as a structure file. The file type extension is ***.sps**.

The .sps file saves all the data visible in Stylesheet Designer, as well as the associated XML and Schema/DTD files.

Please note:

Only template files (all *.sps files) saved from within Stylesheet Designer, can be edited in Authentic View! These documents are created/opened by selecting the **File | New** menu option and clicking the "**Select an Authentic view template...**" in the Create new document dialog box.

To define the data that should appear in the template file, please see Authentic | Assign Template XML file.

Save as...

The "Save As..." command shows the familiar Windows "Save as..." dialog and prompts for the name and location of the .sps file to be saved.

Please note:

Only **template files** (all ***.sps** files) saved from within Stylesheet Designer, can be edited in Authentic View!

Assign working XML file...

The "Assign working XML file" command assigns an existing XML file to the currently open DTD or schema file.

The XML file is used to preview the XSLT file using the XML data. Clicking the HTML Preview tab without having assigned an XML file, opens a message box prompting you to select one.

Please note:

The name and folder of the XML working file is displayed in the **title bar** of Stylesheet

Designer! If a file has not been assigned, only the *.sps name is displayed.

Save generated XSLT file as...

The "Save generated XSLT file as..." command allows you to save the current version of the XSLT file visible in the XSLT Stylesheet tab.

Save generated XSL-FO file as...

The "Save generated XSL-FO file as..." command allows you to save the current version of the XSL-FO file visible in the "XSL-FO" tab.

Please see PDF processing and page layout for more information.

Most recently used files

The list of most recently used files, shows the file name and path information for the nine most recently used files, which you can select with the mouse.

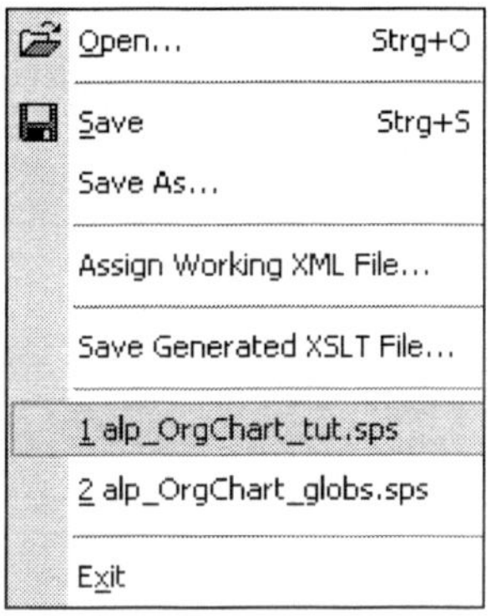

To access these files using the **keyboard**, press:
ALT+F,1 to open the File menu, and select the first file in the list.

Exit

The "Exit" command is used to quit Stylesheet Designer. If you have an open file with unsaved changes, you will be prompted to save these changes.

Edit

The Edit menu contains the undo and redo commands which allow you to discard or restore your previous actions.

Undo

 Hotkey: **CTRL + Z**

The "Undo" command contains support for unlimited levels of Undo! Every action can be undone and it is possible to undo one command after another. The Undo history is retained after using the "Save" command, enabling you go back to a state the document was in before you saved your changes.

Redo

 Hotkey: **CTRL + Y**

The "Redo" command allows you to redo previously undone commands – thereby giving you a complete history of the work you have completed. You can step back and forward through this history using the Undo and Redo commands.

Select all

Selects the entire contents of the Design Document window.

Insert

The Insert menu provides commands enabling you to insert various items into the Design view.

Image...

The "Image..." command allows you to insert a .GIF, .JPG or .PNG graphics into the Design tab.

Paragraph

The "Paragraph" command inserts an HTML paragraph <p> at the current cursor position.

Format

The "Format" command allows you to **insert** or **change** existing nodes to the HTML formats available in the flyout menu.

The entries available here, can also be directly selected from the combo box in the standard icon bar.

Bullets and Numbering

The "Bullets and Numbering" command allows you to **insert** a bullet or numbering symbol. The symbol is inserted at the beginning of the line containing the cursor or node that you marked. The menu options have the same effect as clicking either of the icons in the icon bars.

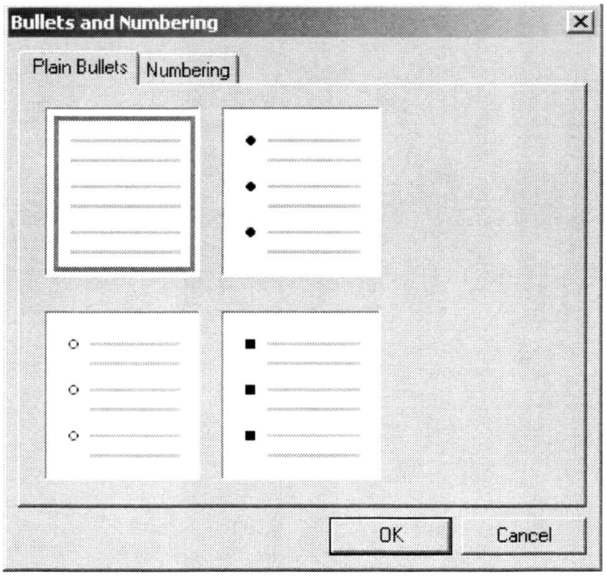

The "Numbering" command changes the paragraph to a numbered list and back again. The numbers are automatically incremented if you add more paragraphs. Clicking this icon always inserts the default numbering - digits starting with 1.

Automatic numbering for dynamic data in Authentic View:
This is only possible when using the para tab.

1. Right click the **para** tab which should have auto numbering.
2. Select "**Change to List**".
   This inserts a bullet in front of the contents placeholder.
3. Click the **contents** placeholder, and click the Numbering icon in the title bar.
   This changes the bullet to a number.

   Opening the document in Authentic View and hitting the Enter key while in the para tab, automatically adds a new paragraph with correct auto numbering sequence.

The "Bullets" command changes the paragraph to an unordered bulleted list and back again. Bullets are automatically inserted if you add more paragraphs. Clicking this icon always inserts the default bullet - a solid round bullet.

The symbols used for bullets and numbering can be changed using the menu option **Properties | Bullets and numbering**. The changes made in this dialog box only apply to the currently selected list or list item.

Horizontal Line

The "Horizontal Line" command inserts a horizontal rule at the location of the text insertion cursor. It is not available when a block of content, an entire element, or a tree fragment is selected. By default, the inserted rule is black and has a thickness of 1pt. You can change these default values by right-clicking the inserted rule and selecting "Edit Properties".

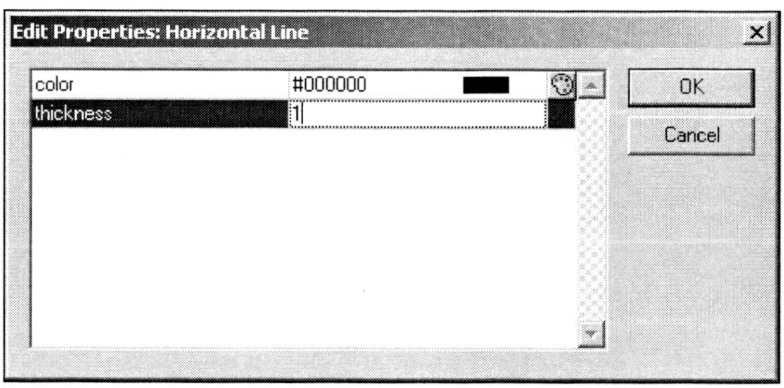

Edit the color and thickness values as required and then click "OK".

Contents

The **(contents)** command insert the "contents" placeholder in Design view. The Contents "text" between two tags, is the Design view symbol for an XML data **placeholder**.

The placeholder is filled with data when you switch to the HTML Preview tab. The data is supplied by the XML file assigned to the currently visible schema visible in the tree view. Use the menu option **File | Assign working XML file...** to assign the XML file to the schema.

To (re) insert a placeholder:

1. Click between the two tags where you want to insert the placeholder.
2. Click right (at the cursor position) to open the context menu, and select "Insert Contents".

The placeholder is inserted at the cursor position.

To delete a placeholder:

1. Click the placeholder and press the keyboard Del. key.

   This deletes the placeholder in the Design tab, and causes the XML data to be suppressed in the HTML Preview.

See also:
Insert Contents

Rest of Contents

The **Insert Rest of Contents** command inserts the **unused child elements** (of the current parent) at the cursor position. This option only applies to elements, attributes are not inserted.

The unused child elements are those child elements (of the current parent element) that occur in the schema, but have not been inserted in the Design Document window.

The placeholder is filled with data when you switch to the HTML Preview tab. The data is supplied by the XML file assigned to the currently visible schema visible in the tree view. Use the menu option **File | Assign working XML file...** to assign the XML file to the schema.

To (re) insert the placeholder:

1. Click between the two tags where you want to insert the placeholder.
2. Click right (at the cursor position) to open the context menu, and select "Insert Rest of Contents".
   The placeholder is inserted at the cursor position.

To delete the placeholder:

1. Click the placeholder and press the keyboard Del. key.

   This deletes the placeholder in the Design tab, and causes the XML data to be suppressed in the HTML Preview.

This option is especially useful when using Docbook DTD/schema(s).

Date Picker

The Date Picker command allows you to insert a Date Picker at the cursor insertion point. This command is enabled only when the cursor is placed within the tags of an (XML Schema) `xs:date` datatype element.

The Date Picker is a graphical calendar in Authentic View, with which the Authentic View user can enter the date for that `xs:date` datatype element. This date is entered in the standard XML Schema format for dates.

For a description of how to include the Date Picker in the Authentic Stylesheet, see Date Picker in the How To section of this documentation.

Page

With the "Page" command you can insert a page break or page number. These insertions are possible only at those locations where the cursor turns into a text insertion cursor.

Page Break
Click **Page | Break** to define a page break at the location of the text insertion cursor. The page break is displayed as a dashed line across the whole of the Design window. In HTML output, while the page break has no effect in the browser view, a page break *will* be inserted when browser view of the HTML file is *printed out.* In PDF output, a page break is caused at the point where the page break is inserted.

Page Number
Click **Page | Number** to insert the current page number in the PDF output. The page number appears as a block (i.e. as a separate line) or as an inline (embedded in text), depending on where in the document the page number has been inserted. For example, if the page number is inserted within a paragraph element, then the page number appears inline within the paragraph. If, on the other hand, the page number is inserted, say, between two elements, then it appears on a separate line by itself.

Bookmark

The "Bookmark" command allows you to define a bookmark from an element in Stylesheet Designer.

E.g.
1. Double click the text (free standing or table header text) from where you want to start.
2. Go to the **Menu** bar, click **Insert** and select **Insert Bookmark** (or use the shortcut CTRL+G)
3. The name of the bookmark is shown in the **Bookmark name** field. You can change it to a name of your choice. If there are more bookmarks on the same page, they are displayed in the "Other bookmarks on this page" window.
4. Click "OK". The bookmark has been set.

See also:
Inserting bookmarks and hyperlinks in the Tutorial section.

Hyperlink

The "Insert Hyperlink" command/icon allows you to define a hypertext link from an element in Stylesheet Designer.

E.g.
1. Click the text (free standing or table header text) from where you want to start.
2. Click the Hyperlink icon in the title bar.
3. Select the **Static** tab.
4. Enter the address you want to navigate to e.g. http://www.altova.com
5. Click the HTML Preview tab, and then click the header to jump to the link destination.
6 The Altova home page now appears in the HTML Preview window.
7. To go back to the HTML Preview pane, right-click and select Back.

A hyperlink or bookmark element (or group) can be both a hyperlink <u>and</u> a bookmark. They are however, single level structures, it is not possible to create a hyperlink inside a hyperlink, or a bookmark inside a bookmark.

Static vs. dynamic hyperlink
A hyperlink entered in the **Static tab** Address field remains fixed. The Absolute Path check box does not have to be selected in this case.

The "Dynamic" and "Static and Dynamic" tabs, allow you to use XPath expressions to dynamically select specific nodes. The dynamic data, is supplied by the associated XML file.

See also:
Inserting bookmarks and hyperlinks

Auto-Calculation

An Auto-Calculation uses an XPath expression to generate a result that is placed in the document at the point where you insert the Auto-Calculation. Note the following points:

- An Auto-Calculation can be inserted anywhere in the Design Document.
- The point at which you insert the Auto-Calculation determines the context node for the XPath calculation.
- An Auto-Calculation result is non-editable.
- Any node in the XML document can be updated with the result of the Auto-Calculation.

To insert an Auto-Calculation, do the following:

1. Place the cursor in the Design Document at the point where you wish to insert the Auto-Calculation.
2. Click **Insert | Auto-Calculation**. The following sub-menu appears:

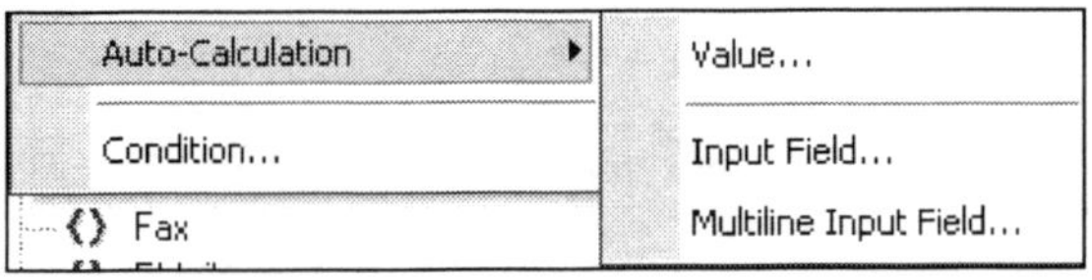

3. Click an option according to what you wish to create the Auto-Calculation as. Note, however, that the Auto-Calculation is non-editable in Authentic View, even if created as an input field. This pops up the Auto-Calculation dialog:

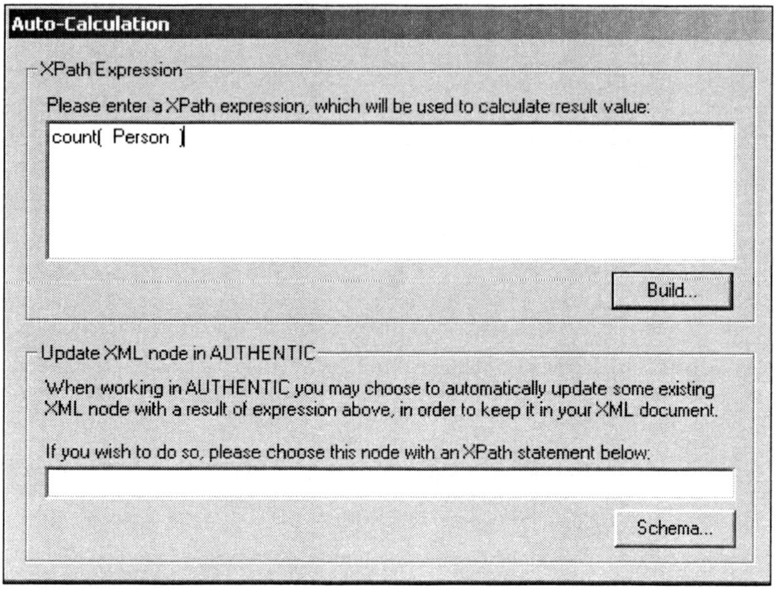

4. Build or enter the XPath expression.
5. If you wish to update a node, select the node by clicking the Schema... button and then the required node.

For examples of how to use Auto-Calculations, see Using Auto-Calculation.

Condition

This command enables you to insert a condition template at the cursor point or around the selection.

The use conditional templates is described in Conditional templates.

Table

The Table menu provides commands enabling you to change table characteristics; append, insert, delete and join rows and columns. The table commands available to you depend on the type of table and the current cursor position. To prepare for the insertion of CALS or HTML tables in Authentic View, please see the CALS / HTML Table properties section.

To change table characteristics:

- You must have previously inserted a table using the **Insert | Table** menu command (a fixed table), or
- Dragged an element into the Design window and selected **Create Table** from the popup menu (a dynamic table).
- Click in a table cell and select the specific command from the menu or toolbar.

Navigating in tables:
Use the keyboard Tab as well as the arrow keys, to navigate the table cells.

Adding text in tables:
Text can be entered in any table cell, this includes the table headers as well.

Insert Table...

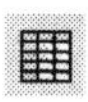

The "Insert Table..." command inserts an empty table into the design tab. A dialog box opens allowing you to define the size of the table. The inserted table is of a **fixed type** and does not automatically change size with varying XML data in the HTML Preview.

To insert a **dynamic table** please see the section **Context menus | Create... context menu | Create table.**

Delete table

The "Delete table" command deletes the currently active table.

Append row

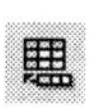

The "Append row" command appends a row to the end of the currently active table.

Append column

The "Append column" command appends a column to the end of the currently active table.

Insert row

The "Insert row" command inserts a row above the current cursor position in the currently active table.

Insert column

The "Insert column" command inserts a column to the left of the current cursor position in the currently active table.

Delete row

The "Delete row" command deletes the row where the cursor is currently positioned.

Delete column

The "Delete column" command deletes the column where the cursor is currently positioned.

Join cell left

The "Join cell left" command joins the current cell (current cursor position) with the cell to the left. The tabs of both cells remain in the new cell, the column headers remain unchanged.

Join cell right

The "Join cell right" command joins the current cell (current cursor position) with the cell to the right. The tabs of both cells remain in the new cell, the column headers remain unchanged.

Join cell below

The "Join cell below" command joins the current cell (current cursor position) with the cell below. The tabs of both cells remain in the new cell, the column headers remain unchanged.

Join cell above

The "Join cell above" command joins the current cell (current cursor position) with the cell above. The tabs of both cells remain in the new cell, the column headers remain unchanged.

Split cell Horizontally

The "Split cell Horizontally" command creates a new cell to the right of the currently active cell. The size of both cells, is now the same as the original cell.

Split cell Vertically

The "Split cell Vertically" command creates a new cell below the currently active cell.

View cell bounds

This command displays or hides table boundaries in the Design [Document] tab.

To display the table boundaries:

1. Set the table **border** to **0** (zero) in the Table Properties dialog box, in the Table tab.
2. Click the View table cell bounds icon.
   This switches the dashed table borders of all tables on or off.

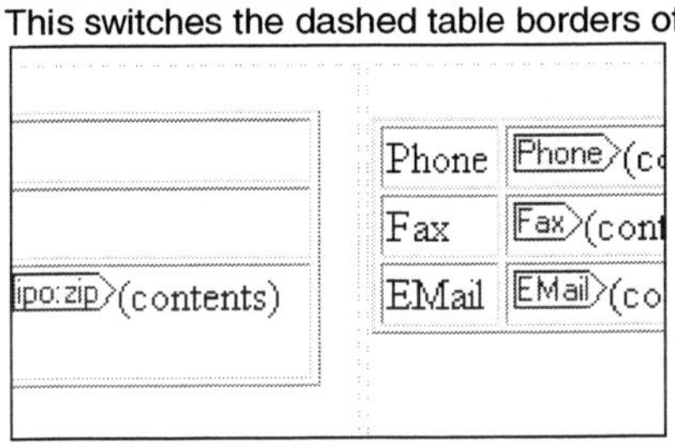

This method allows you to see hidden table borders and easily change the table size using the mouse.

- Move the mouse pointer over the dashed line, until the double-headed arrow appears, then click and drag the mouse. A popup appears showing the dimensions while you drag the mouse.

Table properties

The "Table properties" command opens the Table Properties dialog box. This allows you to customize your table.

Cell content alignment

These commands allow you to format the cell content of individual cells in a table.

Align Top
This command aligns the cell contents to the top of the cell.

Center vertically
This command centers the cell contents.

Cell bottom
This command aligns the cell contents to the bottom of the cell.

Authentic

The Authentic menu allows you to define special settings for further processing of the resulting HTML document with the **Authentic View**. These settings only apply when using the Authentic View!

Node Settings...

The "Node Settings..." command allows you to define the properties of a node (element, attribute, or contents) for display and processing **in Authentic View**.

To define node settings:

1. Click a node (element or attribute start or end tag; or contents).
2. Select the menu option **Authentic | Node Settings...** (or right click the tag and select "Authentic Node settings..." from the popup menu). When an element or atribute is selected as the node, the following dialog appears:

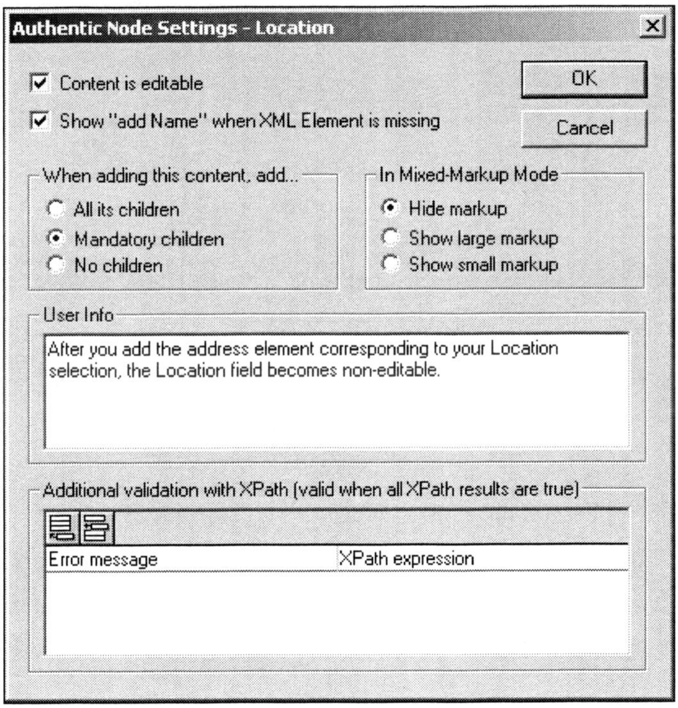

When the selected node is contents, the following dialog appears:

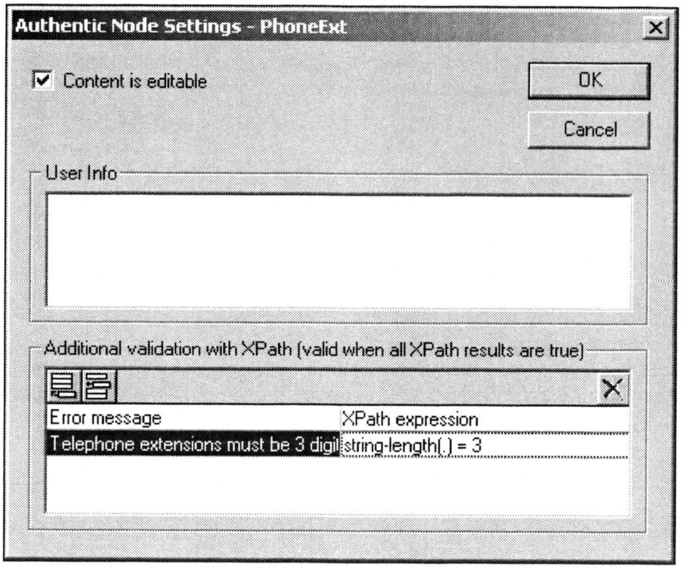

Notice the difference between the two dialogs. The dialog for contents nodes does not have element-specific settings.

Content is editable
This check box lets you define whether the XML content of the node can be edited in Authentic View. This setting is available when the selected node is an element, attribute, or contents.

Show "add Name" when XML Element is missing
This check box lets you specify whether a prompt ("Add [element name]") appears in Authentic View when the element is missing. This setting is available when the selected node is an element.

When adding content, add...
This setting is available when the selected node is an element. It allows you to define what child elements of the selected element node are added when the selected node is added in Authentic View.

In Mixed-Markup Mode
This setting is available when the selected node is an element or attribute. It allows you to define what kind of tags are displayed for the selected node when Authentic View is in mixed markup mode.

User Info
Text entered in this text box appears as a tool tip when the mouse pointer is placed over the node. It is available when the selected node is an element, attribute, or contents. If both the element/attribute node as well as the contents node has User Info, then the User Info for the contents node is displayed as the tooltip when the mouse is placed over the node.

Additional validation with XPath
This setting is available when the selected node is an element, attribute, or contents. You can set an XPath expression to define the validity of the node's XML value. An XML value that falls outside this defined range is invalid.

If the XML value of the node is invalid, this is made known to the Authentic View user by means of an error message when the XML document is validated (**F8**). The error message that is displayed is the text you enter into the Error message field of the Additional validation setting. Additionally, if the selected node is contents, invalid data is dsplayed in red in Authentic View, and the error message displayed on a mouseover.

Text State icons

The "Text State icons" command allows you to define an icon for each global element (that can contain text) present in the schema. A global element is one that appears under the "Global Templates" element in the schema tree view. You have total freedom to apply any styles, formatting etc. to XML documents using this command.

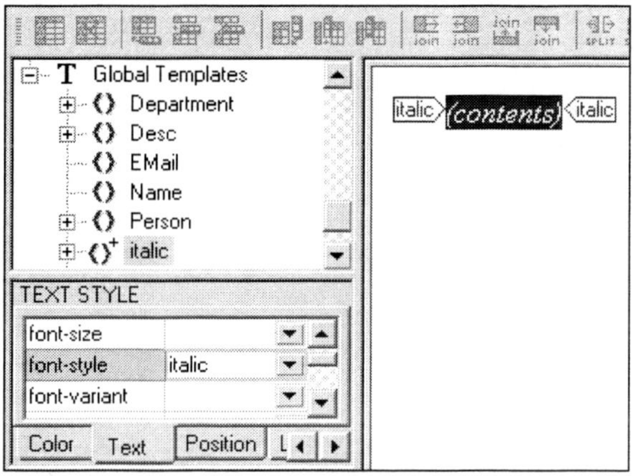

Defining text state icons

1. Make sure the element type you want to define as an icon is available as a global element in the schema (e.g. italic). The entry will be visible under Global Templates in the schema tree view in Stylesheet Designer.
2. Click the **italic** element under Global Templates, and define the attributes you want it to have in the Text style window e.g. font-style = italic.
3. Select the menu option **Authentic | Text State Icons.**

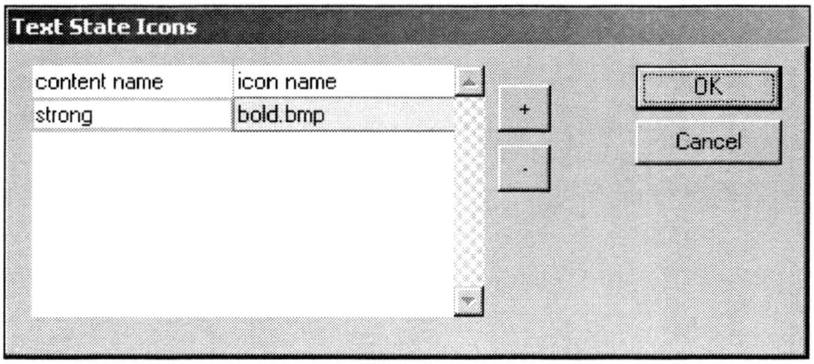

This opens the "Text State Icons" dialog box.

4. Click the "+" button to add a new line.
5. Click the combo box that is made available at this point.
The drop down list contains all the elements that can contain text in the Global Templates list.

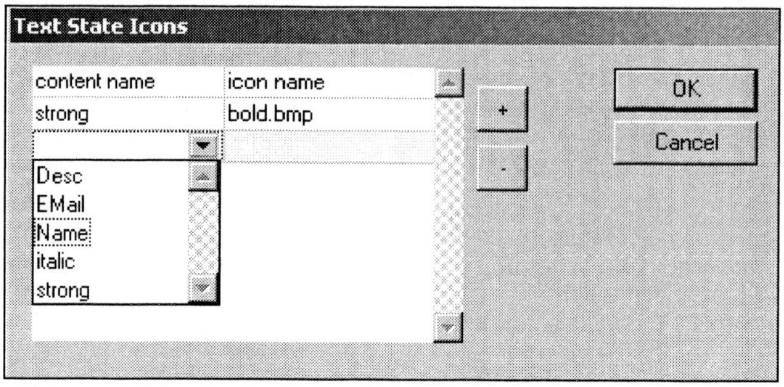

6. Click the **italic** entry and confirm with Enter.
7. Double click in the **icon name** column, and enter the name of the icon that should represent the attribute e.g. italic.bmp, in the Authentic View toolbar.

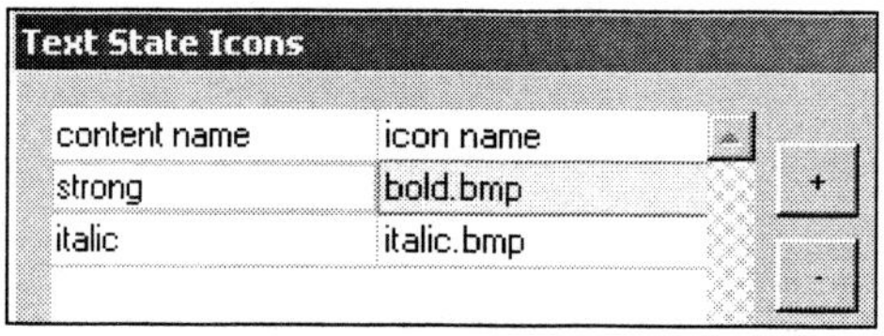

8. Click OK to confirm.

Making Text state icons available to Authentic View

1. Design the icon you want to represent "italic" in your graphic program (as a windows .BMP), and give it the same name as entered in the Text State Icon dialog box (italic.bmp)
2. Place the italic.bmp in the installation folder of STYLEVISION 2004 which is your installation folder **..\sps\Picts.**
3. Start Authentic View and open or create a new template file (*.sps). The italic.bmp icon you defined is now visible in a toolbar.
4. Mark some text in the Authentic View and click the italic icon to apply the formatting.

CALS / HTML Table properties...

The CALS/HTML table properties define the following:

- Whether the Authentic View user can insert XML tables (tables that use schema elements to define the table's structure) or not
- If XML tables are enabled, you can then define what schema elements correspond to what elements in either the CALS or HTML table model.

When you click **Authentic | CALS / HTML Tables...**, the following dialog appears:

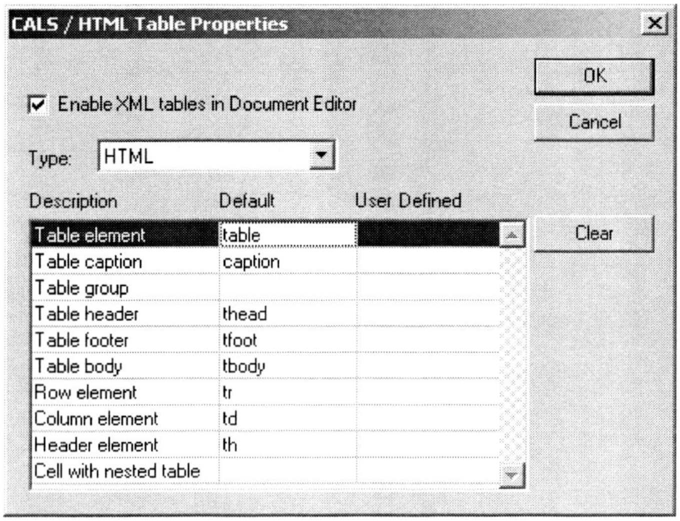

Enabling XML Tables in Authentic View
To enable XML tables in Authentic View, check the box marked Enable XML tables in Document Editor. You still have to define schema elements to correspond to the CALS table model or the HTML table model.

Defining schema elements for the selected table model
In the combo box, select the table model (CALS or HTML) with which you want your schema table structure to correspond.

If you have a schema element called `table`, this is taken to correspond to the CALS/HTML `table` element, and the `table` element in the dialog is shown in black. If there is no schema element called `table`, then, in the User Defined column, enter the name of the schema element that corresponds to the `table` element. Do the same for all the other elements of the selected table model.

Once you have done this, XML tables are properly enabled. When the Authentic View user inserts an XML table in the XML document, the table is created as the schema elements you have specified to correspond to the selected table model. In Authentic View, the table data structure is displayed as a table.

Please see Tables, in the How To section of this documentation.

Assign Template XML file

The "Assign Template XML" command allows you to define which XML file is to act as a template, when you select the **File | New** menu option in the Authentic View and select an Authentic template file (*.sps).

The option allows you to **insert data** from any XML file into the **template file** created when using the **File | New** option in STYLEVISION 2004. The data does not have to originate from the working XML file currently in use, but it must conform to the currently loaded schema.

1. Open the XML file that is to supply the template data in STYLEVISION 2004. Use **DTD/Schema | Assign schema** to assign the correct schema file to it.

2. Edit the XML file to suit your needs, e.g. create a table containing all your boilerplate company text.
3. Save the file, switch back to Stylesheet Designer and select the menu option **Authentic | Assign Template XML file**. Select the XML file you just edited.
4. Save the .sps file and switch back to STYLEVISION 2004.
5. Select **File | New**, click the **Select an Authentic view template** button and select the .sps file you created in Stylesheet Designer.
   The new template opens and now contains the company boilerplate text you defined.

Please note:

If you want **non-editable** data to appear in a template, right click the node containing/representing the data in the Design window, and select **Authentic Node Settings...** from the popup. Then deselect the **Content is editable** check box.

Auto-add Date Picker

This is a toggle command that switches the Auto-add Date Picker ON and OFF. When the Auto-add Date Picker is ON, any `xs:date` datatype element that is created as contents or as an input field will have the Date Picker automatically inserted within the element tags and after the `(contents)` placeholder or input field.

See also: Date Picker in the How To section.

HTML Import

The HTML import menu enables you to convert HTML files to XML, and auto-generate the XML Schema/DTD, XSLT stylesheet, and XML content files.

Open HTML file

Opens an HTML file. The familiar Windows "Open" dialog is opened and allows you to select the HTML file you want to convert to XML.

Having selected the file you want to import, it then appears in the Design [Document] window. You then drag the elements you want to convert to XML into the schema window at left. Please see the HTML to XML Migration documentation for further information.

Add to Parent

Adds the selected item, in the Design window, as a **child item** to the currently active element/attribute in the Schema window.

1. Select the XML **parent item** by clicking it in the schema window (not necessary if the root element is the only visible element in the schema view).
2. Select the HTML item (e.g. header or text) you want to define as the child item (in the **Design [Document]** window), and
3. Select the specific menu item from the list below.

Convert selection to elements
Converts the HTML selection(s) in the Design [Document] window, into an XML element.

Convert selection to attributes
Converts the HTML selection(s) in the Design [Document] window, into an XML attribute.

Surround selection with element
Embeds the current HTML selection between an XML start and XML end tag.

Convert selected Table/List to elements
Converts the HTML selection (even if the text cursor is only set in a table), into an XML table where all HTML items are converted into XML elements.

Convert selected Table/List to attributes
Converts the HTML selection (even if the text cursor is only set in a table), into an XML table where all HTML items are converted into XML attributes.

Insert

Inserts the selected item, in the Design window, **above** the currently active element/attribute in the Schema window.

1. Select/click the XML item **above** which the element/attribute is to be inserted in the **schema window**.
2. Select the HTML item (e.g. header or text) you want to insert and convert to XML, in the **Design [Document]** window.
3. Select the specific menu item from the list below.

Convert selection to elements
Converts the HTML selection(s) in the Design [Document] window, into an XML element.

Convert selection to attributes

Converts the HTML selection(s) in the Design [Document] window, into an XML attribute.

Surround selection with element
Embeds the current HTML selection between an XML start and XML end tag.

Convert selected Table/List to elements
Converts the HTML selection (even if the text cursor is only set in a table), into an XML table where all HTML items are converted into XML elements.

Convert selected Table/List to attributes
Converts the HTML selection (even if the text cursor is only set in a table), into an XML table where all HTML items are converted into XML attributes.

Append

Appends the selected item, in the Design window, to the currently active element/attribute in the Schema window.

1. Select an XML item to which the element/attribute is to be appended in the **schema window**.
2. Select the HTML item (e.g. header or text) you want to append and convert to XML, in the **Design [Document]** window.
3. Select the specific menu item from the list below.

Convert selection to elements
Converts the HTML selection(s) in the Design [Document] window, into an XML element.

Convert selection to attributes
Converts the HTML selection(s) in the Design [Document] window, into an XML attribute.

Surround selection with element
Embeds the current HTML selection between an XML start and XML end tag.

Convert selected Table/List to elements
Converts the HTML selection (even if the text cursor is only set in a table), into an XML table where all HTML items are converted into XML elements.

Convert selected Table/List to attributes
Converts the HTML selection (even if the text cursor is only set in a table), into an XML table where all HTML items are converted into XML attributes.

Settings...

The "Settings..." command allows you to define the specific HTML import settings.

Import whitespace text:
Imports and preserves the whitespace of imported text.

Import empty cells from table/list:
Imports empty cells from HTML tables or lists.

Properties

The Properties menu allows you to change the properties of the various objects in Stylesheet Designer.

HTML Page...

The "HTML Page..." command allows you to define the HTML page properties. The properties defined here take precedence over the individual HTML element settings.

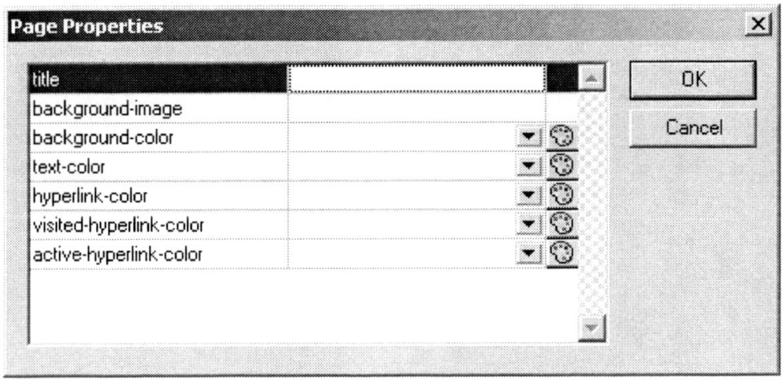

PDF Page...

The "PDF Page..." command allows you to define the PDF page properties, paper size and margins. These settings only apply when printing the document.

Table...

The "Table properties" command opens the Table Properties dialog box. This allows you to define the specific table properties.

Bullets and Numbering...

The "Bullets and Numbering" command allows you to **change** the symbols of existing bullets and numbering in the Design window.

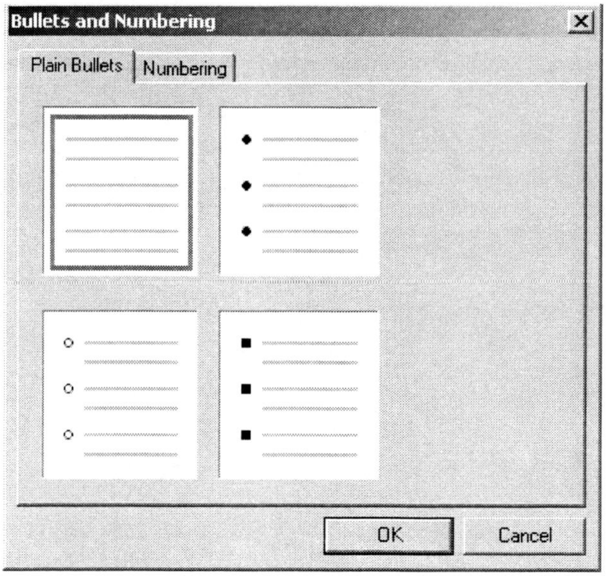

Selected object

The "Selected object" command opens the dialog box of the specific object you select. This command only becomes active if you select a **combo box**, **check box** or **radio button**.

Tools

The Tools command allows you to select the customize option, from where you can customize Stylesheet Designer.

Spelling

This command (hotkey Shift+F7) opens the Spelling dialog box, and automatically starts checking the currently active XML document in this case the NanonullOrg.sps document.

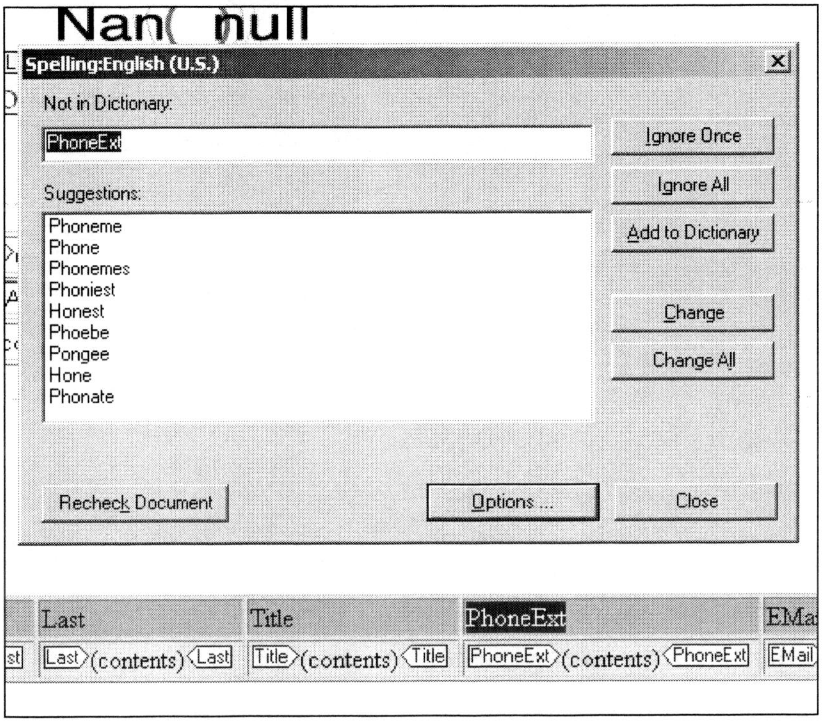

Not in Dictionary
This text box contains the word that cannot be found in any of the existing dictionaries (default and custom dictionaries). You can also edit the text here. The word is also highlighted in the XML document. The command buttons become active at this point and allow you to decide which action to take.

Suggestions
This list box displays a list of words that resemble the unknown word (supplied from all dictionaries). Double clicking a word in this list automatically inserts it in the document and continues the spell checking process.

Ignore once
This command allows you to continue checking the document while ignoring the first occurrence of the unknown word. The same word will be flagged again if it appears in the document.

Ignore all
This command ignores all instances of the unknown word in the whole document.

Add to dictionary
This command adds the unknown word to the currently active **custom dictionary**. This is the dictionary containing the check mark in the Custom Dictionaries dialog box (custom.tlx).

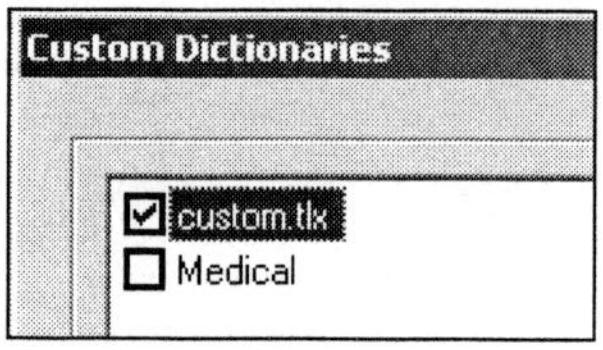

Change
This command replaces the currently highlighted word in the XML document, with the selected word in the Suggestions list box.

Change all
This command replaces all occurrences of the currently highlighted word in the XML document, with the selected word in the Suggestions list box.

Recheck
The Recheck button restarts the check from the beginning of the document.

Close
This command closes the Spelling dialog box.

Options...
This command opens the Options dialog box.

Spelling options

This command opens the **Options** dialog box which defines the global spelling checker options.

Always suggest corrections:
Activating this option causes suggestions (from all of the dictionaries) to be displayed in the Suggestions list box. Disabling this option causes no suggestions to be shown.

Make corrections only from main dictionary:
Activating this option causes only the default dictionary to be used, none of the custom dictionaries are scanned for suggestions. It also disables the Custom Dictionaries button, preventing any editing of the custom dictionaries.

Ignore words in UPPER case:
Activating this option causes all upper case words to be ignored.

Ignore words with numbers:
Activating this number causes all words containing numbers to be ignored.

Dictionary Language
Use this combo box to select the dictionary language for the spelling checking. The default installation allows you to select English. Other language dictionaries will be made available on the Altova download web site.

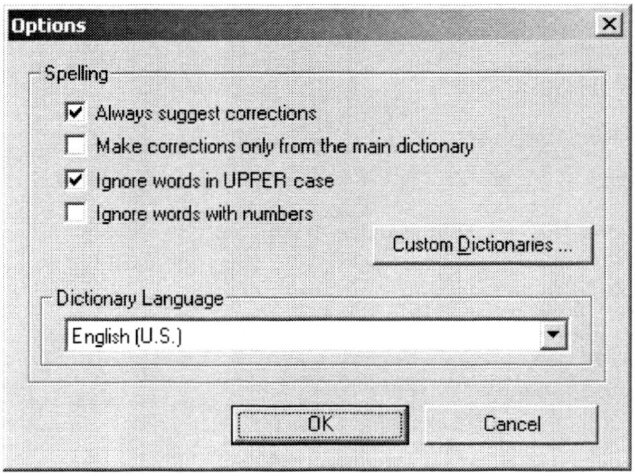

Custom dictionaries
The Custom Dictionaries... button allows you to:

- modify an existing dictionary (add or delete dictionary entries)
- create a totally new dictionary
- add an existing dictionary
- remove an existing dictionary

When you start the spell checking process, all dictionaries listed in the Custom Dictionaries list box are searched. If you want to limit the search to specific dictionaries, use the Remove command to delete those you do not want searched.

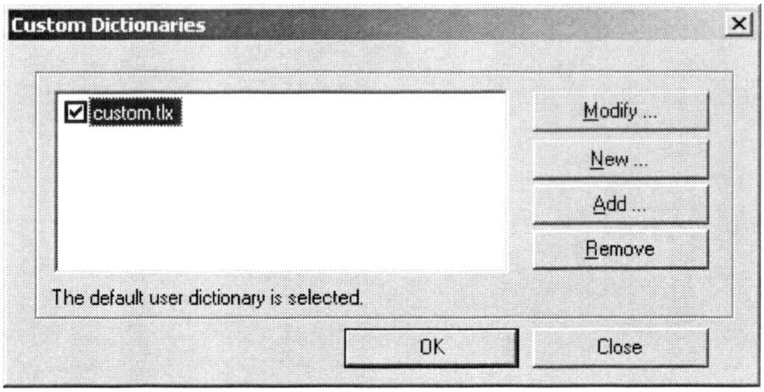

To modify dictionary entries:

1. Click the custom dictionary name whose entries you want to change, and click Modify...
   This opens the dictionary highlighted in the list box (custom.tlx in this case). A prompt appears if none of the dictionaries has been selected.

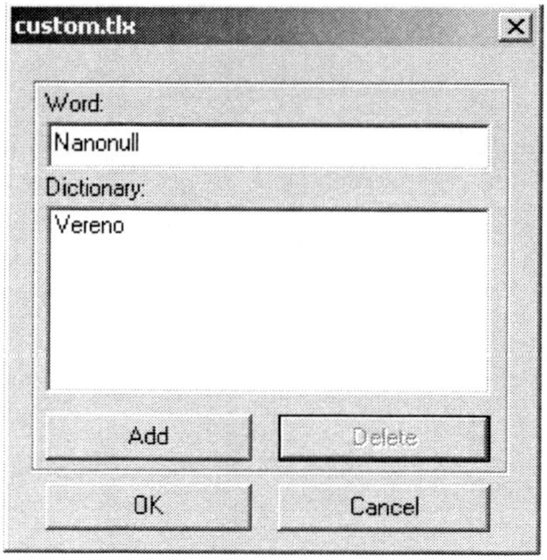

2. Click in the Word: field and enter the new dictionary entry (this automatically activates the Add button).
3. Click Add to add it to the dictionary.

To delete an entry from the dictionary:

1. Click the word in the Dictionary list box to highlight it, and click Delete.
2. Click OK to confirm the changes made in this dialog box.

To add a new dictionary:

1. Click New, and enter the name of the new **custom dictionary** in the File name... field.
2. Click Save to save the dictionary.
3. You can now add entries to the dictionary using the Add button, or the Add to Dictionary button while performing a spell check.

To add an existing dictionary:

Use this option to add previously removed (or third party dictionaries).

1. Click Add and select a dictionary from the list box. Dictionaries have a *.**tlx** extension.
2. Click Open to add the dictionary to the Custom dictionary list.

Please note:

It is not mandatory for a dictionary to have a *.tlx extension. It can have any, or no extension at all, and still be added to the dictionary list box.

To remove a dictionary:

- Click the dictionary name in the list and click Remove. This removes the dictionary from the list, it does not physically delete it from your hard disk.

Customize

The customize command lets you customize Stylesheet Designer to suit your personal needs.

Commands

The Commands tab allows you customize your menus or toolbars.

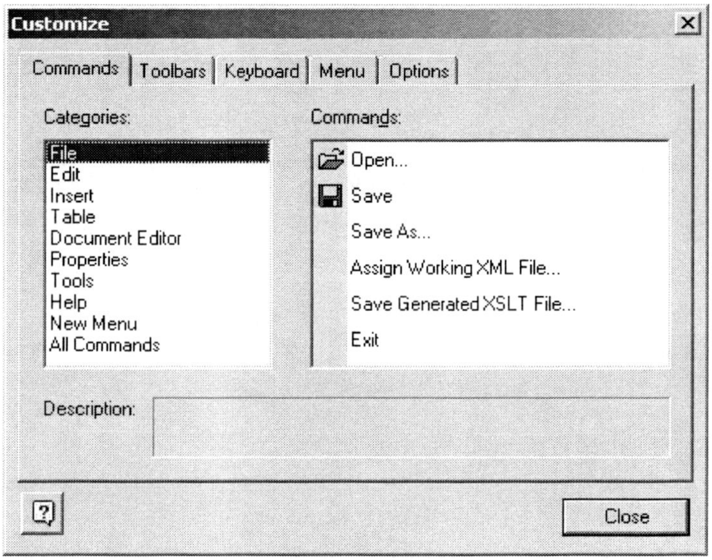

To add a command to a toolbar or menu:

1. Open this dialog using **View | Customize.**
2. Select the command category in the Categories list box. The commands available appear in the Commands list box.
3. Click on a command in the commands list box and drag "it" to an to an existing menu or toolbar.
4. An I-beam appears when you place the cursor over a valid position to drop the command.
5. Release the mouse button at the position you want to insert the command.

- A small button icon appears at the tip of mouse pointer when you drag a command. The check mark below the pointer means that the command cannot be dropped at the current cursor position.
- The check mark disappears wherever it is possible to drop the command (over a tool bar or menu).
- Placing the cursor over a menu when dragging, opens it, allowing you to insert the command anywhere in the menu.
- Commands can be placed in menus or tool bars. If you created you own toolbar you can populate it with your own commands/icons.

Please note:

You can also edit the commands in the **context menus** (right click in Stylesheet Designer opens a context menu), using the same method. Click the Menu tab and then select the specific context menu from the Context Menus combo box.

To delete a command or menu:

1. Open this dialog using **View | Customize.**
2. Click on the menu entry or icon you want to delete, and drag with the mouse.
3. Release the mouse button whenever the check mark icon appears below the mouse pointer.
   The command, or menu item is deleted from the menu or tool bar.

Toolbars

The Toolbars tab allows you to activate or deactivate specific toolbars, as well as create your own specialized ones.

Stylesheet Designer toolbars contain symbols for the most frequently used menu commands. For each icon you get a brief "tool tip" explanation when the mouse cursor is directly over it. The status bar (at the bottom of the application window) displays a more detailed description of the command.

You can drag the toolbars from their standard position to any location on the screen, where they appear as a floating window. Alternatively you can also dock them to the left or right edge of the main window.

To activate or deactivate a toolbar:

1. Click the check box to activate (or deactivate) the specific toolbar.

To reset the Menu Bar

- Click the Menu Bar entry and
- Click the **Reset** button, to reset the menu commands to the state they were in when Stylesheet Designer was installed.

To reset all toolbar and menu commands

- Click the **Reset All** button, to reset all the toolbar commands to the state they were when Stylesheet Designer was installed. A prompt appears stating that all toolbars and menus will be reset.
- Click Yes to confirm the reset.

Show text labels:
This option places explanatory text below toolbar icons when activated.

Keyboard

The Keyboard tab allows you to define (or change) keyboard shortcuts for any Stylesheet Designer command.

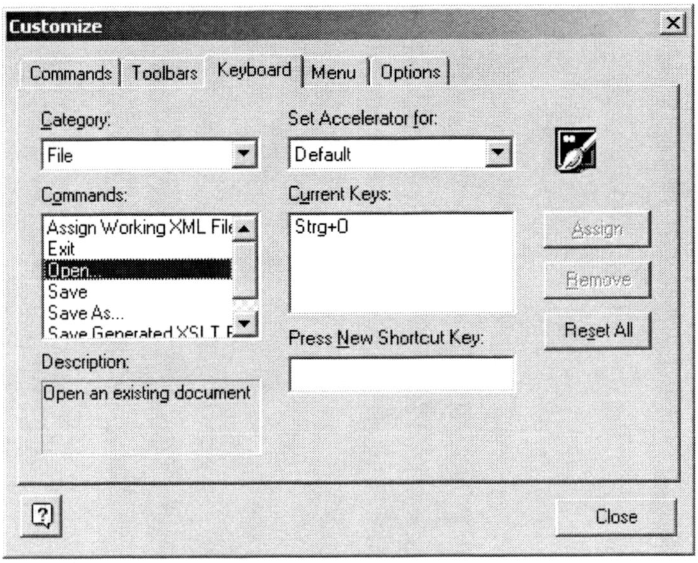

To assign a new Shortcut to a command:

1. Select the commands category using the **Category** combo box.
2. Select the **command** you want to assign a new shortcut to, in the Commands list box
3. Click in the "**Press New Shortcut Key**:" text box, and press the shortcut keys that are to activate the command.
   The shortcut immediately appears in the text box. If the shortcut was assigned previously, then that function is displayed below the text box.
4. Click the **Assign** button to permanently assign the shortcut.
   The shortcut now appears in the Current Keys text box.
   (To **clear** this text box, press any of the control keys, CTRL, ALT or SHIFT).

To deassign (or delete a shortcut):

1. Click the shortcut you want to delete in the Current Keys list box, and
2. Click the **Remove** button (which has now become active).
3. Click the Close button to confirm all the changes made in the Customize dialog box.

To reset all keyboard assignments:

1. Click the Reset All button.
   A dialog box appears prompting you to confirm if you want to reset all keyboard assignments.
2. Click Yes if you want to reset all keyboard assignments.

Set accelerator for:

Currently no function.

Menu

The menu tab allows you to customize the main menu bars as well as the context menus (right click anywhere).

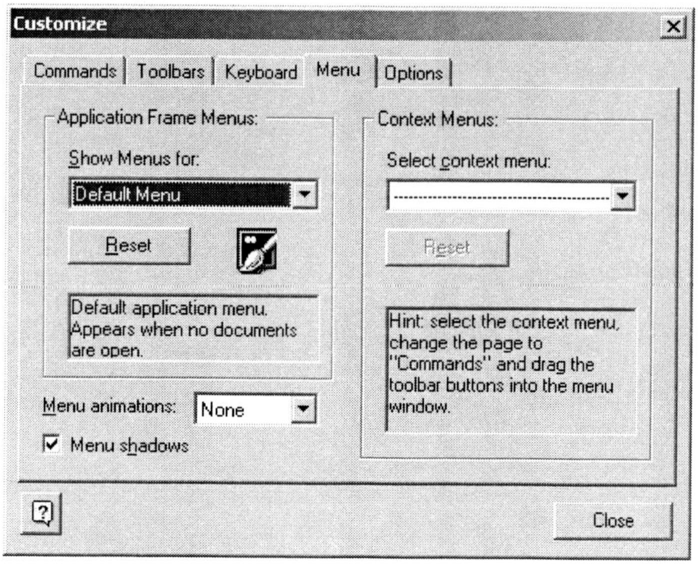

To customize a menu:

1. Select the menu bar you want to customize (Default Menu currently).
2. Click the **Commands** tab, and drag the commands to the menu bar of your choice.

To delete commands from a menu:

1. Click right on the command, or icon representing the command, and
2. Select the **Delete** option from the popup menu,

or,

1. Select **View | Customize** to open the Customize dialog box, and
2. Drag the command away from the menu, and drop it as soon as the check mark icon appears below the mouse pointer.

To reset either of the menu bars:

(Select the Default Menu entry in the combo box)

1. Click the **Reset** button just below the menu name.
   A prompt appears asking if you are sure you want to reset the menu bar.

To customize any of the Context menus (right click menus):

1. Select the context menu from the combo box.
2. Click the **Commands** tab, and drag the commands to context menu that is now open.

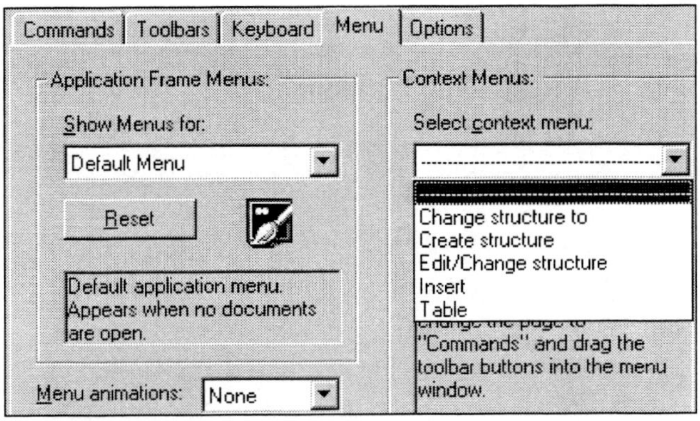

To delete commands from a context menu:

1. Click right on the command, or icon representing the command, and
2. Select the **Delete** option from the popup menu

   or

1. Select **View | Customize** to open the Customize dialog box, and
2. Drag the command away from the context menu, and drop it as soon as the check mark icon appears below the mouse pointer.

To reset any of the context menus:

1. Select the context menu from the combo box, and
2. Click the **Reset** button just below the context menu name.
   A prompt appears asking if you are sure you want to reset the context menu.

To close a context menu window:

1. Click on the **Close icon** at the top right of the title bar, or
2. Click the Close button of the Customize dialog box.

Menu animations

- Select one of the menu animations from the combo box, if you want animated menus.

Menu shadows

- Click the "Menu shadows" check box, if you want all your menus to have shadows.

XSL-FO Options

The Options command allows you to define the global XSL settings.

XSL-FO Generation

FOP 0.20.4 compliant

Selecting this option filters out those FOP properties that cannot be processed without stopping the transformation. Any elements or properties that cannot be processed will stop the transformation and display an error message.

Full XSL-FO standard

Selecting this option enables the full XSL-FO standard. Any elements or properties that cannot be processed will stop the transformation and display an error message.

FO Processor

Enter the batch file name which starts the XSL FO processor when you click the PDF Preview tab.

Help

The Help menu contains all commands required to get help or more information on Stylesheet Designer, as well as links to information and support pages on our web server.

Stylesheet Designer includes a online help system that is based on the Microsoft HTML Help Viewer, and let you currently access the table of contents, index and search function of the supplied help file.

The Help menu also contains the Registration dialog, which lets you enter your license key-code, once you have purchased the product.

Table of contents...

This command displays a **hierarchical representation** of all chapters and topics contained in the online help system. Use this command to jump to the table of contents directly from within Stylesheet Designer.

Once the help window is open, use the three tabs to toggle between the table of contents, index, and search panes. The Favorites tab lets you bookmark certain pages within the help system.

Index...

This command accesses the **keyword index** of Stylesheet Designer Online Help. You can also use the Index tab in the left pane of the online help system.

The index, lists all relevant keywords and lets you navigate to a topic by double-clicking the respective keyword. If more than one topic matches the selected keyword, you are presented a list of available topics to choose from.

Search...

The Search command performs a **full-text search** in the entire online help system.

- Enter your search term into the query field and hit the Return key. The online help system displays a list of available topics that contain the search term you've entered.
- Double-click on any item in the list to display the corresponding topic.

Registration...

When you start Stylesheet Designer for the first time, you are automatically presented with the Registration dialog box, which lets you register your software product in order to be eligible for technical support and activate your license, which is done by entering a unique key-code to unlock the software.

FREE Evaluation Version

If you have downloaded the Stylesheet Designer from our web server and would like to activate your **FREE** 30-day evaluation version, please enter your name, company, and e-mail address and click on the "Request FREE evaluation key..." button. Stylesheet Designer then uses your Internet connection to transmit the information you have just entered to our web server, where a personal unique evaluation license will be generated for you. The license key-code, which is necessary to unlock your software, will then be sent to the e-mail address you have entered - it is therefore important, that you enter your **real e-mail address** in the registration dialog box!

Once you have clicked the request button, please go to your favorite mail software and retrieve the license key-code from our e-mail message, which you should be receiving in a matter of a few minutes (depending on transient Internet conditions).

If you requested a key-code and it didn't arrive in a short space of time, the process may have failed due to Firewall restrictions in your network. If this is the case, please send a short message with your information via e-mail to our website and our support staff will generate a key-code for you manually.

When you have received your evaluation key-code, please enter it into the key-code field in the registration dialog box and click on OK to start working with Stylesheet Designer.

Whenever you want to place an order for a licensed version of Stylesheet Designer, you can also use the "Order license key..." button in the registration dialog box or the Order form menu command to proceed to the Secure Altova Online Shop on the Internet.

Licensed Version

If you have purchased a *single-user* license for Stylesheet Designer, you will receive an e-mail message from us that contains your license-data and includes your name, company and key-code. Please make sure that you enter **all fields** from your license e-mail into the registration dialog box. The key-code will only be able to unlock your software installation, if the entries in the name and company fields match the name and company entered into our order form.

If your company has purchased a *multi-user* license for Stylesheet Designer, you will receive an e-mail message from us that contains your license-data and includes your company name and key-code.

Please make sure that you enter the company name and key-code from your license e-mail into the registration dialog box and also enter your personal name into the name field. The key-code will only be able to unlock your software installation, if the value in the company field match the company name entered into our order form.

Please note that the Stylesheet Designer License-Agreement does not allow you to install more than the licensed number of copies of Stylesheet Designer on the computers in your organization (per-seat license).

Order form...

When you want to place an order for a licensed version of Stylesheet Designer, use this command or the "Order license key..." button in the registration dialog to proceed to the Secure Altova Online Shop on the Internet, where you can choose between different single- and multi-user license packs.

Once you have placed your order, you can choose to pay by credit card, send a check by mail, or use a bank wire transfer.

Support Center...

If you have any questions regarding our product, please feel free to use this command to query to our support center on the Internet at any time. This is the place where you'll find links to the FAQ, support form, and e-mail addresses for contacting our support staff directly.

FAQ on the web

To help you in getting the best support possible, we are providing a list of Frequently Asked Questions (FAQ) on the Internet, that is constantly updated as our support staff encounters new issues that are raised by our customers.

Please make sure to check the FAQ before contacting our technical support team. This will allow you to get help more quickly.

We regret that we are not able to offer technical support by phone at this time, but our support staff will typically answer your e-mail incidents within one business day.

Components download

The Components download option, currently lets you to download the latest Microsoft XML Parser, as well as an alternate XSLT Transformation System, and will be expanded in the future.

Altova on the Internet...

This command takes you directly to the Altova web-server http://www.altova.com where you can find out about news, product updates and additional offers from the Altova team.

Japanese distributor...

If you are located in Japan, you may prefer to contact our Japanese distributor on the Internet by using this menu command.

About Stylesheet Designer

This command displays the current Stylesheet Designer splash window and version number.

Context menus

Context menus are opened by right-clicking on an object in the Design window of the user interface. The object could be a Schema component, a (contents) placeholder, or some static content (such as an image, a hyperlink, or text).

What menu items are displayed in the context menu is determined by what object you right-click. Right-clicking on an element produces context menus as below. The context menu at left is for an element that has text and block styles applied. If no text or block styles have been applied, then the last section does not appear (below, right).

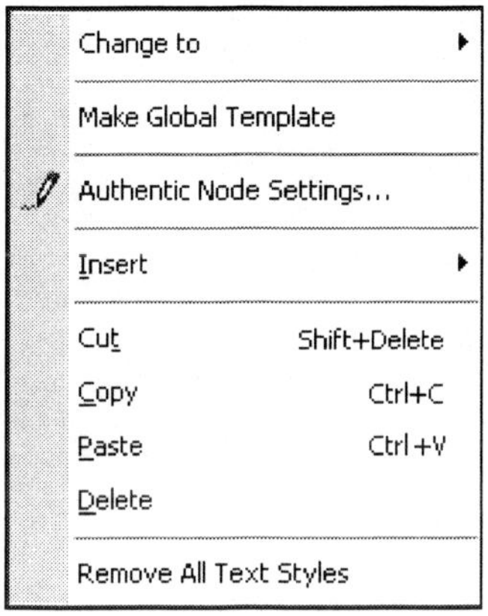

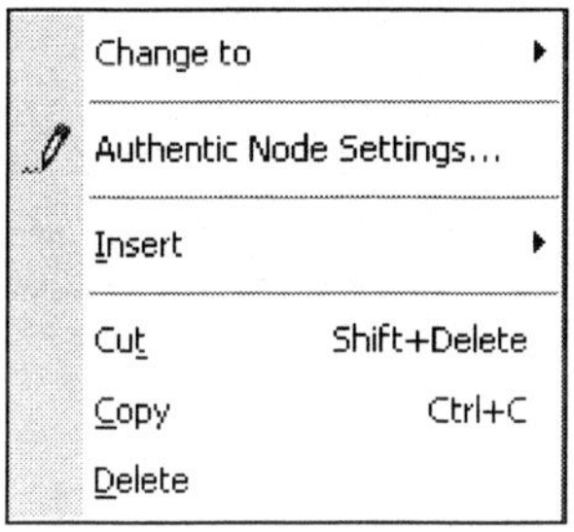

Right-clicking on a (contents) placeholder or static content produces a smaller context menu. These menus differ slightly from each other depending on the object selected. The two context menus below are for a (contents) placeholder (figure at left) and for an image (figure at right).

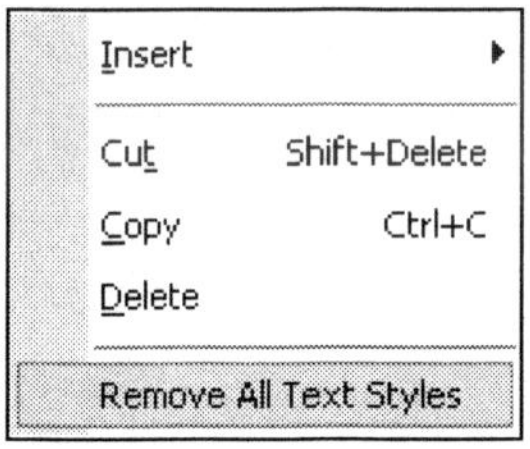

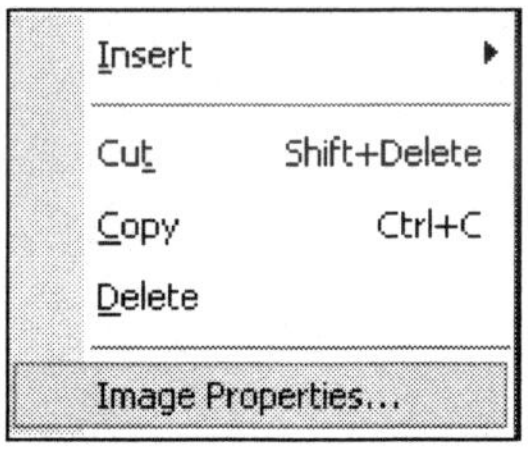

There is one other context menu you will encounter. This context menu pops up when you drag an element from the Schema tree view and drop it into the Design window. It enables you to specify how the element is to be used.

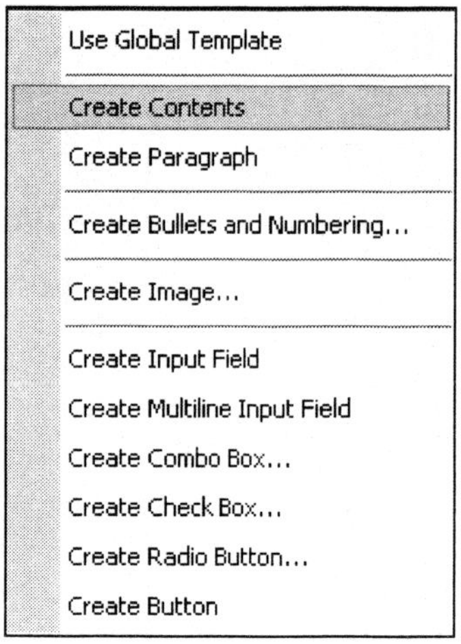

A detailed description of the Change to context menu commands follows. These commands also describe the corresponding commands in the context menu that pops up when drag an element from the Schema window into the Design window.

Change to

The Change to item of the context menu has a number of subitems. These are shown in the figure below, and described below.

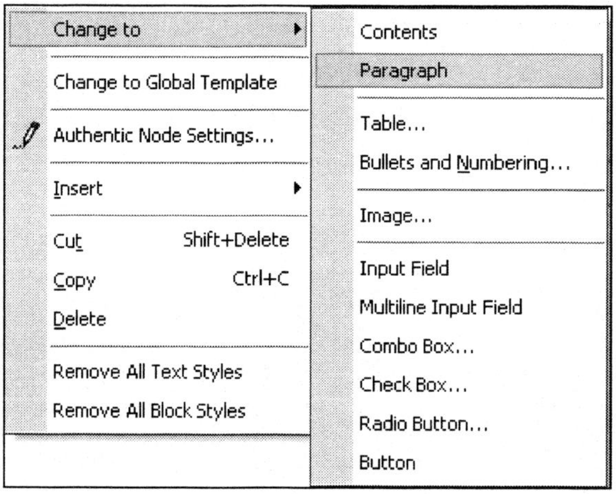

The Change to command enables presentation of the selected element to be changed into another presentation. The command also allows you to create data entry objects for interactive forms, such as input filelds, check boxes, radio buttons, etc, from a selected object. Using the Authentic view of XMLSpy, these data entry objects can be used in interactive forms that allow the use to enter data directly into the XML file. The Change to command is not available when the (contents) placeholder or the text content of an element is selected.

Change to Contents, Paragraph
The Change to Contents option causes the text content of the selected element and of all its

descendants to be output *in document order*. There will be no whitespace between descendant elements, and the output document structure and all local inline formatting will disappear. If, however, a global template is in use for the selected element or any of its descendants, the inline properties of that template will be retained for that element.

The Change to Paragraph option causes the text content of the selected element and of all its descendants to be output *in document order* and within a single paragraph. No new paragraph will be generated for any descendant element. There will be no whitespace between descendant elements, and the output document structure and all local inline formatting will disappear. The inline formatting of global templates will, however, be retained.

With both the above options, it is important to note that only the text content of the XML file are output. Any text content that is contained in the XSLT file (i.e. inserted in the Design view of Stylesheet Designer) will not be output.

Change to Table
The Change to Table option creates a two-dimensional table. One dimension of the table is formed by the "columns" of child elements. There can be as many columns to the table as there are children of the selected element. Only the child elements -- and no other descendant -- can form the columns of the table. The second dimension of the table is formed by the instances in the XML document of the selected element.

Selecting the Change to Table option causes a dialog to pop up that allows you to configure the table. The "columns" can be set out vertically (as columns) or horizontally (as rows). Child elements can be selected or deselected to be output as columns, in the figure below "Established" has been deselected. The content of child elements can be output in any of a variety of formats, each of which is described in this section.

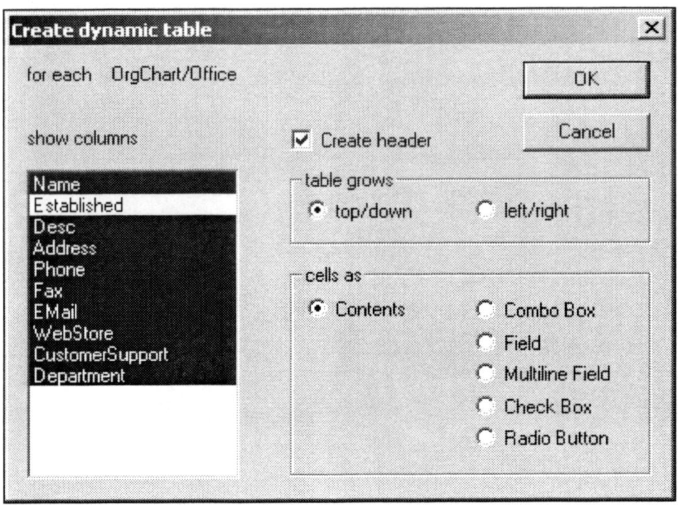

After the table is created, it can be edited in the Design window just as any other dynamic table.

Change to Bullets and Numbering
The Change to Bullets and Numbering option creates an itemized or a numbered list. A new list item is created for each instance of the selected element. Depending on the content model, the output will be as follows:

- If the selected element contains only element content, the text content of all the element's descendants is output as described in the "Change to Contents, Paragraph" section above.

- If the selected element contains mixed content, the text content of the selected element and descendant elements will be output. Text that has been inserted into the XSLT document will not be output.
- If the selected element contains text content only, then the text content is output.

Note that, in all of the above cases, the inline formatting of global templates will be retained.

Selecting the Change to Bullets and Numbering option causes a dialog to pop up that allows you to select what kind of list to output.

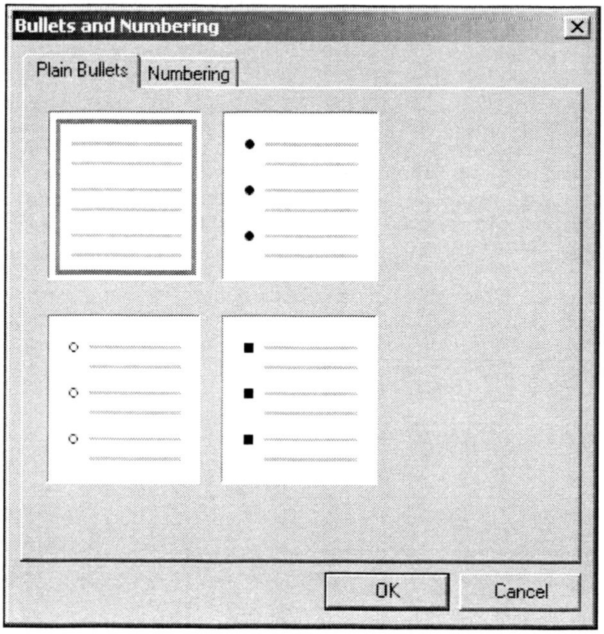

After the list type is specified, it can, in the Design window, be edited and assigned formatting properties.

Change to Image
The Change to Image option replaces the element with an image you browse for.

Change to Input Field
An Input Field is a data entry field in an interactive form. Selecting Change to Input Field in the Design view replaces the selected element's content with a text box. The HTML Preview displays a text box for each instance of the selected element. The text box is intended for data entry on the user side.

Change to Multiline Input Field
A Multiline Input Field is a data entry field. Selecting Change to Input Field replaces the selected element's content with a multiline text box in the Design view. The HTML Preview displays, for each instance of the selected element, a multiline text box with a scrollbar.

Change to Combo box
A Combo box is a data entry field in which the user selects the entry from a finite list of pre-

defined options. Selecting Change to Combo box causes the following dialog to open, in which you define the values the combo box is to contain.

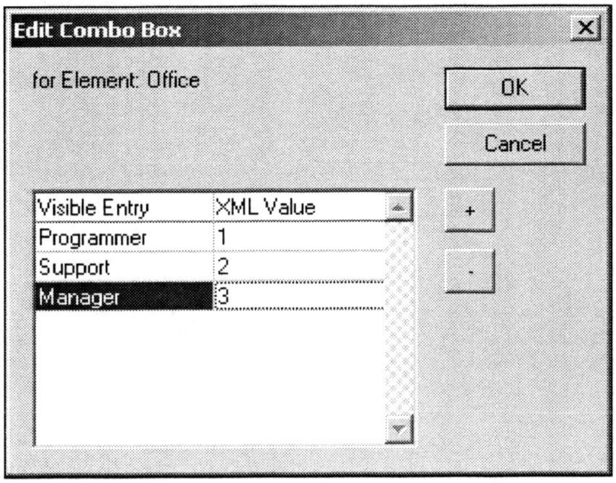

Click the "Plus" button to add a list entry line to the combo box. Double click in the "Visible entry" column and enter the list entry you want to have appear in the combo box. Double click in the "XML value" column to add combo box return values. The visible entry is used as a descriptor, the XML value is what is actually saved. For example:

Visible entry	XML value
Programmer	1
Support	2
Manager	3

Click the "Minus" button to delete a selected row from the list of entries.

Clicking OK replaces the selected element's content with a combo box. The HTML Preview displays a combo box for each instance of the selected element, and each combo box will have a drop-down menu containing the entries entered under "Visible entry". The user selects an item from the drop-down menu, and the corresponding XML value becomes the content of the selected element in the XML file.

To **reopen and edit** this dialog box, in the Design window, right-click the combo box (not the element containing it), and select the menu option **Edit Properties.** Alternatively, **click Properties | Selected object...** to reopen the Dialog box.

Change to Check box

A Check box is a Boolean data entry field. Selecting Change to Check box pops up a dialog box with which you can configure the Check box.

Click the "Plus" button to add an entry line to the "Checked values" column. Double click in the column and enter the checked value you want to appear. Double click in the "Unchecked value" text box to change the unchecked value. The unchecked value represents the unchecked status of a check box, and is the XML value when unchecked (a check box must always have a distinct state).

Click the "Minus" button to delete a row from the checked values.

Clicking OK inserts the element/attribute tags with a check box between the start and end tags in the Designer view. The HTML Preview displays a check box for each XML data instance.

To **reopen** this dialog box, click the check box and select the menu option **Properties | Selected object...**

Change to Radio button
A dialog box opens the moment you select the check box entry.

Click the "Plus" button to add an entry line to the "Checked values" column. Double click in the column and enter the "Checked value" you want to appear. The checked value is the XML value that represents checked.

Click the "Minus" button to delete a row from the checked values.

Clicking OK inserts the element/attribute tags with a radio button between the start and end tags in the Designer view. The HTML Preview displays a radio button for each XML data instance.

To **reopen** this dialog box, click the radio button and select the menu option **Properties | Selected object...**

Change to Button
Selecting Button inserts the element/attribute tags with a button named "Button text" between the start and end tags in the Designer view. The HTML Preview displays a button for each XML data instance.

Change... context menu

Change...
Right-clicking in the Design view, opens this context menu. If you right-click a tag, you can change the tag into any one of the other types available in this list.

The Authentic Node Settings... item, opens a dialog box enabling you to define the current node properties for further editing in the Authentic View. (A node in the Design view, means an element or attribute tag.)

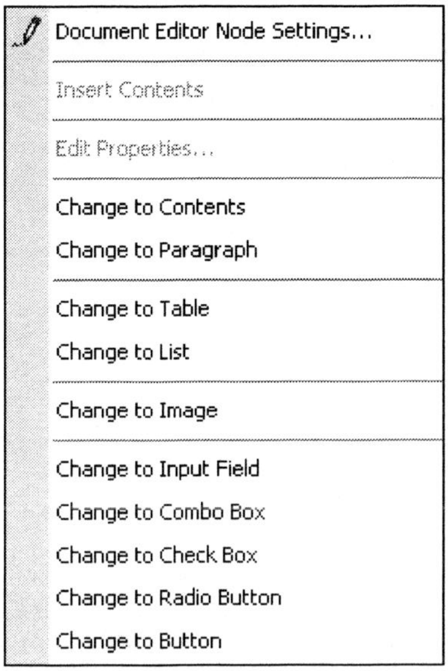

See also: Insert

Create... popup menu

Create...
Not exactly a context menu. This menu is automatically opened when you **drag** an element from the schema tree view into the Design view pane. It allows you to decide how the schema component is to be used in the XSLT stylesheet.

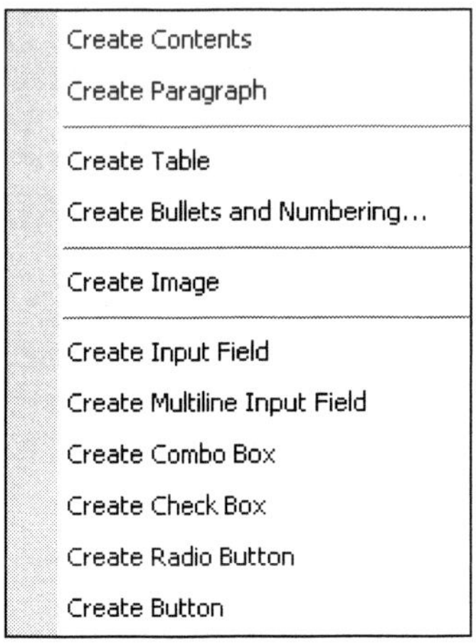

Create Contents:
Selecting Create Contents inserts the respective tags, and displays them in the same line in the Design tab. The HTML Preview tab displays the XML data as text in a single line without delimiters.

Create Paragraph:

This command encloses the contents in a paragraph. Selecting Create Paragraph, inserts the respective tags, and displays them over three lines. The first line contains the start tags, the second the (contents) placeholder, and the third all the end tags. The HTML Preview tab displays the XML data as text, one line for each instance.

Create Table

Selecting Table allows you to create a dynamic table which automatically adjusts its size according to the data supplied by the working XML file. You can define how the table expands as well as the specific controls: check box, combo box, input field, button etc.

Create Bullets and Numbering:

Selecting Bullets and Numbering, inserts the respective tags and displays them over three lines in the Design view. The first line contains the start tags, the second a "bulleted" (contents) placeholder, and the third the end tags. The HTML Preview tab displays the XML data as bulleted text, one line for each instance.

Create Image:

Selecting image inserts the image referenced in the image path.

Create Input Field:

Selecting Input Field inserts the element/attribute tags with a text box between the start and end tags in the Designer view. The HTML Preview displays a text box for each XML data instance. Input fields can be resized by clicking the right or lower border and dragging. A popup appears displaying the current dimension.

Create Multiline Input Field:

Selecting Multiline Input Field inserts the element/attribute tags with a multiline text box between the start and end tags in the Designer view. The HTML Preview displays a multiline text box with scroll bar for each XML data instance. Input fields can be resized by clicking the right or lower border and dragging. A popup appears displaying the current dimension.

Create Combo box:

Selecting Combo box allows you to define a combo box and the values it contains for the element/attribute you insert. A dialog box opens the moment you select the Combo box entry.

Click the "Plus" button to add a list entry line to the combo box. Double click in the "Visible entry" column and enter the list entry you want to appear. Double click in the "XML value" column to add combo box return values. The visible entry is used as a descriptor, the XML value is what is actually saved.

E.g.	Visible entry	XML value
	Programmer	1
	Support	2
	Manager	3

Click the "Minus" button to delete a row from the list entries.

Clicking OK inserts the element/attribute tags with a combo box between the start and end tags in the Design view. The HTML Preview tab displays a combo box for each XML data instance.

To **reopen** this dialog box, click the combo box and select the menu option **Properties | Selected object...**

Create Check box:

A dialog box opens the moment you select the check box entry. To open this dialog box at a later time right-click the element to change and select **Change to Check Box**.

Click the "Plus" button to add an entry line to the "Checked values" column. Double click in the column and enter the checked value you want to appear. Double click in the "Unchecked value" text box to change the unchecked value. The unchecked value represents the unchecked status of a check box, and is the XML value when unchecked (a check box must always have a distinct state).

Click the "Minus" button to delete a row from the checked values.

Clicking OK inserts the element/attribute tags with a check box between the start and end tags in the Designer view. The HTML Preview displays a check box for each XML data instance.

To **reopen** this dialog box, click the check box and select the menu option **Properties | Selected object...**

Create Radio button:
A dialog box opens the moment you select the check box entry.

Click the "Plus" button to add an entry line to the "Checked values" column. Double click in the column and enter the "Checked value" you want to appear. The checked value is the XML value that represents checked.

Click the "Minus" button to delete a row from the checked values.

Clicking OK inserts the element/attribute tags with a radio button between the start and end tags in the Designer view. The HTML Preview displays a radio button for each XML data instance.

To **reopen** this dialog box, click the radio button and select the menu option **Properties | Selected object...**

Create Button:
Selecting Button inserts the element/attribute tags with a button named "Button text" between the start and end tags in the Designer view. The HTML Preview displays a button for each XML data instance.

Insert Contents

The **Insert Contents** item only becomes active if you have previously clicked and set the text cursor in the Design view, and subsequently right-clicked at that position. The (contents) placeholder is inserted at the position of the cursor.

The **Insert Rest of Contents** item inserts the **unused child elements** (of the current parent) at the cursor position. This option only applies to elements, attributes are not inserted.

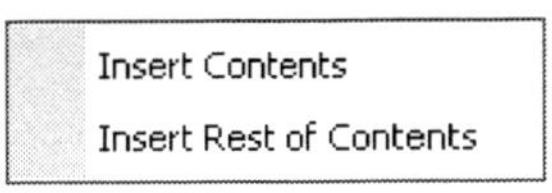

Part VIII

8 Technical Background Information

This chapter contains useful background information on the technical aspects of STYLEVISION 2004. If you run across a technical term in the remainder of this help system you may occasionally find a link to some of the background materials provided here.

XML Parser

When opening any XML document, STYLEVISION 2004 uses its built-in incremental validating parser to both check the document for well-formedness and validate it against any specified DTD, DCD, XDR, BizTalk, or XSD Schema.

The same parser is also used while editing a document that refers to a DTD, DCD, XDR, BizTalk, or XSD Schema to provide intelligent editing help and immediately display any validation error that is encountered.

This is possible through the incremental design of the new parser that is optimized for the special needs of an integrated development environment.

The built-in parser implements the new May 2nd Final Recommendation XML Schema from the W3C and we are constantly tracking the W3C Schema Group's efforts and are actively participating in all Schema-related discussions to provide you with a state-of-the-art development environment.

Schema Dialects

An important aspect of XML is the area of schemas and DTDs that define the logical structure (or content model) of an XML document - STYLEVISION 2004 is the ideal tool that integrates schema and DTD creation while working with XML instance documents.

STYLEVISION 2004 supports both editing and schema-validation of the following schema kinds:

- Document Type Definitions (DTD)
- Document Content Descriptions (DCD)
- XML-Data Reduced (XDR)
- BizTalk
- XML Schema Definition (XSD) draft April 7, 2000, CR Oct. 24 2000, May 2nd 2001 Final Recommendation

and can validate an XML instance document against any of the above schema dialects.

OS & Memory Requirements

STYLEVISION 2004 is a modern 32-bit Windows application that runs on Windows 98, NT 4.0, Windows 2000 and Windows XP. It requires a fair amount of memory to be installed in the system, because it loads each document fully into memory.

On the other hand it typically requires less memory than many Java-based applications, because it is written entirely in C++ and thus does not require the overhead of a Java runtime environment.

Having documents in main memory is necessary to completely parse and analyze each document, and to also improve the viewing and editing speed during normal work. While editing a small to medium sized document (up to 512kB) is possible in as little as 2MB of RAM, opening a 5MB document can consume up to 50MB during the initial parsing process.

Memory requirements are also influenced by the unlimited Undo history. When repeatedly cutting and pasting large selections in large documents, memory can rapidly be depleted.

Internet Usage

STYLEVISION 2004 is an integrated development environment for XML and as such will, also initiate Internet connections on your behalf in the following situations:

a) if you click the "Request evaluation key-code" in the registration dialog the three fields in the registration dialog box are transferred to our web server by means of a regular http (port 80) connection and the free evaluation key-code is sent back to the customer via regular SMTP e-mail.

b) if you use the Open URL... dialog box to open a document directly from a URL, that document is retrieved through a http (port 80) connection.

c) if you open an XML document that refers to an XML Schema or DTD and the document is specified through a URL, it is also retrieved through a http (port 80) connection, once you validate the XML document. This may also happen automatically upon opening a document, if you have instructed STYLEVISION 2004 to automatically validate files upon opening in the File tab of the Tools | Options dialog.

d) if you are using the Send by mail... command, the current selection or file is sent by means of any MAPI-compliant mail program installed on the user's PC.

All this communication is, of course, only initiated in response to a direct request from you! XML is, after all, related to the Internet and thus any XML development tool must have access Internet protocols to provide an efficient environment for the everyday duties of any XML developer.

Unicode Support

Unicode is the new 16-bit character-set standard defined by the Unicode Consortium that provides a unique number for every character,

- no matter what the platform,
- no matter what the program,
- no matter what the language.

Fundamentally, computers just deal with numbers. They store letters and other characters by assigning a number for each one. Before Unicode was invented, there were hundreds of different encoding systems for assigning these numbers. No single encoding could contain enough characters: for example, the European Union alone requires several different encodings to cover all its languages. Even for a single language like English, no single encoding was adequate for all the letters, punctuation, and technical symbols in common use.

These encoding systems used to conflict with one another. That is, two encodings used the same number for two different characters, or different numbers for the same character. Any given computer (especially servers) needs to support many different encodings; yet whenever data is passed between different encodings or platforms, that data always runs the risk of corruption.

Unicode is changing all that!
Unicode provides a unique number for every character, no matter what the platform, no matter what the program, and no matter what the language. The Unicode Standard has been adopted by such industry leaders as Apple, HP, IBM, JustSystem, Microsoft, Oracle, SAP, Sun, Base and many others.

Unicode is required by modern standards such as XML, Java, ECMAScript (JavaScript), LDAP, CORBA 3.0, WML, etc., and is the official way to implement ISO/IEC 10646. It is supported in many operating systems, all modern browsers, and many other products. The emergence of the Unicode Standard, and the availability of tools supporting it, are among the most significant recent global software technology trends.

Incorporating Unicode into client-server or multi-tiered applications and web sites offers significant cost savings over the use of legacy character sets. Unicode enables a single software product or a single web site to be targeted across multiple platforms, languages and countries without re-engineering. It allows data to be transported through many different systems without corruption.

Even though XML is clearly defined to be based on the Unicode standard, STYLEVISION 2004 is still one of the few XML development tools that *fully* implements Unicode!

Windows NT 4.0 & Windows 2000

Starting with version 2.0 STYLEVISION 2004 provided full Unicode support in the Windows NT and Windows 2000 version of the software. To edit any XML document from a non-roman writing system you will, however, also need a font that supports the Unicode characters being used by that document.

Windows NT typically includes support for all common single-byte writing-systems in its Arial, Times, and Courier New fonts and will additionally include all required fonts for the writing-system in your own country (i.e. if you install the Japanese version of Windows NT you will automatically have fonts that support the Katakana, Hiragana, and Kanji writing-systems as well as the input-methods and dictionaries to enter Kanji and to switch between Katakana and Hiragana). If you wish to edit any document from a foreign writing-system, you may want to install additional Windows NT components for that writing-system or purchase special Unicode fonts for these writing-systems (such fonts are available from all leading type vendors).

Please note that most fonts only contain a very specific subset of the entire Unicode range and are therefore typically targeted at the corresponding writing system. Consequently you may encounter XML documents that contain "unprintable" characters, because the font you have selected does not contain the required glyphs. Therefore it can sometimes be very useful to have a font that covers the entire Unicode range - especially when editing XML documents from all over the world.

The most universal font we have encountered is a typeface called "Arial Unicode MS" that has been created by Agfa Monotype for Microsoft. This font contains over 50.000 glyphs and covers the entire set of characters specified by the Unicode 2.1 standard. It needs 23MB and is included with Microsoft Office 2000.

We highly recommend that you install this font on your system and use it with STYLEVISION 2004, if you are often editing documents in different writing systems. This font is not installed with the "typical" setting of the Microsoft Office setup program, but you can choose the Custom Setup option to install this font.

In the "Examples" folder you will also find a new XHTML file called "Unicode-UTF8.xml" that contains the sentence "When the world wants to talk, it speaks Unicode" in many different languages ("Wenn die Welt miteinander spricht, spricht sie Unicode") and writing-systems (" Unicode ") - this line has been adopted from the 10th Unicode conference in 1997 and is a beautiful illustration of the importance of Unicode for the XML standard. Opening this file will give you a quick impression on what is possible with Unicode and what writing systems are supported by the fonts available on your PC installation.

Windows 98/ME

These Windows versions do not include full Unicode capabilities on the operating system layer. Instead support for non-roman writing-systems is provided through so-called code-pages that contain all the required characters mapped to either the available byte-values in the range of 0x80 to 0xFF (in case of single-byte systems, such as Cyrillic or Hebrew) or as double-byte values, where the first most significant bit of the first byte is typically used to indicate that this is a so-called "wide character" (in case of CJK writing-systems).

We therefore provider a special Windows 98/ME version of STYLEVISION 2004 that is automatically installed whenever you are using the Setup program on these operating systems. This version of STYLEVISION 2004 supports the following code-pages for viewing and editing XML documents (for excellent background information about code-pages please refer to http://czyborra.com/charsets/codepages.html):

Code-page	**Equivalent XML Encoding**
1252	ISO-8859-1 (Western, Latin-1)
1250	ISO-8859-2 (Eastern Europe, Latin-2)
1251	ISO-8859-5 (Cyrillic)
1253	ISO-8859-7 (Greek)
1254	ISO-8859-9 (Turkish)
1255	ISO-8859-8 (Hebrew)
1256	ISO-8859-6 (Arabic)
874	ISO-8859-11/TIS-620 (Thai)
932	Shift-JIS (Japanese)
936	GB2312 (Chinese)
949	EUC-KR (Korean)
950	Big5 (Taiwanese)

Whenever you open an XML file, STYLEVISION 2004 detects the character-set encoding used in that file, expands the file to an internal full Unicode representation and then transforms the document to a code-page supported by Windows 98 in order to enable viewing and editing of the document.

In most cases this process will be entirely automatic, as the available ISO-8895-x encodings as well as some of the CJK encodings often correspond with a certain code-page. However, if you open a Unicode encoded file (e.g. UTF-8 or UTF-16) STYLEVISION 2004 will be unable to determine which code-page to use and will thus bring up a dialog box that asks you to specify a code-page to be used for editing.

In order to correctly view and edit a Unicode file under Windows 98/ME it is extremely important that you use this dialog box to:

a) choose the correct code-page that includes all characters contained in the file and
b) later select a font and script from the settings dialog box that also supports the same code-page.

If the file contains any characters that are not available in the selected code-page, the user will receive an error message including a detailed list of offending characters before they will be replaced by a '_' (underscore).

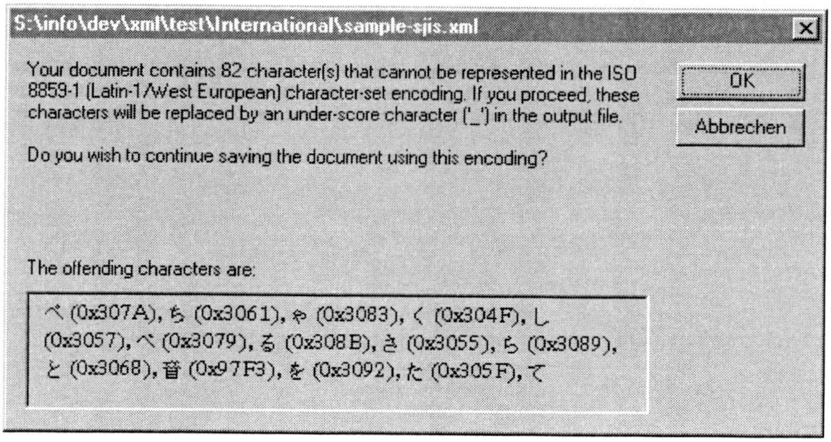

We therefore highly recommend using only the Windows NT/2000 version of STYLEVISION 2004 for editing XML files that make full use of Unicode!

Right-to-Left Writing Systems

Please note that even under Windows NT 4.0 any text from a right-to-left writing-system (such as Hebrew or Arabic) is not rendered correctly except in those countries that actually use right-to-left writing-systems. This is due to the fact that only the Hebrew and Arabic versions of Windows NT contains support for rendering and editing right-to-left text on the operating system layer.

RichEdit Component

STYLEVISION 2004 uses the Microsoft-supplied "RichEdit" component for editing documents in the Text View. The version of RichEdit that is available in Windows 98 and Windows NT 4.0 is called RichEdit 2.0 and contains many known limitations.

Windows 2000 contains a new and vastly improved version called RichEdit 3.0, that not only fixes most known bugs, but also contains special support for finer Undo-Control as well as better international capabilities with foreign writing systems.

STYLEVISION 2004 already contains full support for RichEdit 3.0 and takes advantage of the new features, if it detects the presence of RichEdit 3.0.

Altova is a registered MCSP (Microsoft Certified Solution Provider), we are unfortunately not allowed to distribute the RichEdit 3.0 component to our customers (RichEdit is only available as part of the operating system and is not redistributable).

We are, however, allowed to suggest that if you have access to a Windows 2000 CD-ROM you should install Windows 2000 on some machine and copy the file "riched20.dll" from the Windows\System directory of that machine to the Windows NT 4.0 or Windows 98 Windows installation (thereby replacing the old RichEdit 2.0 version) that you wish to use STYLEVISION 2004 on.

This will get you all the benefits of RichEdit 3.0 now and will - in our experience - not cause any compatibility problems, since the RichEdit 3.0 component is fully compatible with Windows 98 and Windows NT 4.0.

License Metering

STYLEVISION 2004 has a built-in license metering module that helps you in avoiding any unintentional violation of our license agreement. STYLEVISION 2004 can be licensed either as a single-user or multi-user software and depending on your license, this license-metering module makes sure, that no more than the licensed number of users are using STYLEVISION 2004 concurrently.

This license-metering technology uses your local area network (LAN) to communicate between instances of STYLEVISION 2004 running on different computers.

Single license
When STYLEVISION 2004 starts up, it sends a short broadcast datagram to find any other instance of the product running on another computer in the same network segment. If it doesn't get any response, it will open a port for listening to other instances of STYLEVISION 2004. Other than that, it will do nothing at all in a single-user situation. If you are not connected to a LAN or are using dial-up connections to connect to the Internet, STYLEVISION 2004 will NOT generate any network traffic at all.

Multi license
If more than one copy of STYLEVISION 2004 is used within the same LAN, they will briefly communicate with each other on startup, to exchange their key-codes to ensure that the number of concurrent licenses purchased is not accidentally violated, as additional copies of the product are launched by more users.

This is the same kind of license metering technology, that is common in the Unix world and with many other database development tools and allows our customers to purchase reasonably-priced concurrent-use multi-user licenses (see http://www.xmlspy.com/order for our price list).

Please note, that STYLEVISION 2004 is at no time attempting to send any information out of your LAN, or over the Internet. We are also deliberately sending very few and small network packets so as to not put a burden on any network. The TCP/IP ports (2799) used by STYLEVISION 2004 are officially registered with the IANA see http://www.isi.edu/in-notes/iana/assignments/port-numbers for details) and our license-metering module is a proven and tested technology.

If you are using a firewall, you may notice communications on port 2799 between the computers that are running STYLEVISION 2004. You are, of course, free to block such traffic between different groups in your organization, as long as you can ensure by other means, that your license agreement is not violated.

You will also notice, that STYLEVISION 2004 contains many useful functions that make use of your Internet connection, but these are unrelated to the license-metering technology.

Part IX

9 Licensing and Distribution

This appendix contains important legal information concerning your rights to use this software product. Please read carefully - this information is binding, as you have agreed to these terms upon installation of this software product.

Electronic Software Distribution

We are making STYLEVISION 2004 available through electronic software distribution only, because this method offers many unique benefits for our customers:

- you can freely evaluate the software before making a purchasing decision
- once you decide to buy the software, you can place your order online and immediately get a fully licensed product within minutes
- you can be sure to always get the latest version of our software
- we include both a comprehensive integrated online-help system and an electronic manual that you can also print out, if you prefer to read your documentation on paper

Once you download this software product, you may evaluate the STYLEVISION 2004 for a period of up to 30 days free of charge. During this evaluation period the software will start to remind you after about 20 days that it has not been licensed yet. The reminder message will, however, only be displayed once every time you start the program.

If you would like to continue using the program after the 30 day evaluation period, you have to purchase a SOFTWARE PRODUCT LICENSE, which is delivered in the form of a key-code that you enter into the Registration dialog to unlock the product.

You can register and purchase your license on-line by directing your browser to access our web-shop at http://www.xmlspy.com/order. On this page you will get detailed pricing information (including multi-user discounts) and also find a list of authorized distributors and resellers.

If you want to share STYLEVISION 2004 with others, please make sure that only the installation program is ever distributed. It contains the application program, grammar description, sample files, and this online manual as well as a quick Read-Me file in one neat package. Any person that receives the STYLEVISION 2004 software from you is also automatically entitled to a 30 day evaluation period. After the expiration of said period, any other user must also purchase a license in order to be able to use STYLEVISION 2004.

For further details, please refer to the SOFTWARE PRODUCT LICENSE at the end of this manual.

Copyright

Software Product License

THIS IS A LEGAL DOCUMENT -- RETAIN FOR YOUR RECORDS

ALTOVA END USER LICENSE AGREEMENT

Licensor:

Altova GmbH
Rudolfsplatz 13a/9
A-1010 Wien
Austria

Important - Read Carefully. Notice to User:

This End User License Agreement ("Software License Agreement") is a legal document between you and Altova GmbH ("Altova"). It is important that you read this document before using the Altova-provided software ("Software") and any accompanying documentation, including without limitation printed materials, 'online', or electronic documentation ("Documentation"). By clicking the 'Next' button below, by installing, or otherwise using the Software, you agree to be bound by the terms of this Software License Agreement including without limitation the warranty disclaimers, limitation of liability and termination provisions below, whether or not you decide to purchase the Software. If you do not agree, you are not licensed to use the Software, and you must destroy any downloaded copies of the Software in your possession or control. Please go to our Web site at http://www.altova.com/eula to download and print a copy of this Software License Agreement for your files.

1. **SOFTWARE LICENSE**

(a) **License Grant.** Upon your acceptance of this Software License Agreement Altova grants you a non-exclusive, non-transferable (except as provided below), limited license to install and use a copy of the Software on your compatible computer, up to the Permitted Number of computers. The Permitted Number of computers shall be delineated at such time as you elect to purchase the Software. During the evaluation period, hereinafter defined, only a single user may install and use the software on one computer.

(b) **Server Use.** You may install one copy of the Software on your computer file server for the purpose of downloading and installing the Software onto other computers within your internal network up to the Permitted Number of computers. No other network use is permitted, including without limitation using the Software either directly or through commands, data or instructions from or to a computer not part of your internal network, for Internet or Web-hosting services or by any user not licensed to use this copy of the Software through a valid license from Altova.

(c) **Concurrent Use**. If you have purchased a "Concurrent-User" version of the Software, you may install the Software on any compatible computers, up to ten (10) times the Permitted Number of users, provided that only the Permitted Number of users actually use the Software at the same time. The Permitted Number of concurrent users shall be delineated at such time as you elect to purchase the Software.

(d) **Backup and Archival Copies.** You may make one backup and one archival copy of the Software, provided your backup and archival copies are not installed or used on any computer and further provided that all such copies shall bear the original and unmodified copyright, patent and other intellectual property markings that appear on or in the Software. You may not transfer the rights to a backup or archival copy unless you transfer all rights in the Software as provided under Section 3.

(e) **Home Use.** You, as the primary user of the computer on which the Software is installed, may also install the Software on one of your home computers. However, the Software may not be used on your home computer at the same time as the Software is being used on the primary computer.

(f) **Key Codes.** Prior to your purchase and as part of the registration for the thirty (30) - day evaluation period, as applicable, you will receive an evaluation key code. You will receive a purchase key code when you elect to purchase the Software. The purchase key code will enable you to activate the Software beyond the initial evaluation period. You may not relicense, reproduce or distribute any key code except with the express written permission of Altova.

(g) **Title.** Title to the Software is not transferred to you. Ownership of all copies of the Software and of copies made by you is vested in Altova, subject to the rights of use granted to you in this Software License Agreement. As between you and Altova, documents, files, stylesheets, generated program code and schemas that are authored or created by you via your utilization of the Software, in accordance with its Documentation and the terms of this Software License Agreement, are your property.

(h) **Reverse Engineering.** Except and to the limited extent as may be otherwise specifically provided by applicable law, you may not reverse engineer, decompile, disassemble or otherwise attempt to discover the source code, underlying ideas, underlying user interface techniques or algorithms of the Software by any means whatsoever, directly or indirectly, or disclose any of the foregoing, except to the extent you may be expressly permitted to decompile under applicable law, if it is essential to do so in order to achieve operability of the Software with another software program, and you have first requested Altova to provide the information necessary to achieve such operability and Altova has not made such information available. Altova has the right to impose reasonable conditions and to request a reasonable fee before providing such information. Any information supplied by Altova or obtained by you, as permitted hereunder, may only be used by you for the purpose described herein and may not be disclosed to any third party or used to create any software which is substantially similar to the expression of the Software. Requests for information should be directed to the Altova Customer Support Department.

(i) **Other Restrictions.** You may not loan, rent, lease, sublicense, distribute or otherwise transfer all or any portion of the Software to third parties except to the limited extent set forth in Section 3. You may not copy the Software except as expressly set forth above, and any copies that you are permitted to make pursuant to this Software License Agreement must contain the same copyright, patent and other intellectual property markings that appear on or in the Software. You may not modify, adapt or translate the Software. You may not, directly or indirectly, encumber or suffer to exist any lien or security interest on the Software; knowingly take any action that would cause the Software to be placed in the public domain; or use the Software in any computer environment not specified in this Software License Agreement. You will comply with applicable law and Altova's instructions regarding the use of the Software. You agree to notify your employees and agents who may have access to the Software of the restrictions contained in this Software License Agreement and to ensure their compliance with these restrictions. you agree that you are solely responsible for the accuracy and adequacy of the software for your intended use and you will indemnify and HOLD harmless ALTOVA from any 3rd party suit to the extent based upon the accuracy and adequacy of the software in your use. without limitation, The Software is not intended for use in the operation of nuclear facilities, aircraft navigation, communication systems or air traffic control equipment, where the failure of the Software could lead to death, personal injury or severe physical or environmental damage.

(j) **License Metering**. Altova has a built-in license metering module that helps you to avoid any unintentional violation of this Software License Agreement. Altova may use your internal network for license metering between installed versions of the Software.

(k) **Software Activation**. Altova may use your internal network and internet connection for the purpose of transmitting license-related data entered by the user at the time of installation or registration to an Altova-operated license server and validating the authenticity of the license-related data in order to protect Altova against software piracy.

(l) **LiveUpdate**. Altova provides an optional new LiveUpdate notification service to you, which is free of charge. Altova may use your internal network and internet connection for the purpose of transmitting license-related data to an Altova-operated LiveUpdate server to validate your license and determine if there is any update available for you. This transmission typically takes place at a specified interval (e.g. only once per week) and you are free to deactivate this service in the Software settings.

2. **INTELLECTUAL PROPERTY RIGHTS**
Acknowledgement of Altova's Rights. You acknowledge that the Software and any copies that you are authorized by Altova to make are the intellectual property of and are owned by Altova and its suppliers. The structure, organization and code of the Software are the valuable trade secrets and confidential information of Altova and its suppliers. The Software is protected by copyright, including without limitation by United States Copyright Law, international treaty provisions and applicable laws in the country in which it is being used. You acknowledge that Altova retains the ownership of all patents, copyrights, trade secrets, trademarks and other intellectual property rights pertaining to the Software, and that Altova's ownership rights extend to any images, photographs, animations, videos, audio, music, text and "applets" incorporated into the Software and all accompanying printed materials. You will take no actions which adversely affect Altova's intellectual property rights in the Software. Trademarks shall be used in accordance with accepted trademark practice, including identification of trademark owners' names. Trademarks may only be used to identify printed output produced by the Software, and such use of any trademark does not give you any right of ownership in that trademark. XMLSPY, AUTHENTIC, STYLEVISION, MAPFORCE, MARKUP YOUR MIND, AXAD, NANONULL, and ALTOVA are trademarks of Altova GmbH (registered in numerous countries). Unicode and the Unicode Logo are trademarks of Unicode, Inc. Windows, Windows 95, Windows 98, Windows NT, Windows 2000 and Windows XP are trademarks of Microsoft. W3C, CSS, DOM, MathML, RDF, XHTML, XML and XSL are trademarks (registered in numerous countries) of the World Wide Web Consortium (W3C); marks of the W3C are registered and held by its host institutions, MIT, INRIA and Keio. Except as expressly stated above, this Software License Agreement does not grant you any intellectual property rights in the Software.

3. **LIMITED TRANSFER RIGHTS**
Notwithstanding the foregoing, you may transfer all your rights to use the Software to another person or legal entity provided that: (a) you also transfer each of this Software License Agreement, the Software and all other software or hardware bundled or pre-installed with the Software, including all copies, updates and prior versions, and all copies of font software converted into other formats, to such person or entity; (b) you retain no copies, including backups and copies stored on a computer; (c) the receiving party secures a personalized key code from Altova; and (d) the receiving party accepts the terms and conditions of this Software License Agreement and any other terms and conditions upon which you legally purchased a license to the Software. Notwithstanding the foregoing, you may not transfer education, pre-release, or not-for-resale copies of the Software.

4. **PRE-RELEASE PRODUCT ADDITIONAL TERMS**
If the product you have received with this license is pre-commercial release or beta Software ("Pre-release Software"), then this Section applies. To the extent that any provision in this Section is in conflict with any other term or condition in this Software License Agreement, this Section shall supersede such other term(s) and condition(s) with respect to the Pre-release Software, but only to the extent necessary to resolve the conflict. You acknowledge that the Software is a pre-release version, does not represent final product from Altova, and may contain bugs, errors and other problems that could cause system or other failures and data loss. CONSEQUENTLY, THE PRE-RELEASE SOFTWARE IS PROVIDED TO YOU "AS-IS", AND ALTOVA DISCLAIMS ANY WARRANTY OR LIABILITY OBLIGATIONS TO YOU OF ANY KIND, WHETHER EXPRESS OR IMPLIED. WHERE LEGALLY LIABILITY

CANNOT BE EXCLUDED FOR PRE-RELEASE SOFTWARE, BUT IT MAY BE LIMITED, ALTOVA'S LIABILITY AND THAT OF ITS SUPPLIERS SHALL BE LIMITED TO THE SUM OF FIFTY DOLLARS (U.S.$50) IN TOTAL. You acknowledge that Altova has not promised or guaranteed to you that Pre-release Software will be announced or made available to anyone in the future, that Altova has no express or implied obligation to you to announce or introduce the Pre-release Software, and that Altova may not introduce a product similar to or compatible with the Pre-release Software. Accordingly, you acknowledge that any research or development that you perform regarding the Pre-release Software or any product associated with the Pre-release Software is done entirely at your own risk. During the term of this Software License Agreement, if requested by Altova, you will provide feedback to Altova regarding testing and use of the Pre-release Software, including error or bug reports. If you have been provided the Pre-release Software pursuant to a separate written agreement, your use of the Software is governed by such agreement. You may not sublicense, lease, loan, rent, distribute or otherwise transfer the Pre-release Software. Upon receipt of a later unreleased version of the Pre-release Software or release by Altova of a publicly released commercial version of the Software, whether as a stand-alone product or as part of a larger product, you agree to return or destroy all earlier Pre-release Software received from Altova and to abide by the terms of the license agreement for any such later versions of the Pre-release Software.

5. **LIMITED WARRANTY AND LIMITATION OF LIABILITY**

(a) **Limited Warranty and Customer Remedies.** Altova warrants to the person or entity that first purchases a license for use of the Software pursuant to the terms of this Software License Agreement that (i) the Software will perform substantially in accordance with any accompanying Documentation for a period of ninety (90) days from the date of receipt, and (ii) any support services provided by Altova shall be substantially as described in section 6 of this agreement. Some states and jurisdictions do not allow limitations on duration of an implied warranty, so the above limitation may not apply to you. To the extent allowed by applicable law, implied warranties on the Software, if any, are limited to ninety (90) days. Altova's and its suppliers' entire liability and your exclusive remedy shall be, at Altova's option, either (i) return of the price paid, if any, or (ii) repair or replacement of the Software that does not meet Altova's Limited Warranty and which is returned to Altova with a copy of your receipt. This Limited Warranty is void if failure of the Software has resulted from accident, abuse or misapplication. Any replacement Software will be warranted for the remainder of the original warranty period or thirty (30) days, whichever is longer.

(b) **No Other Warranties and Disclaimer.** THE FOREGOING LIMITED WARRANTY AND REMEDIES STATE THE SOLE AND EXCLUSIVE REMEDIES FOR ALTOVA OR ITS SUPPLIER'S BREACH OF WARRANTY. ALTOVA AND ITS SUPPLIERS DO NOT AND CANNOT WARRANT THE PERFORMANCE OR RESULTS YOU MAY OBTAIN BY USING THE SOFTWARE. EXCEPT FOR THE FOREGOING LIMITED WARRANTY, AND FOR ANY WARRANTY, CONDITION, REPRESENTATION OR TERM TO THE EXTENT WHICH THE SAME CANNOT OR MAY NOT BE EXCLUDED OR LIMITED BY LAW APPLICABLE TO YOU IN YOUR JURISDICTION, ALTOVA AND ITS SUPPLIERS MAKE NO WARRANTIES, CONDITIONS, REPRESENTATIONS OR TERMS, EXPRESS OR IMPLIED, WHETHER BY STATUTE, COMMON LAW, CUSTOM, USAGE OR OTHERWISE AS TO ANY OTHER MATTERS. TO THE MAXIMUM EXTENT PERMITTED BY APPLICABLE LAW, ALTOVA AND ITS SUPPLIERS DISCLAIM ALL OTHER WARRANTIES AND CONDITIONS, EITHER EXPRESS OR IMPLIED, INCLUDING, BUT NOT LIMITED TO, IMPLIED WARRANTIES OF MERCHANTABILITY, FITNESS FOR A PARTICULAR PURPOSE, SATISFACTORY QUALITY, INFORMATIONAL CONTENT OR ACCURACY, QUIET ENJOYMENT, TITLE AND NON-INFRINGEMENT, WITH REGARD TO THE SOFTWARE, AND THE PROVISION OF OR FAILURE TO PROVIDE SUPPORT SERVICES. THIS LIMITED WARRANTY GIVES YOU SPECIFIC LEGAL RIGHTS. YOU MAY HAVE OTHERS, WHICH VARY FROM STATE/JURISDICTION TO STATE/JURISDICTION.

(c) **Limitation Of Liability.** TO THE MAXIMUM EXTENT PERMITTED BY

APPLICABLE LAW, IN NO EVENT SHALL ALTOVA OR ITS SUPPLIERS BE LIABLE FOR ANY SPECIAL, INCIDENTAL, DIRECT, INDIRECT OR CONSEQUENTIAL DAMAGES WHATSOEVER (INCLUDING, WITHOUT LIMITATION, DAMAGES FOR LOSS OF BUSINESS PROFITS, BUSINESS INTERRUPTION, LOSS OF BUSINESS INFORMATION, OR ANY OTHER PECUNIARY LOSS) ARISING OUT OF THE USE OF OR INABILITY TO USE THE SOFTWARE OR THE PROVISION OF OR FAILURE TO PROVIDE SUPPORT SERVICES, EVEN IF ALTOVA HAS BEEN ADVISED OF THE POSSIBILITY OF SUCH DAMAGES. IN ANY CASE, ALTOVA'S ENTIRE LIABILITY UNDER ANY PROVISION OF THIS SOFTWARE LICENSE AGREEMENT SHALL BE LIMITED TO THE AMOUNT ACTUALLY PAID BY YOU FOR THE SOFTWARE PRODUCT. Because some states and jurisdictions do not allow the exclusion or limitation of liability, the above limitation may not apply to you. In such states and jurisdictions, Altova's liability shall be limited to the greatest extent permitted by law.

(e) **Infringement Claims.** Altova will indemnify and hold you harmless and will defend or settle any claim, suit or proceeding brought against you that is based upon a claim that the content contained in the Software infringes a copyright or violates an intellectual or proprietary right protected by United States or European Union law ("Claim"), but only to the extent the Claim arises directly out of the use of the Software. You must notify Altova in writing of any Claim within ten (10) business days after you first receive notice of the Claim, and you shall provide to Altova at no cost with such assistance and cooperation as Altova may reasonably request from time to time in connection with the defense of the Claim. Altova shall have sole control over any Claim (including, without limitation, the selection of counsel and the right to settle on your behalf on any terms Altova deems desirable in the sole exercise of its discretion). You may, at your sole cost, retain separate counsel and participate in the defense or settlement negotiations. Altova shall pay actual damages, costs, and attorney fees awarded against you (or payable by you pursuant to a settlement agreement) in connection with a Claim to the extent such damages and costs are not reimbursed to you by insurance or a third party, to an aggregate maximum equal to the purchase price of the Software. If the Software or its use becomes the subject of a Claim or its use is enjoined, or if in the opinion of Altova's legal counsel the Software is likely to become the subject of a Claim, Altova shall attempt to resolve the Claim by using commercially reasonable efforts to modify the Software or obtain a license to continue using the Software. If in the opinion of Altova's legal counsel the Claim, the injunction or potential Claim cannot be resolved through reasonable modification or licensing, Altova, at its own election, may terminate this Software License Agreement without penalty, and will refund to you on a pro rata basis any fees paid in advance by you to Altova. THE FOREGOING CONSTITUTES ALTOVA'S SOLE AND EXCLUSIVE LIABILITY FOR INTELLECTUAL PROPERTY INFRINGEMENT. This indemnity does not apply to infringements that would not be such, except for customer-supplied elements.

6. SUPPORT AND MAINTENANCE

Altova offers an optional "Support & Maintenance Package" which you may elect to purchase in addition to your Software license. The Support Period, hereinafter defined, covered by such a package shall be delineated at such time as you elect to purchase the package. Your rights with respect to support and maintenance depend on your decision to purchase this optional package:

(a) If you have **not** purchased the Support & Maintenance Package, you will receive the Software AS IS and will not receive any maintenance releases or updates. However, Altova, at it's option and in it sole discretion on a case by case basis, may decide to offer maintenance releases to you as a courtesy, but these maintenance releases will not include any new features in excess of the feature set at the time of your purchase of the Software. In addition, Altova will provide free technical support to you for thirty (30) days after the date of your purchase (the "Support Period" for the purposes of this paragraph a), and Altova, in its sole discretion on a case by case basis , may also provide free courtesy technical support during your thirty (30) -day evaluation period. Technical support is provided via a web-based support form only, and there is no guaranteed response time.

(b) If you have purchased the Support & Maintenance Package, you will receive the Software and all maintenance releases or updates for the duration of the Support Period, which may or may not include additional features. Updates and maintenance releases only cover the minor releases within the same major version of the software that you have purchased, and upgrades to the next major version are specifically not included in this maintenance. However, Altova will offer you an "upgrade advantage", by providing you with a special upgrade price for the next major version of the Software, which is guaranteed to be lower than the future upgrade price to the next major version that customers without a current Support and Maintenance Package will have to pay. In addition, Altova will provide Priority Technical Support to you for the duration of the Support Period. Priority Technical Support is provided via a web-based support form only, and Altova will make commercially reasonable efforts to respond via e-mail to all requests within forty-eight (48) hours during Altova's business hours (MO-FR, 8am UTC – 10pm UTC, Austrian and US holidays excluded) and to make reasonable efforts to provide work-arounds to errors reported in the Software.
During the Support Period you may also report any Software problem or error to Altova. If Altova determines that a reported reproducible material error in the Software exists and significantly impairs the usability and utility of the Software, Altova agrees to use reasonable commercial efforts to correct or provide a usable work-around solution in an upcoming maintenance release or update, which is made available at certain times at Altova's sole discretion.
If Altova, in its discretion, requests written verification of an error or malfunction discovered by you or requests supporting example files that exhibit the Software problem, you shall promptly provide such verification or files, by email, telecopy, or overnight mail, setting forth in reasonable detail the respects in which the Software fails to perform. You shall use reasonable efforts to cooperate in diagnosis or study of errors.
Altova may include error corrections in maintenance releases, updates, or new major releases of the Software. Altova is not obligated to fix errors that are immaterial. Immaterial errors are those that do not significantly impact use of the Software.

Whether or not you have purchased the Support & Maintenance Package, technical support only covers issues or questions resulting directly out of the operation of the Software and Altova will not provide you with generic consultation, assistance, or advice under any circumstances.
Updating Software may require the updating of software not covered by this Software License Agreement before installation. Updates of the operating system and application software not specifically covered by this Software License Agreement are your responsibility and will not be provided by Altova under this Software License Agreement.
Altova's obligations under this Section 6 are contingent upon your proper use of the Software and your compliance with the terms and conditions of this Software License Agreement at all times. Altova shall be under no obligation to provide the above technical support if, in Altova's opinion, the Software has failed due to the following conditions: (i) damage caused by the relocation of the software to another location or CPU; (ii) alterations, modifications or attempts to change the Software without Altova's written approval; (iii) causes external to the Software, such as natural disasters, the failure or fluctuation of electrical power, or computer equipment failure; (iv) your failure to maintain the Software at Altova's specified release level; or (v) use of the Software with other software without Altova's prior written approval.
It will be your sole responsibility to: (i) comply with all Altova-specified operating and troubleshooting procedures and then notify Altova immediately of Software malfunction and provide Altova with complete information thereof; (iii) provide for the security of your confidential information; (iv) establish and maintain backup systems and procedures necessary to reconstruct lost or altered files, data or programs.

7. TERM AND TERMINATION

This Software License Agreement may be terminated (a) by your giving Altova written notice of termination; or (b) by Altova, at its option, giving you written notice of termination if you commit a breach of this Software License Agreement and fail to cure such breach within ten (10) days after notice from Altova. Upon any termination of this Software License Agreement, you must cease all use of the Software, destroy all copies then in your possession or control and take such other actions as Altova may reasonably request to ensure that no copies of the Software remain in your possession or control.

8. **RESTRICTED RIGHTS NOTICE.**
The Software was developed entirely at private expense and is commercial computer software provided with RESTRICTED RIGHTS. Use, duplication or disclosure by the U.S. Government or a U.S. Government subcontractor is subject to the restrictions set forth in this Agreement and as provided in FAR 12.211 and 12.212 (48 C.F.R. §12.211 and 12.212) or DFARS 227-7202-1 (48 C.F.R. §227-7202-1) as applicable.

9. **GENERAL PROVISIONS**
If you are located in the European Union and are using the Software in the European Union and not in the United States, then this Software License Agreement will be governed by and construed in accordance with the laws of the Republic of Austria (excluding its conflict of laws principles and the U.N. Convention on Contracts for the International Sale of Goods) and you expressly agree that exclusive jurisdiction for any claim or dispute with Altova or relating in any way to your use of the Software resides in the Handelsgericht, Wien (Commercial Court, Vienna) and you further agree and expressly consent to the exercise of personal jurisdiction in the Handelsgericht, Wien (Commercial Court, Vienna) in connection with any such dispute or claim. If you are located in the United States or are using the Software in the United States then this Software License Agreement will be governed by and construed in accordance with the laws of the Commonwealth of Massachusetts, USA (excluding its conflict of laws principles and the U.N. Convention on Contracts for the International Sale of Goods) and you expressly agree that exclusive jurisdiction for any claim or dispute with Altova or relating in any way to your use of the Software resides in the federal or state courts of Massachusetts and you further agree and expressly consent to the exercise of personal jurisdiction in the federal or state courts of Massachusetts in connection with any such dispute or claim. If you are located outside of the European Union or the United States and are not using the Software in the United States, then this Software License Agreement will be governed by and construed in accordance with the laws of the Republic of Austria (excluding its conflict of laws principles and the U.N. Convention on Contracts for the International Sale of Goods) and you expressly agree that exclusive jurisdiction for any claim or dispute with Altova or relating in any way to your use of the Software resides in the Handelsgericht, Wien (Commercial Court, Vienna) and you further agree and expressly consent to the exercise of personal jurisdiction in the Handelsgericht Wien (Commercial Court, Vienna) in connection with any such dispute or claim. This Software License Agreement will not be governed by the conflict of law rules of any jurisdiction or the United Nations Convention on Contracts for the International Sale of Goods, the application of which is expressly excluded. This Software License Agreement contains the entire agreement and understanding of the parties with respect to the subject matter hereof, and supersedes all prior written and oral understandings of the parties with respect to the subject matter hereof. Any notice or other communication given under this Software License Agreement shall be in writing and shall have been properly given by either of us to the other if sent by certified or registered mail, return receipt requested, or by overnight courier to the address shown on Altova's Web site for Altova and the address shown in Altova's records for you, or such other address as the parties may designate by notice given in the manner set forth above. This Software License Agreement will bind and inure to the benefit of the parties and our respective heirs, personal and legal representatives, affiliates, successors and permitted assigns. The failure of either of us at any time to require performance of any provision hereof shall in no manner affect such party's right at a later time to enforce the same or any other term of this Software License Agreement. This Software License Agreement may be amended only by a

document in writing signed by both of us. In the event of a breach or threatened breach of this Software License Agreement by either party, the other shall have all applicable equitable as well as legal remedies. The Software and its related documentation may not be exported or reexported in violation of the U.S. Export Administration Act and its implementing regulations or the laws of the jurisdiction in which the Software was obtained. Each party is duly authorized and empowered to enter into and perform this Software License Agreement. If, for any reason, any provision of this Software License Agreement is held invalid or otherwise unenforceable, such invalidity or unenforceability shall not affect the remainder of this Software License Agreement, and this Software License Agreement shall continue in full force and effect to the fullest extent allowed by law. The parties knowingly and expressly consent to the foregoing terms and conditions.

Last updated: 2003-08-04

Index

- . -

.sps file 257
    definition of 257

- A -

Abort 181
About Stylehseet Designer 450
Access 79
    elementTypes 47
Activate 217, 448
    license 217, 448
Active Server Pages 92
Add 138
    active and related files 138
    active file to project 138
    child element 26
    elements with drag and drop 29
    external folder to project 138
    external web folder to project 141
    files to project 70, 137
    folder to project 138
    node & child nodes 429
    project to source control 132
    sequence compositor 26
    to source control 132
    URL to project 137
Add Child 151, 152, 153
Add Child | Sequence 88
Add to parent 435
    HTML import 435
Add to source control 69
Additional Validation 362
    in Authentic View 362
    setting in Authentic Stylesheets 362
Agreement 478, 479
Align 427
    cell content 427
    cell content 427
Align top 427
    cell content 427
Anchors 337
    in Authentic Stylesheets 337
Annotation 103
    appinfo 88
    editing 88
Append 99, 146, 148, 149, 150, 151, 157
    attribute 40, 100
    attribute / element 57
    child elements schema 85
    column 425
    HTML import 436
    row 425
    row (Document Editor) 172
Appendix 476
Appinfo 88
    inserting 88
Apply 205
    formatting 410
    in Authentic View 279
April 7 464
Arabic 471
Arial Unicode MS 468
Ascending 157
ASCII 110
ASP 92
Assign 98
    DTD 166
    DTDs to folders 98
    Schema 166
    shortcut to a command 196
    template 433
    XSL 66, 170
    XSL transformations to folders 98
    XSL:FO 171
Assign DTD 147
Assign DTD/Schema 105
Assign file 220
Assign XML file 416
Attachment 113
ATTLIST Declaration 148
    Add Child 153
    Appending 150
    Convert To 155
    Inserting 148
Attribute 146, 149, 151, 464
    Add Child 151
    adding 40
    append 40

Attribute 146, 149, 151, 464
- Appending 100, 149
- Convert To 154
- Definition 167
- drag & drop 82
- element 40
- entry helper 50, 57
- enumerations 40
- icon 76
- insert / append 82
- Inserting 100, 146
- limiting contents 40
- mandatory 100
- namespace prefix 164
- order 76
- window 40

Attribute List 148
- Add Child 153
- Appending 150
- Convert To 155
- Inserting 148

Attribute preview 208

Attribute values 280
- entering in Authentic View 280
- in Authentic Stylesheet 314

AttributeGroup 464

Attributes 155
- how to use in Authentic View 280
- in Authentic View 267

Authentic 310
- dynamic table editing 262
- markup display 262

Authentic node settings 362
- additional validation 362
- dialog box 364

Authentic Stylesheet 257
- and Authentic View 257
- creating 310
- definition of 257
- generating from HTML 237
- in document creation 255
- opening schema for 310
- saving 310
- and Authentic View 297
- and document creation process 297
- Auto-add Date Picker 434
- Block Style 413
- closing 305
- conditional templates 384
- creating dynamic tables 378
- creating lists 371
- creating static tables 377
- data-entry devices 369
- Date Picker 386
- design process 307
- for HTML and PDF 299
- formatting of numeric fields 388
- formatting tables 410
- formatting text and components in 414
- generating XSLT from 299
- in document creation process 296
- input formatting 388
- overview of tables in 375
- table formatting 380
- terminology 300
- Text Style 413
- uses of 296

Authentic View 275
- adding element content in 275
- adding elements in 275
- and Authentic Stylesheet 255, 257
- and content editing 255
- applying (replacing) an element 279
- Attributes entry helper 267
- benefits of 253, 258
- changing view to 262
- clearing an element 279
- concepts 257
- context menu 267
- context menus 267, 291
- data entry devices 275
- document display 264
- documentation 252
- editing dynamic tables 262
- Elements entry helper 267
- entering attribute values 280
- entering data in 274
- entering text in 275
- Entities entry helper 267
- entry helpers 267
- entry helpers in 261
- features 258
- formatting text in 262
- in Altova products 252
- in document creation process 257
- inserting an element 278

Authentic View 275
  inserting entities in 281
  interface 260
  introduction to 253
  main window 264
  main window in 261
  markup display in 262, 264
  menu bar in 261
  opening an XML document in 273
  overview of GUI 261
  printing an XML document from 282
  project window in 261
  removing elements in 291
  SPS Tables 284
  static table example 275
  tables 284
  terminology 257
  toolbar icons 262
  toolbar in 261
  tutorial 272
  tutorial requirements 272
  usage of important features 283
  usage of XML tables 285
  XML table icons 288
  XML tables 285
Auto-add Date Picker 434
Auto-Calculation 340
  in Authentic Stylesheets 340
  insert 423
Auto-complete 207
  text view enable/disable 207
Auto-completion 92
Automatic validation 206

- B -

Back 96, 181
  in Authentic tables 340
Background Information 462
Base 34
  element 34
  in input formatting 388
Batch manipulation 98
Batch-processing 170
bgcolor 340
  in Authentic tables 340
Big-endian 210
BizTalk 163, 164, 166, 463, 464
Block components 323
  in Authentic Stylesheets 323
Block formatting 413
  in Authentic Stylesheets 413
Block Style Window 323
  for formatting in Authentic Stylesheets 323
Block styles 414
  in Authentic Stylesheets 414
Bookmark 216, 422, 448
  in Authentic Stylesheets 337
Border 427
  view table border 427
Break 422
  insert page break 422
Broadcast 473
Browser 208
  back 181
  font 181
  forward 181
  Menu 181
  referesh 181
  separate window 181
  stop 181
  View 177, 181
Browser and XML 14
Browser menu 96
Browser view 66, 96
Bullet 419
  insert 419
  symbol types 437

- C -

C++ 465
Cache 167
CALS 432
  inserting table 432
  in Authentic Stylesheets 381
Cancel 181
Cascade 214
  Window 214
Catalog 164
  CustomCatalog 164
CDATA 147, 149
  Add Child 152
  Appending 149
  Convert To 154
  Inserting 147

Cell 427
- align content 427
- join above 426
- join below 426
- join left 426
- join right 426
- split horizontally 427
- split vertically 427
- view 427

Center vertically 427
- cell content 427

Change 419
- HTML format 419
- button 456
- check box 456
- combo box 456
- contents 456
- image 456
- input field 456
- list 456
- multiline input field 456
- paragraph 456
- radio button 456
- table 456

Changing view 262
- to Authentic View 262

Chapters 216, 448

Character 179
- position 179

Character-Set 107, 110, 469
- encoding 210

Character-set encoding 469

Check 92
- spelling checker 182
- validity 53
- well-formedness 53

Check in 131

Check Out 130

Check spelling 439

Check well-formedness 162

Child element 158
- adding 26
- insert 85

Child nodes 429
- add with node 429

Choices 103

CJK 469

Clearing an element 279
- in Authentic View 279

Clipboard 118
- copy 118
- cut 118
- paste 119

Close 110

Close All 110

Close project 125

Code fragments 113
- send by mail 113

Code page 208

Code-page 469

Collapse 76
- unselected 179

Color 208, 209
- tab 209
- table 209

Column 425
- append 425
- delete 426
- insert 426
- resizing 76

Columns 79, 155

COM 473
- Com(plex) tab 34
- customize 442

Command 104
- add to toolbar/menu 193
- context menu 200
- delete from menu 200
- reset menu 200

Comment 147, 149
- Add Child 152
- Appending 149
- Convert To 154
- Inserting 147

Comments 103, 122

Common Dialog 220

Compare source files 135

Comparing directories 189

Comparing files 187
- options 191

Complex 34
- type 34
- type extending 34
- referenced 85

ComplexType 464

Component 170
Download XSLT 170
global 34, 88
icon 26
insert / append 82
inserting 82
navigator 23, 82
Component download 218, 450
Component navigator 99
Components 318
moving in Authentic Stylesheets 318
Compositor 26
sequence 26
Compositors 88
Concurrent-use 217, 448, 473
Condition 424
insert 424
insert 424
how to use 384
in Authentic Stylesheets 347
Conditions 347
in Authentic Stylesheets 347
Constraint 82
schema 82
Content editing 255
in Authentic View 274, 275
Content model 15, 82, 103, 169, 464
display 85
sizing 169
Contents 420, 459
Context menu 200
commands 200
during customize 203
for HTML to XML conversion 247
in Authentic View 267, 291
Context-menu 76, 92
Contract 476
Conversion 240
HTML to XML reference 240
Convert 166
HTML to XML 435
Convert To 153
ATTLIST 155
Attribute 154
CDATA 154
Comment 154
DOCTYPE 155
Element 154, 155
ENTITY 155
externalID 155
NOTATION 155
PI 154
Text 154
XML 154
Copy 118, 119
data to/from 3rd party prod. 59
Structured Text 119
to clipboard 118
XML-Text 119
XPath 121
Copyright 219, 476, 478, 479
Core presentation 76
Courses 218
training 218
Cover page 405
designing for PDF 405
CPU 465
CR&LF 205
Create 70
addtnl. project folder 70
button 457
check box 457
combo box 457
contents 457
image 457
input field 457
list 457
multiline input field 457
new schema 23
new XML document 47
paragraph 457
project 70
radio button 457
XPath expression 158
CSS 96
Custom 182
dictionary 182
CustomCatalog 164
Customize 442
comands 442
context menu 200
customization contex menu 203
Enhanced Grid View 76
keyboard 444
menu 200
options 447

Customize 442
    toolbar/menu commands 193
    toolbars 444
    XSLT menu 445
Cut 118
    and copy in Designer 410
CVS 125

- D -

Dashed 427
    cell boundaries 427
Data entry devices 275
    in Authentic View 275
Data Exchange 79
    Table view 79
Database 119, 155
Database / Table view 59
    sort data 59
Database/Table View 76, 79, 155, 156, 157
Data-entry devices 369
    how to use 369
    in Authentic Stylesheets 314
Datatype 82
Date 388
    formatting of 388
    creating the Date Picker 386
Date Picker 434
    auto-add 434
    how to use 386
    insert 421
    using in Authentic View 292
DCD 163, 164, 463, 464
Decimals 388
    formatting of 388
Declarations 40
    global 40
Default 200
    menu 200
    schema settings 168
Default editor 206
Delete 119
    column 426
    command from context menu 200
    command from toolbar 193
    element 47
    file from project 70
    icon from toolbar 193
    row 426
    row (Document Editor) 173
    shortcut 196
    table 425
    toolbar 194
Delete particle 88
Demote 158
Descending 157
Details 26
    entry helper 26
    tab 30
Diagram 169
    Display 169
Dialog 220
Dictionary 182
    adding custom 182
    modifying existing 182
    spelling checker 182
Direction 122
Directories 98
    comparing two 189
Disable source control 130
Display 76
Display All Globals 15, 169
    icon 26
Display as Table 59
Display diagram 169
Display Settings 209
Distribution 477
Distributor 218, 450
Dockable window 214
DOCTYPE 105, 147
DOCTYPE Declaration 147
    Add Child 152
    Appending 150
    Convert To 155
    Inserting 147
Document 75, 107
    save invalid doc. 53
    save to URL 111
    Spelling checker 182
Document Content Description 464
Document creation process 255
    illustration of 255, 257
Document design 255
Document Type 147, 150, 152
Document Type Declaration 147
Document Type Definition 166, 167, 464

Documentation 103
  Annotation 88
Download 218, 450
  components 218, 450
Download source control project 127
Drag & drop 82
  attributes and ID constraints 82
Drag and drop 29
  add elements with 29
Drag&drop 101
  enumerations and patterns 101
Drag-and-drop 231
DTD 105, 155, 463, 464
  add child ATTLIST 153
  add child DOCTYPE 152
  add child ELEMENT 153
  add child ENTITY 153
  add Child ExternalID 152
  Add child NOTATION 153
  append DOCTYPE 150
  append ExternalID 150
  assign 166
  ATTLIST Declaration 148
  DOCTYPE declaration 147
  generating from HTML 237
  go to 167
  go to definition 167
  NOTATION Declaration 148
DTD / Schema 47
DTD/Schema 166
  Menu 166
DTDs 205, 206
Duplicate 173
  row (Document Editor) 173
Dynamic (SPS) tables 284
  description of 284
Dynamic components/content 307
Dynamic images 316
  in Authentic Stylesheets 316
Dynamic tables 262
  editing 262
  how to create 378
  how to format 380
  in Authentic Stylesheets 328, 375
  modifying properties of ,in Authentic Stylesheets 328

- E -

EBCDIC 110
Edit 50
  intelligent editing 50
  macro button 203
  Menu 118
Edit with XMLSPY 227
Editable content 429, 433
  node settings 429, 433
Edited with XMLSPY 205
Editing 76
Editing element/attribute names 76
Electronic Software Distribution 477
Element 464
  Add Child 151
  adding 26
  Appending 99, 149, 157
  attributes 40
  base 34
  Convert To 154
  Definition 167
  definition view 88
  deleting 47
  display (shortcut) 43
  facet 30
  Inserting 99, 146, 156
  inserting in Authentic Stylesheet 310
  make global 88
  mandatory 53, 99
  namespace prefix 164
  optional 30
  reference 40
  restricting definition 34
  and global templates 396
ELEMENT Declaration 148
  Add Child 153
  Appending 150
  Convert To 155
  Inserting 148
Element icon 76
Element types 85
Elements 318
  inserting in Authentic Stylesheet 318
  search for 122
  how to use in Authentic View 275, 278, 279
  in Authentic View 267

ElementTypes 47
  accessing 47
Elm 23
  Element (global) 23
E-Mail 113, 217, 448
Empty elements 206
Empty File 105
Enable source control 130
Enclose in Element 158
Encoding 107, 110, 469
Enhanced Grid 59
  Database / Table view 59
  Tree view 177
  view 50
Enhanced Grid View 155, 174, 206
  customization 76
Entities 281
  inserting entities in Authentic View 281
  how to use in Authentic View 281
  in Authentic View 267
Entity 101
  append 101
  entry helper 101
  insert 101
ENTITY Declaration 148, 166
  Add Child 153
  Appending 150
  Convert To 155
  Inserting 148
Entry helper 21
  attribute 50, 57
  component navigator 23, 82
  Details 26
  facet 30
  insert attribute / element 57
  update 57
Entry-Helper 99, 100, 101, 164, 214
  info 103
  Schema Design View 99
Enumeration 103
  attribute 40
  drag & drop 101
Error 162
ESD 477
EUC-JP 110
EUC-KR 110
Evaluate 158
  XPath 158
Evaluation Version 217, 448
Example files 20
  tutorial 20
Excel 79, 119
  copy data to/from 59
Exchange 119
  xml text 119
Exit 116, 417
Expand 76
  fully 179
Explorer 206
Extend 34
  complex type definition 34
Extensible Markup Language 146
Extensible Stylesheet Language 170
External parsed entites 206
External parsed entity 166, 167
External XSL processor 210
ExternalID Declaration 148
  Add Child 152
  Appending 150
  Convert To 155
  Inserting 148

- F -

F5 181
Facet 30
  element 30
  entry helper 30
  updating schema 59
Facets 464
FAQ 218, 449
Favorites 216, 448
Fetch file 130
  source control 130
File 105
  add active and related 138
  add to project 138
  Close 110
  Close All 110
  Encoding 110
  Exit 116
  Menu 105
  MRU 116
  New 105
  new - create template 105
  Open 107, 116, 416

File 105
- Open URL 108
- opening options 205
- Print 114
- Print Setup 115
- Reload 110
- Save 111
- Save All 112
- Save As 111
- Save to URL 111
- Send by Mail 113
- tab 205

File import 241
File types 105, 206
Files 187
- comparing two 187
- comparison options 191

Find 122, 123
Find Defintion 167
Fixed text 433
- node settings 433

Flush 167
FO 171
- Assign XSL:FO 171
- compliance levels 303
- full standard 447
- processor 447
- setting up in Stylesheet Designer 303

FO processors 401
Folder 163
- add external folder 138
- add external web folder 141
- create addtnl. project folder 70

Folders 98
Folder-tree 98
Font 181, 468
- schema 209
- Schema Documentation 209

Font Size 181
Footers 356
- in Authentic tables 356

FOP 401
- compliance 447
- in Stylesheet Designer 303

Format 419
- HTML 419
- marking 410
- XML doc in text view 121
- in Authentic Stylesheets 323, 414
- in Stylesheet Designer 413
- of numeric fields 388
- in Authentic Stylesheets 414

Formatting text 360
- in Authentic Stylesheets 360

Forward 96, 181
Fragments 113
- send by mail 113

Full-text 216, 448
- search 216, 448

- G -

GB2312 110
Get latest version 130
Getting started 5, 227
Global 467
- component 34
- declarations 40
- settings 205
- reference 88

Global templates 396
- and mixed content 396
- creating and using 396
- for Authentic text formatting 360
- in Authentic Stylesheets 360

Globals 82
- show 169

Go to 167, 170, 171
- Element definitions (schema) 43
- Schema definition 167
- XSL 66

Go to Definition 167
Go to File 180
Go to line/char 179
Grammar 206
Graphic view of component 169
Gray bar 178
Grayed-out 50
- attribute / element 50

Grid fonts 208
Grid View 76, 174, 178
Grouping files 69
- project 69

- H -

Hebrew 471
Help 216, 448
  contents 216, 448
  index 216, 448
  Menu 216, 448
  search 216, 448
Help system 216, 448
Hide 214
  markup 172
Hide markup 262, 264
Hierarchical Display 76
Hiragana 468
History 118, 418
  redo 118, 418
  undo 118, 418
Homepage 227
Horizontal line 420
  inserting 420
Hotkey 196
  view element 88
HTML 170
  add to parent 435
  and Authentic Stylesheets 299
  append 436
  conversion to XML 231, 243
  formats in Designer 419
  from XML doc. 66
  generating XML ,schema ,XSLT ,Authentic Stylesheet 237
  importing into Stylesheet Designer 230
  importing into Stylesheet Dewsigner 242
  insert 435
  inserting table 432
  open file 435
  settings 436
HTML import 230, 242, 435
HTML Import menu 245
HTML tables 381
  in Authentic Stylesheets 381
HTML to XML Tutorial 226
Http:// 227
Hyperlink 422
  in Authentic Stylesheets 337

- I -

IANA 473
ICComNet 473
Icon 193
  add to toolbar/menu 193
  show large 203
  for Authentic View text 360
  in Authentic Stylesheets 360
  text state 431
IDE 4
  drag & drop 82
Image 419
  insert 419
  in Authentic Stylesheets 316
Import 241
  HTML 435
Incremental validating parser 99
Index 216, 448
  help 216, 448
Info 21
  window 21
Info window 103, 214
Info windows 164
Input fields 314
  in Authentic Stylesheets 314
Input-methods 468
Insert 99, 146, 147, 148, 156
  attribute 100
  attribute / element 57
  auto-calculation 423
  bookmark 422
  bullets an numbering 419
  CALS table 432
  column 426
  conditional template 424
  contents 420, 459
  data into template 433
  Date Picker 421
  horizontal line 420
  HTML import 435
  HTML table 432
  hyperlink 422
  image 419
  page break 422
  page number 422
  paragraph 419

Insert 99, 146, 147, 148, 156
processing instruction 147
Rest of contents 421, 459
row 426
row (Document Editor) 173
table 425
table row 79
attribute 82
particle 82
Insert child elements 85
Insert row (table view) 156
Inserting an element 278
in Authentic View 278
Installation 217, 448
Instance 163
Instance document 166
Integer 388
formatting of 388
Intelligent editing 50, 76, 92, 99, 166, 207
Attribute window 100
element window 99
Entity window 101
info window 103
update entry helper 164
Intermediate version 162
Internal Subset 150, 151, 152, 153, 155, 166
ATTLIST 148
DOCTYPE 147
ELEMENT 148
ENTITY 148
ExternalID 148
NOTATION 148
Internet 4, 108, 111, 217, 218, 448, 449, 450, 466
Internet Explorer 96
Introduction 4, 6
Stylevision 1
Invalid 53
document - save 53
ISO/IEC 10646 467
ISO-8859-x 110
ISO-8895-x 469
isRef 40
reference 40

- J -

Japan 218, 450
Join 426
cell below 426
cell left 426
cell right 426
JScript 92

- K -

Kanji 468
Katakana 468
Keyboard 92
customize 444
Keyboard shortcut 196
Key-code 217, 448, 477

- L -

LAN 473
Large markup 172
show 172
Last project 145
open 145
Left 158
Legal information 476
Liability 479
Limitation of 479
License 116, 217, 448, 476, 477, 478, 479
Agreement 478, 479
Metering 473
Licensed Version 217, 448
License-metering 217, 448
Limit 40
attribute contents 40
Line 179
go to 179
word wrap in text view 179
Line-breaks 205
Links 337
in Authentic Stylesheets 337
Lists 371
creating in Authentic Stylesheets 371
Little-endian 210
Local project 127
Low-level 92

- M -

Macro 203
edit button 203
Mail 466
Main 164
MainCatalog 164
Main window 21, 76, 163
MainCatalog 164
Make global 88
Mandatory 53, 99
element 53, 99
Mandatory attribute 100
MAPI 113, 466
Marking 410
table data 410
Markup 172
hide 172
in Authentic View 262, 264
show large 172
show mixed 172
show small 172
Marquee 29
drag and drop 29
Maximum cell width 208
maxIncl 30
facet 30
maxOcc 26, 30
details 26, 30
Memory 163, 167, 465
Menu 104
add/delete command 193
Browser 181
Commands 104
customize 200
Default/XMLSPY 200
delete commands from 200
DTD 166
Edit 118
File 105
Help 216, 448
Project 124
Schema 166
Schema design 168
Table 155
View 174
Window 214
XML 146
XSL 170
XSLT customized 445
Menu Command 104, 220
Microsoft Excel 119
MIME 206
minOcc 26, 30
details 26, 30
Mixed content 396
and global templates 396
Mixed markup 172
show 172
Model | Sequence 88
Modify 146
Modifying table properties 328
in Authentic Stylesheets 332, 340
Modifyng table properties 356
in Authentic Stylesheets 356
Most recently used project 145
Mouse 92
Move 158
Left 158
Right 158
row (Document Editor) 173
Move up 173
row (Document Editor) 173
Moving components 318
in Authentic Stylesheets 318
MS Visual Source Safe 125
MSXML 210
MSXML3 96
Multi-user 205, 217, 448, 473

- N -

Namespace 23
schema 23
Namespace declaration 166
Namespace Prefix 164
Navigating 76
Navigation 43
shortcuts in schemas 43
Network 116, 466
communications 466, 473
traffic 466, 473
New 105
create personal template 105
New Project 124

Next occurrence 122
Nippon 450
Node set 158, 159
 window 158, 159
 edit/fixed content 429
Noneditable content 429, 433
 node settings 429, 433
Non-roman writing system 468
Non-XML 92
Non-XML files 206
NOTATION Declaration 148
 Add Child 153
 Appending 151
 Convert To 155
 Inserting 148
Numbering 419
 insert 419
Numbers 388
 formatting of 388
Numeric fields 388
 formatting of 388

- O -

OASIS 164
 xml catalogs 164
Object 438
 settings 438
Online help 4, 5
 for HTML to XML conversion 249
Online Shop 218, 449
Open 107, 116
Open 416
 HTML file 435
 last project 145
 recently used files 417
Open project 124
 source control 127
Open URL 108, 227
Opening options 205
 file 205
Optimal widths 179, 208
Optional 30
 element 30
Options 447
 customize 447
Order 477
Order Form 218, 449
OrgChart.sps 272
 in Authentic View tutorial 272
OrgChart.xml 272
 in Authentic View tutorial 272
OrgChart.xsd 272
 in Authentic View tutorial 272
Origin 159
 XPath 159
OS 465
Outlook 113
Output formatting 205
Overview 21
 HTML to XML 225

- P -

Page 405
 headers and footers in PDF output 405
 HTML properties 437
 insert page break 422
 insert page number 422
 numbering in PDF output 404
 PDF properties 437
 setting margins of for PDF output 404
 setting size of for PDF output 404
 inserting 422
Page properties in PDF 404
Pane 225
Panes 225
Paragraph 419
Parameter entities 101
Parent element 158
Parsed entity 166
Parser 463
 XSLT 210
Parser download 218, 450
Password protection 108, 111
 URL 108, 111
Paste 119
 cut and copy in Designer 410
Paths 124
 in project files 124
Pattern 101
 drag & drop 101
Patterns 464
PDF 299
 and Authentic Stylesheets 299
 defining page headers and footers 405

PDF 299
  defining page properties 404
  designing cover page of 405
  formatting 401
  layout elements 405
  processing 401
  processing via FO 401
  setting up in Stylesheet Designer 303
PI 147, 150, 152, 154
  Add Child 152
  Appending 150
  Convert To 154
  Inserting 147
port 473
  2799 473
  80 466
Position 179
  Character 179
  Line 179
Pre-defined formats 323, 414
  in Authentic stylesheets 323, 414
Premium 164
Presentation 208
Pretty print 121
  in text view 121
Preview 96, 114
  in Stylesheet Designer 310
Price list 477
Print 115
  Command 114
  Preview 114
  Setup 115
Print Setup 115
Printing 282
  from Authentic View 282
Processing instruction 170
  Add Child 152
  Append 150
  Convert To 154
  Insert 147
Processing instructions 122
Processor 447
  FO 447
Program settings 205
Project 166
  Add active and related files 138
  Add External folder 138
  Add External web folder 141
  Add file 138
  Add files to project 137
  Add folder 138
  Add local/network folder 138
  add to source control 132
  Add URL to project 137
  adding files to 70
  advantages 69
  assigning DTDs 98
  assigning XSL transformations 98
  Close Project 125
  create 70
  create addtnl. folder 70
  delete file from 70
  management 124
  Menu 124
  Most recently used 145
  New 124
  Open project 124
  properties 69, 143, 163
  Reload project 125
  remove from source control 134
  save 70
  Save Project 125
  window 21
  paths in 124
Project open 127
  source control 127
Project window 18, 124, 214
Promote 158
Properties 143
  and source control 143
  HTML page 437
  PDF page 437
  Project 143
  source control 136
  table 427, 437
Protocols 5
Provider 127
  select 127
  source control 125
PVCS Version Manager 125

- Q -

Quit 116

- R -

RAM 465
Recently used files 116
  open 417
Recommended links 5
Redo 92, 118, 418
Reference 74
  complex type 85
  element 40
  HTML to XML 240
  to global particle 88
Refresh 96, 181
  entry helper 57
  source control 137
Registration 217, 448, 466, 477
Registry 205
  settings 205
Reject source edits 132
Reload 110, 181, 205
  entry helper data 164
Reload project 125
Remove 134
  from source control 134
Rendering 471
Repeated elements 79, 155, 156, 157, 207
Replace 123
  All 123
Replacing an element 279
  in Authentic View 279
Repositories 108, 111, 125
Requirements 465
Reseller 477
Reset 200
  menu commands 200
  shortcut 196
  toolbar & menu commands 194
Rest of Contents 421, 459
Restriction 34
  element 34
Result 158
  node set 158
Resume 162
Revalidate 53
RichEdit 118, 418
RichEdit 3.0 209
RichEdit component 472
Right mouse button 92
Right-to-left 471
Root element 105, 147
  schema 23
  selecting 47
Row 157, 425
  Append 157, 425
  append (Document Editor) 172
  delete 426
  delete (Document Editor) 173
  duplicate (Document Editor) 173
  Insert 156, 426
  insert (Document Editor) 173
  move down (Document Editor) 173
  move up 173
Rule 420
  inserting 420
Run native interface 137

- S -

Save 111, 416
  and well-formedness 111
  anyway 53
  generated XSL-FO file 417
  generated XSLT file 417
  invalid document 53
  project 70
  Save All 112
  Save As 111
  Save URL 111
Save as 416
Save project 125
Schema 105, 163, 164, 166, 167, 464
  adding elements 26
  constraints 82
  creating new 23
  CustomCatalog 164
  defaults 168
  definition 22
  design view 82
  Design view 174
  Design View - entry helper 99
  dialect 163, 164
  dialects 464
  Documentation font 209
  DTD/Schema menu 166
  Editing 15

Schema 105, 163, 164, 166, 167, 464
go to 167
namespace 23
opening to create Authentic Stylesheet 310
root element 23
Schema / DTD 47
settings 23, 168, 205
shortcuts 43
view 23
Display all globals 169
Display diagram 169
menu 168
zoom 169
Schema fonts 209
Schema overview 15, 23, 169
(Globals) 82
display all globals 26
Script language 212
Scripting 212
Search 122, 123
for attributes ,elements ,text 122
help 216, 448
Secure Online Shop 218, 449
Select All 121, 418
Select file 220
Selected object 438
Selection 113
Selector 121
Semantic 98
Send by Mail 113
Separate window 181
Browser 181
Sequence 155
compositor 26
unbounded 26
Set Namespace prefix 164
Settings 205
HTML 436
schema 23, 168
scripting 212
Settings for file comparison 191
SGML 5
Shift-JIS 110
Shortcut 196
assigning/deleting 196
show in tooltip 203
in schema documents 43
Show 214
Database / Table view 59
Show differences 135
Show globals 15
displays all globals 15
icon 169
Show history 134
Show large markup 262, 264
Show mixed markup 262, 264
Show small arkup 262, 264
Side-by-side 181, 208
Simple type 30, 85
SimpleType 464
Single-user 217, 448, 473
Size 209
Sizing content model 169
Small markup 172
show 172
SMTP 466
Software Product 473, 478, 479
Sort 157
Ascending 157
Descending 157
elements 79
table columns 59
Source 88
appinfo 88
send by mail 113
Source control 125
add to source control 132
changing properties 143
Check In 131
Check Out 130
enable 130
get latest version 130
open project 127
properties 136
refresh status 137
remove from 134
run native interface 137
show differences 135
show history 134
Undo Check out 132
Spellchecker 439
Spelling checker 182
custom dictionary 182
Spelling options 184, 440
Splash screen 208

Split cell 427
horizontally 427
vertically 427
Spreadsheet 119, 155
SPS 432
making CALS/HTML tables available 432
definition of 257
SPS table 275
static table example in Authentic View tutorial 275
description of 284
editing dynamic tables 262
in Authentic Stylesheets 375
Start 4, 5
Start 227
add (context menu) 203
StarTeam 125
Static (SPS) tables 284
description of 284
Static components/content 307
Static images 316
in Authentic Stylesheets 316
Static table 275
example in Authentic View tutorial 275
how to create 377
how to format 380
in Authentic Stylesheets 332, 375
joining cells in 332
modifying properties of ,in Authentic Stylesheets 332
specifying column widths 332
Static text 314
in Authentic Stylesheets 314
Stop 96, 181
Structured Display 76
Structured Text 119, 207
Structuring 98
Style 208, 209
in Stylesheet Designer 413
Stylesheet 96, 170, 171
adding/deleting placeholders 410
and Authentic View 297
and document creation process 297
and tables 375
Block Style 413
Block Style Window 305
closing 305
closing an Authentic Stylesheet 305
creating lists 371
data-entry devices 369
description of interface 305
description of Schema Window 305
document design 307
documentation 294
FO compliance levels 303
formatting in 414
getting started 302
How to use... 368
Icons 410
icons in Design Document 410
icons in schema tree 410
in Altova products 294
in document creation 257
in document creation process 296
insert Date Picker 421
introduction 295
setting up 303
setting up FO processor 303
Symbols 410
Tags 410
terminology 300
Text Style 413
Text Style Window 305
Stylesheet Designer Tutorial 309
files used in 309
introduction 309
Sub-Element 79, 155, 158
Support 218, 449
Support Center 218, 449
Suspend 162
Symbol types 437
bullets 437
numbering 437
Synchronize 177
Tree and Grid view 177
Syntax 159
XPath 159
well-formedness 53
Syntax-coloring 92, 118, 206, 208, 418

- T -

Tab 34
Com(plex) element 34
details 30
Elm (global element) 23
Tab characters 205

Table 425
build automatically 206
cell alignment 427
colors 209
delete 425
display as 155
insert CALS / HTML table 432
insert row 79
Menu 155
properties 437
Sort 157
Table view 79
View 157
view border 427
Table boundaries 427
Table footers 356
in Authentic Stylesheets 356
Table of contents 216, 448
Table properties 328, 427
in Authentic Stylesheets 332, 340, 356
Table View 79, 156, 157, 207
Tables 262
editing dynamic (SPS) tables 262
formatting in Stylesheet Designer 380, 410
icons for editing XML tables 288
overview in Authentic Stylesheets 375
using SPS (static and dynamic) tables 284
using XML tables 285
TargetNamespace 166
TCP 473
Technical Information 462
Technical Support 218, 449
Template 105
create personal 105
directory 105
inserting data from XML 433
making CALS/HTML tables available 432
saving XSLT files 310
Template folder 20
Template XML 433
assign 433
Template XML file 300
Terminate 116, 181
Text 147, 149, 170
Add Child 152
Appending 149
Convert To 154
editing text files 92
find text string 122
font 209
Inserting 147
pretty print 121
in Authentic Stylesheets 360, 413
in Authentic Stylesheets 323
Text state icons 431
for Authentic View 360
in Authentic Stylesheets 360
Text Style Window 323
for formatting in Authentic Stylesheets 323
Text styles 414
in Authentic Stylesheets 414
Text view 50, 92, 176
auto-complete enable/disable 207
of Working XML file 309
RichEdit component 472
schema fonts 209
Tile 214
horizontally 214
vertically 214
Toggle 214
Toolbar 194
activate/deactivate 194
add command to 193
button 220
create new 194
reset toolbar & menu commands 194
show large icons 203
customize 444
Tools 182
menu 182
Tooltip 203
show 203
show shortcuts in 203
Topic 216, 448
view on TOC 216, 448
Training 218
courses 218
Transfer 119
data from Grid view 119
Transformation 66
XSL - HTML 66
Transformation XSL 170
Tree view 177
Enhanced Grid 177
Turn off automatic validation 206
Tutorial 5

Tutorial 5
 example files 20
 goals 20
 HTML to XML 226
 see Stylesheet Designer Tutorial 309
Type 34
 AddressType 34
 complex 34
 simple 30

- U -

UCS-2 110, 210, 467
UCS-4 110, 467
UDP 473
Unbounded 26
 element 26
Undo 92, 118, 418
 history 118, 418
Undo Check out 132
Unicode 107, 110, 467
 capabilities 469
 consortium 467
 standard 467
 support 468
Unicode characters 468
Universal font 468
Unlimited levels of Undo 118, 418
Unlock 217, 448
Unselected 179
Update 57
 entry helper 57
 schema facet 59
Updates 4
URL 108, 111, 227, 466
 add to project 137
US-ASCII 110
Use 473, 479
 license 473, 479
 in Authentic Stylesheets 364
Using Global Templates 396
Using XML 13
UTF-16 210, 469
UTF-8 110, 467, 469

- V -

Valid 53
 invalid document - save 53
 check validity 53
 DTD 164
 files in a folder 138
 files in a web folder 141
 marks incorrect data 59
 revalidate 53
 Schema 164
 XML 163
 XML document 53, 163
Validating parser 99, 463
Validation 166
 projects 98
Validator 463
VBScript 92
Version Number 219
View 178, 179
View 178
 Browser view 66, 177
 Collapse 178, 179
 content model (shortcut) 43
 Database / Table view 59
 element definition 88
 Enhance Grid view 174
 Enhanced Grid 50
 Expand 178, 179
 Go to File 180
 Go to line/char 179
 Grid 76
 Menu 174
 Optimal widths 179
 Schema Design view 174
 Schema view 23
 Synchronize 177
 Text view 50, 176
 Tree 177
 XSL 17
View element definition 88
View table cell bounds 427
Visualizer 158
 XPath 158

- W -

W3C 5, 164, 463, 464
Warranty 479
Watch for changes 205
Web 108, 111
    add to project 141
Web Server 218, 449, 450
Web Shop 218, 449
Web solution 92
Web-server 4
Welcome 4
Well-formedness 53, 92, 162
    and saving 111
Where 122
Window 215
    Cascade 214
    Entry-Helper 214
    Info 214
    Menu 214
    node set 159
    Open 215
    Project 214
    Tile horizontally 214
    Tile vertically 214
    select file 220
Windows 75
    overview 21
Windows 2000 465, 468, 472
Windows 95 465, 472
Windows 95/98 469
Windows 98 465, 472
Windows NT 465, 468, 472
WML 170
Word wrap 179
    enable/disable 179
Working directory 127
    source control 127
Working XML file 300, 416
    assigning for Authentic Stylesheet 310
Wrap 179
    word wrap enable/disable 179
Writing-systems 471
Wwriting-system 468
www 227

- X -

XDR 163, 164, 166, 463, 464
XHTML 96, 105, 170
XML 4, 5, 467
    Add Child 152
    Appending 150
    convert HTML to 435
    Convert To 154
    copying to 3rd party prod. 59
    create template 105
    document and icons 46
    Inserting 147
    Introduction 6
    Menu 146
    new document 47
    Parser 463
    reformat doc in text view 121
    Schema 166
    sorting data 59
    spelling checker 182
    standards 11
    using 13
    validate document 53
    why 9
    in Authentic Stylesheets 364
XML data 92
XML declaration 147
XML Diff 189
    comparing directories 189
    comparing files 187, 191
XML document 255
    content editing 255
    creation process 255
    design of 255
    opening in Authentic View 273
XML Document creation process 296, 297
XML document in Authentic View 257
    definition of 257
XML File 107
    send by mail 113
XML instance 163
XML instance document 163
XML overview 14
XML Schema 103, 163, 164, 166, 463, 464
    generating from HTML 237

XML tables 285, 381
description of 285, 381
editing 285
editing the properties of 285
enabling in Authentic Stylesheets 381
icons for editing 288
in Authentic Stylesheets 375
usage of 285
XML-Conformance 206
XML-Data 163, 164, 464
XMLSPY 4, 74, 218, 219, 450
Authentic 310
training 218
XML-Text 119, 207
XPath 121
copy 121
examples 160
for additional validation 362
in Auto-Calculation 340
in conditional templates 347
origin 159
syntax 159
visualizer 158
xs 40
xs:boolean 40
xs:date 30
xs:integer 30
xs:positiveInteger 34
xs:string 26, 30
XSD 164, 166, 463, 464
xsd:annotation 103
xsi 47
xsi:type 47
XSL 96, 170, 171
Assign 171
assigning to an XML doc. 66
FO options 447
go to XSL 66
Menu 170
transformation 66
XSL stylesheet 170
XSL Transformation 98, 170
XSL views 17
XSL-FO 303
compliance levels 303
save file 417
XSLT 96, 121, 170, 171, 179
generating from HTML 237
processor 210
save file 417
brief description 295
from Authentic Stylesheet 310
from Authentic Stylesheets 299
insert auto-calculation 423
insert conditional template 424
XSLT Transformation System 218, 450
download 218, 450

- Z -

Zoom 169
schema design 169